3

The Inner American

THE INNER AMERICAN

A *Self-Portrait*

from 1957 to 1976

Joseph Veroff
Elizabeth Douvan
Richard A. Kulka

Basic Books, Inc., Publishers

NEW YORK

Library of Congress Cataloging in Publication Data

Veroff, Joseph, 1929–
   The Inner American.

   References: p. 619
   Includes index.
   1. Mental health—United States.   2. Mental health—
United States—Statistics.   3. United States—Statistics,
Medical.   4. United States—Social conditions—1945-
I. Douvan, Elizabeth Ann Malcolm, 1926-
II. Kulka, Richard A.   III. Title.
RA790.6.V47   973.92   81–68127
ISBN: 0–465–03293–1   AACR2

This book is dedicated to

Professors Daniel Katz and Gerald Gurin,

esteemed colleagues, models of skill,

integrity, and humanity

Contents

Acknowledgments

LARGE SCALE social research is by nature collaborative. It depends on the specialized contributions of many individuals, coordinated and integrated with each other.

We have enjoyed an exceptional series of collaborations in the course of conducting our research and writing this book. We have learned and increased our understanding in all of these relationships. We have found great personal pleasure in them as well.

In designing the 1976 replication study we consulted Gerald Gurin and Sheila Feld, co-authors of the 1957 study, our friends and colleagues over the years. Their advice, encouragement, and collegial support, given graciously and generously, are among the very great rewards the project held for us. Angus Campbell, long time director of the Survey Research Center (SRC) and distinguished social scientist, urged us to do the replication study and shared findings as they came in with characteristic enthusiasm.

Colleagues in SRC's service sections made their critical contributions with the professionalism and helpful personal styles we are lucky enough to be able to assume—Irene Hess in sampling, John Scott and Tracy Berckmans in the field section, Joan Scheffler in Coding.

David Klingel and Mary Ellen Colten helped through the whole process of the study as active discussants and constructive, keen critics. Dave also managed data, solved incredible technical problems, taught us and our students the latest analytic techniques, and maintained morale in tough times.

The study was funded by NIMH, under Grant MH26006. Herbert Coburn, who headed the section that reviewed and advised us on the proposal, was always constructive and thorough in his work and was extraordinarily helpful to us.

We applied for and received an NIMH training grant, MH14618, for doctoral and postdoctoral scholars to work on the project as they developed survey skills. With this group of remarkable young colleagues we shared for five years a seminar and a working life that was rich in intellectual and personal rewards, perhaps the most ideal work situation imaginable. This book owes much to their enspiriting talk and we thank all of them: Helen Weingarten, Charlene Depner, Toni Antonucci, Steven Dubnoff, Anne Locksley, Alfreda Iglehart, Lynn Kahle, Fred Bryant, Janet Kohen, Sandra Stukes, Jeanne Lemkau, James McRae, Karen Mikus, Aloen Townsend, Betty Jones, Lois Tamir, Luis Rubalcava, Kathleen Pottick, Elysse Sutherland, Robert Taylor, Susan Goff, David Reuman and Susan Contratto.

Other colleagues who contributed in various significant ways include: Michael Gorodetsky, David Featherman, Richard Price, Kenneth Heller, Joann Veroff, and Warren Norman.

Mary Loewen, Toby Teumer, and Sue Ellen Hansen typed, coordinated, formatted and corrected various versions of the manuscript. They kept things organized and sane which could easily have gotten out of control. They brought care and creative solutions to numerous problems; they offered spirit and good will throughout.

The Inner American

Chapter 1

INTRODUCTION

THIS BOOK presents findings from two national studies of the American population which focused on questions of well-being and satisfaction, life experience, and performance in major roles, psychological stress, and the methods people use to manage stresses that life presents. The studies permit an assessment of the life experience of Americans at two time points: 1957, when the first study was conducted, and 1976, when we replicated it. Having the two time points provides us the rare opportunity to speak of changes in life experience which have occurred over the intervening generation.

In 1957 Congress established a Joint Commission on Mental Illness and Health to evaluate "national resources for coping with the human and economic problems of mental illness." The commission staff, recognizing "at the outset that no nationwide information was available on what the American people themselves [think] of their mental health," asked the Survey Research Center at the University of Michigan to design and conduct an intensive interview survey with a sample of 2,500 normal adults in order to obtain such information. The results of this study were reported by the study staff in two major monographs[1] and numerous articles.

The study was designed to answer a series of questions about normal men and women: "How well or badly adjusted do they consider themselves to be? Are they happy or unhappy, worried or unworried, optimistic or pessimistic in their outlook? Do they feel strong or weak; adequate or inadequate? What troubles Americans, as they see themselves? And what do people do about their troubles? Do they solve their problems by themselves? Do they learn to live with them? Do they turn to

[1]Gurin, G., Veroff, J., and Feld, S., *Americans View Their Mental Health.* New York: Basic Books, 1960 and Veroff, J. and Feld, S. *Marriage and Work in America.* New York: Van Nostrand, 1970.

someone for help? When they feel the need for help, where do they turn? What kind of help do they get? How effective do they think this help is?" (Gurin et al., 1960, p. ix.)

The commission staff and the research staff recognized that answers to such questions about psychological well-being constitute only one set of measures of "mental health" or "mental illness." People may clearly diagnose their own mental health differently from friends or experts. Nevertheless, such information from a national sample of "normal" people living in households added a good deal to the commission's understanding of needs and resources in the field of mental health. The sample survey was seen as a supplement to community studies and analysis of records which plot the epidemiology of mental illness as assessed by psychiatrists and other diagnostic experts. The look at people's own reports of their experience and functioning was seen as having more than "simple human interest" for, in the commission's view "the needs of the people—as they themselves feel them, come to understand them, and express them—ultimately determine [in a democracy] the ways in which organized efforts will be made to meet these needs." (Gurin et al., 1960, p. ix.)

In 1976, with funding from the National Institute of Mental Health, we replicated the 1957 study. In the preceding decade, social scientists had developed a keen interest in "the quality of life" and "social indicators" of that quality. The social-indicator movement arose in recognition of the fact that economic indicators like gross national product, the index of consumer prices, and per capita income were used widely to guide social policy and that they were at best only partial and indirect measures of life quality. Political developments of the late sixties—in particular, the demonstrated disaffection of middle-class youth and the growing distrust of government among the electorate—indicated that economic growth and affluence could not be read directly as indicators of people's satisfaction or contentment. Something more was needed to reveal the level of ease, comfort, fulfillment, and satisfaction (or their opposites). Numerous social scientists and politicians suggested that in addition to economic indicators, we needed psychological measures to assess the quality of American life and to inform national policy aimed at enhancing the life of the nation.

Several commentators noted that older studies might be used for base-line information; by repeating questions in the future in occasional national studies we could provide ongoing social indicators to assess changes in the quality of American life as well as what has remained stable. Among the past studies frequently mentioned for this purpose was the 1957 study by Gurin, Veroff, and Feld.

We, too, had been eager to redo the study. With the growing impetus of the social-indicators movement as stimulus, we proposed the study to the National Institute of Mental Health and in 1975 were awarded the funds to proceed. Thus, we set out to exploit this unique opportunity to explore social change and social stability in American society from the perspective of people's own subjective experience.

In the years between the two studies, there were clear upheavals in the state of the country and the world as technologies for transportation and communication changed the nature of American politics and economics from a limited international basis of operation to a clear multinational interdependence. These changes could not have occurred without concomitant upheavals in the way people articulated their values and goals, and encountered their frustrations. We hope to identify these changes.

Despite these upheavals, we are also convinced that American people in 1976 were basically as adaptable as they were in 1957. Certain settings in which we operate have clearly become less viable—cities do not inspire as much sense of community as they once did; jobs have perhaps become even more specialized and bureaucratized. Nevertheless, people learn to evaluate their experience within the terms of their present lives. They adapt to changes even if we, as social critics, view these changes as unhealthy. Thus, as much as we are interested in social change, we are equally interested in social stability. We will focus particularly on how much people's sex, age, or education are important factors affecting their evaluation of their own mental health, *regardless* of historical era: are there persistent sex differences, adult development differences, social status differences in well-being, in spite of changes that have occurred in the world? Are there social psychological principles about subjective experience that *transcend* particular historical circumstances?

Therefore we highlight stability in the pattern of findings as much as change. To account for both enables us to have a more integrated perspective on the forces in the social environment that are more or less powerful in their impact on dimensions of subjective experience. To know which type of psychological reaction changes and which does not, what groups change and what groups do not, may also bring us closer to a theory of social change.

Because the studies we will compare are based on two national surveys, giving us a representative sample of 2,460 adults (twenty-one and older) in 1957 and a comparable sample of 2,267 in 1976, we are freer to talk about change and stability in the *country*. Nevertheless, we are dealing with a standard survey research interview, with all its limitations and advantages. Clearly, when an unknown interviewer asks a question as personal as "What things about your marriage are not quite as nice as you would like them to be?" responses will not always be candid or spontaneous. We have to train ourselves to diagnose the significance of people's reactions in the context of the method we used. At the end of this chapter, we will detail methods of our survey and the particular precautions we used in formulating questions, drawing a sample of respondents, interviewing, coding answers, and analyzing the information to allow us some security in our assessments. We feel we have valid appraisals of people's subjective experiences within the limits of these methods. These appraisals enable us to detect what has remained stable and what has changed in the critical evaluations that people make of their own lives.

The Areas of Subjective Life Investigated

The studies on which this report is based included two quite distinct purposes:

1. To assess the subjective mental health, the life experience of American adults.
2. To determine in some detail how American people cope with problems of adjustment which arise in their lives.

The second purpose served a specific practical interest of Congress: to assess the availability of mental-health resources and the degree to which adults in our society were likely to use such resources if they were made more widely available. Did people know about mental-health professionals? Had they ever consulted such persons? Would they for a pressing problem? If not, why not? Were people inhibited by fear of being stigmatized for using available professional help? Or did they have alternative sources of counsel and support in their families and friendship groups?

To deal adequately with people's readiness to seek professional help, especially when that help might carry certain elements of fear or stigma, demands considerable subtlety and a complex series of overlapping and interrelated questions. The information we gathered about help seeking is extensive, complicated, and intricately analyzed to yield reliable information about the readiness of people to use professional help, the particular helpers they use, the referral mechanisms by which they reach professional helpers, and their evaluation of the help they receive. We analyze all of these aspects of help seeking separately for subgroups in the population to come closer to an understanding of the availability of resources and the process that leads people to use them.

In a word, the analysis of professional help-seeking is a book in itself, and we have made the decision to treat it in a separate volume. While the original Gurin, Veroff, and Feld book dealt with both aspects of their study in a single volume, the addition of time comparisons to our present analysis increased the bulk of our discussion by half and meant that the size of a one-volume report would be discouraging in both size and cost. In addition, it seems to us now that the two parts of the study are quite different and appeal to quite different audiences. While detailed analysis of help-seeking behavior is critically interesting to mental-health professionals and to a segment of the social science community, the analysis of American adults' subjective experience of their lives will probably interest a broader group of social scientists, historians, journalists, and many people who are simply curious to know how we as a nation are faring in our adventure with life.

In this book, then, we will merely refer to some of the findings about professional help-seeking and will focus on how people cope informally with their problems—particularly on how much help they receive from family and friends. Informal support—the use of other people as listening posts, sympathizers, counselors for problems—is, after all, an important feature of life experience which relates closely to life satisfaction and adjustment. To know that most of us have people we can talk to about our worries and unhappiness and that talking things over is one of the key mechanisms we use in times of trouble tells us something critical about the social integration of Americans. Following our assessment of the subjective mental health in the life experiences of Americans, therefore, we will present a chapter devoted to the ways Americans cope with their everyday problems. The specialized focus on professional help-seeking will be examined in Book 2.*

SUBJECTIVE MENTAL HEALTH

In this volume, then, we first focus on the subjective mental health of the American people. The topics we discuss consist of different points of entry to people's experience of life, their evaluations of their own lives and adjustment:

Feelings and sources of well-being
Self-perceptions
Marriage
Parenthood
Work
Symptom patterns

This variety of topics deals not only with traditional assessments of psychological adjustment (e.g., feelings of well-being and symptoms of distress), but also reflects four special emphases that we and the authors of *Americans View Their Mental Health* gave to considering adjustment: a multiple-criteria approach, the analysis of psychological experience for positive as well as negative feelings, evaluation of the salience and experience in social roles, and measurement of people's psychological involvement with their own experience.

*References to Book 2 refer to *Mental Health in America* by Joseph Veroff, Richard Kulka, and Elizabeth Douvan (Basic Books, 1981), which is a companion volume to *The Inner American.*

The Multiple-Criteria Approach

First and most important, we adopted one of the suggestions made by Jahoda (1958) in her monograph which explored conceptions of mental illness and health for the Joint Commission that sponsored the 1957 study. She cogently argued that social scientists and psychiatrists should use not one but multiple criteria in evaluating mental health (which in our particular case, should be considered *subjective* mental health). People evaluate their own mental health in many different ways, not all of which are necessarily consistent. They can be very happy, but can experience some problems in raising their children. They can be very discontented in marriage, but generally be free of symptoms of anxiety or ill health. Different people may emphasize one or another of these criteria as being *the* critical issue in evaluating their own subjective mental health. We neither wanted to identify which was the *key* factor, nor develop any weighting procedures that would enable us to combine these factors into one overall assessment of subjective mental health. This decision makes our analyses very complex and our conclusions less pointed but, we assume, closer to reality.

There was also considerable pressure on the authors of the 1960 volume to come up with an epidemological assessment of the mental health in the population; some way to classify a given proportion of the population as being especially needy of psychological help given their evaluations of their own subjective adjustment. Those authors refrained from doing so, and we are following suit.

This was not the decision of the researchers in the well-known *Midtown* study (Srole et al., 1962) who had psychiatrists evaluate the mental-health status of respondents in a New York City residential sample. Psychiatrists judged the sickness or health of a sample of respondents in their survey through a personal interview. The pattern of responses in the larger survey interview that predicted the psychiatric evaluation was used as the index of mental-health status for the entire sample.

The strategy of the *Midtown* study can be seriously questioned. Blum's (1978) work shows that psychiatric evaluations in the 1950s depended on different criteria than parallel evaluations made in the 1970s. The concepts of mental illness and mental health held by psychiatrists and social scientists change. In different historical periods, different general concepts of psychological functioning, different attitudes toward which deviants should be institutionalized, different attitudes toward help seeking will all affect the rates of "disturbance" assessed by any technique proposed. Dohrenwend and Dohrenwend (1974) carefully present the accumulated evidence in researches purported to give an epidemiological portrayal of a society or a subgroup in a society and conclude that the methods used to assess mental health or illness are all biased one way or another. No clearer picture of this exists than in their own work, which shows that one ethnic group may report experiencing a symptom more than another not because they are *absolutely* more distressed, but because that symptom fits their general cultural style. The fact that more women than men report a high rate of physical and psychological symptoms of distress should not necessarily be read as greater overall disturbance in women. Women may find it more acceptable to perceive such symptoms in themselves.

Thus, we feel that the original strategy of using multiple criteria and avoiding any external or single overall criterion has been vindicated. We sometimes wish we had a single criterion for ease of presentation. Some of the tables in this book will overwhelm a reader who quickly wants to know how this country has changed from 1957 to 1976. There will be some consistent patterns in these tables; but for every consistent one, there will be exceptions, not all of which we can rationalize. Nevertheless, we feel that the complexity is warranted.

The Emphasis on Both Positive and Negative Experiences in Psychological Adjustment

In the 1960 volume, the authors used many measures, recurring in this volume, that asked people to think about their positive experiences. As examples, people are asked the following: what kinds of things make them happy; the nicest thing about their marriage and having children; their strong points. These questions are then coded for the type of positive feeling people have about life in general, marriage, their children, themselves. It is hard to read our analysis of the presence or absence of any one type of response as potential indicators of subjective mental illness, as one might read the reports of symptoms or being unhappy with life in general, or feeling inadequate about the way one is conducting one's marriage. Rather, responses to questions that asked people to depict their positive feelings tell us more about the presence or absence of certain sources of positive mental health, albeit in subjective terms. We can see whether a person mentions interpersonal sources of happiness, which we and others feel are paramount in overall positive feelings of adjustment. We can see whether or not a person can articulate positive feelings at all, which may be our best clue about whether he or she experiences life positively. In other words, we will continue to take Jahoda's advice and strive to portray aspects of *positive* subjective mental health along with aspects of *negative* subjective functioning.

The Analysis of the Salience and Experience of Social Roles

If there was a single general theoretical framework that implicitly shaped *Americans View Their Mental Health*, it was the traditional social-psychological emphasis on the importance of social roles. Not only did that perspective guide the areas assessed within the multiple-criteria approach, but it also shaped much of the analysis.

Each of three chapters of *Americans View Their Mental Health* is devoted to a different significant social role: marriage, parenthood, and work. Satisfactions, feelings of adequacy, problems experienced within each of these roles were assumed to be shaped not only by some stable core self that is more or less competent, unhappy, or unhealthy, but also by the person's interaction with expectations from others who define the role. A person's reference group helps shape what s/he is supposed to do or feel about work, marriage, or raising children. So do the specific people a worker shares a workplace with, the particular spouse a person shares bed and board with, the particular offspring a parent shares love, values, and income with. Roles as expectations from others are critical contributors to well-being and distress because self-identity does not exist in any clear way apart from the way s/he is embedded in these roles. Roles and the self are so intertwined that they are more often than not fused concepts. George Herbart Mead (1934) and Charles Cooley (1902) long ago introduced this way of thinking about the social self. It was implicitly part of the way the authors of *Americans View Their Mental Health* developed their measures of subjective experience. We will continue to use that framework, but even more explicitly. Our theoretical integration of results is essentially a role analysis.

In another way we will be even more explicit in the use of the role conceptualization for this volume. A major guiding strategy in *Americans View Their Mental Health* for analyzing how different subgroups of the population may differ in their feelings of adjustment and in their styles of coping with personal problems was to make systematic comparisons of men and women, as well as different age and educational groups. And again, more implicitly than explicitly, the authors of *Americans View Their Mental Health* interpreted the results within a framework consistent with a role analysis.

Differences between men and women in their reports of subjective mental health are easily interpretable as reflections of different expectations for men and women. We have already offered such an interpretation of their differential symptom reports.

We can offer similar interpretations of age and education differences. Since the 1960 volume, there has been a growing recognition that age differences in any psychological process may reflect how young and older people are conforming to age roles. Neugarten and Datan (1973) have given us such a sociological perspective on the life cycle. The so-called "mid-life crisis" may be an instance of psychological crisis generated not from long-term personal problems coming to a head at mid-life, but from people fulfilling expectations about personal upheaval and reevaluations at mid-life.

We will also find consistent education differences that are profitably interpreted as role differences. Particularly in our discussion of education differences in reports of marital difficulties, we will argue that the college educated belong to reference groups which emphasize relationship satisfactions in marriage, and that they differ from the less educated in this respect.

In structuring our questionnaire and in analyzing our data, we were heavily immersed in thinking of human experience within a role context. It therefore should be no surprise to find that much of our analysis of social change reflects the same thinking.

People's Psychological Involvement with Experience

Also woven into our analysis of change is still another way of thinking about subjective adjustment, one that the authors of the original volume explicitly used. They delineated it in this way:

> We are concerned not only with how positively or negatively a person evaluates different areas of his life—how "happy" he feels, how "satisfied" he is in his job, how positive or negative in his self-percept—but also in looking at these feelings in relation to the person's expectations and demands. In our descriptions of various demographic groups, we try to distinguish the contentment that is a concomitant of limited aspirations and demands of life from the gratification that represents the realization of maximal expectations, to distinguish the dissatisfaction which represents a lack of gratification in life from the tensions and problems that do not reflect any unusual deprivation but are rather a natural consequence of an investment and involvement in life. . . . (Gurin, Veroff, and Feld, 1960, p. 12)

Psychological involvement with one's experience was assumed to reflect positive mental health. This was a clear perspective in the 1960 study. Not only did the authors believe that people who have a psychological investment in their experiences are those who are ready to seek outside professional help—and they tend to be—but they also saw psychologically involved people as men and women who are committed to personal growth and self-actualization. These are goals of positive mental health that were just being articulated in the 1950s, but have become commonplace in the 1970s.

We will continue to analyze people's interpretations of their gratifications and frustrations in these terms. We will ask: are they using external or internal definitions of problems? Are they seeing psychological aspects of either strong points or weaknesses in their own selves? Are they reporting "ego"—or external—satisfactions or dissatisfactions with work? The psychological versus nonpsychological approach to one's experience is still an important distinction to make. It will be critical to our analysis of people's connections to their social roles and critical to our interpretation of social change. We hope, however, that in making this distinction about people's subjective experience, we can keep in mind that it is, after all, perhaps just one way of looking at life. It is a perspective that we find useful and meaningful, but is one that perhaps we, as psychologists, have been especially socialized to use in evaluating experiences. Although we will not blatantly state that people who view their own lives from the psychological vantage point are living fuller lives, perhaps this hidden assumption is implicitly woven into our analyses and interpretations.

COPING WITH PROBLEMS AND SOCIAL SUPPORT

When men and women experience distress, what do they do about it? How do they characterize their own ways of coping with problems in their daily lives? Some handle difficulties by forgetting about them; some pray; some try to take direct action or talk to family or friends about worries or unhappiness they encounter; some seek professional counsel. The last strategy will be the major focus of the second volume. The others will be topics of a major chapter in this volume and Book 2. In this book we will be interested in how people cope with problems and their social support as facets of their experience of well-being.

In the second volume, we will use the data on informal coping and social support to illuminate issues of formal help-seeking. Do people seek professional help because they do not have friends and family from whom to gain informal support? Or do people develop consistent styles of seeking counsel so that those who use professionals are also likely to talk to friends? Thus, in Book 2, we will use the information about coping and informal support to understand the context and alternatives to formal help-seeking.

There clearly are other steps besides consulting professionals that people take about their problems—whether they be seen as personal or situational—and the clearest and most commonly used alternative is to talk things over with a loved one or a friend. Another common problem-solving method is prayer. Another is to just forget about the source of strain and carry on as if everything were okay. We want to pay special attention to these coping strategies: how their use has changed in American life, and what such change tells us about shifts in the experiences of the people.

In social-scientific circles, there has arisen a widespread interest in informal social-support networks as a panacea for the isolation and general psychological difficulties that are presumed to have intensified over recent social history. How prevalent and extensive are these helping networks in people's everyday experience? In more religious circles, there would be more than casual interest in an analysis of the importance of prayer as a way to handle problems. Who uses this alternative? What psychological service does it seem to perform? How has its use increased or decreased over the generation? We will be examining these questions (and others) in some detail.

Social Change: 1957–1976

The comparative analysis of the two surveys presented in this book can be used to evaluate hypothesized directions of social psychological change in the general population. We use the plural "directions of social change" advisedly. As we have already noted, the subjective dimensions of adjustment in American society are multiple and are not necessarily perfectly correlated. We will find, for example, that Americans as a whole have become more aware of psychological support from friendships at the same time that they have become more clearly attuned to their own independence from others as a source of basic happiness. These results are not necessarily contradictory; as we shall see, they speak to different levels of adjustment.

Change occurring for one group may not occur for another. Our society is organized complexly. Differentiation in status or roles leads to differentiation in subjective experiences of adjustment. Men and women may well have reacted to the upheavals of the era between the 1950s and 1970s very differently. The renaissance of women's political consciousness forced men and women to become more polarized in the ways they structure experience, perhaps just as often as it forced them to become more alike. The college educated, and especially young people who were college educated in the 1960s and early 1970s might well have been just an avant garde that got considerable media publicity but who outside of the world of fashions and entertainment did little to lead other people in changing their ways of evaluating the quality of their lives.

There is another sense in which we will speak of changes. While we can most easily see change or stability in a direct social indicator like "happiness," "marital happiness," or "extent of worries," these are only the more readily apparent indices of change. A more subtle index is a change in how *one subjective indicator relates to another.*

For example, we will find that people who reported being "not too happy" in 1976 were much more optimistic about their future happiness than were comparable people in 1957. The result speaks of an important change in Americans' inner experience: people in the 1970s who were unhappy did not necessarily see that state as coloring their future; they could anticipate change. This result tells us a great deal about psychological changes in the significance of unhappiness in people's lives between 1957 and 1976.

Thus our assessment of change will not be as easily summarized or as neatly integrated as that of a social commentator who picks and chooses what is observed. We will see multiple changes, not always consistent, and not always apparent in all groups. We will see changes in *relationships* of measures we use. This will add considerable depth but also dizzying complexity to ready-made diagnoses of what has happened to American society.

What did we anticipate might change and what remain stable, and why? We can lay out only our very general preconceptions about the psychological milieu in the country that might have shifted sufficiently during the era in question to register a change in how people view their own lives. The analysis to follow develops in two stages: first, a brief presentation of some of the common assumptions about changes in American social character during the past era; and second, a preview of critical integrative themes that emerged from our analysis of change and stability from 1957 to 1976. We consider both the contents of people's psyches and how these contents depend on certain social facts about their lives.

SOME COMMON ASSUMPTIONS

Between 1957 and 1976, our culture underwent what can reasonably be described as a psychological revolution. The establishment of the joint commission which sponsored *Americans View Their Mental Health* was in itself a signal and symptom of the shift toward a psychological orientation in our culture. A congressional commission took on itself the task of assessing the psychological health and well-being of the American people! This act as well as the programs and policies launched in the wake of the commission's extensive series of studies and reports revealed, among other findings, a faith in mental-health services, a belief that psychological well-being could be reasonably assessed, and that psychological technology (i.e., mental-health services), properly applied, could increase well-being. This sanguine assertion by Congress may not have initiated the "therapeutic age," but it certainly signaled the fact that this new era was abroad in our world.

Other signs of the psychological revolution have been noted and documented by sociologists and historians. Child raising, which had always been permissive in America compared to Europe, took a new turn after the Second World War. Women were attracted back to full-time work in the home (from their work in the market world where they had gone to help the war effort) by the prospect of raising perfect children (Slater, 1976). Impelled by this goal and the advice of child-raising experts, women sought to mold children's attitudes and motives to a degree previously unheard of. Where in earlier times parents sought obedience/compliance from children and left their internal psychological world alone, they now aimed at creating the attitudes and motives that would lead the child to behave properly on the basis of her/his own desires. They invested the child with "potential" and took the goal of socialization to be the realization of that unique potential. The child was invested with unique value, and to a real degree, the world (and primarily the world of the family) was to be judged by the criterion of realizing or releasing that value.

This system led inevitably, according to Philip Slater and others, to a significant gap between generations, reflecting in the younger generation a shift away from allegiance to institutions and forms toward the significant investment of individuals and feelings.

> For any generation born before World War II, rituals, ceremonies, and social institutions have an inherent validity that makes them intimidating—a validity that has priority over human feelings. One would hesitate to disrupt a serious social occasion for even the most acute and fateful need, unless it could be justified in social rather than personal terms. Doris Lessing and Shelley Berman have both observed (in the case of people confronted with aircraft whose integrity has been cast in doubt) that most people would die quietly rather than make a scene.
>
> Many younger people no longer share this allegiance. They don't see social occasions as having automatic validity—social formality is deferred to only when human concerns aren't pressing. Stoicism is not valued. Thirty years ago, on the other hand, a well-brought-up young man like the hero of *The Graduate* would have stood passively watching while his personal disaster took place. Cinematic comedy often made use of this meek deference—think of the cops-and-robbers chases in which both participants would briefly interrupt their frantic efforts in order to stand at attention while flag or a funeral procession passed by.
>
> This change was responsible both for the character of radical protest in the sixties and for the angry responses of older people to it. Sitting-in at a segregated restaurant, occupying a campus building, lying down in front of vehicles, pouring blood in office files—all depended heavily on a willingness to make a scene and not be intimidated by a social milieu. And this was precisely what so enraged older people. They were shocked not so much by the radicalism of young people as by their bad form. That students could be rude to a public figure was more shocking to parents than that the public figure was sending their children to their deaths in an evil cause. (Slater, 1976, pp. 63–64)

Finally we can contrast themes which dominated social criticism in the periods of our two surveys. David Riesman et al.'s *The Lonely Crowd* (1950) struck the keynote of the fifties—that Americans had become slavish conformers who guided their behavior by the expectations of others, hoping thereby to win approval, to "fit in." By 1976, on the other hand, we had become, in Christopher Lasch's view a "culture of narcissism" (1979). While both of these theses contrasted contemporary society with the golden age of the Victorian era when men were men and behavior was dictated by strong moral principles internalized during childhood and operating autonomously through individual conscience and standards of taste, the pass we had come to, according to the two visions, differ dramatically. According to Riesman, in the 1950s we had become too social, guided by the compass of social norms; in Lasch's view by the 1970s we didn't care at all about social norms and were entirely preoccupied with looking out for "Number 1." While American social criticism tends to the hyperbolic, these assertions undoubtedly picked up and reflected themes that had some base in reality. Though they may have relied too heavily on and generalized too widely from observations of special groups in the population (particularly intellectuals and the media elites), both Riesman and Lasch were probably on the trail of something real.

At least some thoughtful critics would see the two themes as stages of a single process: secularization. When religious authority waned, the autonomous, well-internalized moral code no longer served to guide behavior. The individual, then, looked to others for direction, and finally, recognizing the relativity of all judgment, came to measure all things by their ability to provide individual gratification, narcissistic pleasure. Family historians described a parallel process in the relation between family and the larger society; whereas in Colonial America family and state were integrated closely, the public and private aspects of life deeply interpenetrating and family life accessible to public scrutiny, by the nineteenth century, an adversarial, compensatory relation between the two spheres had become dominant. The world was now cast as a dangerous, competitive jungle, and the private family world a protective haven that held all that was warm, supportive, moral, and sustaining. It may then be, as one observer notes, that the family has taken a further move in this line of development:

> [The family] is no longer seen as a compensatory institution, but as a community whose end is the support, the fulfillment, and the health and satisfaction of its individual members. The family no longer serves mainly to nurture the citizen, the religious person, or even the economic person. It is there to serve "psychological man"—persons who are "born to be pleased." ... Therapeutic values are privatistic values, and they are probably even anti-institutional. This may be an era, according to some observers, when individuals will be experiencing their families increasingly as a burden—as a network of responsibilities, roles, and traditions that can be tedious, boring, and inhibiting. (Orr, 1980, p. 380)

The problem with much of this social criticism and prediction is that it is based on limited information; it is a problem of generalization. Facts are observed correctly: the divorce rate has increased; women have left families in order to realize their individual talents or needs; the best-seller lists are dominated by books on self-improvement, personal growth, narcissistic preoccupation. But the facts are then interpreted too broadly, accorded a centrality and power in the broad population which they may in fact hold only for a part, for a highly articulate, "leading," powerful subgroup—but a subgroup all the same.

Our analyses of two national studies permit us to depict broad changes in American society with considerable confidence; they also permit us to isolate phenomena occurring only in certain social groups. As we approach these analyses, we can preview some of the general themes about social-psychological changes in the American population that occurred between 1957 and 1976. We will also describe changes that are especially characteristic of one group or another.

SOME CENTRAL THEMES ABOUT SOCIAL CHANGE

Reduced Social Integration

A central theme of the book concerns what we judge to be a *reduced integration of American adults into the social structure.* Social organization, social norms, the adaptation to and successful performance of social roles all seem to have lost some of their power to provide people with meaning, identity elements, satisfaction. In fact, role and status designations have become objects of suspicion, as Slater suggests. The feminist movement objects to the use of "Miss" and "Mrs." as titles, pointing to the fact that marital status is used in a nonsymmetrical way to define women but not men. Ths use of status titles like Doctor or Professor, and inquiry about the vocation/profession of an individual on first encounter are considered bad form, somehow contravening genuine response to and interest in the core of the person so designated or questioned. Any allusion to status is taken as a preoccupation with status and a disregard for personal, egalitarian, human values. Reflecting an interest in what a person does (in the vocational realm) is taken as preoccupation with status and a disinterest in the authentic, the essential, the personal qualities and style of that person.

This reduced tie to the structural givens of the social order represents a potential psychological loss. Knowing what a person does can reveal a good deal of information about the personal organization, the essential and authentic aspects of a person. Knowing that a man works in a factory will not tell you whether he is gathering material for a book on automation or earning money to support a passion for painting, or never thought about work except as a means of earning a living. But it will tell something about his organization of life and experience and will open the door to further questions which may reveal more telling aspects of himself. Knowing that a woman is a physician, an inventor, or a professor of French literature will reveal more and more detailed information about her, and not only about prestige and wealth. Since Veblen's time, the connection between what people do for forty or more hours a week in work and the ways in which they will structure perception, knowledge, meaning, and relationships has been noted and studied by social scientists of various disciplines and persuasions. If a man spends most of his waking, attending hours thinking of human beings as resources to be deployed in the winning of wars, or as objects to be manipulated in the service of business profit, this activity will in all likelihood influence the way in which he relates to his children, his wife, his friends. What a person does is related to what he is—in his core.

The paradoxical truth is that disregard for status, which is urged as a counterthrust to formalism and status consciousness out of desire to reduce obstacles to close interaction between people, actually *increases* distance between people by insisting that they turn inward for the derivation of meaning and self-definition, by placing the burden of self-definition entirely on the individual—and making it a matter of individual achievement rather than a consensual and shared reality. No longer do we allow the individual to derive some of his sense of self and legitimacy from a position in a social structure. Rather, he must rediscover meaning in the spring of his individual detached self each day. Individual achievement becomes the whole story, and it urges distance from rather than connections to structure or to others.

None of this is to deny that preoccupation with status can be dehumanizing. The person who can see others only as representatives of status categories, who cannot see or relate to the personhood, the reality of a secretary or plumber or grocery clerk, or refers to "my little seamstress" or "little butcher," surely dehumanizes those others with whom s/he interacts. If *all* we ask is what people do in the occupational world, we fail to know them. If we *judge* people by the criterion of status, we lose the color and richness of human personality.

But the misuse of knowledge does not contradict its validity. Status, position in a social structure, connections to groups and to other people are all valid and informing and have traditionally signified meaning to the individual and to others about the individual's self. People do not play roles in quite the way that the implied analogy to theater conveys. We play roles, but our roles also enter—and alter—our selves. In a real sense, we *become* our roles, not just to an audience but also to ourselves. Aspects of the self which are role-derived (an American, a painter, a husband and father) are no less authentic and are usually more central to self-definition than those aspects based on extra-role dimensions (tall, nearsighted, melancholy, cheerful). They are aspects of the self, and they are facts of interest to anyone who would know the self.

When status and roles are discredited as legitimate information about people, as we believe they increasingly are in our society, they lose their meaning and their capacity to lend meaning to people's own lives and self-definitions. When being a doctor carried connotations of humanity and generosity, position in the community, respect and trust, as well as wealth, authority, and achievement, a man's whole self-definition was marked and relatively settled by accession to that role. It satisfied many needs, including the need to feel legitimate and accepted as fully adult in the community of adults. Today the role of physician has lost much of this defining force. Being a doctor ensures income and envy, but little else. While the medical profession itself has contributed to this breakdown in meaning and prestige by a single-minded pursuit of self-interest, broader movements in the culture questioning the validity of status and roles as sources of meaningful information have also loosened the hinges on the system of meaning. In earlier eras, the doctor who turned poet or novelist was a curiosity, an oddity in his rareness. Today doctors become writers, but they also become real estate investors, congressmen, financiers. Whereas being a doctor was formerly assumed to carry meaning enough for a lifetime, today, for many men, it carries meaning for perhaps fifteen years, after which point they are likely to look for other sources, other goals.

The role of physician is an extreme one. It requires long preparation and is thus an unusual test of the reduction in significance attached to any role. On the other hand, it is also a position with very large financial rewards which on the one hand act as adhesive but also offer wide freedom to choose. Affluence allows choices which are not possible when people must work hard simply to survive.

What about other work roles and roles outside of the occupational sphere entirely? Have they also suffered an attrition in meaning? As we shall see in our analyses, we have to conclude that they have, although perhaps not as profoundly as the popular press would lead us to believe. They are no longer adult roles which are acquired and settled and then automatically give one meaning and stability. They depend on performance and achievement, and they have lost their implication of permanence, their unidirectional conferring of adult status and identity elements.

There are paradoxical consequences for the subjective experiences of people in a social system in which the binding power of roles has been diluted. On the one hand, there is a larger freedom to work out a legitimate life without conforming to rigid prescription or without comparing one's efforts to overidealized standards that so often demoralize. On many counts, Americans now feel better about themselves because they are more self-reliant and less dependent on social rules. On the other hand, the comforts of the social system are also given up when social roles lose their moral force. Although we obviously have not given up all role demands—or else we could no longer exist in a cooperative society—we have given up some easy rules that would guarantee legitimacy among those we know and among those we do not know. Without these easy guarantees, we have become a somewhat more anxious people. We see more problems in many parts of our lives. As many people have learned, it is often difficult to discover the authentic self. Freedom from a constraining authority often becomes a burden; the freedom to choose often a haunting personal problem.

An Increased Search for Intimacy

Related to this thinning of the social commitment and social investment, we note an increased sensitivity to interpersonal relations—a desire for friendship, warm relationships at work and in the family, a desire for personal impact in everyday encounters. In all of the major life
roles we looked at—work, marriage, and parenthood—respondents in
1976 stress interpersonal aspects in their definitions and in describing
their satisfactions, problems, and inadequacies. The search for satisfying warm relationships which was primarily a feature of middle-class,
educated life in 1957 has spread more broadly in 1976.

Men, in particular, seem to have suffered a loss of meaning from this
shift in cultural emphasis from social integration and role performance
to interpersonal and individual sources of meaning. The traditional
male role depended critically on status differentiation, role performance, legitimate authority—more so than the traditional female role.
Head of household, ultimate authority, breadwinner, and worker all
took their meaning and criteria for performance from their integration
into a structured set of reciprocal roles. They carried status, power, and
the implication of uniqueness. As authority has come more and more to
be questioned and challenged, it no longer comes automatically with a
particular position, but must be achieved and legitimized on the basis
of performance. As a result, people—and men in particular—began to
emphasize more personal needs in their relationships with others. A
search for intimacy was launched by a people who had traditionally
depended on interaction rituals to guide their behavior and feelings.
This happened both in the workplace and in the family.

At work, many forces coalesce to reduce the automatic meaning for
men in attaining a secure job. Women and minorities have entered the
boardroom as well as the factory. While occupational segregation is
still a dominant pattern, these previously marginal groups assert their
right to an equal share of any work. Given recent history and their successes, however restricted, even the highest levels of managerial and
professional jobs are less immune to the possibility of democratization.
Dominant majority males must lose some measure of their assured
uniqueness at work.[2] For women and minorities, on the other hand, the
yielding of traditional discriminatory barriers has opened up new
fields and contributed new stimulus for work aspirations which up to

[2] This sense of uniqueness based on history and experience is still commonly assumed
by white males in high administrative positions. When a women's delegation asks to
have women candidates considered for these jobs, they are patiently lectured about the
difficulties attending such consideration: women simply do not have the experience that
would make them reasonable candidates. One administrative officer naïvely expressed
his view of the problem more directly at a dinner party. He turned to the chief financial
officer of the university and asked with palpable disbelief "Can you imagine a woman or
black doing your job?" The fact that a black woman administrator was present apparently
did not strike him as contradicting his view; but surely if three or four marginal types
had been present, he would not have assumed its obviousness.

now would have been impossible fantasies. The promise of meaningful work, opportunities for advancement, and material rewards commensurate with talent and effort leaven the work motivation and achievement strivings of the disadvantaged. Our data yield evidence of the meaningfulness of work to women that is not so clearly shared by men. For many women, even those who start working to meet the needs of a family, merely assuming the role of worker contributes to a sense of resourcefulness that compensates for problems experienced on the job.

Other forces have contributed to the questioning of uniqueness in work for majority males. The counterculture movement of the sixties mounted a frontal assault on the work ethic. The term "workaholic" entered our vocabulary. Sons of workaholics rejected the "rat race" and confronted their parents with the irony that they had won the world but lost their own children. These young men swore that they would not trade life for financial success.

The development of social-welfare policy slipped one more support from under the work ethic. If welfare legislation, insurance programs, and workmen's compensation provide for minimal subsistence without work, then clearly work is not necessary for survival. And welfare—traditionally associated with the poor and degraded—became just another source of income as graduate students applied for food stamps. The shock and anger expressed by high officials and professionals at the idea of welfare for "able-bodied" persons, must surely stem in part from the threat they experience to their core values. If one can survive without work, how then justify their sixty hours a week at activities they claim (and truly feel in many cases) to find burdensome and unfulfilling?

If work has lost savor for many men, some of its automatic payoff in the sense of a unique contribution and significant impact, what then? Within the workplace itself, an emphasis on relationships developed. No small factor in this focus was the intensification of the bureaucratic organization of most people's work. More jobs required that people negotiate a web of hierarchical distinctions that were very unreal. The popularity of the T-group and sensitivity training in the 1960s originated in the resocialization of managers often embedded in a tangle of overbureaucratized organizations. Neophytes in focusing their attention on the interpersonal life, men approached their search for meaning in relationships as they did everything else. They objectified it as a commodity, a skill that could be packaged and taught to consumers hungry for interpersonal meaning. This approach only made matters worse for many people. We will find in our data that there is a growing dissatisfaction with the nature of interpersonal relationships at work.

If the workplace itself is inadequate for most people's search for intimacy, interpersonal exchange in family life may offer an alternative in which people can find meaning and validate their sense of significance. The family arena had gone through its own disruptions, as we noted earlier, and these disruptions often accentuated the search for intimacy. In addition, the nature of family life made it a far easier arena for people's search for closeness and impact than the workplace.

The shift in the meaning of family roles occurred over a fairly brief period of our recent social history. Returning from World War II, chastened about the possibilities of personal influence in the larger world of affairs, American men—and the women they married—launched an era of familism and family building in reaction to their loss of hope for significant influence on the world. If they lacked the hope to affect congressional decisions, they could still hope to influence their children and the local school board. Men and women at the end of the 1940s and 1950s launched the baby boom and reinforced traditional concepts of sex roles. Both were severely questioned in the late 1960s and 1970s.

Gratifications automatically generated from being the authoritative breadwinner/husband/father fell apart during the period between our two studies. The feminine mystique as a guide for mothers and wives was clearly demystified. The role of breadwinner was soon shared, and the husband/father could not assume a *unique* contribution in this role. As wives assumed a greater economic role in family support, they acquired more equal power in family decision making as well. Decisions became subject to more negotiation and debate, and the traditional pattern of unquestioned authority associated with both the father's and the husband's role yielded to a more interactive, shared authority. Wives who may once have wielded subtle feminine power on significant family choices came to expect direct participation.

Power and authority no longer automatically redound to those who parent—the positions of father or mother, the head-of-household, the final authority—all have lost the element of power ascription. Children have come to expect rationalized authority and the possibility of participating in decisions. Evaluation of performance and satisfaction in parenting have increasingly come to depend on the development of warm interpersonal relationships with one's children. It is not enough for a man to support his children and see that they obey him and learn to live by society's rules. It is not enough for women to say to their children, "Be nice." They have to justify their demands. Mothers have learned to listen harder for their child's idiosyncratic feelings and goals in their desire to raise ideal children. Both fathers and mothers have come to want and need warm relationships with their children and to feel inadequate without them. Love and warmth form the new basis for socializing children—the basis to substitute for the unquestioned authority which previously came with the role of parent. Men and women now feel guilty if they get angry with their children.

As family roles have undergone this transformation they have become fertile arenas for people's search for intimacy, particularly for men who have found their newly generated interpersonal goals largely unfulfilled at the workplace. The emphasis on relationship issues in fathers' and mothers' discussions of parenting and in husbands' and wives' discussions of marriages is one of the clearest trends we see in our study.

Experts perceptive of the changes we have been discussing tell men—and men feel on their own—that they will succeed as fathers to the extent that they develop warm, close, "meaningful" relationships with their children. But who is resocializing them with the skills they need to realize such relationships—skills in openness to feelings and fantasy, skills in self-disclosure and emotional sharing, the capacity to play, ease and expressiveness? Most of today's adult males were not taught such skills as they were growing up. They interacted within traditional authority-based families with fathers who were themselves models of task orientation and emotional repression. The only experience of fathering they know from their own lives is one specifically designed to make them emotionally retentive and interpersonally cool, inept in all the behaviors now asked of them in the contemporary ideal of the warm, sharing, expressive father.

In school and the peer group rewards attached to "manliness," toughness, and competitive achievement. The stress on competitive achievement—which trains young men to keep their eyes on the golden ring or main chance and to leave their feelings at home—urges them to see themselves and other people as objects to be used in the scramble to succeed. These pressures simply reinforce all of the qualities which inhibit warm, emotional, expressive, and sharing interaction with their own children.

So we find that men are sensitive to the interpersonal criteria of parenthood, they want warm relationships with their children, but they feel that such relationships elude them. The lack of warmth and closeness with their children is what men think of most often when asked what kinds of problems they have had with their children and what inadequacies they have experienced in the parent role. They don't refer to warm, loving relationships as often as mothers do when they are asked in the surveys to think of the "nicest things about having children" or the ways in which "having children change(s) a person's life."

The Increasing Dependence of Men on the Institution of Marriage

What do men do with all of their unmet needs for interpersonal warmth? With both work and parenthood somehow falling short of providing these needs, where do they turn? Predictably— and entirely in keeping with traditional expectations of "masculine" behavior, they look to marriage for the warmth and expressiveness they fail to find (or develop) in the rest of their lives. Men look to their wives for warmth, nurturance, emotional sharing, expressiveness. Many adult men in our society experience emotional expressiveness only vicariously through the expressiveness of the women in their lives. When asked in the surveys how they handle problems, worries, or periods of unhappiness, married men often talk about the support they experience *only* from their wives. The wife represents the only resource short of formal help. Women—whether married or unmarried—have more informal resources to use in troubled times. When asked whether they are close enough to friends or relatives to talk over problems and troubles with them, men—more than women—say that they are not so close.

This series of themes reflecting men's needs for warm interpersonal relationships, their inability to satisfy such needs at work or in their parenting functions, and their exclusive reliance on marriage as an arena for emotional sharing and satisfaction of needs for interpersonal warmth and expressiveness—casts light on statistical data about marriage and divorce. It clarifies findings that seem to indicate that marriage is more crucial to the health and well-being of men than women and that men almost always remarry after divorce or widowhood. If marriage provides the only access to warmth and emotional statisfaction, it is both highly desirable and salutary to people's experience of life.

But this emphasis may also place an impossible burden on a single relationship, and in this sense it may contribute heavily to increased divorce rates. If men need so much and are so undeveloped in the skills of interpersonal sharing and emotional expressiveness, they may ask too much and give too little to support marriage. It is not surprising that in the 1976 survey more wives than husbands say that they wish their spouse understood them better and shared more of their thoughts and feelings.

During the early days of the recent women's movement, a good deal was said about women's vicarious living. Women were seen as depending on their husbands and children for vicarious realization of achievement needs and success experience. Our data reveal that men also use marriage vicariously to experience warmth and expressiveness. As women have moved into the occupational world and experienced achievement directly, they may have less need to use marriage for vicarious achievement. And they may be less available and willing to supply their husbands' needs for vicarious experience of emotionality. The symbiosis which had served mutual expression has been unhinged and dislocated.

A General Increase in Taking a Psychological Orientation to Experience

The increased orientation toward interpersonalism in work and family roles, the diminution of the importance of roles, can be seen as part of a broader cultural change, the introduction of the "era of psychology." The 1957 report spoke of a psychological orientation, as distinguished from material or moral orientations, and suggested that this way of looking at life experiences and life problems might increase significantly in the future.

By 1976 we have evidence that this shift had indeed occurred. In all areas covered by the studies, psychological orientation is palpably greater in 1976 than it was in 1957. American people are more likely to frame their satisfactions, problems, and inadequacies in psychological and relational terms—whether they speak of work or marriage or parenthood. In 1976 they less often attribute inadequacies or satisfactions to external and material conditions. They less often externalize problems and less often attribute blame. The psychological and interpersonal orientation, which was almost exclusively a characteristic of the highly educated in 1957, had become common coin by 1976.

Methods

DESIGN OF THE INTERVIEW SCHEDULE

The 1976 interview schedule appears as appendix A. Wherever possible, the exact wording of questions and structure of interviewing from the 1957 schedule were retained on the 1976 schedule. The first schedule followed the researchers' interest in obtaining multiple assessments of multiple areas of subjective well-being and ways of handling problems. The flow of questions was from general open-ended feelings of well-being in the first part[3] to more specific topics relevant to mental health and help seeking toward the end. Every section of the interview was designed for the same funneling from general questions to very specific ones. Furthermore, very personal questions (such as probing for things about a person's marriage that are "not quite as nice as you would like them to be" were cushioned by asking for positive responses first (such as the "nicest things" about the person's marriage).

The funneling procedure means that responses to open-ended questions about well-being are not influenced by the content of more specific questions. Researchers can never totally control the bias that inevitably exists in the order of questioning, but funneling over the entire interview from very general to very specific mental-health ques-

---

[3] The study was introduced as a study of modern living. The very first questions are quite neutral in both studies: inquiries about use of leisure time and socializing. For a random two-thirds of the sample in both years, a story-telling procedure designed to measure human motives (Veroff, Atkinson, Feld, and Gurin, 1960) intervened between these questions and the first ones asking about general feelings of well-being (worries, happiness, etc.). The story-telling procedure is neutral. Most people enjoy it. It is rationalized to the respondents as a measure of how people interpret situations as they come up in everyday life.

tions and funneling within a given topic from open-ended to specific questions maximizes the validity of spontaneous responses.

Obviously people may be defensive in response to questions that ask them to evaluate their own lives. The strategy of using multiple assessments, besides conforming to the multiple-criteria approach, helps us estimate how much defensiveness may be operating. We would expect some correlation between multiple measures of adjustment in a given area. If one type of question provoked too much defensiveness, we would be alerted to it from its pattern of relationship with other measures. There should be some convergent validity.

To offset defensiveness, we asked some questions in written form when it was clear that respondents could read and use a checklist. This was true for the symptoms and for certain personal questions asked about marriage on the 1976 survey (see appendix A, question D4).

The many open-ended questions are unique to a national survey of this kind and permit us to evaluate the spontaneous reactions of people to general questions about their lives. What a difference it makes to ask someone "What are some of the things you're not too happy about these days?" in contrast to offering them a 5-point scale to evaluate how unhappy they are about a variety of features of their lives. Many people would tell us they were unhappy about their work situation if we asked them specifically about it, but it comes up infrequently as a spontaneous source of unhappiness. We believe the latter may be closer to the phenomenology of unhappiness.

Because they were irrelevant to some of the mental-health issues of the 1970s, some of the questions asked in the 1957 survey were not reported in the 1976 questionnaire. In spite of lack of clarity, other questions of 1957 were retained for the 1976 survey because they were so important to our evaluation of change. For example, one of the 1957 symptom items, "Do you ever drink more than you should?" is very ambiguous, but we did not change it because we wanted comparative information.

New questions were devised for the 1976 survey after consultation with social scientists about the topics about subjective well-being or styles of coping with problems that were absent from the 1957 survey and should be included in the 1976 even if no comparison between the two survey years would be possible. Our inclusion of questions about help seeking for situational crises (appendix A, questions M7–M10) is the most important example of this new type of question. Another example is a set of items designed to assess feelings of depression (appendix A, question D4). As these new questions are introduced in discussion, they will be presented in detail.

THE INTERVIEWING SITUATION

The procedures in these two studies followed the standard ones used by the Survey Research Center. Interviewers have a backlog of experience on other surveys; they are permanent employees who are enlisted for different surveys as they come up. Most of them are women (97 percent), white (87 percent) and over thirty-four years of age (87 percent). The typical interviewer is thus a white middle-aged woman. They are trained to convey a sense of legitimacy to the process, and they are given further legitimacy by a letter that precedes their direct contact for an interview. While critics can raise questions about what self-presentations men have to fashion when being interviewed by a woman, even more questions can be raised about such self-presentation to a male interviewer when questions focus on personal problems and distress. There might be reason to think that a female interviewer will elicit more honest responses to such questions. Especially in 1976, there was an effort to match black interviewers with predominantly black sampling areas.

All interviewers are provided with question-by-question instructions which inform them of special probing that may be required for a given question or special answers to make to a respondent's questions about a particular item; they are also intended to help establish a working alliance between the interviewer and the researchers.

While regional conferences were held throughout the country for all the interviewers involved in the 1957 survey, only a conference at the University of Michigan was held for the field supervisors in the 1976 survey. The personal nature of this survey was new to interviewers in 1957; by 1976, they were used to asking personal questions. Both sets of interviewers were impressed with the unusual value of the survey; the interviewers for the new (1976) survey were especially aware of the potential to assess social change. Consequently, rapport among the interviewers themselves was good, and judging from the answers to a questionnaire sent to respondents after the interview, we conclude that rapport between interviewers and respondents was perhaps higher than it is in the standard Survey Research Center interview. Outright refusal to be interviewed in 1957 was 9 percent of the designated sample. This figure nearly doubled by 1976 and reflects the general trend in the population to be more reluctant to participate in any interview. All surveys in the 1970s encountered this problem. We will discuss this issue in more detail in the section on sampling.

As a way to introduce the interview, the following statement was read to respondents in both 1957 and 1976:

> The Survey Research Center has been asked to make a study of the stresses and strains of modern living. There have been a lot of changes in our way of

living over the past fifty years or so. These changes have brought this country to the highest standard of living in the world. But a great many people are concerned about whether or not there are problems involved in the rapid pace of our present life. Doctors, educators, religious leaders, and other experts are interested in finding out how people feel about this question.

Of course, this interview is completely voluntary. If we should come to any question you don't want to answer, let me know and we'll skip over it. I think you'll find the questions interesting and will want to give them careful thought.

It is of some interest that the same preparatory set was as applicable in 1976 as it was in 1957.

Interviewing for both studies occurred during the summer months and during years where many people were conscious of an economic recession. The economic outlook for 1957 and 1976 was not exactly comparable, but the general moods reflect depressed phases of the economic cycle.

Only a handful of interviews were cut short because of the unusual length for a national survey interview; the average length was ninety minutes. There might have been a slightly higher refusal rate in the two studies compared to other national surveys because of the length of the interview. When respondents heard the anticipated amount of time required for interviewing, they may have been slightly more prone to refuse in both 1957 and 1976. We have no way to tell how many nonresponses were outright refusals to be interviewed because of time or general unwillingness. The respondents did note in their postinterview questionnaire that the interview was lengthy but most found it interesting, probably because of its personal nature. In an effort to make the interview shorter, we confined certain more exploratory questions to only two-thirds of the sample. The same procedure was used in 1957. In all but a few cases, the questions discussed in this report are those asked of the total population. Exceptions are indicated as they appear in the tabulations.

SAMPLING

The national samples interviewed for the two studies were drawn by a multistage probability area design (see Kish and Hess, 1965).[4] This procedure identifies primary sampling points within the coterminus United States. These consist of standard metropolitan areas, single counties, and certain county groups within each region of the country.

[4] Details are available in appendix 3. Note that the sampling standard error is somewhat larger than conventional ones because a study of this sort is based upon a multistage area sampling design as opposed to simple random sampling. The design effect for this survey is minimal; the ratio of variances of the complex to the simple random sampling is close to one.

Successive subdivisions of these sampling points are conducted in keeping with the sampling probabilities proportionate to their populations initially, and with equal probabilities in the final stages. At the last stages, addresses are identified and selected; finally, a single household resident among eligible members is chosen randomly to be interviewed. No substitutions are permitted.

Since the sampling procedure restricts the survey to private households, it excludes the following people: residents of military establishments, hospitals, educational, penal and religious institutions, hotels, larger rooming houses, logging and lumber camps. Thus we omit from our sample a great many people who are transient and probably a good many who would select responses to our questionnaire that would be indicative of considerable distress.

For the initial survey, 84 percent of the designated respondents were successfully interviewed; for the 1976 survey, 71 percent were interviewed. This reduced rate is a serious problem. When the original study was made, national surveys had remarkably small nonresponse rates. By 1976, however, all surveys were having significant problems meeting those standards. In our case, nonresponse rate comes close to being intolerable. When response rates get over 20 or 25 percent, the representativeness of the sample must be questioned. While we will analyze our sample against census data and find that the sample does not deviate radically from the population on critical demographic factors, in the final analysis we cannot reassure ourselves completely of the sample's representativeness because the variables on which it is most likely to deviate are ones which are not measured by the census.

All surveys are now in serious trouble. Our world has changed in many ways which militate against the household survey's success. Americans have become much less trusting and open with strangers, and, even more important, most American households are deserted during the daytime hours ordinarily used to interview or at least to contact households and arrange interview appointments. With wives and mothers at work, no one is home to be contacted. And evening hours when respondents are more likely to be at home are not the most desirable times for interviewers to be alone on the streets or making first approaches unannounced to strange households. Nonresponses have been found most frequently in densely populated metropolitan centers. The nonresponse rate for New York City in the 1976 survey was 40 percent. It was 55 percent in Los Angeles. Refusals also tend to come more often from these same areas. More older than younger people refuse to be interviewed. And people living alone often refuse to be interviewed.

The problem is formidable and, in light of these changes in the culture, the decision of many survey research workers to shift from personal face-to-face interviews to telephone surveys is understandable.

TABLE 1.1
Comparison of Respondent Characteristics of the 1976 Study Sample with the 1978 Current Population Survey Estimate of the United States Population

Respondent Characteristic	1976 Study Sample		1976 Current Population Survey Estimate of United States Population[a] (%)
	Unweighted Sample (%)	Weighted[b] Sample (%)	
Sex			
Women	58	56	53
Men	42	44	47
	100%	100%	100%
Age			
21–24	11	11	11
25–34	25	25	23
35–44	17	17	17
45–54	14	16	17
55–64	15	16	15
65 and over	18	15	17
	100%	100%	100%
Race			
White	86	87	88
Black	11	10	10
Marital Status[c]			
Married, Separated	67	74	72
Single	11	11	14
Widowed	14	9	9
Divorced	8	6	5
	100%	100%	100%
Regions[d]			
New England	6	6	6
Middle Atlantic	15	16	18
East N. Central	18	18	19
West N. Central	10	11	8
South Atlantic	15	15	16
East S. Central	8	7	6
West S. Central	11	10	10
Mountain	3	3	4
Pacific	14	14	13
	100%	100%	100%
Education[e]			
Grade school	19	18	21
Some high school	15	15	15
High-school graduate	34	35	36
Some college	17	16	13
College graduate	15	16	15
	100%	100%	100%
Household Income			
Under 3,000	8	—[f]	8
3,000–4,999	10	—	10
5,000–6,999	9	—	9
7,000–9,999	14	—	12
10,000–14,999	21	—	19
15,000–24,999	26	—	27
25,000 and over	12	—	15
	100%	—	100%

[a] Unless otherwise noted, the U.S. population figures are for adults twenty-one years and over, which matches the age range of the 1976 study sample for sex, age, race, and region; the CPS data came from the July 1976 Current Population Surveys. For marital status and education, they came from the March 1976 survey. For household income, the estimate was from March 1977 FPS because at that time this was the respondent's estimated family income for "the previous year" and thus would overlap with the family income estimates for our survey which asked for estimates of "this year."

[b] Weighted by number of eligible respondents in the dwelling unit.

[c] CPS Data for persons twenty years and over.

[d] Excluding Alaska and Hawaii.

[e] Data for persons twenty-five years and over in all estimates.

[f] It is not appropriate to weight Household Income by the number of eligible respondents in the household, or dwelling unit.

We conducted analyses of our sample in comparison to 1976 Current Population Survey[5] data and have assured ourselves that the sample in the 1976 study does not deviate grossly from these census data in any of the critical social characteristics for which comparisons can be made: sex, age, race, marital status, region, education, and family income. Details of these comparisons are presented in table 1.1.

CODING

The choice of highly detailed, elaborate coding schemes for open questions in 1957 stood us in good stead when the 1976 coding began. For example, there were fifty-five coding distinctions drawn in the coding of the responses to "What are some of the things you feel pretty happy about these days?" Had a different choice been made in 1957— for example, for more abstract, general, or inclusive code categories, the problem of comparability of coding in the two studies would have been considerably more thorny and would have required specific training to ensure that coders could reproduce the judgments made in 1957. In the scoring of motives from projective responses, we *did* face this problem and accordingly employed special training procedures (Veroff, Depner, Kulka, and Douvan, 1980).

But in coding the interview questions, coders could follow the detailed categorization scheme established in 1957 with no apparent difficulties or problems. The specificity of the code designations assured comparability over time as well as high intercoder agreement.

In all open questions, the code provided a general "other" category for responses that could not be fitted into one of the more specific categories. Whenever an answer was thus coded, the answer was recorded verbatim on a card. In those instances where "other" cards accumulated in unusual numbers, we perused them carefully to see whether new categories could be formed to accommodate frequent answers. And in a few cases, new categories clearly emerged from the 1976 interviews. Some answers were common enough in 1976 to warrant a category that had not been necessary in 1957.

One example (and there were only a handful of such cases in all) will illustrate this situation. In answer to a question about problems respondents had encountered in raising their children, a new response category was necessary to accommodate answers about the special problems of raising children without the help of a father. The increased number of female single-adult households in 1976 has clearly raised the incidence of such problems to the point where we needed a category that had not been apparent or necessary in 1957.

[5] The Current Population Survey, carried out monthly by the Bureau of the Census for the Bureau of Labor Statistics, samples 55,000 households in a multistage sampling of an updated listing from the latest census (1970). For each variable, we used the monthly statistic available that was closest in time to the months that our survey began.

ANALYSIS STRATEGY

The authors of the 1960 volume resisted making overall evaluations of the nation with respect to any of the measures of subjective mental health. Much as it would have been tempting to say something like "35 percent of Americans in 1957 were very happy," (because that proportion selected that alternative in overall evaluations of their well-being), the authors were cautious about emphasizing such a result. With a subtle change in wording, the percentages could easily have shifted. Rather, they emphasized two other kinds of analyses: (1) the interrelationships between pairs of measures as a way to gauge their psychological significance; and (2) the differential distribution of these measures in different subpopulations with particular emphasis on sex, age, and education differences. In these analyses, *relative* differences between groups are emphasized.

With a 1957–1976 comparison we are less pressed to focus on absolute percentages, the change or lack of change in percentages becoming interesting and important in its own right. And this can apply as much to analysis of help seeking as it does to the analysis of subjective mental health.

The 1976 analyses, therefore, reflect this critical new focus, the effect of time and the multiple events which occurred and altered our society and Americans' experience of life. In each of the central areas, we were interested in determining whether the 1957 descriptive findings remained stable or changed in 1976, and whether relationships established between sex, age, education, and other demographic factors to well-being, role experience, problems, and methods of dealing with stress were replicated or altered in the 1976 results.

In all chapters, therefore, the very first presentation will be year comparisons. A cautionary note should be made about all results comparing 1957 to 1976. When we discuss them, we will often talk about the change or stability of results as if there were no intervening fluctuations. It could very well be that had we sampled the population in the 1960s or the early 1970s, we would have seen change between 1957 and the 1960s, but no change thereafter. Or, where we saw lack of change, there may have been change between 1957 and the 1960s but a reversion to the 1957 distribution in 1976. Without data for the 1960s and early 1970s, we are actually in some technical error in referring to change or lack of change. For ease of analysis and interpretation, we ignore these possibilities, although we may be wrong in some instances.

After we present comparisons for 1957 to 1976, we ask a more analytic question: can we attribute change or stability to critical demographic shifts from 1957 to 1976? We are a much more highly educated population in 1976; we also now have proportionately more very young and very old birth cohorts in 1976 than we had in 1957, when the middle-aged cohort was proportionately larger. These substantial education and age shifts may be correlated with changes in psychological reactions that we uncover. Furthermore, if we controlled for these demographic shifts, maybe some new year changes would come to light that were not apparent in the overall year comparisons.

As a result, we need some technique for analyzing year changes while simultaneously controlling for age and education differences. We used for this purpose a relatively new multivariate analysis technique, log-linear hierarchical modeling (Goodman, 1978), which allows us to test the effect of time on a measure of well-being or of the use of informal help, *net of demographic changes which have occurred in the population during the same time period.*[6]

The necessity of such a technique will be clarified by an example. In analyzing the methods people employ in handling periods of unhappiness, we find that in 1976 American men and women are much less likely to turn to prayer than they were in 1957. This is an interesting and important finding, of special concern for religious institutions and their leaders. But the finding does not tell us whether the decreased use of prayer is the result of general desacralization, secularization in our culture which has affected all groups, or the failure of religion to attract and bind only certain groups like the young or highly educated people. We are uncertain because the decrease in use of prayer occurs at the same time that other changes have also occurred in the population which are closely related to (and confounded with) religious adherence. Both age and education relate to the use of prayer as solace— young people and highly educated people refer to prayer less than do older and less educated people. Since the population has changed in both of these factors—including in 1976 more young people and many more college-educated people than it did in 1957—the decreased use of prayer may simply reflect these demographic changes.

Of course, even if this were the case, the finding is real and reflects an important change in the centrality of religion in our national life. It will still spur efforts by religious leaders to increase and enlarge their attraction, to seek out ways in which they can serve people in supportive functions that will bind them to religious institutions.

But the more refined question—whether dilution of religious commitment is culture-wide or reflects a more specific, localized disaffection among the young or the highly educated—is crucial to social theory and also provides directives for programs religious institutions mount to increase their base of attraction. It may be that such programs need to appeal only to the very young.

In order to answer this question, we needed a technique which would allow us to detect the effect of time (1957–1976) net of changes in age and education. Log-linear hierarchical modeling is designed exactly for this purpose.

[6]The technique is described in detail in chapter 2, pp. 66–72, when results of its use are first reported.

In each of the chapters, we follow our analysis of overall year differences with a presentation of the log-linear hierarchical modeling via
Everyman's Contingency Table Analysis (ECTA) which looks at year
differences in a given measure of subjective mental health in a further
cross-classification by education and age differences. (In addition, we
cross-classify the data by sex differences to see whether some of the results were more or less true for men or women.) This will allow us to
do two things: (1) qualify results in our report of year differences either by saying that they are not apparent when the controls are introduced, or by seeing that they are only apparent in certain groups; (2)
see year differences that emerge only when controls are introduced.

The multivariate analysis permits us to see *interaction effects:* results
that hold only for or are especially strong in certain subgroups based
on sex, age, education, or year. For example, we will find that although
overall reports of job satisfaction have not changed much between 1957
and 1976, there is a substantial year increase in reported job dissatisfaction among young college-educated women. These interactions are
complicated to think about, but at times are among our most exciting
results because they point to changes in some groups and not others.
These differential results are often better understood than some overall
effect.

Multivariate analyses are also the launching points for our discussion of sex, age, and education differences within each chapter. They
alert us to results we should highlight in talking about how these social characteristics are related to general well-being (chapter 2), self-
perceptions (chapter 3), marriage (chapter 4), parenthood (chapter 5),
work (chapter 6) symptoms (chapter 7), and ways of coping with problems (chapter 9).

Overview of the Book

The next six chapters, each devoted to a different way of partitioning
subjective mental health, follow the same plan for analysis: a presentation of basic year differences; qualifications to the year differences in
light of multivariate analyses; sex, age, and education differences in
that area of subjective mental health. Interspersed in these presentations, we present information about measures available only for the
1976 sample when findings amplify general themes developed in the
chapter and round out our understanding of the psychological climate
of 1976.

In chapter 8 we select twenty-three measures of subjective mental
health culled from the most useful analyses in the preceding chapters
and plot their differential distribution in 1957 and 1976 in certain de-

mographic groupings, other than those based on sex, age, and education. Thirteen such critical social characteristics are considered for their possible relevance to subjective mental health: occupation, income, region, place of residence, race, religion, church attendance, broken-home background, father's occupation, childhood place of residence, marital status, employment status, and parental status. Analyses are done with and without multivariate controls for sex, age, education, and year.

Chapter 9 summarizes analyses of the coping styles Americans use to handle their problems. Not only will we present the methods of adaptation that differentiate men and women, 1957 and 1976, older and younger respondents, the less educated from the more educated, but we will explore the styles that differentiate people within each of the demographic groupings assessed in chapter 8.

A brief concluding chapter will attempt a broad integration of the major trends in this systematic examination of our recent social-psychological history.

Chapter 2

FEELINGS AND SOURCES OF WELL-BEING

WE BEGIN with analysis of the way people in the two generations evaluate their overall emotional adjustment and well-being. How happy are people's day-to-day lives? How much do Americans worry? Have they suffered crises that made them feel they were having a nervous breakdown or that required help from some formal resource? Do they expect their future to be happier, about the same, or less happy than their current lives? In answering such questions, we will cover *present* evaluations of well-being, reports of *past* crises and thoughts about the *future*. We clearly assume a multiple-criteria approach to subjective mental health since we inquire not only about present feelings of well-being, but also about reports of past and anticipated future well-being. Despite a limited appraisal of each time orientation, we seek to delineate the phenomenology of well-being across the individual's time perspective both in 1957 and 1976.

Feeling good about the present does not necessarily imply satisfaction with past experiences nor optimism about the future, though we do expect some correlations among them. As much as we can assume that appraising one time dimension of life with positive warmth would generalize to another time dimension, we could assume as well that contrast phenomena may occur. People who see their present as very happy might not be able to see their past or future in as glowing terms; people who see their present as unhappy might be unwilling to see their state of mind as a condition extending far back into the past or continuing long into the future. Only by differentiating people's sense of their past, present, and future well-being will we get a rich, textured perspective of the nation's feelings of well-being.

Multiple criteria for feelings of well-being abound *within* each time orientation. That is, feelings of present and past well-being are assessed in a number of different ways, and we find, as we did in 1957, that conclusions about feelings of well-being will differ depending on the criteria adopted.

What follows are analyses of several measures of well-being. Most of these deal with evaluation of the *degree* of *distress* or *well-being* experienced in the present, past, and anticipated future. We will call these *feelings of well-being.* Those that deal with the *kinds* of *experiences* people mention when they are asked to pinpoint the bases of their present well-being will be called *sources of well-being.* All the measures to be discussed are listed in table 2.1. Before we proceed with the absorbing question of which Americans in 1957 and 1976 experienced more feelings of distress or well-being of different kinds, let us examine the measures listed in table 2.1.

Measures of Well-Being

FEELINGS OF PRESENT WELL-BEING

We will be looking at five measures that help assess people's evaluation of their present well-being. Each emphasizes a different perspective about people's reaction to their ongoing lives.

Worries

One of the critical distinctions we made in *Americans View Their Mental Health* was between reports of unhappiness and reports of worries. While an evaluation of unhappiness was seen to reflect an ongoing affective morale in one's life—a barometer of resigned passive feelings— a report of being worried was interpreted to be responsive to ongoing coping with life problems—a personal investment in change for the future. Both types of feelings were seen as states of discomfort, but worries alone seemed to implicate a future orientation. We asked about worries in the following direct question:

> Everyone has some things he worries about more or less. What kinds of things do you worry about? Do you worry about such things a lot or not very much?

TABLE 2.1
Questions Assessing Feelings and Sources of Well-Being: 1957–1976

Measure	Questions
Feelings of Present Well-Being	
Worries	Everyone has some things he worries about more or less. What kinds of things do you worry about? Do you worry about such things a lot or not very much?
Happiness	Taking things altogether, how would you say things are these days—would you way they're very happy, pretty happy, or not too happy these days?
Present happiest	Now I'd like you to think about your whole life—how things are now, how they were ten years ago, how they were when you were a little (boy/girl). What do you think of as the happiest time in your life? (IF R MENTIONS SINGLE EVENT, PROBE: I don't mean just a particular day or single happening, but a whole period of your life.)
Satisfaction	In general, how satisfying do you find the way you're spending your life these days? Would you call it *completely satisfying, pretty satisfying,* or *not very satisfying?*
Zest[a]	Now I'd like you to look at the first page of this booklet which tells about some of the ways in which different people describe themselves. After each statement, would you please check the category that applies to you.

Measure

Questions

How often do you feel:	A Little or None of the Time	Some of the Time	A Good Part of the Time	All or Most of the Time
a. My mind is as clear as it used to be.				
b. I find it easy to do the things I used to.				
c. My life is interesting.				
d. I feel that I am useful and needed.				
e. My life is pretty full.				
f. I feel hopeful about the future.				
Score value	(1)	(2)	(4)	(5)

(Zest score = Sum of score value of a, b, c, d, e, f)

Feelings of Past Well-Being

Nervous Breakdown

Problem Relevant for Professional Help

Have you ever felt that you were going to have a nervous breakdown?

a. Sometimes when people have problems like this, (referring back to question about personal problem—very unhappy, nervous, irritable, marriage, children, etc.) they go someplace for help. Sometimes they go to a doctor or a minister.

TABLE 2.1 (continued)

Questions Assessing Feelings and Sources of Well-Being: 1957–1976

Measure	Questions
	Sometimes they go to a special place for handling personal problems—like a psychiatrist or a marriage counselor, or social agency or clinic. How about you—have you ever gone anywhere like that for advice and help with any personal problems?
	b. Can you think of anything that's happened to you, any problems you've had in the past, when going to someone like this might have helped you in any way?
	[Yes to (a) or no to (a), yes to (b).]
Childhood Unhappiest Time	Mentioning childhood, adolescence or "youth" as opposed to adult periods in response to:
	Thinking now of the way things were in the *past*, what do you think of as the most unhappy time in your life? (PROBE FOR A WHOLE PERIOD OF R'S LIFE.)
Evaluation of Past Compared to Present[a]	Compared to your life today, how were things 5 or 6 years ago—were things happier for you than they are now, not quite as happy or what?
How Frequently Bad Things Have Happened[a]	Over their lives most people have something bad happen to them or to someone they love. By that I mean things like getting sick, losing a job, or being in trouble with the police. Or like when someone dies, leaves, or disappoints you. Or maybe just something important you wanted to happen didn't happen. Compared with most other people you know, have *things like this* happened to you *a lot, some, not much, or hardly ever.*
Frequency Felt Overwhelmed[a]	When things like these have happened to you, have there been times when you found it very hard to handle? That is, when you couldn't sleep, or stayed away from people, or felt so depressed or nervous that you couldn't do much of anything? (If yes) Would you say you felt that way many times or just once in a while.

Measure	Questions
Feelings of Future Well-Being	
Morale about Future	Compared to your life today, how do you think things will be 5 or 10 years from now—do you think things will be happier for you than they are now, not quite as happy, or what? (Coded pattern response to this question plus the happiness question, listed below)

Patterned Coding

	Response on the Happiness Question	Response on the Future Question
Level 1		
"Very happy about future"	Very happy	Same
	or	
	Pretty happy	Happier
	or	
	Not very happy	Very much happier
Level 2		
"Happy about future"	Very happy	Little less happy
	or	
	Pretty happy	Same
	or	
	Not too happy	Happier
Level 3		
"Not happy about future"	Very happy	Very unhappy
	or	
	Pretty happy	Less happy
	or	
	Not too happy	Same
NA	Anything	I don't know; I won't be here.

TABLE 2.1 (continued)
Questions Assessing Feelings and Sources of Well-Being: 1957–1976

Measure	Questions
Sources of Well-Being	
Sources of Happiness	(If mention present time as happiest in response to a previous question) Why is this a happy time—what are some of the things you feel pretty happy about these days? *or* (If mention past times as happiest in previous question) How about the ways things are today—what are some of the things you find pretty happy? (Categories grouped responses that were related to: *economic and material, children, marriage, interpersonal—other than children or marriage, job, R's health, family's health, sense of independence or absence of burdens, personal characteristics, other.*)
Sources of Unhappiness	Everyone has things about their lives they are not too happy about. What are some of the things that you're not too happy about these days? (Categories were the same as above for happiness except the independence category was nonexistent, and a category called *Community, National and World Affairs* was added.)
Sources of Worry	Everyone has some things he worries about more or less. What kinds of things do you worry about? (Same as categories for sources of unhappiness)

[a] Question asked only in 1976.

Happiness

The question used in 1957 to measure feelings of happiness is shown below:

Taking things altogether, how would you say things are these days—would you say they're very happy, pretty happy, or not too happy these days?

This item has been used in a number of surveys since 1957. It is only a three-point scale, but it has been significantly related to many other social indicators and demographic characteristics.

Present Happiness

Adjustment is a cumulative process. We all have misfortunes and calamities, and we have high points in everyday life. When we reflect on our experience, the very process of reflection must be influenced by the moving stream of emotional perspective. We skew the past perhaps even more sharply than the present. Psychotherapists often use these distortions to diagnose unconscious motivation. Nevertheless, one can ask whether there are not gross differences in how people evaluate their present compared to their past, because, however distorted, their evaluations do reflect some overall sense of present states of well-being.

How might these comparative evaluations of well-being be helpful in understanding measures of *present* well-being? The question asked for this evaluation is:

Now I'd like you to think about your whole life—how things are now, how they were ten years ago, how they were when you were a little boy/girl. What do you think of as the happiest time of your life?

Here, we can use a person's selection of the present over the past as "happiest" as a direct indicator of relatively great present well-being.

Satisfaction (1976 only)

The terms "happiness" and "worries" have strong affective connotation. However, researchers measuring feelings of well-being also are interested in the more cognitive evaluations of contentment: has life been measuring up to expectations? Such an evaluation is captured in measures of satisfaction. Unfortunately, we did not have a measure of overall satisfaction with life in 1957, but in order to connect with ongoing research about the quality of life, we introduced one in the 1976 survey. It read:

In general, how satisfying do you find the way you're spending your life these days? Would you call it completely satisfying, pretty satisfying, or not very satisfying?

The question was adapted from Campbell, Converse, and Rodgers (1976).

This measure is relatively highly correlated with the happiness measure (.39), and with zest (.28), the next measure we will be discussing. Although Campbell, Converse, and Rodgers identify satisfaction as a cognitive appraisal of well-being, it no doubt also entails some affective orientations. In this connection, we introduced the measure of zest. We consider zest a measure of pleasurable involvement with ongoing life. The fact that our measure of satisfaction correlates moderately with zest would suggest that satisfaction is not purely a cognitive appraisal of domains that have to do with how life is going, but that it also bears some kind of affective orientation to that experience. Depner (1978) has done some interesting explorations relating the overall measure of satisfaction to domains of satisfaction which we, too, measured in our study. The results of her work suggest that one of the major components of our measure of overall satisfaction with life is satisfaction with marriage, more than with work or parenting.

Since fewer people in 1976 own up to feeling "completely satisfied" with their lives (16 percent), as opposed to being "very happy" in response to the happiness question (35 percent), we understand *satisfaction* to reflect standards of "ideal" lives rather than standards of general well-being. If you ask people whether they feel completely satisfied with life, you risk alerting them that *all* the ideal goals of their lives have not been completely met. Saying that they are pretty satisfied indicates perhaps that they are generally very satisfied, but not *completely* satisfied. Probably the reason why we have fewer people in the "completely satisfied" compared to the "very happy" category is that the first category is a function of the semantic set established by the word "completely." We would claim that if we had structured the happiness measure similarly and suggested an alternative such as "completely happy" with the way life is going, we would have elicited a similar distribution. For this reason, we have much more of the measure of cognitive appraisal of *ideal* well-being in the satisfaction measure than in the happiness measure.

Zest (1976 only)

One of the features of well-being that we failed to measure directly in 1957 was "depression." Many psychologists, particularly those dealing with clinical populations, have noted a syndrome of distress that reflects a withdrawn, negatively tinged retreat from ongoing experience correlating with a general lack of energy. A scale developed by Zung (1965) has been employed by researchers to assess this condition, although it is not often used in survey studies. Blumenthal, Dielman, and Bongort (1974) used the scale in one study along with a variety of other measures also used in the original study, *Americans View Their Mental Health*. In order to determine which of the items in the Zung scale to include in the 1976 study to assess depression, we reanalyzed their data set and intercorrelated the items with other measures drawn from the 1957 study for this replication volume. Many items in the Zung scale correlate very highly with certain items in the symptom-factor scales we discuss in chapter 7. That is, many questions that ask about feeling depressed, feeling blue and the like, overlap considerably with measure of nervousness, tension, and physical symptoms that we assess as "symptoms." One group of items, however, was *not* very highly correlated with symptom scores: the set of questions that asked people about their positive experiences of well-being. These are listed below, and they form the components of the scale that we are calling zest. Respondents were asked the frequency of these feelings:

My mind is as clear as it used to be.
I find it easy to do the things I used to.
My life is interesting.
I feel that I am useful and needed.
My life is pretty full.
I feel hopeful about the future.

With each of these items, the respondent was shown a card which allowed four responses: a little or none of the time; some of the time; a good part of the time; or most of the time. (See table 2.1 for explicit coding.)

Since these items had relatively high intercorrelations in the 1976 population, ranging from .37 to .57, we developed a zest scale summing across the items. The higher the score, the more likely that the person is finding life experiences zestful—that is, he/she finds life interesting, feels useful and needed, sees life as full and hopeful, the mind is operating clearly, and the person is working efficiently. Forty percent of the 1976 American population responded either with "a good part of the time" or "all of the time" to each of the items on the scale. Taking a "depressed" reaction to life experience as being one where a person responded to each of the items by saying he/she felt that way some of the time or a little or none of the time, only 3 percent of the American population in 1976 provided a pattern that could be labeled a depressed syndrome. This suggests that the strength of this measure in relation to other variables comes more from differentiating people who say that they find experience pleasurable compared to those who feel bland about their experience. Hence, we call this measure of positive experiences of well-being a zest scale.

It is interesting to compare responses to this scale with responses to the precending measures of satisfaction. In table 2.2 we present the relationships between those who saw their experiences as having little zest (Low), moderate zest (Moderate), and a lot of zest (High) with how much satisfaction they say they obtain from life. We find that a good

TABLE 2.2
Interrelationship of Satisfaction to Zest
(1976 only)

	Satisfaction		
Zest	Completely Satisfied (%)	Satisfied (%)	Not Very Satisfied (%)
Low	18	33	71
Moderate	24	32	16
High	58	35	13
	100%	100%	100%
Total Number	368	1,621	227

	Zest		
Satisfaction	Low (%)	Moderate (%)	High (%)
Completely Satisfied	8	14	26
Satisfied	7	8	70
Not Very Satisfied	21	5	4
	100%	100%	100%
Total Number	767	638	807

proportion of the people who say that they are highly zestful are not completely satisfied with what their life is like (74 percent). Furthermore, those who are completely satisfied are not necessarily highly zestful; only 58 percent of the "completely satisfied" respondents have a high zest score. With *satisfaction* and *zest*, we are measuring interrelated but different feeling aspects of well-being. *Zest* accentuates the evaluation of positive experience. *Satisfaction* seems to reflect meeting one's expectations for life.

FEELINGS OF PAST WELL-BEING

In various guises, we sought from respondents in both generations a review of their lives which would give us some indication of their feelings of adjustment over the years. Measures available for both years are feelings of having a *nervous breakdown;* having had a *problem relevant for professional help;* perceiving *childhood* as the *unhappiest time* of one's life.

In 1976, three additional measures were constructed for past well-being which were not included in 1957. These are: how does the person *evaluate* his/her *past compared to* his/her *present;* how *frequently* does the person think that *bad things have happened* to him/her, and how often does he/she *feel overwhelmed by bad things* that have happened. We discuss these measures, along with the replicated ones, below.

Nervous Breakdown

Four of the measures tap the respondent's perception of the past as having presented some kind of mental-health problem. We have asked about issues of mental health in a number of ways. In the first question, we asked whether or not respondents have experienced an impending *nervous breakdown:*

Have you ever felt you were going to have a nervous breakdown?

Note that the question asks only for a simple yes or no and that it does not ask whether the respondent thought he/she *had* a nervous breakdown—only that he/she thought he/she was going to have one.

Experienced Problem Relevant for Professional Help

A second mental-health-related question asked whether at any time in the past the person perceived her/himself as experiencing the kind of problem for which professional help might have been relevant. We will discuss this measure in greater detail in Book 2. We apply it here as an appraisal of past well-being because it clearly involves a measure of the person's perceptions of his or her own past adjustment represented by whether the person thought he/she might have had a problem for which professional help could profitably have been used. The explicit questions used for this assessment were:

Sometimes when people have a problem like this [referring to personal problems in a previous question] they go someplace for help. Sometimes they go to a doctor or a minister, sometimes they go to a special place for handling personal problems like a psychiatrist, a marriage counselor, or a social agency or clinic. How about you—have you ever gone anywhere like that for advice and help with your personal problem? (If no, the person was asked further: Can you think of anything that has happened to you, any problems you have had in the past, where going to someone like this would have helped you in any way?)

People were categorized as having seen the problem relevant for help by saying either that yes, they had gone for help, or that they saw that they had a problem for which help would have been relevant.

Childhood unhappiest

This assessment attempts to get at a person's reaction to earlier socialization experiences. Does the person refer to some time before adulthood (childhood, youth, adolescence) as the *unhappiest* time in response to the question:

Thinking now of the ways things were in the *past*, what do you think of as the most unhappy time?

Evaluation of the Past Compared to the Present (1976 only)

This measure and the next two were asked only in 1976. The measure is designed to parallel another we will discuss soon: future morale. In the latter, we asked respondents to compare their future well-being with that of the present. In this measure we ask them to compare their past well-being with their present: Compared to your life today, how were things five or six years ago—were things happier for you than they are now, not quite as happy, or what? The responses were coded into three major categories: things being either happier in the past, the same as in the past, or happier in the present.

Frequency of Bad Events (1976 only)

Much of the 1957 "mental-health" questionnaire was directed at assessing perceived "personal" problems. The questions oriented the respondents to consider things about the inner self that were troubling. Note especially the tone of the questions used to assess *Experienced Problems Relevant for Professional Help*. Over the generation since the 1957 study, very many more mental-health practitioners and theorists have shifted the focus from "personal" problems that depend primarily upon helping institutions and therapy to "situational" problems—or crises—that require a different approach to help giving. Accordingly, in 1976 we asked respondents whether they had experienced bad things *happening* to them in specifiable ways. Response to the following question was used to obtain a measure of *perceived frequency of bad events happening in the past:*

> *Over their lives, most people have something bad happen to them or to someone they love. By that I mean getting sick, losing a job, getting in trouble with the police. Or like when someone dies, leaves, or disappoints you. Or maybe just something important you wanted to happen didn't happen. Compared to most other people you know, have things like this happened to you a little, some, not much, or hardly ever?*

With this question, we sought a shorthand appraisal of persons' perceptions of stressful life events that have occurred (Holmes and Rahe, 1967). The result was not an exact measure of the number of such events, but rather a perception of the perceived frequency with which stressful events have occurred.

To what events do people refer when they feel bad things happen to them? For many respondents, the *last* bad thing that happened was someone's death (30 percent). Another sizable group (19 percent) referred to a health problem, and a third large group (16 percent) referred to interpersonal disruption, as shown in table 2.3. What is clear from these responses is that "bad things" rarely refer directly to mental-health problems.

TABLE 2.3

*Last "Bad Thing" Reported to Have
Happened to Person (1976 only)*

Event	Last Bad Thing to Have Happened to Person %	
Economic Difficulty	3	
Work-Related	8	
Legal Trouble	3	
Interpersonal Disruption	16	
Marriage		8
Other—love relationship		3
Other—interpersonal		5
Physical Separation	1	
Other Interpersonal Difficulty	3	
Death of Significant People	30	
Spouse		7
Parent		9
Other		14
Health Problem	19	
Self		9
Other		10
Mental Health Adequacy	4	
Self		2
Other		2
Other	1	
Never Had Bad Experience	6	
Not Ascertained	7	
	100%	
Total Number	2,264	

Frequency Felt Overwhelmed (1976 only)

Another question followed up that of the frequency of bad things happening:

When things like these have happened to you, have there been times when you found it very hard to handle? That is, when you couldn't sleep or stayed away from people, or felt so depressed or nervous that you could not do much of anything? (If the person said yes, we followed up with the question, "Would you say you felt that way many times or just once in a while?")

FEELINGS OF FUTURE WELL-BEING

Morale About the Future

To measure morale, we used a question about anticipated happiness in conjunction with a measure of present happiness. Hence the question:

> Compared to your life today, how do you think things will be five or ten years from now—do you think things will be happier for you than they are now, not quite as happy, or what?

From the pattern of responses to these two questions, as reported in table 2.1, we constructed a four-level index called Future Morale. A number of people's future evaluations—more often older people's—were not ascertainable because their response to the question about the future did not compare it to the present: e.g., "I won't be here," or "I'll be dead." These phrases carry different meanings for different people. They could mean feeling "resigned," "demoralized," or they could even mean something positive for those who believe in an afterlife. The four levels reported in table 2.1 are defined as *very happy about the future, happy about the future, not happy about the future, not ascertainable* (I don't know; I won't be here).

When examining this measure, we should remember the built-in psychological correlation between it and the measure of present happiness. No respondents said they were very happy now and that their future was going to be very much unhappier; nor were there any respondents who said they were not too happy now and that they were going to be very much happier. If such patterns represent logically possible combinations of responses, they do not seem to be psychologically possible. In some ways, the possibility of such patterns was constrained by the wording of the question.

SOURCES OF PRESENT WELL-BEING

Three separate questions were the source of information about people's reported sources of well-being. One asked about happiness, another about unhappiness, and another about worries.

Sources of Happiness

Content analysis of the following questions gave us categories of happiness people reported:

> If [respondent] mentions present time as happiest in response to a previous question) Why is this a happy time—what are some of the things that you feel pretty happy about these days? Or (if respondent mentions past times as happiest in previous question) how about the way things are today—what are some of the things you find pretty happy?

The responses were coded just as they were in 1957 and summarized in a parallel manner for all three questions (table 2.1). In two instances, parallel categorization could not be made for sources of happiness and unhappiness: i.e., people mentioned independence as a source of happiness but did not mention dependence as a source of unhappiness or worry; and they mentioned the community, national, or world problems as sources of unhappiness or worry, but never as sources of happiness. This lack of symmetry in type of sources of unhappiness (worries) and happiness is interesting and worth exploring by people interested in the phenomenology of happiness and unhappiness.

Sources of Unhappiness

For sources of unhappiness, people were asked:

Everyone has things about their lives they are not happy about. What are some of the things you're not too happy about these days?

Except for the instance noted above, there was parallel categorization of sources of unhappiness and sources of happiness (table 2.1).

Sources of Worries

In 1957 and 1976 Americans were asked:

Everyone has some things he worries about more or less. What kinds of things do you worry about?

This question preceded the evaluation of how much the person worries; thus, there may be some connection between extent of worrying and what the person has presented to the interviewer as his/her source of worry. As noted above, the categories for worries duplicated categories for unhappiness.

INTERCORRELATION OF MEASURES OF WELL-BEING

We can now look systematically at interrelationships among various measures of present, past, and future feelings of well-being. We interrelated all measures separately for 1957 and 1976. In addition, we correlated sources of happiness and unhappiness with the measure of happiness, and the source of worries with extent of worrying. These data will be presented subsequently.

Interrelationships of Feelings of Well-Being

Two general conclusions about the intercorrelation of measures of feelings of well-being are remarkable. First, the correlations are quite small. Second, there is considerable consistency across the generation.

Let us look at the first conclusion: the intercorrelations of feelings of well-being are generally of small order.

TABLE 2.4

*Relationship of Extent of Present Happiness to Anticipation
of Future Happiness (by year)*

	Evaluation of Present Happiness					
	Very Happy		Pretty Happy		Not Too Happy	
Anticipation of	1957	1976	1957	1976	1957	1976
Future Happiness	(%)	(%)	(%)	(%)	(%)	(%)
Happier	43	38	43	45	34	51
About the same	38	37	39	22	17	7
Less happy	6	8	10	14	14	14
Don't know,						
won't be here	11	10	16	13	31	19
Not ascertained	2	6	2	5	4	8
	100%	100%	100%	100%	100%	100%
Total Number	849	690	1,326	1,291	275	244

Only one set of correlations stands out as being at all sizable. Future morale and happiness were highly correlated (.57 in 1957; .48 in 1976). Recall that there was a built-in correlation between the two, and thus these correlations are spuriously high. We should note, however, that the correlation between *happiness* and *future morale* is slightly lower in 1976 than in 1957; a significant difference, given our large samples. What might account for this difference? In table 2.4 we plot levels of future morale reported by people who are "very happy," "pretty happy," and "not too happy" for 1957 and 1976. People who rated themselves as "not too happy" in 1976 were much more optimistic about their future than were comparable people in 1957. Fifty-one percent of demoralized people in 1976 thought life would get happier, compared to only 34 percent in 1957. These trends hold true at each age level. Thus, we see that while the measure of happiness still reflects morale, it has a slightly different force at the two points in time.

Correlations between any other pair of measures ranged from .00 to .38, with most of the higher correlations occurring between measures with the same time reference. For example, *happiness* and *present happiest* correlated .33 (1957) and .29 (1976). *Nervous breakdown* and *problem relevant for help* correlated .31 (1976). These are not high correlations, and most of the others were of even lower order. Such findings confirm our decision to analyze the measures one by one rather than to combine them into an overall scale of well-being.

Our second general conclusion concerning the pattern of intercorrelations of feelings of well-being is that there is a near-perfect matching of correlations from the 1957 period to the 1976 period, the biggest difference being the slightly reduced correlation between present happiness and future morale noted above. Americans seem to have been generally unchanging over the generation in regard to the bearing that present, past, and future evaluations have on one another.

The summary statements below elaborate on these results:

1. *Present worrying relates to having evaluated one's past in terms of a mental-health crisis rather than to imagining or anticipating bad things happening in the future.* Our expectation was that worries would have specific orientations to a future perspective rather than to the past. We can, however, think of "worrying" in the reverse: it can be interpreted as an indication that the person is apprehensive of a pressing danger signal of something bad happening in the future *as it did in the past.* Having experienced a minor or major disruption in the past either as a stressful bad event or as a nervous breakdown can alert people to parallel situations in the future—which may be averted by behavioral adjustment. Not that all worriers have encountered catastrophes; indeed, some of the proverbial "worrywarts" are people who in spite of having had benign experiences are perpetually warding off doomsday by magical worrying. Nevertheless, people who are aware of their past vulnerability evidently cope with the future by "worrying"; perhaps such background conditions lead to the positive coping characteristics of "worrying."

2. *Present well-being as "happiness" or "zestfulness" generalizes to anticipated future well-being but partakes little of nostalgia for the past.* Happiness seems to imply anticipatory feelings of well-being as well as satisfaction and zest with one's present lot. Zest also associates with positive feelings about the future, more so than with absence of negative feelings about the past. These findings may reflect merely the glow of well-being generalized to the future without a highly differentiated future perspective on life: recall that there may be a methodological bias in the association of these two measures. Nevertheless, people seem to assume that if they are happy or zestful they will continue to be happy or zestful. Self-evident as it may be that "happy" people do not emphasize past happiness, it is important to bear in mind that people's memories of past happiness are not likely to sustain them at a high level of present happiness if their present or future life circumstances seem actually or potentially disruptive.

3. *Well-being (satisfaction) is correlated more with present happiness than with future morale or past evaluations.* Satisfaction thus seems to be an evaluation of *current* capacity to get what one has hoped for in the past. Nevertheless, like the happiness index, it is clearly different from a strong affective involvement in the present. One indication of this is the higher correlation of zest to happiness (.38) than to satisfaction (.28).

4. *People who think the present is the happiest time of their life seem to have rejected the past (youth is seen as unhappy) and to be hopeful (optimistic) about the future.* Unlike the other happiness measure, this one reflects very little on past involvement with mental-health problems. If someone

has experienced mental-health problems in the past, perhaps he/she tends to be cautious about calling the present "very happy" in any absolute terms. It may have little to do with saying that the present is the happiest period of one's life. Calling the present the happiest compared to periods in the past also suggests a momentum which carries over into optimism about future well-being.

5. There is a less than perfect correlation between having felt overwhelmed by a "nervous breakdown" that occurred in the past and having felt that one could not handle stressful life events (.41). This finding indicates that we get different results from people's evaluation of their past mental-health difficulties when the question is phrased as "nervous breakdown" and when it is phrased as not being able to cope with bad stressful events. Nonetheless, the pattern of intercorrelations of these two items with other measures is very similar. Therefore, even though different people report feelings of mental-health difficulties as an internal problem (nervous breakdown), or as an overwhelmed reaction to a particular stressful external event, both states of being overwhelmed have parallel effects on present and future well-being.

INTERCORRELATION OF FEELINGS OF WELL-BEING
WITH SOURCES OF WELL-BEING

Any attempt to gauge the psychological bases that men and women use to evaluate their well-being is of interest to observers of the quality of life. What then is the relationship of the *extent* of happiness to

TABLE 2.5

*Correlations (r)[a] of Happiness With Mentioning Various
Sources of Happiness and Unhappiness 1957 vs. 1976*

Sources	Sources of Happiness		Sources of Unhappiness		Sources of Worry	
	1957	1976	1957	1976	1957	1976
Economic and material	.04	.06	−.05	−.07	.09	.20
Children	.05	.02	−.10	−.05	.10	.08
Marriage	.21	.16	−.10	−.10	.06	.05
Other interpersonal	.10	.03	−.10	−.09	.06	.01
Job	.02	.03	−.02	−.05	.05	.14
R's health	−.07	−.07	−.11	−.05	.08	.04
Family's health	.02	.01	−.07	−.03	.11	−.01
Independence	.02	.04	—	—	—	—
Personal characteristics	.01	.04	.03	.05	.06	.05
Community, national, and world problems	—	—	.03	.04	.02	.01

[a] Since the correlations are based on a large number of respondents, very small correlations are statistically significant. A correlation of .05 is significant at <.05 level of confidence; a correlation of .06 at <.01 level; a correlation of .07 at <.001 level; and so on.

sources of happiness and unhappiness? The relationship of extent of worries to *sources* of worry? These data are presented in table 2.5.

It is clear from the table that the indices of *happiness* and *worries* do not correlate highly with any one type of source of well-being in either year. Only marriage-related sources of justification are *consistently* mentioned more often in both years by people who say they are very happy (.21 in 1957; .16 in 1976),[1] and even these relationships are very weak. The range of correlations of happiness or worries with sources of well-being is .01 to .21. This makes it hard to pin down any particular source of happiness, unhappiness, or worry as normatively central to the population's feelings of well-being in either 1957 or 1976. Marital sources of happiness come close to being a normative basis of happiness in both 1957 and 1976. Economic and job worries come closest to being normative bases of worrying in 1976. We will discuss this shift in our generation comparison.

Well-Being in American Society: 1957 and 1976

Having explicated our measures, we can proceed to examine the changes that have occurred in two national samples separated by a generation of considerable social upheaval. All these data are presented in table 2.6, which reports changes in feelings of well-being and table 2.7, which reports changes in perceived sources of well-being. Information about measures available only in 1976 are excluded from these tables and will be presented later. To begin with, we will look at the American population as a whole, applying a global perspective to our analysis of change and stability. Subsequent sections will elaborate analyses of how differences in sex, age, and educational level of respondents qualify our picture of well-being in 1976 and how it has changed since 1957.

Feelings and Sources of Well-Being in 1957 and 1976

Only two indices of well-being (table 2.6) show any remarkable changes from 1957 to 1976 at the national level: *worrying* and having experienced *problems relevant for help*. Worrying a lot (or all the time) increased from 32 percent to 42 percent; having experienced a problem relevant for help increased from 23 percent to 36 percent. Otherwise, differences between the 1957 and 1976 population's evaluation of their well-being are minimal.

Regarding reported sources of present well-being (see table 2.7)

[1] Sex, age, and education controls do not appreciably change the pattern of correlations. Nor does using only married respondents make a difference.

TABLE 2.6
Year Differences in Feelings of Well-Being

Measure of Well-Being	1957 (%)	1976 (%)
Present	(N=2,460)	(N=2,264)
Worries		
Always, a lot	32	42
Sometimes, not never	52	46
Never	11	6
Not ascertained	5	6
	100%	100%
Happiness		
Very Happy	35	30
Pretty Happy	54	57
Not too Happy	11	11
Not ascertained	<1	27
	100%	100%
Present Happiness		
Yes	62	66
No	35	31
Not ascertained	3	3
	100%	100%
Past		
Nervous Breakdown		
Yes	19	21
No	81	79
Not ascertained	<1	<1
	100%	100%
Problem Relevant for Help		
Yes	23	36
No	71	58
Not ascertained	6	6
	100%	100%
Childhood Unhappiest		
Yes	24	29
No	72	67
Not ascertained	4	4
	100%	100%
Future		
Future Morale		
Very Happy	51	48
Happy	22	21
Not Happy	9	11
Don't know; won't be here	16	14
Not ascertained	2	6
	100%	100%

TABLE 2.7

Year Differences in Sources of Happiness and Unhappiness[a]

Sources	Sources of Happiness		Sources of Unhappiness	
	1957 (%)	1976 (%)	1957 (%)	1976 (%)
Economic and material	35	28	27	20
Children	29	24	7	7
Marriage	17	15	5	5
Other interpersonal	16	18	3	13
Job	8	9	11	20
R's health	9	11	7	9
Family's health	8	6	5	3
Independence; absence of burdens	8	16	—	—
Personal characteristics (problems)	2	5	13	8
Community, national and world problems	—	—	13	24
Miscellaneous	12	8	4	4
Not happy (unhappy) about anything	5	3	18	10
Not ascertained	2	4	2	3
Total Number	2,460	2,264	2,460	2,264

[a] Percent responding with a given source of happiness or unhappiness in their first two mentions of each.

there are again only minimal shifts in most dimensions. Nevertheless, there are important changes in a few domains of happiness, unhappiness, and worries which are discussed in the forthcoming section.

Let us amplify these findings. While two large shifts in these measures of well-being have occurred over the generation, others, though less striking, are worth noting. In addition, some correlational analyses speak of shifts in the generation not so apparent in tables 2.6 and 2.7. Before we discuss these findings, let us state that, on the whole, we are impressed with the remarkable stability of these measures of the affective life of the American population. Since it will be easy to lose perspective on this fact as we get engrossed in teasing out generational differences, let us at the outset emphasize that *American well-being generally has remained constant from 1957 to 1976.* Subjective dimensions of experience of overall life quality are evidently extremely stable. We will see in subsequent chapters that reactions to certain specific life circumstances—such as experiencing problems in marriage or perceiving one's adequacy in work—change quite dramatically; but more global evaluative feelings represented by the measures in this chapter are far less susceptible to changing historical circumstances.

Worries and Sources of Worry. In 1976 people worried more about economic or job issues than they did in 1957. It is not that more people worried about such matters in 1976—in fact, more people worried about economic matters in 1957—but when they did focus their concerns on jobs or economic matters in 1976, respondents worried about such problems a great deal. It is not hard to reason that when people in 1976 worried about the future of their jobs or their economic situation, they projected a very uncertain future which caused a great deal of worry, whereas people in 1957 were in the beginning of a projected boom. The Great Society was a viable image in the next decade for the country at large and for individuals' lives. They might be concerned about the future, but not deeply worried. By 1976 the future had become more uncertain and much more worrisome as the baby-boom cohort entered a shrinking job market, inflation increased, and national productivity slackened.

Happiness and Sources of Happiness and Unhappiness. Looking again at table 2.7, we find that in both years while economic and material concerns are prevalent in the list of reasons for respondents' happiness and unhappiness, they have dropped somewhat in 1976 as sources of happiness and unhappiness, as well as sources of worry. Economic concern is no longer the leading source of unhappiness in 1976 that it was in 1957. It is being replaced by a focus on community, national, and world problems. For a significant proportion of the population, increased affluence over the generation seems to have had an impact on expressed feelings of happiness and unhappiness and worries.

On the other hand, structuring well-being in terms of work has increased: there has not been a shift away from mentioning one's job as a source of happiness, but there has been a shift toward mentioning it as a source of unhappiness. These shifts in orientation toward financial concerns and jobs as the foci of well-being exemplify a theme that surfaces repeatedly in this volume. Financial well-being or distress is not as salient an issue in people's lives in the current generation as it was twenty years ago, but occupational concerns have become more critical issues. Though both 1957 and 1976 were recession years and the general state of the economy was similar, it seems that people's jobs have come to guarantee them enough money, but not enough social integration in their present lives or guarantees about future security.

Other bases of well-being shifted in important ways. Many more people in 1976 mention distress with community, government, or world problems as a source of personal unhappiness. And many more people are now unhappy about interpersonal issues. Both of these changes in response can be read as indicators of some disintegration of social bonding in American life over the generation which is indirectly reflected in feelings of distress.

Perhaps also reflective of this loosening of people's integration in their social world is the greater mention of the pleasures of being independent (from 8 percent to 16 percent) and the pleasures taken in one's *own* characteristics (from 2 percent to 5 percent) as sources of happiness in the 1976 populations compared to the 1957. The latter finding is paralleled by a decrease (13 percent to 8 percent) in the report of one's own personal traits as a source of unhappiness. We can read these changes as movements away from the pleasures of social ties with one another and a greater absorption with personal resources for gratification. Although such survey evidence has been viewed as supporting the idea that we are moving into a new era of narcissism (Lasch, 1979), we tend to interpret the data as a movement away from the social world rather than absorption with the self. In terms of attribution theory, we could speculate that people are blaming the system more for their discontent (e.g., seeing community problems as a source of unhappiness), and, in the process, are actively seeking self-involvement as a way to compensate for inadequate social anchors. While this pattern is more common now than it was in 1957, we want to emphasize that it is by no means characteristic of *most* Americans.

We may ask whether this shift from a more social to a more personal/individual conception of happiness is reflected in sources of happiness or unhappinesss. Do those who say they are very happy and those who are unhappy mention different sources of happiness and unhappiness in 1957 compared to 1976? The correlations of the extent of people's happiness and unhappiness with the mention of particular sources do not support such a contention (see table 2.5). Nothing from this analysis supports the view that there have been dramatic changes in the bases of personal happiness or unhappiness in our society.

By and large, Americans are as happy in 1976 as they were in 1957, and they generally report similar sources of happiness and unhappiness. The trend we observe (from a social to an interpersonal interpretation of happiness), though important, is relatively small.

One other change about happiness merits reiteration. Currently, saying that one is "not too happy" does not seem to be as demoralized a response as it was a generation ago. More "unhappy" people in 1976 are optimistic about the future. People in the 1976 sample are much more confident about their own capacity to work out the tasks they have set themselves than the 1957 population was. Asked how true the following statement is of them:

> I have always felt pretty sure that my life would work out the way I wanted it to

25 percent of the adults in 1957 said "not true at all" or "not very true," compared to 16 percent in 1976. Furthermore, the shift is most apparent among those who said they were "not too happy." Experiencing unhappiness in 1976 still reflects demoralized feelings, but these feelings seem to relate more to distress about immediate circumstances with the promise of alleviation through future dealings with the world.

Present happiest. In both years there is a clear tendency to avoid see-

TABLE 2.8

Happiest and Unhappiest Time of Life: 1957 and 1976

Happiest Time of Life	Year	
	1957 (%)	1976 (%)
Past Time	59	63
Early childhood	15%	17%
Adolescence	10	10
Young adulthood	7	9
Youth	7	4
No specific time		
Marriage	11	10
Parenting	7	7
Job	2	2
Other		4
Present Time	35	31
Happy All My Life	4	5
Never Happy	<1	<1
Not ascertained	2	1
	100%	100%
Unhappiest Time in the Past		
Early childhood	6	5
Adolescence	7	10
Young adulthood	6	10
Youth—not ascertained specific	4	3
Marriage—related time	12	15
Children—related time	3	4
Work—related time	9	7
Death of a loved one	22	22
Illness or potential danger to self or loved one	11	10
No specific time unhappy	0	1
Never unhappy	10	8
Not ascertained	11	5
	100%	100%
Total Number	2,460	2,264

ing the present as happiest and to locate the happiest time of one's life in the past. Sixty-three percent of the population in 1976 and 59 percent in 1957 pinpoint some past time as the happiest of their life—a slight shift. The past time referred to was some period in youth (see table 2.8). About 20 percent of Americans in both 1957 and 1976 define the happiest past time of their life by some adult role status, such as some time in early marriage, or a time when they were raising their children, or when they held certain jobs.

Past well-being: 1957–1976. There is not much change from 1957 to 1976 in reports of having felt one might have a nervous breakdown.

There is a clear rise in readiness to see past problems as having been relevant for seeking help. Notwithstanding the obvious increase in the availability of professional resources that occurred over the generation, there must be a psychological readiness to see one's problems as needing the attention of an outsider. The 1976 population is not any more likely to see past problems as mental disorders ("nervous breakdown"), but they are more likely to translate their problems as potentially responsive to expert assistance. The important distinction that seems to have increased over the generation is that going for help does not necessarily mean one is going crazy. Many clinicians report that clients often need to be reassured on initial contact that seeking help does not necessarily mean that they are suffering from a mental disorder. A number of results throughout this volume will suggest that the American population has become more willing to talk about the personal problems they face in a range of circumstances. This reflects a kind of psychological awareness, but not necessarily a change in people's perception of their own mental health. The increased readiness is probably best understood as a change in the social phenomenology of perceived problems; that is, occurring at a societal rather than a deep personal level. Sanctions against seeking formal help have loosened, and help seeking as a coping strategy has been encouraged and has increased across the entire spectrum.

Interestingly, there is an increase in the correlation between having experienced a nervous breakdown at one time or another and seeing past problems as relevant for help. The correlation between these two indices, which was .24 in 1957, increased to .31 in 1976. This is not a substantial increase, but nevertheless one that commands attention. It may be attributable to a shift from 1957 to 1976 in what people identify as indications or precipitant causes of nervous breakdown (table 2.9). The 1957 population sees nervous breakdown based on external matters somewhat more than the 1976 population: in 1957, 39 percent of those who said they had felt they might have a nervous breakdown referred to some external cause, such as death of a loved one, work-related tension, or financial or other circumstantial conditions. This percentage decreased somewhat in 1976 to 32 percent. More impressive is the decrease from 18 percent to 9 percent in seeing one's physical illness or disability as the precipitant of a nervous breakdown. In 1976, seeing one's own personality problems, or an interpersonal difficulty increased as major precipitants. The increase in mentioning interpersonal difficulties was especially substantial.

The overall impression is that what constitutes a nervous breakdown in 1976 is subjectively different from what it was in 1957. More people now see interpersonal issues as sources of nervous breakdowns, and fewer people see external events as precipitants. Again this seems to reflect an increased psychological orientation to perceived distress, within which formal helpseeking is more clearly relevant.

TABLE 2.9

Problems Mentioned in Feeling of Impending Nervous
Breakdown (first-mentioned reasons only)

	1957 (%)		1976 (%)	
External	39		32	
Death or illness of loved one; other separation		16		14
Work-related tension		12		13
Financial or other circumstantial conditions		9		5
Own physical illness or disability	18		9	
Personality problems, general tensions	18		23	
Interpersonal difficulties	16		32	
Menopause	4		1	
Not ascertained	5		6	
	100%		100%	
Total Number	464		472	

Finally, there is not much shift in the population's location of unhappy periods of their lives except for the slight rise seen in table 2.8 in references to unhappiness in adolescence or young adulthood.

Future Well-Being: 1957–1976

Most Americans in both years are optimistic about their future well-being: 73 percent in 1957 thought their future was going to be "very happy" or "happy," and 69 percent thought so in 1976. We seem to have been an optimistic people in 1957 and we continue to be so in 1976.

Does optimism mean something different in the two eras? The scale shows no striking differences in relationships to other measures in 1957 and 1976. In both years, those who are optimistic, compared to those not particularly optimistic about the future, are happier and are more likely to see their youth as the unhappiest time of life. Optimism is not systematically related to other measures of well-being, although there are some slight trends that differ in each year. It remains to be seen whether there is differential optimism in various subgroups in 1957, compared to 1976.

The 1976 Population: Feelings and Sources of Well-Being

We enriched our repertoire of questions about well-being in 1976 by including a variety of additional measures. Let us look now at the responses given by the 1976 population to these questions to see whether they put any perspective on the results noted in the last section. What more do they tell us about the state of psychological well-being of the American population in 1976?

TABLE 2.10

*Feelings of Well-Being Assessed in Question
Asked Only in 1976*

Feelings of Well-Being Total Number = 2,264	Percentage
Feelings of Present Well-Being	
Satisfaction	
Completely satisfied	16
Pretty satisfied	73
Not very satisfied	10
Not ascertained	1
	100%
Zest	
Scores:	
6–18 (low or "depressed")	19
19–22	20
23–25	23
26–27	17
28–30 (high)	19
Not ascertained	2
	100%
Feelings of Past Well-Being	
Frequency of Bad Things Happening:	
A lot	8
Some	31
Not much	27
Hardly ever	34
Never	<1
Not ascertained	<1
	100%
Past Compared to Present	
Past happier	24
Same	30
Past not happier	41
Not ascertained	5
	100%
Frequency Felt Overwhelmed by Bad Things Happening	
Many times	8
Sometimes	6
Once in a while	28
Never	58
Not ascertained	4
	100%

Table 2.10 shows the distributions of five new indices of well-being. A large majority of the population (89 percent) felt relatively satisfied with their lives, gave very few "depressed" responses to the zest questions, and did not regard the past five to ten years as happier than the present. They could not think of many bad things that had happened to them. Only 8 percent of the population said "a lot" of bad things happened to them and 31 percent said some. Fifty-eight percent denied ever feeling overwhelmed by bad events.

How do these results fit in with what other things we know about the 1976 population—in particular, with how it has changed or remained stable since 1957?

In regard to present well-being, the new measures suggest that a relatively satisfied nondepressed population of men and women in 1976, although more "worried" than the previous generation, did not translate worrying into an abundance of negative perceptions. Taking satisfaction as an affective evaluation of how much life has fulfilled expectations, and zest as an affective appraisal of positive involvement with life experiences, we can further state that worrying seems not to have diminished positive experiences or fulfillment of aspiration.

Looking at past well-being, the 1976 measures offer some new insights about the change we have observed. Many more men and women in 1976, compared to 1957, say they have had a personal problem for which they could or did use professional help. Since feelings of impending nervous breakdown correlate relatively well with having had a problem relevant for help, we might have expected a significant shift in people reporting that they felt as if they were going to have a nervous breakdown, but there was no change in such reported feelings. This suggests that people over the generation learned to see problems other than an impending nervous breakdown as relevant for help seeking.

Frequency bad things happened and *frequency feeling overwhelmed* did correlate with seeing *problem relevant for help* in 1976; the correlations were .23 and .32 respectively. Nearly everyone agrees that bad things happen, and 42 percent admit to feeling overwhelmed at least once in a while when bad things happen. Did these psychological feelings become facilitative of help seeking in 1976? Help seeking probably has come to be seen as relevant for crises stemming from *outside* circumstances more than it once was, as the psychology of crisis intervention became a therapeutic discipline in the last decade. We will be discussing this further in Book 2.

The fact that only 24 percent of the 1976 population said that their past was happier compared to the present suggests that we are not an overly nostalgic people. Since we found no dramatic shifts in people's use of the past or present as happiest, we would assume we would have found little shift from 1957 to 1976 had we asked in 1957 for this more limited evaluation comparing the relatively recent past with the present.

Multivariate Analyses of Measures of Well-Being

Thus far we have examined differences between 1957 and 1976, as well as information solely available in 1976 as if the nation were a single entity. Such large-scale social indicators have important implications, as does descriptive information for any group, small or large. In this case, it is clearest that more Americans are worrying in 1976 than were in 1957, but there has been little overall shift in reported happiness within the United States as a whole. And that, too, speaks forcefully about the lack of change in the country.

Nevertheless, we can probe such results more carefully. Are they more descriptive of certain groups than others? Men? Women? Does the same level of worry mean something different in different groups? For example, how does worry compare among the more educated and the less educated? In the young compared to the elderly? Does any year change reflect only the fact that we have become a much more highly educated society? Does lack of change reflect the fact that the 1976 population has proportionately more older and younger members than the 1957 population?

By taking into account such features of the American population, we can begin to perform two much-needed functions in our analyses of subjective well-being. First, information about the different responses of various education and age groups for men and women taken separately in 1957 and in 1976 will help us qualify and understand the changes or stability just highlighted in our generational comparison. Was an apparent generational shift prevalent in only one group? Would an apparent generational shift "disappear" if we controlled for the differential composition of age and educational groups in 1957 and 1976? Perhaps measures that show no overall change from 1957 to 1976 will emerge as significant "changes" when we control for these factors.

We will perform a second function by looking more closely at year differences. Information about men and women of different ages and education groups in both years would help us depict how sex, age, and education by themselves affect subjective well-being. These were powerful analytic variables in the 1957 study, and we have adopted them as standard analysis filters for all our data. Having measures from two different years separated by a twenty-year period of momentous change involving increased formal education levels for most groups in the society and the consciousness raising of women, youth, the elderly, and the oppressed, adds richness to our study of sex, age, and education differences of subjective well-being. In effect, this affords us the opportunity in these analyses to evaluate not just the generation difference, per se, but how generational differences might amplify sex, age, and educational comparisons of subjective well-being. For example, women in 1957 "worried" more than men. If that difference has disappeared or diminished over the generation, one might suspect that attitudinal shifts about sex roles during the 1960s and 1970s could and did have some effect on how women react to their life situations. On the other hand, if it remained stable, then we might begin to think of more profound sex-role determinants of "worrying," ones that are not so amenable to consciousness raising.

We can include measures used only in 1976 for analyses of sex, age, and education differences. Despite losing year differences and interactions, the results will still allow us to depict crucial demographic comparisons in well-being.

For our two next immediate goals—amplifying year comparisons and depicting sex, age, and education comparisons—we needed a way to look more closely at measures of well-being. We followed a number of steps we shall mention below, to aid us in this task; this strategy will apply not only to this chapter but to subsequent chapters as well.

We first divided respondents into thirty-six groups cross-classified by the *two* years, the *two* sexes, *three* age groups (21–34, 35–54, 55 and older), and *three* educational levels (no high school, some high school, some college).[2]

Second, we subjected each of the measures of well-being to log-linear cross-classification analysis (Goodman, 1978). Thus, for *worries, happiness, future morale,* and other variables, we cross-classified the level of well-being (sometimes grouped for simplicity) by the various year $\times$ sex $\times$ age $\times$ education groups noted above. (For measures used only in 1976, the year classification was left out.) The log-linear cross-classification technique asks what is the most parsimonious "model" or set of variables (among sex, year, age, and education, and their interactions) needed to reproduce reliably the cross-classifications with regard to the specific psychological response (e.g., extent of worrying cross-classified by sex by age by education by year). The power to detect interaction in cross-classification tables is one of the technique's strong points. In this chapter, for example, the technique provides the key generalization that the increased worrying we observed in the year comparison is most strongly evidenced by younger people in 1976, compared to 1957.

Again, the "model" might say that with education differences alone, we could successfully reproduce the observed frequencies in a given

---

[2] We used these gross categories in order to maintain reasonably sized groups. We naturally would have preferred more refined groupings of age and education, and for descriptive purpose we will present some data for these narrower groups.

table under scrutiny, or it might point to an interaction between year and age, in addition to an effect by education. Complex interactions involving four or five variables can also be part of the model.[3] Significance tests are generated for these models to indicate where the power of the variables is coming from. The technique is fully explained in appendix C. Since we are not interested in how sex × age × education × year interact with each other *apart from their relationships* to the psychological variables, we asked in our model testing what effects involving the psychological reactions were needed *over and above* the demographic variables' interrelationships.

Further, we looked more closely at each of the effects in the model required for a given psychological reaction, to see where the specific effect was occurring. We find, for example, that age differences are needed in the model to reproduce the *future morale* cross-classification by year × sex × age × education. We wanted to know which reaction by which age group is responsible for the importance of age differences in the model. Further statistical analyses (lambdas) permit such assessments. Lambdas test the impact of knowing the frequency of a given cell of a given cross-classification effect. The significance tests (lambdas) applied to the example, to each of the levels of age and each of the levels of the *future morale* assessment tell us that the youngest group is *significantly*[4] more likely to have cases in the "happier" levels, and the oldest groups significantly less likely to have cases at that level.

Finally, we listed these observations of significant differences in tabular form. The summary of these analyses of measures used in this chapter appear in tables 2.11 through 2.14. Table 2.11 is a summary of the multivariate analysis of feelings of well-being; tables 2.12, 2.13, and 2.14 are summaries of the multivariate analyses of sources of happiness, unhappiness, and worries, respectively. These data helped guide our further discussion in this chapter. In each table we present whether there is a "main effect" for age, education, year or sex required, and/or an interaction effect to reproduce the observed cross-classification of each of the measures. If there is a main effect, we symbolically summarize it in the table. If an interaction occurs, we simply state what variables are involved. Otherwise a blank is indicated.

Let us illustrate the use of this type of table. Looking at table 2.11, "Main effects" for age, education, year, and sex are listed as columns.

---

[3] In the specific computer analysis used (ECTA), assumption of hierarchical effects is made—that is, if an interaction is needed, a variable that is part of the interaction is automatically used in the model as a simpler effect. For example, if age and education are interactively necessary to reproduce the cross-classification of a given psychological variable, then age alone and education alone are included as parts of the "model" being tested.

[4] At the technical level this significance should be interpreted as a difference in odds-ratios about cases being in a certain cross-classification. See Davis (1974) and Duncan and Duncan (1978) for a clear explanation of odds-ratio.

TABLE 2.11
Summary of Multivariate Analyses of Feelings of Well-Being

	Relationship(s) Required[a] to Reproduce Observed Cross-Classification of Measures by Age × Education × Year[b] × Sex[c]				
	Main Effect[d]				
Measures of Well-Being	Age	Education	Year	Sex	Interaction
Happiness	—	G<H<C	57>76	—	Age × Sex
Worries	Y>MA>O	G>H>C	57<76	M<F	Age × Year
Present Happiest	—[e]	—[e]	—[e]		—[e]
Men	Y>MA>O	—	—	***	
Women	Y>MA>O	G<H<C	57<76	***	
Satisfaction	Y<MA<O	—	—[b]	—	
Zest	MA>Y,O	G<H<C	—[b]	M>F	
Nervous Breakdown	Y,MA>O	—	—	M<F	
Experienced Problem Relevant for Help	Y>MA>O	G<H<C	57<76	M<F	
Childhood Unhappiest	Y>MA>O	G<H<C	—[b]	M>F	Age × Education × Year
Past Happier	Y<MA<O	G<H<C	—[b]	M<F	
Frequency of Bad Things	—	G,H>C	—[b]	M<F	
Frequency Overwhelmed	Y>MA>O	G>H>C	—[b]	M<F	
Future Morale	Y>MA>O	G<H<C	57>76	—	

[a] In this and subsequent tables, a listed relationship is "required" in one of two possible senses: (1) any "Main Effect" indicated by an entry or any interaction(s) listed, is part of a log-linear hierarchical model (Goodman, 1978) which produces expected frequencies that do not significantly deviate from those actually observed (x^2, $p > .05$); or (2) main effect listed, although contained within a required interaction listed in (1) has a significant effect (lambda, $p < .01$, see page 67 for explanation) above and beyond its role in the interactions. The elements of the log-linear hierarchical model listed represent the most parsimonious model over and above a base model which includes all the two-way relationships for the demographic variables (age, education, year, sex), plus all the interactions of these demographic variables.

[b] Year excluded in measures assessed only in 1976.

[c] Sex effects inappropriate in disaggregated data.

[d] In this and subsequent tables, entries describe relationships by following designations: for age groups, Y=21–34, MA=35–54, O=55+; for education groups, G=grade school, H=high school, C=college; for year, 57=1957, 76=1976; for sex, M=men, F=women. Group(s) to left of the < symbol are less than the group(s) to the right of that symbol; group(s) to the left of the > symbol are greater than the group(s) to the right of that symbol.

[e] Cross-classification is run separately for men and women because a complex four-way interaction involving both the measure of well-being and sex is needed to explain the five-variable cross-classification.

TABLE 2.12

Summary of Multivariate Analyses of Sources of Happiness

Relationship(s) Required[a]
to Reproduce Observed Cross-Classification of Measures
by Age × Education × Year × Sex[b]

Sources of Happiness	Main Effect[c]				Interaction
	Age	Education	Year	Sex	
Economic and Material	—	H>G,C	57>76	M>F	
Children	—	—	—	M<F	Age × Year
Marriage	Y>MA>O	G<H,C	57>76	—	
Other Interpersonal	—[d]	—[d]	—[d]	M>F	—[d]
Men	Y>MA>O	—	—	—[b]	
Women	—	G<H,C	—	—[b]	
Job	Y>MA>O	—	—	M>F	
R's Health	Y<MA<O	—	—	—	Age × Education
Family Health	MA>Y,O	—	57<76	M<F	
Independence	Y,MA<O	—	57<76	—	
Personal Characteristics	—	G>C>H	57<76	M<F	Age × Year

[a] See Footnote[a] of Table 2.11 for an explanation of "Required."

[b] Sex effects inappropriate in disaggregated data.

[c] See Footnote[a] of Table 2.11 for description of "Main Effects."

[d] Cross-classification is run separately for men and women because a complex four-way interaction involving both the measure of well-being and sex is needed to explain the five-variable cross-classification.

TABLE 2.13

Summary of Multivariate Analyses of Sources of Unhappiness

| Sources of Unhappiness | Relationship(s) Required[a] to Reproduce Observed Cross-Classification of Measures by Age × Education × Year × Sex[b] | | | | Interaction |
| | Main Effect[c] | | | | |
	Age	Education	Year	Sex	
Economic and Material	Y>MA>O	—	—	—	
Children	MA>O>Y	—	—	M<F	Age × Education
Marriage	Y,MA>O	—	—	M<F	
Other Interpersonal	MA<Y,O [d]	G<H<C [d]	57<76 [d]	M>F	*
Job Men	Y>MA>O	G<H<C	—	—[b]	
Women	Y>MA>O	G<H<C	57<76	—[b]	
R's Health	Y<MA<O	—	—	M<F	
Family Health	Y<MA,O	—	57>76	M<F	
Community, National and World Problems	Y<MA,O	—	57<76	M>F	
Personal Characteristics	—	G<H<C	57>76	—	

[a] See Footnote[a] of Table 2.11 for an explanation of "Required."

[b] Sex effects inappropriate in disaggregated data.

[c] See Footnote[a] of Table 2.11 for description of "Main Effects."

[d] Cross-classification is run separately for men and women because a complex four-way interaction involving both the measure of well-being and sex is needed to explain the five-variable cross-classification.

TABLE 2.14
Summary of Multivariate Analyses of Sources of Worries

Relationship(s) Required[a]
to Reproduce Observed Cross-Classification of Measures
by Age × Education × Year × Sex[b]

Sources of Worries	Main Effect[c]				Interaction
	Age	Education	Year	Sex	
Economic and Material	Y>MA>O	G>H>C	—	—	
Children	MA>Y,O	—[d]	—[d]	M<F	Education × Age; Age × Year
Marriage					
Men	—[d]	—	—[d]	M<F	—[d]
Women	Y>MA>O	—	—	—[b]	
Other Interpersonal					
Men	—[d]	—[d]	—[d]	M>F	—[d]
Women	—	—	—	—[b]	Age × Education × Year
Job	Y,MA<O	G,H<C	57<76	M>F	
R's Health	Y>MA>O	G,H<C	—	M>F	
Family Health	Y<MA<O	—	57>76	M>F	
Community, National and World Problems	Y<MA<O	G<H<C	—	—	
Personal Characteristics	Y>MA>O	C>G>H	—	M<F	

[a] See Footnote[a] of Table 2.11 for an explanation of "Required."

[b] Sex effects inappropriate in disaggregated data.

[c] See Footnote[a] of Table 2.11 for discussion of description of "Main Effects."

[d] Cross-classification is run separately for men and women because a complex four-way interaction involving both the measure of well-being and sex is needed to explain the five-variable cross-classification.

There is an additional column for interaction effects. Different measures of well-being are listed as rows. Look at the *happiness* row. The results listed in the columns for happiness show a blank under the main effect for age and sex—thus we know that age and sex do not relate to happiness when all the variables in the cross-classification and their interaction are taken into account. They are not needed in a model which can reproduce the observed frequencies. As it turns out, there is an age × sex interaction which is needed, and it is listed under the interaction column. (As will soon become clear, younger men state they are "very happy" less often than younger women, but this result is reversed for older men and women.) The fact that in the year column we indicate that 1957 is significantly "less happy" than 1976 indicates that *over* and *above* the interaction effect, year differences were also needed in the model that reproduces the frequencies.[5]

These analyses become laborious when complicated interactions are needed in the model; thus we simplified our procedure by occasionally running analyses separately for males and females when complex interactions that involved sex as a variable were needed. This happened in trying to find a model for sex × year × age × education differences in *present happiest*. Thus, in table 2.10, the models are run separately for males and females. No interactions with sex are computed, but they are implied in the comparison of effects needed for males and females. Straightforward sex differences are tested with the model in which all interactions are included. The footnotes in table 2.11 clarify these points and apply to all such summaries of multivariate analyses that appear in parallel tables in other chapters.

QUALIFICATIONS OF YEAR COMPARISONS AS RESULT OF MULTIVARIATE
ANALYSES

We can now look at the summary tables for evidence that might cause us to qualify or expand on any of the differences highlighted, or to clarify changes that were previously ignored.

Results Not Previously Highlighted

All the results we have highlighted as year differences in the previous section show up as *year* main effects, but a few more year effects appear in the summary tables that were not previously highlighted. The first two emerge as straightforward year effects; the next four emerge from interaction effects. They are listed below.

The straightforward new year effects are:

1. *There is a significant year difference in happiness and future morale.*
There is a slight tendency for people in 1957 to say they are "very hap-

---

[5] Lambdas were at $p < .01$. We adopted a more stringent criterion for significance of "main effects" of a variable if that variable was also part of a needed interaction.

TABLE 2.15
Year Differences in Happiness and Future Morale (by education)

	Educational Level									
	Grade School		Some High School		High School Graduate		Some College		College Graduate	
	1957	1976	1957	1976	1957	1976	1957	1976	1957	1976
Happiness Percent: "Very Happy"	23	24	30	24	46	32	43	36	44	37
Future Morale Percent: Very happy, happy	30	22	55	42	64	55	67	57	66	60
Total Number	802	380	511	347	674	766	247	411	210	347

py" and to say their future will be happy more often than people in
1976 when education, age, and sex are controlled. This can be readily
seen in table 2.15, where we present separate results for the 1957 and
1976 responses to happiness and morale about the future for different
educational levels. The differences are not large but are very consistent
with one exception (grade school only with regard to happiness). People in 1957 expressed more extreme happiness and optimism for the future than did people in 1976 at each educational level. That more educated people in general are more happy and optimistic, and that there
were more educated people in 1976 masked these findings when we
looked at overall year differences.

2. *Women seem to have been somewhat more likely in 1957 to talk of their
present life as happiest compared to women in 1976.* The same trends existed for men. (See table 2.16, which introduces age, education, and sex
controls.) What becomes clear in these results is that the controls bring
to light a somewhat greater nostalgia in most groups of women of the
later generation: more women in 1957—especially young women—
said the present was happiest; more women in 1976 said their past was
happiest. This finding was true also for some groups of men, but not
significantly so.

Four further year differences not previously highlighted occur as interaction results in tables 2.11 through 2.14: the interaction of age ×
education × year is needed to reproduce the cross-classification of
whether childhood is mentioned as the unhappiest time; the interaction of age × year is needed to reproduce the tabulation of whether
children are mentioned as a source of happiness and as a source of worries; an age × education × year interaction is needed for men only to
reproduce the cell frequencies regarding interpersonal sources of worry. The results reflect the following facts:

3. *Mentioning childhood as the unhappiest time is especially prevalent in
young college-educated people of 1976 (59 percent) compared to all other
groups (24 percent).*

4. *Children as a source of happiness are mentioned more among young people
in 1957 and among middle-aged people in 1976.*

5. *Children as a source of worries are mentioned most frequently by middle-
aged people in 1976.*

6. *Young college-educated men in 1976 are more likely than their counterparts in 1957 to worry about interpersonal matters.*

Result 3 above may be a function of the psychological orientation in
the high school and college classrooms of the 1960s and 1970s that
taught people to attribute difficulties encountered in living as reflections of problems in early socialization. Result 6 might reflect the deeper immersion of young college-educated men into a psychological orientation to interpersonal relationships, again, recently taught more
vigorously in college classrooms; women have long held that orienta-

TABLE 2.16
Year Differences in Reporting Present Life as Happiest Time (by age × education × sex)

		Men				Women			
		1957		1976		1957		1976	
Education	Age	Total Number	Percent-age	Percent-age	Total Number	Total Number	Percent-age	Percent-age	Total Number
Grade School	21–34	48	48	20	15	54	35	20	15
	35–54	134	35	25	32	158	25	19	42
	55+	183	19	28	107	222	12	14	169
High School	21–34	163	47	41	150	310	51	42	254
	35–54	215	41	37	149	296	38	27	253
	55+	83	30	25	125	113	18	11	180
College	21–34	100	43	41	180	78	59	46	197
	35–54	100	39	39	131	100	34	47	91
	55+	36	33	21	37	34	12	15	92

tion. The more recent college-educated men might have been the first group of men to focus heavily on interpersonal experience, per se.

With a control for parental status results 4 and 5 listed above are less clear-cut and thus seem to be a function of the smaller proportion of parents among the young of 1976. It seems to have been a cohort phenomenon that young people of the 1950s became very invested in being parents. Children were a major source of happiness for them in 1957. The same cohort as middle-aged people—remaining child centered in 1976—were forced into a lot of worrying about their offspring facing the complexities of settling into the 1970s as adults.

Qualifications to Previously Described Year Differences

In scanning Tables 2.11 through 2.14, we discovered evidence of three qualifications to previously mentioned year differences.

First, increased reporting of job unhappiness seems clearest among women. Twenty-three percent of men in 1957 mentioned job sources of unhappiness and 25 percent did so in 1976. The parallel results for women are 11 percent in 1957 and 20 percent in 1976. When we control for employment status, results are almost identical: for working men—24 percent in 1957, 25 percent in 1976; for working women—14 percent in 1957 and 25 percent in 1976. The group registering a considerable increase in reports of job unhappiness from 1957 to 1976 are women. As more women have begun careers or joined the work force to bring in more money, evidently they have been able to voice more discontent than they once did. The women's movement may have lowered the threshold of complaint about work as a salient feature of ongoing life. Evidently, for men, the salient feature of work unhappiness has not shifted much. This problem will be discussed in more detail in chapter 6.

Of the other two qualifications involving interaction of age and year, one has to do with the increase in worrying between 1957 and 1976; the other with the increase in mentioning personal sources of happiness. While a significant year effect remains for these responses, there is also an important interactive effect with year and age. Younger groups in 1976 are just more likely to express a lot of worry—whatever they worry about—compared to both young people in 1957 and older groups in either year. In addition, younger people in 1976 are more likely than younger people in 1957 to focus on personal sources of happiness, though not many people of any age in either year give such a response. These data are displayed in table 2.17. More will be said on these results when we present age differences in a later section. For the moment, we need only point out that *in addition* to the significant differences in 1957 vs. 1976 in *worrying* and *mentioning personal characteristics* as sources of happiness, there is an even stronger increase in such responses for young people. Thus, the generation changes seem to have had interesting effects on the young in particular—it has made

TABLE 2.17

*Percent Worrying Always or A Lot and Mentioning
Personal Characteristics as Source of Happiness
(by age × year)*

Age	Total Number		Worrying Always or A Lot		Mentioning Personal Characteristics as Sources of Happiness	
	1957	1976	1957 %	1976 %	1957 %	1976 %
21–29	453	546	32	51	1	6
30–39	584	463	32	53	2	7
40–49	514	341	34	47	2	4
50–59	390	342	35	39	3	4
60–64	153	166	33	42	5	3
65+	353	397	36	39	3	3

them particularly vulnerable to worry and at the same time more able to turn inward to seek sources of happiness. These may be related phenomena: as the future becomes more uncertain, people may seek internal support to compensate for what they perceive as inadequacies in their social world. It may be equally plausible to think of the data as separate phenomena. Increased worry in the young may be a reaction to unsettling economic conditions and a fast-changing social world. Among other pressures, young people now face very uncertain expectations for family roles. Their increased focus on personal happiness may be something quite separate—perhaps a response to the self-oriented movements of the 1960s which developed in times of affluence as opposed to a period of economic and social constraint.

Our brief scanning of the summary multivariate tables, and how they may have affected our analysis of year differences, reveals a rich vein of information about the social characteristics in our range of focus: sex differences, age differences, and education differences. We will discuss each in turn, highlighting results that are significant main effects or interactive effects in the summary tables.

Sex Differences in Feelings of Well-Being

Here we explore the differential responses of men and women in 1957 and 1976 to questions that assess sources of well-being as well as overall evaluations of well-being.

TABLE 2.18

Selected Sex Differences in Reported Sources of Well-Being[a] (by year)

Sources of Well-Being	1957		1976	
	Males %	Females %	Males %	Females %
Happiness				
Economic or material	38	33	32	26
Job	12	5	11	7
Children	20	36	18	39
Unhappiness				
Job	23	8	25	17
Community, national, world problem	15	8	32	19
Worries				
Job	20	6	24	10
Children	8	22	12	27
Family's health	11	23	10	16
Total Number	1,077	1,383	960	1,304

[a] Percentage of respondents with a given source of well-being or worries in their first two mentions.

We find patterns that conform to clear sex-role expectations when we examine how men and women in the two generations respond differently to questions about sources of happiness, unhappiness, and worry. Hochschild (1975) has forcefully argued that there are norms in society not only for how people in different positions behave and act, but also how they should *feel*; rules that regulate *when* people are supposed to feel something and *what* the quality of that experience should be. The unwritten rules that prevail in our social system are doubtless fairly well known in relation to how men and women are supposed to *feel* about their life experiences. Our findings conform very well to such expectations and are summarized in table 2.18. Men are more likely than women to say that they are happy about economic and material matters; they are more unhappy about jobs and worry more about jobs than women do. This fits with standard sex-role expectations of our society in which men are expected to focus their affective gratifications within the provider roles. By contrast, women report that they are happy about their children, they worry about their children, and they worry about their family's health significantly more than men do—again in correspondence with rules that women are supposed to focus on their children and their families.

It could be argued that men report affective experiences in the provider role and that women report affective experiences in family roles because these are their respective spheres. When we control for whether or not a person was employed or was a parent, most of the sex differences remain, but some change. In particular, working men and women report equal happiness through their jobs (12 percent men; 12

TABLE 2.19

*Sex Differences Among Employed People's Reports
of Work-Related Sources of Unhappiness (by year)*

	1957		1976	
	Men %	Women %	Men %	Women %
Total Sample	24		28	
		13		25
Total Number	924	457	753	599
21–29 only	27		33	
		22		34
Total Number	164	87	207	187

percent women). This is true in both 1957 and 1976. Employed men still report more job *unhappiness* than employed women do in 1976, but there is clearly a generational narrowing of the gap between the sexes on this dimension. This pattern, seen in table 2.19, shows many more employed women in 1976 reporting that they are unhappy about their work. Sex-role expectations seem to exist for men and women regardless of whether they are in roles or not, but as they take on a role, some of the norms shift. Indeed, with consciousness raising, women in 1976 were much more likely to see sources of unhappiness in work than women in 1957—facets of experience they may have been taught to overlook in 1957. If anything, young female workers complain about work more than the young male workers in 1976 (see table 2.19), suggesting that the rule for women *not* getting actively involved in jobs as a source of gratification or frustration is becoming much less clear, perhaps even disappearing in the youngest generation.

The above results which we have interpreted as a conventional tendency for men and women to report affective experiences in terms of the salient life roles to which they are assigned can also be interpreted as merely different time spent in particular roles. That is, more men are actively engaged in the provider role and more women are actively engaged in family roles. The degree of affective involvement in their sex-specific role gratifications and frustrations could be a function entirely of time involvement, rather than of *rules* that men and women have learned. Both explanations seem plausible, and indeed they may be different facets of the same positions; that is, men are supposed to be more active as well as more involved in the job and provider role, and women are supposed to be more involved and more feeling about the parental role. It is interesting to note that men and women refer to their marital roles as sources of happiness at about the same rate. However, since many more men in our samples are "currently married," we reran

TABLE 2.20

Sex Differences in Reporting Marital Sources of Happiness and Unhappiness (married respondents only)

| | Marriage as Source of Happiness | | | | Marriage as Source of Unhappiness | | | |
| | Men | | Women | | Men | | Women | |
Year	Percentage	Number	Percentage	Number	Percentage	Number	Percentage	Number
1957	19	908	25	963	2	908	9	963
1976	18	697	27	739	3	697	6	739
Total	19	1,604	26	1,702	2	1,605	8	1,702

the analysis for married men and women only (table 2.20). The trends are clear: more women than men spontaneously focus on marriage as a source of their affective lives. If our lines of reasoning are accurate, we can conclude either that there are clearer role expectations for wives than husbands about how much they are supposed to find happiness or unhappiness in a marital role, or that wives devote more time to their marriages than their husbands. Of course, both may be true.

One other point of difference between men and women seems important: more men than women report feeling unhappy about their community, their nation, or world affairs. Though it is a less obvious sex-role stereotype, this type of response could be classified as one that fits certain conceptions of how men and women are supposed to differ. Ortner (1974) cogently argues that men are perceived cross-culturally as more related to culture and women more connected to nature. Part of the association, she argues, is that men relate more to the wider civic order and women are more related to the insular family bond. Our results substantiate Ortner's contention that men seem to be more absorbed in issues in the world than women in considering sources of unhappiness.

Overall, the findings about sex differences in sources of happiness, unhappiness, and worries, show remarkably similar patterns of well-being for men and women. Other than the sources clearly connected with men and women's roles, the sexes seem to structure the quality of their well-being very similarly.

How do men and women differ in evaluations of their affective life? Women report that they are leading or have led more difficult lives than men; they report much more frequent experience of distress. Table 2.21 presents the results upon which we base these conclusions. Most dramatically, more women than men in both 1957 and 1976 report that they worry a lot, that some time in their life they have experienced the feeling of having a nervous breakdown, that they have had a problem for which they used or could have used help, and that some time in the past (rather than the present) was the happiest of their life. The pattern is corroborated in the 1976 assessment for which no comparable measure was available in 1957: more women (45 percent) than men (31 percent) say that bad things have happened to them a lot or some of the time, and that they have been overwhelmed when such bad things have happened to them. Furthermore, in 1976 men are more likely to score higher on zest.

Are men simply more likely to avoid thinking about negative feelings either in their past or present life? Sex-role expectations enter this interpretation: men are not supposed to feel as sad about life events as women do; they are supposed to cope with those events when they occur, take action to change negative events. If nothing can be done about fate, men should not cry or experience deeply depressed reac-

TABLE 2.21
Sex Differences in Measures of Well-Being (by year)

Measure	1957 Men %	1957 Women %	1976 Men %	1976 Women %
Present Well-Being				
Worries:				
Always, a lot	28	38	39	50
Sometimes, not much	57	54	52	46
Never	15	8	9	4
	100%	100%	100%	100%
Happiness:				
Very happy	33	30	36	31
Pretty happy	57	60	52	57
Not too happy	10	10	12	12
	100%	100%	100%	100%
Present Happiest Time:				
Yes	38	36	34	30
Satisfaction:[a]				
Completely satisfied			17	16
Pretty satisfied			73	72
Not satisfied			9	11
Not ascertained			1	1
			100%	100%
Zest:[a]				
Low score			31	38
Moderate score			31	27
High score			38	35
			100%	100%
Past Well-Being				
Nervous Breakdown:				
Yes	12	24	14	26
Experienced Problems Relevant for Professional Help:				
Yes	18	27	32	40
Childhood Unhappiest Time:				
Yes	30	20	35	27
Evaluation of Past Compared to Present:[a]				
Past happier			24	25
Same			32	28
Not as happy			39	42
Not ascertained			5	5
			100%	100%
Frequency of Feeling Overwhelmed:[a]				
Never			66	52
Once in awhile			25	31
Sometimes; many times			9	17
			100%	100%
Future Well-Being				
Morale for Future:				
Very happy	52	50	51	48
Happy	22	21	20	21
Not too happy	10	9	10	11
Not ascertained	16	20	19	20
	100%	100%	100%	100%
Total Number[b]	1,077	1,383	960	1,304

[a] Measure not available for 1957 sample.

[b] Numbers vary depending on whether nonascertained responses are categorized.

tions. Women are permitted such experiences; indeed, implicit social rules say that women are *supposed* to react in these ways.

Another interesting result bears on the foregoing discussion: men more than women locate the unhappiest time in their childhood or their "youth." Such a response can be interpreted as coping with unhappy feelings by admitting to strong negative feelings that have occurred far in the past. Men engage this coping strategy more than women. It is as if men purposefully locate the *distant* childhood past as an unhappy period because at that time they were presumably less in control of their lives. As men are prodded into questioning the quality of their *present* life circumstances, they may avoid thinking of their affective life, especially the unhappy part of it. If men are experiencing distress, they may wish to avoid blaming themselves for their fate, for not preventing this fate, or extricating themselves from it.

All of these results might be interpreted as reflecting "real" life circumstance differences between the sexes. Although social researchers (Phillips and Segal, 1969; Dohrenwend and Dohrenwend, 1974) have alerted the social-psychiatric researcher to the differential responsiveness of men and women to questions about well-being which may be a function of sex-role expectation, one could also argue that women *do* face more difficult life events in their experience, that they indeed do have more bad things happen to them, that they are confronted with things that would produce the strain that would lead to feelings of a nervous breakdown or to cause them to worry. Equally, in this line of reasoning, one could argue that men do in fact have unhappier childhoods than women, that the transition to adulthood is generally more difficult for men than for women, but that as both sexes move through adulthood, men find life circumstances easing more than women do, and find a gradually enhanced quality of life. Jessie Bernard (1972) has argued that marriage is an institution well set up for men but not for women. Certainly the occupational world is one that is stacked in favor of men in our society. The obligations of the parent role for maintaining family comfort and health are burdens that traditionally are seen in the woman's domain more than the man's. Role changes that occur soon after early adulthood can be seen as changes that burden the life of the woman and *lighten* the load for the man. Again, the shorter life span of men might suggest that women are more often confronted with handling the problem of solitude than men are. The adult life span may in fact be more difficult for women than for men. Locksley and Douvan (1979) have presented evidence from a study of high school students for the fact that high schools are generally geared to men's goals more than to women's. A cross-over in ease of adaptation to the social structure may begin during this transition period. As young women are channeled into parenthood, in particular, the sexist bias in adult institutions may enliven men's joy in the present and engage women's nostalgia for the past.

TABLE 2.22

Relation of Age to Happiness (by sex and year)

| | Age | | | | | |
| | 21–34 | | 35–54 | | 55+ | |
Happiness	Men (%)	Women (%)	Men (%)	Women (%)	Men (%)	Women (%)
1957						
Very Happy	33	45	35	38	30	24
Pretty Happy	64	48	54	51	55	57
Not Too Happy	3	7	11	11	15	19
	100%	100%	100%	100%	100%	100%
Total Number	317	440	447	556	306	373
1976						
Very Happy	29	35	33	31	30	28
Pretty Happy	62	55	58	59	58	58
Not Too Happy	9	10	9	10	12	15
	100%	100%	100%	100%	100%	100%
Total Number	340	467	306	383	294	433

To an important extent, this latter hypothesis about developmental transformations in quality of life for the two sexes as they take leave of early adult roles and enter more mature stages is confirmed in some of our survey evidence. While there is no overall sex difference in the mention of happiness, there is a very interesting interaction with age. In table 2.22 we see that young women are relatively more happy than young men and old men are relatively happier than old women. There is a steady increase in feeling not too happy with each succeeding age for both sexes, but the interaction indicates that women's reports of being very happy diminish with each group in both years while the percentage of men's reports of being very happy remains relatively constant.

It seems plausible that there are elements of truth to both interpretations we have offered for the differential report of well-being for men and women: that men disclaim their bad affective experiences, and that the institutional arrangement of our society has generally favored the adult male more than the adult female. Both interpretations recognize that the conscious experience of well-being in our society is not as favorable for women as for men. The measures for which we did not get very clear evidence of sex differences were those that implied more cognitive evaluation of experience: in the evaluations of satisfaction with life, and of expectations of the future. When asked for such evaluations, men and women give similar responses.

More will be said about men's apparent denial of negative feelings in our interpretation of the results of sex differences in the report of psychological and physical symptoms in chapter 7. Men report fewer symptoms of physical and psychological distress. To the degree that such denial allows men to cope actively with their lives, denial may be a positive adjustment. To the degree that denial is a negative experience which suppresses feelings that need attention, men's reactions may be more problematic. Indeed, there is reason to believe that the denial of symptoms may ultimately be detrimental to men's health, insofar as unwillingness to recognize bad physical or psychological conditions stands in the way of getting the help that would alleviate them.

Age Difference in Feelings of Well-Being

We turn now to the examination of how men and women of different ages respond to questions of well-being and evaluate their overall adjustment. The different age groups in each of the years are compared on the various measures of general sources of well-being in table 2.23. We present parallel data for the measures of evaluations of well-being in table 2.24. The age groups are differentiated: 21–29, 30–39, 40–49, 50–59, 60–64, 65 and older, to facilitate analysis of the ages in the two generations that serve as *comparable cohorts*. We can examine the group 21–29 in 1957, which became approximately 40–49 in 1976; the group 30–39 in 1957 which became the group 50–59 in 1976; and the group 40–49 in 1957 which became the group 60–69 in 1976; and so on. We present cohort comparisons when they are particularly meaningful. As we indicated in chapter 1, cohort analyses generally duplicated age analyses. As each cohort matured, they generally followed the same developmental trends indicated by cross-sectional analyses in each year.

What are the important differences in age groups in both generations with regard to sources of worries, unhappiness, and happiness and their general feelings of well-being?

YOUNG PEOPLE

First, young people generally report worries and unhappiness and happiness that are connected to the new social roles of early adulthood. We find, for example, that younger respondents report economic and job worries, economic and job sources of unhappiness, and job sources

TABLE 2.23
Selected Age Comparisons of Sources of Well-Being and Distress (by year)

	Age											
	21-29		30-39		40-49		50-59		60-64		65+	
Source of Well-Being (Distress)	1957 (%)	1976 (%)	1957 (%)	1976 (%)	1957 (%)	1976 (%)	1957 (%)	1976 (%)	1957 (%)	1976 (%)	1957 (%)	1976 (%)
Happiness												
Marriage	31	22	18	16	18	17	12	14	6	8	6	5
Other interpersonal relationships	16	22	20	22	18	18	15	16	9	8	10	14
Unhappiness												
Respondent's health	2	4	3	4	7	6	10	9	11	14	16	20
Worries												
Economic/material	52	48	44	39	41	31	31	23	24	26	17	19
Job	15	26	14	19	12	13	12	14	10	13	7	4
Respondent's health	2	7	6	5	10	11	13	15	13	25	21	25
Community, national, world problems	7	9	7	8	10	11	11	11	10	13	14	10
Total Number	453	546	584	463	514	341	390	342	153	166	358	392

of happiness much more than older groups do. The results are best illustrated by looking at the figures for the different age groups in their worrying regarding both economic/material matters and worrying about their job in table 2.23. Economic worries were in the minds of 52 percent (1957) and 48 percent (1976) of those 21–29. Parallel data for those 40–49 are 41 percent (1957) and 31 percent (1976). For those 65 and older, they are 17 percent (1957) and 19 percent (1976). Worries about jobs show a similar decline: 15 percent (1957) and 26 percent (1976) in the 21–29 group, 12 percent (1957) and 13 percent (1976) in the 40–49 group, 7 percent (1957), and 4 percent (1976) in those 65 and over. The challenge of finding their socioeconomic station, especially through work, becomes the focal point of well-being in young people's reports of worries, as well as their source of happiness and unhappiness. As men and women grow into their social position, symbols of success, economic and job well-being become less central and are thus mentioned less often. It is in considering their future that the young become worried, happy, or unhappy about the course of their economic role-building efforts. Contrasted to older people, they are generally more willing to admit to worries, but as we recall from our previous discussion of year differences, the young in 1976 are especially worried compared to the young in 1957 and they are much more worried than older groups in both eras. The role-building efforts of young people in 1976 appear to be in much greater jeopardy than ever before. The economic and job outlook for the young does not allow them to feel comfortable about role-building efforts. Anxiety about inflation has been omnipresent in the past few years and exaggerated because of the very high unemployment in the country.

The challenge of adult social tasks to be transacted by the young in the realm of family roles is reflected in the greater mention of marriage as both a source of happiness and unhappiness. Young people in 1957 also mentioned children as a source of happiness more than older people did at that time, but the parallel 1976 group does not mention children as often as middle-aged people. When we control for marital and parental status, we find that marital happiness and unhappiness are more salient among the young married. Among the married, 31 percent (1957) and 32 percent (1976) of young people (21–34) mention marital sources of happiness. Parallel figures diminish to 20 percent (1957) and 19 percent (1976) among the middle-aged (35–54), and to 13 percent (1957) and 16 percent (1976) among the older groups (55+). Parental happiness was a particular focus of young parents in 1957 (40 percent), about 10 percent more than most other groups. Young (34 percent) and middle-aged (33 percent) parents in 1976 are equally likely to report parental happiness. This finding supports the widespread perception that young parents in 1957 were heavily invested in parenting.

More than any other age groups, young people tend to mention interpersonal relationships as a source of happiness: friends, parents,

TABLE 2.24
Selected Age Comparisons of Feelings of Well-Being (by year)

	Age											
	21-29		30-39		40-49		50-59		60-64		65+	
Measure of Well-Being	1956 (%)	1976 (%)	1957 (%)	1976 (%)	1957 (%)	1976 (%)	1957 (%)	1976 (%)	1957 (%)	1976 (%)	1957 (%)	1976 (%)
Present Well-Being												
Worries:												
Always, a lot	32	51	32	53	34	47	35	39	33	42	36	39
Zest:												
Highest third	—	37	—	43	—	41	—	39	—	31	—	23
Present happier than past:												
Yes	—	53	—	50	—	39	—	33	—	30	—	24
Past Well-Being												
Childhood unhappiness:												
Yes	38	52	31	34	22	26	18	20	11	20	12	13
Nervous breakdown:												
Yes	17	24	21	25	21	23	20	18	16	23	14	14
Experience problems relevant for help:												
Yes	30	43	29	40	23	42	19	32	12	26	14	19
Overwhelmed by bad things:												
Yes	—	48	—	44	—	42	—	39	—	39	—	37
Future Well-Being												
Morale about future:												
Very happy	76	69	65	65	53	48	40	42	27	28	17	17

family in general (see table 2.23). There is the interesting sex difference that young men are more likely to talk about these interpersonal sources of happiness (26 percent) than young women (18 percent). This may reflect the fact that young men are less pressed into the marriage roles as *the* sole appropriate source of happiness. They can obtain gratification from interpersonal relationships other than marital and parental ties without feeling uneasy that they have not yet reached full adulthood.

The young were clearly more happy than older groups about their future, felt that their present was happier than their past, and felt that sometime in their past was the unhappiest time in their life (see table 2.24).

With the bulk of their life ahead of them, young people are clearly worried, yet quite optimistic that the future is going to be very happy. These points are underscored in table 2.24, where we see that 76 percent (1957) and 69 percent (1976) of 21–29 year-olds think their future will be very happy. This compares with 53 percent (1957) and 48 percent (1976) among 40–49 year-olds and only 17 percent (1957) and 17 percent (1976) among those 65 and older. This is a phenomenal age difference in future optimism and is clearly tied to age rather than cohort. The young are both worried (especially in 1976) and optimistic. This contradiction may arise from their recognizing both the potential and the limitations of their futures.

It is important to point out that while the pattern of results shows younger people to be more optimistic, they are also more likely than older people to define their past problems as relevant for help. Readiness for help may reflect their optimism about change in the future. Young people seek help to *change* the future; older people are probably more pessimistic about the effectiveness of such efforts.

In a cohort analysis, we find that the effects of the broad socialization to see personal problems in mental-health terms may have been confined to the young in 1957, since only cohort 1 (21–29 in 1957)

TABLE 2.25
Cohort Changes in Experiencing Problem
Relevant for Help

		Percent Change		
Cohort	Total Number	1957 (%)	1976 (%)	Total Number
Cohort 1 (21–29 — 40–49)	453	30	42	341
Cohort 2 (30–39 — 50–59)	584	29	32	342
Cohort 3 (40–49 — 60–69)	515	23	24	311

shows any appreciable change in readiness to view problems in mental-health terms (table 2.25). Cohorts 2 and 3 show negligible change. Thus, the young not only seek help and are prepared to see themselves as needing help, but also seem to be easily socialized to these ways.

MIDDLE-AGED PEOPLE

In light of the many positive indicators of well-being favoring the young, it was somewhat surprising to find that it is not the youngest but the middle-aged group that reports greater zest. The results show slight peakings at middle age, but nonetheless these are significant results in multivariate analyses. Evidently, statements endorsing present happiness do not measure the identical things as items assessing zest. In answering a question about happiest time of life, we are measuring general affective tone, but not the keener consciousness of experiencing life's pleasures. It would seem appropriate to say that as men and women consolidate their lives at middle age, they are less happy overall because they become aware that the future as a time for experiencing the real bounties of life is diminishing. With this increased understanding of the narrowing future, many middle-aged people may become more aware of the specific richness of their *present* life. Hence the middle-aged, while not as "happy" as the young, may be more "zestful."

It is clear that of the particular sources of well-being and distress mentioned by the middle-aged, the 1976 group is more likely to worry about its children than either the middle-aged group of 1957 or the young parents of 1976. There is some evidence of an interaction such that the young parents of 1957 were worried about their children as were the middle-aged parents of 1976, suggesting that this may be a cohort phenomenon. The experiences of the 1976 generation of middle-aged parents could reflect difficulties in raising children through the 1960s, including the adolescent stage at the end of the sixties and in the seventies.

There is another possible interpretation of these results. Middle-aged parents are also happier about their children in 1976 than younger or older people in 1976. Since, as a cohort, they were also happy about their children in 1957, this group would seem to have experienced generally more involvement with their children rather than particular problems with their children. That cohort of parents became terribly invested in child rearing as a new revolution for a better society, and their involvement can find expression in happiness or in worry.[6]

[6] The results about the middle-aged cohort of parents is one of the few that touches on variation in age differences between 1976 and 1957. Another was that younger groups worry more relative to older groups in 1976 compared to 1957. Otherwise all of the age results we have discussed apply equally to 1957 and 1976.

OLDER AGE GROUP

In the older group, we find the mirror-image of certain patterns of affective experience that were positive in the young: older people are less happy, less optimistic about their future, less able to say that the present is the happiest time of their life, and tend to locate some time in their past life as happier (see table 2.24). On the other hand, there are responses in the older group to indicate that consolidation of life experiences occurs and enables them to dismiss feelings of distress that troubled younger groups. Specifically, they are less likely to say that they have experienced a nervous breakdown and less likely to say that they felt overwhelmed by bad things happening to them (see table 2.24), and more likely to say that they are completely satisfied with life. Twenty-four percent of those sixty-five and older say they are "completely satisfied." Their older age has thus put some perspective on what it means to be unable to cope with bad experiences in life. Even though older people have probably had more "bad things" happen to them, they are not more likely to report them. What is defined as a bad event may shift as the person gets older. Being overwhelmed by a bad event is clearly taken more in stride. For example, we can think of older people having adapted to more deaths of significant people in their lives. For these reasons, older people are the least ready to define a problem they have had in the past as one that required outside help. Only 14 percent of the oldest group (65+) in 1957 and 19 percent in 1976 say they have ever experienced problems relevant for help compared with 30 percent (1957) and 43 percent (1976) among the youngest age group. It is not known whether older people blot out "help" they have received from their own memories, or whether they restructure helping situations as some other phenomenon. In reviewing their lives, they may easily distort experiences to enhance perceived self-sufficiency—a dynamically crucial self-identity in older people, as we shall see below.

There is evidence (table 2.23) that older people focus more on their own health as a source of happiness and unhappiness. It is as if pulling away from their former social roles refocuses concern about physical well-being, especially as people begin to anticipate their own death or perhaps begin to fear invalidism. "At least I have my health!" is commonly heard among the elderly. Since that response can be seen as a disconcerted distressed response, or as an affirmation, there is no correlation ($r=.00$) between mention of one's own health as a source of happiness and the evaluation of one's happiness among the older group. Interpersonal sources of gratification remain the basic focus for elderly people who say that they are happy. For example, the correlation between happiness and their marriage as a source of happiness is .14 for older married people.

Older people also report somewhat greater worry than younger peo-

TABLE 2.26
Selected Education Comparisons in Sources of Well-Being (by year)

	Educational Level									
	Grade School		Some High School		High School Graduate		Some College		College Graduate	
Source of Well-Being Being Discussed	1957 (%)	1976 (%)	1957 (%)	1976 (%)	1957 (%)	1976 (%)	1957 (%)	1976 (%)	1957 (%)	1976 (%)
Happiness										
Economic/material	31	26	37	29	38	30	35	30	34	26
Marriage	10	10	18	15	23	16	21	15	19	19
Unhappiness										
Job	10	8	16	16	16	22	19	25	21	32
Other interpersonal	9	8	11	16	12	22	14	23	14	32
Personal characteristics	6	4	10	6	15	9	17	11	14	13
Worries										
Community, national, world problems	8	8	8	8	11	9	10	13	12	12
Total Number	807	380	511	347	674	766	213	411	210	347

ple about community, national, and international affairs (see table 2.23). Perhaps this finding reflects the fact that older people invest in a system outside their personal sphere of control. They may have more conscious understanding about the community as a system independent of their specific place in it.

We get a less clear picture about middle-aged people going through a specific life stage that conditions the quality of experience. Some middle-aged people continue to be involved in the same role issues as younger people, while others are more concerned with the transition problems faced by older people. Perhaps situations occur less normatively for the middle-aged; they respond to life crises specific only to themselves individually or to very specific reference groups. Neugarten (1968b), for example, has pointed out that there are clear norms for the time when a person in a given occupation should reach a peak in his/her career, but that the peak will vary widely in different occupations. Premature experiences of death of spouse or friend, serious illness, or marital disruption can color the middle-aged person's evaluation of well-being and perceptions of happiness, unhappiness, and worries. Older people become adapted to events more uniformly and tend to react as older people are "supposed" to feel and think. Such phenomena of norms being reestablished in their cohort may become even more striking if we move into social arrangements where older people are even more segregated from the young than they are now.

Education Differences in Feelings of Well-Being

Educational attainment was a critical factor in responses to questions of well-being in the 1957 sample, and it continues to be in 1976. Selected results appear in table 2.26 for sources of well-being and in table 2.27 for evaluations of well-being. More limited sets of data appear in tables 2.28 and 2.29.

Looking at table 2.27 and comparing various educational levels on measures of well-being, we conclude that the more educated in our society are much better off psychologically than the less educated. The better educated in both years report greater happiness in absolute evaluation, in comparison to the past, and in the selection of the happiest time of their lives. They also show greater confidence in the future.

The additional assessments carried out only in 1976 support the general impression that men and women of higher educational attainment experience greater well-being. College-educated people are higher in zest. Fifty-two percent of college graduates rank in the highest third of the measure. The college educated are also less likely to say that bad things have happened to them frequently and are less overwhelmed by

TABLE 2.27

Selected Education Comparisons in Feelings of Well-Being (by year)

	Educational Level									
	Grade School		Some High School		High School Graduate		Some College		College Graduate	
Measure	1957 (%)	1976 (%)	1957 (%)	1976 (%)	1957 (%)	1976 (%)	1957 (%)	1976 (%)	1957 (%)	1976 (%)
Present Feeling										
Happiness: very happy	23	24	30	24	46	32	43	36	44	37
Worries: sometimes, not much	48	44	65	35	58	47	54	57	61	55
Present Happiness: yes	25	21	37	25	45	35	41	36	39	42
Satisfaction: completely satisfied	—	19	—	17	—	16	—	14	—	16
Zest: high third	—	22	—	28	—	39	—	39	—	52
Past Feelings										
Experienced Problems Relevant for help: yes	16	20	25	37	25	38	27	42	36	44
Childhood Unhappiest: yes	17	18	23	22	29	27	32	38	34	49
Past Compared to Present: Not as happy	—	24	—	39	—	43	—	48	—	46
Frequency Bad Things: Happier: a lot, some	—	40	—	43	—	41	—	34	—	36
Frequency Felt Overwhelmed: Sometimes, many times	—	16	—	19	—	15	—	9	—	9
Future Feelings										
Morale about Future: Very happy	30	22	55	42	64	55	67	57	66	60

bad events when they occur. They are more likely to pinpoint child-hood as the unhappiest time in their lives. The whole pattern of results in table 2.27 suggests that the college educated as a group, especially in contrast to people with minimal education, are very optimistic, happy, and oriented to the future—but not necessarily with heightened wor-ry. In fact, the more educated groups tend to be *moderately* worried rather than extremely worried or not worried at all. They view their present life experience as happier than their past.

The one deviant finding we have from all our analysis of education is that the more educated tend to seek professional help. In contrast to the series of results showing the more educated to be more glowing about their psychological well-being, in both years the more educated report having experienced a problem relevant for help in the past. Thirty-six percent of the 1957 college graduates say they have experi-enced a problem for which they sought or could have sought help. This contrasts with 16 percent of the grade school educated. The overall fig-ures for 1976 are 44 percent for the college educated and 22 percent for the grade school educated. This general trend differs somewhat for men and women. Among women, the high school educated and the college educated are equally oriented to help seeking—more so than the grade school educated. Among men, however, all education levels differ in help-seeking readiness; the college educated are clearly more ready than the high school educated who are, in turn, more ready than the grade school educated (see table 2.28). Thus, all women who go be-yond a grade-school education become considerably more oriented toward professional help-seeking. (This is especially true in 1976.) There is little difference between high school– and college-educated women in this regard. With each increment in education for men, how-ever, there seems to be a stronger orientation toward help seeking, both in 1957 and 1976. If, as we previously discussed, we see profes-sional help-seeking as a mechanism of coping with problems as they arise, these findings seem to be consistent with the overall impression that more educated people are better off.

We thus have clear evidence that people's social status has some bearing on how they react to life. The higher the status, the higher the morale about the present and future, and the lower the distress report-ed about the past. The predisposition of the more educated to see their past as having personal problems relevant for help suggests a general readiness to see problems in mental-health terms and to cope with them in that way, rather than seeing one's past as "troubled." Since some of this pattern is true of younger as well as older respondents, and since age is strongly related to education, we should emphasize that the age and education effects are independent phenomena. The re-sults emerge from multivariate analyses controlling on age and educa-tion simultaneously.

How do we interpret the fact that status is so clearly related to mea-

TABLE 2.28

Relationship of Education to Help Readiness (by year × sex)

Ready to Use Professional Help for Personal Problems

	1957				1976			
	Men		Women		Men		Women	
Educational Level	Total Number	Percentage	Total Number	Percentage	Total Number	Percentage	Total Number	Percentage
Grade School	365	11	434	26	154	18	226	22
High School	461	18	719	30	424	28	299	44
College	242	30	212	31	378	41	380	45

sures of adjustment? Does status give a person the resources for feeling competent about the future and dispassionate about bad past experiences? Do these resources—both economic and psychological—help the more educated assume that they can overcome future problems as they have overcome past experiences? Institutions in this society are no doubt arranged felicitously for the more educated. Lack of status achievement can make people question their past, especially in trying to account for lack of achievement. Furthermore, persons with lower educational attainment quickly come to recognize that things are likely not to get better for them in a competitive, evaluative social structure.

In this regard, it is curious that there are no differences between education groups on reported level of satisfaction. We have surprisingly high frequencies among less educated groups in the "completely satisfied" category (table 2.27). We interpret these results to signify that many less educated people are defensive about their lot in life. Under the press of evaluating their satisfaction with life, they may report they are satisfied, primarily because their thoughts about the future are not very optimistic. If people think that the future is limited, it is hard to admit present dissatisfaction. People tend to adjust their standards and feel "satisfied" when they are confronted with the difficulties of *ever* achieving higher standards. On the other hand, among the better educated, there is optimism that what is happening to them right now may not be permanent, and they can accept not being completely satisfied.

Certain very interesting differences between educational levels hold up under multivariate scrutiny in *sources* of well-being and distress. (See the results in table 2.26.) The results seem to follow a particular pattern in which at each educational level—grade school, high school, and college—there is a particular quality of experience which focuses sources of happiness and unhappiness, or both, and a particular quality of experience which focuses worry. We will argue that the quality of experience that becomes the focus of happiness and/or unhappiness is that area of life in which the person had every expectation of finding fulfillment. The focus of worries, however, is that area of life where expectations are more doubtful, but where there is optimism for fulfillment. We will examine each educational group with this model in mind, assuming that for each group there is a focus of happiness and/ or unhappiness where the standard of expectations for the good life were relatively high, and a focus of worries where there are unsure expectations but a clear hope for change.

Among the grade school educated, in contrast to other educational groups, there is a greater focus on happiness derived from physical health. We find in table 2.29 that the middle-aged grade school educated, contrasted to the middle-aged high school or college educated, say that they are happy about their present health. Thirteen percent of all grade school educated in 1957 report their own health as a source of happiness. This contrasts with 5 percent of all college graduates who

TABLE 2.29

Selected Education Comparison in Sources of Well-Being (by age × year)

		21-34			35-54			55+		
Sources of Well-Being (Distress)		Grade School (%)	High School (%)	College (%)	Grade School (%)	High School (%)	College (%)	Grade School (%)	High School (%)	College (%)
Happiness										
R's health	1957	5	3	5	11	9	5	17	15	19
	1976	0	4	3	16	8	5	20	23	17
Worries										
Economic	1957	46	49	47	45	39	38	21	23	24
	1976	53	48	38	43	35	28	21	21	18
Total Number	1957	102	473	184	292	511	200	405	196	70
	1976	30	404	377	74	402	222	276	305	159

report physical health as a basis of happiness. In 1976, the parallel result in the grade school educated is 18 percent, and for the college educated 6 percent. Furthermore, these results are evident when age is controlled, and they are particularly striking in the middle-aged group (see table 2.29).

Again, where age is controlled, grade school educated people worry about their economic and material well-being a good deal more than other groups. Within our model, we would thus suggest that physical survival is the domain the grade school educated take for granted, and economic well-being is the domain for which they have hopes for change. Hence, health becomes a focus of happiness and unhappiness, and economic and material well-being becomes a focus of worrying.

Moving to the high school educated groups, we find a greater focus on economic and material happiness among the high school educated in contrast to other groups (see table 2.26). The differences are not large, but they become significant when age enters the multivariate analysis. High school–educated people in our society take for granted that their economic and material well-being will be satisfied. Thus, when they encounter difficulty, they are "unhappy" about it; in addition, the high school–educated group, compared to the grade school educated (see table 2.26) seem to focus on marital satisfaction in discussing their happiness. One might argue that high school–educated people assume that role functioning through work and/or marriage will provide easy anchors for their lives. The young high school–educated group seems to "worry about" its children more in contrast to the other groups. Twenty-eight percent of young high school–educated parents mention worries about children compared to 21 percent among other parents. This is an interesting trend to contemplate within our model since it may be vicariously through children that the high school educated in our society demonstrate optimism about a change in their social status. To the degree that their children do not fulfill achievement expectations, high school–educated parents would see their own hopes for achievement dashed.

Among the college educated, we find that it is in the job domain that their quality of experience seems to be strikingly different from other groups. This group most often mentions their experiences with job unhappiness (see table 2.26). It is as if college-educated people find particular frustrations from their expectations in this area of work. These results are confirmed in analysis of the job role in chapter 6. We find, in addition, that the college educated differ from other educational levels in speaking of interpersonal and personal sources of unhappiness (see table 2.26). It may be that expectations for fulfillment among the college educated are unique in the areas of psychological and interpersonal well-being. Their college experience may have encouraged them to think in terms of ultimate fulfillment through interpersonal success and the development of character. Such expectations among the college educated may spawn frustration when the elite discover after college that they are not so special. This response is not entirely typical of the college educated, but it is more prevalent in that group compared to the others.

The college educated are slightly more worried than the other educational levels about community, national, and international affairs. Again we would argue that the college educated worry about fulfilling their moral and civic duties more than other groups. They also worry more about their jobs. Within the framework being developed, we would say that there are aspirations in the college educated for work as a source of internal gratification. Many college-educated people are taught to aspire to highly personalized fulfillment through work. Indeed, most college-educated people regard impact through their jobs as the epitome of self-actualization. Many college-educated people worry about whether their jobs really fulfill that expectation. Thus, as a source of happiness, a job is a domain for feeling successful in the social structure; as a domain for worries, a job is probably a domain for individuation as well.

Summary

It is impressive in summarizing our analysis of well-being over a generation how few interactions by year occur. Only in the following important results does the *pattern* of well-being seem to differ for 1957 and 1976: worries are more prominent in the young in 1976 contrasted with other groups; childhood as the unhappiest time of life is especially prominent among the college-educated young in 1976; children are mentioned as a source of happiness more among young people in 1957 than for any other age groups. Both worrying about and expressing happiness about their children are especially characteristic of the 1976 middle-aged. With control for parent status, however, the latter two results are less clear-cut and emerge more as a function of the higher proportion of nonparents among the young in 1976.

Aside from these results, we found straightforward and clear year differences occurring across sex, age, and education level, the most important being: increased worrying and readiness to state that one has problems relevant for help; increased experience of independence as a source of happiness; community, national, and world problems as a greater source of unhappiness; and concern about jobs as a source of worry. We found other trends of some importance: slight decreases in experienced happiness and future morale and decreased attention to self as a source of unhappiness with a corresponding increase in attending to the self as a source of happiness.

These key changes over the twenty years seem to be independent of the obvious increases in people's educational level, as well as changes in age distribution. We often find education and age main effects occurring at the same time that we get universal changes between 1957 and 1976. This gives rise to the assumption that the generational shift we have been discussing in feelings of well-being (e.g., increases in worries, decrease in being "very happy," decrease in morale) may be a function of specific historical changes that have occurred, independent of the changes in demographic characteristics of the American population itself. People certainly react to the problems of the 1960s and 1970s on specific historical issues such as the role transitions for women and environmental problems or shifts in our economy which have had global effects. These larger uncertainties are reflected in the greater concern about community and international issues, greater concern about job problems, self-realization, and less concern about material problems. The generational shift from concerns about health to more interpersonal matters suggests that we have moved from uncertainties about physical well-being to uncertainty about more psychological aspects of our lives.

The press for advancing women's status in American society seems to have had minimal consequences in the experienced well-being of men and women. There are still clear differences in how men and women approach their psychological well-being. Specifically, women are more negative than men in assessments of their well-being. However these findings are interpreted, they are probably among the most important findings in this chapter—or indeed in this book.

Education differences in well-being are persistent and not peculiar to one or the other generation. Most of our results suggest that the better educated, though more likely than the less educated to seek professional help, perceive themselves as fairly well off in most other measures of well-being. In examining the particular qualities of experience, the better educated focus on personal aspects of happiness and unhappiness and sources of worry while the less educated focus more on the economic and specific role factors in happiness and unhappiness. The least educated (grade school) in our society still focus on the basic issues of survival, perhaps even more intensively than in 1957, as fewer and fewer people obtain such minimal education.

Important as the idea of differences in educational status are in helping us understand how men and women look at their experiences of well-being, we are even more impressed with the extent to which life-cycle factors structure experiences of happiness, unhappiness, and worry. Further, most life-cycle differences are parallel in 1957 and 1976. We see little evidence of cohort effects. We find fairly strong differences in how young, middle-aged, and old people, regardless of year, experience the quality of their lives, regarding both evaluation of well-being and sources of gratification and frustration.

Older people are clearly less happy than middle-aged or young people, although the pattern of differences is different in men and women. Older people clearly are not as oriented toward evaluating their past life as one in which they felt overwhelmed at any point, either by nervous breakdown or by bad things happening to them. They evaluate their past in very different terms than younger people, who see their past as sources of distress and see the present and future as times for recouping, maintaining, and establishing their happiness. Older people do not anticipate the future as a better or happier time. Their life is here and now, or in the past. Middle-aged people are particularly sensitive to ongoing experiences as rich and interesting. It remains to be seen whether these general evaluative differences among different age groups will hold up as we approach more specific domains of subjective experience in the chapters that follow.

Chapter 3

PERCEPTION OF SELF

IN chapter 1 we described the psychological revolution which occurred in American society in the years between our two studies. This revolution expressed itself specifically and dramatically in a heightened salience of self-concern. The personal-growth movement flourished. Booksellers' shelves and best-seller lists filled with self-improvement literature of many persuasions. One observer feared that with so much personal growth occurring, we might become a land of psychic behemoths.

The shift is neatly symbolized by the most popular books of social criticism which dominated the national scene in the periods of our two studies: David Riesman et al.'s *The Lonely Crowd* and Christopher Lasch's *The Culture of Narcissism.* In the fifties, according to Riesman, we were a nation of conformers who had lost touch with the inner voice. By the mid-seventies, Lasch perused the landscape of American Character and decided that the inner voice was all that was left. In his view, we had abandoned commitment to the family and other institutions, or had at least downgraded their command on our loyalties and actions. All of reality and social exchange was now dominated by the sole criterion of its capacity to gratify individual, narcissistic appetites.

The problem with such social criticism is that it is based on limited information, an issue of generalization. If Henry VIII had been a social critic in the grand style, he would have based his generalizations on observations of behavior at his court. He would have concluded that the world was a teeming mass of egoism despite the fact that most of the population, preoccupied with scrabbling for the next meal, had not yet discovered the ego.

So with our modern social critics. Facts are observed correctly: the divorce rate has increased; women have left their families in order to realize individual talents or needs; the best-seller lists are dominated by books on self-improvement, personal growth, narcissistic preoccupation. But the facts are then interpreted too broadly, accorded a centrality and power in the broad population which they may in fact hold only for a part, for a highly articulate, "leading," powerful subgroup—but a subgroup all the same.

What do we learn about self-concepts and self-perceptions when we go to the larger population? Do American people reflect the self-concern, the narcissism attributed to them? Has the self moved to center stage since the 1950s? Has the personal-growth literature and the psychological revolution influenced us in large and important ways?

In *Americans View Their Mental Health,* results pertaining to perceptions of the self were perhaps the most tentative and perplexing reported. Open-ended questions about respondents' sense of identity, strengths, and weaknesses yielded no dramatic differences between groups for whom we might anticipate large effects. Sex and age differences appeared, but were minor. Furthermore, variations in self-perceptions were not very predictive of readiness for self-referral for professional help. One of the major reasons the original study focused on perceptions of self was that such psychological orientations were thought to be bases for seeking psychological help. A degree of self-awareness or a degree of experienced difficulty in the self were hypothesized to be preconditions for seeking help from professionals. Though a few results relating aspects of self-perception to professional help-seeking confirmed the hypothesis, they represented minor trends throughout.

Despite the tentative results from measures of self-perception in 1957, two consistent and important themes ran through the findings. People differed in significant and predictable ways in (1) willingness to attend to the self as an object of evaluation; and (2) the choice of *external* vs. *internal* bases of self-definition. While we had hoped to develop estimates of self-esteem from the questions, these two themes dominated the structure of the responses. They are not, however, without interest. Indeed, they represent important parameters of self-consciousness and are critical for understanding subjective adjustment. Nevertheless, although these two dimensions seemed clear in the data, the findings used as evidence for them were not large or striking.

As we began to plan the replication study, however, we realized that we might obtain more information about parameters of self-consciousness when we contrasted responses across the generation. Despite the fact that results in 1957 were not decisive, we thought there might be dramatic changes in the phenomenology of self-perception over the generation and that we would discover them only through the kind of open-ended questions asked in 1957. The psychological revolution witnessed during the past generation might indeed have much more impact on the words and concepts people use in self-definitions than on their choice of scale positions on such matters as personal efficacy or self-worth. In addition, we hoped to get better assessment of self-esteem by introducing new questions developed since the first study.

What follows, therefore, is our attempt to obtain insights about changes in self-consciousness that occurred over the generation; in what people think about themselves, their weaknesses, strong points, and identities. We will focus on the two thematic conceptualizations noted earlier and ask whether people use the same or different attributes and constructs when they think about the self. We will also look at evidence of changes in self-esteem in people's evaluation of the self-concept.

Measures

Our discussion in this chapter will focus on the first three questions listed in table 3.1. The first asks about perceived differentiation of the self from other people, the second about changes desired in the self, and the third about perceived strong points. The questions prompt a rich array of responses. The extremely detailed coding developed in 1957 was used in 1976 to ensure coding reliability across the generation, and to allow us to regroup perceived aspects of self into different categories if desired.

Let us look at the measures derived from each of these questions.

PERCEIVED DIFFERENTIATIONS

First we asked respondents how they differed from other people. Since we did not specify particular arenas of difference, a respondent might say that s/he was not different from other people, or might mention social role characteristics, moral factors, personality characteristics, or any combination of these. Furthermore, since the question is a neutral question asking people only to think about their differences from other people, the tone of responses could reveal a respondent's general positive or negative orientation to her or himself. Therefore we asked coders to make judgments about how positive or negative the affective orientation seemed to be. Thus, in addition to yielding a measure of willingness to give some differentiation of the self from others (*per-*

TABLE 3.1

Measures Used to Assess Changes in Self-Perception

Measure	Questions	Code
Perceived Differentiation	People are the same in many ways, but no two people are exactly alike. What are some of the ways in which you're different from most other people?	Mentions some way that self is different vs. Don't know; not different

Sources of Perceived Difference		External:
		
		A. Social Role Reference
		  (1) occupation related
		  (2) housewife related
		  (3) marriage related
		  (4) parenthood related
		  (5) other role related
		
		B. Physical Attributes
		Internal:
		
		A. Moral-religious (e.g., religious, honest)
		B. Other virtue (e.g., dependable)
		C. Personality-related
		  (1) achievement (e.g., persistent)
		  (2) adjustment (e.g., well-balanced)
		  (3) affiliative skill (e.g., friendly)
		  (4) altruistic (e.g., helpful)
		  (5) autonomy-influence (e.g., independent, stubborn)
		  (6) anger-related (e.g., quick tempered, slow to anger)
		  (7) general competence (e.g., intelligent)
		  (8) other

Measure	Questions	Code
Positive-Negative Orientation		Coder evaluation of dominance of positive-negative characteristics mentioned
Perceived Shortcomings	Many people when they think about their children, would like them to be different from themselves in some ways. If you had a (son/daughter—SAME SEX AS R), how would you like (him/her) to be different from you?	Explicitly mentions way in which wants child to be different; vs. Don't know; doesn't want child to be different
Sources of Perceived Shortcomings		External: A. Occupational Attainment (e.g., have better job) B. Economic Condition (e.g., have more money) C. Educational Attainment (e.g., be better educated) D. General, Better Life (e.g., "easier life") E. Other Internal: A. Moral-religious (e.g., go to church more often) B. Other virtues (e.g., have more will-power) C. Personality (1) achievement (e.g., accomplish more) (2) adjustment (e.g., be more relaxed) (3) affiliative (e.g., be less shy)

TABLE 3.1 (*continued*)
Measures Used to Assess Changes in Self-Perception

Measure	Questions	Code
		(4) autonomy-independence (e.g., be less dependent)
		(5) anger traits (e.g., be better tempered)
		(6) general competence (e.g., be better organized)
		(7) other
Perceived Strengths	How about your good points? What would you say were your strong points?	Explicitly mentions a strong point vs. Don't know; explicitly say has no strengths
Sources of Perceived Strengths		External:
		A. Role-related
		(1) occupation reference
		(2) housework reference
		(3) marriage reference
		(4) parenthood reference
		B. Physical Attributes
		Internal:
		A. Moral-religious Traits (e.g., lead a clean life)
		B. Other Virtuous Traits (e.g., unselfish)
		C. Personality
		(1) achievement (e.g., don't give up)
		(2) adjustment (e.g., take things in my stride)
		(3) affiliative skill (e.g., has lots of friends)
		(4) altruistic (e.g., do what I can to help)
		(5) autonomy-influence (e.g., self-

Measure	Questions	Code
		(6) anger related (e.g., don't get angry easily)
		(7) general competence (e.g., capable)
		(8) other
Self Needing Friends	Do you feel you have as many friends as you want, or would you like to have more friends?	Would like more friends vs. As many friends as wants
Self as Efficacious Planner	I have always felt pretty sure my life would work out the way I wanted it to... very true—pretty true—not very true—not true at all	Very true → not true at all
Self as Needing Power	I often wish that people would listen to me more... very true—pretty true—not very true—not true at all	Very true → not true at all
Self Needing Acceptance	I often wish that people like me more than they do... very true—pretty true—not very true—not true at all	Very true → not true at all
Self-Esteem[a]	How often are these true for you:[a] a. I feel that I am a person of worth, at fsv1least as much as others. b. I am able to do things as well as most other people. c. On the whole, I feel good about myself.	Summarized index of alternatives: (scores range 3 to 12) 4=often true: 3=sometimes true 2=rarely true 1=never true
Internal Control[a]	Some people feel that they can run their own lives much the way they want to; others feel that the problems of life are sometimes too big for them. Which one are you more like?[a]	Can run life vs. Problem too big

[a] Question asked only in 1976.

ceived differentiation) and a measure of *sources of perceived differences*, the question also provided a rating of the person's *positive-negative orientation to her/himself.*

The scale of positive-negative orientation ran from very positive (e.g., "I'm a very competent person") to very negative (e.g., "I'm the kind of person that most people don't like"). There were two kinds of midpoints: neutral (e.g., no indication of self-evaluation: as in "I am a bookkeeper") and ambivalent (e.g., a balanced combination of positive and negative attributes). A summary of measures derived from this question of perceived self-differentiation is given in table 3.1.

To assess the contents of perceived differentiations, we established a set of categories parallel but not identical to those used in the 1957 survey. These appear in table 3.1 under the measures of perceived differentiation of the self. They include distinctions based on role performance (occupation, housewife, marital, parental, or other role designations); distinctions concerning physical attributes; moral aspects of self (e.g., being a religious person); stereotypic virtues (e.g., "I am sincere," "honest"); achievement (e.g., "I'm a good worker"); adjustment (e.g., "I am a pretty well adjusted person"); competence (e.g., "I am pretty smart"); affiliative skills (e.g., "I get along well with other people"); autonomy or influence attributes (e.g., ""I am able to get my way about things"); anger-related characteristics (e.g., having a hot temper or not); altruistic characteristics (e.g., "I am a helpful person"). These specific categories were then grouped into major categories: external characteristics of the self (social roles, physical attributes, or social status); and internal characteristics of the self (with a distinction drawn between moral or virtuous stereotypes as opposed to morally neutral personality attributes). These larger groupings are indicated by major headings in the description of this measure in table 3.1.

PERCEIVED SHORTCOMINGS

The second question asked indirectly about *perceived shortcomings* in the self: "If you had a (son/daughter—SAME SEX AS R) how would you like (him/her) to be different from you?" We assumed that respondents specifying a difference would view the characteristic as a limitation or shortcoming in the self.

Some respondents said they *wouldn't* want their child to be different from themselves. Others said they didn't know or alluded to a characteristic which clearly did not represent a difference from self (e.g., "I would want him to marry" when the respondent himself was married). We distinguished three groups: those who specified ways they would want their children to be different, those who said they didn't want their children to be different, and those who said they didn't know or gave a nondistinguishing characteristic. This three-category system constituted our measure of *perceived shortcomings.*

Sources of shortcoming. As in the measure of self-differentiation, we distinguished between external and internal shortcomings. External shortcomings focus on role functioning (e.g., wanting the child to marry when respondent is unmarried, or wanting the child to have a better job or not to work in a factory). Or they focus on status issues as, for example, the hope that the child would obtain more education than the respondent had.

Internal shortcomings focused on personality-based difficulties the person saw in her or himself; for example, "have better self-control" or "be more ambitious." Although in 1957 we made a further distinction among types of internal characteristics (moral-virtuous as opposed to personality characteristics), in analysis we found that the critical issue was whether a person mentioned *any* internal characteristic rather than the *type* alluded to. Coding of shortcomings appears in table 3.1.

PERCEIVED STRENGTHS

The third question asked about people's perceived strengths. One infrequent but important answer was that the respondent felt s/he did not have *any* strong points. A complete categorization of distinctions made in *Perceived Strengths* appears in table 3.1. Again we grouped responses into the larger categories of external and internal strengths. Among internal characteristics, we distinguished between stereotypic/moralistic responses (e.g., "I am a sincere person" or "I'm easygoing") and more individualized psychological responses (e.g., "When I get into an argument with someone, I know how to calm things down quickly"). We realize that this distinction may reflect stylistic aspects of the response rather than specific content. The person who says s/he is able to cool down arguments may be referring to the same behavior as the person who says s/he is easygoing. Nevertheless, the distinction seems important. It is easy to offer clichés to describe one's strengths. Such responses may reflect less introspective capacity than more individualized answers do.

These, then, were the ways we coded the three major questions about the structure of self-perception. In 1957 we also asked four questions about specific self-perceptions which were not analyzed in *Americans View Their Mental Health*, primarily because the results were not striking. In 1976 we used the questions again, since although analysis of 1957 responses had not yielded much, we hoped that a 1957–1976 comparison might uncover interesting changes.

SPECIFIC SELF-PERCEPTIONS: NEEDING FRIENDS, NEEDING POWER, NEEDING ACCEPTANCE, AND SELF AS EFFECTIVE PLANNER

These more objective questions are also listed in table 3.1. The first asks whether respondents have enough friends, the second asks whether they feel they are effective in planning their lives, the third asks whether they wish people listened to them more, and the fourth asks whether they wish people liked them more. The four questions allow us to assess four other aspects of self-perception: needing friends, efficacy, needing power, and needing acceptance (see table 3.1).

Three of the closed questions focus on perception of self in relation to other people. Questions 4, 6, and 7 ask in one way or another how much self-definition depends on other people. Question 4 asks respondent whether s/he needs more friends, question 6 asks whether s/he needs more power, and question 7 asks whether s/he has enough acceptance from other people. Question 5 goes to another issue: whether respondent feels in control of (able to plan effectively) her or his life. The question allows either a retrospective or prospective time orientation and is, in this sense, somewhat ambiguous. Nevertheless, it focuses on a crucial issue: confidence in the self as planner.

We will want to ask whether these questions relate to each other and to the more open-ended questions about self-perception in the same or different ways in 1957 and in 1976.

SELF-ESTEEM AND PERCEIVED INTERNAL CONTROL

Two additional indices used only in 1976 will be discussed since they are germane to the topic. The first consists of three items from a modified version of Rosenberg's self-esteem scale (1965), listed in table 3.1. The second index is a 2-point measure of internal control derived from the question: "Some people feel that they can run their own lives much the way they want to; others feel that the problems of life are sometimes too big for them. Which one are you more like?" (see table 3.1). This item encapsulates the general meaning of Rotter's concept of internal control (Rotter, 1966).

Thus we have data available from both years on four objective questions and three open-ended ones and, in addition, two indices for 1976 only. Responses to most of these questions were coded on ordinal scales: the presence or absence of perceived differentiation, shortcomings, and strengths; positive-negative orientation to the self; perception of self as needing friends, having efficacy, needing power, and needing acceptance. Other scales are nominal: sources of differentiation, shortcomings, and strengths. In order to run intercorrelations among the various measures, we converted sources of self-perception into separate critical categories and considered each a separate variable. For example, we might select "personality shortcoming" and build a variable which asks whether the individual mentions a personality shortcoming or not. In other words, we divided each qualitative variable into a series of yes/no responses indicating presence or absence of a particular self-perception.

To get a sense of how the various measures are similar and different from one another, we intercorrelated all measures for each year. A remarkable consistency appears in correlations among this large and varied group of indices over the generation. For example, in both years, people who do not see themselves as different from other people tend not to adduce any personal strengths but do admit shortcomings. Another important example of stability across time: people who take a positive view of themselves when asked how they differ from other people also tend to mention personal strengths and to say that they do not want their children to differ from themselves. These results are true in both 1957 and 1976, with only slight variation in the relationships. A further consistent pattern: in both years, people tend to approach shortcomings and strengths with parallel psychological sets. If they mention role strengths, they also tend to give role shortcomings. If they mention moral flaws, they also mention moral strengths. This is an interesting finding and suggests that people use consistent, general schemas in self-perception, irrespective of evaluative direction.

Some differences do appear in the pattern of intercorrelations in 1957 and 1976, and these involve mainly closed-ended questions about the self. The following differences are worth noting:

1. In 1957 respondents who said they wish people listened to them more were more likely than their 1976 counterparts to describe themselves as differing from other people in stereotypical moral or virtuous characteristics. This results suggests that in 1957 people who wanted to influence others may have been self-righteous people trying to impose moral standards on others, or at least more so than those expressing a desire to influence others in 1976.

2. In 1957 there was no relationship between perceived effectiveness and the desire for more friends, but in 1976 there is a clear relationship: people who see themselves as not very effective also report wishing for more friends. The closer connection in 1976 between perceived efficacy and having friends may stem from the increasing importance of intimacy as a goal in our society.

3. The relationship between wanting people to like one more and seeing oneself as lacking some stereotypic virtue is stronger in 1957 than in 1976. This suggests that mentioning personality characteristics as a shortcoming in 1976 means something different than it did in 1957. In 1976 it has become more common to structure self-perceptions, including shortcomings, in personality terms. More frequent allusion to personality attributes in 1976 may thus reflect increased cultural usage rather than a more individual, dynamic change in self-perception. Furthermore, not being liked was evidently a more critical feature of the self in 1957, since at that time it seems to have reflected a preoccupation with shortcomings.

Taken together, these findings suggest that the structure of self-perception may be somewhat different in 1976 than it was in 1957. There has been a decided cultural shift in the understanding and value of interpersonal relationships in self-definition. The meaning of the word "friend," what "being listened to" means, what it means to "be liked by others" seem to have changed between 1957 and 1976. One hypothesis to consider is that people have pressed for greater social intimacy, and particularly for intimacy that entails being liked and listened to in more individuated and personalistic ways. In 1976 people are regarded for *what they are* rather than for *what they ought to be*. In 1957 the cultural values were geared to having people define themselves and judge others by normative expectations, the way they performed roles, by social position, and consensually based ideals of social power and acceptability. In 1976 we have a greater sense of *personal* identity structured in idiosyncratic ways. More people use individuated personality concepts to describe themselves and think about intimate relationships as a standard of social ability to aim for.

In comparison to 1957, friends make people feel effective in 1976 (result 3 above). In 1957 the person who used moral attributes (rather than more neutral personality characteristics) to define the self also felt socially empowered (listened to). Having specific stereotyped "good" qualities was thought to win friends and influence people. The connection was stronger in 1957 (result 1 above) probably because moral standing had more effect on social relationships in 1957 than it does now. These results support Lasch's view that morality has diminished as the basis of evaluation and self-evaluation in our society.

In spite of these few year differences, we are impressed with the fact that the pattern of intercorrelations among self-perception measures remains relatively constant. In this sense we think Lasch's assertions about the change in focus from society to self in the American population are overstated and perhaps reflect his preoccupation with a limited elite subgroup in the population. The self-perceptions of most Americans are quite similar in 1957 and 1976.

It is also important to recognize that correlations among measures are not very high. This reminds us again of the value of analyzing measures separately rather than combining them into larger scales. Being able to report strengths, a positive view of one's difference from others, and seeing oneself as an effective planner and having internal control can all be considered aspects of a general assessment of self-esteem. We might have been tempted to combine them for an overall measure. Nonetheless, we are impressed that the responses reflect different facets of self-esteem and that they have responded differently to the changes in our culture over the last twenty years. Intercorrelations are still relatively low among the various measures, and it thus seems important to examine them individually.

Let us turn now to the central question of this chapter: how does the

1976 population differ from the 1957 population in their perceptions of self?

Year Differences in Self-Perceptions

Table 3.2 presents a summary of comparisons between self-perceptions of the population in 1957 and 1976. Tables 3.3, 3.4, and 3.5 expand on the more specific differentiations in perceived differences, weaknesses, and strengths respectively. Some of these results are striking; some show very little change.

With regard to the two themes that emerged from the 1957 analysis, we can say that in 1976 men and women are more inward-looking, or intraceptive, and that they have a more highly differentiated view of the inner world of self. In addition, we find evidence that the 1976 population evaluate themselves more positively than the 1957 population did. Let us turn to findings which support these conclusions.

1. In 1976 American people are more articulate about their own identities. This conclusion is based on a 7 percent increase (from 1957 to 1976) in the proportion of people who respond to the question asking how they differ from most people. In 1976 men and women are more willing to talk about their uniqueness. Though we find no significant change in the percentage of people listing two or more distinctive features (39 percent in 1957; 41 percent in 1976), there was some indication that the perceptions of difference from others were more positively tinged in 1976. The changed willingness to discuss one's distinctiveness indicates, we feel, that American men and women are more intraceptive now than they were twenty years ago.

This increased willingness to distinguish the self does not generalize to an increased willingness to talk about one's strengths or shortcomings. Indeed, we will see below that there is a decrease in allusions to shortcomings. Rather than seeing this as a counterindication of intraceptiveness, however, we think it reflects an increased positive self-evaluation.

2. The 1976 population more often structure their more intraceptive self-perceptions as personality characteristics rather than as stereotypic moral characteristics or as role performance. This conclusion is based on a number of findings in table 3.2. In 1976, nine percent more people differentiate themselves from others on the basis of personality traits or qualities. Table 3.3 shows that no single personality characteristic stands out as more prevalent in 1976. Rather, there is a general increase in orientation to personality characteristics. There is only a slight and insignificant tendency for the 1976 population to mention more personality

TABLE 3.2
1957–1976 Comparisons in Measures of Self-Perception

Measure	1957 (%)	1976 (%)
Perceived Differentiation[a]		
Mentioning difference	69	76
"Not different from others"	16	11
DK	14	12
Not ascertained	1	1
	100%	100%
Sources of Perceived Difference		
External	7	6
Internal		
Moral, virtuous	14	13
Personality	52	61
Other	9	3
DK	7	8
Not ascertained	1	1
Not different	10	8
	100%	100%
Positive-Negative Orientation to the Self		
Very positive	4	6
Positive	64	62
Neutral	13	18
Ambivalent	5	3
Negative	13	10
Not ascertained	1	1
	100%	100%
Perceived Shortcomings[a]		
No shortcomings	10	10
DK	10	18
Shortcomings mentioned	75	66
Not ascertained	5	6
	100%	100%
Sources of Perceived Shortcomings		
External	38	28
Internal		
Moral, virtuous	4	5
Personality	36	40
Other	2	<1
DK	3	5
Not ascertained	5	8
No shortcomings	12	13
	100%	100%
Perception of Strong Points[a]		
No strong points	3	3
DK	10	9
Strong points mentioned	86	87
Not ascertained	1	1
	100%	100%

TABLE 3.2 (Continued)

Measure	1957 (%)	1976 (%)
Sources of Strong Points		
External	13	9
Moral	32	27
Personality	45	55
Other	1	1
DK	5	5
Not ascertained	1	2
No strong points	2	1
	100%	100%
Self Needing Friends		
No	59	55
Yes	40	44
Not ascertained	1	1
	100%	100%
Self as Efficacious Planner		
Very true	21	21
Pretty true	53	58
Not very true; not true at all	25	19
Not ascertained	1	1
	100%	100%
Self Needing Power		
Very true	15	9
Pretty true	26	27
Not very true	39	42
Not at all true	19	20
Not ascertained	1	2
	100%	100%
Self Needing Acceptance		
Very true	13	6
Pretty true	23	18
Not very true	38	42
Not at all true	25	32
Not ascertained	1	2
	100%	100%
Self-Esteem		
Feel I am Person of Worth:		
Often true	—[b]	72
Sometimes true	—	24
Rarely true	—	2
Never true	—	<1
Not ascertained	—	2
		100%
Feel I am Able to Do Things as Well as Others:		
Often true	—[b]	56
Sometimes true	—	36
Rarely true	—	5
Never true	—	1
Not ascertained	—	2
		100%

TABLE 3.2 (Continued)

Measure	1957 (%)	1976 (%)
On the Whole Feel Good about Myself:		
Often true	—[b]	67
Sometimes true	—	28
Rarely true	—	3
Never true	—	2
		100%
Sum Across Above Items		
All items, often true (High)	—[b]	43
Two items, often true (Med.)	—	23
One item sometimes true		
One item often true (Med.)	—	13
Two items sometimes true		
All items, sometimes true (Low)	—	10
One but not all items rarely, never true (Low)	—	8
All items rarely, never true (Low)	—	1
Not ascertained	—	2
		100%
Internal Control		
Can run life the way one wants	—[b]	80
Problem life sometimes too big	—	15
DK; in between	—	4
Not ascertained	—	1
		100%
Total Number	2,460	2,264

[a] Initial reaction to the question.

[b] This question not asked in 1957.

shortcomings than did people in 1957, but they clearly give more personality traits when they think of their strong points. Again, increased allusion to personality attributes as strong points cuts across the range of characteristics rather than concentrating in any single category (see table 3.5).

This increase in personality-based sources of strengths supports our conclusion that in 1976 the population is more positively oriented toward the self. When respondents think about their strong points, they are more likely to think of personality characteristics than moral stereotypes or role designations (e.g., "good husband" or "good parent"). Increases occur in personality characteristics: more deep-rooted, internal sources of self. The shift from moral-virtuous terms in 1957 to personality terms in 1976 seems a clear shift from normative concepts of morality to more individuated and morally neutral bases of self-conception.

We see this shift away from moral virtues toward more individually based characteristics as reflecting both a more highly developed intra-

TABLE 3.3
Sources of Perceived Differences in Self Compared to Others: 1957 vs. 1976

Perceived Differences	1957 (%)	1976 (%)
External		
Social Role Reference:		
Occupational-related	1	1
Housewife-related	1	1
Marriage-related	1	<1
Parenthood-related	2	1
Other role-related	1	1
Physical Attribute	2	3
Internal		
Moral-Religious Characteristic	8	6
Other "Virtues"	8	7
Personality-Related:		
Achievement	4	5
Adjustment	6	9
Affiliative	21	22
Attributive	1	2
Autonomy-Influence	8	12
Anger	4	3
General competence	13	14
Other	10	4
DK	8	8
Not ascertained	1	1
	100%	100%
Total Number	2,213[a]	2,077[a]

[a] Excludes 247 in 1957 and 187 in 1976 who explicitly said they were not different from others.

TABLE 3.4
Sources of Perceived Shortcomings: 1957 vs. 1976

Perceived Shortcomings	1957 (%)	1976 (%)
External		
Occupational Attainment	3	3
Educational Attainment	25	18
Economic Insecurity	2	2
General Life Conditions	5	6
Physical Attributes	7	4
Other	1	<1
Internal		
Moral-Religious Characteristic	4	4
Other Lack of "Virtue"	1	2
Personality-Related:		
Achievement	7	10
Adjustment	8	12
Affiliative	10	10
Autonomy-independence	4	7
Anger-related	4	2
General competence	6	5
Other	2	1
DK	4	6
Not ascertained	5	9
	100%	100%
Total Number	2,159[a]	1,966[a]

[a] Excludes 301 in 1957 and 298 in 1976 who do not want child to be different from self.

TABLE 3.5
Sources of Perceived Strengths:
1957 vs. 1976

Perceived Strengths	1957 (%)	1976 (%)
External		
Occupational	2	2
Housewife	3	2
Marriage	3	2
Parent	5	4
Physical	1	1
Internal		
Moral-Religious	17	11
Other Virtues	16	17
Personality-Related:		
Achievement	7	8
Adjustment	7	10
Affiliative-skilled	14	15
Altruistic	8	8
Autonomy-influence	3	5
Anger-related	3	2
General competence	5	8
Other	1	1
DK	5	5
Not ascertained	1	1
	100%	100%
Total Number	2,418[a]	2,778[a]

[a] Excludes 42 in 1957 and 36 in 1976 who explicitly say they have no strong points.

ceptive sensitivity (i.e., greater awareness of internal qualities) and also a more positive evaluation of self (i.e., higher self-esteem reflected in personal strengths). Structuring personal strengths in normative moral categories means the ever-present possibility of failure to meet the norm and the consequent negative self-evaluation, while the more neutral personality categories imply an aesthetic distance and an appreciation of self.

Let us caution the reader again that we may be dealing here mainly with a labeling difference: the 1957 generation, having been socialized to use moral categories for describing the self, might use these categories to refer to the same characteristic which the 1976 population describes as a personality trait (because they have been socialized in a more psychological era). Thus, when the 1957 respondent says that s/he is "thrifty," s/he may refer to the same quality in the self that the 1976 respondent describes as being "well-organized."

It is nonetheless our view that the personality phrasing of strengths is more likely to reflect and lead to more positive self-evaluation than the morally phrased attribution. We have some confirmation of this view: there is a slight negative correlation between perceiving one's source of strength in personality terms and self-esteem.

3. *The 1976 population is less likely to phrase shortcomings as external characteristics, particularly as lack of education.* Many fewer people in 1976 mention wanting a child to have more education than they themselves have. It may seem obvious that a population which has become more educated would no longer see education as a deprivation or shortcoming in their own lives. Yet people in 1976 might still have focused on lack of education if they had used a *relative* social comparison. The college educated might have seen their lack of professional or advanced training beyond college as a shortcoming and a way they would like their children to differ from themselves. But they clearly do not. Having obtained a college education, people are not apparently chafed by the levels of education beyond the bachelor's degree acquired by professional elites in our society.

4. *The 1976 population is more positive in their view of themselves.* This generalization is based on a number of results from table 3.2. In the measure of positive/negative orientation to the self, 5 percent fewer respondents in 1976 gave *any* ambivalent or negative differentiation of the self from others. Second, 9 percent fewer respondents in 1976 said they would want their child to be different from them in some way, as we noted above. In addition, 43 percent of Americans in 1957 gave two or more ways in which they would want a child to differ from themselves, compared to 35 percent in 1976. Third, as also noted and discussed above, more people in 1976 gave individuated, personality-based strengths. Fourth, there is a large decline in perceiving the self as needing social acceptance and a small decrease in the proportion wishing that other people liked them more. Finally, in 1976 there is an increase in the proportion of people who feel they are effective planners. We take both of the last two results as indications that people feel more positive about themselves. Not needing other people for self-validation and being able effectively to control the future are important features of high and independent self-esteem.

We did not directly measure either self-esteem or internal control in 1957. However, when we consider the distribution of these items for 1976, we are impressed with how much of the population is on the positive side of self-perception. Forty-three percent say it is "often true" that they feel they are persons of worth, able to do things as well as other people, and feel good about themselves. Another 23 percent respond "often true" to two of these items and "sometimes true" to one. Another 13 percent say "sometimes true" to two and "often true" to one. Only about 20 percent give any indication of negative self-perception. The 43 percent who say "often" to all three questions are labeled "high self-esteem" in later analyses. Any other combination of responses we label either "moderate" or "low." Very few people hold a depressed self-picture: only 9 percent of the population say "rarely true" or "never true" to one or more of these questions. Nevertheless, the fact that a large proportion answer "sometimes true" to one or more suggests that we have a sizable group with "moderate" self-esteem which may contrast with the "high" group in important ways.

On the measure of internal/external control, we find that 80 percent of the population say they feel they can run their lives the way they want to and only 15 percent say that problems in life are sometimes overwhelming. Four percent fall somewhere in between or say they do not know. By and large, then, we have, as a people, moved to a more positive view of self between 1957 and 1976, and the new questions asked in 1976 corroborate the view that we are a people who take a positive view of our own capacity to cope and to place ourselves securely in the social world.

As a population, we seem to be moving in the direction of positive self-perception. This is perhaps not surprising in a time period that has witnessed great normative stress on the self as a major source of strength. We have become more psychological and in the process have attended to and selected competences rather than shortcomings in self-attribution. Since, as we have suggested, the meaning of some of the questions may have changed over twenty years, we must use caution in interpreting this change and the pattern of self-attribution as absolute shifts rather than shifts in cultural phrasing.

To clarify gross year differences reported, we turn next to multivariate analyses.

Multivariate Analysis

QUALIFICATIONS OF YEAR DIFFERENCES

Except in a few instances, the year differences reported proved robust when tested against our multivariate criterion (see table 3.6). That is, most year differences held up when we took the effects of age, education, and sex into account along with year of interview. Despite differences in the distributions of age and education in the 1957 and 1976 populations and net of the effect of these differences, the 1976 population show greater intraceptiveness, greater use of personality characteristics in defining the self, and higher self-esteem than the 1957 population did.

However, a few findings need to be conditioned in the wake of multivariate analyses. The modest tendency noted in 1976 to phrase shortcomings as personality characteristics does not withstand the mul-

TABLE 3.6
Summary of Multivariate Analyses of Self-Perception

Measures of Self-Perception	Relationship(s) Required[a] to Reproduce Observed Cross-Classification of Measures by Age × Education × Year[b] × Sex[c]				
	Main Effects[d]				Interaction
	Age	Education	Year	Sex	
Perceived Differentiation	—	G<H<C	57<76	—	Age × Education; Age × Year
Sources of Differentiation:					
External	—	—	—	—	Education × Year
Internal					
Moral-virtuous	—	G>H>C	—	—	
Personality	Y>MA,O	G<H<C	57<76	—	
Positive/Negative Orientation	Y<MA<O	G<H<C	57<76	M>F	
Perceived Shortcoming					
Sources of Shortcoming:					
External	MA>Y>O	G>H>C	57>76	M>F	
Internal					
Moral-virtuous	—	G<H,C	—	M>F	
Personality	Y>MA>O	G<H<C	—	M<F	
Perceived Strength					
Sources of Strength:					
External	Y,MA>O	G>H>C	—	—	Age × Education; Education × Year
Internal					
Moral-virtuous	Y<MA<O	—	57>76	M>F	
Personality	Y>MA>O	G<H<C	57<76	—	
Self Needing Friends	Y>MA>O	—	—	—	
Self as Efficacious Planner	Y>MA>O	G,H<C	—	M>F	Age × Year
Self Needing Power	Y,MA>O	G<H<C	—	—	
Self Needing Acceptance	—[e]	—[e]			—[e]
Males	—	—	57>76	—[c]	
Females	Y>MA,O	G>H>C	57>76	—[c]	
Self-Esteem	—	G<H<C	—[b]	M>F	
Internal Control	—	G<H<C	—[b]	M>F	

[a] See Footnote [a] of Table 2.11 for an explanation of "Required."

[b] Year excluded in measures assessed only in 1976.

[c] Sex effects inappropriate in disaggregated data.

[d] See Footnote [a] of Table 2.11 for description of "Main Effects."

[e] Cross-classification is run separately for males and females because a complex four-way interaction involving both the measure of self-perception and sex is needed to explain the five-variable cross-classification.

tivariate test. In all likelihood, it is an effect produced by changes in the age and educational status of the 1976 population.

The small decline noted in the wish to have more friends (between 1957 and 1976) also washes out in analysis when age and education are taken into account. And the year effect in efficacy—the sense of being able to plan for the future—turns out to be a year-by-age interaction. While we noted a year change for the population as a whole in the direction of greater efficacy, those respondents under forty years of age show little or no increase in efficacy, while those over forty show a much larger shift. Year does not have an effect on this response net of education and age effects.

Year by education findings, while not significant beyond the education main effect, are provocative. Table 3.13 shows that while grade school- and high school-educated people have a greater sense of efficacy in 1976, those who have graduated from college actually show a decrease in the sense of their own effectiveness.

A few other interaction effects emerge from multivariate analyses. For example, in allusions to unique or distinguishing characteristics of the self, we find a year by age effect in addition to the main year effect. Respondents aged fifty or under are much more willing to distinguish the self from others in 1976 than they were in 1957, but those over fifty have changed little, if at all. While most groups show a decrease in external sources of differentiation from 1957 to 1976, the grade school educated actually give such sources more often in 1976.

ADDITIONAL YEAR DIFFERENCES

Finally, in sources of personal strength, no year difference appeared in allusions to external sources (where we might have expected a *decrease* over time), but the multivariate analysis reveals that there is in fact a year by education effect such that grade-school respondents use external references slightly more in 1976 than in 1957, while more educated people are notably *less* likely to phrase their strong points as external characteristics in 1976.

The fact that so many of the year differences in self-perception withstand the multivariate test (e.g., willingness to distinguish the self, the use of personality dimensions in thinking about the self and its strengths, a reduced need for social acceptance) indicates that changes in self-perception have occurred across the board and are not only the product of an increased proportion of highly educated people in our society. The sources of increased intraceptiveness, more psychologically framed and articulate self-concepts, and more positive self-regard must, we think, be located in broad cultural currents which have affected the young and old, men and women, the educated and uneducated in similar ways. Certain subgroups may be particularly sensitized to the currents and show their effects in a heightened degree. But by and large, they diffuse through the society by means of the media, the schools, churches and other organizations, and interpersonal exchange.

To clarify year differences further, we will now present sex differences, age differences, and education differences within each of the years. These results will provide further insight about conclusions we have drawn from generational shifts.

Sex Differences in Self-Perception

We began with a general hypothesis that differences that existed between men's and women's self-perceptions in 1957 would be muted in 1976 because of changes in our society's orientation to sex roles. This hypothesis was generally not supported by multivariate analyses. While some of the sex differences by year shown in table 3.7 show such trends, only two are large enough to warrant discussion. The others fall away when we take into account the fact that in 1976 there are proportionately more older and educated women in the population.

The two results which show the hypothesized muting of sex differences in 1976 are found in perceived shortcomings, the ways in which one would like a son or daughter to differ from the self. Relatively more women than men in 1957 referred to physical attributes in describing shortcomings, but the difference has diminished by 1976. And while men alluded to lack of education as a shortcoming much more than women in 1957, this sex difference has decreased sharply in 1976. Both of these results are emphasized in table 3.7 by boxes drawn around them. (In subsequent tables throughout this book, certain other results will also be highlighted by such boxes.)

Our evidence thus indicates that women are now less oriented to physical appearance as a shortcoming and that men are less oriented to educational status than they once were. In spite of these two findings, we must reject the hypothesis and conclude that there has not been much change in differential basis of self-perception for men and women. Sex differences which appeared in 1957 maintain their strength in 1976.

What are these differences? In what ways do the sexes continue to differ, despite marked differential shifts in education and age distributions?

Consistent and clear sex differences in responses to questions about the self reveal that women have a more negative orientation than men. We note this in a number of responses. More men than women give positive differentiations of the self from other people; more men than women give answers coded high in self-esteem; more men than women see themselves as effective planners and as having control over

TABLE 3.7

Sex Differences in Self-Perception (1957 vs. 1976)

Measure	Year	Men (%)	Women (%)
Perceived Differentiation			
Mentioning Difference	1957	70	69
	1976	76	76
Sources of Differentiation			
External	1957	6	7
	1976	6	6
Internal			
Moral-Virtuous	1957	13	14
	1976	12	13
Personality	1957	53	51
	1976	61	61
Positive-Negative Orientation			
Negative or Ambivalent	1957	14	21
	1976	10	15
Perceived Shortcoming: yes	1957	76	73
	1976	67	65
Sources of Shortcomings			
External			
Physical Attributes	1957	4	10
	1976	3	5
Lack of Education	1957	37	16
	1976	23	14
Other	1957	7	12
	1976	7	9
Internal			
Moral-Virtuous	1957	6	2
	1976	6	5
Personality	1957	25	43
	1976	34	44
Perceived Strengths: yes	1957	84	86
	1976	87	87
Sources of Perceived Strength			
External	1957	12	15
	1976	8	10
Internal			
Moral-Virtuous	1957	35	30
	1976	30	24
Personality	1957	43	46
	1976	53	48
Adjustment Characteristics	1957	7	7
	1976	8	11
Altruistic Characteristics	1957	4	10
	1976	7	9
Other	1957	32	29
	1976	38	28

TABLE 3.7 *(continued)*

Measure	Year	Men (%)	Women (%)
Self Needing Friends			
More Friends	1957	38	41
	1976	44	44
Self as Efficacious Planner			
Very True, Pretty True	1957	80	71
	1976	84	79
Self Needing Power			
Very True, Pretty True	1957	43	40
	1976	29	39
Self Needing Acceptance			
Very True, Pretty True	1957	34	38
	1976	26	23
Self-Esteem: very high	1957	—	—
	1976	48	40
Internal Control: high	1957	—	—
	1976	86	75
Total Number	1957	1,077	1,383
	1976	960	1,304

their lives. In all of these ways, men indicate a more positive sense of self. None of the differences are large—less than 10 percent in most cases as can be noted in table 3.7. Yet the consistency across varied domains and the centrality of the differences to theories of sex roles make them important. Nevertheless, their meaning can easily be exaggerated. Most women have relatively high self-esteem despite the fact that men as a group have somewhat more positive self-regard.

Two other sex differences in self-perception clarify the meaning of women's lower self-evaluation. Women more often than men mention personality shortcomings in answering the question about how they would like a child of theirs to be different from themselves. And men more often mention either role/externally based shortcomings or moral/virtuous stereotypes. Thus women seem to judge their shortcomings on the basis of deeper, more individuated qualities and characteristics, to hold more internal aspirations for identity.

Such aspirations may be subtle and difficult to realize. External criteria may be clearer and easier to meet: one has either reached a certain level of education or not; one is honest or not. But how does one judge one's outgoingness or personal organization? How extroverted is extroverted enough? Women may hold more abstract and ill-defined expectations for themselves, whereas men have more clear-cut external bases for judging themselves. Women may thus have more ambiguity and doubt about their own adequacy.

Another way to look at these findings is that women may rely on others for confirmation of their adequacy more than men do. Standards like "independence" and "adjustment" may be more social in definition. Thus women, holding such standards, may be less directly in control of their own sense of adequacy, depending to a larger degree on evaluation by others.

The more socially dependent quality of women's self-esteem is subtle and not easily captured in survey questions. We found, for example, no sex difference in the wish that other people liked one more. Multivariate analysis uncovered one significant interactive effect involving sex: young women in 1957 were especially high on the desire to be liked. The reduction in young women's need for social acceptance in 1976 is evidently closely linked to their greater education. Many more young women in 1976 are college educated, and highly educated women are less likely to express the need for social acceptance.

But no overall sex difference appeared in these responses. Similarly, we found no difference between men and women in the wish that people listen more to them or the desire to have more friends. The more social reference of women's self-evaluation we have posited is evidently more subtle than these direct questions tap. The social cues women rely on—the well-being of a child, husband, or parent—may be susceptible to other kinds of measures. We looked at answers to 1976 questions about the use of time for clues about women's standards of altruism. Men and women were asked: "How much of your free time do you usually spend doing things to help or please other people? Would you say you spend a lot, some, little, or none of your free time doing such things?" Seven percent more women than men say they spend most or a lot of their free time helping or pleasing other people (37 percent of men and 44 percent of women). Yet more women than men say that they would *like* to spend even more time pleasing and helping others (25 percent of men and 31 percent of women). This illustrates nicely the pattern we suggested above: women orient their behavior and self-definition toward other people more than men do—and yet they do not fully meet their own standards of altruism.

Another interpretation of many of the sex differences we have reported is possible. Research on social motivation (Veroff, 1969) suggests that men are more likely than women to take high risks, anticipating that they will succeed. Some men, however, take risks out of a strong concern about failure: they engage in defensive risk taking to deny the possibility of failing. It is possible that sex differences in personal efficacy and positive orientation to self result from this same pattern: some men may say that they can plan their own lives or are unique in positive ways because such responses serve a defensive purpose. At some level of awareness, men may feel just as (or even more) uncertain as women do about their ability to cope with life on their own. But men have difficulty admitting any failure of auton-

TABLE 3.8
Age Differences in Self-Perception (1957 vs. 1976)

Measure	Year	Age 21-29 (%)	30-39 (%)	40-49 (%)	50-59 (%)	60-64 (%)	65+ (%)
Perceived Differentiation	1957	75	70	65	71	65	70
Mentioning Difference	1976	84	79	79	72	70	70
Sources of Differentiation							
External	1957	9	9	5	5	8	4
	1976	6	5	8	7	8	6
Internal							
Moral-Virtuous	1957	11	10	15	16	13	21
	1976	10	12	12	13	13	17
Personality	1957	54	53	55	50	51	47
	1976	67	64	62	58	57	52
Positive-Negative Orientation							
Negative or Ambivalent	1957	24	21	17	18	17	8
	1976	14	13	15	12	15	9
Perceived Shortcoming: yes	1957	90	87	82	72	65	57
	1976	83	80	76	66	57	43
Sources of Shortcomings							
External	1957	36	40	41	38	35	32
	1976	28	29	33	30	30	21
Internal							
Moral-Virtuous	1957	4	5	3	3	5	6
	1976	7	7	4	4	6	5
Personality	1957	48	40	37	30	26	20
	1976	51	48	42	35	28	21
Perceived Strength: yes	1957	89	87	88	89	75	84
	1976	92	89	91	89	86	81
Sources of Strength							
External	1957	17	15	12	13	10	9
	1976	9	10	13	9	5	9
Internal							
Moral-Virtuous	1957	27	26	32	35	42	42
	1976	20	25	26	33	38	31
Personality	1957	48	50	49	42	33	37
	1976	66	58	55	51	45	47
Self Needing Friends							
More Friends	1957	45	42	42	37	37	32
	1976	53	43	43	37	49	36
Self as Efficacious Planner							
Very True, Pretty True	1957	82	80	71	74	67	69
	1976	85	80	80	78	76	81
Self Needing Power							
Very True, Pretty True	1957	42	42	44	42	39	42
	1976	39	37	37	35	38	33
Self Needing Acceptance							
Very True, Pretty True	1957	41	36	36	34	37	36
	1976	26	23	25	19	32	28
Self-Esteem: very high	1957	—	—	—	—	—	—
	1976	46	'50	47	42	36	33
Internal Control: high	1957	—	—	—	—	—	—
	1976	82	84	79	81	69	75
Total Number	1957	450	580	513	388	150	351
	1976	540	461	338	388	163	391

omy. Sex-role prescriptions inhibit men from admitting weakness or inadequacy. Such defensive orientation in self-perception may also contribute to sex differences in help-seeking behavior. More women than men have sought and used both formal and informal help. Women are freer to use available resources in time of stress because they have less stake in appearing to be independent and effective. Indeed, Veroff (in press) has shown that women who perceive themselves to be effective are *more* likely to say they would seek help in times of personal difficulty. In males only among the college-educated young men—a group for whom traditional sex-role stereotypes are breaking down—does efficacy relate to help seeking in the same way that it does in women.

In spite of the sex differences observed in self-percepts, we are impressed primarily with the modesty of the differences. We have found differences which are consistent and mesh with differential social expectations imposed on men and women. Nevertheless, they are small, and we again conclude that sex differences have been exaggerated in much popular discussion.

Age Differences in Self-Perceptions

Age differences are presented in table 3.8. Young, middle-aged, and older respondents differ from each other in a number of ways in the kinds and qualities of their self-perceptions. Surprisingly, however, we found no age variation in the 1976 measure of self-esteem. Young, middle-aged, and older respondents differ in the bases on their self-percepts, but not in their overall evaluation of the self. Young people are self-critical, are able to focus on certain negative features of the self, but this does not lead to negative self-esteem. And older people focus on certain positive aspects of the self—a kind of consolidation of life experience—but this does not lead them to overvalue the self. What are the specific findings that lead us to these conclusions? Let us look at each of the three age groups in turn.

YOUNGER PEOPLE'S SELF-PERCEPTIONS

In younger people's responses we detect two important themes: younger people, in the process of identity development, are willing to speak of shortcomings, willing to focus on aspects of the self which are not as ideal as they would like. The second notable aspect of self-perception in the young is a strong sense of efficacy, the feeling that they can handle whatever may arise in life.

TABLE 3.9

Mentioning Social Skill Strengths by People of Different Ages (by year)

Those Mentioning Social Skill Strengths	Age					
	21–29 (%)	30–39 (%)	40–49 (%)	50–59 (%)	60–64 (%)	65+ (%)
1957	18	18	15	14	10	9
	(421)	(540)	(478)	(364)	(131)	(317)
1976	23	18	16	13	7	13
	(521)	(429)	(320)	(320)	(149)	(348)
Both Years	21	18	15	13	9	11
	(942)	(909)	(798)	(684)	(280)	(665)

NOTE: Numbers in parentheses are total numbers of persons in each group.

TABLE 3.10

Percentage of "Very True" "Pretty True" Wanting Acceptance Among Different Age and Education Groups (by sex, by sex × year)

Year	Age			Education		
	21–34 (%)	35–54 (%)	55+ (%)	Grade School (%)	High School (%)	College (%)
1957						
Men	34	36	34	30	35	34
	(316)	(448)	(303)	(363)	(458)	(242)
Women	42	36	37	40	40	28
	(440)	(555)	(371)	(429)	(723)	(215)
1976						
Men	26	26	29	37	26	25
	(341)	(307)	(289)	(149)	(416)	(370)
Women	23	22	25	35	23	16
	(465)	(380)	(434)	(222)	(678)	(379)
Both Years						
Men	30	32	32	36	30	29
	(657)	(755)	(592)	(512)	(874)	(612)
Women	33	30	30	39	32	20
	(905)	(935)	(805)	(651)	(1401)	(594)

NOTE: Numbers in parentheses are total number of persons in each group.

The following pattern of findings informs these generalizations. Young respondents are less likely than older people to deny that they are unique or different from other people. Furthermore, they focus more often on personality factors in describing *how* they differ from others. They speak of personality shortcomings in response to the question about changes desired in a child, and they also offer personality characteristics as their strong points. They seem to be actively working out identity issues, to be intensely aware of their unique qualities, shortcomings, and strengths. It is interesting to note that young women—more than older women—say they wish people liked them more. Young people—both men and women—more often than older people, wish they had more friends. Yet, in listing sources of strength, young people also more often allude to their social skills (see table 3.9). Thus, they are not reflecting a deep sense of social insecurity in their wish to be liked more and have more friends. Rather, they are in the process of building social networks and are striving to enlarge their circles. They are able to take a self-critical stance, but this does not imply deep or corrosive negative self-evaluation.

One group stands out among the young: the least educated. Young respondents with less than a high school degree very frequently say that they are not different from other people, not unique in any way. Evidently to develop a sense of distinction or begin building an identity, the young person must have certain prerequisite competences. In modern American society, one of these prerequisites is a high school education.

The fact that young people are more likely than older people to feel that they can plan effectively suggests that identity building does not disrupt essential self-conceptions in the young. It should be pointed out that while results in table 3.8 suggest that young people are higher in overall self-esteem than older people, multivariate analyses that control for education dissipate all relationships between age and self-esteem. Young people are more often college educated compared to middle-aged and older people, and it is their higher education which stimulates higher self-evaluation. The same may be said about the measure of internal control. More highly educated people feel they control their lives more than the uneducated do. With education controlled, no age difference remains.

We conclude that young people's self-schemas are in process and in transition. The young seek unique ways of defining themselves, particularly those aspects of self which connect them to other people. Young people need and want other people more than older people do. Yet they also focus on social skills in self-attributions of personal strengths (see table 3.9). Thus, we get a picture of young people setting aspirations for themselves, being aware of their flaws and limitations, but not being overwhelmed by them in self-evaluation. The heightened concern with social acceptance (i.e, wish to be liked more) which young women expressed in 1957 has more or less disappeared in 1976 (see table 3.10). A strong sense of identity does not apparently require social acceptance.

MIDDLE-AGED PEOPLE'S SELF-PERCEPTIONS

Few findings distinguish middle-aged self-pictures from those of other age groups. The one pattern that emerged, particularly in multivariate analyses controlling for education, year, and sex, was that middle-aged people focus on role status and role performance in considering both their strong points and their weaknesses. Asked about shortcomings, middle-aged people (compared to younger and older groups) spoke of role or status inadequacies, particularly the lack of educational attainment. These results can be seen only when education is controlled. For example, see table 3.11. The middle-aged were also most likely of any group to describe their strong points in role terms; to allude to being good mothers or fathers, good at their jobs, and so on. Other than these two findings, middle-aged people fall between the younger and older groups on all questions about the self. These results suggest that beyond holding self-concepts between those of the young and the old, middle-aged people are at a point of stock taking, evaluating their progress toward life goals they set at some earlier point in their lives. Evaluating role status speaks of the importance of meeting normative expectations and fulfilling responsibilities.

TABLE 3.11

Middle-Age College-Educated vs. Other
College-Educated Groups on Mentioning
Role-Related Strengths of Self-Perception

	College Educated	
Age Group	Percentage	Total Number
Young	6	542
Middle-Aged	11	415
Old	4	223

OLDER PEOPLE'S SELF-PERCEPTIONS

Perhaps the single most important finding from the age analysis of self-perceptions is the shift that occurs in older people's capacity to plan for the future. In 1976 many more older people say it is true or very true that they can plan ahead effectively (compared to older people in 1957). This result is important because it suggests that things have improved specifically for older people in our society over the generation. Increased Social Security and medical services which have become available to older people must surely be counted among the

factors which have improved and have allowed older people this greater sense of effectiveness.

Another explanation might be offered. Older people in the 1957
study were part of a generation that experienced particular disruption
in middle adulthood because of the economic dislocation of the Great
Depression. For many, career plans and life plans were disrupted. Such
experiences might indeed create a sense of personal ineffectiveness.

Older people in 1976 show an increased differentiation of self from
others. They have a greater sense of their own uniqueness and identity
than older people had in 1957.

Nevertheless, findings from both years indicate that the old are less
willing than the young to focus on the self as a point of introspective
concern. Older people are less articulate about their shortcomings, saying that they do not know how they would like a child to be different
from themselves or giving only generalized responses. This result,
however, may reflect a methodological problem. The question about
shortcomings asks in what ways the respondent would like a child of
hers/his to be different from her or himself. As people get older, there
may be a tendency to accept the way one's child *is*. To say that you
would like her/him to be different in some way may have a very concrete reference for the older person and (s)he may be reluctant to specify aspects of the self very different from the child as being too critical
of what the child *is*. Thus, the inarticulateness of older people may re-

TABLE 3.12
*Age Difference in Reporting "Moral" and "Virtuous"
Strong Points (by year)*

	Age					
Year	21–29 (%)	30–39 (%)	40–49 (%)	50–59 (%)	60–64 (%)	65+ (%)
1957						
Moral	12	13	16	21	29	30
Virtuous	16	16	18	17	20	17
	(421)	(540)	(478)	(364)	(131)	(317)
1976						
Moral	7	8	13	12	18	19
Virtuous	14	19	14	24	24	16
	(524)	(429)	(320)	(320)	(149)	(348)
Both Years						
Moral	9	10	15	16	23	24
Virtuous	15	17	16	20	22	16
	(947)	(969)	(798)	(684)	(280)	(655)

NOTE: Numbers in parentheses are total number of persons in each group.

flect a methodological problem in that the question has a very different meaning for them.

Nevertheless, the finding can also be seen as substantive. Older people have probably resolved many of their doubts about their own selves. In some ways, raising questions and criticisms about the self in old age is a meaningless activity. The same kind of interpretation can be offered for the fact that older people do not often wish for greater social acceptance or want more friends. They have already negotiated social adaptations and are not about to question them now. To do so would negate or devalue their previous lives and the self.

A related finding indicates that older people do not refer to social roles in defining their strengths or shortcomings. Older people are disengaging from roles; often they are forced to disengage by the growth of children, the death of a spouse, mandatory retirement clauses. They have loosened connections to the social structure, and roles are no longer salient for self-definition.

Older people focus on moral qualities as strong points. This finding corroborates many life-span developmental studies which suggest that as people age they turn to the spiritual life as a way to construct identity and find meaning. They speak of themselves as moral or religious rather than having stereotyped virtues (see table 3.12). It seems that older people do not become more self-righteous, but that they turn to the spiritual side of life as a way to enhance their self-evaluation.

Young people focus on developing social skills and social roles, middle-aged people measure themselves by their social role attainments, and older people focus on spiritual aspects of the self. This developmental shift helps us to understand the fact that there is no relationship between age and self-esteem. The basis for self-esteem varies across the life cycle, but evaluation of self remains stable. For young people, meeting goals of self-development and identity leads to positive self-esteem. Having reached certain role statuses yields self-esteem in the middle-aged. In later life, consolidating the self around certain general values apart from role performance serves as the basis of positive self-regard.

Education Differences in Self-Perception

As we turn to the question of whether grade-school, high-school, and college-educated respondents vary in their perceptions of strong points, weaknesses, and differentiation of self, we face a critical methodological problem which pervades our research but is especially salient in the study of self-perception. Many of the results that differentiate educational levels are interpretable as differences in the ability of more highly educated people to articulate answers to questions about self-perception. For example, in table 3.13 we find that grade school–educated people in both years are more likely to say they do not know how they differ from others or to mention fewer specific shortcomings and strong points (compared to high school– and college-educated respondents). On the other hand, in both years, college-educated people more often give personality qualities as differentiating the self, more skill-oriented strong points such as achievement skills, and more personality shortcomings (e.g., general adjustment or achievement) than either high-school or (especially) grade-school respondents. Furthermore, college-educated men and women more often present positive differentiations of the self.

Are these results due simply to the greater articulateness of the college educated? Are they more likely to give *any* response—not just individuated psychological responses—compared to less educated people? We do not think that verbal ability accounts entirely for our findings. We credit them as substantive findings as well. While the criticism suggests caution, we would defend our view by noting that certain responses—for example, role characteristics and certain moral-spiritual qualities—are actually mentioned *less* frequently by the college educated. If all we were observing was the operation of verbal ability, these answers should also be higher among the well educated. One can phrase role adequacy in more or less articulate and verbally complex ways. The fact that the highly educated do *not* refer to such characteristics seems to us a substantive finding—that such characteristics are not as salient in their thoughts about themselves as are certain personality traits.

More critically, the college educated endorse responses to closed-ended questions that reflect the same greater self-awareness that the open-ended responses do. The college educated in both years are the most likely to see themselves as efficacious planners, as people who do not need more power or social acceptance. (The latter result is clearly apparent only in women, as indicated by table 3.10). On measures introduced in the 1976 survey the more educated are highest in both self-esteem and internal control. In table 3.13 we see these dramatic results. While only 27 percent of the grade school educated respond to the self-esteem items in a way that puts them in the "high" category, the figure rises at each higher educational level, until 60 percent of college graduates are in the "high" category. The same pattern occurs for the measure of internal control that asks people whether they think they can run their own lives. There is a 20 percent increase from the least to the most educated in their feelings that they can run their own lives.

We are thus convinced that we are dealing with a very palpable phenomenon: the college educated examine who they are, their strengths, their uniqueness with more interest than people at the other educa-

TABLE 3.13
Education Differences in Self-Perception (1957 vs. 1976)

Measure	Year	Education				
		Grade School (%)	Some High School (%)	High School Graduate (%)	Some College (%)	College Graduate (%)
Perceived Differentiation						
Mention Difference	1957	71	71	78	80	84
	1976	68	68	72	70	76
Sources of Differentiation						
External	1957	6	9	9	8	10
	1976	12	5	6	6	8
Internal						
Moral-Virtuous	1957	23	17	15	9	10
	1976	23	18	13	11	10
Personality	1957	59	64	63	70	69
	1976	53	64	73	75	76
Positive-Negative Orientation						
Negative or Ambivalent	1957	14	19	20	23	18
	1976	14	10	15	13	9
Perceived Shortcomings: yes	1957	69	82	84	86	83
	1976	53	70	74	74	75
Sources of Shortcomings						
External	1957	49	47	40	32	25
	1976	42	45	34	27	14
Internal						
Moral-Virtuous	1957	8	5	3	3	1
	1976	6	6	6	8	5
Personality	1957	24	37	46	57	63
	1976	23	33	48	52	69
Perceived Strengths: yes	1957	83	88	88	89	92
	1976	79	87	88	92	96
Sources of Strength						
External	1957	15	17	14	11	9
	1976	17	14	9	7	4
Internal						
Moral-Virtuous	1957	42	33	30	34	25
	1976	35	31	28	26	25
Personality	1957	39	47	53	51	66
	1976	43	50	62	66	70
Self Needing Friends						
More Friends	1957	37	43	39	45	45
	1976	41	42	45	44	46
Self as Efficacious Planner						
Very True, Pretty True	1957	71	74	76	80	86
	1976	79	75	82	80	81
Self Needing Power						
Very True, Pretty True	1957	49	41	38	35	36
	1976	46	44	36	36	22
Self Needing Acceptance						
Very True, Pretty True	1957	38	40	36	32	30
	1976	36	25	24	21	20
Self-Esteem: very high	1957	—	—	—	—	—
	1976	27	38	45	48	60
Internal Control: high	1957	—	—	—	—	—
	1976	66	69	83	86	89
	1957	796	508	670	247	209
Total Number	1976	375	343	757	408	344

tional levels. Their advantages in the society put them in a good position to emerge from self-inquiries feeling very good about themselves.

In the last twenty years, the self has attracted increasing attention in our society. The "narcissism" some critics detect in our character has probably affected the literate, college-educated segment of our population more than other groups. They are subjected on all sides to pressure to examine their identities and life positions. Intraceptiveness as a value has burgeoned under the press of psychoanalysis and the personal-growth movement. Psychology courses are extremely popular on the campuses. The more educated are undoubtedly most affected by this push to psychologize and examine the self.

Summary

The findings in this chapter support one major conclusion: the increased pressure for intraception in a nation which has become much more highly educated, has encouraged a stronger view of the self as a differentiated being. Most of the changes over the generation reflect positive effects on self-perception. Many more people take a positive view of the self and are sensitive to more psychological aspects of their strengths and unique qualitites. One can think of these changes as reflecting a more integrated identity, a stronger sense of the self as an individual being with individuated ways of responding to the world. Whereas we were a society somewhat more bound and defined by social roles in 1957, we seem to have moved toward a more personalized self-consciousness in 1976.

Sex differences were not very large in either era. We found slight evidence of muting of six differences between 1957 and 1976. Age roles continue to affect people's view of themselves; not so much in specific social role terms, but in the aspects of life experience integrated at different stages in the life cycle. Older people are less concerned than young people about affiliative issues and more concerned about the moral side of life. Middle-aged people are very aware of role achievements.

Educated people in our society now seem to be somewhat less concerned than they were in 1957 about social aspects of identity. The college educated, in particular, are less likely to see themselves needing social power or social acceptance in 1976 than they were in 1957. These results suggest that as the more educated develop individuated, personalized integrations, they also turn away from social relationship as the base of self-definition. These changes may have some negative consequences, but they do not emerge in measures of self-esteem used in our study. There was a tendency for college-educated respondents to be somewhat more ambivalent—as well as more positive—about their self-presentations. This ambivalence may stem from turning too much to the self as a measure of adjustment and turning away from the rewards so clearly available through roles. Thus, we see some cost for growing self-integration. Nevertheless, our data suggest that in the main in 1976 people hold more integrated concepts of themselves— and of their strengths and weaknesses—than did the population in 1957.

Chapter 4

MARRIAGE

DURING the last twenty years, marriage has been profoundly challenged and changed. Divorce rates accelerated steeply. One anthropologist dubbed the ascending pattern "omnigamy" and claimed that divorce had become the dominant institution organizing our social life—the building block, as it were, of our social organization. No anthropologist stranger, he claimed, could understand our kinship system without taking primary account of the dissolution and reformation of families. Our language, which has always been sparse in kinship terms, now has need of a whole new system to designate kin acquired when one's parents remarry or when one remarries. Children have a mother, a mother's husband, father's wife or girlfriend, new grandparents—the parents of their parents' spouses, and so forth. Life is complicated, and family obligations paradoxically proliferate. There is some possibility that divorce and remarriage represent our society's answer to the shortcomings and disadvantages of the nuclear family: a mechanism for building an extended family by choice rather than ascription.

Bruno Bettelheim (1976) attributes the disruption of families to release from survival preoccupations. When the family's survival was at stake, he says, it usually took precedence over individual whim but "if only psychological benefits are involved, why should those of a parent weigh less heavily than those of his child in reaching a decision?"

When, finally, individual happiness becomes the criterion by which all things are measured, when the ability to withstand, strength of character, position in a community, the good of the group, exemplary and responsible adult behavior, and/or the welfare of one's children are all subjugated to individual happiness and "self-realization," then social arrangements weaken. And the calculus assumes a market quality: all things are measured by hedonic coinage. Fullness of life—the satisfactory experience and performance of all the roles available to an adult in one's society—loses significance. The question becomes: how much individual satisfaction does each of the roles offer? When all experiences are judged by a single metric—whether that be "happiness" or "cost benefit" or ease—none has unique rewards, and all become exchangeable.

One other trend in the culture will appear frequently in the discussion of findings from this research. That is a decrease in sensitivity and allusion to status and roles in various aspects of life. Meaning and self-definition no longer derive primarily from the accession to adult status and the adequate or outstanding performance of adult roles. In fact, role and status disignations have become objects of suspicion, as though they were different from—and even contradictory to—the core self, the essential person.

Does knowing that a person is married tell us something important about the authentic self of that person? It probably does, but we have become increasingly unwilling to admit it. In our society, with wide dissemination of statistical data about marriage and divorce rates, it means at least that the person is probably an optimist about the future of social arrangements and has a significant capacity to commit her/himself to human relationships which on their face are full of risk. Whereas, in other eras, security needs might be inferred from the act of marrying, at the moment it is probably closer to the truth to read verve, omnipotence, and bouncy optimism into the act.

Along with the occupational roles, family roles have traditionally carried the weight of defining individuals as full adult members of our society. Marrying and having children signal adulthood in all societies, but their significance is exaggerated when occupational preparation prolongs economic dependency. For many women in our society, marriage still represents the major path to legitimate adulthood and autonomy vis-à-vis their own parents. For all young people, the birth of a first child ushers in a new relationship to the parent generation; a new uniting with their own parents in the generation responsible for historical continuity and for raising the young. Marriage and parenting are reserved to adults and are rich with possibilities for meaning and self definition.

Yet family roles have also been depleted of meaning in our times. They have certainly lost meaning in a normative sense and the sense that their assumption automatically implies either problem-free bliss or long-term personal commitment. They have become more stressful.

Nevertheless, we will find that both men and women are extraordinarily certain that marriage is of central importance to them—perhaps not in the status it confers, but in the interpersonal support it provides. That fact about marriage is more clear-cut for men than for women. In

The Future of Marriage (1972), Jessie Bernard persuasively argues that the institution of marriage is felicitously arranged for men, but much less so for women. She implies that marriage may even be bad for the psychological well-being of women. Our data do not support this extreme argument but will support her more general position.

In this chapter we will look first at findings about the salience of marriage in 1957 and 1976: how strongly people feel that everyone should marry and stay married, how morally indignant they are about violation of that norm, how positive they feel about the change that marriage brings in people's lives, and how much they think marriage fulfills their life values. We will follow the discussion of these attitudes and norms with a look at respondents' own experience of marriage in 1957 and 1976: how satisfied they are with their marriages, what they find to be the most significant gratifications and disadvantages of their own marriages, how they evaluate their own adequacy as spouses, and what problems they have encountered in marriage. In both of these analyses, we will focus on changes which have occurred between 1957 and 1976, although in some critical instances we have data only for the 1976 respondents. In addition to year changes in the salience and experience of marriage, we will continue our investigation of sex, age, and education as they affect marital attitudes.

The Salience of Marriage

MEASURES

All of the assessments of marital salience that we will analyze are listed in table 4.1. Unfortunately, some were available only in the 1976 sample. The measures used in both years include the respondent's *attitude toward the nonmarrying person,* an evaluation that gives us considerable insight about the norms for marrying; the respondent's *positive/ negative orientation to marriage* and *nonrestrictive/restrictive orientation to marriage,* both of which are based on the respondent's perception of the changes that marriage introduces in a person's life. In 1976 only we also have *attitudes toward divorce,* based on a question asking married people about the effectiveness of divorce as a solution to marital problems; *value fulfillment through marriage (and other roles);* and *social validation through marriage (and other roles).* The last two need some explanation.

Value fulfillment through marriage (and other roles) was derived from a series of questions that asked respondents to choose from a list of nine values culled from Milton Rokeach's end values (1973) the two they would rate as most important in their own lives. From these two, each

Measures of Marital Salience

Measure	Question	Code (Examples)
Both 1957 and 1976		
Attitude Toward Nonmarrying Person	Suppose all you knew about a man (for man)/woman (for woman) was that he/she did not want to get married. What would you guess he/she was like?	*positive* (unmarried state seen as legitimate and happy) *neutral* (independent, self-sufficient, interested in career) *negative* (selfish, immature, peculiar)
Positive/Negative Orientation to Marriage	Think about a man's (woman's) life. How is a man's (woman's) life changed by being married?	*positive* (get companionship; fuller life; makes person more happy) *neutral* (have to get along, share; settles you down; more responsibility) *negative* (lose your freedom; ties you down; life harder)
Restrictive/Nonrestrictive Orientation to Marriage	Same as above	*All responses restrictive* (restrictive-responses indicating greater responsibility, concern for another, having children, etc.) *some responses restrictive* *no responses restrictive*

TABLE 4.1 (continued)
Measures of Marital Salience

Measure	Question	Code (Examples)
1976 Only		
Attitude Toward Divorce	Some people think divorce is often the best solution when people can't seem to work out their marriage problems. Other people think divorce is never the best solution. Would you say divorce is often, sometimes, rarely, or never the best solution?	as is
Social Validation Through Marriage (and other roles)	Now for each pair of statements I read, please tell me which one you would rather overhear a friend say about you. First which of these: She/he is a fine mother/father. She/he is excellent at her/his work. How about these two: She/he is a good wife/husband. She/he is excellent at her/his work. And which of these two would you rather overhear: She/he is a good wife/husband. She/he is a fine mother/father.	*For each role:* —most preferred (2 choices) —moderately preferred (1 choice) —least preferred (0 choices)
Value Fulfillment Through Marriage and Other Roles 1. Measurement of primary value orientation:		
Sociability	Here is a list of things that many people look for or want out of life. Please study the list carefully, then tell me which *two* of these things are most important to you in *your life.* (a) of these two, which *one* is more important to you in your life? (1) sense of belonging	Choice of *either* in (a): —sense of belonging —warm relations with others
Hedonism		Choice of *either* in (a): —excitement

Measure	Question	Code (Examples)
Self-actualization	(3) warm relations with others (4) being well-respected (5) fun and enjoyment in life (6) security	Choice of *either* in (a): —self-fulfillment —sense of accomplishment
Moral respect	(7) self-respect (8) a sense of accomplishment	Choice of *either* in (a): —being well-respected —self-respect
Security		Choice of "security" in (a)
2. Measurement of fulfillment of values through roles:	Now I'd like to ask you how much various things in your life led or would lead to (MOST IMPORTANT VALUE CHOSEN IN PRIMARY VALUE QUESTION).	
Leisure-value fulfillment	First, how much have the things you do in your leisure time led to (MOST IMPORTANT VALUE) in your life—*very little, a little, some, a lot, or a great deal?*	as is
Work in house—value fulfillment	How much has the work you do in and around the house led to (MOST IMPORTANT VALUE) in your life—*very little, a little, some, a lot, or a great deal?*	as is
Job value fulfillment	How much (has/would/did) work at a job (led/lead) to (MOST IMPORTANT VALUE) in your life?	as is
Marriage value fulfillment	How about being married? How much (has/would/did) being married (led/lead) to (MOST IMPORTANT VALUE) in your life?	as is
Parenthood value fulfillment	How about being a (father/mother)? How much (has/would) being a parent (led/lead) to (MOST IMPORTANT VALUE) in your life?	as is

respondent was then asked to name the *most* important. Finally s/he was asked how much each of the major life roles (work, marriage, and parenting) and leisure activities and "work around the house" contributed to the realization of this crucial value.[1] If, for example, a respondent chose "a sense of accomplishment" as her most important value, she was then asked: "Now I'd like to ask you how much various things in your life either have led or would lead to *a sense of accomplishment*. First, how much have the things you do in your *leisure* time led to *a sense of accomplishment* in your life—very little, a little, some, a lot, or a great deal? And subsequently: "How much has the work you do in and around the house led to a sense of accomplishment?" "How much has your work (being married, being a father/mother) led to a sense of accomplishment?" People not currently married were asked either to think of a past time when they were, or what the role would provide if he/she were in it.

Social validation through roles was derived from another series of questions which asked respondents to choose between two fixed alternatives in answer to: "Which of these would you rather overhear someone say about you?" Being good at work, being a good husband, and being a good father were pitted against each other in pairs. Because the respondent was asked to think of these as public views of himself/herself, we consider the responses as measures of the salience of each of the roles for *social* validation in critical reference groups.

INTERCORRELATIONS OF MEASURES

When the measures of marital role salience were intercorrelated, we found little evidence that the measures tapped highly similar issues. They generally were not very highly correlated, except for the .54 correlation between the measure of *positive/negative orientation to marriage* and *restrictive/nonrestrictive orientation to marriage*, which were slightly different coding schemes applied to responses to the same question. All other correlations varied between .00 and .18, but most of them were significantly positive. Among the highest of these correlations were the ones between *attitudes toward a nonmarrying person* and the *positive/negative orientation toward marriage*. As expected, the more positive respondents were to a nonmarrying person, the more negative they were to marriage (−.14 in 1957; −.16 in 1976). The attitude toward divorce was quite unrelated to attitudes toward marriage. This suggests that Americans who are certain that marriage is good for people do not also believe that marriage should be saved at all costs.

---

[1] This series of questions appears in table 4.1. Values were grouped as indicated in the table.

1957 AND 1976 COMPARED

On the issue of generational change in attitude toward people who reject the marital imperative, the evidence is rich and remarkably consistent (see table 4.2). In 1957 fifty-three percent of all respondents gave answers which indicated that they thought such a choice bad— the person was seen as either sick or immoral, too selfish or too neurotic to marry; 37 percent gave reasons which were relatively neutral. In 1976 these figures had shifted to 34 percent negative and 51 percent neutral. Only one-third of the population now think that a person who chooses not to marry must be sick or morally flawed. The weight of public opinion is now clearly on the side of neutrality. There is even a small minority of respondents in 1976 (15 percent) who view the choice positively.

Further analysis of this attitude in 1957 revealed that it operated as a very powerful norm at that period of American history. The majority of respondents in 1957 took this sanctioning attitude toward the refusal to marry *irrespective of their own marital status.* Even people who had them-

TABLE 4.2
Year Difference in Measures of
Marital Role Salience

	Year	
Measure of Marital Role Salience	1957 (%)	1976 (%)
Attitude Toward Nonmarrying Person[a]		
Positive	10	15
Neutral	37	51
Negative	53	34
	100%	100%
Positive/Negative Orientation Toward Marriage		
Positive	43	30
Neutral	34	42
Negative	23	28
	100%	100%
Restrictive/Nonrestrictive Orientation to Marriage		
All responses restrictive	44	59
Some responses restrictive	34	27
No responses restrictive	22	14
	100%	100%
Total Number	2,460[b]	2,264

[a] Question asked only one-third of respondents in 1957.

[b] Total numbers vary depending on number of nonascertainables.

selves not married and respondents who had had bad marriages which ended in divorce (who might reasonably be expected to take a jaundiced view of the institution) tended to evaluate the choice not to marry negatively. The smallest proportion of any marital status group giving a negative evaluation occurs among single men: 34 percent. Fifty percent of single and divorced women and 70 percent of divorced men answered the question in ways indicating a negative view of people who do not marry. The uniformity of response across groups is, we think, evidence of a strong societal norm.

Other evidence investigating the *positive/negative orientation to marriage* and the *restrictive/nonrestrictive orientation to marriage* reflects the moral force of promarriage norms in 1957, compared to 1976. Table 4.2 shows that in 1957 the dominant concept of marriage was a positive and enlarging one in response to the question: "How is a man's (woman's) life changed by being married?" Of the whole population—irrespective of marital status—over 40 percent gave answers indicating a view of marriage as enlarging the individual, opening new opportunities, and about 20 percent responded negatively to the changes brought by marriage. Among respondents who had not experienced marriage, a positive view was even more common, accounting for more than half of all responses given by married, widowed, and divorced people. In 1976, in contrast, less than a third of all respondents (29 percent) offer such a positive view of marriage and almost as many reveal a distinctly negative view of the changes marriage brings (26 percent). In 1976, respondents are much more likely to answer in ways that emphasize the burdens and restrictions marriage imposes rather than the opportunities it offers.

Further analysis of the above data reveals the poignant circumstance that single women felt when confronted with these powerful norms in 1957. In that sample, for every marital status in which people had experienced marriage—that is, among the married, widowed, divorced, and separated—women were always more negative about marriage than men were. This certainly corroborates Jessie Bernard's theory that marriage was good for men but bad for women. Only among those who had never been married were women *more positive* about marriage than men. And they were extraordinarily positive—more so than married women, and more than any group except widowed men. By 1976 their positive evaluation of marriage had dropped more dramatically than any other group.

We read these findings as a reflection of the normative climate of 1957, in which marriage was defined as the only legitimate status for a woman. While married women knew that marriage was no miraculous solution to life's problems and had its own share of burdens and restrictions, women who weren't married tended to think of marriage as a blissful, desirable state. By 1976 much fresh air and openness had been injected into discussions of marriage, and single women's idealization of marriage had disappeared. Two factors may have contributed to the idealization: if marriage is the only status valued by a society (particularly for women) and refusal of marriage is thought to reflect on one's good sense or morality, then obviously unmarried people will want to marry. But some women who in fact preferred the single state might also be reluctant to admit their preference or reveal in any way that they reject the idea of marriage. In 1957 women were certainly under intense normative pressure to marry in order to realize legitimate femininity, and women who were not married idealized the married state because they wanted very much to achieve it. Once normative pressure relaxed, they could look at marriage as one possible course, but certainly not the only or ideal way to live.

In a smaller sample used for pretesting, we also asked people whether a young person could have a happy life by remaining single. Over two-thirds of these respondents said yes. When we gave these respondents a list of reasons a young person might have for not marrying, the ones most often seen as good reasons were "not in love" (75 percent) and "needs a lot of freedom" (50 percent). Women more often thought love was crucial; men more often alluded to freedom. Another reason thought valid by about half the respondents was "It's hard to think of living with one person for your whole life." Women more often thought this reason made sense. In all, it is an interesting response which is probably a modern response. A hundred years ago, people married, had children, and raised them. By that time, a large proportion of wives died. Couples often did not go through the empty-nest period or retirement because the partners did not both survive together that long.

One derivation and series of findings we would like to add before leaving the data on the normative imperative to marry: if norms soften and people are more tolerant toward a variety of life-styles, one might expect that the negative effect of choosing a deviant (i.e., nonnormative) life-style would also diminish. However, our evidence indicates that this is not so. In 1957 two groups in the population showed notable symptoms of stress: divorced women and single men. We had thought some of this stress—any part attributable to a sense of deviance and normative pressure—might have ameliorated with a change in norms. But in fact our data reveal that in 1976 single men and divorced women are still exceptionally stressed. Table 4.3 presents the relationship between marital status and various measures of well-being (happiness, nervous-breakdown, anxiety, immobilization, and ill health symptoms). This topic will be discussed extensively in chapter 8, but a few of the results are relevant here. Single men are less likely to express being very happy and to report high immobilization symptoms and that they had at some time felt as if they might have a nervous breakdown. Relative to others, divorced women are particularly unhappy, high in anxiety and ill health symptoms, and likely to report

TABLE 4.3
Relationship Between Marital Status and Selected Measures of Well-Being

Measures of Overall Well-Being	Percentage of Married Men		Percentage of Married Women		Percentage of Single Men		Percentage of Single Women		Percentage of Divorced Men		Percentage of Divorced Women	
	1957	1976	1957	1976	1957	1976	1957	1976	1957	1976	1957	1976
Happiness												
Very Happy	36	34	43	40	11	26	27	24	22	15	18	13
Not too Happy	8	8	7	6	12	11	11	14	20	19	27	20
Nervous Breakdown												
Yes	11	12	25	25	13	19	17	24	15	23	28	37
Anxiety Symptoms[a]												
Very Low (5 + 6)	34	24	25	14	35	28	27	20	43	17	24	10
Very High (12)	13	10	24	25	5	15	15	25	13	16	28	33
Immobilization Symptoms[a]												
Very Low (3)	50	36	45	40	36	26	55	33	53	24	49	38
Very High (7)	14	18	18	18	20	34	19	23	28	29	24	21
Health Symptoms[a]												
Very Low (6)	47	35	35	32	44	42	49	39	45	33	39	25
Very High (15)	16	20	24	28	20	16	19	28	15	20	24	32
	(883)	(451)	(948)	(489)	(65)	(78)	(70)	(73)	(38)	(49)	(107)	(113)

NOTE: Numbers in parentheses are total number of persons in each group.

[a] To be discussed fully in chapter 7.

having feelings of impending nervous breakdown. Either a time lag is required for changed norms to affect the individual's evaluation of his/her psychological state or—more likely—the stress of these positions comes from forces other than social norms. The divorced woman—particularly if she is raising children alone—faces realities like poverty and role overload which are so oppressive that they make social stigma pale by comparison.

The unmarried male in our culture has still not experienced a socialization which prepares him with adequate social and interpersonal skills to create and maintain a reasonably integrated and satisfying life with people on his own—without a wife to initiate and maintain friendships and kinship ties.

SALIENCE OF MARRIAGE: 1976

One indication that the norms for marriage are neither as strong nor as absolute as they once were is seen in responses to a 1976 question which asked whether divorce was ever a good solution to marital problems (table 4.4). Thirty-one percent of the respondents said that divorce is never or only rarely a good solution—apparently they believed that marriage is an absolute and indissoluble commitment. But 89 percent think that at least under some conditions, divorce is the best path. While we have no data on this question from 1957, it seems likely that sanctions against divorce would have been much greater at that time.

Whereas in 1976 there were less binding attitudes toward the imperatives of marrying, more skeptical feelings about marriage, and an openness to dissolving marriages, we have no general evidence that marriage and family roles have become unimportant to people in 1976. Quite the contrary. In response to 1976 questions about how roles fulfill primary values and how much people get social validation through marriage and other roles (see table 4.4), family roles are clearly very important. Table 4.4 shows that more than 50 percent of married men and women think that marriage leads to their primary value a great deal, 34 percent say "a lot." This is a sizable majority of married people who see marriage as salient in their lives. It is interesting to contrast married and unmarried people in this regard, as shown in table 4.5. Single and divorced men and women in our sample clearly do not often see marriage as the route to fulfilling their values. The absence of the role probably does not make them long for it as it does for widows. It would have been interesting to have had this measure a generation ago. Our guess is that it would have shown a greater longing in the single and the divorced/separated groups.

Family roles almost uniformly rate higher in enhancing personal values than work or leisure roles do. (See tables 4.6 and 4.7 where we show how men [table 4.6] and women [table 4.7] evaluate how much various life roles lead to fulfillment of primary values.) There are few

TABLE 4.4

Distribution of Responses to 1976 Measures of Marital Role Salience
(for total sample and married respondents separately)

	Distribution	
Measure of Role Salience	Married Only (%)	Total Sample (%)
Attitudes Toward Divorce		
Divorce Best Solution to Problem:		
Often	12%	—[a]
Sometimes	57	—[a]
Rarely	20	—[a]
Never	11	—[a]
	100%	—[a]
	(1,437)	—[a]
Value Fulfillment Through Marriage		
Very little, a little	4%	10%
Some	9	12
A lot	34	30
A great deal	53	48
	100%	100%
	(1,410)	(2,173)
Social Validity Through Marriage		
a. Marriage >		
Parenthood	58	52
	(979)[b]	(1,519)[b]
b. Marriage >		
Work	76	68
	(979)[b]	(1,519)[b]
c. Marriage > Work *and* Parenthood	46%	40%
Marriage > One Role		
(Work *or* Parenthood)	34	34
Marriage < Work *and* Parenthood	6	13
Not Ascertained	14	13
	100%	100%
	(979)[b]	(1,519)[b]

NOTE: Numbers in parentheses are total number of persons in each group.

[a] Question asked only of married respondents.

[b] Question asked of only two-thirds of sample.

exceptions to the greater importance attached to family roles. One important exception is that older women who are not married say that the job allows them a lot of self-actualization, more so than marriage would. And it is partly the rarity of this ordering which lends it a certain weight. But even in this case, parenting yields more self-actualization than the job, and when the same analysis is restricted to people who occupy all three roles, women never rate the job more fulfilling than family roles and men (and only older men) do so only for self-ac-

TABLE 4.5
Marital Status Differences on 1976 Measures of the Salience of Marriage (by sex)

| | Marital Status | | | | | | | |
| | Married | | Single | | Widowed | | Divorced/Separated | |
Measures of Salience of Marriage	Men (%)	Women (%)	Men (%)	Women (%)	Men (%)	Women (%)	Men (%)	Women (%)
Value Fulfillment Through Marriage								
A great deal of value fulfillment through marriage	50	53	24	30	57	52	22	21
Total Number	637	739	130	126	46	262	87	175
Social Validity Through Marriage								
Marriage>parenthood	57	60	42	42	61	39	42	29
Marriage>work	74	79	49	42	61	68	42	47
Marriage>work, parenthood	43	50	25	25	46	31	21	23
Marriage>one role only	37	31	40	32	29	35	42	27
Marriage<work, parenthood	6	7	19	29	7	19	35	43
Total Number	484	495	85	83	28	172	52	119

TABLE 4.6

Married Working Father's Evaluation of How Much Five Life Roles Lead to Fulfillment of Primary Value Orientation[a] (by age and value orientation)

Primary Value	Age	Total Number	Leisure (%)	Work in House (%)	Job (%)	Marriage (%)	Parenthood (%)
Sociability	21–39	42	19	17	29	48	60
	40+	43	28	28	40	58	60
Hedonism	21–39	20	30	10	30	50	60
	40+	8	25	12	50	88	87
Self-Actualization	21–39	64	17	25	41	41	52
	40+	59	33	28	56	25	67
Moral Respect	21–39	55	22	11	44	47	47
	40+	102	18	13	50	51	55
Security	21–39	54	7	9	52	46	48
	40+	50	18	10	60	44	36
Total	21–39	235	17	15	41	46	53
(Across values)	40+	263	23	18	52	57	56

[a] Percentage of people of a given value orientation who report that a given life role leads to that value orientation "a great deal."

TABLE 4.7

Married Working Mothers' Evaluation of How Much Five Life Roles Lead to Fulfillment of Primary Value Orientation[a] (by age and value orientation)—1976 only

Primary Value	Age	Total Number	Leisure (%)	Work in House (%)	Job (%)	Marriage (%)	Parenthood (%)
Sociability	21–39	40	25	25	20	68	70
	40+	32	22	9	3	62	75
Hedonism	21–39	4	0	0	0	25	25
	40+	2	0	0	0	50	100
Self-Actualization	21–39	25	16	8	24	52	52
	40+	19	37	42	47	79	84
Moral Respect	21–39	35	23	20	29	51	65
	40+	43	23	16	30	51	51
Security	21–39	25	4	12	24	48	64
	40+	29	3	21	38	52	48
Total	21–39	129	18	17	23	55	63
(Across values)	40+	125	20	19	34	58	62

[a] Percentage of people of a given value orientation who report that a given life role leads to that value orientation "a great deal."

tualization and security (see table 4.6). In most cases the job is only half or two-thirds as high as one or the other of the family roles.

With regard to the measure of *social validity in roles,* in which we asked respondents which role competence is most important to their social presentation, we find in table 4.3 that either family role, pitted against work, yields a ratio in favor of the family role of more than 3:1. This dominance of family roles over work is the same for males and females. Within the family sphere, the spouse role dominates over the parent role in a ratio of 3:2 for men and slightly less for women. This series seems to us to touch very close to the core sense of self, that aspect which carries central significance or meaning. Clearly, for both men and women, that significance attaches to family more than it does to work, and slightly more to the marital than to the parental role.

Critics might object that social desirability is at work here, that it is simply harder for people to admit that they do not care how they are evaluated as parents or marriage partners whereas such an admission is possible about work. Married and widowed people have a harder time rejecting social validation through marriage because it means rejecting a specific person. As table 4.5 shows, single and divorced people clearly have less trouble in rejecting social validation through marriage.

Critics might also interpret the data from this series—especially from married people—to mean simply that people know they are good at their work and are less certain about their adequacy as parents or marriage partners, because of an inherent ambiguity in the criteria for family roles. Following such reasoning would mean that people need more social, consensual validation of their adequacy in family roles especially when they are ongoing rather than imagined roles for people or previous roles which they have rejected, as is the case for the divorced.

Both of these counterviews have merit. Social desirability and norms probably do contribute to the desire to be thought of as very good in one's family role performance. And certainly evaluation in these roles is more difficult and ambiguous—thus adding value to social validation. It seems to us nonetheless that in conjunction with other evidence we have presented, the responses also support the interpretation that family roles in 1976 are highly salient for most people, even if norms about them have softened.

The 1957 study built a strong rationale for the reasons that marriage organized and conditioned much of life:

> Being married or not married is an all-pervasive life condition which sets up certain requirements for human conduct, certain channels for the gratification of important human needs, and certain inevitable blocks to these needs. Furthermore, the marriage role can, in a sense, set the pace of other important life roles—friendship, parenthood, work.... Scientific theorists and inspirational leaders have ... looked to the institution of marriage for keys to general ... well-being and the roots of discontent; similarly, they

have looked for extreme psychological problems in the . . . person deprived of the marriage role. (Gurin, Veroff, and Feld, 1960, pp. 91–92.)

Certainly marriage remains a critical area of gratification and problems. We have seen that married people look to the role of spouse for realization of their central values and attribute great salience to the role. But it can hardly be said in 1976 that we automatically assume that "the person deprived of the marriage role" will have "extreme psychological problems." It can't even be said without conditioning that we think of the unmarried person as "deprived." The individualization—or desocialization—of the concepts of mental health and happiness is perhaps most palpable just here, in the fact that mental health is no longer assumed to depend on the realization of all possible normal adult roles. In 1957 psychologists and the population at large assumed that not being married or not having children would make a person unhappy at least and probably psychologically ill-adjusted. We have seen in the normative data that this is no longer the case. Most people think that an unmarried person can have a happy life. And it ill behooves anyone to attribute "extreme psychological problems" to all those people who choose not to marry or who give up the married state. Such a position would require labeling too many of one's friends and neighbors "pathological"—perhaps even one's parents or oneself. While in 1957 failure to assume and maintain the spouse role was taken to be a symptom of psychological problems, by 1976 marriage has come to be seen as only a potential mechanism for increasing happiness and psychological well being. Individual marriages are judged by the criterion of their realization of these individual outcomes. In 1957 it was rather the individual who was judged by his/her ability to form and maintain a marriage.

In any case, nonmarried statuses have increased. There are more people represented in categories other than "married" in our 1976 data (37 percent) than in our 1957 data (24 percent). Larger proportions of respondents are single, divorced, or widowed than was true in 1957, and a somehat larger proportion of married people have been divorced at some time in the past than was true in 1957 (see table 4.8).

Experience in Marriage

The fact that people value their family attachments and hold them central to self-definition does not mean that marriage and parenthood are without problems and conflict. We know from divorce statistics that problems abound. And in 1976 our findings reveal a significant increase in people's awareness of marital stress and of the fact that family

TABLE 4.8
Marital Status: 1957 vs. 1976

Marital Status	1957 (%)	1976 (%)
Married	76	63
First Marriages	65	52
Previously Divorced[a]	7	9
Previously Widowed[a]	4	2
Single	6	11
Widowed	12	14
Divorced/Separated	6	12
	100%	100%
Total Number	2,460	2,264

[a] The 1957 and 1976 percentages for previously divorced and previously widowed are not completely comparable. The 1957 question about previous marriage(s) asked about the "first marriage"; the 1976 question asked about the "last marriage."

roles involve problems and burdens. Yet, as we shall see, the 1976 findings show an *increase* in people's report of marital happiness. Before we discuss these results, let us clarify the measures used to assess the experience and perceived performance in the marital role.

MEASURES

Tables 4.9 and 4.10 present the measures used in our analysis to tap the experiences men and women have in adjusting and structuring their marriages. Table 4.9 describes measures which will allow year comparison; table 4.10 describes measures available only in the 1976 survey but which enlarge our analysis of the year comparisons. Many of the open-ended questions are coded with the distinction critical to our analysis of change; that is, do people use role references or very personal references when discussing their gratifications, frustrations, or feelings of inadequacy. Although the 1957–1976 measures cover a wide gamut of experience (perceived marital happiness, unhappiness, problems, and inadequacy, together with their perceived sources), the new questions in 1976 permitted a more specific focus on dimensions of marital well-being that have become critical in studies of marriage since the 1957 survey (conflict, resentment, tension about sex, and so forth, as listed in table 4.10).

INTERCORRELATIONS OF MEASURES OF EXPERIENCE IN MARRIAGE

We added a great many measures in 1976 to the study of people's experiences in marriage. From the intercorrelation of these new measures

TABLE 4.9

Measures of Experience in Marriage Available in Both 1957 and 1976 Surveys

Measure	Question	Code (Frequent Examples)
Marital Happiness	Taking things all together, how would you describe your marriage—would you say your marriage was *very happy, a little happier than average, just about average,* or *not too happy?*	As is
Nicest Thing About R's Marriage	We've talked a little about marriage in general. Now, thinking about your own marriage, what would you say are the nicest things about it?	*Companionship* doing things together, closeness *Situation* nice house having children *Spouse* my husband (wife); he (she) is nice *Love* the love; we love each other *Other Needs* equality *Nothing*
Not So Nice Things About R's Marriage	Every marriage has its good points and bad points. What things about your marriage are not quite as nice as you would like them to be?	*Relationship* we fight sometimes; not enough companionship *Spouse* my husband (wife) not considerate *Respondent* I lose my temper too quickly *Situation* He doesn't make enough money *Nothing; NA; DK* *Everything*

Measure	Question	Code (Frequent Examples)
Marriage Problem?	(Not asked of married person who said marriage was not too happy, for whom the admission of problem was assured.) Even in cases where married people are happy there have often been times in the past when they weren't too happy, when they had problems getting along with each other. Has this ever been true for you? (yes/no)	As is (People who said marriage was not too happy were coded as admitting to a problem)

Source of Marital Problem	(referring to "yes" response to above question) What was that about?	*Relationship*
		   Not enough love
		Spouse
		   My husband (wife) drinks
		Respondent
		   I get angry too quickly
		Situation
		   The kids take too much time
		General
		Not ascertained

Ever Feel Inadequate as Spouse	Many (men/women—SAME SEX AS RESPONDENT) feel that they're not as good (husbands/wives) as they would like to be. Have you ever felt this way? (yes/no)	As is

Source of Inadequacy as Spouse	(referring to the above question) What kinds of things make you feel this way?	*Role performance*
		   I can't keep up with housework
		   I don't make enough money
		Traits, personality
		   I'm too inconsiderate; bossy
		Health, mental health
		   I've been sick a lot
		Sexual Issue
		Other

Frequency of Inadequacy as Spouse	(again referring to the above question) Do you feel this way a lot of the time or only once in a while?	*A lot, often* *Sometime* *Rarely, Never* (Includes people who deny feeling inadequate above)

TABLE 4.10

Measures of Experience in Marriage Available Only in 1976 Survey

Measure	Question	Code
Resentful Feelings	How often have you been irritated with or resentful toward what your spouse did or didn't do? often/sometimes/rarely/never[a]	as is
Upset about Sex	How often have you been upset about how you and your spouse were getting along in the sexual part of your life? often/sometimes/rarely/never	as is
Felt Conflict	How often have you felt tense from fighting, arguing or disagreeing with your spouse? often/sometimes/rarely/never	as is
Wish for More Understanding	How often have you wished that your spouse understood you better? often/sometimes/rarely/never	as is
Wish for More Communication	How often have you wished your spouse talked more about how he/she feels or thinks? often/sometimes/rarely/never	as is
Perceived Individualism/ Interdependence	Some married people think of themselves as two separate people who make a life together. Others think of themselves as a couple, it being very hard to describe one person without the other. Which best describes your marriage—the "two separate people" way/or the "couple" way?	as is
Perceived Equity	All in all, who would you say gets more out of being married—you, your (husband/ wife), or both about equal?	as is
Frequency of Chatting	Now I'm going to read you a couple of things that married couples sometimes do together. First, how often have you and your (husband/wife) chatted with one another in the past two weeks? Would you say *many times, sometimes, hardly ever,* or *never?*	as is
Frequency of Physical Affection	(read after item above) How about: Been physically affectionate with one another? How often have you and your husband/wife been physically affectionate with one another in the past two weeks? (Would you say *many times, sometimes, hardly ever,* or *never?*)	as is

[a] This item and the next four comprised a series asked in the order listed.

with the ones available in both years, we can get some perspective on the meaning of both the new measures and the old ones.

First, it is important to note that not all the original measures of marital well-being correlated highly with one another. There were clear but relatively low positive correlations between marital problems and both marital happiness (-.22 in 1957; -.24 in 1976) and feelings of inadequacy as a spouse (.20 in both years). Interestingly, however, the latter measure was relatively independent of the measure of marital happiness (-.06 in 1957; -.08 in 1976). This suggests that people's doubts about their own role performances do not automatically translate into general distress about their marriages. Of the 1976 measures of marital experiences, none stood out clearly as being closely related to any of the 1957–1976 measures. Frequency of chatting and physical affection had clearer correlations with marital happiness than they did with the experience of problems or inadequacy. We thus should see these measures of reported interactions as closely allied with the affective well-being of the marriage. The frequency of reported resentments, conflicts, tensions about sex, desires for more understanding and talk, all correlated with each of the measures of felt problems, and marital happiness at about the same strength (varying between .22 and .38), but they tended to relate less strongly to reported feelings of inadequacy. Most of these new measures reflected experiences of tension between husband and wife. To the degree that the measure of felt inadequacy is not an appraisal of actual tension between husband and wife, but a measure of not meeting one's own standards in marriage, we can comprehend the low correlations that exist between the 1976 measures and the measure of felt inadequacy.

The most unusual measures introduced into the 1976 battery of assessments of marital experience—*perceived equity* and *perceived individualism/interdependence in marriage*—had interesting correlates with other measures of marital experience. The more one saw one's spouse as getting relatively more than oneself from marriage, the less inadequate one felt (−.11), but the less happiness one reported (.13). These are low correlations, but they are provocative. Whether one is pleasing one's spouse may be the critical question a person asks about his/her evaluation of competence in marriage. Perceived-individualism in marriage seems to be slightly correlated with *positive* experiences in marriage (.19 with *marital happiness*, −.18 with *marital problems*). This suggests that individualism rather than interdependence has more positive subjective consequences in marriage.

TABLE 4.11
Evaluation of Marriage in 1957 and 1976

Marital Evaluation	Year 1957 (%)	Year 1976 (%)
Marital Happiness		
Very happy	47	53
Above average	21	27
Average, not happy	32	20
	100%	100%
Nicest Things about R's Marriage		
Relationship:		
Companionship	42	56
Love	32	41
Other needs: security, power	5	7
Spouse, special characteristic	5	8
Situation (noninterpersonal)	22	16
Other	27	18
No things: not ascertained	7	8
	2	2
	100%	100%
Not so Nice Things about R's Marriage		
Relationship	11	20
Spouse's personality, role functioning	19	24
R's personality, Role functioning	7	4
Situational factors	30	24
Everything: things in general	1	3
No things	31	23
Not ascertained	1	2
	100%	100%
Marriage Problems?		
Yes	46	61
No	54	39
	100%	100%

Marital Evaluation	Year 1957 (%)	Year 1976 (%)
Source of Marriage Problem		
Relationship	14	18
Spouse's role, personality	10	10
R's role, personality	5	5
Situation	12	18
General	2	4
Not ascertained	3	6
No problems	54	39
	100%	100%
Ever Feel Inadequate as Spouse?		
Yes	57	55
No	43	45
	100%	100%
Frequency—Inadequacy as Spouse		
A lot, often	12	12
Sometimes	42	41
Rarely	1	1
Never	45	46
	100%	100%
Source of Inadequacy		
Role performance	24	21
Traits: too domineering, protective	4	2
Health, mental health	10	12
Sex	3	2
Other	1	1
Inappropriate, no inadequacy, not ascertained	45	46
	100%	100%
Total Number	1,872[a]	1,437[a]

EXPERIENCE IN MARRIAGE: 1957 AND 1976 COMPARED

Table 4.11 compares the reported evaluations of marriage for 1957 and 1976. Two results stand out: the *decrease* in reported "average" or "not too happy" marriages in the assessment of marital happiness and the *increase* in reported marital problems. At first blush, these results seem paradoxical.

What accounts for the rather strong trend toward increased happiness in marriage? One might immediately think that the increase is an artifact of the higher divorce rate in 1976—that people who are really unhappy in marriages are less likely to stay in those marriages today than they were twenty years ago. Undoubtedly that is so, but it must be even more complicated. An analysis of first and later marriages (table 4.12) indicates that the increase occurs equally in each kind of marriage from 1957 to 1976. That second marriages also look "happier" in 1976 suggests that people who did divorce and remarry at the earlier time might have had more guilt about their second marriages than they do today. In a number of ways, then, the modern institution of divorce may be a force not weakening but strengthening marriages in American society. Of course, if divorce becomes even more normative than it is now, it would, by definition, raise questions about the viability of the marital role. Bane's analysis (1976) would suggest that the divorce rate may have stabilized.

If marriages are happier, then what accounts for the large reported increases in marital problems? Among people who are currently married the question about marriage problems draws the largest difference over time. Respondents in 1976 are more likely to say that they have at some point had problems in their marriage. The change is larger for

TABLE 4.12

Marital Happiness Reported by People in First and
Later Marriages Compared (by year)

	First Marriages		Later Marriages	
Marital Happiness	1957 (%)	1976 (%)	1957 (%)	1976 (%)
Very Happy	48		43	
		53		51
Above Average	21		22	
		28		22
Average	29		30	
		17		26
Not Too Happy	2		5	
		2		2
	100%	100%	100%	100%
Total Number	1,599	1,167	258	254

men than for women (38 percent to 58 percent, for men; 49 percent to 62 percent, for women), but it seems to be a very general cultural change. This finding—that respondents, and particularly men, are more likely to say they have experienced problems in their marriage, might mean several things. It might indicate that men have come to be more open—with themselves and with interviewers—about negative feelings, complaints, and problems. In general we know—from our own studies and from other research about health and mental health— that women are more aware of the internal world, of the reality of feelings and fantasy. Yet the increase in men's reports of marriage problems stands out: they do not show the same large increase in reporting problems in either parenting or work. Thus the increase seems to be a significant finding which reflects real stress.

Despite increased recognition of problems in marriage in 1976, respondents do not report more feelings of inadequacy as spouses than they did in 1957. This combination of reporting more problems and no greater sense of inadequacy clearly implies that problems are attributed to some source other than personal failure to perform adequately as spouses. A failure in the relationship, the interpersonal aspects of marriage, or some external condition are the responses that appear more often as sources of marriage problems in 1976, compared to 1957 (see table 4.11).

Thus, with increased happiness in marriage, we find increased recognition of problems in marriage. This is not necessarily contradictory; indeed, throughout the earlier study, awareness of problems and gratification in a role tended to be associated, as though recognition of problems reflected in part a more articulated and larger set of expectations in various roles—as though holding more demanding criteria also implied a larger capacity for gratification in the role. If all people want from a marriage is lack of conflict—a bland, smooth interaction— they can achieve this by reducing interaction to a minimum.

In addition to questions which asked for evaluative responses—how happy is R's marriage, how adequate or inadequate is he/she as a spouse, have there been any problems in the marriage—we asked open questions designed to yield information about how respondents structure marriage. We looked at some of these questions and their answers in discussing normative changes—How does marriage change a person's life? What does R think of a young person who chooses not to marry?—but in these cases we were still interested in evaluative dimensions which could be coded from the plethora of contents the questions elicited. We wanted to know how positive or negative respondents' attitudes were toward marriage and toward people who remain voluntarily single.

There are other ways to look at responses to open questions, other interesting things to learn from their varied contents. We learn, first of all, that in 1976 more respondents have a more differentiated concept of marriage and are more open about both the negative and positive aspects of marriage. We know already that in 1976 fewer respondents say they have *no* problems, but it is also important to note that fewer say they can't think of anything which is not so nice about their marriage. These latter results are small but consistent.

Only in the question about problems in marriage do we note a small increase in 1976 in the number of people refusing to specify the source of the problem, but even here they were willing to say that a problem exists. Even in the normative questions—How is a person's life changed by getting married? What would you think of a young person who decided never to marry?—responses in 1976 are more differentiated in the sense that they are more varied. Respondents in 1976 are more likely to say that marriage both enlarges *and* restricts life, and they are more likely to see both sides of the decision not to marry. In general, questions about marriage, both about its salience and experience in it, stimulated more responses in 1976 than in 1957.

Beyond people's greater differentiation about marriage, are there any differences in *what* people in 1957 and 1976 highlight in answering open-ended questions? Before presenting results, let us step back and consider the ideas behind this more qualitative analysis.

In the 1957 study, a distinction was drawn between marriage as an interpersonal, intimate relationship and marriage as an institutional arrangement of interacting mutual roles. The distinction derives from those theories which delineate traditional and modern forms of marriage: the traditional depending on division of functions and reciprocity, and the modern focusing on intimacy between individuals whose roles are less clearly differentiated. In the traditional marriage, the male provides material support and contact with the outside world through his employment and the female provides services—both material and socioemotional—required for the internal functioning of the family group. She organizes the work of the home—cleaning, laundry, food preparation and serving, health care, and leisure activities—and tends the critical social and emotional development of the dependent children.

The modern arrangement reduces differentiation of roles and division of labor. Partners in a modern marriage perform parallel functions, both holding jobs and sharing home responsibilities. With this dedifferentiation comes greater ambiguity in criteria for performance and also a focus on the relationship between the partners, which serves as the medium for negotiating distribution of work. When functions are clearly divided, negotiation is reduced and performance is relatively clearly evaluated. When both partners perform all functions in tandem, each task—at least at home—needs to be assigned and negotiated.

The original analysis of the 1957 data distinguished these two orientations in respondents' answers to open questions. Did R give *relational* responses or *role* responses in answer to questions like "What are the nicest things about your marriage?" "What are the things that aren't so nice about your marriage?" "What was that (problem you faced in marriage)?" "What makes you feel that you're not as good a husband/wife as you'd like to be?" Further analysis revealed that the way in which Rs structured their conception and definition of marriage varied by education and age (younger and more educated respondents gave more relational responses) and related to marital happiness.

We assumed that the conception of marriage as an intimate, interpersonal relationship between partners performing parallel functions would be more prevalent in 1976 than it had been in 1957. The increasing movement of married women into the labor market and the growth of feminism during the twenty years between studies led us to anticipate a shift toward the modern form. And the psychologizing of our culture—a critical cultural trend which we document in chapter 2 and have reported in analysis of the use of formal help for personal problems (Kulka, Veroff, and Douvan, 1979)—clearly supports the prediction.

Table 4.11 offers evidence to support our expectation. In reporting *the nicest things about marriage*, 56 percent of respondents in 1976 allude to relational aspects of marriage—some aspect of the interaction or emotional support or understanding they realize with their spouse. This figure compares to 42 percent in 1957 who gave similar answers. This increase is fairly large, holds for nearly all subgroups in the population (age, education, and sex), and is very large in certain subgroups.

A comparable shift occurs in response to the question about the things about marriage that are not so nice, and smaller differences (though still consistent with the prediction) occur in responses to the questions about the marriage problems and sources of inadequacy. The second of these questions—about inadequacies—was coded for particular aspects of the relationship stressed. When we restrict analysis to those relational answers which have to do with intimacy—e.g., thoughtfulness, sensitivity, responsiveness to the spouse—the change from 1957 to 1976 is apparent, but slight. The most interpersonal and most sophisticated relational responses have increased most.

Experience of Marriage: 1976 Only

Questions added to the schedule in 1976 contribute other information about the experience of marriage reported by American people. The information these questions yield is in table 4.13.

We asked one series of questions which address respondents' expectations and experience of the interaction between marriage partners; responses support the view that interpersonal exchange represents a central focus of people's experiences in marriage. On the descriptive side, most married people report a high level of social exchange. Three-fourths of the sample reported chatting with their spouse "many times," and half said they had been physically affectionate "many

Marital Experiences Reported in Measures Used Only in 1976

Measure	Percentage	Measure	Percentage
Resentful Feelings		*Perceived Individuation/Interdependence*	
Often	10	"Two separate people" describes marriage	27
Sometimes	51	"A couple" describes marriage	71
Rarely	33	In between, some of both	1
Never	4	Not ascertained	1
Not ascertained	2		100%
	100%		
		Perceived Equity	
Upset About Sex		Self gets more from marriage	7
Often	5	About equal, NA	86
Sometimes	22	Spouse gets more from marriage	6
Rarely	42	Not ascertained	0
Never	27		100%
Not ascertained	4		
	100%	*Frequency of Chatting*	
		Many times	75
Wish for More Communication		Sometimes	20
Often	20	Rarely	3
Sometimes	36	Never	1
Rarely	29	Not ascertained	1
Never	13		100%
Not ascertained	2		
	100%	*Frequency of Physical Affection*	
		Many times	48
Felt Conflict		Sometimes	40
Often	7	Rarely	6
Sometimes	28	Never	3
Rarely	44	Not ascertained	3
Never	19		100%
Not ascertained	2		
	100%	Total Number	1,437
Wished for More Understanding			
Often	15		
Sometimes	36		
Rarely	31		
Never	16		
Not ascertained	2		
	100%		

times" (table 4.13). To put the case even more clearly, only tiny groups report *never* chatting (1 percent) and never expressing affection physically (3 percent) during the previous two weeks. Most people experience exchange and affection in marriage.

Yet we find that this experience of marriage does not completely meet people's expectations or desires for interaction. In answer to the question "How often have you wished that your spouse understood you better?" 51 percent answer "often" or "sometimes." For this sizable group, then, the interaction in marriage, though quite active, is not up to expectations and does not fully meet their needs. Only 13 percent and 16 percent respectively say that they "never" wish for more talk or more understanding. While we by no means assume such expressions to reflect deep dissatisfaction or a sense of serious deprivation, we think they reflect the fact that Americans' conceptions of a fully satisfactory marital relationship have been influenced by a modern, intimate, highly interactive ideal communicated in the self-development literature. Despite active exchange in marriage, most people hold an ideal for marital interaction which is grander than they are able to realize in their own marriages.

Most respondents are not seriously upset about their sex lives. Only 5 percent say they are "often" upset about sex ("how you and your spouse were getting along in the sexual part of your lives"); 22 percent say they feel this way "sometimes" (table 4.13). And most respondents say they rarely or never feel conflict ("tense from fighting, arguing, or disagreeing with [their] spouse."). Only 7 percent of the sample report often having such feelings about conflict. A somewhat larger group say that they often (10 percent) feel irritated or resentful toward their spouse, and in this case a majority of respondents report feelings of resentment or irritation at least "sometimes" (55 percent).

The impression we have from these data in table 4.13 is that marriages in America are, by and large, relatively harmonious and unruffled by disruptive impulses and conflict. If we think of a major task of the family as the regulation of sex and aggression through socialization and social control of resources, then clearly we must see American marriages as largely succeeding in this realm. Most married people are relatively satisfied with their sexual experience in marriage, and the social interaction of partners is relatively free of disruptive aggression, hostility, and conflict. Most people say that their marriages are very happy or happier than average.

Yet we find that for most people there are expectations and ideals of social exchange in marriage which their own marriages do not completely fulfill. This seems to us a testimonial to the influence of the self-improvement, self-realization movements of the last generation: movements which urged an experimental attitude toward marriage and touted the benefits and enrichment to be realized for oneself and one's marriage through open marriage or various forms of sexual exploration. Most people are satisfied with their sexual fulfillment in marriage, but the advertising has left them with a vague sense that their marriages could be larger and richer in social exchange. We can see the expression of occasional irritation and of aspirations incompletely fulfilled as another sign of increased sophistication, complexity, and articulation in attitudes toward marriage. Though most people are happy in their marriages, they are willing to speak of problems and negative feelings as well, as though to say, "Of course nothing in human interaction is perfect." We can read such realism as a base for marriage which reflects greater strength than a defensive denial of problems or a romantic insistence that marriage is and must be perfect.

We have two assessments designed to tap people's conception of the space and exchange between partners. The first, *perceived individualism/ interdependence in marriage,* asked what best describes a person's marriage better—"as two separate people (individualism) or as a couple (interdependence)?" How much does the reality of the marriage bond enter and alter the identities of the partners? Nearly three-quarters of all respondents (71 percent) think of their marriage as couplehood. The force of the bond or of interdependence is assumed by most people.

The second assessment, *perceived equity,* asked, "All in all, who would you say gets more out of being married—you, your husband/wife, or both about equal?" Responses to this question can be thought of as potential reflections of conflict or impending trouble in a marriage. According to a strict exchange-theory interpretation of marriage (or any relationship, for that matter) people remain in the relationship as long as their opportunities for a more advantageous exchange position are minimal and the exchange within the marriage is reasonably equal. If, then, people feel that they are getting from the relationship less than they give, they will begin to chafe under the inequality and look for other options. However, the question can also be thought of as reflecting the reality and force attributed to the marriage bond. If couplehood affects the identity of the marriage partners, then each partner derives from the marriage something so crucial—an element of her/his self— that cost-accounting specific gains and losses has little to contribute to calculation of the marriage's utility. If it is crucial to both partners, then relative terms like "more" or "less" add nothing to the calculation. And, indeeed, most respondents (86 percent) choose the "about equal" response to this question, assessing the value of their marriage to be about the same for themselves and their spouses.

TABLE 4.14
Summary of Multivariate Analyses of Marital Reactions for Measures Used in Both 1957 and 1976

Measure of Marital Reaction	Relationship(s) Required[a] to Reproduce Observed Cross-Classification of Measures by Age × Education × Year × Se				
	Main Effects[b]				Interaction
	Age	Education	Year	Sex	
A. Marital Role Salience					
Attitude toward nonmarrying person					
negative	Y<MA<O	G<H,C	57>76		
neutral	Y>MA>O		57<76	M<F	
Positive/negative orientation to marriage					
positive	Y<MA<O	G<H<C	57>76		
Restrictive/nonrestrictive orientation to marriage					
all restrictive	Y>MA>O		57<76		Age × Year × Sex
B. Experiences in Marriage					
Marital happiness					
very happy		G<H<C	57<76	M>F	
Nicest thing about respondent's marriage					
relationship		G<H<C	57<76	M<F	
Not so nice thing about respondent's marriage					
spouse	—[d]	—[d]	57<76	M<F	
self	—[d]	—[d]	—[a]	M>F	
relationship[c]	—[d]	—[d]	—[a]	M<F	
men				—[a,d]	Age × Education × Year
women		G<H<C	57<76	—[a,d]	
Marriage problem	Y>MA>O		57<76		
Source of marriage problem					
relationship		G,H<C			
spouse, spouse's characteristics		G>H>C		M<F	
respondent's self, respondent's characteristics				M>F	
external situation					
Inadequacy as spouse	Y>MA>O	G<H<C			Age × Education
Source of inadequacy					
role functioning[c]	—[d]	—[d]	—[d]	M>F	—[e]
men		G<H<C		—[a,d]	Age × Education
women	Y>MA>O			—[a,d]	
lack of protectiveness		G<H<C	57<76	M>F	
dominance			57>76	M<F	
other relational faults					Age × Education

[a] See Footnote[a] of Table 2.11 for an explanation of "Required."

[b] See Footnote[a] of Table 2.11 for description of "Main Effects."

[c] Cross-classification is run separately for males and females because a complex four-way interaction involving both the measure of self-perception and sex is needed explain the five-variable cross-classification.

[d] Sex effects inappropriate in disaggregated data.

TABLE 4.15

Summary of Multivariate Analyses of Marital Reactions for Measures used Only in 1976

Measures of Marital Reaction	Relationship(s) Required[a] to Reproduce Observed Cross-Classification of Measures by Age × Education × Sex			
	Main Effects[b]			
	Age	Education	Sex	Interaction
A. *Marriage Role Salience*				
Attitude toward divorce:				
Divorce often best solution (married only)		G<H<C	M<F	
Value fulfillment through Marriage:				
A great deal (All R's)	Y,M<O			
Social validity through Marriage:				
All R's	complex		M>F	
Married only	complex			
B. *Experiences in Marriage*				
Resentful feelings		G<H<C	M<F	
Upset about sex (often, never)		G,H>C		
		G,H>C		
Wish for more communication			M<F	
Felt anger	Y,M>O			
Wish for more understanding		G,H>C		
Perceived individualism/ interdependence:				
in-between		G<H,C	M>F	
Perceived equity				
self gets more	—[c]	—[c]	—[c]	
men	Y<M<O		—[d]	
women	Y,M>O		—[d]	
Frequency of chatting	Y<M<O			Sex × Age × Education
Frequency of physical affection	Y<M<O			

[a] See Footnote [a] of Table 2.11 for an explanation of "Required."

[b] See Footnote [a] of Table 2.11 for an explanation of "Main Effects."

[c] Cross-classification is run separately for males and females because a complex four-way interaction involving both the measure of self-perception and sex is needed to explain the five-variable cross-classification.

[d] Year excluded in measures assessed only in 1976.

Multivariate Analyses of Marital Salience and Experiences

Since many new questions about marriage were introduced in 1976, we will separate multivariate analyses that controlled for year (table 4.14) from those which controlled on sex, age, and education only (table 4.15). The former will be used to ask whether year differences discussed in previous sections need qualifying; it will also be the springboard for discussing sex, age, and education differences in subsequent sections.

QUALIFICATIONS TO YEAR COMPARISONS

Multivariate analysis shifts our statements and interpretations about changes in marital attitudes over time very slightly. Nearly all of the year differences we have discussed withstand analysis which simultaneously takes year, sex, age, and education into account (table 4.13). All of the normative shifts hold, indicating that they are net of demographic changes in the population. The fact that the 1976 population is both older and more highly educated does not explain the change in norms. These changes also reflect critical events in the twenty years between our two studies, and they hold across all the demographic subgroups in the analysis.

In a few cases, our interpretation of year changes in married respondents' experience in their own marriages must be conditioned by findings from multivariate analyses. First and most important, we had concluded that men showed a greater increase in problems in marriage than women. In the multivariate analysis, however, we find that year and age are the only variables required to account for the distribution of responses on this question. The interaction of sex by year—which would indicate that men shifted more than women—does not emerge as a highly significant contributor to the distribution, though a separate test of the contribution it makes indicates that it adds somewhat to the "goodness of fit" we achieve with a model that excludes the interaction. This, however, is the only major year result we highlighted that was questioned by the multivariate analysis.

Other results in table 4.14 do make us qualify our overall analyses of year differences. First, we find on the index of *not so nice things about marriage*, only women show an increase in relational responses when multivariate controls are applied. Second, in descriptions of their own inadequacy as spouses, only protectiveness and dominance—of all the relational responses possible and given—turn out to be real changes for both men and women over the twenty years. Protectiveness ("not sensitive enough to partner's needs," "not thoughtful enough") increases and dominance ("I'm too bossy," "I'm too demanding") decreases; these time changes hold even when age and educational changes in the population are accounted for. Third, role sources of inadequacy decrease over the twenty years only for certain age groups among men. And finally, when the three demographic variables are entered in analysis along with year, the year change in relational answers to the question about *problems* in marriage washes out entirely. Evidently, it was the large increase of more educated and younger people in the 1976 sample that is critical to that result.

The new measures of marital salience and experiences were also subjected to cross-classification analyses (controlling for sex, age, and education). These results are shown in table 4.15. Using this table and the previous one, we will proceed with a discussion of sex, age, and education differences in marital reaction.

Sex Difference in Marital Salience and Experience

The multivariate analyses will ferret out the consistent sex differences in marital reactions in both 1957 and 1976, and any sex differences that occur in one survey that are discrepant from parallel comparisons in the other. Finally, we will look at sex differences in the new measures for 1976.

Overall, we find remarkable similarity in men's and women's response to marriage in both years. Two results stand out as sex differences more apparent in one year than another. The first was one that fits with our assumption of dramatic changes in norms about the single woman. There was a complex interaction of age, sex, and year in how much people conceive marriage as restrictive. The finding is presented as a sex by year by marital status effect—that unmarried males were quite likely to take a restrictive view of marriage in 1957 (63 percent report nothing but restrictive changes that marriage brings) and show little change (68 percent) in this respect over the twenty years, but that unmarried women (thus also relatively young women) were very unlikely in 1957 to conceive of marriage as restrictive (36 percent) and have shifted dramatically by 1976 to a recognition of marriage at least carrying some cost in restrictiveness, a position more like the single men. On another normative question—response to someone who decides not to marry—men and women are clearly different, with more women taking a neutral view of such a choice. These results are shown in table 4.16.

Other than these two results, sex differences—or lack of them—are parallel in 1957 and 1976. In the experience of their own marriages, men and women are about equally happy, and they are similar in their sense of adequacy in the marital role. The experience of problems in marriage has increased for both men and women, and while women

TABLE 4.16
Selected Sex Differences in Marital Reactions in Measures
Used in 1957 and 1976 (by year)

	Men		Women	
Measure	1957 (%)	1976 (%)	1957 (%)	1976 (%)
Marital Role Salience (all respondents)	(1,077)	(960)	(1,383)	(1,304)
Attitude toward nonmarrying person				
percent neutral	31		39	
		42		52
	(302)[a]		(479)[a]	
Positive/negative orientation to marriage				
percent ambivalent, negative, very negative	20		26	
		27		29
Restrictive/nonrestrictive orientation to				
marriage: percent all responses restrictive	43		46	
		60		58
Experience in Marriage (married only)	(908)[b]	(697)[b]	(963)[b]	(740)[b]
Marital Happiness:				
Very happy	49		45	
		55		51
Above average	23		20	
		27		27
Average, not too happy	28		35	
		18		22
Nicest Thing about Respondent's Marriage:				
Relationship mentioned	40		44	
		51		60
Not So Nice Thing about Respondent's Marriage:				
Spouse	12		24	
		14		29
Relationship	12		14	
		21		24
Nothing	37		23	
		27		16
Marriage Problem?				
Yes	38		49	
		58		62
Source of Marriage Problem:[c]				
Spouse	13		30	
		9		21
Self	13		8	
		11		7
Felt Inadequacy as Spouse?				
Yes	56		58	
		55		57
Frequency of Felt Inadequacy as Spouse				
A lot, often	12		12	
		11		12
Sources of Inadequacy[d]				
Role functioning	48		37	
		41		35
Lack of protectiveness	19		15	
		26		17
Too domineering, bossy	5		9	
		3		5

NOTE: Numbers in parentheses are total number in each group.

[a] Questions asked of only one-third of sample in 1957.

[b] Numbers will vary among measures somewhat depending on the number of not ascertainable responses. These were for a given measure. In some instances percentages are based on an even more selective group, as indicated.

[c] Percentages based on only those who admitted to marriage problem.

[d] Percentages based on only those who admitted to feeling inadequate.

are more likely to report problems in both years and men have increased slightly more than women have, these results are not significant in the multivariate analyses. This is so because married women are distinctly younger than married men in our sample (9 percent more wives than husbands are 21–25), and there is a strong relationship of age to reporting marital problems. As we will discuss in the next section, younger married people are much more alert to marital difficulties than older ones. Thus, in multivariate analyses, age differences absorb the sex differences in reporting marital problems. Nevertheless, it is clear that women see more problems in marriage than men do.

While evaluation of the marriage experience is similar for men and women, the context and sources of their evaluations show some interesting differences. Men more often than women attribute their inadequacy as spouses to their lack of sensitivity and responsiveness (or protective traits) and women more often than men to their dominance or bossiness. Furthermore, in women we note an age relationship in attributions to role functioning. Young women say that they feel inadequate as housekeepers-homemakers, whereas this response decreases in the older groups of women.

The most interesting sex differences concern the attribution of problems and dissatisfaction in marriage. Women are much more likely than men to say that their marriage problem stems from some characteristic or problem behavior of their husbands whereas men more often attribute the problem to themselves. The same pattern exists for the "not so nice things" about marriage. These differences occurred in 1957 and appear again in 1976.

This finding—that women more often blame their husbands for problems in marriage—runs counter to a great deal of reported research and requires some discussion. Research on achievement behavior has found that women tend to externalize success and internalize failure. Thus, a woman will attribute her success in a task to luck or chance, but will see failure as the result of some personal failing or shortcoming. Men, on the other hand, tend to reverse the pattern; attributing success to their own skill and failure to bad luck or bad breaks.

Why, then, do we find this interesting reversal in attributions about "not so nice things" or problems (i.e., a failure) in marriage? Two possible explanations can be offered. The first is that the shift in attribution of failure in marriage reflects reality: since men have more power and resources in traditional marriage, they also may be in a better position to make or break the relationship. If they bring problems to the marriage or behave disruptively, it is simply more critical to the relationship. The fact that men less often blame their wives and are more likely to attribute problems in marriage to some inadequacy of their own can be seen as supporting this explanation. Less powerful people are expected to accommodate eccentricities and negative traits of the more

TABLE 4.17
Sex Differences in Marital Reactions on Measures Used Only in 1976

Measure	Men (%) (697)		Women (%) (740)	
Marital Role Salience				
Attitude Toward Divorce				
Divorce is best solution:				
often	73		78	
sometimes	22		18	
rarely	3		2	
never	1		1	
not ascertained	1		1	
	100%		100%	
Marriage Fulfills Values		*All R's*[a]		*All R's*[a]
very little	2	5	2	7
little	2	3	3	4
some	10	13	8	10
a lot	34	30	33	29
great deal	50	45	53	46
not ascertained	2	4	1	4
	100%	100%	100%	100%
		(960)		(1,304)
Social Validity Through Marriage				
more than work, parenthood	43	39	50	40
more than one role only	37	37	31	31
less than work, parenthood	5	10	7	16
not ascertained	15	14	12	12
	100%	100%	100%	100%
Experience in Marriage				
Resentful Feelings				
often	6		14	
sometimes	47		56	
rarely	41		26	
never	6		2	
not ascertained	—		2	
	100%		100%	
Upset About Sex				
often	5		5	
sometimes	23		22	
rarely	42		41	
never	26		29	
not ascertained	4		3	
	100%		100%	
Wish for More Communication				
often	13		26	
sometimes	38		34	
rarely	33		25	
never	12		13	
not ascertained	4		2	
	100%		100%	

TABLE 4.17 (continued)

Measure	Men (%) (697)	Women (%) (740)
Felt Conflict		
often	5	9
sometimes	27	29
rarely	46	42
never	20	17
not ascertained	2	3
	100%	100%
Wish for More Understanding		
often	13	18
sometimes	32	39
rarely	36	25
never	17	15
not ascertained	2	3
	100%	100%
Individuation/Interdependence in Marriage		
"Two separate people" describes marriage	22	32
"A couple" describes marriage	76	66
in between	1	1
not ascertained	1	1
	100%	100%
Perceived Equity in Marriage		
self gets more from marriage	8	6
about equal	85	87
spouse gets more from marriage	5	6
not ascertained	2	1
	100%	100%
Frequency of Chatting		
often	73	78
sometimes	22	18
rarely	3	2
never	1	1
not ascertained	1	1
	100%	100%
Frequency of Physical Affection		
often	44	52
sometimes	43	36
rarely	5	6
never	3	2
not ascertained	5	4
	100%	100%

NOTE: Numbers in parentheses are total number of persons in each group.

[a] Includes both married and non-married respondents.

powerful, and traditionally women have adapted and been expected to adapt to their husbands.

A second interpretation is that people tend to externalize blame and internalize success in those areas in which they are skilled, expert, and invested, and will show the reverse pattern of attribution in areas not claimed as their own field. So, in the achievement area—defined as competing against a standard of excellence, usually in an occupational context—men feel competent and at home and take full credit for their achievements while externalizing failures. Women, on the other hand, feel less able in this sphere and reverse their attributions. But in interpersonal relations women are the experts, and thus may be able to take credit for their successes and externalize problems or failures—just as men do with achievement.

Questions added in 1976 yield a few additional and important differences. Because these questions are new to a national survey, all comparisons between husbands and wives are presented in table 4.17, even if there are no significant sex differences. Women report chatting with their husbands slightly more than men report chatting with their wives, although with controls the result is muted. Women also say they wish their husbands talked more about their thoughts and feelings— more often than men express comparable feelings about their spouses. Both of these findings reflect traditional sex-role socialization and a common source of marital problems. Women are raised to be the socioemotional experts and are skilled in the verbal interaction and sharing which contribute to rich interpersonal intimacy. Men, on the other hand, are socialized to attend to reality and suppress feelings and self-disclosure. In marriage, then, women talk and want verbal responsiveness of the kind they have had with other women, but their men are often silent partners, unable to respond in kind. Rubin (1976) has described the problems that this difference creates in working-class marriages, especially around issues of conflict and sex. And our data indicate that the gap in expressiveness is not restricted to the working class.

Women also experience much more resentment and irritation with their husbands than husbands do with their wives. Seventy percent of women report such feelings compared to 53 percent of the men. These results confirm our earlier findings that women are more likely to find fault with husbands than vice versa in American marriages. Some of this resentment might come from women's higher expectations for communication in marriage, and hence their greater unmet need in this regard. Some of it may arise from the inequitable distribution of child care and housework responsibilities that typically fall on women's shoulders—even when both they and their husbands work.

Because a few additional questions asked in 1976 about family roles might help us interpret some of these differences, let us digress for a while and look at them. One asked about the interference of work and

TABLE 4.18
Sex Differences in Perceived Conflict of Roles, Housework, and Child-care Behaviors
(for all married people and for dual career couples)

Role Measure	All Married People		Dual-Career[a] Couples	
	Men (%)	Women (%)	Men (%)	Women (%)
Conflict of Roles				
Demands of respondent's work interfere with demand of family (working respondents only):				
yes	29		29	
		21		22
sometimes	19		18	
		22		22
no	52		53	
	100%	57	100%	56
	(575)	100%	(253)	100%
		(320)		(294)
Housework Behavior				
Who does more work around the house (cooking, cleaning, laundry)?:				
husband	3		2	
		2		1
equal	12		17	
		13		16
wife	85		81	
	100%	85	100%	83
	(694)	100%	(252)	100%
		(736)		(314)
How often husband helps (if wife is major housekeeper):				
often	14		17	
		16		24
sometimes	45		4	
		39		36
hardly ever	40		36	
		40		37
never	1		1	
	100%	5	100%	3
	(590)	100%	(205)	100%
		(624)		(260)
Child-care Behavior				
Who does more child-care (parents of children 12 years old or younger only):				
husband	2		2	
		2		3
equal	18		31	
		23		36
wife	80		67	
	100%	75	100%	61
	(298)	100%	(103)	100%
		(341)		(151)
How often husband helps (if wife is major child caretaker):				
often	43		45	
		35		33
sometimes	54		53	
		52		51
hardly ever	3		2	
		13		16
never	0		0	
	100%	0	100%	0
	(235)	100%	(68)	100%
		(255)		(92)

NOTE: Numbers in parentheses are total number of persons in each group.

[a] Both husband and wife work twenty hours per week or more.

family roles for working men and women ("Do you feel that the demands of your work ever interfere with the demands of your family?") and the others asked about the relative contribution of husbands and wives to housework and to child care if children were younger than twelve. Table 4.18 shows that working husbands more often than working wives report that work interferes with family demands. Our traditional norms so clearly require women to take the major—if not total—responsibility for family needs (cooking, washing, child care, and general emotional support) that to recognize any interference that work produces is undoubtedly much more threatening to a woman's perception of her adequacy than to a man's. Women are perceived to do most of the housework by more than 80 percent of men and women, *whether or not they both work* (see table 4.18). The same pattern applies to care of young children, although there is somewhat more perceived equal sharing of child care when both husband and wife work (31 percent of the husbands and 36 percent of the wives in dual-career couples say they share equally in care). Compared to helping with housework, there is more frequent perceived helping with child care by husbands. In these instances husbands perceive they help more than wives think they do.

There is thus an obvious greater burden of family roles placed on women in their marriages, even in dual-career couples. Could this burden be related to their greater expressed unhappiness and resentment in marriage? Some hint that this may be so came from the positive correlations between wives' unhappiness and felt resentment in marriage and the reported help they receive from their husbands in housekeeping and child care (see table 4.19). With one exception, the results are even stronger for women in dual-career marriages. No parallel comparisons are significant for men, except that there is a trend for men to report being happier in marriage if their wives take the major responsibility for child care (r=.15, p < .01, N=296). This result does not hold up for men in dual-career families. It is also important to note that wives' perception of who has major responsibility for housework and child care is *not* related to the two measures of well-being. It is evidently not the assignment of the major responsibility for child care and housework that contributes to women's feelings of discomfort with their marriages, but it is the lack of support from their husbands in these responsibilities.

Let us return to analyses of other 1976 measures of marital reactions that may differentiate husbands and wives. Aside from differences in verbal expression and desire for rich interpersonal exchange, already noted, women, more than men, hold more modern and liberal views of marriage. They are somewhat more likely than men to approve of divorce, and they more often characterize their marriages as "two separate people" and to see marriage as less important to their social validity than men, stressing individual identity rather than couplehood.

TABLE 4.19

Correlation (r) of Two Measures of Marital Well-Being
(Marital Happiness and Resentment Feelings) in
Women with Measures of Perceived Role Assignment
and Degree of Husband Helping
(for all wives and for "dual-career" wives)

Measure of Perceived Role Assignment and Degree of Husband Helping		Marital Happiness		Resentful Feeling	
		r	Total Number	r	Total Number
Degree of Husband	All wives	.03	730	.03	726
Responsibility for	"Dual-career"	.02	312	.04	314
Housework					
Degree of Husband	All wives	.21[b]	730	.13[a]	618
Helping with	"Dual-career"	.25[b]	258	.06	260
Housework (when					
wife has major					
responsibility)					
Degree of Husband	All wives	.05	340	.08	341
Responsibility for	"Dual-career"	.16	150	.13	150
Child Care (for					
parents of 12-year-					
olds or younger)					
Degree of Husband	All wives	.30[b]	255	.25[b]	255
Helping with Child	"Dual-career"	.38[b]	92	.29[b]	92
Care (when wife has					
major responsibility)					

[a] $p < .001$.
[b] $p < .0001$.

With these new questions for 1976, however, we are still as impressed with the similarity of men's and women's reports as we are by the differences. Both men and women see marriage as equally fulfilling their major life values and equally contributing to their general social validity. They generally register an equal number of complaints and express equal harmony. Perhaps we should especially stress that wives are as likely as husbands to perceive equity in their relationships. If Bernard (1972) is accurate about marriage as an institution set up for men more than for women, then neither men nor women perceive this inequity in their relationships, in spite of women assuming so much of the household and child-care roles. Perhaps the norm for equity is so pervasive that it forces people to say their commitments are equitable even if the outside observer can see an imbalance. Perhaps even if women feel more resentful toward their husbands than husbands feel toward their wives, they do not allow themselves to translate these feelings into a full-blown recognition of inequity.

Age Differences in Marital Salience and Experience

The youngest group in 1957—respondents between the ages of 21 and 29 who were 40–49 in 1976—came into adulthood at a time when ideas of family life, togetherness, and large families were cresting. Betty Friedan's book *The Feminine Mystique* (1963)—the signal for rethinking many of those values and ideals—was not published until 1963; the feminist movement had not begun, and no one had yet read alarm into demographic data which clearly held the word on overpopulation. Although birth-control technology, the sexual revolution, feminism, and the movement for population control eventually reverberated through the population, we would expect that their greatest force would be felt among those who became adult after 1957, those who are in the youngest age groups in our 1976 sample. After all, they are in the generation which begins family formation in the face of high divorce rates, the assertion of women's rights to independent identities, and concerted assaults on family values from many quarters. Alternative life-styles, experimental sexual programs, and the glamorizing of the single life provide a variety of options to the current generation unknown and unimagined in earlier eras. Surely the opening of alternatives and diminished promarriage and pronatal norms must have a very great effect on the attitudes of young adults in our society, on the conceptual structure with which they approach the issue. We expected, then, that age would be a critical variable in analysis of marital responses.

Indeed, in questions dealing with norms and general attitudes toward marriage, we find that the young are distinguished by their skepticism about marriage and their neutrality and tolerance toward alternative life paths (table 4.20). In both years, age is related to a positive general attitude toward marriage: middle-aged and older respondents most often think that marriage enlarges a person's life, and they think of marriage as restrictive less than young respondents do. When asked what they would think about a person deciding never to marry, the youngest group are much more likely to respond neutrally to such a choice than either middle-aged or older respondents. The increase in neutral responses (and the *decrease* in negative evaluations) to this question are among the largest changes occurring in any area of the study over the twenty-year period. The shift is particularly striking among the youngest groups: from 46 percent negative in 1957 to 22 percent negative in 1976 among people in their twenties. For respondents in their thirties, the change is from 52 percent to 28 percent.

While the youngest groups are highly skeptical and tolerant in their general reactions to marriage, they do not stand out so distinctly in the experience and conception of their own marriages in the measures available in both surveys.

Age as such does not show strong or significant relationships to

Measure	Age Groups											
	21-29		30-39		40-49		50-59		60-64		65+	
	1957 (%)	1976 (%)	1957 (%)	1976 (%)	1957 (%)	1976 (%)	1957 (%)	1976 (%)	1957 (%)	1976 (%)	1957 (%)	1976 (%)
Marital Role Salience (All respondents)												
Attitudes toward nonmarried persons:[a]												
Neutral	41	59	35	53	33	46	38	44	37	40	28	34
Total Number	294	533	399	443	352	328	271	323	111	155	234	358
Positive/Negative Orientation to Marriage Positive, Very Positive	35	21	46	28	46	32	52	35	42	45	48	37
Restrictive/nonrestrictive Orientation to Marriage All Restrictive	51	67	48	62	41	57	39	53	51	44	38	56
Experience in Marriage (Married Respondents only)												
Marriage Problems? Yes	52	70	54	67	44	64	42	56	30	52	28	39
Ever felt Inadequate as Spouse? Yes	65	63	59	61	56	55	46	52	40	58	37	35
Total Number	369	331	512	344	438	269	285	249	100	94	160	148

[a] Question was asked of only one-third of the 1957 sample.

marital happiness or to the reported sources of pleasure in marriage or sources of dissatisfaction and problems. There is a complicated age effect with marital happiness that is not apparent in our multivariate analysis, but is in a simpler treatment of age difference for men and women separately. While younger, middle-aged, and older men's reports of being very happy in marriage remain constant in both years (50 percent, 48 percent, 47 percent in 1957; 54 percent, 53 percent, and 57 percent in 1976) the relationships of age to reports of being very happy in marriage shifted from 1957 to 1976 for women. In 1957 women had a very clear inverse relationship between age and marital happiness, but this relationship has disappeared in 1976. (In 1957, reports of a very happy marriage were 48 percent in young women, 45 percent in middle-aged women, and 37 percent in older women; in 1976, parallel reports were 53 percent, 50 percent and 50 percent, respectively.) We have interpreted this finding (Douvan, 1978) along with similar findings about self-esteem in older women as reflecting certain gains realized by older women from the women's movement.

In other important ways, age seems to condition both sexes' reports of their marital well-being. Young people in both years more often admit to having had problems in marriage compared to middle-aged or older married people and to experiencing feelings of inadequacy in their marriages. Indeed, these results are very compelling (see table 4.20). Young married men and women undoubtedly are more alerted to difficulties in their marriages because they are still in the process of building a relationship. As couples mature together, they accommodate to many things that were once perceived to be problems or personal failings. They may even defensively not see existing problems because their long-term commitment may be psychologically undermined by recognition of problems in the marriage or in their own performance.

There were some complicated results about what younger vs. older husbands and wives report as sources of their own inadequacies. Young women more often feel inadequate in role functions of marriage: they feel less adequate as housekeepers and homemakers. In middle age and later, homemaking functions are taken in stride and apparently no longer cause women as much insecurity or sense of inadequacy.

Among men, however, role functioning as a source of inadequacy varies with age in complicated ways. One complication is conditioned by education. Essentially, the finding indicates that in our society men with minimal education have the greatest difficulty meeting the provider role. Young married men with grade-school education are particularly sensitized to that (83 percent in 1957; 100 percent in 1976; compared to no more than two-thirds in any other group) and evidently lose their sensitivity to it as they age, unlike the men of more educational attainment. In 1957 83 percent of the young grade school-educated men spoke of inadequate provision as a husband. Among that

TABLE 4.21
*Selected Age Differences in Marital Reactions on Measures
Used Only in 1976*

Measure	Age					
	21-29 (%)	30-39 (%)	40-49 (%)	50-59 (%)	60-64 (%)	65+ (%)
Marital Salience	(553)	(463)	(341)	(342)	(166)	(397)
Value fulfillment through marriage (all respondents): A great deal	43	40	48	51	50	48
Social validity through marriage (all respondents): Don't know (cannot choose)	97	12	12	17	14	18
Marital Reactions	(231)	(345)	(269)	(249)	(94)	(148)
Felt conflict: Never	11	14	19	23	23	36
Perceived equity: Self gets more (men)	66	7	8	12	9	7
	(141)	(165)	(133)	(113)	(57)	(88)
(women)	4	9	11	4	0	5
	(190)	(180)	(136)	(136)	(37)	(60)
Frequency of chatting (in past two weeks): Many times	74	71	76	77	85	80
Frequency of physical affection (in past two weeks): Many times	60	57	45	39	45	28

NOTE: Numbers in parentheses are total number of persons in each group.

cohort in 1976 (middle-aged men with a grade-school education) only 30 percent report inadequate provision as a personal shortcoming in their marriage. No other group of men show this age shift in perceiving role-functioning inadequacies.

The other complication has to do with a year difference in how age affects men's perception of their shortcomings as a provider. Middle-aged men generally have become more acutely aware of their lack of provision for their wives in 1976 than were middle-aged men in 1957. In 1976, 48 percent of middle-aged men with a college degree report role-functioning inadequacies compared to 39 percent of the comparable group in 1957. This was a rise of 9 percent. For high school–educated men in 1976 there has been a rise of 14 percent over the 44 percent reporting these inadequacies in 1957. In cohort terms, the young men with either a high school or college education in 1957 who became middle-aged in 1976 did not show any dropoff in their concerns about being good providers. Instead, they showed increases. All of this suggests that men of middle age in America in 1976 felt a constant press for providing, unlike the middle-aged men of a generation ago. The spiraling pressure for increased consumption, the increasing norm to send children to college, the cost of which, in turn, has become higher, no doubt take their toll on men's images of themselves as good family providers at middle age.

From the 1976 questions, we learn that while young people by and large have more physically interactive marriages than older people, they also have more conflictful tensions between them. Young people report more physical affection than middle-aged people, who in turn report more than older people. (See results in table 4.21.) Older couples, on the other hand, apparently argue less than middle-aged or young couples, and they less often feel irritated with each other, although this latter finding seems mainly a function of the lower educational level of older respondents. The older men are, the more they see themselves as getting more out of marriage than their wives, while the reverse is true for women; this perception results in a fairly significant difference between older men and women. Ten percent of men fifty-five and older see themselves as receiving more benefits in marriage compared to 2 percent of the women; who, in turn, are more likely to see equity in the relationship. We might see these results as confirming a general accommodation in older marriages—a greater recognition of the benefits of marriage in men as they age; a greater sense of equity in older women.

In examining reports about chatting between husbands and wives, we discovered an interesting interaction: generally, older people say they chat more with their spouses than do younger people, as table 4.21 indicates, but the multivariate analysis indicates that for college-educated women, the reverse is true. This interaction can be seen in table 4.22. Thus, older people generally converse in a companionate way with their husbands and wives more than younger people, who perhaps are geared to more active pursuits or to talking in a style more intense than "chatting." This is not so with college-educated women. We can speculate that the younger college-educated women have been primed to making their marriages companionate when their children are young; but given freedom from children, they are particularly active in companionate relationships with people other than their spouse. Even so, most older college-educated women say they chat frequently with their husbands.

We can interpret these findings about interaction and conflict in two ways. We might say that older couples aspire to less richness in their marital exchange; they chat but they don't fight or argue, simply be-

TABLE 4.22
Age Related to Reporting Chatting with
One's Spouse "Many Times"
(by education × sex)

| | Reports of chatting "many times" with spouse during last two weeks | | |
| | Age 21–34 (%) | Age 35–54 (%) | Age 55+ (%) |
Education			
Men			
Grade School	33	62	86
	(12)	(21)	(66)
High School	70	74	78
	(112)	(120)	(94)
College	72	72	79
	(99)	(112)	(53)
Women			
Grade School	73	77	84
	(11)	(26)	(50)
High School	73	81	80
	(172)	(180)	(71)
College	85	80	73
	(114)	(69)	(33)

NOTE: Numbers in parentheses are total number of persons in each group.

cause they have reduced the intensity of their interactions. Or we can look at the relationship the opposite way and say that since they have settled their differences and accommodated to each other, older couples have less need to fight. Older women perceive more equity; older men own up to the special benefits they receive from marriage. The reduction in physical affection with age would argue for some thinning out of the relationship rather than a settling in. Even among the oldest group, however, a large majority (75 percent) say that they are "often" or "sometimes" physically affectionate with their spouses.

Nowhere in our analysis do we have any evidence that middle-aged marriages are distinctly different from younger or older marriages. We might have expected such a pattern from Campbell, Converse, and Rodgers' (1976) results showing that couples in the throes of early parenting are worse off in overall well-being than young married couples without children or older parents whose children have moved into adulthood. Perhaps a refined family life-cycle analysis might corroborate their results on our data, but a straightforward analysis does not.

Education Differences in Marital Salience and Experience

In contrast to the effects of age, which concentrate on normative attitudes, the effects of education show their largest force in respondents' experience of their own marriages. From multivariate analyses, we know that there are significant education differences in how people respond to questions about the salience of marriage; but a look at table 2.23 shows that these findings are minimal. The striking education differences show up in respondents' feelings about their own marital relationships. Highly educated respondents more often report inadequacies in their marriages as well as exceptional happiness. They more often allude to relational aspects of marriage in answering contextual questions and probes—nicest and least nice things about their own marriages,[2] the sources of marital problems and inadequacies. In answers to the 1976 questions, more educated respondents also differ from the less educated in two almost paradoxical ways. (See results in table 2.24.) On the one hand, they are less likely to describe themselves as wishing for more understanding from their spouse or as being often upset about sex. On the other hand, they are less likely to deny certain bad feelings that come up about marriage: feeling irritated and resentful toward their spouse, feeling upset about sex, and feeling that divorce is sometimes the best solution for marital problems. They are thus more open to seeing conflict and difficulties in their married lives, yet they are also aware that they are not experiencing extreme problems. Perhaps their alertness to problems in relationships makes the highly educated more able to manage conflicts when they do occur. Education can be thought of as effecting changes in people which allow them greater facility in relationships—facility in the open exchange in daily interaction which encourages a rich, rewarding relationship, greater skills with which to handle and resolve marital conflict when it develops.

One other striking difference in the responses of the more highly educated men and women in the 1976 survey occurred in responses to the question of individualism vs. interdependence in their marriages. A powerful result emerges (see table 4.24), with many more highly educated seeing their marriages as the coexistence of two separate people rather than as the bond of a couple. Of the grade school–educated respondents, 11 percent see their marriages as "two separate people"; this compares to 40 percent of college graduates who see their marriages in this way. These findings seem to us powerful in the light they

---

[2] The multivariate analysis in table 4.14 indicates that the report of relationship difficulties as a source of things not so nice about one's marriage is more complex for men than for women. This is so because young high-school husbands in 1957 were particularly alert to these difficulties (15 percent), and male high-school graduates particularly increased in these reports in 1976 over 1957. Nevertheless, the overall education effect in table 4.23 is as apparent for men as it is for women.

TABLE 4.23

Selected Education Differences in Marital Reactions on Measures Used in Both 1957 and 1976

	Education									
	Grade School		Some High School		High School Graduate		Some College		College Graduate	
Measure	1957 (%)	1976 (%)	1957 (%)	1976 (%)	1957 (%)	1976 (%)	1957 (%)	1976 (%)	1957 (%)	1976 (%)
al Role Salience	(802)	(380	(511)	(347)	(674)	(766)	(247)	(411)	(210)	(347)
tude Toward nmarrying Person:										
ˈegative	42		52		54		47		56	
		33		32		31		36		31
itive/Negative entation to rriage										
ꞏositive	40		43		44		50		44	
		33		29		30		28		34
ience in Marriage	(551)	(188)	(408)	(220)	(543)	(535)	(193)	(247)	(169)	(238)
ꞏital Happiness:										
ery happy	38		37		54		55		64	
		51		42		51		58		64
est thing about R's riage:										
elationship	37		37		45		50		58	
		42		49		56		60		67
so nice thing about Marriage: elationship										
(Men)	10		9		8		13		18	
		5		13		22		25		31
(Women)	3		13		11		19		8	
		12		12		20		26		31
ꞏce of Problem in riage[a]										
elationship	10		12		16		23		18	
		10		13		16		23		27
ꞏouse	13		13		10		8		7	
		7		9		11		8		8
ꞏequacy as Spouse										
ꞏever	57		41		45		39		31	
		56		53		44		44		39
ꞏce of Inadequacy ꞏck of protectiveness	16		29		31		27		36	
		16		28		27		33		39

: Numbers in parentheses are total number of persons in the group.

ꞏtion was asked of only one-third of the 1957 sample.

TABLE 4.24

Selected Education Differences in Marital Reactions on 1976 Measures

	Education				
Measure	Grade School (%)	Some High School (%)	High School Graduate (%)	Some College (%)	College Graduate (%)
Marital Role Salience					
Attitude Toward Divorce: Never best solution	27	11	10	6	4
Marital Experience: Resentful feelings Never	12	3	4	2	2
Upset about sex Often	8	6	5	4	6
Sometimes	14	21	22	24	29
Never	39	30	29	22	21
Wish for more understanding Often	22	24	14	14	10
Perceived individualism/ interdependence in marriage Sees marriage as two separate people	11	20	26	36	40
Total Number	188	220	535	247	238

shed on the nature and requirements of "ideal" marriages as they are realized in our society. Some theories hold that differentiation of the experiences of marriage partners can lead to stress. Our findings about highly educated marriages suggests this is not so. The more educated see their marriages as a coalescence of two separate people and also express considerable happiness in marriage and a sense of open communication and understanding.[3] This differentiation of experience evidently does not jeopardize happiness and adjustment in marriage or create stress since it seems to be combined with the capacity to communicate and work through conflicts.

The pattern of these results suggests that marriages among the more educated members of our society are particularly "healthy." Locksley (1978) was impressed with the same pattern of findings, and wrote a persuasive interpretation of these education differences:

Education is accompanied by a progressive secularization of attitudes. This

---

[3] The correlations between seeing one's marriage as "two separate people" and *marital happiness, resentful feelings, wish for communication, wish for understanding* and *in conflict* are .13, −.10, −.09, −.13, and −.15, respectively—highly significant correlations with a sample size of over 1,000.

could have the effect of enabling people to express problems in areas otherwise viewed as beyond the bounds of decent discourse (for example sexual frustrations), and also the effect of enabling people to think of problems as potentially solvable. Education forces people to become increasingly verbally adept, thereby facilitating interpersonal communication in general. Education involves the public evaluation of one's ideas, thereby inculcating relative dispassion about one's beliefs, opinions, and inclinations. All of these tendencies could enhance an individual's ability to handle marital conflict in the medium of discourse rather than of physical violence, display of affect, stubbornness, and so on. Disagreements would take longer to reach the boiling point; partners could be more capable of flexible and equitable solutions.

    These points provide a possible explanation for the pattern of results. More educated respondents acknowledge having in the past felt unhappy and inadequate in their marriages, whereas less educated respondents do not. On the other hand the more educated respondents have happier marriages in the present and indicate much less misunderstanding and disaffection than do the less educated respondents. These findings are certainly consistent with the notion that education facilitates verbalization and resolution of conflict which, over time, enhances marital adjustment and furthers marital companionability. (Locksley, 1978, pp. 164–65)

Among the points she raises are the possible increased range of marital choices that might exist for people who go to college and the possible indoctrination that college gives people about presenting themselves to others in an interview such as ours. We find these additional interpretations possible, but less compelling than Locksley's initial view that higher education socializes people to verbalize conflict and to be flexible about solutions to problems. Both of these styles enhance marital compatibility.

In addition to interpretations of education differences in marital well-being that emphasize ways in which education affects the minds of men and women, we cannot ignore the other, more structural interpretation of these findings: high educational attainment is a credential for obtaining both high-paying jobs and high-status spouses in our society. Status attainment in the larger social world undoubtedly creates an aura of well-being in marriage that affects the marriage relationship itself.

Summary

Perhaps nowhere in the book will we see such a dramatic change from 1957 to 1976 as we have in men and women's increased tolerance of people who reject marriage as a way of life. This loosening of the normative necessity of being someone's wife or husband in order to be a valid adult undoubtedly has had and will continue to have profound effects on other reactions to marriage. The number of divorced people who stay divorced and do not remarry has clearly increased. Divorce has become more than a peripheral institution. It has come to be a much more viable alternative to marriages that are not successful. Our 1976 married people are open to divorce as a solution to problems, although husbands, who continue to feel somewhat better about their marriages than their wives do, are less positive about divorce than women.

The increased understanding that marriage can be bad and restrictive for people does not mean that Americans in 1976 felt that marriage was unimportant in their own lives. Along with parenthood, marriage is held to be a more central source of value realization than either work or leisure pursuits. We have seen in chapter 2 that reports of marital happiness and unhappiness are more critical than any other sources of well-being and distress in accounting for people's overall evaluation of well-being. Thus, while Americans have increased their awareness of alternatives to marriage, they have not by any means lost sight of the psychological importance of marriage.

Indeed, the fact that the alternative of divorce has become more available can help account for the finding that compared to 1957, marriages in 1976 are judged to be happier. In fact, most people see their marriages as being happy. Our 1976 measures suggest that while married people recognize conflict, are sometimes upset about sexual issues, feel resentment, and want more understanding, these feelings are not very frequent. So, while trouble is recognized, it seems not to be corrosive. Perhaps as a result, marriage is seen as equitable for both parties by more than 85 percent of American husbands and wives.

Sex, age, and education differences in marital reactions that were apparent in 1957 generally persist in the 1976 responses. Comparison of men and women speaks much more to their similarities than to their differences, although there are some findings that point to greater marital well-being in husbands than in wives. In the 1976 measures, this was most clearly highlighted in the greater irritation and resentment felt by wives. Analyses of age differences continue to show reduced awareness of problems and conflicts in older married couples, but, as the 1976 measures show, there is an accompanying reduction in reports of physical affection. As couples get older, they seem to reduce the intensity of their relationships, perhaps because of both reduced sexuality and reduced requirements for accomplishment when men and women are no longer struggling with child rearing or juggling family and work roles.

Education differences in marital well-being are strong. Compared to their less educated counterparts, more educated husbands and wives evaluate most aspects of their marriages more positively. At the same time, the more educated less often deny the presence of a number of marital difficulties. Thus we see the more educated in our society as more sensitive to issues of interpersonal accommodation in marriage, and, thus more able to enhance the quality of their marriages. The less educated may be in double jeopardy in their marriages. Their lack of education often bars them from the jobs and money which can contribute to marital well-being, and also often bars them from the interpersonal psychological perspective that seems to enhance married life.

Chapter 5

PARENTHOOD

THE YEARS between 1957 and 1976 witnessed the introduction and spread of modern birth-control technology, the first technology which made the absolute separation of sex and reproduction widely available. The effects of this change have been profound, and we have probably not yet seen the full working through of its effects and implications. The breakup of traditional sexual norms and morality was made possible by modern birth control. The recasting of parenthood as an act of choice rather than a combination of fate and biology has opened up new patterns of life for adults in our society. An adult can now be sexually active and childless, married and childless—alternatives which in earlier times were unavailable or chancy, at best. In combination with other events, the spread of cheap birth control has led to the sexualization of marriage, a revaluing of sex for its own sake aside from its role in reproduction, and an undermining of traditional religious authority which held that legitimate sexual enjoyment was necessarily linked with marriage and the desire to procreate. As a facilitator of change, birth control combined with reaction against post–World War II domesticity and idealization of family life to produce an active movement to reassess family life and the value of parenthood. In combination with population problems, it produced a reassessment of the value of children and childbearing.

We expect, then, that our national sample in 1976 will hold attitudes toward parenthood which are significantly different from those reported for the population in 1957. As in the case of marriage, we suspect that changes will be more impressive in attitudes about parenthood than in the way people experience and value their own children and their roles as parents. In part, of course, this difference between attitudes and personal encounter will be a function of selection: people who are most negative about children or parenthood or who feel most strongly about the need for population control will not be parents. The absolute ability to impose one's will in the issue will lead, first of all, to self-selection out of the role. Those who become parents now more than ever before are people who actively want to be parents. In all likelihood, their response to parenthood will be at least as positive as the attitudes of parents as a group at any time in the past.

At the same time that these developments were occurring, other cultural changes affecting the role of parent also evolved. The most crucial of these had to do with a dilution of traditional authority. As religious adherence waned, the sway of absolute religious authority over the spheres of morality and individual conduct diminished. Alternative codes based on humanistic values, mental-health criteria, or extreme individualism ("doing one's thing") surfaced and were urged by adherents as *the* meaningful and sensible bases for organizing life and action. If one no longer had children because the church (or nature or biology) insisted on an indissoluble link between sex and procreation, the choice was now made in order to experience the whole range of life's variety or to assert one's legitimate status as a "mature" adult or because children were seen as a source of pleasure, value, and meaning.

But the crisis of authority, which began with a loss of religious faith and the dilution of religious authority, was not limited to religion. It spread to secular authority, appearing as a questioning and challenging of the legitimacy of governmental power, a loss of faith in the processes of government. And, according to many observers, the crisis spread even to the family, with children and youth rejecting parental authority in greater numbers and with a force previously unimaginable. Conservative political and religious groups saw these changes as somehow all interrelated, tied both to the abandonment of religious faith and to a growing "permissiveness" on the part of parents: a form of collaboration by parents in the questioning of their unique authority.

While this conservative formulation can be faulted as overly facile and concrete, the reduction of parental authority does seem real and probably stems from a complex of cultural changes beyond the diminution of religion as an organizing focus of life in our society. To point to a few of these changes, we can cite as an example the enlarged influence of child-raising "experts," which Lasch (1977) claims resulted in parents' losing faith in their own ability to judge and make decisions affecting their childrens' lives without confirmation from experts.

The very great increase in expert power depended on the growth and power of mass communication. When parents depended on word of mouth or printed words for their advice, styles of parent-child interaction and family organization were likely to be more continuous from one generation to the next and less standardized across a whole society.

Experts became more important and powerful as our society became more mobile, and access to the media became universal.

The media also provide children and youth with a vastly enlarged view of life's possibilities and of varied styles of action and family life. Simply the fact that the media informs us all about the large number of runaway youth and the existence of shelters for runaways offers youngsters a view and concrete model of action different from life in their families. Alternative models have always been developed or discovered by youth faced with impossible home situations. But they have never been so broadly publicized, so universally available as they have now become.

Finally, the change in family forms—from a nuclear family with a single breadwinner to a family in which both adults work and share household tasks—must be seen as reducing authoritarian relations in the family. When wives work, they acquire greater power to influence family decisions and family interaction. By itself, this represents a dislocation in traditional power relations and a redistribution of authority.

All of this complex pattern of change, then, argues for both changes in attitudes about parenthood and changes in the day-to-day experiences of parents. We expected that the necessity of becoming a parent, like the necessity of getting and staying married would have lost some of its clear moral force and dominance as a norm, and that respondents in 1976 would look at parenthood with greater realism—recognizing both its positive rewards and its costs and problems—than people did in 1957. We also expected that difficulties encountered in raising children in the 1960s and 1970s would be qualitatively distinct from those in the 1940s and 1950s.

The Salience of Parenthood

The simplest indication of the decline of pronatal norms would be a larger proportion of nonparents in our 1976 sample, compared to 1957. When normative pressure diminishes, behavior which follows from the norm will also decrease. But we find that this has happened very little: 20 percent of the 1957 sample were not parents, while 23 percent of the 1976 sample did not have children (see table 5.1). When we look beyond this roughest measure to ask where childlessness has increased, when we analyze parent status by various demographic characteristics, we find that the slight increased size of the childless group occurs mainly in the youngest age group and is in part an artifact of the larger proportion of 21- to 29-year-olds who are single, but not entirely. There is a 5 percent rise in childlessness for the youngest age group

TABLE 5.1

ercent Ever Married with No Children and Percent Single in Various Demographic Groups (by year)

emographic Group	Total Number	Percentage Ever Married with No Children		Percent of Single		Total Percent Having No Children	
		1957	1976	1957	1976	1957	1976
ɔtal	2,460	14		6		20	
	2,264		12		11		23
ɣ Sex							
Men	1,077	14		8		22	
	960		12		14		26
Women	1,382	15		6		21	
	1,303		12		10		22
ɣ Age							
21–29	453	17		12		29	
	553		22		28		50
30–39	584	10		5		15	
	463		7		9		16
40–49	515	15		4		19	
	341		4		3		7
50–59	390	16		6		22	
	342		8		4		12
60–64	153	14		5		19	
	166	11		8		19	
65+	352	14		7		21	
	396		15		6		19
ɣ Age (Two Youngest Groups)							
Education							
21–29							
Grade school	55	6		9		15	
	17		12		18		30
High school	274	16		8		24	
	269		17		20		37
College	124	25		20		45	
	265		28		36		64
30–39							
Grade school	103	17		5		22	
	29		3		14		17
High school	356	8		4		12	
	247		5		5		10
College	124	7		6		13	
	186		10		13		23

who were married at one time or another. When we restrict analysis to respondents who are currently married, we again find that it is the youngest group of married people who show a significant increase in childlessness. Among currently married 21- to 29-year-olds, 31 percent in 1976 have no children, compared to 19 percent in 1957. In the oldest group (65 and over) there has been essentially no change over the two decades, and in all other age groups parenthood is more common in 1976 than it was in 1957. Among married respondents who are between 40 and 60, the decrease in childlessness is actually quite marked: 19 percent to 7 percent for the 40–49 year-olds and 22 percent to 12 percent for the 50–59 year-olds. These age groups in 1976 correspond to the generation most crucially affected in childhood and youth by the depression years and the Second World War. They are the parents of the baby boom.

The fact that it is only the young who have not married—or, if married, have remained childless—means that the returns are not in. We can't tell whether the observed changes reflect a postponement of family roles or a more final decision *not* to assume them. That determination awaits a later study. But we can at least conclude from our data that while norms may have softened somewhat in this realm, the choice to become parents is still clearly dominant among people who marry. Even among 21- to 29-year-olds, 50 percent have been married and have children. And among ever-married people in the next age decade (30 to 39), the proportion of parents is very large and has remained stable across the generation, although the college-educated among them are not reproducing as fast (7 percent were childless in 1957; 10 percent in 1976). In the 1976 sample, these young marrieds certainly experienced all of the cultural changes that would argue against parenthood, and it is clear that the college educated were those most responsive to such an argument. Despite all of this, most young people in their thirties have children. We can reasonably conclude that increased choice about pregnancy has not dramatically led to a strong new norm against having children, although we should keep special watch on the college-educated youngest group.

MEASURES OF SALIENCE OF PARENTHOOD

Only one question used in both 1957 and 1976 addressed the salience of parenthood, and that question, listed in table 5.2, asks about how a man or woman's life is changed by having children. Answers were coded for both the positive-negative quality of the attitude expressed and also for the extent to which parenthood was seen as restricting. These measures are highly correlated (.63 in 1957; .60 in 1976) but nonetheless conceptually different, as were parallel measures about the salience of marriage.

TABLE 5.2
Measures of the Salience of Parenthood

Measure	Question	Code
1957 and 1976		
Positive/Negative Orientation Parenthood	And now I'd like to ask you some questions about children. First, thinking about a (man's/woman's—same sex as respondent) life, how is a (man's/woman's) life changed by having children?	(examples) positive (brings happiness; children are a fulfillment; give love; make you less selfish) neutral (more responsibility; you have to support some-one; busier) negative (children tie you down; you have no free time)
Restrictive/Nonrestrictive Orientation to Parenthood	Same as above	all responses restrictive (examples of restrictive responses are: you have to think of someone else; more responsibility; you give up your freedom) some responses restrictive no response restrictions
1976 Only		
Attitude Toward Voluntary Childlessness	How do you feel about couples who decide to have no children at all	negative— selfish; immature; strange pity— they are missing some-thing; it's their loss neutral— it's up to them; it's okay if they both agree; they don't like children positive admire them
Value Fulfillment Through Parenthood	Same set of questions found in Table 4.1 [p. 144] to measure most important value Followed by: What about being a (father/mother)? How much (has/would) being a parent (lead/led) to (most important value) in your life? Very little, a little, some, a lot, a great deal?	(as is) parent fulfills major value: a great deal a lot some a little very little
Social Validity Through Parenthood	Same set of questions found in Table 4.1 [p. 144] to measure social validity through marriage and other roles	See Table 4.1

In 1976 a number of questions were added to measure the significance of parenthood in people's lives. Two series have already been discussed in chapter 4: one having to do with how much people see various roles fulfilling their major values and the other having to do with how much social validity people see in performing well in various roles. From the first we derive a measure of the *Value Fulfillment Through Parenthood* and from the second a measure of *Social Validity Through Parenthood* (see table 5.2). Finally, there was a direct question asking people how they felt about couples who decided not to have children (*Attitude Toward Voluntary Childlessness*). The question was coded for negative, neutral, and positive responses, and then there was a group of responses which could best be called "feeling pity for the couple." (Examples of the codes are given in table 5.2.)

Intercorrelations of these various new measures from the 1976 questionnaire yield a generally low positive matrix among them and with the measures from 1957–1976. The highest (.17) indicates that those who find parenthood fulfilling values are likely to see parenthood as critical to social validity. Again, as in the previous chapter, the low intercorrelations suggest that each of them may produce distinct patterns of results with other variables.

YEAR DIFFERENCES IN SALIENCE OF PARENTHOOD

Two different ways of assessing attitudes toward parenthood based on the same question were *Positive/Negative* and *Restrictive/Nonrestric-*

TABLE 5.3

Year Differences in the Salience of Parenting (By Parental Status)

Measures	All Respondents		Nonparents		Parents	
	1957 (%)	1976 (%)	1957 (%)	1976 (%)	1957 (%)	1976 (%)
Positive/Negative Orientation Toward Parenthood						
Positive	58	44	56	33	58	47
Neutral	20	28	23	34	20	26
Negative	22	28	21	33	22	27
	100%	100%	100%	100%	100%	100%
Total Number	2,346	2,139	445	471	1,901	1,668
Restrictive/Nonrestrictive Orientation Toward Parenthood						
All responses restrictive	30	45	34	53	30	42
Some responses restrictive	34	34	25	32	36	35
No responses restrictive	36	21	41	15	34	23
	100%	100%	100%	100%	100%	100%
Total Number	2,338	2,134	445	471	1,893	1,666

tive Orientations to reported changes that the role produces in people. In both schemes, 1976 responses are less positive toward parenthood and children than were those given by the population in 1957 (table 5.3). Unconditional positive response to parenthood has decreased by about 14 percent. The change has been relatively modest in parents (11 percent) but stronger in nonparents (23 percent). The same pattern applies to changes in perceived restrictiveness of parenthood. Whereas 11 percent more parents' answers in 1976 are coded as "some or all responses

TABLE 5.4
1976 Measures of the Salience of Parenting
(By Parental Status)

Measure	All Respondents	Non-parents	Parents Only
Attitude Toward			
Voluntary Childlessness			
Negative	18	12	20
Pity	18	9	20
Neutral	60	74	56
Positive	4	5	4
	100%	100%	100%
Total Number	2,127	503	1,620
Value Fulfillment			
Through Parenthood			
A great deal	55	40	59
A lot	28	28	28
Some	10	17	9
A little	3	7	2
Very little	4	8	2
	100%	100%	100%
Total Number	2,131	445	1,686
Social Validity Through			
Parenthood (and Other Roles)			
Parenthood Preferred to			
Work Role	74	42	84
Parenthood Preferred to			
Marriage Role	36	30	38
High—Parenthood Preferred			
to Both Roles	29	19	32
Moderate—Parenthood			
Preferred to One Role	47	36	50
Low—Parenthood			
Less Preferred Than Both Roles	14	38	7
Can't Decide	10	7	11
	100%	100%	100%
Total Number	1,519[a]	303[a]	1,159[a]

[a] Questions asked of only two-thirds of the 1976 sample.

restrictive," this is true for *26 percent more* childless respondents in 1976. Clearly there is a much stronger sense of the difficulties of being a parent for childless men and women in the 1970s than there was a generation ago. Aside from normative shifts about the acceptability of saying that parenthood has problems, it may indeed be the case that raising children in the 1970s is substantially more difficult and restricting for parents. Increased urbanization, the rapid introduction of new technologies, the impoverishment of schools are some of the many social changes that could make parents feel greater stress in the role.

In 1976 we asked a question about voluntary childlessness. Since the question was asked only in 1976, we cannot speak of changes which have occurred over the generation. But we can conclude from the distribution in table 5.4 that in 1976 there is no clearly dominant negative moral judgment about the choice not to have children. Over half of all respondents answer the question in morally neutral ways, saying that it probably reflects a decision for other activities or a judgment about one's talents and capacities for the particular activity of child raising. Even when we look at the answers of only parents, this neutral response is the most common one (74 percent). About a third of our respondents indicate that they think the decision is undesirable, but even among this third, many say that they pity or feel sorry for people who don't have children rather than assuming a moral, judgmental stance. This pattern is especially true for parents, much less true for nonparents. They think such a choice a bad one, but do not judge the people who make it to be bad people. While we can only guess what the responses would have been in 1957, it seems reasonable to assume that a larger proportion of the population would have viewed voluntary childlessness negatively even among those who themselves were childless, and that the framework for this judgment would more often have been explicitly moral.

Two other types of judgmental issues about parenthood were assessed as aspects of the salience of parenthood: value fulfillment and social validity through parenthood. Table 5.4 indicates that most nonparents conclude that parenthood would give them a lot or a great deal of fulfillment of their major value; less so than parents, clearly, but still quite a bit considering their highly neutral stand about voluntary childlessness. This pattern suggests there must be an underlying value conflict in most childless people in our society. The general normative values for obtaining life fulfillment through parenting must be so high that coming to a neutral position about childlessness for oneself is probably still a marginal position. Compared to parents, childless people clearly are much more invested in work as a way to define their validity as other results in table 5.4 indicate. And 84 percent of parents compared to only 42 percent of childless men and women would rather overhear that they are fine fathers (mothers) than that they are excellent at the work they do.

In general, the parent role seems only moderately relevant for most people's social selves. Marriage is more salient in the same assessments; work somewhat less so.

In summary, we begin to see some shakeup in the dominance of parenthood in Americans' view of the important things in life. Not that it is unimportant. In the previous chapter, we reported that family roles hold a central position in the experience and values of the American population. Parenthood figures prominently in sources of well-being and worries. We have seen that most adults report that parenthood contributes significantly to value realization. And when we limited analysis to those respondents who actually hold all three of the major life roles (spouse, parent, worker), family roles are more critical than occupational roles for almost all groups. Women rarely rate jobs more fulfilling than parenthood. Only older men rate their jobs more important than parenthood, and then only when they choose self-actualization or security as their critical value. When we ask what they would most like to overhear someone say about them, most respondents clearly want to be thought of as good marriage partners and parents, choosing either of these alternatives over "excellent at the work s/he does."

But as the sanctions against remaining childless become less severe, as they seem to have, nonparents seem to be breathing easier and making the absence of children less figural in their lives—perhaps a boon rather than a curse. We seem to have lost some of the 1957 overinvestment in the importance of the role. In 1957 we used no scale to measure satisfaction-dissatisfaction or happiness-unhappiness with parenthood. In preparing for the 1957 study, it was found that parents almost never gave negative answers to a direct question. It was apparently not possible in the normative climate of that time for a parent to say s/he was dissatisfied or unhappy with her/his experience of parenthood. It now seems that by 1976 the normative climate has changed and parents are more open to seeing negative features of parenthood. Our interpretation is that parents are no longer *overly* invested in the role and more often think of it as a major but not all-encompassing aspect of their lives.

The Experience of Parenting

While we have tried to disentangle the salience of parenthood from the actual experiences of the role, they are clearly intertwined in the subjective evaluation of mothers and fathers. When we ask people to think about the changes that parenthood brings a man or woman, we indirectly ask them to think about their own satisfactions or difficulties. When we ask people to consider how much being a parent fulfills a

TABLE 5.5

Measures of Experience in Parenthood

Measure	Question	Code (examples)
Both 1957 and 1976 Satisfactions from parenting	What would you say is the nicest thing about having children?	general happiness they make you happy; give fun; are fulfilling affiliation love and affection; they are company achievement sense of accomplishment; challenge teaching guiding them; you have someone who takes after you
Parental Problem?	Most parents have had some problems in raising their children. What are the main problems you've had in raising your child(ren)?	yes—discusses a problem no—denies ever having a problem
Type of parental problem	Same as above.	physical, material financing; home; physical care obedience getting them to obey affiliation we aren't close non-home problems type of neighborhood health health difficulty of child; illness

Measure	Question	Code
Parental Inadequacy	Many (men/women—same sex as respondent) feel they're not as good (father/mothers—same sex as respondent) as they would like to be. Have you ever felt this way?	yes—has at some time felt inadequate no—has never felt inadequate

Sources of Parental Inadequacy	(following above question) What kinds of things have made you feel this way?	physical/economic care
		    not enough money;
		    giving them enough affiliation
		    don't spend enough time; not close enough
		lack of tolerance
		    lose my temper; impatient obedience
		    I can't get them to obey; don't discipline

Frequency of Parental Inadequacy	(referring to above two questions) Have you felt this way a lot of times or only once in a while?	a lot; often sometimes; once in a while never
1976 Only Felt interference from parenthood	Some people say that having children does not leave them enough time for other things they want to do. Would you say that having children prevents (prevented) you from doing things you want(ed) to do *often, sometimes, rarely, or never?*	as is
Effects of Parenthood on Own Marriage	Some people say that having children brings a husband and wife closer together. Others feel that having children makes a husband and wife less close. How do you feel about that? Do you feel that children have brought you and your (husband/wife) *closer together or farther apart?*	closer some of both farther apart

TABLE 5.6

Selected Correlations of 1976 Measures of Parental Experience

	Measure of Parental Experience[a]			
Measure	Parental Problems? (1)	Frequency of Parental Inadequacy (2)	Felt Inter-ference from Parenthood (3)	Effect of Parenthood on Marriage (4)
(2)	.20[b] (1,616)	—	—	—
(3)	.21[b] (1,642)	.19[b] (1,671)	—	—
(4)	.08[c] (1,457)	.14[b] (1,485)	.11[b] (505)	—

[a] Each measure coded such that higher codes indicate more subjective difficulty.

[b] $p < .0001$

[c] $p < .01$

major life value, they respond partially by some evaluation of their own encounters as a parent. Nevertheless, these evaluations are only indirectly speaking of experience. In this section we consider direct assessments of experienced adjustment to parenthood.

MEASURES OF THE EXPERIENCE OF PARENTING

Three sets of questions were used to assess parenting experiences in both 1957 and 1976: one to assess the satisfaction, one to ask about the sense of adequacy in the role, and one to ask about problems encountered in the role. The six measures listed in table 5.5 were derived from these questions. The first, *satisfactions from parenting,* is based on responses to a question asking about the nicest things about having children.[1] The codes that will be extensively analyzed in the chapter are listed in table 5.5. A more detailed analysis will be made only in the year comparison to be presented in the beginning of the next section. The second and third measures summarize parents' response to a question about their problems in raising children: *Parent Problem* (whether or not they deny having had a problem raising children) and *Type of Parent Problem* (a content analysis of the problems discussed, the code for which appears in table 5.5). The fourth, fifth and sixth measures summarize parents' responses to questions about felt adequacy as a parent: *Parental Inadequacy* (whether the parent recognizes having felt inadequate at some time); *Sources of Parental Inadequacy* (a content analysis of sources mentioned, a code for which is listed in table 5.5); and *Fre-*

---

[1] This question was asked of all respondents but will be analyzed only for parents.

quency of Parental Inadequacy (how often inadequacy as a parent is felt). The latter is a more elaborate version of parental inadequacy.

Two questions from the 1976 survey expand our understanding of the experience of parenting. These are *Felt Interference from Parenthood* (how much having children interferes or interfered with doing what the respondent wants or wanted to do); and *Effect of Parenthood on Own Marriage* (whether parenthood is perceived to have brought the respondent and his/her spouse closer together or further apart). Table 5.5 presents the questions.

In both years, the correlation between *Parental Problem* and *Frequency of Parental Inadequacy* was .20. Some parents clearly refer to the same issues as problems and as factors affecting their own adequacy, but there are some people whose parenting problems do not reflect their own perceived adequacy. Then there are some people who feel inadequate in what they have been doing, but do not see it as a problem. We nevertheless expect somewhat parallel results from these two measures.

The new 1976 measures are only moderately correlated with *Parental Problem* and *Frequency of Parental Inadequacy* and with each other. These are reported in table 5.6. While they are low, the correlations are higher than parallel intercorrelations assessed in the chapter on marriage. Evidently there is more coherence in the way people evaluate their experiences as parents than the way they evaluate their experiences as husbands and wives. Perhaps more psychological dimensions make up the experience of marriage than the experience of being a father or mother.

YEAR COMPARISONS OF EXPERIENCE IN PARENTING

In 1957 a distinction was drawn between an interpersonal orientation toward parenting and other ways of looking at the role of parent:

> Some parents focus on the quality of the interaction between themselves and their children, thinking about their parent experience and judging their parent performance primarily by the richness and satisfaction of the interpersonal relationship. Other parents, equally concerned with the welfare and growth of their children, focus much more on providing physical care or the opportunities for education and other resources which will ensure their children mobility and a good life. But they are not especially concerned with the quality of relationship or interpersonal exchange they have with their children. (Gurin, Veroff, and Feld, 1960, pp.117–125)

An unspoken assumption residing in this distinction seems to be that an interpersonal orientation is a more "modern" way of looking at parenthood. It is probably true that such an orientation did not develop until relatively late in human history. In earlier eras, the role aspects of parent-child interaction were dominant: the parent obligation consisted primarily and crucially of ensuring the child's physical survival.

Role distinctions between parent and child were exaggerated by certain theologically based assumptions about "human nature": the infant was held to be invested with all of nature's evils—aggression, untamed impulses of all kinds—unsocialized and uncivilized. The role of the parent was to fight nature and impose civilization on the little beast.

In preliterate and rural cultures, children and their development are taken for granted and are socialized casually. If parents manage to provide food and minimal insurance of survival, the child takes care of his/her own growth and development with casual assists from older children and adults when they happen to be around and paying attention.

But with the development of modern child-raising technique and ideology, a much greater weight of responsibility fell on the adults. If the child was father of the man, modern psychology also urged the view that the parent had enormous power to mold the child. And it was the parent's responsibility not only to provide nurturance and ensure survival, but also to develop a warm and rich interaction with the child, to ensure stimulation of curiosity and growth, to instill morals, character, and achievement motives, and to teach the child that "healthy" balance of competitive and cooperative behavior which would ensure acceptance, popularity, and success with peers and in the larger society. A large order this, and a role prescription for parenting which was almost certain to lead to anxiety, attentiveness to experts, and some measure of disappointment and failure for many parents. It would probably also eventually lead to greater skepticism about the experts, a development which we are beginning to see in books like Bronfenbrenner's *The Ecology of Human Development* (1979), in which a noted expert questions the whole enterprise of "scientific" child-development research and along the way debunks much of the knowledge base of the "experts."

Notwithstanding this latest development, we expected that between 1957 and 1976, American parents would have bought a good deal of modern child-raising ideology and that they would have become more concerned with and focused on the parent-child relationship as the key to successful parenting. We expected that relational aspects of parenting would figure prominently as the context within which people would evaluate their parenting practices and parent experience.

We were therefore surprised by our results. Some results did support this expected change, but they were few and slight. Indeed, the 1957–1976 comparisons on the experiences in parenting yield remarkably parallel findings for both years (see table 5.7). Especially remarkable is the fact that detailed analysis of satisfactions from parenting in table 5.7 reveals almost identical percentages for the two years. The value of children to parents (see Hoffman, Thornton, and Manis, 1978) has been constant from 1957 to 1976. Overall, we are impressed with the fact that although we hypothesized considerable change in the responses about

TABLE 5.7
Year Differences in the Experiences in Parenting

Measure	1957 (%)	1976 (%)
Satisfactions from Parenting		
General:	45	44
General happiness	15	15
Fun	8	7
Fulfillment	10	7
Watch kids	12	15
Affiliation:	39	39
Give love	9	10
Receive love } love	5 15%	7 20%
Love, general	1	3
Companionship	21	17
Improve relationship with spouse	3	2
Influence	4	6
Achievement	5	5
Change in R	1	1
Help R	2	1
Other	2	1
Not ascertained	2	3
	100%	100%
Total Number	1,919	1,698
Parent Problem?		
Yes	75	77
No	25	23
	100%	100%
Total Number	1,843	1,652
Types of Parental Problems		
Physical, material	16	16
Obedience	18	20
Affiliation	6	11
Non-home problem	13	15
Health	12	7
Other	10	8
No Problem	25	23
	100%	100%
Total Number	1,843	1,651
Parental Inadequacy?		
Yes	49	55
No	51	45
	100%	100%
Total Number	1,209[a]	1,712
Sources of Parental Inadequacy		
Physical, material	10	10
Affiliation	13	20
Lack of tolerance	11	10
Obedience	8	7
Other	7	8
No inadequacy	51	45
	100%	100%
Total Number	1,201[a]	1,683
Frequency of Parental Inadequacy		
A lot, often	16	16
Once in a while; sometimes	31	37
Rarely	1	1
Never	52	46
	100%	100%
Total Number	1,180[a]	1,697

[a] Question was asked of only two-thirds of 1957 sample.

experiences in parenthood, no strong differences emerge. There are some minor trends. Let us look at them, bearing in mind the overall lack of change.

First, there has been a slight increase in reports of feeling inadequate as a mother or father, and this increase seems largely due to a greater tendency in 1976 to discuss affiliation inadequacy. It is worth noting that in the question about inadequacy the change comes in the number of people who say they have felt inadequate "once in a while." The same proportion (16 percent) in both years say they feel inadequate "a lot of times" or "often" but a larger proportion in 1976 say they feel inadequate "once in a while," or "sometimes" (37 percent compared to 31 percent in 1957). These differences suggest either that we have become slightly more introspective about our role in child rearing, as we hypothesized, or that parents face greater threats to their adequacy in rearing children now than they once did. We rather think that it is the modern child-rearing ideology that has sensitized mothers and fathers.

Second, we should note that while admitting to problems in child rearing remains at about the same level in 1976, reports of affiliative problems have nearly doubled from 6 percent to 11 percent. Putting this together with the fact that the emphasis on "love" as the satisfaction from parenting has gone up slightly (15 percent in 1957 to 20 percent in 1976), we have some evidence for an increased emphasis on the emotional tie between parent and child in both the satisfactions and problems mentioned by parents in 1976. Thus they feel that they are not as close to their children as they would like to be, that they do not enjoy the kind of warm, open, sharing relationship which they ideally would have.

Clearly the focus on relationship aspects of raising children was not absent from the 1957 parental responses. The authors of *Americans View Their Mental Health* noted that practically all the replies to the question about the nicest things about parenthood could be construed to imply a concern with parent-child relationships. In itself, this is an interesting finding. Unlike the reports on the nicest thing about marriage, responses on the nicest thing about having children deal amost exclusively with some aspect of an interpersonal relationship with the children. When respondents talk about the nice things about a marriage, they are able to mention situational factors extrinsic to the actual marital relationship (a nice house, financial security, the children). This is apparently not as possible when a parent thinks of the nicest things about having children, and gratifications become more completely focused in the relationship itself. (Gurin, Veroff, and Feld, 1960, p. 121)

At the time, however, it was noted that some answers nonetheless indicated more involvement than others (e.g., "there is someone to love") and when we restrict analysis to these most involved, love-centered responses, we find that they have increased somewhat over the period from 1957 to 1976. So have the influence-related responses, while the less intense references to the companionship that children provide have decreased. Thus, people in 1976 are slightly more sensitized to the warm interpersonal aspects of parent-child interaction and to power elements in that exchange, and less focused on non-affective affiliative satisfactions. *On the whole, however, it would be hard to say that 1976 parents are any more concerned with parent-child relationships than were 1957 parents.*

1976 MEASURES OF EXPERIENCES IN PARENTING

One question discussed under the topic of the salience of the parent role also examines satisfactions from parenthood—how much fulfillment of values does the respondent find in parenthood? We concluded from the responses that parenting remains a central anchor of satisfaction for most people. A large majority of our respondents in 1976 (87 percent) say that parenthood has provided them with a "great deal" or "a lot" of fulfillment. Only 4 percent of the sample have realized only "little" or "very little" satisfaction from the role.

The general positive evaluations of parental experiences also emerge in the pattern of responses to *Felt Interference from Parenthood* and *Effects of Parenthood on Own Marriage* (see table 5.8).

When respondents are asked about the effect children have on parents' lives, they generally recognize that having children, like any other choice and activity in life, carries some cost in eliminating other

TABLE 5.8

1976 Measures of Experiences in Parenting

Measure	Percentage
Felt Interference from Parenthood	
Children Interfere with What One Wants to Do:	
Often	5
Sometimes	32
Rarely	30
Never	33
	100%
Total Number	1,707
Effects of Parenthood on Own Marriage	
Children Bring Husband/Wife:	
Closer together	71
Both together and apart	9
Apart	9
No difference	11
	100%
Total Number	1,690

TABLE 5.9
Summary of Multivariate Analyses of 1957–1976
Measures of Parental Reactions

Measures of Parental Reactions	Relationship(s) Required[a] to Reproduce Observed Cross-Classification of Measures by Age × Education × Year × Sex				
	Main Effect[b]				Interactio
	Age	Education	Year	Sex	
Parental Role Salience					
Positive/Negative orientation toward parenthood					
Parents: Percent positive	Y<MA<O	G<H,C	57>76	M>F	
Nonparents: Percent positive			57>76	M>F	
Restrictive/Nonrestrictive orientation toward parenthood					
Parents: Percent nonrestrictive	Y<MA<O	G<H<C	57>76	M>F	Age × Se
Percent some restricting					
Nonparents: Percent nonrestrictive		G<H<C	57>76		Sex × Ye
Experience in Parenting					
Satisfaction from Parenting:					
Affiliation	Y<MA<O			M<F	
—Companionship		G>H>C	57>76		
—Love		G<H<C	57<76	M<F	
Achievement					
Influence			57<76	M>F	
Change in R				M>F	Age × Ye
Parent Problem?					
Yes	MA>Y>O	G<H<C		M<F	Educ × Ye
Type of Parental Problem:					
Physical	Y<MA<O	G>H>C			
Obedience	Y>MA>O	G<H,C		M>F	
Affiliation	Y>MA>O	G<H<C	57<76	M>F	
Nonhome					
Health			57>76		
Parental Inadequacy?					
Yes	MA>Y>O	G<H<C	57<76	M<F	Age × Ed
					Age × Se
Source of Parental Inadequacy:					
Physical, Material		G>H>C		M>F	
Affiliation		G<H<C	57<76		
Lack of Tolerance	Y>MA>O	G<H<C		M<F	
Obedience					
Moral Training	MA>Y>O				
Frequency of Parental Inadequacy:					
often	MA>Y>O				

[a] See footnote [a] of Table 2.11 for an explanation of "required."
[b] See footnote [a] of Table 2.11 for a description of "main effects."

choices that might have been made. The majority of people recognize that "having children interferes with other things [a person might] want to do" at least sometimes. Only a third of the sample say this is "never" true. Very few (5 percent), however, think it is often true. Most respondents say it is true only "sometimes" or "rarely."

When asked about the specific effect children have on the marriage relationship, most respondents (71 percent) choose an alternative which says that "children bring a couple closer together" rather than one which holds that children push a couple further apart. Small percentages say that children have both effects (9 percent) or that they have neither effect (11 percent).

These 1976 measures reinforce the impression we have that most people are either faring well in their evaluations of their parental experiences or are unwilling to discuss grievances they may have in the role. Our guess is that both interpretations are accurate. Perhaps analy-

TABLE 5.10
Summary of Multivariate Analyses of 1976
Measures of Parental Reactions

Measures	Relationship(s) Required[a] to Reproduce Observed Cross-Classification of Measures by Age × Education × Sex			
	Main Effects[b]			Interaction
	Age	Education	Sex	
Parental Role Salience				
Attitude Toward Voluntary Childlessness (Negative)				
Parents	Y<MA<O	G>H>C		Educ × Sex
Nonparents	Y<MA<O	G>H>C		Age × Education
Value Fulfillment Through Parenthood				
Parents		G<C<H	M<F	
Nonparents	Y>MA>O		M<F	
Social Validity Through Parenthood				
Parents				
Nonparents	MA>Y>O	C<G<H		
Experience in Parenting				
Felt Interference from Parenthood	Y>MA>O	G<H<C		
Effects of Parenthood on Own Marriage				
Percent Closer		G,H>C	M>F	

[a] See footnote [a] of Table 2.11 for an explanation of "required."
[b] See footnote [a] of Table 2.11 for a description of "main effects."

ses of sex, age, or education differences in subsequent sections will help us judge the relative importance of each.

Multivariate Analyses

When we apply log-linear hierarchical classification analysis to the response distributions, entering age, education, year, and sex, along with responses to parenting questions, none of the year effects we have described turns out to be by-products of other relationships, or of shifts in demographic characteristics of the population rather than primary year effects (table 5.9). Slight trends discussed turn out to be significant effects. In responses to the question about the nicest thing about having children, the slight increase in power/influence allusions is a stable main effect of year of interview, as is the increase in love-related allusions and the decrease in companionship allusions.

In this regard it is important to note that for the context questions about feelings of inadequacy or problems in the parent role, increases in affiliative responses from 1957 to 1976 clearly meet the multivariate test. Thus multivariate analyses support our conclusion that the salience of the parent-child relationship as an intense affective bond has increased somewhat over the generation. The less intense affiliative response—companionship—has decreased somewhat.

The remaining year differences discussed in the previous section also withstand the multivariate test—the increased negative salience of parenthood as well as the increased admission to inadequacies felt in the parent role.

No big surprises about the year differences emerged from examining interaction effects, except that there was a tendency for college-educated parents to be even more aware of parenting problems in 1976 (83 percent) than they were in 1957 (75 percent) while grade school–educated parents showed the reverse change: 72 percent in 1957 to 63 percent in 1976. We thus have evidence for a general phenomenon that reappears in other areas of this study. While college-educated Americans are becoming more oriented to psychological problems in their lives, poorly educated Americans are becoming less so. This polarization seems to occur as more Americans are college educated while fewer remain with only a grade-school education.

One additional qualification to results across the generation must be made because of the multivariate analyses: the increase in perceived restrictiveness from 1957 to 1976. This was less apparent in childless men compared to childless women. (These results are in table 5.11.) We suspect that they do not think much about the responsibilities of fatherhood and so have been less affected by the increasing skepticism

TABLE 5.11

Selected Sex Differences in Response About Parenthood in Measures Used in Both 1957 and 1976
(By Year × Parental Status)

	Parents Only				Nonparents			
	Men		Women		Men		Women	
Measures	1957 (%)	1976 (%)	1957 (%)	1976 (%)	1957 (%)	1976 (%)	1957 (%)	1976 (%)
Parental Role Salience[a]								
Positive/Negative Orientation Toward Parenthood:								
Positive	63	49	54	45	57	45	55	27
Restrictive/Nonrestrictive Orientation Toward Parenthood:								
All responses restrictive	27	43	31	41	35	48	33	58
Experiences in Parenting								
Satisfaction from Parenting:								
Affiliation	32	33	40	40				
[Love-related]	[12][b]	[16][b]	[19][b]	[22][b]				
[Companionship]	[20][b]	[17][b]	[21][b]	[18][b]				
Influence	5	8	2	4				
Parental Problem?								
Yes	70	74	78	78				
Type of Parental Problem								
Obedience	18	22	18	18				
Affiliation	7	12	6	11				
Providing[c]	14	12	14	16				
Parental Adequacy?								
Yes	43[d]	53	54[d]	57				
Sources of Parental Inadequacy								
Physical, material	11[d]	11	10[d]	8				
Affiliation	16[d]	26	10[d]	17				
Lack of tolerance	6[d]	5	15[d]	13				
Total Number	848	711	1,105	1,012	204	215	241	253

Size of sample will vary somewhat because number of nonascertained responses will vary.

This percentage is a subpercentage of percent Affiliation.

Sum of "Inadequate Finances" and other resources.

Based on two-thirds of sample who were asked the question of parental inadequacy.

TABLE 5.12

*Selected Sex Differences in Responses About Parenthood
in 1976 Measures (by parental status)*

Measures	Parents Only		Nonparents	
	Men (%)	Women (%)	Men (%)	Women (%)
Parental Role Salience				
Attitude Toward Voluntary				
Childlessness:				
Negative	23	18	12	12
Positive	18	22	8	10
	(668)	(956)	(232)	(271)
Value Fulfillment Through				
Parenthood:				
Great deal	54	62	36	43
	(692)	(994)	(207)	(238)
Social Validity Through				
Parenthood:				
High (parenthood preference	30	34	21	18
to marriage, work identity)	(404)	(656)	(159)	(182)
(Would rather overhear:				
Fine parent > good at work	84	84	46	39
Fine parent > fine husband/wife	33	41	31	30
	(483)	(674)	(166)	(196)
Experience in Parenting				
Felt Interference from				
Parenthood:				
Often	6	5		
Never	33	34		
	(700)	(1,007)		
Effect of Parenthood				
On Own Marriage:				
Closer	76	67		
Both closer and apart	8	10		
Farther apart	8	11		
No difference	8	12		
	100%	100%		
	(690)	(1,000)		

NOTE: Numbers in parentheses are total number of persons in each group.

about the joys of parenting that has occurred in women who were childless.

Together with the results in table 5.10—the summary of multivariate analyses of the 1976 measures—we will now use the results of the multivariate analyses to feature the critical sex, age, and education differences in the experience of parenthood. While a few results for these social characteristics depend on the year in which the assessment occurred, the differences we will discuss seem to represent stable phenomena across our recent social history.

Sex Differences in the Salience and Experience of Parenthood

Women and men differ in practically every dimension of parenting investigated. The sex differences we find (presented in tables 5.11 and 5.12) are not enormous, but they are ubiquitous and significant and reflect the fact that definitions of motherhood and fatherhood still differ in our society. For all of the publicity and pressure brought to bear on cultural distinctions in parenting for men and women, traditional definitions of father as material provider and moral authority, and mother as socioemotional provider and daily caretaker still hold sway and infuse people's conceptions, performance, and experience of parenthood.

In normative attitudes, women are somewhat less enthusiastic about parenthood than men are. When they describe the changes in a person's life effected by having children, women are more negative and more often see the changes as restricting the adult's freedom. It is important to note that while generally men and women are equally likely to take a nonjudgmental and neutral stance toward voluntary childlessness, this is not true among the less educated in our society. Fifty-four percent of the grade school–educated men in our society are neutral or positive about the choice not to have children. This compares to 35 percent of the grade school–educated women. More importantly, reverse trends are apparent in the more educated men and women. More edu-

TABLE 5.13
Sex Differences in Parents' Attitude Toward Voluntary
Childlessness (By Education, 1976 Only)

Attitude Toward Voluntary Childlessness	Highest Educational Level Attained					
	Grade School Only		High School		College	
	Men (%)	Women (%)	Men (%)	Women (%)	Men (%)	Women (%)
Negative	28	31	28	18	14	10
Pity	18	34	17	20	19	18
Neutral	51	33	52	58	62	68
Positive	3	2	3	4	5	5
	100%	100%	100%	100%	100%	100%
Total Number	111	170	313	544	242	236

cated women are very much more neutral than less educated women. These results are summarized in table 5.13. They suggest that less educated women are highly invested in motherhood as a significant factor in their lives much more than other women, and more than comparably educated men who may view their role as provider for children with some ambivalence because of the handicaps produced by their lack of education.

Among those who are negative about the choice of voluntary childlessness, men more often phrase their negative view as a moral judgment ("they're selfish, self-centered," "they're childish"), while women more often say that they feel sorry for a young couple who don't have children. These trends appearing in table 5.12 are not significant in the multivariate analyses, but they are clearly present and important. The woman's phrasing implies a highly personal value for parenthood—as an experience not to be missed—while the male phrasing implies a societal and moral view in which the childless are seen as selfish and irresponsible, as failing to meet an important obligation of adulthood.

Parenthood is more salient for women than for men. Women are more likely to say that being a parent gives them "a great deal" of fulfillment and less often than men say that they get only "some" or "very little" fulfillment from the role. This applies to both parents and nonparents. Both men and women rank parenthood much higher than work as an area of significant personal investment ("which would you rather overhear someone say about you?") but when we pit parenthood against the role of spouse ("a fine father/mother or a fine husband/wife?") women show greater investment in parenthood than men do (42 percent compared to 35 percent) and a concomitant, lower investment in being a fine spouse (48 percent compared to 55 percent). There are, however, no overall sex differences in *Social Validity Through Parenthood* when the three roles are compared. In all, then, women and men reflect traditional cultural beliefs about the differential role of parenthood in their lives. The male traditionally has defined himself and filled his life with job commitments, while child raising has served similar functions for women. It is important to note, however, that the sex differences we find are modest ones, and that there is a very large overlap in men's and women's evaluation of parenthood. We are not in a position to determine whether the overlap has increased during the last twenty years since these salience items were asked only in 1976. Our guess is that men and women have probably become more similar in their views of parenting (and we have slight evidence for this view which we will present shortly). In any case, we note that while sex differences appear in the parenting data and are consonant with traditional sex-role conceptions, they are very modest and indicate a great deal of similarity between men's and women's views of this crucial life role.

Focusing on the actual experience of raising children, we again find that men and women differ in ways which are predictable and understandable from the perspective of traditional sex roles. Women are closer to the experience and seem both more personal and more realistic about it. Men and women are equally likely to say that having children sometimes interferes with realization of other goals in life, but women more often than men think that children impose some restriction on parents' lives, and they are more likely to admit the possibility that children can create distance between a couple (table 5.12).

When they think of the nicest thing about having children, mothers allude more often to the love and warmth, aspects of affiliative pleasure with their children, while men more often focus on the influence or power implicit in the parent role. Men are more likely to say that having an influence, forming the character of the child, is a major pleasure of parenthood (table 5.11).

Women not only think of the warm interaction with children as the pleasure of parenthood more often than men do; they also *less* often cite affiliation as a source of parenting problems or of their sense of inadequacy in the parent role (see table 5.11). Men say they are not as good fathers as they would like to be because they are not close to their children and do not spend time with them or interact with them enough. And they cite as problems both their lack of closeness and problems of obedience.

Men allude to their ability to provide adequately for their children's lives and well-being as a source of their feelings of inadequacy slightly more than women, who on the other hand, refer to a lack of patience and tolerance as a source of inadequacy (see table 5.11). These sex variations are entirely consonant with traditional role definitions. In the traditional scheme, fathers are expected to be the breadwinners and providers of material resources. They worry about their inadequacy in this function, and their involvement in the work of providing interferes with their time and freedom to interact with children, as much as they think they should in order to be ideal fathers. Women, traditionally responsible for primary child care, do not suffer from lack of involvement or interaction with children, but the demands of daily interaction sometimes strain their equanimity and controls. Therefore they feel that they are not patient enough to be ideal mothers.

One other interesting sex difference should be mentioned. In 1976 women show an increase in mentions of problems of providing adequately for the physical and material needs of children. While it is not a large increase, it contrasts with a decrease for men over a time period that has seen a general increase in affluence. We suspect that it reflects a growing sense among women that they share in the responsibilities of providing for their families. If this is true—that women increasingly assume such responsibility—it would imply there has been some reduction in the sex-linked functions within the family, a significant change in conceptions of the roles of male and female parents.

On the other hand, this change might reflect the increased number of female heads of household. The response may come largely from women who are raising children without a father present and who are assuming provider functions. When we compare responses of mothers who do and do not have husbands, we find that separated and divorced mothers are more likely to allude to problems of support, and that the difference has increased from 1957 to 1976. While 19 percent of married women in 1957 gave such problems compared to 32 percent of the separated and divorced, in 1976 the figures are 18 percent and 39 percent. In both problems and inadequacies, for married men and women the proportion of such responses *decreased* over the generation, but they increased among separated and divorced parents. Given the larger number of single-parent households in 1976—and particularly the female-headed single-parent familes—we conclude that indeed this change does account in large part for the larger proportion of women concerned about material supportive functions of parenting in 1976.

Age Differences in the Salience and Experience of Parenthood

Parenting in its various stages presents opportunities and obligations which vary dramatically. Since these changes depend on the developmental stage of the child as well as the parent's age, and since the two sources vary together, we obviously expect to find significant age differences in responses to parenting. But we also know that the effect of parent aging can never be disentangled from the effects of the child's developmental status.

A special additional complication arises in interpreting age differences associated with parenting. Issues of parenting tend to focus on young children. We do not have a vocabulary for thinking about parenting adult children. As a result, older parents' responses often automatically deal with distant past reactions. Indeed, some of our questions ask them to think of when they were "raising" their children. Hence reports of parental adjustment in older parents will be heavily filtered by the perspective of lifelong accommodations that may occasionally exaggerate points of difficulty in childrearing but more likely will deemphasize strain.

Guided by multivariate analyses, we will focus on age differences that were significant in simultaneous controls for education, sex, and year. The major results appear in tables 5.14 (for 1957/1976 measures) and 5.15 (for measures available only in 1976).

In responses gauging pronatal norms (table 5.15) we find that youn-

TABLE 5.14

Selected Age Differences in Responses About Parenthood in Measures Used in Both 1957 and 1976 (by year, parents only)

	Age											
	21-29		30-39		40-49		50-59		60-64		65+	
Measure	1957 (%)	1976 (%)	1957 (%)	1976 (%)	1957 (%)	1976 (%)	1957 (%)	1976 (%)	1957 (%)	1976 (%)	1957 (%)	1976 (%)
Parental Role Salience												
Positive/Negative Orientation Toward Parenthood:												
Positive	47	42	56	42	56	43	65	49	61	62	65	52
Restrictive/Non-restrictive Orientation Toward Parenthood:												
All restrictive response	36	52	31	44	30	46	23	38	30	30	24	37
Experience in Parenting												
Satisfaction from Parenting:												
Affiliation	37	35	35	35	35	38	34	38	40	32	39	40
Parental Problem:												
Yes	77	79	80	81	76	88	74	77	65	71	65	60
Type of Parental Problem:												
Physical	12	13	10	11	15	17	21	20	25	19	23	21
Obedience	24	26	26	24	15	23	16	18	6	11	9	10
Affiliation	7	16	8	17	7	14	6	9	3	6	3	2
Parental Inadequacy:[a]												
Yes	53	64	52	64	54	60	44	53	44	46	40	38
Sources of Parental Inadequacy:[a]												
Lack of tolerance	18	18	16	16	9	8	6	6	0	2	6	3
Moral teaching	<1	<1	2	3	2	3	3	2	3	2	3	2
Frequency of Parental Inadequacy:												
A lot, Often	17	18	20	19	17	19	15	17	16	18	11	7
Total Number[b]	318	277	497	389	416	315	299	299	212	134	271	310

NOTE: Numbers in parentheses are total numbers of persons in each group.

[a] Only two-thirds of the sample were asked this question in 1957.

[b] Numbers vary somewhat because the number of respondents whose answers are not ascertained vary.

TABLE 5.15
Selected Age Differences in Responses About Parenthood in 1976 Measures
(By Parental Status)

Measure	Age					
	21-29 (%)	30-39 (%)	40-49 (%)	50-59 (%)	60-64 (%)	65+ (%)
Parental Role Salience						
Attitude Toward Voluntary Childlessness:						
Neutral parents	70 (260)	62 (375)	56 (296)	53 (279)	46 (125)	42 (287)
Nonparents	81 (265)	81 (69)	65 (23)	66 (38)	77 (30)	60 (78)
Social Validity Through Parenthood:						
High (parenthood preference to marriage, work)						
Parents	38 (179)[a]	31 (259)[a]	31 (212)[a]	32 (193)[a]	36 (80)[a]	30 (196)
Nonparents	17 (182)[a]	34 (44)[a]	33 (18)[a]	15 (26)[a]	28 (18)[a]	9 (53)
Experience in Parenting						
Felt Interference From Parenthood:						
Never felt interference interference	22 (274)	22 (385)	27 (312)	36 (298)	46 (134)	58 (302)

NOTE: Numbers in parentheses are number of persons in each group.
[a] Questions series asked of only two-thirds of 1976 sample.

TABLE 5.16

Age of Nonparents Related to Perceived Changes
Affected by Parenthood (by year)

| | \multicolumn{12}{c}{Age} | | | | | | | | | | |
| Measure | 21-29 | | 30-39 | | 40-49 | | 50-59 | | 60-64 | | 65+ | |
	1957 (%)	1976 (%)	1957 (%)	1976 (%)	1957 (%)	1976 (%)	1957 (%)	1976 (%)	1957 (%)	1976 (%)	1957 (%)	1976 (%)
Positive/Negative Orientation Toward Parenthood												
Positive	54	32	53	31	56	39	59	47	59	33	64	28
Restrictive/Nonrestrictive Orientation Toward Parenthood												
All Restrictive	39	54	30	58	33	39	34	31	26	60	33	59
Total Number	124	269	76	71	79	23	76	30	23	21	63	57

ger people tend to be more neutral toward a young couple who decide not to have children. Since this result is only for 1976—the only year for which we have data—we might be somewhat skeptical about the results as an age phenomenon and could interpret it only as a historical cohort effect, were it not for the fact that in both years younger people are more negative about the effects of children and parenting than older respondents are. In the question about how having children changes a person's life, age relates to overall positiveness in the answers; as age increases, answers emphasizing restrictive change decline (table 5.14). According to the multivariate analysis, these results do not apply to nonparents in either year, as shown in table 5.16. For parents, however, these age relationships hold for both years and can be thought of as reflecting a difference between retrospectieve evaluation of an experience and evaluation in the thick of the experience. Older parents have finished the hardest work of parenting—the twenty-four-hour tending and responsibility for little children and the turmoil of adolescents struggling to achieve an independent voice. They have managed the challenge of supporting and educating their children. In retrospect, they can look back and say, "Yes, life is mostly enlarged and improved by having children." After all, they are at a period in their lives where they are reaping the rewards of the role and are past most of its burdens and struggles. Thus it would not be surprising if older people in every era would be relatively negative about young people in the society deciding not to have children.

It is important to note, however, that the age differences in these general attitudes toward the effects of parenting are not enormous, and that over the twenty-year period older people have become less enthusiastic about parenthood, just as have younger adults. While 42 percent of the over-65 age group in 1957 saw parenthood as only enlarging—that is, alluded to no restrictions imposed by the role; the comparable figure in 1976 is 29 percent. The decrease in unconditional positive responses is just as large (or larger) for the over-65 group as it is among younger people. The over-65 group in 1976 looks about the same as the 21- to 29-year olds in 1957. Broad cultural changes which have affected the value attached to children and parenthood have affected everyone in the culture, whatever their age. We have little evidence for specific cohort effects in these results.

In spite of social change, the overall developmental results are still clear: older people tend not to see the restrictive or negative aspects of parenting. This is especially highlighted in the very large difference between how often younger and older parents see that parenthood prevents (or, in the case of the older parents, prevented) them from doing what they want (or wanted) to do. Fifty-eight percent of the parents who are 65 and older say "never," compared to 22 percent of the parents who are 21–29. This question was not asked in 1957, so the results could be interpreted as a cohort difference. Nevertheless, it seems compelling to think that age puts perspective on how much personal freedom is violated by attending to the demands of young children.

Contextual questions about the experience of parenthood—the nicest thing about having children and sources of problems and inadequacies in raising children—reveal other interesting age differences. When asked to describe the nicest thing about having children, older respondents more than the young refer to affiliative aspects of the relationship—having someone to love, someone to love you, doing things and sharing things wtih children, the pleasure of companionship. When asked about problems and inadequacies, on the other hand, it is the young who report interaction and affiliation as problematic. Younger parents say they don't spend enough time with their children or are too impatient with their children. They—more often than older parents—allude to a lack of warmth and closeness as the major problem between themselves and their children. It is as though young parents, impressed with expert advice about the crucial need to provide love and warmth to ensure successful child raising, are apprehensive and concerned about whether they are managing the proper spirit and home atmosphere. But older parents, in a position to see that their children have grown up and turned out all right, worry less about the task and are able to take pleasure in the warmth and exchange they either currently share with their children or once shared, in spite of the difficulties. When so much rides on a warm interaction (that is, the health and growth of one's children, the success of one's parenting) and when criteria are ambiguous (how warm is warm enough, how much interaction is enough interaction) it is hard to relax and enjoy the experience. But when the children have grown up and the parents can see that they are all right, they can feel that they have given adequate love and can enjoy the luxury of taking pleasure in their past and present relationship with the child.

Older parents more often focus on external physical sources of problems in child raising: they didn't have enough money to provide adequately or to give their children the advantages they would like to have offered them. This age relationship, which occurs in both years, can be seen as reflecting a change in the requirements of the parent role as children grow older. The financial demands of parenthood are largest when children are in late adolescence and early adulthood, when they enter college or other postsecondary schools, and when they begin families of their own. Parents should therefore experience the heaviest financial pressure during the decade from 40 to 49. In fact, however, references to the financial problems of parenthood increase throughout the later years. Of course the effects of inadequate resources may continue to assert themselves beyond the time when a child has entered adulthood. Older parents may feel that their children would have had better or more successful lives if they had been able to go to college or if they had had the money to start a business, and so on.

On the other hand, the preoccupation of older people with the material side of parenting may simply reflect a distancing from the problematic aspects of parenthood. The psychological or emotional problems of raising their children are not as vivid for parents no longer in the thick of daily child raising, and so when they are asked to think of problems, they think of the more external and emotionally neutral problems of providing material support and comforts. Such answers may also reflect an externalizing of problems which younger parents would cast in a more personal, emotional vocabulary. If children turn out badly or disappointingly, a parent may eventually attribute the problem to the pressure of poverty or the struggle to provide ("I had to be away from them because I was trying hard to earn a living for all of us" or "If only I could have afforded to send him to college") in order to protect the self from the burden of guilt which a more personal attribution would imply ("I wasn't very close to him" or "I never enjoyed raising children").

We might have expected allusions to problems of providing materially for children to be less common in 1976. We have seen evidence in earlier chapters that economic concerns have lessened somewhat over the generation. But in problems of parenting we do not find a significant year effect for reporting economic-material sources. In all of the age categories, we note remarkable stability in the proportions of respondents who allude to such problems. Probably this is so because of a common coping strategy widely used by parents to externalize the locus of parenting problems to less personal sources of difficulty, especially as both parents and children get older. The externalizing function of economic allusions in these answers—their use to avoid more personal sources of problems—gains support from the other age relationships found in answers to this question. Older respondents *less* often allude to problems in their personal interaction with children and problems of closeness (affiliation). In addition, when asked about their *inadequacies* as parents, older respondents do *not* mention failures to provide physical care or material resources any more than younger respondents do. Economic problems are offered in place of the more interpersonal problems young parents give, and they are not cast as personal inadequacies, but as externally imposed problems to which personal responsibility and inadequacy are not attached.

On the other hand, younger parents cast their inadequacies more frequently than older parents as interpersonal or psychological (lack of tolerance). Younger parents seem to take the position of the child and wish they could be more tolerant or more patient with the child. Although the younger parents may not yet have faced the most significant confrontations and conflicts in the role, they are in more immediate contact with day-to-day outbursts of their own anger.

Although most of the results we have discussed thus far speak of change in the subjective evaluation of parenthood during the family life cycle, we should note results in table 5.10 that point to tendencies in *middle-aged* parents to be distinctive in their reactions to parenthood. They are most likely to admit both to problems (see table 5.14) and to feelings of parental inadequacy, and when they do think of their inadequacies, they are most likely to report them as occurring often. These results, though not powerful, are significant. One cannot help interpreting them as the special difficulties of raising adolescents. The fact that the pattern was as true in 1957 as in 1976 suggests that socialization of adolescents may be a difficult task for parents in American society whether it be in a less turbulent and more optimistic time (the 1950s) or in a more disrupted and uncertain era (the 1970s). One result corroborates this interpretation. Middle-aged parents in both 1957 and 1976 are more likely to allude to "moral" issues in inadequacies they feel in raising their children. They more often speak of their concerns about teaching their children to be responsible, good people (see table 5.14). These are the issues parents of adolescents face as their children are launched on their own.

Adolescent children's transition to adulthood may thus be as much a rite of passage for parents as it is for their children. Ultimately this growing up can produce the capacity in parents to distance themselves from their children. Middle-aged parents can emerge as older parents, more comfortable about the significance the role has played in their lives. Many of our results pointing to the positive adaptation of older parents support this interpretation.

Education Differences in the Salience and Experience of Parenthood

Education reflects and is a proxy for economic resources. We therefore expect that economic problems in parenting will be felt more often by our least-educated respondents. We see in table 5.17 that education is negatively related to economic sources of problems and feelings of inadequacy in raising children, more highly educated respondents talking about such problems less than respondents with grade school or only some high school education. From the multivariate analysis, we know that this effect is net of age and cannot therefore be attributed to the fact that older respondents are usually less educated.

But education signifies more than economic position, and we would expect it to have effects on parenting attitudes beyond the experience of economic hardship. More highly educated parents should be more responsive to child-raising literature and should manifest its influence in a more psychological, interpersonal stance toward children. And having access to more powerful and more interesting work roles, the more educated respondents may also have competing interests and activities with which child raising interferes. These effects all gain support from our findings. Thus, we will see that the more highly educated are somewhat more aware of the demands and restrictions of having children and tend to be the most understanding of why a couple might decide not to have children. They nonetheless generally value the parenting experience and find it fulfilling, but perhaps not as much as people with less education. Let us look at the data closely.

In answer to the question, "How is a person's life changed by having children?" more highly educated respondents more often give some but not all answers which recognize restrictions imposed by parenthood (table 5.17). This finding applies to both parents and nonparents. In keeping with this result, grade school–educated parents are slightly less likely to give positive responses to the question. We thus get a picture of the more educated being much more aware of both the positive and the negative aspects of parenting. This kind of finer differentiation of the experience of parenting among the more educated is similar to many other results in our study. Education seems not to be related simply to positive or negative well-being; it is related to increased awareness of *both* positive and negative aspects of roles and other life experiences.

In the case of parenthood, most of the results suggest that education sensitizes parents to difficulties. Compared to the less educated, college-educated parents are more likely to report both problems and felt inadequacies as parents. In the attributions of sources of both problems and inadequacies, more educated respondents more often allude to interpersonal issues. They phrase problems and inadequacies as relational difficulties: they feel that they have not been close enough to their children; they've had problems interacting with them or getting them to obey. They feel that they have lacked tolerance and warmth as parents and that they do not spend enough time with their children (table 5.17). Furthermore, less educated respondents say that children never interfere with other important goals. And on the question which asked whether having children brought parents closer together or tended to separate them, less educated respondents are slightly but significantly more likely to say that children have brought them closer together (table 5.18). The differences are not large but are still significant in the multivariate analysis.

We thus get a picture of college-educated mothers and fathers in contrast to less educated parents as being bothered by their interpersonal

TABLE 5.17
Selected Education Differences in Responses About Parenthood in Measures Used in Both 1957 and 1976 (by education, parents only)

Measure	Grade School 1957 (%)	Grade School 1976 (%)	Some High School 1957 (%)	Some High School 1976 (%)	High School Graduate 1957 (%)	High School Graduate 1976 (%)	Some College 1957 (%)	Some College 1976 (%)	College Graduate 1957 (%)	College Graduate 1976 (%)
Parental Role Salience										
Positive/Negative Orientation Toward Parenthood:										
Positive	56	48	57	47	58	47	64	49	57	43
Restrictive/nonrestrictive orientation toward parenthood										
Some restriction but not all	33	29	34	29	40	37	44	40	38	40
Experiences in Parenting										
Satisfaction from Parenting:										
Companionship	22	23	23	15	20	19	16	14	23	12
Love	13	18	14	22	17	19	19	20	11	29
Parent Problem?:										
Yes	72	63	80	75	74	80	73	78	77	88
Type of Parental Problem:										
Physical, Economic	25	26	16	21	10	14	10	11	6	7
Obedience	11	10	21	15	23	22	17	25	23	27
Affiliation	4	3	5	6	8	14	9	15	8	20
Parental Inadequacy?:[a]										
Yes	39		48		54		61		62	
Sources of Parental Inadequacy:[a]										
Physical, economic	15		11		7		9		2	
Affiliation	6		14		15		20		24	
Lack of tolerance	4		8		17		15		18	
Total Number[b]	610	287	423	272	527	615	182	271	149	215

NOTE: Numbers in parentheses are total number of persons in each group.

[a] Numbers will vary somewhat because number of nonascertained responses vary.

TABLE 5.18
Selected Educational Differences in 1976
Measures of Responses About Parenthood (By Parental Status)

Measure	Grade School (%)	Some High School (%)	High School Graduate (%)	Some College (%)	Co Gra
			Educational Level		
Parental Role Salience					
Attitude Toward Voluntary Childlessness:					
Neutral					
Parents	40	50	59	61	
	(281)	(260)	(597)	(266)	(2
Nonparents	57	75	69	80	
	(56)	(57)	(135)	(127)	(1
Value Fulfillment Through Parenthood:					
"A great deal"					
Parents	58	63	60	56	
	(294)	(279)	(618)	(272)	(2
Nonparents	27	53	48	43	
	(48)	(49)	(118)	(119)	(1
Social Validity Through Parenthood:					
High					
Parents	36	34	35	27	
	(203)[a]	(199)[a]	(400)[a]	(168)[a]	(1
Nonparents	18	32	24	16	
	(29)[a]	(21)[a]	(54)[a]	(36)[a]	(
Experience in Parenting					
Felt Interference from Parenthood:					
"Never"	55	41	26	29	
	(294)	(279)	(618)	(272)	(2
Effect of Children on Couple:					
"Closer"	76	71	72	65	
	(294)	(279)	(618)	(272)	(2

NOTE: Numbers in parentheses are total number of persons in each group.

[a] Only two-thirds of sample were asked this series of questions.

life with their children and families. They perceive problems clearly. The college educated are the major contributors to the particularly strong admission to parental inadequacy among middle-aged parents discussed in the previous section. We have discussed this finding as a special sensitization to adolescent socialization and movement away from the family. Such sensitization may speak of a higher level of aspiration for what family life should be like among the more educated, that they are profoundly concerned with the role of parent as an opportunity to create a brave new psychological world. The fact that college-educated fathers and mothers are more likely to speak of affiliative satisfaction in parenting in terms of giving and receiving "love" rather than in terms of companionship suggests that the college educated are psychologically very involved in the role.

Other results, however, downplay any extraordinary investment the college educated have in parenthood compared to other groups—especially the high school educated. While the majority of all education groups say that parenthood leads to fulfillment of their major life goal "a great deal," it is the high school educated who stand out in this respect rather than the college educated (see table 5.18). Furthermore, the high school educated are most prominent in their choice of parenthood as a way to define their social validity. Thirty-five percent of the high school educated select parenthood over work and the spouse role. This is true for only 26 percent of the college educated. When asked to choose which they would like to overhear about themselves—that they were excellent at work or excellent parents—the college educated more often than other groups choose the work alternative (though it is critical to note that even in this group the parent alternative is chosen by 80 percent of the respondents, thus clearly establishing its primacy). When asked to choose between the parent role and the spouse role, the college educated more often than the high school group find the choice impossible to make, or choose the spouse role.

Parenthood is thus not the pivotal focus of life among the college educated, although it is still one of their major ways of fulfilling life values. The educated members of our society, whether or not they themselves are parents, are far more tolerant of voluntary childlessness than the less educated (see table 5.18). College-educated respondents are much more likely to feel neutral about the choice, and this makes good sense since they see that there are many other goals possible in life and that parenthood may interfere with at least some of them. To the college educated, the young couple who choose childlessness are simply choosing to emphasize certain of these other goals rather than failing to fulfill a role expected of all adults. To the less educated, the young couple are choosing alternatives of less clear moral purpose. We have already noted that age is also a factor affecting this attitude. Thus, when we combine the contributions of both age and education as correlates of the attitude toward voluntary childlessness (see table 5.19),

TABLE 5.19
Attitude Toward Voluntary Childlessness in Various Age × Education Groups (by parental statuses)

Parental Status	Young (21-34)			Middle-Aged (35-54)			Old (55+)		
	Grade School (%)	High School (%)	College (%)	Grade School (%)	High School (%)	College (%)	Grade School (%)	High School (%)	College (%)
Parents' Attitude Toward Voluntary Childlessness									
Negative	25	15	9	29	20	9	31	30	20
Pity	20	13	17	35	23	18	26	21	22
Neutral	45	68	69	34	54	69	41	46	52
Positive	10	4	5	2	3	4	2	3	6
	100%	100%	100%	100%	100%	100%	100%	100%	100%
	(20)	(276)	(170)	(55)	(348)	(188)	(206)	(231)	(120)
Nonparents' Attitude Toward Voluntary Childlessness									
Negative	33	6	6	25	17	18	31	23	12
Pity	—	13	8	12	7	—	14	4	12
Neutral	67	74	80	63	69	78	55	66	76
Positive	—	7	6	—	7	4	—	7	—
	100%	100%	100%	100%	100%	100%	100%	100%	100%
	(6)	(110)	(194)	(8)	(29)	(27)	(42)	(53)	(33)

NOTE: Numbers in parentheses are total number of persons in each group.

we see a particularly accentuated nonjudgmental and even slightly positive view of planned childlessness among younger, more educated men and women in our society. Among the older college-educated groups, there are clearly more remnants of the negative meaning of childlessness for adults. In the multivariate analysis, the combined effect for the nonparents is a significant interaction; the young college-educated nonparents are particularly nonjudgmental about choosing not to have children.

We are thus led to a tentative conclusion that the college educated may have less at stake in the role of parenthood. We say this in spite of the fact that college-educated mothers and fathers have more clearly interpreted parenthood as an arena for working out complicated interpersonal relationships, and in so doing, have discovered new anxieties. We have seen in the last chapter how much involvement and satisfaction college-educated people derive from their marriages. We will see the same factors operating in work in the next chapter. These multiple resources for psychological well-being make parenthood not unimportant to them, but perhaps somewhat less psychologically figural than it is for the less educated, whose self-definitions may depend more on their parental status, their children and grandchildren, and the dreams of what they might become.

Parenthood for the Divorced or Separated

Because of the significant increase in single-parent households as the result of divorce or separation which occurred between 1957 and 1976, and because of the special strains which accompany this family arrangement (Morgan et al., 1977; Sawhill, 1975) it seems important to present at least some modest analysis of the effect of being divorced or separated on attitudes toward and experience of parenthood.

The economic position of the single mother has been described by economists, and it is a bleak picture indeed. Our data corroborate these descriptions (table 5.20). In this analysis, we can assume that divorced mothers are usually raising children alone, whereas divorced fathers generally do not have children in their custody. The data point up the extreme effect of divorce on a woman's income: while divorced fathers have somewhat lower income than married fathers, the difference is not nearly as large as that between married and divorced mothers.

Education has increased throughout the population since 1957, and in general we find the increase reflected in both the married and the divorced/separated groups of parents. There is, however, a slightly larger educational change among the divorced/separated. Whereas this group (both men and women) had somewhat less education in 1957,

TABLE 5.20

Selected Demographic Differences in Married vs. Divorced (Separated) Parents (by sex × year)

Demographic Characteristic	Men Married 1957 (%)	Men Married 1976 (%)	Men Divorced (Separated) 1957 (%)	Men Divorced (Separated) 1976 (%)	Women Married 1957 (%)	Women Married 1976 (%)	Women Divorced (Separated) 1957 (%)	Women Divorced (Separated) 1976 (%)
Income (in 1976 dollars)								
under 4000	11	5	26	17	10	5	34	29
4000–7999	19	13	19	12	22	13	50	35
8000–9900	19	6	4	13	20	9	4	13
10,000–12,499	15	13	22	12	16	13	6	10
12,500–19,999	26	29	22	31	25	34	2	9
20,000 and over	10	34	7	15	7	26	4	4
	100%	100%	100%	100%	100%	100%	100%	100%
Education								
Grade school	33	15	44	21	26	12	34	12
High school	45	48	45	47	58	61	54	58
College	22	37	11	32	16	27	12	30
	100%	100%	100%	100%	100%	100%	100%	100%
Age								
21–29	15	16	4	14	23	21	23	23
30–39	27	25	22	34	21	25	28	29
40–49	23	21	22	16	23	20	23	21
50–59	17	17	19	17	13	20	14	14
60–64	6	9	4	8	5	5	5	7
65+	12	12	29	11	5	9	7	6
	100%	100%	100%	100%	100%	100%	100%	100%
Family Stage								
Preschool children present	37	27	5	10	36	26	20	17
Grade-school children only	12	11	16	17	14	13	19	20
High school + grade-school children	11	11	—	14	11	10	13	11
Grown children + grade-school children	13	18	16	10	12	17	13	20
All grown children	27	33	63	49	27	34	35	32
	100%	100%	100%	100%	100%	100%	100%	100%
Total Number[a]	781	608	27	66	815	650	93	146

[a] Numbers vary because number of respondents not ascertained on a given measure varies.

they look essentially the same as married parents in education in 1976 (table 5.19). This fact stands in striking contrast to the worsened economic situation of divorced/separated mothers, and reminds us of both the devastating economic consequences of divorce for women and also of the lower relationship between education and income among women (compared to men) which exists as a consequence of occupational segregation by sex which still dominates the American workplace.

Age differences between the parent groups reveal one difference: that divorced men are somewhat younger in 1976 than they were in 1957 (table 5.19). And the data on family stages in table 5.19 reflect this same difference: divorced fathers in particular are more likely—in comparison to married fathers—to be represented in family stages with younger children. Overall, there are fewer young children in 1976 than in 1957, but in 1957 the ratio of married to divorced at these stages was larger than is true in 1976. Furthermore, the percentage of parents who are divorced at each of the family life stages, presents a revealing change from 1957 to 1976 (table 5.21). Among fathers and mothers of preschool or grade-school children, the percent divorced has at least doubled between 1957 and 1976. The presence of little children is no longer as significant a deterrent to divorce as it was twenty years ago.

Shifting from demographic factors to attitudes and experience in parenting, we find again that differences between divorced men and women reflect sex role prescriptions quite closely. Raising children alone increases the burdens of parenthood, but since men more often leave child raising to their former spouses when they divorce, the negative effects of parenthood on a divorced parent are likely to be more imposing among mothers than among fathers.

To the question about how children change a person's life, we see the different effect of divorce on mothers and fathers quite clearly (ta-

TABLE 5.21

Percent Divorced (Separated) Among Parents of Children
at Different Family Stages (by sex × year)

| | **Percent Divorced (Separated)** | | | |
| | **Men** | | **Women** | |
Family Life Stage	**1957 (%)**	**1976 (%)**	**1957 (%)**	**1976 (%)**
Has Preschool Child	<1	1	5	12
(<6 years)	(284)	(16)	(319)	(196)
Youngest Child is School Age	1	3	10	21
(6 to 17 years old)	(272)	(228)	(342)	(325)
Youngest Child is	5	10	8	11
18 or older	(273)	(259)	(425)	(449)

NOTE: Numbers in parentheses are total number of persons in each group.

TABLE 5.22

Selected Parental Reactions Among Married vs. Divorced (Separated) Parents (by sex × year)

Measure	Men Married 1957 (%)	Men Married 1976 (%)	Men Divorced (Separated) 1957 (%)	Men Divorced (Separated) 1976 (%)	Women Married 1957 (%)	Women Married 1976 (%)	Women Divorced (Separated) 1957 (%)	Women Divorced (Separated) 1976 (%)
Salience of Parenthood								
Positive/Negative Orientation Toward Parenthood:								
Positive	63	48	69	63	51	43	58	45
Ambivalent, negative	14	20	19	14	31	35	20	31
Restrictive/Nonrestrictive Orientation Toward Parenthood:								
Nonrestrictive	37	24	39	33	30	20	35	16
All restrictive	27	45	23	27	33	43	29	43
Attitude Toward Voluntary Childlessness:[a]								
Negative	—	23	—	21	—	15	—	20
Pity	—	19	—	12	—	21	—	17
Neutral	—	55	—	62	—	61	—	54
Positive	—	3	—	5	—	3	—	9
		100%		100%		100%		100%
Value Fulfillment Through Parenthood:[a]								
Great deal	—	54	—	52	—	61	—	64
Very little, A little	—	6	—	12	—	2	—	6
Social Validity Through Parenthood:[a]								
High	—	28	—	56	—	25	—	56

TABLE 5.22 (continued)

	Men				Women			
	Married		Divorced (Separated)		Married		Divorced (Separated)	
Measure	1957 (%)	1976 (%)	1957 (%)	1976 (%)	1957 (%)	1976 (%)	1957 (%)	1976 (%)
Experience in Parenthood								
Parental Problem:								
Yes	70	76	82	64	80	80	82	88
Type of Parental Problem:								
Physical, material	15	12	14	16	13	14	28	33
Obedience	18	27	24	9	20	22	16	13
Affiliation	7	12	14	20	6	13	6	16
Parental Inadequacy:[b]								
Yes	41	53	73	50	55	62	59	56
Type of Parental Inadequacy:[b]								
Physical, material	10	11	13	14	10	9	11	11
Affiliation	15	26	47	29	10	18	19	19
Lack of Tolerance	6	6	0	2	17	16	8	12
Felt Interference from Parenthood[a]								
Rarely, never	—	63	—	50	—	60	—	61
Felt Effect of Parenthood on Marriage[a]								
Closer	—	80	—	36	—	75	—	31
Total Number[c]	781	608	27	66	815	650	93	146

NOTE: Numbers in parentheses are total number of persons in each group.

[a] Question asked only of the 1976 sample.

[b] Question asked of only two-thirds of the 1957 sample.

[c] Numbers vary because number of respondents not ascertained on a given measure varies.

ble 5.22). Divorced fathers were more likely than any of the other groups in this analysis to stress the positive and enlarging side of parenthood in 1957, and they are again more positive in 1976. While the other three groups show large decreases in positive responses over the generation, the change is much smaller for divorced fathers. They are the only group who offer fewer ambivalent or negative changes in 1976 than in 1957.

When answers are coded for restrictiveness, the pattern of results is similar. Divorced fathers are again the only group of parents who report fewer problems and inadequacies in 1976 than in 1957. Looking closely at the results in table 5.21, we also see they are less likely to report inadequacies or problems than their married counterparts in 1976. What is more, divorced men in 1957 were *especially* likely to speak of their inadequacies and problems in commanding obedience from their children and in relating closely to their children or seeing them enough (affiliation).

These results all suggest that the role of the divorced man vis-à-vis his children has improved markedly. His problems are now not distinctive. Where once he was especially concerned about problems of obedience or of establishing an affiliative relationship with his children, he now uses the same constructs that married men do to structure difficulties. This is an important result. If, compared to 1976, divorce in 1957 was initiated more frequently around paternal neglect and conflict, then the role of the divorced father in relation to his children was objectively a problem, and probably was consistently undermined by his ex-wife. In 1976 more divorces may have been initiated not specifically because of paternal inadequacies, but because of the marital relationship independent of paternal difficulties. If so, then many more divorced fathers in the 1970s could maintain and feel comfortable about a relationship with their children. For 1976 we note that just as many divorced as married men report a great deal of value fulfillment through parenthood. Furthermore, just as many divorced men as divorced women report that they seek social validation through parenthood; 56 percent of both divorced men and women choose being considered a good father or mother above work or marriage excellence. We therefore suggest that divorced men in 1976 are relating much better to their children than they were in 1957.

Nevertheless, the relative decline in allusion to difficulties in the role of parenthood among divorced fathers must be seen at some level as a distancing response and/or the product of distance. Compared to the 1950s, they probably have a more authoritative role in parenting in the 1970s. They may see their children more than they used to. Nevertheless, even in 1976, if divorced fathers take little part in the daily aspects of parenthood and encounter children largely on weekends or holidays, the experience can in all likelihood be enlarging and problem-free—but somewhat distanced. It is a rather partial and rarefied form of parenting, removed from the daily routine, discipline, and restrictions of life with children. It is interesting in this regard that divorced fathers are more likely than married fathers to see their children interfering with what they want to do (see table 5.22). This is not true in the comparable analysis of women. Divorced fathers' lives are clearly less in tempo with the rhythm of their children's activities.

Divorced mothers are very troubled by support issues, particularly when they think of problems. This is even more apparent in 1976 than it was in 1957. In 1957 only 28 percent of divorced mothers talked of physical/material problems in child raising. This figure has risen to 35 percent in 1976. Remembering their financial status, this is not surprising. Divorced mothers generally worry about the same kinds of inadequacies as married mothers do, fitting the picture of problems stemming from continuous and close interaction with children.

In answer to the question of whether children have brought the parents closer together or separated them, both fathers and mothers who are divorced are much less likely than their married counterparts to say that children bring parents closer together. In all, parents who are raising children alone or have lost daily interaction with children have a poignant sense of the special burdens or losses they bear. The care of children is not evidently a communal enterprise for many of them. It probably is often used as a basis for judging inequities or for justifying divorce, rather than as a basis of sharing a common goal.

Summary

Complex changes in our society's norms followed in the wake of universal access to cheap and effective birth control. Among the momentous changes which occurred were a reevaluation of traditional family forms and the framing of marriage, conception, and childbirth as *choices* to be made among alternatives, options to be weighed and balanced against other possible life choices. While earlier generations took marriage and parenthood for granted as necessary parts of adulthood, such unconsidered assumptions now gave way to processes of choice, deliberation, and decision. Once parenthood is cast as a choice, the experience is compared to the outcomes of other possible choices and some metric (personal satisfaction, cost-benefit, etc.) must be found on which alternative outcomes can be scaled.

At the same time that strong pronatal norms were breaking up, secularization of the culture and dilution of traditional authority structures occurred and contributed to a change in orientation toward child raising. While earlier generations stressed role aspects of parenthood and drew sharp lines between the roles of parent and child, later generations adopted the more psychological, interpersonal orientation urged by child-raising experts in which warm interpersonal interaction, empathy, and caring (rather than clear differentiation of authority and power between parent and child) were seen as the medium for ensuring effective socialization.

Parents in 1976 stress relational, interpersonal aspects of parenthood more than their counterparts in 1957. Those parents most actively and closely involved in the work of daily parenting, most directly in "the thick" of parenthood (women, young parents, fathers who are in the family rather than separated or divorced) stress relational aspects of the role, particularly when referring to problems and adequacies in the role. Older parents, at a stage in life where they can see the results of their parenting, allude to the interpersonal pleasures and satisfactions of parenthood, but phrase problems and inadequacies more often as problems of material resources rather than interpersonal difficulties. We interpret these age findings as reflecting both the stringent economic conditions many older parents confronted when their children's economic needs were largest, and also a tendency on the part of older people to distance themselves somewhat from the intense emotional and interpersonal problems of parenthood.

In 1976 women also more frequently allude to problems of supporting and providing for children in material ways—more than they did in 1957. Since this increase runs counter to the change for men and the general trends in our data which reflect a lessening of economic worries, we suggest that in this case the increased economic/material concern shown by mothers might be a reflection of the larger number of women who are raising children in single-parent households. Comparison of mothers who are divorced and separated with those who are married lend support to this interpretation.

Men in our society appear to find close interpersonal relations with their children problematic. They—less often than women—point to this aspect of the role as "the nicest thing" about parenthood, and they more often speak of lack of closeness with their children as a problem they have encountered or a source of inadequacy in their performance as parents. Parenthood seems to have increased as a source of relationship strain for men since 1957—perhaps more than for women. We see this differential change as reflecting the loss of authority which fathers in particular have experienced in family roles.

In traditional families, the father represented ultimate authority. Less involved in the continuous daily interaction of the home because of his commitment to his work, the father had less active emotional engagement with children than the mother had. This meant both that he missed some of the warmth and closeness of relationship which the mother enjoyed, and also that he was advantageously placed to function as a cooler head in controversy, a judge and arbitrator. His was the ultimate authority; his word was law. His authority was legitimized by being above the fray, and his role as breadwinner fueled the power of his position.

When that power diminished—both because his wife joined in the task of support and because of general antiauthority trends in our society which required new sources of legitimacy beyond the unquestioned assumption of position—the father found himself stripped of the old basis of relationship and with no obvious new patterns at hand. Despite the fact that she may work, the mother remained the center of interpersonal and socioemotional exchange, and her socialization prepared her to establish and maintain warm relationships. But the father had no such substitute skills or traditional patterns to bring into play in his relationships with his children.

We do find one exception to this hypothesized erosion of men's parental authority from 1957 to 1976: divorced fathers now seem to be much more involved with their children, more concerned about their personal relationship with them, and less concerned about a capacity to command respect. Nevertheless, even if divorced fathers are in a better position with their children than they once were, they are still very concerned about affiliative issues.

We will see in analysis of the work role that American men in 1976 find less affiliative gratification in work than they did in 1957. They also seem to find parenthood lacking in this same way. Only the marriage role offers men the hope of warm, sharing, emotional exchange. And it may be that in their hope to find a substitute channel for the expression of affiliation in marriage, men overburden or ask too much of that single crucial relationship. Here we may have detected one important source of marital strain that went undetected in the preceding chapter.

Chapter 6

WORK

SINCE the publication of *Americans View Their Mental Health,* many social scientists have become invloved in studying the nature of work in American society and how it affects people's mental health. Among these, several (e.g., Kornhauser, 1965; Braverman, 1975) have spelled out the potential dire consequences of unrewarding and meaningless work for people's physical and psychological well-being. Sounding doomsday predictions about the present quality of the work world, *Work in America* (1973), a provocative political document written by a Special Task Force to the Secretary of Health, Education and Welfare in 1972, sharply criticized the organization of most work settings for American men and women, emphasizing, in particular, effects on people's mental health. Within the industrial sphere, the clerical and management spheres, virtually within all spheres of working life—the quality of employment was found wanting with respect to people's well-being. The report especially stressed that today's workers feel little if any impact on what they are doing.

While the report was based largely on summaries of empirical data, much of it gathered by surveys conducted by the Survey Research Center, it was not always clear what data were being used to draw its dark conclusions. Indeed, a careful reading of the 1969–1970 and 1972–1973 surveys on the Quality of Employment made by the Survey Research Center (Quinn and Shepard, 1975) would not necessarily lead a sophisticated reader to the gloomy conclusion drawn by the authors of *Work in America.* Many results from those studies suggest that most American workers are not particularly dissatisfied with their jobs and do not find their work alienating, although it is also clear that many do express such negative reactions.

The more recent 1977 Quality of Employment Survey (Quinn and Staines, 1979) provided, in fact, the first significant indication that there was *any* decline in job satisfaction for American workers over the past generation. Even so, most workers continue to report being "satisfied." Furthermore, other findings from the 1977 survey indicate that, aside from an increased desire for additional fringe benefits and concerns about exposure to health and safety problems, most American workers over the years of the Quality of Employment Surveys have not experienced any remarkable increases in the frequency and severity of "problems" in their work.

Significantly, only the following types of problems were mentioned by more than 50 percent of American workers in 1977:

1. Difficulty in getting days changed permanently, if so desired (mentioned by 77 percent).
2. Difficulty in getting work hours changed permanently, if so desired (mentioned by 72 percent).
3. Difficulty in getting duties changed, if so desired (mentioned by 54 percent).
4. Shortage of jobs in worker's line of work (mentioned by 54 percent).
5. Inadequate time for leisure activities (mentioned by 55 percent).

Note that these are not complaints about the inherent quality of work. Rather, the perceived inflexibility of the work setting appears to be the dominant concern. The first three are problems in changing job requirements, demands, or expectations; the fourth problem reflects limited job alternatives, which constrain freedom of movement; and the fifth concern involves arranging more time for leisure. Other complaints about inflexibility in working life were frequently mentioned as well: 42 percent of the American workers felt that it would be difficult to find another job with similar pay (even though only 15 percent felt it likely that they would lose their job in the next year); 48 percent of workers said that their stake in their present job was too great to change jobs.

A summary which accounts for all of these results about work problems suggests that while satisfaction with work has clearly decreased to some extent over the past decade, the types of problems that people are experiencing at work are largely unrelated to the kinds of issues raised by the *Work in America* task force. The majority of people were not talking about their lack of impact as a major problem in their work. Rather, they were focusing on other things—the perceived inflexibility of their work, and, in particular, the extent to which they are tied to the specific jobs they hold.

Nevertheless, one must keep in mind that a sizable minority of people in the Quality of Employment Survey *did* talk about difficulties at work that may well imply concerns about impact: 40 percent felt that time dragged at work; 36 percent felt that their skills were underutilized; 32 percent felt that they were overeducated for their jobs; and 13 percent believed that the quality of the product or service provided by their place of work was substandard. Although these responses do not come from a majority of American workers, a sizable group of working men and women are expressing such concerns. Even so, it is hard to detect a dramatic shift in these reports over the time span of the Quality of Employment Surveys. Our two surveys span a longer time period than the Quality of Employment Surveys. Thus, it will be interesting to see whether the period from 1957 to 1976 is one in which we can clearly detect any more profound changes in the quality of working life and, in particular, any changes that bear out the assessments made in *Work in America.*

In our analyses of data comparing workers in 1957 and 1976, we will be focusing on two major questions: (1) whether there have been changes in people's feelings that their work offers them intrinsic gratifications, in particular the intrinsic gratification that people derive from having impact in their work; (2) whether the capacities of American workers to adapt their aspirations to the work demands of their specific job settings have shifted much over the generation.

These two questions are, of course, not unrelated. People's intrinsic involvement in the kinds of things going on in their working lives may provide a satisfactory means of adapting to the work setting itself. Without intrinsic gratification one's adaptation can be considerably more difficult. Attribution of blame for anything going wrong with work is apt to be more externalized when people feel they are not intrinsically involved in the work. In turn, such external blame can reduce identification with an organization, a psychological process which Katz and Kahn (1978) emphasize is critical to successful adaptation to work.

This dynamic relationship between involvement and adaptation can go the other way as well. As people adapt work aspirations to the "realities" of the work situation, they presumably also become more identified with the work itself. And, in turn, various aspects of the work setting can become more intrinsically gratifying. Such an argument was used in our original volume to discuss age differences in reactions to work. Older people were more gratified by work, as indicated by a question on job satisfaction. We interpreted this result to mean that older people were well adapted to the settings that they were in because they were increasingly able to get satisfactions from things seen as more directly tied to their identity. Thus, adaptation can produce intrinsic satisfaction, and intrinsic satisfaction can induce adaptation. Both directions of causality are likely and reflect inextricable processes influencing workers' feelings of well-being.

Other psychological processes to be examined in piecing together styles of workers' adaptation and involvements include a distinction between ego and extrinsic orientations to work, first made in connection with the 1957 survey. We asked: was the worker focused on more *external* (extrinsic) aspects of the work setting as a source of satisfaction or dissatisfaction, or on more *ego* (intrinsic) aspects? We found that an ego orientation to both job satisfaction and job dissatisfaction occurred more often among younger people, more educated people, and workers in higher-status jobs. Note that ego orientation toward work can reflect very high aspirations for work and may thus even be a basis for specific kinds of dissatisfaction. People with high aspirations for work can potentially put forth such great demands that they cannot be fulfilled by *any* work setting. Thus, ego dissatisfactions can result from such very high aspirations. On the other hand, men who have curtailed their work aspirations may very well be "satisfied" only because they do not expect much in the way of ego gratifications from their work. The job may provide a way of making money, structuring time, securing the future, any one of which may be all that is required from work. Thus, adaptation to work has a complex relationship to aspirations, to the frustration of these aspirations, as well as to the objective conditions of a working environment. These issues are even more critical in 1976 than they were in 1957 because the population has become better educated and more affluent, with a large cohort of young "baby boom" workers demanding good jobs, as we will discuss in the next section.

These two questions about the nature of involvement with work and the general adaptation to work demands will be the most important psychological issues to be explored in our examination of changes in reactions to work by the American worker from 1957 to 1976. How have workers adapted to possibilities for achieving or not achieving their goals through their work? What new kinds of ego gratifications do they now obtain from work? How has their involvement with work in general or with their jobs changed, if at all? Seeking answers to such questions will help us plot most recent historical developments in the subjective responses of the American worker.

There is yet another theme that will emerge almost by default in our examination of changes in working life. The nature and role of work in American life have undoubtedly shifted in part because of an emphasis on *new* roles for different groups of people. Tables 6.1 and 6.2 examine some major demographic information relevant to our 1957–1976 comparison of the American work scene. Table 6.1 documents age, education, and occupational shifts in the working force since 1957. Table 6.2 shows the percent of men and women in the 1957 and 1976 samples who were working, retired, and unemployed in different age groups. From these two tables we can see a number of demographic changes which could have dramatic effects on the meaning of work.

First to be reckoned with is the dramatic movement of women into the active work force since 1957. The fact of women entering the labor market has important ramifications for the meaning of work not only for women but also for men. The 1960 monograph did not even discuss women at work, although some relevant questions were asked of em-

TABLE 6.1

*Age, Education and Occupation Comparisons of
1957 and 1976 Samples of Adult Workers (by sex)*

	Men		Women	
Comparisons	1957 (%)	1976 (%)	1957 (%)	1976 (%)
Age				
21–29	18	27	19	30
30–39	27	27	27	24
40–49	25	18	25	18
50–59	18	16	21	17
60–64	6	7	4	6
65+	6	5	3	5
	100%	100%	100%	100%
Education				
Grade School	31	9	26	8
Some High School	20	12	22	14
High School Graduate	26	34	33	43
Some College	11	23	10	18
College Graduate	12	22	9	17
	100%	100%	100%	100%
Occupation				
Professional	13	18	12	19
Managers	13	17	8	7
Clerical	6	6	28	32
Sales	6	6	7	4
Crafts	23	24	2	2
Operative	18	15	16	11
Service	7	6	25	22
Laborer	5	4	<1	1
Farmers	19	4	2	2
	100%	100%	100%	100%
Total Number	924	753	457	599

ployed women. We felt that work was a minor part of the experience of women in our society in 1957 and did not warrant special examination at that time. In our comparative examination of the role of work in the quality of American life, we naturally need to include an analysis of employed women in 1957. But, perhaps more important, we must consider the impact that this change in the sex composition of the work force has had on the meaning of work for everyone.

A second shift in American roles over the same period is an increased orientation toward retirement. In 1957 expectations about what one should feel or do in retirement were not very clear. Such expectations are still not very clear-cut now, but they are much more in evidence in the conscious concerns of people than they once were, primarily because many more Americans are in that paricular status than

TABLE 6.2

Employment Status of Men and Women in 1957 and 1976 Samples (by age)

Age

Employment Status	21-29 1957 (%)	21-29 1976 (%)	30-39 1957 (%)	30-39 1976 (%)	40-49 1957 (%)	40-49 1976 (%)	50-59 1957 (%)	50-59 1976 (%)	60-64 1957 (%)	60-64 1976 (%)	65+ 1957 (%)	65+ 1976 (%)
Men												
Working	88	88	98	94	100	90	93	85	88	68	36	26
Retired	0	0	0	2	0	6	2	11	8	31	62	73
Unemployed	2	8	2	3	<1	4	5	3	4	1	2	1
Student	10	4	0	1	0	1	0	0	0	0	0	0
Not ascertained	0	<1	0	0	0	0	0	1	0	0	0	0
	100%	100%	100%	100%	100%	100%	100%	100%	100%	100%	100%	100%
Total Number	189	235	250	215	231	155	179	139	66	74	161	142
Women												
Working	32	59	37	57	40	57	45	49	25	37	6	12
Housewife	66	30	62	36	57	36	54	41	72	38	79	52
Retired	0	0	0	<1	0	2	0	7	3	22	14	34
Unemployed	2	9	1	6	2	5	1	3	0	3	1	2
Student	0	2	0	<1	<1	0	0	0	0	0	0	0
Not ascertained	0	0	0	0	0	0	0	0	0	0	0	<1
	100%	100%	100%	100%	100%	100%	100%	100%	100%	100%	100%	100%
Total Number	266	318	334	248	284	186	211	23	87	92	192	255

ever before. Not only are increasing numbers of people living for years beyond retirement age, but many more people are retiring earlier than they once did. Table 6.2, which describes the employment status of men and women in 1957 and 1976, shows that there has been an increase in the proportion of Americans who consider themselves "retired" at all age groups over forty. To the extent that these data imply an increased orientation to retirement among older workers, work as a dominant orientation to life among older men and women in our society may have become considerably reduced.

Furthermore, in conjuction with and because of a possible decline in orientation to work among retired people or among people thinking about retirement, we would predict an increased orientation to leisure. Perhaps more than ever, people are beginning to think of work and leisure as compensatory activities. As a result, leisure may have gained some proper status as a *role*: a specific position in our society which has expectations and norms attached to it, expectations about what one should be doing when "not working."

Another demographic feature relevant to work in American society that we must attend to is a greater proportion of young people in the work force today than a generation ago. In table 6.1 we can see that a larger proportion of working men and women in 1976 are aged 21–29 than was the case in 1957. Easterlin, as presented in Collins (1979), has provocatively suggested that this "bulging" cohort of young workers in the current American society, because it compares itself to the successful affluent among its parental cohort, would experience particular trouble in adapting to any limitations within the current work world. In essence, a very large group of people are competing for a shrinking number of slots in the job market, and, at the same time, are expecting to reap "the good life."

This "baby boom" cohort is also highly educated. Whether the demands of the labor market have kept pace with the better education of young workers today is an open question. Formal credentials required for obtaining certain jobs have apparently increased more because the average educational level of potential applicants for such jobs have increased, than because there has been a real upgrading in job requirements. It is not always clear why a college education is necessary for a management position or for certain types of sales positions—or even for certain technical jobs, where on-the-job training can presumably impart the specific knowledge required in the job better than four years of a liberal arts education. The increased education of the American population in 1976 may thus have a critically important impact on the orientation to work among this new generation.

Work in America expressed the major theme that people felt overtrained for their jobs and did not get much chance to express their latent talents. Rubin's (1976) investigation of working-class people in

California suggests that many men and women feel as if they are in a much better position than their parents' generation to get a reasonably good job, but end up with work which is not all that different from that of their parents. They indeed feel frustrated. While only 32 percent of American workers felt as if their "over"-education was a problem in their work, according to the 1977 Quality of Employment Survey (Quinn and Staines, 1979), this is undoubtedly a much larger percentage today than would have been obtained in 1957, when fewer men and women were college educated and many more had only a high school education or less.

Not unrelated to possible changes in the meaning of the work role for people stemming from these demographic shifts within the work force are potential shifts in people's orientation to family roles. As we have seen in chapters 4 and 5, the salience of these family roles in American life still remains quite high, even while normative assumptions about these roles have apparently changed. Indeed, the "psychologizing" of the 1960s and 1970s probably has had a greater impact on thinking about interpersonal experiences within the family context than on conceptions about the work role as we noted in chapter 4. Nevertheless, these forces must also have had some effects on people's interpretations about the meaning of work. Specifically, a plausible accompaniment of this sharpened focus on family roles as issues of particular concern for men and women in our society may have been some deployment of people's concerns *away from the work role*. Salaman (1974), for example, has suggested that there has been an erosion of people's identification with a particular "community" of peers in a given occupation, primarily because people have become less involved with their ongoing work. Such lack of involvement with work can occur not only because people are finding the objective conditions of their work less gratifying, but also because they are shifting their focal concerns to more intimate interpersonal roles, or to their leisure pursuits.

For all of these reasons, we expected that there might have been some substantial changes over the generation in the salience of work in American people's lives. We thus want to know: Who likes to work and why? How important is work to people? And, has there been any shift in how we would answer these questions for the 1976 population as opposed to the 1957 population?

Indirectly, we have already touched upon these questions in other chapters. In the next part of this chapter, therefore, we will review pertinent data from previous chapters on well-being, self-perceptions, and family roles to highlight more systematically any evaluations we can draw about the salience of work in American people's lives and especially about how these may have shifted over the past generation. Next we will present information about the salience of work among housewives. And, finally, we will provide a detailed inquiry about how men and women react to their particular work experiences in the two generations.

The Salience of Work: 1957–1976

A REVIEW OF PERTINENT DATA FROM PREVIOUS CHAPTERS

In a variety of contexts throughout this volume, we have already discussed data pertinent to the salience of work in the lives of Americans. In people's spontaneous responses to questions about their well-being, they disclose what roles are particularly salient to them. We will thus review some data from chapter 2, this time focusing only on working respondents. Since people's spontaneous responses to questions about their picture of themselves, as discussed in chapter 3, reveal how critical the work role may be to self-definition, we will also review some data about self-perceptions, but once again focus only on working respondents. And finally, in discussing the salience of family roles in chapters 4 and 5, the relative importance of work and leisure was indirectly implicated. We will therefore also reiterate those relevant findings here.

The Importance of Work as a Source of Well-Being

In describing sources of well-being in response to questions about happiness, unhappiness, and worries, discussed in chapter 2, many people gave us responses which could indicate that their jobs represented a major source of well-being or distress. For example, one significant finding noted in chapter 2 was that mention of one's job occurred slightly more often in men's and women's responses to the question about worries in 1976 than in 1957. These results are seen in tables 6.3 and 6.4, where we present sources of happiness, unhappiness, and worries for working men (table 6.3) and working women (table 6.4). Seven percent more men and 5 percent more women mention job worries in the current survey. Both tables also clearly indicate that there are no differences between workers in 1957 and 1976 in mentioning their job as a source of *happiness*, but more women in 1976 mentioned their job as a source of *unhappiness* than did working women in 1957 (an 11 percent increase). Thus, many more people in the 1970s than in the 1950s were thinking about their jobs when they considered their overall anxieties and sources of unhappiness, but workers in 1970 were no more or less likely to mention their work as a source of happiness, compared to those of the earlier generation.

From what we are able to glean from changes evident in the Quality

TABLE 6.3

Working Men's Sources of Happiness, Unhappiness, and Worries,[a] 1957 vs. 1976

Sources	Source of Happiness		Source of Unhappiness		Source of Worries	
	1957 (%)	1976 (%)	1957 (%)	1976 (%)	1957 (%)	1976 (%)
Economic and Material	40	34	22	19	44	36
Children	21	18	4	4	8	13
Marriage	17	15	2	4	1	2
Other Interpersonal	20	27	6	8	5	8
Job	12	13	24	25	20	27
R's Health	9	6	4	4	7	9
Family's Health	7	4	3	1	12	10
Independence; Absence of Burdens	7	16	—	—	—	—
Personal Characteristics (Problems)	1	4	10	8	3	4
Community, National and World Problems	—	—	16	34	10	11
Total Number	924	753	924	753	924	753

[a] Percentage responding with a given source in their first two mentions.

TABLE 6.4

Working Women's Sources of Happiness, Unhappiness, and Worries,[a] 1957 vs. 1976

Sources	Source of Happiness		Source of Unhappiness		Source of Worries	
	1957 (%)	1976 (%)	1957 (%)	1976 (%)	1957 (%)	1976 (%)
Economic and Material	38	30	22	20	42	35
Children	27	24	10	8	19	26
Marriage	15	15	8	7	2	3
Other Interpersonal	15	19	17	18	7	10
Job	12	13	14	25	10	15
R's Health	11	12	4	4	11	8
Family's Health	8	8	6	2	16	14
Independence; Absence of Burdens	10	18	—	—	—	—
Personal Characteristics (Problems)	2	6	14	10	5	4
Community, National and World Problems	—	—	7	17	8	8
Total Number	457	599	457	599	457	599

[a] Percentage responding with a given source in their first two mentions.

of Employment data, we would interpret these changes in seeing jobs as a source of worry to mean that people are not necessarily afraid of losing their jobs, but rather are afraid that if they had any inclination to change jobs (which many do), or to achieve greater flexibility in the nature of their work, they would be hard-pressed to effect any change. Their job futures are thus not very clear-cut. Ambiguity about work and lack of control over it have evidently become more central for people over this generation, and hence more people "worry" about their jobs.

The fact that working women are also more likely to talk about their jobs as a source of unhappiness we would interpret differently. There has apparently been a substantial change in women's willingness to mention some grievance about work as a locus of difficulty in their life experience. With the politicalization of women during the 1970s came a greater awareness of women's rights to be considered on an equal footing with men in the work place. Women have not only become more alerted to grievances about work, but are also more willing to talk about them to others.

Table 6.5 shows how often the job is mentioned as a source of worries, unhappiness, and happiness by men and women in different occupational groups within each year. It is clear from that table that women professionals show the largest increase in referring to their jobs in response to the question about unhappiness. Nine percent of professional women said their job was a source of unhappiness in 1957. This percentage had increased to 34 percent among the professional women in 1976. Professional women undoubtedly dominate the awakened political consciousness among working American women. The change observed in reports of job-focused unhappiness among professional women might well reflect this political sensitization rather than an increased and deep-rooted demoralization about work among this group. Note in this regard that 29 percent of professional women in 1976 also spontaneously mention their job as a source of *happiness*, more than any other group—male or female—in either year.

From these data we conclude that, for women, at least, jobs have become much more salient in 1976 than a generation ago. In fact, among working women in 1976, job unhappiness represents the most mentioned source of distress of any sort. Table 6.3 shows that it is also a very salient source of unhappiness among men; mentioned more frequently than any other category except unhappiness about community, national, and world problems in 1976. If we also consider the fact that sources of unhappiness coded as "economic and material" often reflect unhappiness about work even if they are not explicitly stated as such, it is clear that the job domain represents a critical focus of distress for American workers. The job also looms large as a source of worry. Its overall negative salience implies that it is a force to be contended with, something to be adapted to, something which remains as a constant source of discontent in the quality of working people's life experience.

Occupation as a Source of Identity

Chapter 3 examined various responses to questions about the self. We distinguished three types of self-perceptions: differentiation from

TABLE 6.5

Report of Job as Source of Happiness, Unhappiness and Worries in Different Occupational Groups: 1957–1976 (by sex)

Occupation	Total Number				Job as Source of Happiness				Job as Source of Unhappiness				Job as Source of Worries			
	Men		Women		Men		Women		Men		Women		Men		Women	
	1957	1976	1957	1976	1957 (%)	1976 (%)	1957 (%)	1976 (%)	1957 (%)	1976 (%)	1957 (%)	1976 (%)	1957 (%)	1976 (%)	1957 (%)	1976 (%)
Professional	116	132	55	113	24	20	27	29	28	38	9	34	19	37	11	20
Manager	116	122	37	41	17	17	8	22	23	26	16	27	35	30	16	24
Clerical	54	42	129	188	4	12	10	8	22	33	12	24	17	31	8	13
Sales	53	43	33	26	15	7	12	8	28	14	18	19	28	28	9	8
Skilled	210	175	8	11	9	9	—a	9	19	21	—a	18	15	20	—a	9
Operatives	161	114	73	69	10	9	11	6	24	38	22	22	17	20	14	15
Service	60	46	112	133	8	15	8	8	22	26	5	20	18	33	9	9
Unskilled	47	32	2	5	4	12	—a	—a	26	28	—a	—a	11	12	—a	—a
Farmer	86	31	7	11	8	13	—a	0	31	19	—a	—a	26	48	—a	36

a N<10; percent not computed, unreliable.

TABLE 6.6

Percent Mentioning Their Occupation as Source of Differentiation,
Shortcoming, and Strength in Self-Perception: 1957-1976[a]

(by sex, working people only)

Occupation Mentioned as:	Men		Women	
	1957 (%)	1976 (%)	1957 (%)	1976 (%)
Source of Self-Differentiation	4 $(761)^b$	4 $(631)^b$	1 $(376)^b$	2 $(510)^b$
Source of Shortcoming in Self	18 $(776)^b$	13 $(577)^b$	5 $(373)^b$	5 $(480)^b$
Source of Strong Point in Self	6 $(841)^b$	6 $(704)^b$	4 $(431)^b$	4 $(572)^b$

NOTE: Numbers in parentheses are total number of persons in each group.

[a] Across all possible mentions.

[b] Numbers vary because of differential response to questions with a codable response.

others, shortcomings, and strengths. For each of these self-conceptualizations, we may ask whether or not occupational status figures prominently in self-schema, focusing in this instance only on working respondents. Table 6.6 presents the percent of working men and women who explicitly make reference to occupation in response to questions about self-perceptions. These results suggest that occupation does not figure very prominently in self-definitions, although references to work are more common in response to the question about shortcomings than to questions about differentiation or strengths. Overall, while occupation is apparently quite salient with regard to worries and unhappiness, it does not seem to be as readily translated into identity-giving self-perceptions. There is a slight trend for fewer men in 1976 to report wanting their children to have a different occupation from them, but this difference is only 5 percent. From this limited content-analysis of self-description, we conclude that occupation does not figure very highly in the self-perceptions of American working men and women in either 1957 or 1976. Since a different way of questioning about the self might have elicited more occupational references, our conclusion here must be tentative.

The Relative Evaluation of Family, Leisure and Work Roles: 1976 Only

In 1976 we introduced a new series of questions that allowed us to evaluate how much respondents in 1976 valued certain life roles. From a list of life goals respondents were first asked to select the two that were most important to him or her, and then from these to select the *one* most important. Following this selection of values, respondents were asked to judge how much each of five roles (marriage, parenthood, work, leisure, work around the house) contributed to the primary values selected. These data have already been discussed in previous chapters on marriage and parenthood, where we found that both marriage and parenthood are roles most people find to be their primary sources of value fulfillment.

When we reexamine these data with a specific focus on jobs (see tables 4.6 and 4.7), we find that for certain groups work is their primary source of value fulfillment; but, for most people who have all three roles, marriage and parenthood take priority over jobs. Jobs, however, clearly take priority over leisure and work around the house. Only married, working fathers who place primary value on "security" select their job as the major role fulfilling that value. A group of older men who choose self-actualization as a primary value select jobs more than marriage as a source of self-actualization, but they still rate parenthood higher than work. Men who choose moral respect as a major value also find their jobs nearly as fulfilling as marriage and parenthood, suggesting that work is nearly as important as family roles for fulfilling the life goals of men with strong moral or moralistic orientations.

Although the preceding analyses focused on the relative importance of work and family roles, we can examine the same data on value fulfillment through work on an *absolute* basis to derive some additional understanding of the salience of work in America. We will do so in the next section.

ADDITIONAL ANALYSIS OF THE SALIENCE OF WORK

Measures

Three other areas of investigation that provide information about the salience of work in America in both 1957 and 1976 are general work commitment, women's reactions to the housewife role, and people's self-actualizing investments in leisure. In addition, we can analyze more directly people's responses in 1976 to the question about value fulfillment through work, along with people's preferences for being socially recognized as excellent at the work they do, over being either a good spouse or good parent (*Social validity through work*). (This last assessment is similar to *Social validity through marriage* and *Social validity through parenthood*, discussed in previous chapters). All of the items used in these analyses are listed in table 6.7. Let us discuss each in turn.

Year Differences in Work Commitment

One way to assess the salience of work in American society and its potential change over the generation is to look at the way people responded to a question asked in both years about whether or not they would go on working if they did not have to earn a living (and, if they

TABLE 6.7

Measures Related to the Salience of Work

Measure	Question	Code
Both 1957 and 1976		
Work Commitment:	If you didn't have to work to make a living, do you think you would work anyway? (Women 1957 only: if you didn't need the money that you get from working, do you think you would work anyway?) (IF YES) What would be your reasons for going on working?	
Achievement Commitment		Working gives feeling of accomplishment, makes you feel useful
Affiliative Commitment		Likes chance to be with people, friendships, helping people
Work as Habit		Only way of life respondent knows; easier to keep on what you're doing
Moralistic Commitment		Work keeps you healthy, prevents feeling useless or immoral, "good to work"
Time Use Commitment		Avoids boredom, upset if didn't work, go crazy if no work
Escape from Home Commitment		Better than housework, being with family, staying at home
General Like		Like to work; like the work I'm doing
No Commitment to Work		Answer "no" to the first question
Reactions to the Housework Role:		
Liking for Housework	Different people feel differently about taking care of a home—I don't mean taking care of the children, but things like cooking and sewing and keeping house. Some women look on these things as just a job that has to be done—other women really enjoy them. How do you feel about this?	*Expresses liking*: —"I like it." —"I like it" and gives reasons. —I like . . . (mentions particular aspect.) *Other*: —ambivalent —answer or expressed dislike
Career Orientation	Have you ever wanted a career?	Yes No

TABLE 6.7 (continued)

Measure	Question	Code
Plans to Work	Are you planning to work in the future?	Yes No
Challenging Use of Leisure	How do you usually spend your time when your work is done—what kind of things do you do, both at home and away from home?	Leisure challenging if mentions any of the following —gardens —construction —creative arts —homemaking hobby —collecting —fishing —sports —hobbies —political work —youth work

1976 Only

Measure	Question	Code
Value Fullfillment Through Job	How much (has/would/did) work at a job (led/lead) to (MOST IMPORTANT VALUE—see Table 4.1, p. 144)—*very little, a little, some, a lot, a great deal*	As stated
Value Fulfillment Through Leisure	. . . how much have the things you do in your leisure led to (MOST IMPORTANT VALUE, see Table 4.1, p. 144) in your life—*very little, a little, some, a lot, or a great deal*	As stated
Comparative Value Fulfillment of Work and Leisure	Based on two preceding questions.	*Low value fulfillment:* Evaluation for leisure higher than job. *Equal value fullment:* Evaluation for job same as leisure. *High value fulfillment:* Evaluation for job higher than leisure.
Social Validity Through Work	Now for each pair of statements I read, please tell me which one would you rather overhear a friend say about you. First, which of these: (a) She/he is a fine mother/father. (b) She/he is excellent at his/her work. Then: (a) She/he is a good wife/mother. (b) She/he is excellent at his/her work.	Social validation through work: *High:* Two (b) responses selected. *Moderate:* One (b) response selected. *Low:* No (b) responses selected.

TABLE 6.8

Work Commitment Among Working Men and Women in 1957 and 1976

	Men		Women	
Work Commitment	**1957 (%)**	**1976 (%)**	**1957 (%)**	**1976 (%)**
Would not go on working If Money Not Needed	15	16	42	23
Would go on Working If Money Not Needed	85	84	58	77
Reasons for Going on Working				
Achievement Commitment: (Working gives feeling of accomplishment, makes you feel successful)	4	12	1	10
Affiliative Commitment: (Likes chance to be with people, friendships, helping people)	2	3	8	10
Work as Habit: (Only way of life R knows; easier to keep on what you're doing)	2	3	2	2
Moralistic Commitment: (Work keeps you healthy, prevents feeling useless or immoral, "good to work")	9	8	3	4
Time Use Commitment: (Avoids boredom, upset if didn't work, go crazy if no work)	55	43	27	24
Escape from Home Commitment: (Better than housework, being with family, staying at home)	1	1	3	8
General Like: (Like to work, like the work I'm doing)	10	9	14	13
Total Number	924	763	301	612

said they would, why).[1] These questions are reproduced in table 6.7, and responses to them are presented in table 6.8. In particular, responses to the question about reasons for going on working are featured. It is clear that global commitment to work is as high in 1976 for men as it was in 1957. However, the pattern is different for women. Work commitment for women has increased since 1957 and is now almost as high as men's. While only 58 percent of employed women said they would go on working if they didn't need the money in 1957, 77 percent expressed a commitment of that sort in 1976. Reasons given for going on working have shifted noticeably for both sexes from 1957 to 1976, from seeing work as a use of time to avoid boredom or keep from going crazy, toward a conception of work as an arena for meeting challenges, a place where one feels useful and derives a sense of accomplishment.

Overall, these data suggest that the work role has not shifted much in salience for men, but work commitment has apparently increased considerably among women across the generation. Furthermore, work

[1] Note that this question was slightly different for women in 1957. Hence results which compare women across the generation or women to men in 1957 should be treated with some caution. The questions are very close, but are not worded identically.

now seems to be a role that holds somewhat more intrinsic interest than it did a generation ago for both sexes. In contrast, there is little evidence in either year of a strong moralistic commitment to work in the direct responses of our subjects, although the proportion indicating this type of commitment is greater for men than for women. Only about 8 or 9 percent of men in both years are explicitly committed to work as a way to keep healthy, to keep from feeling useless, or to maintain any explicit moral feeling. Such responses are also minimal among women in both survey years. Nevertheless, we hesitate to minimize Americans' moralistic commitment to their work, since "time use" is still the most frequent reason given for continuing to work by both men and women. Such responses come close to invoking the old adage: "The devil finds good use for idle hands." We thus cannot entirely rule out a moralistic pressure to work in our society.

To say that people work to avoid boredom or that they would get upset if they did not work are also responses that could easily be interpreted as reflecting people's shame or guilt if they did not work. A life of leisure is evidently a style of life that is still not an easy one for Americans to assume. However, the observed reduction in that type of response suggests that over the generation we may have become socialized to feel somewhat more comfortable about leisure as a way of life for ourselves. We will be discussing the impact of leisure on the work role more directly in a subsequent section of this chapter.

One final digression about the reasons given by working people for continuing to work in the absence of financial need. Women are clearly more aware of their affiliative bases for work than men. More women in both survey years say they would go on working without financial need in order to have contact with people. Men, never having been sensitized to the absence of social contact associated with not working, are presumably not very aware of the way that work may fill an affiliative void. In contrast, women's firsthand or vicarious knowledge of the potential social isolation of housewives in America makes them sensitive to this sort of investment in work. Having interpreted this result in that way, let us turn now to an analysis of change in perceptions of housewives about their work.

Year Differences in Reactions to the Housewife Role

Over the generation, increasing numbers of women have been turning away from being full-time housewives to the world of paid employment. Thus, as a counterpoint to women's general orientations to work, it is of interest to know how women in the traditional housewife role are reacting to its potential for gratification and frustration. Women's differential reactions in 1957 and 1976 to the role of housewife are assessed using the three questions listed in table 6.7. Table 6.9 presents differential responses to a housework satisfaction question in 1957 and in 1976, along with questions concerning career orientation and plans

TABLE 6.9

Reaction to the Housewife Role Among
Full-Time Housewives (by year)

Measure	1957 (%)	1976 (%)
Satisfaction with Housework		
Unqualified liking	50	46
Qualified liking	19	11
Ambivalent	14	18
Neutral	10	18
Qualified disliking	3	2
Unqualified disliking	3	3
Not ascertained	1	2
	100%	100%
Career Orientation		
Yes	36	39
No	63	60
Not ascertained	1	1
	100%	100%
Plans to Work		
Yes	16	30
No	81	68
Not ascertained	3	2
	100%	100%
Total Number	872	505

for future employment. That table shows that housewives have indeed shifted from a general liking for the role to being more ambivalent or neutral about housework. Our multivariate analyses in a later section of this chapter will show that this shift is evident within every age group except the most elderly, and at every education level except among the grade school educated.

On the other hand, no overall dramatic shift from 1957 to 1976 in career orientation is revealed in table 6.9. Nevertheless, our multivariate analyses will reveal some substantial shifts among young, college-educated housewives in career plans. There is a substantial increase between 1957 and 1976 in plans to work in the future among full-time housewives.

Year Differences in Gratification Through Leisure Activities

One presumed adaptation to a less involving work experience would be to focus one's energies and interests on leisure-time activities. Do we have any evidence from the questions we asked about how people spent their free time that such a shift has occurred?

One approach we used to address this question was to assume that if there has been a shift from work to leisure as a focal domain for feeling competent, then the types of activities that should receive increased emphasis should be those codable as "challenging" leisure pursuits. In both 1957 and 1976 we asked an open-ended question about leisure time (see table 6.7), about what our respondents do when their "work is done." Responses to this question were coded within a complex schema which designated those that use their leisure in ways that have some potential for deriving feelings of accomplishment or a sense of impact while partaking of them. These activities are also listed in table 6.7 and include such pursuits as gardening, homemaking, hobbies, fishing, sports, and political work.

While there has been an overall increase across the generation in participating in these kinds of challenging activities (from 73 percent to 76 percent among men, and from 63 percent to 67 percent among women) the increase is clearly not sizable enough to suggest that there are large groups of workers who feel pressed to compensate for an inadequate involvement with work with a more challenging involvement in leisure. Thus, nothing that we can detect from gross changes in leisure activity leads us to believe that Americans' feelings of accomplishment are now focused on leisure in compensation for felt lack of impact at work.

Value Fulfillment Through Work and Leisure, and Social Validation Through Work: 1976 Only

In previous chapters on marriage and parenthood, we used two measures of salience—value fulfillment and social validation through each role—both of which we will now also apply to the job role. The first depends on the degree of fulfillment that the job is perceived to contribute to a person's major life value (see table 6.7); the other depends on the extent to which work is preferred over the two family roles when a respondent is asked to choose between having a good reputation as a worker as opposed to being a parent or spouse (see table 6.7 for detailed wording).

In this section we will also introduce two other measures of value fulfillment that reflect on the salience of the work role. Since work and leisure pursuits are often paired—sometimes in opposition to each other—any indication that perceived value fulfillment through leisure is more or less than through work would also help us understand the importance of work to people. Thus, two other measures are also considered: the degree of value fulfillment through leisure reported by employed men and women; and, perhaps more important, the comparative value people say they derive from work and leisure (in effect, the value fulfillment through work minus value fulfillment through leisure, with only three distinctions made: work found more fulfilling than leisure, leisure found more fulfilling than work, and work and leisure found equally fulfilling).

These 1976 assessments are reported in table 6.10 for employed men and women, and for housewives. It is clear that most working men and women derive considerable value fulfillment through work. More than three-fourths of both sexes report that their job fulfills their major life value either "a lot" or "a great deal," compared with only about half of each group who say that leisure fulfills their major life value to the same degree. This difference is dramatized by the third measure presented in table 6.10, for which we find only 19 percent of employed men and women think that work fulfills their major life value *less* than their leisure pursuits. This total pattern is in marked contrast to housewives, who do not value their leisure any less, but clearly do value a

TABLE 6.10
Measures of Salience of Work
(by employed men and women, and housewives)

Measure	Employed Men (%)	Employed Women (%)	Housewives (%)
Value Fulfillment Through Work			
Great deal	42	34	20
A lot	37	40	25
Some	14	17	25
A little	3	5	13
Very little	4	4	17
	100%	100%	100%
	(747)	(595)	(461)
Value Fulfillment Through Leisure			
Great deal	21	21	21
A lot	35	33	27
Some	23	25	30
A little	10	10	9
Very little	11	11	13
	100%	100%	100%
	(748)	(596)	(488)
Comparative Value Fulfillment *of Work and Leisure*			
Work > leisure	49	45	34
Work = leisure	32	36	32
Work < leisure	19	19	34
	100%	100%	100%
	(747)	(595)	(461)
Social Validation Through Job			
High (job > parenthood, marriage)	13	15	5
Moderate (job > either parenthood or marriage)	22	32	22
Low (job < parenthood, marriage)	65	53	73
	100%	100%	100%
	(488)[a]	(370)[a]	(326)[a]

NOTE: Numbers in parentheses are total number of persons in each group.

[a] Asked of only two-thirds of the sample.

Working Men's and Working Women's Evaluation of How Much Work and Leisure Lead to Fulfillment of Primary Value Orientation (by age and value orientation, 1976 only)

Primary Value[b]	Age	Total Number		High Value Fulfillment in Work[a]		High Value Fulfillment in Leisure[a]		Value Fulfillment: Work > Leisure[c]		Leisure > Work[c]	
		Men	Women	Men (%)	Women (%)	Men (%)	Women (%)	Men (%)	Women (%)	Men (%)	Women (%)
Sociability	21–39	80	86	24	27	19	23	30	31	38	28
	40+	55	67	38	27	29	27	39	42	19	32
Hedonism	21–39	36	16	22	6	44	31	14	12	53	50
	40+	11	6	36	0	36	25	36	25	55	50
Self-Actualization	21–39	127	89	33	35	17	25	46	25	24	50
	40+	68	40	54	55	32	16	41	44	24	19
Moral Respect	21–39	89	79	38	34	18	30	44	50	18	15
	40+	135	92	51	41	22	21	55	46	10	10
Security	21–39	75	55	49	34	0	30	81	62	0	14
	40+	69	66	55	38	14	9	74	77	6	20
Total Across Values	21–39	407	325	34	31	18	19	46	42	24	6
	40+	338	269	50	38	24	24	53	49	14	21

[a] Percentage of people of a given value orientation who report that work/leisure leads to that value orientation "a great deal."

[b] See Table 4.1 (p. 144) for description.

[c] Percentage of people of a given value orientation who rate work higher or lower than leisure for fulfilling their primary value orientations.

potential job a lot less than employed women value their work. For housewives, then, leisure and work are arenas for value fulfillment that are more nearly on a par than is the case for employed men and women.

In table 6.11 we extend this analysis of the relative evaluation of work and leisure among working people by comparing those who report very high value fulfillment through work and leisure, according to both the primary value they select,[2] then by age[3] and sex. That table also presents the proportion of respondents who rate the value fulfillment of work higher than that of leisure and those who rate leisure higher. It is quite clear from that table that men and (to a lesser extent) women involved in security evaluate their jobs highly as they see their work primarily as a means of sustenance. In contrast, those whose values are either social or hedonistic tend not to rate the job role as highly as others, both with regard to its overall value fulfillment, and with regard to its value compared to leisure activities. Older men and women who value self-actualization also see work as being very fulfilling. We thus see that holding certain values (security, self-actualization) tends to strongly bind people to their jobs, while holding other values (sociability, hedonism) appears to free them to give at least equal weight to leisure. By and large, however, based on this analysis, work seems very important to most Americans.

The measure of *Social validation through work* provides us with a somewhat different picture, one we could deduce from earlier chapters on the family. When men and women are asked to think about how they want to be regarded in their social world, most of them clearly choose a reputation for excellence in their family roles over high regard as a worker. Only a small percentage of men and women select work over both family roles. This result corroborates our view that work is very salient compared to leisure, but not as salient compared to family roles. On an absolute basis, however, work remains a critical arena in American life for enacting one's values.

These conclusions must be tempered, however, by the realization that the majority of working women and working men are married. The relative salience of work and leisure for nonmarried people may be vastly different. Results pertaining to this issue are reported in table 6.12. They reveal a potentially critical difference in the way married and nonmarried people regard their work. Clearly, single men and women derive more of their social validity from work than married people. Without having experienced either family role, they are especially sensitive to their reputation as workers rather than to their hypothetical reputation as spouses or parents. The results further suggest that work is more critical to unmarried women than to unmarried men. For example, single men are more likely to rate leisure over work than

[2] See table 4.1 (p. 000) for a description of the different values.
[3] Contrasting younger (21–39) vs. older (40+).

TABLE 6.12

Marital Status Difference in 1976 Measures of Work and Leisure Salience for Working Men and Women

| | Marital Status | | | | | | | |
| | Men | | | | Women | | | |
Measure	Married (%)	Previously Married (%)	Single (%)	Married (%)	Previously Married (%)	Single (%)
Value Fulfillment Through Work						
Great deal	44	33	33	31	38	40
Value Fulfillment Through Leisure						
Great deal	21	23	18	19	24	23
Comparative Value Fulfillment						
of Work and Leisure						
Leisure higher	17	26	28	20	18	19
Social Validity Through Work						
More than parenthood, marriage	10	23	28	10	17	32
Total Number	383[a]	52[a]	53[a]	200[a]	120[a]	50[a]

[a] Question asked of only two-thirds of sample.

single women. Moreover, single men are more likely to deemphasize the fulfillment of values through work compared to their married counterparts, while the reverse is true for women. As a result, married men are much more likely to report deriving value from their work than married women.

This complex pattern of results suggests that unmarried men are much more in disequilibrium about their unmarried status than single or previously married women. Marital and parental aspirations may be so critical to men's well-being that they may supersede a dominant investment in work. They may instead be heavily involved in their leisure pursuits and meeting women in the ultimate pursuit of family-role status. Once married, the balance for men shifts to being concerned about their work—partially as a way to fulfill their family roles. Forty-five percent of young single men select self-actualizing values as their primary value orientation, compared to only 28 percent of young married men, who are much more likely than the single men to select security as a primary value (20 percent compared to 9 percent).

The shift from singlehood to marriage for young working women is much different. To be working and married in our society still involves different responsibilities for most men and women. The primary role for women is still largely one of maintaining a comfortable home and family life. For men, the primary responsibility is to be a good provider for the family. This traditional sex-role differentiation in dual-worker families may promote a very high salience of family roles for both sexes, but for men, work is more clearly instrumental toward fulfilling their family roles.

As we move into a world where both nonmarried and dual-worker statuses are more normative, we might predict that work will become increasingly salient for women and increasingly less salient for men as family roles become more optional for men and women. We might also predict that as dual-worker families become even more commonplace, and we come to adopt certain new norms about them, that men may well become less involved in work as a prime source of family identity and women more involved.

SUMMARY OF ANALYSES OF SALIENCE OF WORK

Overall, what can we now say about changes in the salience of work among Americans from 1957 to 1976? From two of our exploratory analyses comparing salience of the work role from 1957 to 1976, we derive some evidence suggesting that work may not be as critical today as family roles in Americans' hierarchy of values. We have some evidence that the work role is not particularly critical to self-definition, based on questions we asked about self-perceptions both in 1957 and in 1976. And, from our analysis of how critical work is relative to family roles in fulfilling primary values and as a source of social validity, we have some indication that work is as important as other roles only for certain groups of people.

Nevertheless, other analyses explored in this section all point to the fact that work remains a fairly strong area of concern among Americans. Work appears to underlie much of the anxiety and unhappiness expressed by people today and yet represents an area of life to which men and women are extremely committed—women even more so than twenty years ago. Work is a role that in all likelihood will become increasingly more involving for women as full-time housewives increasingly abandon that role for one involving paid employment. Furthermore, we find no evidence that presumed pressures to seek challenge from one's life from leisure pursuits have had any dramatic effects on the salience of work over the past twenty-five years. Among most working people, work is still preferred over leisure as a primary source of value fulfillment.

In sum, work is extremely salient to many men and women in our society, perhaps more than ever before. One might speculate that many more men and women place their egos on the line in relation to their work than in previous decades. We were indeed somewhat surprised to find that more people in 1976 did not choose to forgo working if they didn't have to. Considering that business enterprises and work settings have become so much larger and complex over the past generation, and that jobs have become increasingly specialized and more subject to control by management, one might speculate that more people would view the job world as something alien to them. A major hypothesis that we propose to account for the unusual commitment to work that seems to have been reinforced among both men and women over the past generation is that the rapid movement of women into the labor force has essentially served to underscore the value of work for both sexes.

Young single women appear to be particularly involved in work. Men and women for whom work provides greatest value fulfillment are those who identify themselves as seeking security or self-actualization as a major value. Among men with these values, work was rated more important than other roles, and for women work came close to marriage and parenthood as a most fulfilling role—at least in comparison with women who selected other primary values. As more women come to identify self-actualization as a primary value, we anticipate that work will become more and more salient to them. Although within the group of married, working mothers, no single-value orientation was perceived as having been better fulfilled through working than through marriage or parenthood, it is important to keep in mind that for women work at a job seems to fulfill most primary values better than either leisure or work around the house. Moreover, we suspect that as more men and women in dual-worker marriages begin to negotiate equity in the balance of work and family roles, the currently higher salience of work for married men vs. married women will diminish.

These data all support the conclusion that the job, while more important than leisure and work around the house for both men and women, achieves as great an importance as family roles only for people with certain value orientations. People with a moral work ethic—particularly those who value self-actualization—seem especially committted to work. Nevertheless, except among people who value sociability and hedonism, work is still of much more importance in people's lives than are their leisure activities.

Reactions to Work

We now turn to our major descriptive task of charting possible changes between 1957 and 1976 in men's and women's involvement with and adaptation to work environments. Reactions to be discussed cover three general topics: satisfaction with work; perceived competence at work; and perceived problems with work. We will consider each one of these topics in turn, although our major emphasis will be on satisfaction.

MEASURES

The questions used to measure each of these topics are presented in table 6.13.

Satisfaction with Work

If you were to ask most people what type of information would provide the clearest understanding of a worker's adaptation to and involvement with work, most would opt for an appraisal of worker satisfaction or affective investment in work. They would want to know whether workers felt *satisfied* or *dissatisfied* with their jobs, *happy* or *unhappy* with their work, *liked* or *disliked* what they were doing in their jobs. Although these terms for workers' affective experiences appear interchangeable, they clearly have different connotations. As discussed in chapter 2, "satisfaction" usually implies a cognitive balancing of aspirations or expectations with experience. "Liking" and "disliking" are less likely to involve an appraisal of standards, although people implicitly may use a cognitive standard. Similarly, appraising a job in terms of "preferences" implies a less clear behavioral commitment than the other terms.

In our surveys, we asked how American people experience their jobs in these three different ways, each involving a slightly different type of affective appraisal: *overall job satisfaction*, which uses the words "satisfied" and dissatisfied"; *perceived sources of job satisfaction and dissatisfac-*

TABLE 6.13
Questions and Codes Used to
Assess Job Reactions in the 1957 and 1976 National Surveys

Job Reaction	Question	Code
Job Satisfaction	Taking into consideration all things about your job, how satisfied or dissatisfied are you with it?	*Very Satisfied:* very good; real good; very happy; love my work; very well satisfied; couldn't be better
		Satisfied: good; pretty good; I like it; pretty well satisfied; basically satisfied
		Neutral: okay; all right, fair, average, so-so
		Ambivalent: mention both satisfaction and dissatisfaction; yes and no; good and bad; like it and don't
		Dissatisfied: not too good; not very well; unhappy; I don't like it; no good, terrible; I hate it
Type of Job Satisfaction	What things do you particularly like about the job?	Presence of:
Economic		—inadequacy of wages, money, salary —lack of job security
Extrinsic—Noneconomic		—nice place to work —easy work —convenience —employee benefits —physical working conditions
Achievement-Related		—responsibility —complexity —use of abilities —feelings of importance —recognition
Affiliation-Related (General)		—contact with people —helping people
Specific People		—satisfaction with particular people —nice people —friends —good boss

TABLE 6.13 (continued)

Job Reaction	Question	Code
Power-Related		—independence —no one pushes me around —leadership, teaching —prestige
Interesting Work		—job, work is interesting —novelty —chance to learn —like kind of work it is
Type of Job Dissatisfaction	What things don't you like about your job?	Presence of:
Economic		—inadequacy of wages, money, salary —lack of job security
Extrinsic—Noneconomic		—not a nice place —hard physical work —inconvenience —lack of employee benefits —hours —dirty place
General: Hard Work		—"hard work" —too much pressure
Lack of Achievement		—lack of responsibility —excess of responsibility —work too complicated —work too simple —nonuse of abilities —feeling of incompetence —lack of recognition
Lack of Affiliation		—no (little) contact with people —dissatisfied with particular people, superiors
Lack of Power		—not enough independence —too much restraint —not enough leadership —not enough prestige
Nothing		—R likes everything about work

TABLE 6.13 (continued)

Job Reaction	Question	Code
Job Commitment	Regardless of how much you like your job, is there any other kind of work you'd rather be doing?	No = commitment Yes = uncommitted
Perceived Ability Required	How much ability do you think it takes to do a really good job at the kind of work you do?	—a lot —some —a little —not much —none
Perceived Ability on Job	How good would you say you are at doing this kind of work, would you say you were: *very good, a little bit better than average, just average,* or *not very good?*	As stated
Work Problem?	Have you ever had any problems with your work—times when you couldn't work or weren't getting along on the job, or didn't know what kind of work you wanted to do? (If yes) What was that about?	
No Problem		No
Problem in Self		—didn't know what to do —was sick —wasn't doing well
Problem in Relationship at Work		—my boss and I could not get along
Problem in Situation		—that kind of work was bad —the hours —the factory was shut down
Problem in Other Person		—my boss, a specific person
General		—just couldn't find work

tion, based on the words "like" and "don't like"; and *job commitment,* which uses the phrase "rather be doing" to describe the kind of work a respondent might *prefer* to do. In our descriptive analyses of these measures, it should be borne in mind that slightly different cognitive schema may be triggered by the particular words or phrases used for each of these measures. Let us just briefly discuss each of these in turn.

1. *Overall job satisfaction.* In 1957, a measure of overall job satisfaction was used to derive a general appraisal of affective life on the job. As shown in table 6.13, responses vary from being "very satisfied" to "dissatis-

fied," with three intervening points: "satisfied," "neutral," and "ambivalent." Unlike a number of similar measures used in research conducted subsequent to the 1957 study, this question was essentially open-ended, allowing a respondent to structure perceptions of the quality of his/her job satisfaction in words most comfortable for him/her.

2. *Sources of job satisfaction and dissatisfaction.* In addition, subjects in both years were asked what things they particularly "liked" about their jobs and what things they did *not* like. These open-ended questions produced myriad responses which were coded with considerable attention to specific details of the quality of experiences of satisfaction and dissatisfaction. In table 6.13 we provide enough examples of responses coded within each category to orient the reader to what the categories mean. For example, under "extrinsic, noneconomic" sources of dissatisfaction we include "not a nice place," "hard physical work," "inconvenience," "lack of employee benefits," "hours," and "dirty place." These are dissatisfactions that are in a sense separate from the individual and his/her particular needs, and are thus coded as being *outside* the person. And, since they are not explicitly economic in focus, such responses are coded in this category. We will rely heavily on this set of categories to help us describe stability or change in the qualitative reactions to jobs from 1957 to 1976.

In particular, we are interested in isolating satisfactions and dissatisfactions that imply the perceived presence or absence of lack of *impact* on the job. "Lack of achievement" and "lack of power" in the work setting are clear dissatisfactions related to impact. Similarly, "achievement-related" and "power-related" satisfactions imply positive feelings about impact. Other categories of satisfaction and dissatisfaction indicate whether workers view affiliative aspects of the job as critical to their work life.

In addition to these specific content categories, dissatisfactions and satisfactions are also grouped along broader psychological dimensions of *ego involvement.* As in 1957, satisfactions and dissatisfactions on the job are classified as either "extrinsic" or "ego" involvements. By "ego" we mean those gratifications or frustrations which are derived directly from the activities that the worker performs at work. By "extrinsic" we mean something quite external to the person, a factor that does not directly implicate his or her ongoing work activity. The nature of the physical plant, structural situations of the organization (e.g., "working hours," "the pay," or "fringe benefits") are examples of extrinsic satisfactions or dissatisfactions, because they do not directly involve the person's ongoing activities while at work. Thus, in the category of ego satisfactions and dissatisfactions are *psychological* benefits or difficulties that a person encounters within the context of his work life.

This distinction is similar to but not identical with that proposed in recent discussions of "intrinsic" motivation for work (e.g., House, 1972) or performance in general (e.g., Deci, 1975; Lawler, 1973; Porter, Lawler, and Hackman, 1975). These more recent approaches have a narrower focus on the motivation for meeting challenges, for deriving recognition or having an impact at work. Such responses are coded as ego satisfactions or dissatisfactions here; but, in addition, we include some of the more social aspects or activities at work which are not considered by others to be intrinsic gratifications or frustrations. In essence, we feel that gratifications or frustrations that depend on the quality of social interactions have as much implication for ego involvement as the more traditional nonsocial sources of gratification or frustration. Therefore, our categories of "ego satisfactions" and "ego dissatisfactions" are much broader than those implied by the term "intrinsic" motivation used by others.

All responses to questions about what people like about work were coded as involving either "ego" or "extrinsic" satisfactions. All responses were then grouped into the following categories for each respondent: (1) all ego satisfactions mentioned; (2) some ego and some extrinsic; and (3) all extrinsic factors mentioned. This measure represents an assessment of *ego involvement with satisfaction*. A parallel measure of *ego involvement with dissatisfaction* was constructed according to the same procedure.

What exactly do these measures of ego involvement with satisfaction and dissatisfaction assess? We posit that a person who mentions ego satisfactions or dissatisfactions is particularly sensitized to psychological aspects of the work environment itself, i.e., psychological incentives to meet certain needs. When these are present, we assume that ego satisfaction occurs; when they are absent, the result is ego dissatisfaction. In contrast, when people are less involved with work, we assume that they would attend more to extrinsic aspects of the job, and more likely report satisfactions and dissatisfactions with "nonpersonal" aspects of the work environment.

Considerable evidence from *Americans View Their Mental Health* is consistent with this assumption. In 1957, the more people reported ego satisfactions about work, the more satisfied they tended to be, and yet they were more likely to report problems in their work. Similarly, the more people discussed ego dissatisfactions with work, the more dissatisfied they felt with their jobs and the more problems they expressed with regard to their work situation. Thus, ego dissatisfactions and satisfactions seem to reflect involvement with work rather than merely satisfaction or dissatisfaction. Such involvement can alert people not only to things that are satisfying about their experience, but also to problems that they are trying to overcome.

Such ego involvements with work were much more common among workers in higher-status jobs in the 1957 study. This finding alerted us to the possibility that our measure of ego involvement may reflect an upper-middle-class bias for what "involvement with work" should mean. We thus cautioned readers of the original volume about this possible bias, and we continue to emphasize that potential bias for readers of the present volume.

3. *Job Commitment.* A more indirect way to examine satisfaction with their jobs is to ask whether people would prefer different ones. Would they rather be doing something else? The job-commitment question does not refer to the specific job, but rather to the particular *kind of work* performed. We can imagine a number of people who are satisfied with their work but not their jobs, and vice versa.

Perceived Competence

Two questions were asked about employed men's perceptions of their work competence in 1957 that were repeated in 1976. Unfortunately, these items were *not* asked of employed women in 1957, but only in 1976. These questions are discussed below.

Perceived ability required. One question asked how much ability the respondent perceived that his/her job required. (See table 6.13 for exact wording.) A question directly preceding this one, which asked, "What does it take to do a really good job at the kind of work you do?" will also be examined to some extent in our discussion, but our focal concern is with responses to the question about perceived ability required. Responses to this open-ended question were categorized into the scale of perceived adequacy presented in table 6.13.

Perceived ability. Following the question about the perceived ability required to do one's job well was a close-ended question assessing the respondent's perception of his/her ability to do the work (see table 6.13). Although the wording of these two questions is not entirely commensurate, these assessments were designed to provide a useful comparison.

Perceived Problems

In addition to asking about job satisfactions, likes, and dislikes, and perceived competencies, we also sought to measures perceptions of problems at work, especially those that might have mental-health implications. The basic question, also listed in table 6.13, assessed whether or not such problems existed among employed men and women. In addition to determining the mere presence or absence of a problem we wanted to delineate the nature of the problems perceived. Thus, table 6.13 also presents one set of categories used to distinguish *types* of work-related problems, coded according to whether the perceived problem is structured in terms of the *self*, aspects of *relationships* with people on the job, *situational* factors at work, characteristics of specific *other people* at work, or some *general* difficulty not specifiable in one of the preceding categories. Of particular interest here is to determine whether, over these twenty years, employed workers are focusing their attention more on situational factors or on personal types of problems experienced at work. We will look at more specific codings of these types of problems mentioned in a subsequent section of this chapter.

Intercorrelations of Measures of Job Reactions

Before we look at the differences between the two survey years in reports of various kinds of job reactions, let us examine how these various measures relate one to another. We examined the intercorrelations of these general measures of job reactions in each year separately for working men and women. None of these intercorrelations are extraordinarily high, but they do bear out some of the assumptions we have been making about the nature of these measures. First, with regard to the meaning of ego involvement with satisfaction and dissatisfaction, we find in both years that the more ego involved people are with either satisfaction or dissatisfaction, the more satisfied or dissatisfied, respectively, they are with their jobs.

Interestingly, however, there is no positive correlation in either year for either sex between ego involvement in satisfaction and ego involvement with dissatisfaction. This result is reassuring because it suggests that these measures represent something more than people's general tendency to respond in a psychologically involved way about their jobs. If each measure primarily reflected such a response style, one would expect that people reporting ego involvement with satisfaction would also tend to do so with regard to dissatisfaction. However, those reporting ego involvement with satisfaction do *not* necessarily respond with ego involvement with dissatisfaction, or vice versa.

Also significant is the fact that, although the overall measure of job satisfaction and the measure of job commitment are positively related, they nevertheless manifest different patterns of correlations with other measures. Evidently, they represent somewhat different ways of assessing job well-being, and hence warrant analysis as two distinct measures. Similarly, the fact that people who mention having experienced some kind of job problem are more likely to express ego dissatisfaction with their work, or less commitment to their kind of work provides a degree of validation for the job-problem measure. Finally, with respect to measures of perceived competence, we find that perceiving one's job as demanding occurred more frequently among people expressing greater overall satisfaction and ego involvement with satisfactions.

These results all serve to corroborate the general logic and set of assumptions which underlie these assessments. Because we observe some degree of intercorrelation among the measures, we may anticipate that some redundant findings will appear in our separate analyses of them. Nevertheless, the correlations are so low that a separate examination of each measure clearly seems warranted.

Underlying this general pattern of intercorrelations are some distinct changes in the way these measures are related to one another in the two survey years. In particular, men's perceptions of their own abilities and of the abilities required of them appear to be differentially related to some of the other measures in 1957 and 1976. We find, for example, that there is a stronger relationship between perceived ability required and job commitment in 1976 (.15) than there was in 1957 (.01). In addition, perceived ability on the job is more highly correlated with expressed ego involved with satisfaction in 1976 (.14) than in 1957 (.01), but *less* correlated with overall job satisfaction in 1976 (.06) than in 1957 (.16). This pattern of results suggests that 1976 perceptions of people's job abilities or the abilities required by the job may be more directly related to ego involvements, and hence more susceptible to dynamic distortion. Several results to be presented in the following section corroborate this hypothesis. Perceptions of competence in work thus seem to be more strongly tied to motivational factors among working men now than twenty years ago. Unfortunately, since measures of perceived ability are not available for women in 1957, no parallel comparison is possible for them.

One differential trend in the pattern of intercorrelations across the two survey years among women that bears mentioning: a woman's commitment to her job in 1976 seems more tied to ego involvement with work than it was in 1957. Job commitment is both more positively related to ego involvement with satisfaction and more negatively related to ego involvement with dissatisfaction in 1976 than in 1957. These differences suggest that women's commitment to their jobs may reflect a much more psychological choice now than it did in the previous generation.

TABLE 6.14

Relationships (r) of Overall Job Satisfaction and Job Commitment
to Specific Source of Dissatisfaction Among Working Men and Women (by year)

	Men				Women			
	Job Satisfaction		Job Commitment		Job Satisfaction		Job Commitment	
Source of Satisfaction/ Dissatisfaction	1957 (%)	1976 (%)	1957 (%)	1976 (%)	1957 (%)	1976 (%)	1957 (%)	1976 (%)
Source of Satisfaction								
Economic	−.07[a]	−.11[b]	−.07[a]	−.03	−.16[c]	−.16[c]	−.03	−.06
Extrinsic–Noneconomic	.00	−.10[b]	−.02	−.09[a]	−.07	−.07	.05	−.05
Achievement-related	.11[c]	.11[b]	−.01	.02	.08	.15[c]	−.07	.05
Affiliation-related	.02	.09[a]	−.02	.07	.09[a]	.08	−.08	.04
Specific People	.04	−.03	−.03	−.13[c]	.08	−.02	−.01	−.01
Power-related	.01	.11[b]	.00	.05	.08	.04	−.03	−.02
Interesting Work	.09[b]	.09[a]	.03	.08[a]	.09	.05	.15[b]	.05
Source of Dissatisfaction								
Economic	−.10[b]	−.10[b]	−.01	.04	−.09	.04	.03	−.04
Extrinsic–Noneconomic	−.07[a]	−.03	−.13[c]	−.09[a]	−.05	−.03	−.07	−.03
General: Hard Work	.00	.06	.02	.00	−.10[a]	−.09[a]	−.05	−.02
Lack of Achievement	−.13[c]	−.09[a]	−.15[c]	−.08[a]	−.05	−.14[c]	−.10[a]	−.18[*]
Affiliative Lack	−.01	−.11[b]	−.09[b]	−.05	−.02	−.13[b]	.01	−.08
Lack of Power at Work	−.13[c]	−.05	−.03	−.03	.02	.03	.0	−.10
Total Number	911	755	916	752	450	608	295	608

[a] $p < .05.$
[b] $p < .01$
[c] $p < .001$

Table 6.14 shows how job satisfaction and job commitment are related to the sources of job satisfaction and dissatisfaction spontaneously mentioned by workers in both survey years. First, what qualities of satisfaction and dissatisfaction are correlated with overall job satisfaction? In both 1957 and 1976, men who express more job satisfaction tend to report more achievement-related satisfactions and more often say that the work is interesting. For women, the most consistent trend across the two survey years is that overall job satisfaction is negatively correlated with reporting economic sources of satisfaction.

In contrast to these consistent relationships, however, is an important difference across the two years in other correlates of job satisfaction. Men in 1976 high on job satisfaction are more likely than their counterparts in 1957 to report *social* types of job satisfaction—affiliative or power-related satisfactions. This difference is not apparent for women. Nevertheless, among women there is a rather sizable increase in the correlation between reports of achievement-related satisfactions and overall job satisfaction between 1957 and 1976. Thus, we might surmise that job satisfaction for men in 1976 is more strongly indicative of their feelings about the social situation of their work than it was a generation ago. By contrast, for women in 1976, feelings about job satisfaction are apparently more strongly indicative of their feelings about their own accomplishments. Each of these modest shifts appear to foreshadow an important change for each sex and to highlight a theme that will become increasingly pivotal in our analyses as our discussion progresses.

When we turn to correlations between job satisfaction and sources of dissatisfactions for men and women, we find that reporting lack of achievement as a source of dissatisfaction consistently relates to feeling dissatisfied with work in both survey years (except among women in 1957). Reports of affiliative dissatisfaction, however, seem to be correlated with overall job satisfaction only in 1976.

When we examine correlations for the measure of job commitment, these same results are not present. For men in 1976, job commitment is related to not mentioning specific people as a source of satisfaction at work. No such relationship is evident in 1957, or for women in either year. In contrast, lack of achievement as a source of dissatisfaction seems to be a consistent basis for reporting lack of job commitment among men and women in both survey years. The only other consistent pattern is that the more men mention extrinsic factors as sources of dissatisfaction, the less committed they are to their work.

Overall, the following pattern seems to emerge: achievement issues seem to underlie many of the specific satisfactions or dissatisfactions that influence people's evaluations of their overall job satisfaction. Women's job satisfaction in particular seems to be more strongly related to achievement issues now than twenty years ago. On the other hand, men's satisfaction seems to be more highly related to affiliative issues now than twenty years ago.

Reporting lack of achievement at work also seems to be the only factor consistently related to how much men and women would prefer another job. In summary, achievement concerns appear to be dominant in responses about job commitment and job satisfaction, but we should also keep in mind that social concerns of men at work are apparently becoming more critical to their feelings about their jobs today than was the case a generation ago.

YEAR DIFFERENCES IN JOB REACTIONS

Table 6.15 presents comparisons between 1957 and 1976 for the variety of measures of job satisfaction that we have been discussing. In subsequent tables we will present year differences in reported job competence and work problems. In each of these tables we report results separately for working men and women. As in previous chapters, we will highlight overall differences here and later present results of log-linear analyses which serve to qualify any of these general statements after partialling out the effects of sex, age, education, year, and their interactions.

Changes in Satisfaction

Overall satisfaction.   Table 6.15 shows that men and women in 1976 express slightly more dissatisfaction than their counterparts in 1957. Such differences are more apparent in women's responses than among men and, as we shall see in subsequent analyses, especially striking among younger, more educated, employed women.

Sources of job satisfaction.   While for both men and women there has been no substantial change from 1957 to 1976 in mentioning economic or extrinsic factors in job satisfaction, there have been some interesting shifts in the psychological types of satisfactions. For both sexes there has been a notable decline in reporting that a job is "interesting" as a basis for one's satisfaction. For men, this decline has been more than offset by increases in the mention of impact-related satisfactions— achievement and power, in particular. For women, a parallel increase is evident for achievement-related satisfactions, but not for power-related satisfactions. In both years, however, the most often reported satisfactions for women are related to affiliation.

Based on these results, it is possible to speculate about what may account for the drop noted in overall levels of satisfaction. Especially worthy of note is the finding that fewer people in 1976 mention that their work is *interesting.* Recalling from table 6.14 that people who regard their work as interesting are especially likely to express high overall job satisfaction, we might interpret the slight decrease evident in overall job satisfaction as a response to decreases in people's perceiv-

TABLE 6.15

Measures of Job Satisfaction in 1957 and 1976 Compared (by sex)

	Men		Women	
Measure of Job Satisfaction	**1957 (%)**	**1976 (%)**	**1957 (%)**	**1976 (%)**
Overall Satisfaction				
Very Satisfied	28	27	38	29
Satisfied	48	47	40	42
Neutral	5	5	5	4
Ambivalent	10	8	8	10
Dissatisfied	8	12	8	14
Not ascertained	1	1	1	1
	100%	100%	100%	100%
Source of Job Satisfaction[a]				
Economic	17	14	13	12
Extrinsic—Noneconomic	26	20	18	20
Achievement-related	17	30	11	22
Affiliation-related (general)	18	22	34	38
Specific people	16	12	26	22
Power-related	14	22	9	10
Interesting work	33	22	29	20
Source of Job Dissatisfaction[a]				
Economic	18	14	10	11
Extrinsic—Noneconomic	31	28	29	22
General: Hard Work	12	13	12	13
Lack of Achievement Potential	6	8	4	9
Affiliative Lack or Problem	10	19	12	20
Lack of Power at Work	4	10	4	5
Ego Involvement in Job Satisfaction				
Only Ego Satisfaction Mentioned	55	64	65	67
Some Ego, Some Extrinsic Satisfaction Mentioned	23	16	16	15
Only Extrinsic Satisfaction Mentioned	16	15	12	14
No Satisfaction	2	2	2	2
Not ascertained	4	3	5	2
	100%	100%	100%	100%
Ego Involvement in Job Dissatisfaction				
Only Ego Dissatisfaction Mentioned	19	35	21	38
Some Ego, Some Extrinsic Dissatisfaction Mentioned	8	8	4	8
Only Extrinsic Dissatisfaction Mentioned	46	40	41	32
No Dissatisfaction	24	15	27	20
Not ascertained	3	2	7	2
	100%	100%	100%	100%
Job Commitment: Not Prefer Other Job	60	50	49[b]	51
Total Number	924	753	457	599

[a] Types of job satisfaction and dissatisfaction do not add up to 100 percent because some respondents mentioned more than one source.

[b] Asked of only two-thirds of the women (N=300).

ing their work as interesting. Sensitization to achievement possibilities at work and sensitization to intrinsically interesting aspects of a job may well be mutually exclusive orientations: people who are highly absorbed in their work as a task to be done, as a process independent of their own accomplishments, may, in a sense, withdraw their attention from specific individual achievements or mastery, and vice versa. A greater focus on individual gratification probably results in a reduced focus on absorption in work as interesting. In assessing the nature of work satisfaction in America today, one might well ask: Are we moving in the direction of being more discontented with work because of an increased stress on achievement motivation?

In a previous volume, Veroff and Feld (1970) found that in 1957, men who were highly achievement motivated in their work more often expressed dissatisfaction in whatever type of work they had. The authors concluded that specific achievement mastery in work often reflected meeting goals that were set with ever-increasing standards of performance. Men and women who are achievement involved in their work often feel restless and tense even after successful accomplishment. One accomplishment induces thinking about another, ad infinitum. A constant press for more individuation, more achievement, and more evaluation of performance in comparison to others might well be the result of a strong focus on achievement orientation in work. And with such pressures may come a decreased intrinsic involvement with work and decreased satisfaction overall.

Overall, evidence presented in table 6.15 suggests that the last twenty years has *not* seen a diminution in people's feelings that they have some impact in their work. On the contrary, an *increase* in the mention of achievement-related and power-related sources of job satisfaction among both men and women across the generation generally holds for all educational levels and all age levels. Apparently there has been a shift either in how jobs themselves are structured for more individuated satisfactions, or in how people have been socialized to structure the satisfactions they derive from work. Increasing numbers of jobs have become more specialized over the generation, a change which could result in more people thinking in *individuated* terms about their job satisfactions. In addition, the generation spanning 1957 to 1976 has been more explicitly socialized to think about gaining individual gratifications from work. In either case, in the process of deriving more satisfaction from work for impact-related incentives, men and women have apparently lost some of their intrinsic investment in work, a loss which may have fostered a decline in overall job satisfaction.

Sources of job dissatisfaction. When we look at changes in sources of job dissatisfaction between 1957 and 1976, we see some evidence that workers are somewhat more conscious of their lack of personal impact, but these changes are very slight. There is an increase among men in perceiving lack of power at work and a slight increase for women in their reporting lack of achievement as a source of dissatisfaction. Overall, however, such sources of dissatisfaction are not very prevalent in the hierarchy of discontent among working people in 1976. In contrast, a response that did increase rather remarkably is seeing something wrong in one's social relationships at work, coded as an "affiliative lack or problem." This appears to reflect an important cultural shift in the nature of expressed dissatisfactions with job settings in America. Furthermore, mentioning affiliative dissatisfactions is consistently correlated with overall job dissatisfaction for both men or women (see table 6.14), along with reports of lack of achievement potential at work. In a sense, there seems to be an "ungluing" of the social integrative bonds that people tend to foster in their work setting. Working men and women complain more about not getting along with people at work, or that people are not nice, or that they have trouble with particular people at work. This trend seems to indicate an increased level of concern about human interaction and its problems in the work setting that was not very apparent a generation ago.

We can only speculate about the causes of this change. One plausible hypothesis is that as we have developed more individuated expectations for job satisfaction, in conjunction with placing a greater emphasis on individual, competitive performance at work, people have become more distrustful of others at work. Greater emphasis on the individual implies less emphasis on the work organization, and a greater emphasis on individual accomplishment implies less emphasis on affiliative relationships with other people at work. Increased specialization in work functioning also results in less bonding among people doing the same thing, even if they work together. In addition, within increasingly hierarchical industrial organizations there is less horizontal concern about work associates, especially if they are seen as competitors for promotion. This phenomenon takes on added significance as many more people enter a glutted job market in the shadows of concern about unemployment.

We feel that this increase in affiliative dissatisfaction is one of the most revealing insights gained from our analysis of these data. Previously, there has been little emphasis in social criticism of the job setting about this particular dimension of the work experience. Although considerable attention has been given to the lack of impact that people seem to feel in their work, there has been little emphasis on reduced feelings of social integration with other workers on the job. To the extent that work represents an occasion for people to come together—to associate and feel part of a social group, whatever work they do—the observed increase in reported dissatisfactions about affiliative aspects of work represents a critical new problem in the lives of American workers. Given current concerns about the loss of community feelings in neighborhoods and towns, and among local groups in general, this apparent breakdown in feelings of community within the work place may well have more devastating consequences for well-being than other feelings of discontent. Working represents a primary way for people to feel connected to others, and, if that connection is breaking down, the prospect of mushrooming alienation within the society at large appears to be distinctly possible.

Ego involvement in job satisfaction and job dissatisfaction. From the distribution of responses categorized as reflecting ego involvement in job satisfaction or job dissatisfaction presented in table 6.15, we observe only a slight increase in both men and women's ego-involved responses to job satisfaction, but a remarkably strong increase in mentioning ego-involved sources of job dissatisfaction. From these results we may conclude that there is greater sense of expressing oneself in the job in 1976 than in 1957, and in that sense jobs have become more psychologically salient for people.

Notable here is the fact that ego involvements with either satisfactions or dissatisfactions are no more nor less correlated with job satisfaction in 1976 than twenty years prior. Therefore, although working Americans have moved in the direction of seeing ego-involved satisfactions and dissatisfactions to a greater extent now than twenty years ago, this shift in cognitive orientation to the nature of job satisfaction and dissatisfaction apparently did not influence how people evaluate their overall job satisfaction. For men, we should recall that there is a larger correlation in 1976 between ego involvement with satisfactions (and dissatisfactions) and perceived competence. Thus, ego involvement in satisfaction and dissatisfaction may well serve to distort perceptions of job ability more so now than a generation ago, but it has little effect on overall satisfaction.

TABLE 6.16

*Relationship of Job Commitment to Work Commitment
Among Employed Men and Women (by year)*

	Men				Women			
	1957		1976		1957		1976	
	Job Committed:		Job Committed:		Job Committed:		Job Committed	
	Yes (%)	No (%)	Yes (%)	No (%)	Yes (%)	No (%)	Yes (%)	No (%)
Work Committed								
Yes	84	86	84	81	67	46	75	78
No	16	18	14	18	31	54	24	21
Not ascertained	<1	1	2	1	2	0	1	1
	100%	100%	100%	100%	100%	100%	100%	100%
Total Number	589	356	379	373	147	148	314	294

Job Commitment. Table 6.15 also shows a 10 percent drop in men's commitment to the kind of work they were doing between 1957 and 1976. Sixty percent of working men said they would *not* prefer another job or kind of work in 1957, compared to only 50 percent in 1976. Among women, however, there is an actual increase. Hence, we observe a decreased job commitment among men over the twenty years and no significant change for women. As a result, women's job commitment in 1976 is essentially equal to that of men.

With regard to differences in commitment between working men and women in 1957, we suspect that at that time more women were working out of necessity rather than out of commitment to work in and of itself. Hence, many of those who said they would prefer other work were likely thinking in terms of not working at all. Evidence presented in table 6.16 basically corroborates this hypothesis. In that table, men and women in both 1957 and 1976 who said they would prefer another kind of work (job) are compared with regard to how committed they would be to working if they had no financial need to do so. Women in 1957 who said they would prefer another kind of work were indeed much more likely than any other group in either year to say they would not work if they didn't have to.

Consequently, if we look only at those men and women who were committed to working, we observe the same decline in job commitment among women between 1957 and 1976 that we previously found for all men. Table 6.17 indicates a 9 percent drop in job commitment among both men and women who were work committed. Thus, when we control for work commitment, we observe the same sort of decline in women's job commitment that we found in their job satisfaction.

Overall, then, from 1957 to 1976 we observe both stability and some striking changes in reports about job satisfaction and commitment. There has been only a slight overall drop in general job satisfaction, and this drop is evident primarily among women. Of greater significance, perhaps, is that reports of impact-related satisfaction have apparently increased for both men and women, while reports of finding

TABLE 6.17

Percent of Employed Men and Women who
Report Preferring Other Work Among Those
who are Committed to Work (by year)

	Prefer Other Work			
	Total Number	1957 (%)	Total Number	1976 (%)
Men	781	60	626	51
Women	109	59	466	50

work interesting have declined. While there has also been some increase in the report of impact-related dissatisfactions, perhaps more striking is a clear increase in the reports of more social integrative types of dissatisfactions. Overall, men and women's commitments to their jobs seem to have declined, especially when we control for their general commitment to work. On the whole, then, positive feelings about work seem to be on the decline, but it is hard to specify the factors behind this trend. Based on the year differences observed here, however, this decline is apparently more a function of changes from a task orientation to a more individuated orientation to work, and to increases in problems with affiliative relationships at work, than to feelings about a lack of personal impact on the job.

Perceived Competence

We turn now to the measures available in 1957 and 1976 for assessing people's sense of their own ability to perform at work: *perceived ability required* and *perceived ability*. The former assesses people's perceptions of how much is demanded of them by their jobs, and the latter how well they think they actually do what is required of them. Unfortunately, these questions were *not* asked of women at all in 1957, and only of one-third of the 1957 male sample.

TABLE 6.18
*Measures of Perceived Job Competence
in 1957 and 1976 (by sex)*

	Men		Women	
Measures	1957 (%)	1976 (%)	1957 (%)	1976 (%)
Perceived Ability Required				
A Lot	39	54	—[a]	45
Some	13	12		11
Little	8	9		9
Not Much, None	14	11		17
A certain kind	16	10		13
NA, DK	10	4		5
	100%	100%		100%
Perceived Ability at Job				
Very Good	30	52	—[a]	59
Better than Average	42	33		30
Average	26	12		11
Not Very Good	1	<1		<1
NA	1	2		<1
	100%	100%		100%
Total Number	312[b]	753	—[a]	599

[a] Question not asked of employed women in 1957.

[b] Asked of only one-third of the 1957 male sample.

As shown in table 6.18, men's perceptions of both the level of ability required in their work and of their own perceived abilities have increased substantially from 1957 to 1976, and fewer workers in 1976 report either that they do not know how much ability is required and what their own ability is. These results are striking. Essentially, employed men in 1976 are not only more likely than male workers in 1957 to perceive their jobs as demanding great ability, but are also more likely to indicate that they are up to the challenge (i.e., that they are very good at their work).

One possible way to gain insight about forces which may underlie this dramatic change is to look at potential differences in specific job requirements mentioned by employed men in the two survey years. Men and women in 1976, and men in 1957, were asked what sort of things are important for doing their job well. The exact question was: "What does it take to do a really good job at the kind of work you do?" The year comparisons in men's responses to this question are presented in table 6.19.

There is a surprising correspondence in the distributions of re-

TABLE 6.19

Perceived Types of Requirements for a Good Job at Work being done by Men and Women (by year, first mention)

Requirement for a Good Job	Men		Women	
	1957 (%)	1976 (%)	1957 (%)	1976 (%)
Training	2	3	—[a]	2
Experience	3	5	—[a]	3
Skill	43	46	—[a]	44
General competence	21	21		19
General social competence	6	8		10
Specific job skill	16	17		15
Interests	14	16	—[a]	18
General achievement interest	6	8		6
General social interest	1	3		5
Specific job interest	7	5		7
Other Traits				
Strengths	6	5	—[a]	4
Hard working orientation	3	5	—[a]	4
Reliability	20	16	—[a]	20
Honesty	1	<1	—[a]	<1
Other	0	2	—[a]	3
DK; NA	2	2	—[a]	2
	100%	100%		100%
Total Number	313[b]	763	—	629

[a] Question not asked of women in 1957.

[b] Question asked of only one-third of the men in 1957.

sponses in both years. Forty-three percent of the men in 1957 responded to the question by mentioning some sort of skill, either general
competence (21 percent), a social skill (6 percent), or a specific job skill
(16 percent). Comparable proportions for 1976 employed men were 46
percent for the overall mention of skills, of which 21 percent were general competence, 8 percent, a social skill, and 17 percent, specific job
skills. The proportion of people mentioning a particular interest that a
person must have to do a good job at his/her work is also nearly identical in the two survey years. Similarly, reliability as an asset for doing a
good job was described by 20 percent of employed men in 1957 and 16
percent in 1976. Thus, there is very little difference between 1957 and
1976 in employed men's perceptions of work requirements: most people answered in terms of skills; a fairly sizable group responded in
terms of specific interests that people might have. Moreover, women's
responses in 1976 also conform fairly well to those given by men.

Thus, one cannot explain the observed increase in perceived capacity
to do one's job on the basis of changes in what men report is required
in their work. The same basic types of skills and interests and traits are
listed by employed men in 1957 and 1976. Hence, we must look for another explanation. One plausible hypothesis is that men have become
more *involved* in perceiving their work as demanding and themselves
as being competent at their work. As a result, many more men today
may distort the amount of ability required or being exercised in their
work.

To evaluate this hypothesis, we examined ratings from the *Dictionary
of Occupational Titles* for the occupations reported by our sample. Our
analysis of those ratings suggests that the jobs held by men in 1976 are
indeed more complex in certain ways than those held in 1957, but
there are also indications that men are distorting the actual difficulty of
their work. For example, in 1957 there was a higher correlation (.42)
between the *Dictionary of Occupational Titles* rating of men's jobs for
"routinization," and their subjective feelings about how much ability
was required on the job than in 1976 (.19). Thus, as men have become
more concerned that their work be ego gratifying and responsive to
needs for expressing their abilities, they are apparently more likely to
distort how much a given job allows them to do just that. As men develop more of a stake in seeing their work as demanding, they may indeed begin to see it that way.

An alternative interpretation might be that as jobs have become more
specialized, more people are seeing themselves as uniquely qualified
for the particular slot they have been assigned. As a result, social comparison with other people becomes somewhat more diffuse and workers begin to inflate their perceptions of both their own abilities and the
requirements of their jobs. The very uniqueness of a job may foster the
perception that the job is demanding; and this same uniqueness may

result in people seeing themselves as very capable in their work, since they have few other people with whom to compare their performance.

Perceived Problems at Work

Once again, comparisons between 1957 and 1976 in the prevalence and types of problems that Americans experience at work can be made only for men, since the questions about work problems was not asked of women in 1957. Tables 6.20 and 6.21 show how men in both surveys (and women in 1976) responded to our question about problems they might have encountered at work. The first table (table 6.20) includes the percentage of people who said they had no problem at all, along with the proportions of those who said that they did have a problem differentiated according to the way they structured these problems in attributional terms. An alternative coding of these problems is presented in table 6.21.

While there has been a significant increase in reporting problems at work, the ways in which men in 1976 tend to structure their problems are not very different from those observed in 1957. The only significant change is in the "general" category which is infrequently used in both survey years. Thus, other than a greater tendency for men in 1976 to structure their work problems in fairly general or vague terms, the increased sensitization to work problems appears to take many forms, none of which are particularly distinctive from the ways in which such problems were described twenty years ago.

The alternative coding of problems reported by men in the two generations in table 6.21 also suggests no remarkable increase in any spe-

TABLE 6.20

Perceived Problem in Work in 1957 and 1976 (by sex)

Work Problem	Men				Women			
	1957 (%)		1976 (%)		1957 (%)		1976 (%)	
No Problem	73		59		—[a]		71	
Has Problem	27		40				29	
In Self		11		17				10
In Relationship at Work		3		4				5
In Situation		9		9				8
In Other Person		2		4				3
General		2		6				3
Not Ascertained	<1		1				0	
	100%		100%				100%	
Total Number	895		742		—[a]		596	

[a] Question was not asked of employed women in 1957.

TABLE 6.21

Perceived Type of Problem at Work

(by sex × year, first mention)

Type of Problem	Men		Women	
	1957 (%)	1976 (%)	1957 (%)	1976 (%)
Holding a Job				
Physical Health Problem	2	4	—[a]	4
Mental Health Problem	<1	2	—[a]	1
Economic Situation	5	4	—[a]	2
Job Choice	8	12	—[a]	6
Difficulties with Achieving	3	3	—[a]	2
Difficulties with Relationship(s)	4	10	—[a]	10
Not Enough Impact in Work	1	1	—[a]	2
Extrinsic Problem	3	3	—[a]	2
No Problem Experienced	74	61	—[a]	71
	100%	100%		100%
Total Number[b]	887	723	—[a]	582

[a] Question not asked of women in 1957.

[b] Those not ascertained excluded.

cific type of problem. There are slight increases in reporting problems of vocational choice and relationship problems. Both of these increases represent a greater psychological orientation to the work setting, suggesting perhaps that more men in 1976 have a psychological perspective on problems at work.

However, since an increased psychological orientation was also observed in men's descriptions of their marital problems, these results may reflect a generalized increase in sensitization to psychological problems, whether it be in work, marriage, or another area. Thus, rather than reflecting a change in the work environments of men over the generation, this finding may result from a change in men's attitudes about the types of problems they are willing to discuss with an interviewer. It has become more normative for men to recognize such problems, to verbalize them to themselves, and to talk about them with another person.

Multivariate Analyses of Work Salience and Job Reactions

Multivariate analyses of information pertaining to the job role are summarized in two tables—one for measures relevant to the salience of work (table 6.22), the other for measures of job reactions (table 6.25).

TABLE 6.22

Summary of Multivariate Analyses of Measures Relevant to Assessing the Salience of Work

Measures Relevant to the Salience of Work	Relationship(s) Required[a] to Reproduce Observed Cross-classification of Measures of Work Salience by Age × Education × Year × Sex				
	Main Effects[c]				Interaction
	Age	Education	Year	Sex	
-1976 Measures					
all Work Commitment:	—[d]	—[d]	—[d]	M > F	—[d]
Men		G,H < C		—[b]	
Women		G,H < C	57 < 76	—[b]	
ons for Working Without nancial Need:					
Achievement		G,H < C	57 < 76		
Bored			57 > 76	M > F	
Affiliation				M < F	
Moral		G,H > C		M > F	
Avoid staying home				M < F	
faction with Housework	Y < MA < O	G > H > C	57 > 76	—[b]	
er Orientation		G < H < C		—[b]	Age × Educ. × Year
s to Work	Y < MA < O			—[b]	Age × Year; Educ. × Year
lenging Use Leisure		G < H < C		M > F	Age × Educ.; Educ. × Sex; Age × Sex × Year
Measures					
e Fulfillment rough Work	Y < MA < O		—[e]		Age × Educ.
e Fulfillment rough Leisure	Y,MA < O	G < H < C	—[e]		
parative Value lment of Work d Leisure:					
Leisure > work	Y,MA < O		—[e]		
l Validation rough Job		G,H < C	—[e]	M < F	Age × Educ.

Footnote a Table 2.11 for an explanation of "Required."

x effects inappropriate in data.

Footnote a Table 2.11 for an explanation of "Main Effects."

oss-classification is run separately for males and females because a complex four-way interaction involving both the measure of job n and sex needed to explain the five-variable cross-classification.

ar effects inappropriate.

We will discuss qualifications to year comparisons resulting from analyses summarized in these two tables separately.

QUALIFICATION TO YEAR COMPARISON: THE SALIENCE OF WORK

Although there are a few exceptions, the multivariate analyses summarized in table 6.22 tend to corroborate findings previously highlighted in our previous analysis of year differences in the salience of work. Thus, the following 1957–1976 changes persist when controls are imposed: (1) increased commitment to work among women; (2) a decreased, but still heavy dependence by both men and women on work to structure their time in 1976, accompanied by an increased commitment to work as an arena for achievement strivings; and (3) decreased satisfaction of housewives with housework.

In contrast, a few qualifications to our previous analyses should be noted. First, whereas we noted a slight increase in housewive's desires to pursue careers by 1976, this increase is evident almost entirely among three specific groups of women highlighted in table 6.23: young, high school–educated women, and middle-aged and older college-educated women. For somewhat different reasons, these particular women entered marriage with more traditional expectations about not working, but in recent years have undoubtedly been socialized to consider a career as a means of social validation. Many housewives in these groups today may feel embarrassed because they are not "doing something" other than housework. This socialization process has not to the same degree filtered down to less educated women—especially to middle-aged and elderly housewives. If anything, these women show a reverse pattern, which may represent increasing polarization among educational groups in our society as more educated people shift the

TABLE 6.23

1957–1976 Comparisons of Housewives' Wish to Have Careers and Plans to Work (by age × education)

		Total Number		Wish for Career		Plans to Work	
Age × Education		1957	1976	1957 (%)	1976 (%)	1957 (%)	1976 (%)
21–34	Grade School	32	6	34	17	47	33
	High School	211	94	40	64	23	69
	College	49	50	55	60	22	66
35–54	Grade School	91	18	32	11	14	11
	High School	167	91	34	25	18	29
	College	52	30	46	73	23	50
55+	Grade School	169	92	27	12	4	2
	High School	78	84	35	32	5	5
	College	16	33	38	55	0	9

standards of the ideal life. A similar phenomenon is also apparent in how lower-status groups in 1976 react to increasing pressures to seek professional help as a way to handle personal problems (see chapter 5, Book 2).

Second, although we noted a striking general increase in plans to work among housewives, this shift is largely accounted for by increases among younger and more educated women. Younger and more educated housewives in both years often plan to work. Moreover, while the year effect is hardly apparent at all among less educated women (see table 6.23), an increase in career plans is quite evident for all college-educated housewives and among the high school-educated young. These women are most likely to have turned to work for gratification of their achievement and social interests. These results may also shed some new light on what men regard as attractive and interesting in their work. As women are increasingly moving onto "their territory," we might speculate that men are becoming more possessive and appreciative of potential or perhaps even illusory satisfactions that can be found in work. All and all, then, our qualifications to previous analyses contrasting women's reactions to being full-time housewives over the generation still imply that men as well as women may have an increased interest in the value of work.

Third, while we observed no general change from 1957 to 1976 in how much Americans spend their leisure in challenging pursuits, one particular group does show a sizable increase: young women (58 percent in 1957 to 76 percent in 1976—see table 6.24). This shift, which is equally apparent for young women in all marital statuses, may reflect the recent socialization of young women to pursue their personal needs for actualization in leisure as well as in work, while they are considering marriage or rearing a family. In the past, younger women were not encouraged to follow such leisure pursuits because they were

TABLE 6.24

Employed Men and Women's Participation in Challenging Leisure Activities (by age by year)

		Year				
		1957		1976		
Age	Total Number	Men (%)	Women (%)	Men (%)	Women (%)	Total Number
Young	292	74		82		315
	144		58		76	269
Middle-aged	445	77		69		281
	235		66		62	220
Old	185	76		66		157
	74		62		57	109

TABLE 6.25

Summary of Multivariate Analyses of Reactions to Jobs

Measures of Job Reaction	Relationship(s) Required[a] to Reproduce Observed Cross-Classification of Measures of Job Reaction by Age × Education × Year × Sex				
	Main Effects[c]				Interaction
	Age	Education	Year	Sex	
Job Satisfaction					
Overall Job Satisfaction	Y < MA < O	G < H < C			Age × Educ. × Year
Ego Involvement in Job Satisfaction	Y < MA < O	G < H < C		M < F	
Ego Involvement in Job Dissatisfaction		G < H < C		M < F	
Job Commitment	Y < MA < O				Year × Sex
Perceived Source of Job Satisfaction:					
Economic		G > H > C		M > F	
Extrinsic—Noneconomic		G > H > C			
Achievement-related		G < H < C	57 < 76		
Affiliation-related	Y < MA < O	G < H < C		M < F	
Specific People				M < F	
Power-related			57 < 76	M < F	
Interesting Work	—d	—d	—d		—d
men			57 > 76	—e	
women		G < H < C	57 > 76	—e	
Perceived Source of Job Dissatisfactions:					
Economic	—d	—d	—d	M > F	
women			—d	—e	Age × Educ. × Ye
Extrinsic—Noneconomic	Y > MA > O	G > H > C			
General Hard Work		G < H,C			
Lack of Achievement Potential	Y > MA > O	G < H < C			
Affiliative Lack or Problem		G < H < C	57 < 76		
Lack of Power		G < H < C		M > F	
Job Competence (Males Only)					
Perceived Ability Required	Y < MA,O		57 < 76	—b	
Perceived Ability	Y < MA < O		57 < 76	—b	
Job Problem (Males Only)					
Problem in Job	Y > MA > O	G < H < C	57 < 76	—e	
Self as Basis of Problems	Y > MA > O		57 < 76	—e	

[a] See Footnote a Table 2.11 for an explanation of "Required."

[b] Sex comparison impossible; 1957 data not available in women.

[c] See Footnote a Table 2.11 for an explanation of "Main Effect."

[d] Cross-classification is run separately for males and females because a complex four-way interaction involving sex was needed to explain variable cross-classification.

[e] Sex comparison inappropriate in desegregated data.

seen as interfering with the pursuit and care of men, motherhood, or housework. This stereotype is not nearly so compelling for young women of today. Thus young working women are able to exploit not only the world of work but also the world of leisure as an avenue for self-actualization. Rather than compensatory outlets for gratification, these roles appear to build on one another for young adult women of the 1970s.

For older working women in both years, a self-actualization orientation to leisure was quite permissible. In fact, the Victorian stereotype of women holds that they *should* develop hobbies and enlarge their civic and church activities once their children are grown and taken care of.

QUALIFICATION TO YEAR COMPARISONS: JOB REACTIONS

All results highlighted earlier in our analysis of year differences in the way employed people react to their jobs were confirmed by the multivariate analyses summarized in table 6.25, with one critical qualification: the increase in overall job dissatisfaction among women is not entirely uniform in all age and education groups. Specifically, it is not apparent at all for older women, and only a modest increase is evident among middle-aged women and young, grade school–educated women. In contrast, increased job dissatisfaction is most dramatic among high school and college-educated young women (see table 6.26).

These young women may speak of job dissatisfaction with an acute political awareness of current inequities for women at work. If so, we

TABLE 6.26
Job Dissatisfaction Expressed Among Employed Women
(by age × education × year)

Age	Education	Reactions to Job: Neutral, Ambivalent, or Dissatisfied			
		1957		1976	
		Total Number	Percentage	Percentage	Total Number
21–34	Grade School	20	25	33	6
	High School	94	18	37	17
	College	27	15	33	25
35–54	Grade School	60	25	29	139
	High School	125	22	24	142
	College	45	13	19	56
55+	Grade School	36	25	20	123
	High School	22	22	20	59
	College	13	23	25	28

may view this increase more as an indicator of political mobilization than as a sign of dramatic changes in the nature of work for young women. Both the achievement expectations of these women and their consciousness about women's issues have been aroused simultaneously over the generation. Such changes will also be apparent in the next major section of this chapter, which deals with sex differences in job attitudes and reactions.

Sex Differences in Work Salience and Job Reactions

In presenting year differences in employed people's reactions to work and their jobs, we routinely segregated the responses of male and female workers. There are good reasons to believe that the reactions of men and women might have been different in both years. In this section, we will reexamine those tables, guided as well by our multivariate analyses, and point out significant differences and similarities in men and women's responses to work and their jobs. Of particular interest are results that reflect some of the transitional experiences that women might have had in entering the labor market with full-fledged vigor and with serious political concerns about equal treatment. Unfortunately, comparisons between men and women over the generation are somewhat limited because some of the questions were not asked of employed women in 1957. Nevertheless, 1976 comparisons are available for all measures. Because men and women are not equally distributed across occupational categories, it is also important to examine sex differences with differences in social status controlled. Since our multivariate analyses include an educational control, we are able to feel some confidence in the importance of the sex differences to be highlighted.

We described several sex differences in work salience in connection with our discussion of year differences. We learned, for example, that due to a remarkable increase in work commitment among women between 1957 and 1976, they are quite similar to men in 1976. Thus, sex differences in work commitment are limited to 1957 (see table 6.27, in which we retabulate major results from the year comparisons to highlight several significant sex differences). This finding is of great significance because many people have argued that women have increasingly entered the labor force over this generation primarily to provide necessary income to maintain an adequate style of family living. This is clearly not the entire story. Most employed women today are similar to working men in their clear commitment to work. The sexes do, however, differ in their stated bases for that commitment. More men in both years say they would be bored without work or that they need

TABLE 6.27
Selected Sex Differences in Measures of the Salience of Work and Reactions to Jobs (by year, employed respondents only)

| | Year | | | |
| | 1957 | | 1976 | |
Measure	Men (%)	Women (%)	Men (%)	Women (%)
Work Salience				
Work Commitment:				
Yes, would work if money not needed	85	58	84	77
Reasons for Working without Money:				
Otherwise bored	55	27	43	24
Affiliative	2	8	3	10
Moral commitment	9	3	8	4
Escape from home	1	3	1	8
Challenging Use of Leisure:				
Yes	73	63	76	67
Social Validity through Work:				
High and moderate[a] (married only)	—[b]	—[b]	28	34
Job Reaction				
Ego Involvement in Job Satisfaction:				
Ego satisfaction only	55	65	64	67
Ego involvement in job dissatisfaction:				
Ego dissatisfaction only	19	21	35	38
Sources of Job Satisfaction:				
Affiliative	18	34	22	38
Specific people	16	26	12	22
Power-related	14	9	22	10
Sources of Job Dissatisfaction:				
Economic	18	10	14	11
Lack of power	4	4	10	5
Perceived Ability Required:				
A lot	39	—[c]	54	45
Perceived Ability:				
Very good	30	—[c]	52	59
Perceived Problems in Jobs:				
Yes	27	—[c]	41	29
Problems in Self in Job:				
Yes	11	—[c]	17	10
Total Number	924	301	763	612

[a] Selects job reputation over one or both family roles.

[b] Measure not assessed in 1957.

[c] Measure not assessed for women in 1957.

work to fill their time. Women's greater mention of needing work as an escape from home might be conceived as equivalent to men's concerns with being bored, but, even if we combine these responses, women still mention them less than men.

Men in both survey years also feel more moralistic about work than women, as if their value as men depended on it. On the other hand, women more than men in both years apparently value affiliative contacts at work, which they say they would not like to give up. Altogether, then, men seem more directly committed to work for structuring their overall lives—both in a moral sense and a more existential sense. A job is what a man should be doing with his time. In contrast, women are more socially committed to work—as a way both to escape felt isolation and to establish social ties with others.

Another consistent sex difference in both survey years is men's greater reported use of leisure time for pursuing activities coded as challenging. This result is further corroborated in a question asked of all respondents in 1976: "How much free time do you spend doing challenging things?" We found that 42 percent of working men said "most" or "a lot" of their free time is spent doing challenging things compared to only 31 percent of working women. This finding reflects a subtle but important sex difference. Apparently women feel less freedom in their "free time" to be self-actualizing. Rather, they tend to use free time in and around their household pursuits. Reading a magazine, talking on the telephone, and visiting neighbors all qualify as leisure pursuits that make women available to others if they are needed, but which clearly do not allow for selfish involvement in their own achievements. Men, on the other hand, are much freer to leave the house to spend their free time—for sports, hobbies, political work, and the like—pursuits that can be challenging and are less interruptible. All of this may well be conditioned by the vestigial sex-role prescription that "a women's place is in the home." Women who do seek self-actualization more likely turn to work rather than leisure pursuits because working brings in money, and thus provides a credible rationalization for spending time away from the family. At this point in our social history, however, most men still do not have to justify time spent in leisure away from the family.

A final sex difference relevant to work commitment is quite surprising. More employed women than men report that they would rather be regarded as excellent at work in contrast to the two family roles. This very substantial difference (35 percent of men and 47 percent of women would select work over at least one of the family roles) is partially a function of the larger proportion of nonmarried women among the employed in contrast to the proportion of nonmarried men. (Nonmarried people value their job roles more in general.) Nevertheless, even when we look only at married employed men and women (see table 6.27), a trend suggestive of women's greater sense of social validity through work is still evident. The only plausible explanation we can think of to account for this result is that women more than men may take for granted the fact that they are good spouses or parents. Consequently, a social reputation for being excellent at work provides a much more distinctive ego boost for a woman. A social reputation for being known as a good spouse or parent might do the same for a man.

Overall, these sex differences suggest that women may not be quite as committed to work as a way of structuring their time or appeasing their moral conscience as men are. They are, nonetheless, clearly committed to working. Work may, in fact, be a better outlet for women for general self-expression and sociability, while men are more attuned to leisure as a way to pursue challenge.

Let us turn next to an analysis of sex difference in job reactions. In trying to summarize overall changes in job satisfaction from 1957 to 1976, it became increasingly clear that one particular group stood out from all others—young employed women in 1957—and in our previous analyses, we found that a significant interaction was accounted for by that group. These differences are highlighted once again in table 6.28, in which we compare men and women in the youngest age group along with those in the two oldest groups combined. Younger employed women in 1957 are distinctly different from all other groups; they are very much more satisfied and much less dissatisfied than others. It may well be that young women in the labor force in 1957 were very accepting of the job positions they held, very satisfied because they were unwilling to see anything they did as being unsatisfying. Recall that these women were not very committed to working at all.

TABLE 6.28

Sex Differences in Reports of Being "Very Satisfied" or Somewhat Dissatisfied (Neutral, Ambivalent, Dissatisfied) About One's Job (by age × year)

Reaction to Job Satisfaction Questions		1957		1976	
		Men (%)	Women (%)	Men (%)	Women (%)
"Very Satisfied"					
	Age: 21–34	26	41	25	26
	35+	29	37	30	33
Some Dissatisfaction: (Neutral, Ambivalent, Dissatisfied)					
	Age: 21–34	29	18	30	35
	35+	21	22	22	22
Total Number	Age: 21–34	287	141	317	272
	35+	602	305	438	335

That being the case, one clear interpretation of these data is that these young women, being not very involved with their work, basically accepted what was "dished out" to them in a stereotypic "feminine" style and avoided trouble by not expressing any dissatisfaction. Young women in 1957 were particularly committed to married life and raising children. It was this generation that spawned the baby boom, a generation that clearly saw the role of women being elsewhere than in the workplace. If we omit that group from the analyses of job satisfaction, men and women's responses to the job satisfaction question are very much alike. There is still a trend for women to be somewhat more satisfied than men, but the differences are very slight.

If we press a little further to examine qualities of satisfaction and dissatisfaction, we find significant but small differences between men's and women's reported dissatisfactions, both in terms of ego involvement and in the particular types of dissatisfactions mentioned. However, we do find very strong differences in what men and women report about satisfactions they gain from work (see table 6.27). Interestingly, more women than men report ego satisfaction from work, and that greater ego satisfaction seems to be located in the affiliative sphere. Only 18 percent of the men in 1957 mention affiliative-related satisfactions compared to 34 percent of the women, a difference which essentially remains the same in 1976 (22 percent of the men and 38 percent of the women). Similar differences are apparent for mentioning specific people at work. Many more women than men report relationships with particular people as being a major satisfaction of work. In contrast, more men talk about power-related satisfactions at work. Twenty-two percent of the men mentioned power-related satisfactions in 1976, compared with only 10 percent of women. Similar differences are apparent for achievement-related satisfactions, but the differences did not withstand multivariate controls.

Therefore, there is a clear sex-stereotyped difference in the way men and women respond to questions about satisfactions at work, with men mentioning impact-related job gratifications—achievement or power as sources of satisfaction—while women mention affiliative gratifications. The very high proportion of women workers who mention affiliative satisfactions probably accounts for why women appear to be so much more ego involved in job satisfaction than men.

A question worth pursuing is whether these sex-linked satisfactions from work reflect a motivated selection corresponding to men's and women's subjective needs to fit sex-role expectations, or whether these satisfactions reflect objective differences in the kinds of potential satisfactions that men and women derive from jobs that are differentially assigned to them within a sexist job structure. Assuming that men are expected to be more power involved in work and women more affiliation oriented, we might infer that men and women are simply fulfilling sex-role expectations by structuring their satisfactions in traditional masculine and feminine terms. Alternatively, however, these may be the satisfactions preeminent within the occupations that each sex is either socialized to seek out or allowed to enter.

One might in fact theorize that affiliative and power (or achievement) motivations are mutually contradictory in the job world. Horner's work on fear of success (1972) is essentially based on this proposition. Thus, we might postulate a positive relationship between impact satisfactions (power and/or achievement) and affiliative dissatisfactions and between affiliative satisfactions and impact dissatisfactions. There is only a little direct evidence for this proposition in our data. Only among women employed in 1976 is there a significant positive correlation between mentioning achievement gratifications *and* mentioning affiliative problems ($r = .16$, $p<.0001$, N = 761). And only among grade school–educated men in 1976 is there a significant association between affiliative satisfactions and mentioning a job's lack of achievement potential as a source of job dissatisfaction.

Nevertheless, some indirect evidence is available in the aggregate data. As men and women have increased their impact gratification from work from 1957 to 1976, they have also decreased their affiliative satisfactions. That men tend to mention feelings of affiliative dissatisfactions at work more than women report lack of achievement satisfaction suggests that this negative tradeoff of achievement for affiliation and vice versa is not entirely symmetrical for the two sexes. Women do not seem to be giving up as much with regard to feelings of achievement at work when they structure their work in affiliative terms as men give up in affiliative relationships when they structure their job in achievement terms.

The general lack of sex differences in overall job satisfaction noted above is further confirmed in the 1976 results for job commitment. Men and women in 1976 appear equally interested in sticking with the job that they have rather than turning to a new one. We have already noted a sex difference on this measure in 1957, but that difference seems to reflect the fact that women in 1957 were not particularly committed to working at all.

Turning now to findings about perceived job competence for men and women, we find two interesting results: one that we expected and one that we did not. As we might anticipate, table 6.27 indicates that women tend to perceive their jobs as not requiring as much ability as men. However, in multivariate analyses controlling for occupation, this sex difference disappears. When we hold constant men's and women's occupations, women are as likely as men to say that their jobs require a lot of ability. In multivariate analyses controlling for educational differences, however, this sex difference remains. Clearly, then, women perceive the fact that they are relegated to jobs requiring less skill than those available to men—perhaps especially so when they are well educated.

TABLE 6.29

Relationship of General Educational Development Required of Job to Perceiving Ability as "Very Good" Among Employed Men and Women (by Education, 1976 only)

General Educational Development Required in Job	Sex	Educational Level							
		Less Than High School Graduate		High School Graduate		Some College		College Graduate	
		Number	Percent "Very Good"	Number	Percent "Very Good"	Number	Percent "Very Good"	Number	Percent "Very Good"
Low[a]	Men	70	44	79	52	40	52	4	75
	Women	79	57	55	62	11	36	3	67
Moderate	Men	70	44	110	42	51	57	29	69
	Women	47	60	136	52	42	57	25	60
High	Men	22	50	54	57	76	62	127	63
	Women	10	60	68	60	56	57	78	77

[a] Low = DOT General Educational Development (GED) Score of 1, 2; moderate = DOT GED Score of 3; high = DOT GED Score of 4–6.

A result we did not anticipate (in table 6.29), however, is the *lack* of a difference between men and women in perceived ability to do their jobs. If anything, women are slightly more likely than men to say that they are "very good" at their jobs, although this difference is not significant when age and education are controlled in a multivariate analysis. Much of the academic literature about perceived competence in men and women would predict a difference in the opposite direction. For example, Crandall (1969) and Parsons et al. (1976) emphasize that, in academic settings from grade school through college, women tend to underestimate their abilities compared to men. However, this seems not to be the case in the current occupational world. An immediately obvious interpretation of this lack of difference is that since women have jobs that are not very demanding, as we noted above, they rate their abilities highly in relation to a lower level of demand.

To evaluate various hypotheses, we introduced a number of different controls to examine this lack of sex difference in perceived job ability. We compared men's and women's perceptions of their abilities in jobs controlling for various *Dictionary of Occupational Titles'* categorizations of occupations:[4] (1) prestige, (2) sex composition, (3) general educational development, and (4) specific vocational preparation required for the job. *In all instances, these controls had little effect on the overall relationship.*

One more complicated control for respondent's occupation did provide some insight. By looking not only at the level of general educational development required by an occupation, but also at the actual education level of the respondent, we were able to assess the issue of under- and overutilization of training. The results of this cross-classification are presented in table 6.29. From that table we see that in almost all instances the general result obtained for all subjects applies within various cross-classifications. Women see themselves, if anything, as *more* able in their jobs than men, regardless of level of educational development required by the job and the respondent's own education.

There are, however, some important discrepancies in table 6.29. Discrepancies are especially apparent for men and women who have *some college* education and who are employed in either low- or high-demand jobs. For those workers, results are consistent with those obtained in classroom settings: Men are more likely than women to judge their abilities at work as high. These results provide some insight into what may be going on here. Men and women who have not finished college are often put in the position of feeling somewhat defensive about their own achievements. Under such circumstances, we find the results consistent with studies of college students. We might speculate that these workers have considerable achievement anxiety, and, under such cir-

---

[4] We used the average weighted coding of the *Dictionary of Occupational Titles'* categorization of jobs within a given census category, based on the work of Temme (1975). Thus, these job ratings are independent of our respondents' perceptions.

cumstances, they tend to fall back on stereotypic behavior—bravado-like overconfidence for men and humble modesty for women. One might also speculate that women who do not finish college have an especially high fear of success, which may result in modest estimates of their own abilities.

Other less defensive people in the job world may have more realistically come to terms with their abilities and their aspirations; they make social comparisons with people in positions similar to their own and derive realistic evaluations of themselves as being competent at what they are assigned to do. Among such people, the slight edge that women apparently have in perceiving themselves as very able at what they are doing may reflect the fact that (in spite of our controls) in most organizational structures women are largely excluded from positions of responsibility and are thereby "protected" from the additional ambiguity about capacity that such responsibility often entails.

Looking at the most educated people in our sample—the college educated—who are generally in high-demand jobs, we find a large proportion of women who think they are very able—more so than the college-educated men. Since women who pass through the educational hierarchy to demanding jobs in our society are given many opportunities to perceive themselves as capable, by overcoming formidable obstacles to arrive in those positions, they indeed come to see themselves as very able. It is also interesting to note that the college graduates who are *not* in demanding occupations manifest a "college-student syndrome": men rate higher in perceived competence than women. These men and women as a group are truly underutilizing their training, and under such conditions they show the more defensive pattern described above.

Another way to examine these interesting results concerning perceived ability in work among employed men and women is to control for *perceived* demand at work (rather than the objectively assessed demand), by taking people's own judgment about how much is required on the job and looking at how much ability they perceive themselves to

TABLE 6.30

Percentage of Men and Women who Perceive Their Ability as "Very Good"
in Jobs Varying in Perceived Ability Required
(1976 only)

Perceived Ability Required	Men		Women	
	Number	"Very Good" (%)	Number	"Very Good" (%)
"A Lot"	406	56	270	63
"Some"	87	52	65	63
"None, Little, Not Much"	151	46	156	47

have within each level of perceived capability required. These results are presented in table 6.30. In none of these comparisons do men perceive themselves as more able than women.

A final difference between men and women's reactions to their jobs can be noted in how they respond to the question about problems at work in 1976. Again we performed a multivariate analysis on the 1976 data only, and a significant sex difference emerged, net of education and age controls. More men than women report having problems at work, particularly problems in themselves (see table 6.27). Looking back at table 6.21 at the types of problems mentioned by men and women, we can see that it is men's greater mention of problems of "vocational choice" that largely accounts for this overall difference.

These results are important in both a specific and a general sense. Specifically, they alert us to the fact that job choice is probably more critical for men in our society today than for women. While family roles are important for both, it is still true that occupational roles tend to play a clearer role in self-definition for men than for women. Therefore, the issue of choice, the issue of which job best fits someone and how adaptive he or she is to a particular work setting, probably remains a more critical issue for men than for women.

In the general sense, these results are important because women are more prone than men to be sensitive to psychological problems in most other life domains. In various chapters throughout this book, we encounter evidence that women are more apt to report difficulties than men. One possible interpretation of these results is that women are simply more oriented toward reporting difficulty of any sort. However, this bias does not seem to be the case with regard to job problems. That men are more likely than women to report job problems argues against attributing sex differences in reported difficulties observed in other domains solely to methodological error or response style.

In summary, with regard to sex differences in reactions to jobs, we conclude that, by and large, men and women react to work quite similarly. Although men and women are not very different in how satisfied they are with their work, they seem to use slightly different criteria as a basis for their satisfaction. Men are more likely than women to see problems at work, but these apparently have less to do with an ongoing work situation than with concerns about whether or not they have made an appropriate job choice.

That women are defining job satisfaction more in affiliative terms and men more in impact-relevant terms are important aspects of these data to keep in mind. We suggested earlier that jobs have increased in achievement potential and decreased in affiliative potential for men and women. This trend may imply that women will have to resocialize or modify their work aspirations and involvements in order to feel more comfortable about their work in general. It also suggests that if men wish to be more comfortable at work, then they have to become more conscious of competing needs at work. Since there is often a conflict between achievement and affiliative possibilities at work, men may have to compromise some of their achievement aspirations at work in order to come to terms with their more submerged affiliative desires. Similarly, women may have to come to terms with some loss in affiliative gratifications as they press toward increasing achievement responsibilities for their work.

Age Differences in Work Salience and Job Reactions

Let us first consider life-cycle differences in the meaning of work, the most important of which occurs among housewives. Younger housewives find housework less satisfying, especially in 1976, and they are more oriented to paid employment at some time in the future (see table 6.31, in which age comparisons are presented for selected measures of work salience and job reactions). The most remarkable change for young women has been a substantial increase in career orientation among young high school–educated housewives, 64 percent of whom in 1976 say they have wanted a career compared to only 40 percent in 1957. In addition, a very strong career orientation has developed among middle-aged college-educated women by 1976, 73 percent of whom say they thought of having a career compared to only 46 percent in 1957. This particular cohort of women—those young and well educated during the baby boom—were likely those most susceptible to the demystification of the traditional housewife role. These middle-aged women are well represented in the labor force today, or, if full-time housewives, are very involved in working.

On measures of work salience assessed for both working men and women, however, few significant age differences are apparent, and those which are suggest that work is more important for *older* than for younger workers. Older people are more likely than the young to report that both work and leisure fulfill their primary values. Of particular importance is the fact that younger people rate leisure higher than work in its potential to fulfill their values (see table 6.31). Furthermore, except among the college educated, older workers are more likely than younger ones to say that they would prefer being known for being good at their work over being good in family roles. This relationship is reversed among the college educated (see table 6.32). In each case, results are the same when we limit our analysis only to married respondents.

Thus, the salience of work, if anything, seems stronger among older people, except among young, college-educated men and women, for whom work is very important relative to other groups. It is important *by Year, Employed Respondents Only)*

	Age Groups											
	21-29		30-39		40-49		50-59		60-64		65+	
Measure	1957 (%)	1976 (%)	1957 (%)	1976 (%)	1957 (%)	1976 (%)	1957 (%)	1976 (%)	1957 (%)	1976 (%)	1957 (%)	1976 (%)
Work Salience												
Housework Satisfaction: Satisfied[a]	61 (115)[b]	42 (96)[b]	54 (207)[b]	43 (89)[b]	71 (162)[b]	58 (67)[b]	79 (114)[b]	62 (84)[b]	85 (62)[b]	64 (35)[b]	71 (149)[b]	70 (134)[b]
Plans to Work	29 (115)[b]	68 (96)[b]	20 (207)[b]	57 (89)[b]	20 (162)[b]	28 (67)[b]	8 (114)[b]	16 (84)[b]	6 (62)[b]	9 (35)[b]	1 (149)[b]	1 (134)[b]
Value Fulfillment through Job: A lot, great deal	—[c]	71	—[c]	74	—[c]	76	—[c]	84	—[c]	86	—[c]	89
Value Fulfillment through Leisure: A great deal	—[c]	18	—[c]	18	—[c]	23	—[c]	24	—[c]	29	—[c]	23
Comparative Value Fulfillment: Leisure > work	—[c]	25	—[c]	20	—[c]	20	—[c]	14	—[c]	10	—[c]	13
Job Reactions												
Job Satisfaction: Neutral, ambivalent, dissatisfied	25	34	25	27	21	21	22	22	18	24	14	12
Ego Involvement in Job Satisfaction: Ego satisfaction	58	64	59	71	66	66	66	73	61	66	65	78
Job Commitment: Do *not* prefer other job	45	36	53	42	61	54	67	69	73	71	77	89
Source of Job Satisfaction: Affiliation-related	22	26	24	27	24	32	25	35	18	29	26	26

TABLE 6.31 (continued)

| | Age Groups | | | | | | | | | | | |
| | 21-29 | | 30-39 | | 40-49 | | 50-59 | | 60-64 | | 65+ | |
Measure	1957 (%)	1976 (%)	1957 (%)	1976 (%)	1957 (%)	1976 (%)	1957 (%)	1976 (%)	1957 (%)	1976 (%)	1957 (%)	1976 (%)
Sources of Job Dissatisfaction:												
Extrinsic, noneconomic	15	15	15	9	16	15	12	14	18	11	29	7
Lack of achievement	6	12	7	11	6	4	5	5	0	6	1	1
Perceived Ability Required:												
A lot	46 (44)d	53	49 (59)d	67	61 (64)d	64	53 (36)d	73	58 (12)d	64	50 (14)d	68
males:		(182)		(174)		(122)		(95)		(45)		(31)
females:		57 (189)		59 (142)		59 (106)		56 (105)		66 (35)		65 (31)
Job Problems:												
Yes	40 (164)e	49	33 (245)e	46	29 (230)e	44	20 (167)e	30	19 (58)e	28	14 (58)e	13
males:		(211)		(202)		(142)		(118)		(50)		(38)
females:		40 (189)		35 (143)		24 (107)		13 (105)		23 (35)		10 (31)
Job Problem in Self:												
Yes	20 (155)e	20	12 (237)e	13	10 (223)e	19	8 (165)e	13	6 (55)e	16	7 (57)e	9
males:		(208)		(200)		(140)		(117)		(50)		(38)
females:		12 (189)		13 (142)		8 (106)		8 (105)		9 (35)		3 (31)
Total Number[f]	251	400	368	345	345	249	261	223	80	85	70	69

NOTE: Numbers in parentheses are total number of persons in each group.

[a] Unqualified liking plus liking.
[b] Reduced N: housewives only.
[c] Measure unvariable for 1957.
[d] Measure obtained on males only and only one-third of the sample.
[e] Measure obtained on males only and only one-third of sample.

TABLE 6.32

Age Differences in Preferring to Be Known as
Excellent in One's Job Over Good Performance in
Both Family Roles (by education)

Education	Preference for Social Validity Through Job Over Family Roles		
	Young (21–34) (%)	Middle–Aged (35–54) (%)	Old (55+) (%)
Grade School	0 (14)	7 (28)	17 (36)
High School	9 (174)	8 (179)	14 (79)
College	29 (180)	14 (122)	9 (45)

NOTE: Numbers in parentheses are total number of persons in each group.

to remember that young people are especially family oriented; they see work and leisure as allied with family roles. As people age and become less involved in family issues, work can take on a more central meaning in their lives quite separate from their family concerns. Indeed, issues of integrity that confront older people, as discussed in chapter 3 (self-perceptions), may stimulate men and women to reevaluate the meaning of their jobs. Whether they are defensively trying to establish meaning where there is little, or whether they react to different aspects of their work as they become more senior, is an open question. In any case, they apparently adapt to changes during the life course by finding more value in work than perhaps they once did. Nevertheless, because the question on which this conclusion is based was asked only in 1976, we must also consider the possibility that this result may reflect a *generational* difference in the value of work in our society, rather than a life-cycle difference in work salience. Our analysis of changes in work salience over the life cycle, however, corresponds well with other results which follow—a discussion of life-cycle changes in how men and women react to their jobs, changes that appear to reflect long-term adaptation to jobs as the patterning of major life roles gradually shifts over the life cycle.

No analysis of the job role illuminates the basic issues of psychological adaptation to work better than our examination of age differences in people's reactions to their jobs. As people get older, possibilities for job mobility decrease greatly, and they generally must adapt to the particular job they have. In this process, many coping mechanisms may be invoked, some of which are injurious to people's overall senses of esteem and some of which are beneficial to the maximization of their potentials. Many people are forced to struggle with a work environment which is not perfectly suited to their own circumstances or preferences. Rarely is an ideal work environment available. Along with potential satisfactions that people can attain from work, there are always a number of dissatisfactions associated with any particular work environment. Hence, the issue of *adaptation* inevitably confronts people at work.

Young people generally enter a work setting with very high aspirations for what they might expect from work, especially the college educated (as we have seen). Many of these expectations are not readily met and may never be. The issue as one gets older then, is, how many of these unachieved aspirations can be dislodged from one's psyche and how many will remain as gnawing sources of discontent? More important, perhaps, is how much the adaptation required of people is below any particular standard for what men and women *should* be doing in the work setting? Without any objective model of what people *absolutely need* in and from work, we are forced to deal only with their subjective job adaptation, which may be either bad or good, depending on how successful that adaptation is in producing overall fulfillment in their lives.

As people get older, another important issue emerges: the relative balance to life roles that people develop as they age. A common assumption is that for men there is a proper sequence of role balance: first, an early role which emphasizes choosing an appropriate career and becoming an adequate provider for the family; then, a middle-aged role of achieving a certain degree of commitment and success in a job or career while enjoying family life to a greater degree; and, finally, a loosening of work commitment as they approach older age. For women, a reverse sequence is often described, whereby commitment to work is less critical in young adulthood, but takes on greater significance after the "real work" of raising children is done. Thus, life-cycle changes in the salience of work for men and women are constrained to be somewhat different according to traditional role expectations for men and women.

Each of these considerations influences our thinking about how relationships between age and reactions to work might differ for men and women. And indeed, the results to be presented in this section suggest that young people do find problematic the issue of accommodating to a job choice, of finding one's "proper" station in life, whereas older people, more comfortable with the jobs they hold, focus on other work issues.

The best indication of this shift over the life cycle for both men and women is that younger people tend more often to see themselves as having had problems at work (see table 6.31). Since concerns about vocational choice are frequently cited as the problems encountered in work, it is not surprising that work "problems" are mentioned more often by young people. Vocational choice is presumably a young person's concern, and, if it is not resolved by middle age or older life, resulting crises can often be overwhelming. Middle-aged and older people protect themselves against such crises by essentially not allowing themselves to think about any question of whether they should do the kind of work they are doing.

These speculations derive some support from the fact that young people are much more likely than older people to say that they would prefer "another kind of work." Young people, whose investments in the work they are doing are not yet as strong, experience less psychological discomfort in admitting to a lack of commitment to a particular job. In contrast, older people who tell an interviewer that they would prefer another job attest to their own lack of adaptation to a job or type of work—which would probably be very hard to change at this junction of their lives.

This assumption that older people are likely to adapt to whatever work they are currently doing may also be used to explain the fact that younger people are generally less satisfied with their work than older people. Surprisingly, however, this is not a *strong* relationship (see table 6.31). We find that older people report more dissatisfaction than we might expect. Apparently, many older people do not successfully suppress their dissatisfaction. That older people express as much dissatisfaction as they do may not reflect a failure in adaptation, but rather the influence of yet another process: disengagement. A comfortable transition from work to retirement may require that older people recognize and focus on some of the difficulties of work as well as on some of the pleasures that they experienced. As a presocialization process for retirement, they must learn to let go. Evidence consistent with this hypothesis is most striking among the least educated men in both survey years, who, unlike the better-educated men show increased job dissatisfaction with age rather than a decline with age in the mention of dissatisfactions (see table 6.33). The same holds true for women generally in 1957.[5] Thus, among less educated older men in both survey years, and for older women in 1957, there is some evidence suggestive of a pressure to disengage, to decrease dependence on occupational identity. Apparently, this disengagement process sensitizes older workers to dissatisfaction rather than satisfaction in the workplace.

Evidence consistent with assumption of an adaptation process, whereby people accommodate to the circumstances of their work as they age, is found in the more frequent report of ego satisfactions among older men and women (see table 6.31). Two explanations may account for this age trend. First, as men and women become increasingly familiar with their jobs, they are able to recognize and appreciate *more* psychologically satisfying aspects of their work. In essence, they

---

[5] As a result, our multivariate analysis reveals a complex sex x age x education x year interaction for this measure.

TABLE 6.33

Age Differences in Reported Job Dissatisfaction, Ambivalence or Neutrality (by sex × education × year)

		Age					
		21-34		34-54		55+	
Sex	Education	1957 (%)	1976 (%)	1957 (%)	1976 (%)	1957 (%)	1976 (%)
Men	Grade School	16 (45)		19 (131)		26 (102)	
			0 (14)		21 (24)		38 (24)
	High School	34 (157)		25 (208)		20 (51)	
			30 (140)		23 (136)		29 (72)
	College	28 (85)		20 (97)		11 (28)	
			29 (163)		20 (123)		17 (48)
Women	Grade School	25 (20)		25 (60)		25 (36)	
			33 (6)		29 (17)		18 (27)
	High School	18 (94)		22 (125)		23 (22)	
			37 (142)		23 (145)		9 (58)
	College	15 (27)		13 (45)		23 (13)	
			33 (124)		19 (59)		28 (29)

NOTE: Numbers in parentheses are total number of persons in each group.

become sensitive to smaller differences. Second, as they get older, people come to "make the best" of any situation, and thereby tend more to *rationalize* psychological satisfactions.

In their analyses entitled "Marriage and Work in America," Veroff and Feld (1970) pointed to similar "distorting" effects in the pattern of relationships between motives of achievement, affiliation, and power with reports of satisfaction in the work role. Their results suggested that people in jobs that did not easily allow for the kinds of gratification that were goals of strong motives they had often defensively *exaggerated* the possibilities for work gratification. Whether such exaggerations are psychologically "real" can be debated. We can say, however, that as people adapt to difficulties at work, they begin to see new gratifications. Even if illusory, they still make the work setting bearable.

Would people who like complexity in work but yet are given very routine jobs enjoy work more if they created their own complexity? Charlie Chaplin's antics on the assembly line in *Modern Times* made his work interesting, and Garson's (1977) book, *All the Livelong Day*, provides a more recent journalistic treatment of the same theme. Each portrays men and women's adaptation to work in very routine jobs by conjuring up fantasies or other playful ways of making the work interesting. And who is to say that no psychologically "real" satisfactions accrue to people who adapt to work in this way, even though these gratifications do not derive directly from the objective structure of work?

There seem to be few reliable differences in the types of job dissatisfactions mentioned by younger and older people. One significant trend is for people to mention achievement dissatisfactions more when they are young than when they are older. At least by implication, there is a peculiar burden on people who report some kind of achievement dissatisfaction to do something about it. This burden can be much heavier on older people than the young. Older workers have to be especially ego dissatisfied to complain, since they can easily come to blame themselves for not getting the credentials needed to obtain jobs permitting more achievement gratification or for not quitting a job and/or finding another before it was too late. Indeed, we might expect a natural tendency among older people to disown dissatisfactions that are psychologically involving, in order to preserve a sense of well-being in their public and private self-identity. Given this line of reasoning, it is surprising that as many older people mentioned ego dissatisfactions in their work as they did.

Finally, one other interesting significant age effect is evident in table 6.31: age differences in perceived ability among men and a similar trend for women. We might reasonably expect that older people would legitimately feel somewhat more confident of their abilities in work than younger people. Seniority brings more responsibilities, more practiced skills, and hence a greater sense of competence. It is perhaps surprising, then, that these results are not even stronger. We could argue, however, that each succeeding cohort of workers being more educated and better trained, poses a significant threat to older cohorts. These younger groups may make older workers feel less capable. Thus, aging in the workplace may be associated with at least two competing tendencies: feeling more competent because of increased seniority and increased responsibilities, and feeling less competent because of the competition with more energetic and better-trained young workers. Although feeling increased competence evidently predominates, a sense of competition with youth may be sufficiently in force to make the older worker feel vulnerable. In a society that does not venerate age and experience, it is likely that this vulnerability constitutes a very real threat to the older worker.

Education Differences in Work Salience and Job Reactions

Table 6.34 highlights selected differences in responses to questions about work salience and job reactions for people from various educational backgrounds. These differences reflect results of multivariate analyses showing significant education effects summarized in tables 6.22 and 6.25. Based on the information provided in table 6.34, we are able to determine the extent to which people from different social groups vary in the ways in which they react to their work.

The use of education as a measure of social status merits some justification in the context of discussing reactions to work, since we could instead use occupational differences as measures of social status. Our reasons for using education rather than occupation are threefold. First, we wanted to use the same measure of social status across various chapters in this book in order to gain a consistent picture of the effect of status on subjective measures of well-being. Thus, conclusions we might draw about status effects in the context of marriage might have potential implications for the nature of status effects on the work context. Second, education as a measure of status reflects not only current social status for most people, but also general background differences that may have profound effects on the initial expectations of men and women for the types of gratifications they seek in work, as well as on their general life goals, both of which may in turn have an impact on people's assessments of their work. Third, occupational measures of status are often imprecise because they are based on incomplete responses that respondents give about the nature of their work. Researchers often need detailed information about an occupation before a clear coding of the status of that occupation can be made. This problem is compounded when we are using data from two different surveys conducted almost twenty years apart, a period during which the occupational structure has shifted. In these analyses, we have assumed that a person's educational credentials are very important in attaining jobs of different status levels, and that education differences reflect critical reference group perspectives that frequently cut across occupational lines.

Nevertheless, in the next section of this chapter, we will also present a brief look at how men and women in different occupational categories reacted to their jobs, as a supplement to our examination of education differences in this section. However, we do not consider that brief

Selected Education Differences in Measures of Work Salience and Job Reactions (by year, employed respondents only)

	Education Groups									
	Grade School		Some High School		High School Graduate		Some College		College Graduate	
Measure	1957 (%)	1976 (%)	1957 (%)	1976 (%)	1957 (%)	1976 (%)	1957 (%)	1976 (%)	1957 (%)	1976 (%)
Work Salience										
Work Commitment: Yes, if money needed	79	73	72	76	78	78	85	83	83	91
Reasons for Work Commitment: Achievement	1	4	1	1	2	6	9	13	8	32
Moral	11	11	5	12	7	6	4	2	4	6
Housework Satisfaction: Satisfied[a]	75 (293)[b]	77 (116)[b]	67 (200)[b]	63 (99)[b]	65 (257)[b]	50 (170)[b]	69 (71)[b]	49 (70)[b]	64 (47)[b]	26 (43)[b]
Career Orientation: Yes	30 (293)[b]	12 (116)[b]	32 (200)[b]	39 (99)[b]	40 (257)[b]	42 (170)[b]	45 (71)[b]	54 (70)[b]	53 (47)[b]	74 (43)[b]
Challenging Use of Leisure: Yes	63	58	71	62	71	75	78	76	73	76
Value Fulfillment through Leisure: A lot, great deal	—[c]	47	—[c]	50	—[c]	53	—[c]	61	—[c]	62
Social Validation through Job: Job>marriage, parenthood	—[c]	10	—[c]	8	—[c]	10	—[c]	22	—[c]	20
Job Reaction										
Job Satisfaction: Very satisfied	22	24	28	20	35	29	34	24	45	38
Ego Involvement in Job Satisfaction: All ego satisfaction	47	51	58	57	60	63	67	66	77	80

TABLE 6.34 (continued)

Measure	Education Groups									
	Grade School		Some High School		High School Graduate		Some College		College Graduate	
	1957 (%)	1976 (%)	1957 (%)	1976 (%)	1957 (%)	1976 (%)	1957 (%)	1976 (%)	1957 (%)	1976 (%)
Ego Involvement in Job Dissatisfaction:										
All ego dissatisfaction	17	20	27	29	31	41	35	58	43	61
Sources of Satisfaction:										
Economic	14	21	16	15	20	14	15	15	9	6
Extrinsic, noneconomic	32	20	24	23	22	22	17	21	12	14
Achievement	81	13	15	12	18	24	18	30	27	40
Affiliation	12	18	22	18	25	31	28	28	41	39
Interest (Men)	33	25	31	27	30	21	42	21	31	20
	(282)	(71)	(186)	(94)	(237)	(252)	(104)	(171)	(110)	(154)
(Women)	21	6	24	19	33	19	40	27	32	24
	(117)	(48)	(98)	(84)	(151)	(257)	(47)	(108)	(40)	(102)
Sources of Dissatisfaction:										
Economic (Men)	23	17	18	16	18	16	16	10	12	13
	(282)	(71)	(186)	(94)	(237)	(252)	(104)	(171)	(110)	(154)
(Women)	8	8	13	12	9	11	8	10	10	12
	(117)	(48)	(98)	(84)	(151)	(257)	(47)	(108)	(40)	(102)
Extrinsic, noneconomic	31	25	35	29	29	27	27	25	25	21
General hard work	8	11	12	9	15	14	13	13	15	15
Lack of achievement	2	3	5	1	6	7	8	11	12	15
Affiliative lack	8		9		13	7	14	11	11	16

Perceived Ability Required:										
A lot (Men)	50 (76)[d]	53 (73)	51 (97)[d]	67 (94)	55 (49)[d]	64 (252)	50 (24)[d]	73 (173)	59 (34)[d]	68 (164)
(Women)	—[e]	35 (34)	—[e]	48 (71)	—[e]	50 (206)	—[e]	61 (92)	—[e]	72 (89)
Perceived Ability:										
Very good (Men)	31 (99)[d]	45 (71)	28 (61)[d]	46 (92)	28 (75)[d]	49 (251)	30 (32)[d]	57 (171)	35 (40)[d]	64 (163)
(Women)	—[e]	50 (50)	—[e]	62 (88)	—[e]	56 (259)	—[e]	52 (109)	—[e]	73 (103)
Job Problems:										
Yes (Men)	21 (282)	29 (73)	31 (186)	33 (95)	29 (237)	40 (255)	39 (104)	47 (173)	36 (110)	48 (164)
(Women)	—[e]	16 (50)	—[e]	23 (88)	—[e]	28 (261)	—[e]	39 (109)	—[e]	34 (103)
Total Number[f]	399	123	284	183	388	516	151	282	150	267

NOTE: Numbers in parentheses are total number of persons in each group.

[a] Unqualified liking plus liking.

[b] Reduced N: housewives only.

[c] Measure unavailable in 1957.

[d] Measure obtained only on males and only one-third of sample.

[e] Measure obtained only on males in 1957.

[f] Numbers will vary somewhat depending on the number not ascertained.

treatment of occupational difference to be the major examination of social status differences in this chapter.

We had anticipated that education differences in job reactions might differ significantly for men and women. Therefore we expected our multivariate analyses to yield several interactions which included sex as a variable. This turned out not to be the case. Very few of our analyses of education differences in job reactions revealed different results for men and women. Differences in points of inflection for certain relationships were evident, but the overall patterns of relationships between educational status and job reactions are pretty much the same for each sex. Therefore, differences are presented here with results for men and women combined.

A careful examination of table 6.34 reveals that college graduates are distinctly more committed to working, especially for achievement reasons, derive more social validity through work, more value fulfillment in leisure, and are much more satisfied with their jobs than people with less education. Furthermore, the more educated people are, the more they express ego satisfactions and ego dissatisfactions in their work. Thus, more educated people are apparently more ego involved in their jobs. In mentioning specific ego-involved satisfactions in work, college-educated workers, in contrast to the less educated, focus particularly on affiliation- and achievement-related satisfactions and place less emphasis on financial and other extrinsic rewards. Other results indicate that the college educated are more likely to report problems in work, feel that their jobs are demanding, and consider themselves very good at their work—this last evaluation especially in 1976.

In seeking a general interpretation of the effect of educational status on men's and women's reactions to their jobs, the most consistent findings seem to indicate that as social status increases, involvement with work becomes more central. This pattern is even evident for housewives, among whom the higher educated are more dissatisfied with housework, more oriented toward a career, and, in 1976, especially committed to future paid employment (61 percent of college-educated housewives in 1976 plan to work sometime in the future compared to only 25 percent in 1957).

We might well interpret this pattern of results to reflect that men and women with appropriate educational credentials are obviously better able to obtain jobs with potential for achievement satisfaction. However, there are other aspects of these results, which suggest that college-educated men and women feel more involved with their work, not only in the realm of achievement mastery, but also in their social relationships. These two sources of job satisfaction (achievement-related and affiliation-related satisfactions) are considerably more apparent in the responses of higher-educated men and women in both years. Thus, more-educated people are evidently at an advantage in getting into jobs that are not only more demanding, but also more socially gratifying.

The fact that more-educated people are also more attuned to ego dissatisfactions in work rather than to extrinsic ones makes us somewhat cautious about this interpretation. Higher-educated workers report greater affiliative and power dissatisfactions in their work, which reflects a greater concern with problems of social integration at work. These results present a paradox: college-educated people are more responsive to both affiliative satisfactions and affiliative (or power) dissatisfactions at work. We conclude that a college background sensitizes people to the nature of social relationships on the job, both to when they go well and when they do not. The less educated are perhaps somewhat less involved in such issues, although more so in 1976 than they were in 1957. Overall, then, the apparent effect of education in our society is to alert people to both social possibilities and social disruptions in the workplace. A cultural shift in the last generation, however, has made people of all educational statuses somewhat more aware of this difficulty in the workplace than they once were, although, as we noted in the previous section, this orientation may be particularly strong among college-educated young women in 1976.

This greater involvement in work among more educated members of our society is also reflected in their reporting more work problems than the less educated. The less educated seem to have less conscious concern about their own adaptation to work, such as finding the right spot to fit their personal needs, a problem which may be a luxury of the more educated.

Let us look now at a few results which suggest that the effects of education on reactions to work are different for men and women. One provocative result is that while education is minimally related to men's seeing their work as interesting, the more educated a woman is, the more likely she is to perceive her work in that way. This critical result suggests that women moving through institutions of higher education may be particularly socialized to attend to the intrinsic aspects of doing the kind of work they choose to do. Or, women who become aware of the power-achievement aspects of work, those who become sensitive to the competitive nature of the workplace and what it may imply for their feminine status, may opt out of the job market altogether, or at least the educational institutions whose credentials are needed to advance to higher-status competitive positions. Primarily, then, only those women who have enough intrinsic interest in their work, only those who have survived the "fear-of-success-challenges" that exist within our educational institutions, finish college.

An alternative explanation for these results is that women whose educational credentials qualify them for potential competition with men for power within the workplace, when faced with such a struggle for power, tend to retreat from mentioning achievement aspects of work as a source of gratification and structure their gratification in noncompetitive terms. According to this perspective, college-educated women conceive of their work as "interesting" because they are fearful of admitting to themselves that they are achievement oriented in their work.

Mentioning their work as interesting, however, was actually most prevalent among men and women who had *some* college, yet did not finish. For women in this group, mentioning interesting work may reflect a fear of success that also impelled them to drop out of college. Mentioning interesting work among college-educated men who lack a college degree may reflect a sense of failure about not getting proper credentials and hence be a rationalization for not having a more achievement-demanding job. Although these interpretations are highly speculative, the phenomenon that reported joy of working for "interest" is positively related to education among women but unrelated to education for men is an important interaction that merits additional investigation in future research.

Another job reaction differentially related to education for men and women is perceived job ability.[6] For men there is a straightforward linear relationship: the more educated a man is the more likely he is to perceive that he is very able in the work that he does. For women this is also generally true, but there is a surprising dip in perceived ability among women who have had some college experience but no college degree. We have already alluded to this result in our previous discussion of sex differences in perceived competence. This interactive trend highlights the possibility that among women who do not finish college may be a substantial number who are fearful of success, who rush into marriage and/or do not wish to finish school because of worries that college graduation may put them into a more competitive orientation vis-à-vis men, or cast some doubt on their femininity. Thus they withdraw from the educational world and seek jobs where their work is less demanding and where they are less likely to be perceived as unfeminine. These are the women who are particularly modest about their job abilities compared to those from other educational backgrounds.

In light of other results we have discussed in this section, it is surprising to find that there is no consistent relationship between education and job commitment. One reason for this lack of consistency is that relationships between education and job commitment for men and women in 1976 essentially constitute mirror images of one another, as shown in table 6.35. For women, job commitment seems to go down with increasing education, except at the college-graduate level, at which point job commitment appears to rise again. For men, although

---

[6] These results are apparent only for the more detailed classification of educational level. The three-level classification used in our multivariate analyses does not yield these results.

TABLE 6.35

*Percent who are Job Committed[a] Among Men and Women
with Different Educational Levels (1976 only)*

	Men		Women	
Education	Total Number	Percent Job Committed	Total Number	Percent Job Committed
Grade School	71	38	48	67
Some High School	94	47	84	65
High School Graduate	252	48	257	51
Some College	171	65	108	39
College Graduate	154	40	102	50

[a] Say "no" to the question: Would they prefer other work?

job commitment increases with education, college graduates are particularly low in job commitment.

How can we account for these very discrepant patterns? A number of the results we have been discussing with respect to college-trained men and women's perceptions of themselves seem pertinent here. Women who overcome formidable sexist obstacles that occur in educational environments are probably unusually committed to intrinsic involvement with their work. This intrinsic involvement may in turn translate more readily to high job commitment. By contrast, extrinsic involvement in work may reduce job commitment, because it alerts them to potential positive benefits of alternative jobs.

As college graduates come to recognize how achievement fulfilling and competitive work is supposed to be for them, they often initiate a lifelong search for just the right job, one that will allow them to have a substantial degree of personal impact. We have already noted how often college-educated men in 1976 mentioned having experienced a job problem, frequently a problem of vocational choice, (i.e., finding just the right job). Among college graduates, however, the two sexes may have very different orientations to the achievement aspects of work. Women graduates seem to have a much clearer dedication to the *intrinsic* nature of work, while male graduates seem to have developed a clearer commitment to individuated aspects of work.

This distinction has been highlighted by Dorothy Kipnis (1974) in her discussion of achievement motivation differences between men and women. She emphasizes that in internalizing achievement orientation in early childhood, women become more intrinsically involved in achievement, while men become more oriented toward the social-competitive aspects of work. Her theory derives from the assumption that goals for achievement behavior are more family based and develop earlier among women, while among men they are more peer based and come later. Her basic thesis appears to have some application to the findings presented here. Women who withstand social pressures *not* to be a successful achiever in school and become college graduates are likely those who have highly internalized intrinsic orientations to work by the time they enter the labor force. On the other hand, men who scale the academic ladder and achieve success through school and college graduation are more likely to enter the job market with a highly developed social-competitive achievement orientation. These two distinct achievement orientations are hard to relinquish and may well be the basis for the very different patterns of involvement with work evident for male and female college graduates. They account for male college graduates being surprisingly lower in job commitment than one might expect, and for female college graduates being surprisingly high.

To this point in our examination of the effect of educational status on job reactions, we have perhaps attended too much to the differential *psychological* reactions of college graduates as a basis for explaining these results. Essentially ignored in this presentation is the fact that college graduates generally end up in jobs that pay better, give them more prestige in the society, and allow for greater responsibilities in the workplace itself. The refined psychological differentiations we have been making with regard to people in different educational groups, may in fact reflect the fact that college graduates have elite jobs while less educated people occupy lower status jobs. As a way of gaining some perspective on this question of how educational status is related to occupational reactions, we turn in the next section to a brief examination of *occupational* differences in the job reactions of men and women.

OCCUPATIONAL DIFFERENCES IN JOB REACTIONS

Tables 6.36 and 6.37 present 1957–1976 comparisons of reactions to work among various occupational groups for men and women. These tables encompass a great deal of information, and multivariate analyses of these data are difficult to describe because the large number of occupational categories result in a small number of cases in any particular cell. Consequently, results tend to be ambiguous and scattered across a number of different categories, in spite of the presence of an overall significant main effect or interaction. Therefore we present these data primarily for descriptive purposes, to provide basic information to readers who would like reactions to work among particular occupational groups in 1957 and 1976. Several other studies conducted during the last decade, such as the Quality of Employment Surveys (Quinn and Staines, 1979), provide much more detailed information about how people in specific job categories currently react to their work. The value of tables 6.36 and 6.37, then, lies primarily in its comparison of two

Job Reaction	Year	Professional (%)	Manager (%)	Clerical (%)	Sales (%)	Skilled (%)	Operative (%)	Service (%)	Laborer (%)	Farmer (%)
I. Measures of Job Satisfaction										
Overall Job Satisfaction:										
Very satisfied	1957	42	40	13	26	25	24	25	19	22
	1976	33	37	24	28	26	18	22	19	32
Neutral, ambivalent, dissatisfied	1957	16	16	30	26	20	16	20	21	16
	1976	21	20	26	19	27	32	28	35	6
Ego Involvement in Job Satisfaction:										
Only ego satisfaction	1957	77	70	43	64	53	44	37	40	58
	1976	80	73	71	67	57	46	70	44	61
Ego Involvement in Job Dissatisfaction:										
Mentioning some ego dissatisfaction	1957	25	37	39	28	12	25	30	8	15
	1976	58	48	38	56	35	32	41	41	10
Job Commitment: Not prefer other job	1957	65	72	39	53	55	55	57	66	79
	1976	56	62	45	56	39	40	52	41	87
Perceived Source of Job Satisfaction:										
Economic: Yes	1957	9	16	24	19	17	25	20	21	6
	1976	3	12	10	16	18	22	9	31	13
Extrinsic—Noneconomic: Yes	1957	12	14	37	15	30	37	45	28	29
	1976	16	13	21	19	19	33	17	31	29
Achievement-related: Yes	1957	28	27	11	15	21	10	7	8	10
	1976	52	38	26	23	33	10	11	12	23
Affiliation-related: Yes	1957	26	38	17	64	5	14	20	6	1
	1976	27	36	29	40	7	12	48	9	6
Specific People: Yes	1957	10	10	24	8	21	19	18	32	1
	1976	11	4	14	14	11	17	15	19	6
Power-related: Yes	1957	16	15	41	11	8	14	12	13	6
	1976	25	28	14	37	17	22	15	12	33
Interesting Work: Yes	1957	46	28	33	24	41	31	15	15	39
	1976	21	20	26	12	27	18	17	25	35

TABLE 6.36 (continued)

Job Reaction	Year	Professional (%)	Manager (%)	Clerical (%)	Sales (%)	Skilled (%)	Operative (%)	Service (%)	Laborer (%)	Farmer (%)
Perceived Source of Job Dissatisfaction:										
Economic: Yes	1957	14	14	18	17	18	16	15	28	36
	1976	8	14	17	5	13	17	24	12	29
Extrinsic—Noneconomic: Yes	1957	23	22	22	36	36	40	30	36	24
	1976	24	18	17	21	36	37	22	25	42
General Hard Work: Yes	1957	14	24	20	11	10	6	5	4	12
	1976	14	22	19	14	9	9	11	0	20
Lack of Achievement Potential: Yes	1957	9	5	11	11	6	8	7	2	2
	1976	9	10	14	5	7	10	4	16	0
Affiliative Lack or Problem: Yes	1957	11	20	13	8	9	9	8	2	4
	1976	27	22	21	30	14	12	13	12	10
Lack of Power: Yes	1957	6	6	7	4	1	2	7	0	5
	1976	22	15	7	12	6	4	11	9	0
II. Measures of Perceived Competence										
Perceived Ability Required: A lot	1957[a]	54	42	21	25	46	21	28	25	51
	1976	65	60	50	56	51	43	46	31	58
Perceived Ability at Job: Very good	1957[a]	37	32	43	31	26	23	56	19	23
	1976	60	57	52	63	44	50	65	50	26
III. Measure of Perceived Problem										
Work Problem:										
Yes	1957[a]	36	35	32	38	27	26	25	17	24
	1976	48	36	42	49	42	37	41	53	16
In Self	1957	17	12	14	12	11	11	10	4	8
	1976	11	16	22	29	15	14	11	22	6
Total Number	1957	116	116	54	52	210	161	60	47	86
	1976	132	122	42	43	175	114	46	32	31

TABLE 8.3
Occupational Differences in Women's Job Reactions, 1957–1976

Job Reaction	Year	Professional (%)	Manager (%)	Clerical (%)	Sales (%)	Skilled (%)	Operative (%)	Service (%)	Laborer (%)	Farmer (%)
I. Measures of Job Satisfaction										
Overall Job Satisfaction:										
Very satisfied	1957	56	30	39	36	—[a]	22	38	—[a]	—[a]
	1976	43	20	29	27	27	19	29	—[a]	9
Neutral, ambivalent, dissatisfied	1957	11	19	16	18	—[a]	26	12	—[a]	—[a]
	1976	25	32	31	38	27	25	24	—[a]	27
Ego Involvement in Job Satisfaction:										
Only ego satisfaction	1957	87	84	65	73	—[a]	38	64	—[a]	—[a]
	1976	80	83	66	73	40	46	65	—[a]	46
Ego Involvement in Job Dissatisfaction:										
Mentioning some ego dissatisfaction	1957	31	34	29	33	—[a]	19	23	—[a]	—[a]
	1976	58	52	53	50	18	33	32	—[a]	27
Job Commitment: Not prefer other job	1957[b]	61	36	38	52	—[a]	50	53	—[a]	—[a]
	1976	58	46	48	54	27	52	52	—[a]	36
Perceived Source of Job Satisfaction:										
Economic: Yes	1957	2	5	12	12	—[a]	29	11	—[a]	—[a]
	1976	3	7	13	12	46	23	10	—[a]	46
Extrinsic—Noneconomic: Yes	1957	9	8	19	6	—[a]	37	14	—[a]	—[a]
	1976	17	12	20	15	0	29	23	—[a]	18
Achievement-related: Yes	1957	11	16	16	6	—[a]	7	7	—[a]	—[a]
	1976	38	30	22	12	27	16	16	—[a]	0
Affiliation-related: Yes	1957	54	54	25	58	—[a]	14	37	—[a]	—[a]
	1976	50	54	34	81	9	7	41	—[a]	9
Specific People: Yes	1957	16	5	33	18	—[a]	34	26	—[a]	—[a]
	1976	13	17	27	15	18	26	23	—[a]	27
Power-related: Yes	1957	13	16	10	6	—[a]	5	6	—[a]	—[a]
	1976	17	15	13	8	0	6	6	—[a]	0
Interesting Work: Yes	1957	36	27	38	21	—[a]	22	20	—[a]	—[a]
	1976	25	15	24	15	46	23	10	—[a]	18

TABLE 6.37 (continued)

Job Reaction	Year	Professional (%)	Manager (%)	Clerical (%)	Sales (%)	Skilled (%)	Operative (%)	Service (%)	Laborer (%)	Farmer (%)
Perceived Source of Job Dissatisfaction:										
Economic: Yes	1957	9	11	9	12	—[a]	10	10	—[a]	—[a]
	1976	12	10	12	15	27	9	10	—[a]	0
Extrinsic—Noneconomic: Yes	1957	27	32	23	33	—[a]	40	27	—[a]	—[a]
	1976	20	29	16	23	27	22	27	—[a]	46
General Hard Work: Yes	1957	11	19	16	12	—[a]	12	9	—[a]	—[a]
	1976	10	17	12	15	27	12	13	—[a]	18
Lack of Achievement Potential: Yes	1957	7	3	7	3	—[a]	0	1	—[a]	—[a]
	1976	20	5	12	4	9	4	3	—[a]	0
Affiliative Lack or Problem: Yes	1957	13	14	15	15	—[a]	10	9	—[a]	—[a]
	1976	26	17	26	12	0	14	18	—[a]	9
Lack of Power: Yes	1957	4	3	4	6	—[a]	1	5	—[a]	—[a]
	1976	8	10	4	12	0	5	3	—[a]	0
II. Measures of Perceived Competence										
Perceived Ability Required: A lot	1957	—[c]	—[c]	—[c]	—[c]	—[c]	—[c]	—[c]	—[c]	—[c]
	1976	66	51	42	31	36	36	38	—[a]	18
Perceived Ability at Job: Very good	1957	—[c]	—[c]	—[c]	—[c]	—[c]	—[c]	—[c]	—[c]	—[c]
	1976	69	66	57	31	27	54	59	—[a]	82
III. Measure of Perceived Problem										
Work Problem:										
Yes	1957	—[c]	—[c]	—[c]	—[c]	—[c]	—[c]	—[c]	—[c]	—[c]
	1976	36	37	28	27	27	22	31	—[a]	0
In Self	1957	—[c]	—[c]	—[c]	—[c]	—[c]	—[c]	—[c]	—[c]	—[c]
	1976	11	15	9	12	9	4	15	—[a]	0
Total Number	1957	55	37	129	33	8	73	112	30	7
	1976	113	41	188	26	11	69	133	5	11

[a] Numbers less than 10; percent would be very unreliable.
[b] Question asked of two-thirds of working women in 1957.

surveys conducted two decades apart. In general, we find results presented in the previous section on education differences more compelling as an analysis of the effects of social status on work and job reactions. Hence, we will highlight here primarily those results which indicate that relationships observed in the general population between 1957 and 1976 occur either most dramatically or entirely within specific occupational groups. These results are:

1. The increased dissatisfaction previously reported for younger and more educated women in 1976 cannot be attributed to any particular occupational category. Thus, increased expectations that young, well-educated women have had over the generation for what work should be, and yet have found wanting, are apparently not specific to any particular occupational group. However, professional men and women are consistently more likely than others to report being very satisfied with their jobs.

2. When we examine ego involvement expressed in satisfactions and dissatisfactions among men and women in different occupational groups, we notice that the observed sex differences tend to break down. Thus, ego involvement with work seems to be more apparent among women than for men due to the kinds of jobs they are assigned, rather than to distinctive differences in the ways in which the two sexes work.

    A comparison of clericals and operatives provides a dramatic illustration of this effect. Men and women in these jobs seem to be equally ego involved in their work, but clerical workers seem to be more ego involved than operatives. Since women are more likely to be clerical workers than operatives, ego involvement appears to be greater for women than for men. In 1976 men and women in professional groups are about equally likely to mention ego involvements with their satisfactions and dissatisfactions, both clearly being very ego satisfied in their work, as were the managers of both sexes.

3. Job commitment appears to be particularly strong among American farmers in both 1957 and 1976. Since farming is an occupation which is fast fading from the American scene, we might anticipate that people who remain farmers do so out of a very conscious and deliberate choice, one that seems to be very binding.

4. The increase in achievement-related satisfactions expressed by men in 1976 seems to be primarily among professionals, but is also relatively strong among men in clerical jobs. Increased use of the computer in clerical settings over the generation may have helped to preserve achievement investments among male clerical workers.

5. The increased mention of power-related satisfactions among employed men between 1957 and 1976 seems to be most dramatic among salespeople. This does not seem to be so for women in that group.

6. The decrease in mentioning "interesting" work as a source of job satisfaction appears to occur within all occupational groups, but is most dramatic in men's reactions to professional and sales jobs. Curiously, then, in those jobs where there has been an increase over the generation in achievement (professionals) and power one also finds a *decrease* in reports of the job being interesting. This is consistent with our hypothesis

that an orientation to self-satisfactions in work decreases the potential of being absorbed in that work for its inherent task interest.

7. The increased mention of affiliative difficulties at work is evident in most occupational groups, and occurs clearly in both a high-status group (professional) and a low-status group (service for women, and laborers for men). Thus, decreased social integration at work is evident at both ends of the occupational spectrum.

8. Increases in perceived job abilities between 1957 and 1976 are common to *all* occupational groups.

9. Increased perceptions of problems at work, while occurring in all white-collar occupations to some extent, appear most dramatically for blue-collar jobs. Surprisingly, among laborers we find the most dramatic rise between 1957 and 1976 in reports of problems in the self as a basis for work difficulty. One might suspect that, as the country went into an era of expansion and affluence, during which a plethora of jobs existed, people in low-status jobs might read their inability to move out of poor jobs as a function of their own inadequacies.

From this examination of differences in occupational reactions to work in the two survey years, it is clear that differences are not profound. We are thus impressed with how much more education contributes to our understanding of differential job reactions than does this analysis by general occupational categories. In future analysis, we intend to derive more specific job categorizations that will help us analyze the nature of work settings more clearly than we can with these gross occupational classes. We have presented these tables specifically for readers who have an interest in the occupational classifications used in social science research over several decades. In chapter 8 we will return to these same categories again to determine the extent to which they distinguish men and women in their more generalized patterns of well-being, and in their problem-solving behaviors outside the work setting.

Summary

The results presented here describing year, age, sex, and educational differences in work salience and job reactions are fairly straightforward. While men's and women's involvement with individual accomplishment in work has increased over the generation, their involvement with the intrinsic nature of work has declined, as has their contentment with the affiliative climate of their work settings. Along with a distinctly greater commitment of women to work in the new generation, these are the critical year differences.

There are several consistent differences between the younger and older respondents in the ways they react to work; education also seems to have a profound effect on the way people react to work. A number of sex differences, some which vary dramatically by year, are also discussed in some detail.

We may now ask, how does this pattern of results help us answer the questions originally put forth at the beginning of this chapter? How do people adapt to their work settings? How do they adjust their aspirations? How does their involvement in work situations come to reflect those aspirations? Quite clearly, younger workers seem to be more distressed with work, more aware of their own shortcomings, and more sensitive to the difficulties that they experience. This pattern presumably reflects a pressure in the young to not accept the work as it is, but rather to demand more from it in order to achieve an ideal balance of gratifications in their work life. In contrast, older workers are essentially locked in to a set of circumstances which they have already adapted to, and hence tend to make the best of what they have.

Our results suggest that the adaptation to work dovetails with other roles. For example, there is some indication that older people are now more aware of their discontents at work. This situation may reflect a phasing out of the work role and a renewed commitment to leisure, a process triggered by an increased emphasis on retirement.

The profound differences noted between the college educated and the less educated in their reactions to work also give us some insight into the general questions raised above. Probably all people in our society hope that their work will serve to fulfill their inner desires for interesting and exciting experiences. But the college educated are perhaps especially oriented to viewing their work in this way, to reflect upon their experiences and to savor them. As a result, such expectations may be even more deeply rooted among the college educated than among less educated people. The more educated may also be more ego involved in what they experience as satisfaction or dissatisfaction in their work because they have been socialized to feel that one should expect *very personal* satisfactions from the job experience.

An interesting question is whether, in the process of becoming very ego involved in work, the more educated come to expect *too much* from that role. Do they develop such high expectations for individuation through a job that job gratification may be possible only in rare settings? Achieving a realistic balance between having some ego involvement in work and a perspective that work should not be the only focus of life, may be more easily accomplished by less educated people. That is, the less educated may be able to benefit from the interest there is at work, ignore the achievement aspects of it, and return to their nonwork life with a greater sense of equilibrium than men and women who get so achievement involved with their jobs that they tend to ig-

TABLE 6.38

Education Differences in Perceiving Work Interfering with Family (by sex)

Perception of Work Interfering with Family	Men Education			Women Education		
	Grade School (%)	High School (%)	College (%)	Grade School (%)	High School (%)	College (%)
Yes	10	23	33	6	16	19
Sometimes	11	15	19	12	17	17
No	79	62	48	82	67	64
	100%	100%	100%	100%	100%	100%
Total Number	200	121	431	50	348	210

nore intrinsic interests in their work and bring their driving aspirations for success home with them. Their concern may, in turn, disrupt their family lives.

We have some evidence consistent with this interpretation in responses to a question asked only in 1976. College-educated men and women are more likely than less educated workers to say that their work interferes with family life. (The exact question was "Do you feel that the demands of your work ever interfere with the demands of your family?") These data are presented in table 6.38. The results are more pronounced for men than women, but the same trend is evident for both sexes.

That we found sex differences in certain stereotypic reports of job satisfactions and dissatisfactions (men are more oriented to power, achievement, and economic matters, and women more to affiliation) is not particularly surprising, but nevertheless is important to emphasize because these findings derive from national survey data. These differences suggest that men and women adapt to work in characteristically different ways. Perhaps the most surprising result found in our compilation of these results is that men are *less* ego involved in work than women, from the standpoint of both satisfactions and dissatisfactions. This is a striking result in light of the other interpretations that have been given to men's greater involvement in work.

At the heart of this apparent discrepancy, of course, is our broader definition of ego involvement, conceived as *any* aspect of work which clearly engages one's sense of self. Having no special bias in using only achievement or power aspects of work to define "ego involvements," we included affiliative pleasures from work in our definition of ego involvement, and it is clear that women are *more* involved in the social fabric of work. Women are well aware that work allows them to achieve a better adaptation to the larger social order than staying at home with children and/or being a housewife. Demoralization frequently accrues to the housewife role, because in modern society we seem to overvalue performance at work. If anything, this recognition makes women *more* ego involved with work, despite their general assignment to lower-status jobs. Men rather routinely accept the fact that their place is at work, and hence are perhaps somewhat less ego involved in work once they are there.

At the same time, men may be learning more about the affiliative nature of work. One of the most important differences in expressed satisfactions in work across the generation is that men as well as women are more uncertain about their affiliative relationship at work. Men's greater attention to the affiliative nature of their jobs may foreshadow a critical new psychological adaptation to work in the future: one that may foster a true egalitarian exchange between men and women as they teach one another the joys of individuation *and* communion in the workplace.

Chapter 7

SYMPTOM PATTERNS

IN INTRODUCING the chapter on symptoms nearly twenty years ago, the authors of *Americans View Their Mental Health* expressed considerable bewilderment about the lack of a well-developed conceptual and theoretical framework for the creation and use of checklists or scales of psychological, physical, or psychosomatic symptoms as measures of "mental health" or "mental illness" in both research and clinical applications. Unfortunately, during the period between that first survey and the present study that theoretical void, though repeatedly decried (e.g., Seiler, 1973; Tousignant, Denis, and Lachapelle, 1974), is still very much in evidence. By now there is a very extensive methodological literature bearing on the validity of these scales, but there has still been relatively little research concern with the conceptual ramifications of these measures. While much important methodological work has raised the question about whether such checklists can appropriately be used to diagnose "mental disorder," very little research addresses the important theoretical question of what precisely *is* fruitfully measured by these widely used scales.

The Stirling County Study (Leighton, Harding, Macklin, MacMillan, and Leighton, 1963), using the Health Opinion Survey (MacMillan, 1957), and the Midtown Study (Srole, Langner, Michael, Opler, and Rennie, 1962), using the Langner Scale (1962), both of which include a core of items taken in part from the Army's Neuropsychiatric Screening Adjunct (Star, 1950), set the stage. These studies, perhaps unwisely, used such symptom lists as general indicators of mental illness or psychiatric impairment because they were particularly interested in identifying patterns of undetected or untreated mental disorder in the general community. In these two pioneering studies, more extensive psychiatric evaluations of respondent protocols served as the ultimate criteria of "case identification" against which these symptom lists were validated, thereby giving at least tacit endorsement to their subsequent use as screening devices for mental disorders in a general population. Because of that extensive preliminary work, in conjunction with the obvious practical and economical advantages of using such measures, epidemiologists and other researchers quickly adopted versions of those symptom checklists as quick and easy means of identifying cases of untreated psychiatric disorder in any population (Dohrenwend and Dohrenwend, 1974).

Unfortunately, however, the validity of these scales for that purpose was more often assumed than empirically established, and a solid body of methodological research conducted over the past fifteen to twenty years raises many critical questions about the wisdom of that strategy. For example, the potential influence of serious response biases in these symptom checklists has often been noted. Such biases may be found in the fact that different ethnic and social groups may regard the content of the symptoms as more or less undesirable or congruent with their styles (Dohrenwend and Dohrenwend, 1969). Other potential biases are inherent in results which show women reporting higher numbers or levels of symptoms than do men, since such sex differences may be interpreted not as "real" differences in psychiatric disorder, but rather as differences in how culturally "appropriate" or "acceptable" it is in our society for men and women to perceive such symptoms in themselves and/or to reveal their existence to others (e.g., Phillips and Segal, 1969; see also, however, Clancy and Gove, 1974).

Perhaps more important, however, psychiatric evaluations as the ultimate criteria for pinpointing psychiatric disorder may also reasonably be called into question (Dohrenwend, 1975). In this regard, problems associated with the heavy reliance upon the "known groups" research procedure for the validation of these scales have repeatedly been raised (Norland and Weirath, 1978; Seiler, 1973). While psychiatric judgments are necessarily pragmatic criteria, since psychiatrists are ultimately heavily involved in judging "disorder" in institutional settings, work by Blum (1978) suggests that these judgments may in fact be highly influenced by the fashions of thinking within psychiatry which happen to be au courant.

Overall, then, a substantial research literature has established beyond a reasonable doubt that the Langner Scale, the Health Opinion Survey, and variations thereof, are clearly inadequate as general measures of mental illness appropriate for the quick assessment of overall mental disorder or psychiatric impairment in a population (Dohrenwend, 1975; Schwartz, Myers, and Astrachan, 1973; Seiler, 1973; Spiro, Siassi, and Crocetti, 1972; Tousignant et al., 1974). In addition to the methodological and theoretical liabilities noted above, critics have emphasized that (1) all such scales include a substantial number of items which are physiological in content and are thereby confounded with physical illness; (2) even questions which are more clearly relevant to psychological impairment tend to measure only certain types of neurotic symptoms, namely aspects of anxiety and depression; and (3) the majority of items included in such indices deal only with rather mild forms of psychological disorder or distress (cf. Gove and Geerken, 1977).

Let us not, however, make the all too common error of throwing out the proverbial baby with the bath water. To acknowledge that symptom scales are not adequate as screening devices for mental illness or psychiatric impairment in the community is not to say that they lack significant value as indicators of how Americans *view* their mental health. Symptom patterns are interesting and important indicators of psychological experience in their own right; they represent the presenting complaints that people have, ones that they commonly use in conversations about the everyday stresses and strains of modern living. As such, they should play a critical role in any comprehensive assessment of the quality of subjective adjustment among adult Americans.

Since the emphasis adopted in *Americans View Their Mental Health* and in the present volume is on the theoretical and practical utility of using *multiple* indicators of well-being rather than one particular diagnostic criterion of good or poor mental health, we feel relatively immune from the barrage of theoretical and methodological criticism directed at these symptom measures over the past two decades. We look at the symptom list as just one among several ways of tapping people's feelings about their life experiences, as merely one means of assessing the degree to which one feels in relatively good or poor mental health. Although many of the items used in the original symptom checklist for *Americans View Their Mental Health* were, in fact, derived from the Health Opinion Survey and the Langner Scale, for both of which the stated purpose was to identify mental illness and psychiatric impairment in the general community, we categorically deny any interest in using the symptom measures in that way, in spite of the fact that other investigators have in recent years used the so-called "Gurin Mental Status Index" or "Gurin Scale" for that purpose (e.g., Gove and Tudor, 1973; Myers and Bean, 1968; Myers, Lindenthal, and Pepper, 1971; Schwartz et al., 1973).

We do not, however, disclaim the symptom checklist's potential for measuring certain aspects of well-being in our society. These symptoms are indeed signs of distress, bodily and psychological conditions which seem to characterize people under stressful conditions, and the symptom measures presumably do a reasonably good job of distinguishing between those who experience a large number or greater frequency of such symptoms and those who experience a smaller number or lesser frequency. Nevertheless, we would caution against giving greater weight to the incidence of these symptoms than to other dimensions of subjective well-being discussed in other chapters of this book. Within the "multiple criteria" paradigm, the symptom checklist is simply one of many potential indicators of psychological adjustment, no more or no less appropriate for the study of subjective mental health than any other measure in our arsenal.

In point of fact, we regard the symptom checklist itself not as *one* indicator of psychological adjustment or distress, but rather as a *composite* of different aspects or dimensions of subjective adjustment. Thus, in the 1960 volume, we reported not one symptom measure, but four. Based on factor analysis (a statistical technique often used in the social sciences to identify clusters of measures that theoretically reflect common "factors"), four distinct clusters of symptoms were isolated and named: (1) *Psychological Anxiety*, based on feelings of nervousness or not being able to sleep; (2) *Physical Health*, reflecting reports of pains and ailments or not feeling healthy enough to do things one would like to do; (3) *Immobilization*, a mystifying combination of finding it difficult to get up in the morning and being troubled by hands sweating so that they feel damp and clammy; and (4) *Physical Anxiety*, which included experiencing shortness of breath or rapid heartbeat. These four factors appeared to represent distinctly different though interrelated components of felt distress, and a number of subsequent studies have provided further evidence that these widely used mental-health indices possess multidimensional characteristics (e.g., Butler and Jones, 1979; Jegede, 1977; Seiler and Summers, 1974; Spiro, Siassi, and Crocetti, 1972). And yet, the bulk of research conducted with these measures has essentially assumed their unidimensionality (see Seiler, 1973) by simply summing across all symptom items to derive a global score, rather than attending to potential differences in patterns of relationships among items or in their relationships to other variables of interest.

Perhaps the most serious liability of this strategy has been a failure to explicitly take into account the substantial number of physiological symptoms among the checklist items. While factor analytic studies of these symptom lists, based on different sample populations and/or different mixes of symptom items, rarely produce identical dimensions, they rather consistently reveal the presence of at least two basic subscales: one dealing with aspects of psychological distress and another representing symptoms of physiological malaise (see Butler and Jones, 1979; Crandell and Dohrenwend, 1967; Meile, 1972; Phillips and Segal, 1969; Seiler, 1973; Seiler and Summers, 1974; Spiro et al., 1972; Tousignant et al., 1974). Indeed, we were well aware in our analyses of the 1957 data that there was a distinct physical-health component to the symptom checklist, as clearly indicated by our factor analyses. By isolating that component, we are able to use the physical-health subscale of the symptom checklist as a control variable when examining relationships involving the more psychologically oriented symptoms, thereby helping to clarify the potential confounding of physical and psychological symptomatology in the total scale.

In doing so, however, we wish to emphasize that even if we are able to separate aspects of physical health and psychological reactions contained in the checklist, we still strongly suspect that physical and psychological health are inextricably interwoven (see Eastwood and Trevelyan, 1972; Hinkle and Wolff, 1957; Shepherd, Cooper, Brown, and Kalton, 1966). Since physical ill health may be either a cause of psychological distress or a consequence of it (see Gove and Hughes, 1979), physical symptom items on the checklist may often represent useful indicators of psychological distress in their own right rather than extraneous content which serves to bias total scores or relationships (see Thoits and Hannan, 1979).

In general, however, we still strongly advocate the derivation and use of separate factors or dimensions of psychological or psychophysiological distress in research with these symptom scales: a multidimensional approach not unlike the clinical use of tests like the MMPI, which consists of a number of separate subscales, presumably diagnostic of certain specific psychiatric categories. Thus, in this volume, we continue to follow such a strategy because we feel that the derivation and use of different symptom measures can aid substantially in pinpointing sources of observed differences between population subgroups and in gaining a better theoretical understanding of the precise meaning of people's acknowledged complaints, experienced and reported in the course of everyday living.

A related and important methodological insight emerging from the substantial body of research on these symptom checklists accumulated over the past two decades raises questions about potential differences in the meanings of symptoms to members of different social groups. The Dohrenwends (1969, 1974), in particular, have been influential in demonstrating that different groups of people may have different ways of expressing felt disturbance, depending on the social context within which symptoms emerge. For example, they have presented data suggesting that Puerto Ricans may score higher on certain kinds of symptoms (e.g., somatic or psychophysiological symptoms) than other ethnic groups because their subculture tends to recognize such symptoms as part and parcel of everyday living and/or as the "appropriate" way to express psychological distress (Dohrenwend and Dohrenwend, 1969).

Earlier in this book, we referred to Hochschild's (1975) cogent analysis of social rules which may affect feeling states as well as behaviors. In recognizing the potential influence of such phenomena on reported symptomatology, the Dohrenwends have made us aware that certain subgroups of the population may view certain expressions of bodily complaints as natural to the ongoing social fabric of their community. As such, reports of such symptoms by members of those groups reflect not so much an admission of disturbance, but rather an awareness of the social rules governing how people are supposed to feel in that particular society. As a result, in using any one symptom, or even a commonly derived set of scales from one symptom checklist, researchers are bound to make some substantial errors in attributing felt disturbance to certain subgroups of the population. This is clearly an important insight with regard to the symptom list per se, but is also relevant to any question used in a national survey intended to apply to all people. Recall, for example, that we have already discussed such phenomena in connection with differences in the expression of happiness and unhappiness among different population subgroups and in connection with subgroup differences in describing oneself.

The pertinent question, however, is how to deal with the problems of social desirability and subcultural differences in symptomatic responses. Can we interpret the reporting of symptoms as reflecting anything more than an awareness of facets of experiences that people perceive as acceptable within the groups to which they belong? For example, how should one interpret the phenomenon of sex differences in symptomatic responses; i.e., that more women than men tend to report most of these symptoms? Should we interpret these differences as indicating that women experience more of the types of distress measured by these symptom items than men do, or that women simply see such distress as less undesirable than men do—or, at least, are less willing to view the *admission* of such distress as undesirable (see Phillips and Segal, 1969)? This active debate regarding sex differences is probably best resolved by assuming that, above and beyond these sources of response bias, there may indeed be some "real" differences between men and women in experiencing such symptoms.

Although there is some evidence that perceptions of the social desirability of symptom items are indeed related to symptomatic responses (e.g., Dohrenwend and Dohrenwend, 1969; Gove and Geerken, 1977; Phillips and Clancy, 1970, 1972), equally compelling evidence presented by Gove and others (Clancy and Gove, 1974; Gove and Geerken, 1977; Phillips and Clancy, 1972) suggests that sex differences do not account for much in the way of conscious social desirability of these items, and, in turn, that differences in response bias do not seem to account entirely for the sex differences consistently observed in studies using these symptom scales. More generally, Gove and his colleagues (Gove and Geerken, 1977; Gove, McCorkel, Fain, and Hughes, 1976) have recently reported systematic evidence that, while these types of response bias are indeed often statistically associated with indicators of mental health and/or traditional demographic variables, measures of response bias appear to have little impact on the observed relationships between mental-health measures and demographic variables commonly used in community surveys of mental health.

Nevertheless, because researchers cannot yet assume with confidence that such sources of response bias *never* act systematically to distort the patterns of relationships between reported symptoms and variables of interest, we still think it advisable to take reasonable precautions to guard against the potential influence of social desirability on measures derived from the symptom checklist. In addition to reiterating our avowed lack of interest in identifying the "mentally disturbed" or "impaired" and underscoring our interest in using the symptom list to make relative comparisons among certain groups, as opposed to conceiving of reported symptoms as "absolute" indicators, we suggest two other precautions to minimize possible distortions due to response bias. First, we should be particularly wary of interpreting a persistent choice of the "never" response to symptom items as a "true" indicator of lack of experienced symptomatology or distress, since among the group of respondents who manifest that pattern may well be a substantial number of conscious and unconscious "deniers." Accordingly, in our own analyses, we take the precaution of separating those respondents who reply "never" to an entire set of symptom items from those who are willing to admit experiencing at least one of the symptoms at one point or another. By doing so, we attempt to differentiate low symptom scores from *extreme* reports of the absence of symptomatology.

A second way to minimize the potential influence of response bias in our interpretations involves scores at the other extreme, whereby we take care to *distinguish extremely high scorers* on a symptom index from those reporting more moderate levels of experienced distress. For example, people who report "feeling nervous or tense" or experiencing certain other bodily symptoms "a great deal of the time" presumably constitute a very distinct group, one which is likely to contain very few "false positives." In comparisons involving these extreme scores, false negatives may well still be present, but should serve merely to dampen rather than obliterate observed relationships.

In this chapter we will present analyses of our 1976 replication of the same list of twenty symptom items used in 1957, in spite of the flurry of criticism about its use which has developed in the interim. In addition, however, this chapter will include a discussion of three other items concerning the use of alcohol and drugs as a way of handling difficulties, which were added to the end of the original symptom checklist. As we approached our analyses of the twenty items common to both survey years, we realized the exciting possibility of replicating the original factor analysis conducted with these items two decades ago. By repeating that analysis, we were able to determine whether the factor structure or patterns of symptoms found in 1957 remained essentially the same in 1976. Indeed, as we shall soon see, these analyses provide considerable evidence that the factor structures of symptoms for men and women are strikingly similar in both survey years. Because of this remarkable parallelism in factor structures across the two surveys for both sexes, we feel justified in using indices based on these factors in differential analyses with demographic characteristics and with other measures related to subjective mental health.

What follows in the next section, therefore, is a description of the factor analyses conducted with the symptom items, with an emphasis on factors found common to both sexes in both survey years. (Here we will be presenting many technical details about these analyses. Some readers may want to skip this section and proceed to a less technical summary on p. 346.) Indices based on those factors will then be examined for year differences and for differences among sex, age, and education groups in 1957 and 1976. At the end of the chapter we will then present additional data on the three items concerning substance abuse, asked only in the 1976 survey.

Factor Analyses of Twenty Symptom Items

Table 7.1 lists the twenty symptom items asked of all respondents in both 1957 and 1976. As described in the 1960 volume (Gurin et al., 1960), most of these items were taken from survey interviews of the Stirling County (MacMillan, 1957) and/or the Midtown (Srole et al., 1962) sudies, although revisions in wording were made and four items (3, 6, 10, and 16) were developed specifically for the 1957 study. In 1957 the questions were asked in the order listed; except for the last item, which had been asked in a series of questions immediately prior to the others in the questionnaire. The same questionnaire sequence was followed in 1976, but the three items (asked only in that survey) on the use of alcohol and medicines or drugs (see table 7.17) intervened between items 16 and 17. In both studies, the first sixteen items in Table 7.1 were presented in a respondent booklet checklist, which the interviewers were instructed to give respondents to fill in themselves, except where respondents were unable to read, in which case the interviewer read each item and the alternative replies. Except for the last four items in table 7.1, all items had four alternatives arbitrarily assigned scale values of 1, 2, 3, or 4; the last four yes/no questions were assigned scale values of 2 and 4. Where necessary, scale values were then reversed prior to analyses, so that a high value would indicate a greater frequency of experiencing the symptom for each item.

As in 1957, these symptom items were intercorrelated separately for men and women, and the resulting intercorrelation matrices were then

TABLE 7.1
Twenty Symptom Items Asked in 1957 and 1976

Items	Alternatives
1. Do you ever have trouble getting to sleep or staying asleep?	Nearly all the time. Pretty often. Not very much. Never.
2. Have you ever been bothered by nervousness, feeling fidgety or tense?	Nearly all the time. Pretty often. Not very much. Never.
3. Are you ever troubled by headaches or pains in the head?	Nearly all the time. Pretty often. Not very much. Never.
4. Do you have loss of appetite?	Nearly all the time. Pretty often. Not very much. Never.
5. How often are you bothered by having an upset stomach?	Nearly all the time. Pretty often. Not very much. Never.
6. Do you find it difficult to get up in the morning?	Nearly all the time. Pretty often. Not very much. Never.
7. Has any ill health affected the amount of work you do?	Many times. Sometimes. Hardly ever. Never.
8. Have you ever been bothered by shortness of breath when you were not exercising or working hard?	Many times. Sometimes. Hardly ever. Never.
9. Have you ever been bothered by your heart beating hard?	Many times. Sometimes. Hardly ever. Never.
10. Do you ever drink more than you should?	Many times. Sometimes. Hardly ever. Never.
11. Have you ever had spells of dizziness?	Many times. Sometimes. Hardly ever. Never.
12. Are you ever bothered by nightmares?	Many times. Sometimes. Hardly ever. Never.
13. Do you tend to lose weight when you have something important bothering you?	Many times. Sometimes. Hardly ever. Never.
14. Do your hands ever tremble enough to bother you?	Many times. Sometimes. Hardly ever. Never.
15. Are you troubled by your hands sweating so that you feel damp and clammy?	Many times. Sometimes. Hardly ever. Never.
16. Have there ever been times when you couldn't take care of things because you just couldn't get going?	Many times. Sometimes. Hardly ever. Never.
17. Do you feel you are bothered by all sorts of pains and ailments in different parts of your body?	Yes. No.
18. For the most part, do you feel healthy enough to carry out the things you would like to do?	Yes. No.
19. Have you ever felt that you were going to have a nervous breakdown?	Yes. No.
20. Do you have any particular physical or health problem?	Yes. No.

TABLE 7.2
Intercorrelation Matrix for Symptom Checklist in 1957 (by sex)[a]

Symptom Items	1	2	3	4	5	6	7	8	9	10	11	12	13	14	15	16	17	18	19	20
1. Trouble sleeping	—	.49[b]	29	29	21	11	31	29	24	04	27	23	16	28	16	22	17	18	19	24
2. Nervousness	.47[b]	—	33	25	28	16	32	31	34	09	33	26	21	37	34	34	25	16	30	25
3. Headaches	30	37	—	25	26	14	25	20	16	03	33	20	10	22	21	25	23	13	15	22
4. Loss of appetite	26	26	28	—	31	18	31	25	18	05	31	20	29	28	25	22	24	16	12	20
5. Upset stomach	23	29	26	24	—	13	22	17	15	07	22	18	15	17	15	19	17	09	12	20
6. Difficult getting up	03	20	13	14	18	—	07	06	06	15	06	10	14	11	26	26	-01	-01	05	01
7. Ill health interferes with work	34	38	27	23	29	10	—	42	37	-04	36	16	18	31	19	38	36	40	17	50
8. Shortness of breath	24	32	27	20	23	06	48	—	51	-02	37	10	15	28	22	29	29	31	17	36
9. Heart beats hard	26	36	28	20	25	09	41	57	—	08	36	16	14	26	20	26	25	20	16	27
10. Drinking	04	11	07	07	05	21	00	02	05	—	02	14	02	08	08	12	-03	-07	06	-07
11. Dizziness	31	37	36	27	28	09	41	38	43	06	—	26	19	27	19	30	30	24	20	29
12. Nightmares	18	24	17	10	21	16	20	18	19	11	19	—	16	25	20	20	20	12	18	11
13. Losing weight	14	24	12	25	15	10	16	08	13	11	17	20	—	19	24	16	09	02	17	15
14. Hands tremble	24	33	18	18	22	14	29	30	30	12	33	23	17	—	37	30	20	18	19	21
15. Hands sweat	16	29	18	20	21	16	21	19	28	15	29	16	22	33	—	33	15	08	21	11
16. Can't get going	26	35	27	27	26	25	47	33	35	08	41	21	19	30	32	—	20	20	15	24
17. Pains and ailments	24	27	25	17	21	04	32	28	28	01	28	17	11	19	19	26	—	32	15	28
18. Healthy enough to do things	16	16	13	09	10	01	39	29	20	-07	17	06	03	16	08	23	29	—	10	29
19. Nervous breakdown	22	34	18	17	16	10	29	23	28	08	30	15	17	19	24	31	18	13	—	19
20. Health trouble	28	30	21	14	18	-01	50	33	29	-03	34	13	06	19	12	28	30	34	23	—

[a] Intercorrelations for 968 men who answered all items are listed *above* the diagonal; intercorrelation for 1,228 women who answered all items are listed *below* the diagonal. Decimal points are omitted in all other figures. All correlations are positive unless otherwise indicated.
[b] Figures in table are product-moment correlations.

TABLE 7.3

Intercorrelation Matrix for Symptom Checklist in 1976 (by sex)[a]

Symptom Items	1	2	3	4	5	6	7	8	9	10	11	12	13	14	15	16	17	18	19	20
1. Trouble sleeping	—	.47[b]	29	28	25	12	31	23	23	11	24	21	17	28	19	29	28	13	26	23
2. Nervousness	.45[b]	—	34	27	29	18	35	29	38	15	30	27	24	45	31	37	30	13	35	19
3. Headaches	28	33	—	30	28	19	29	25	25	05	33	23	21	30	19	25	26	12	13	16
4. Loss of appetite	26	28	33	—	38	16	23	21	14	09	26	21	31	26	20	28	18	09	13	06
5. Upset stomach	23	31	32	34	—	20	28	20	19	11	23	21	22	28	24	26	16	02	18	15
6. Difficult getting up	13	20	18	12	24	—	14	03	07	18	06	14	19	13	18	26	04	-03	10	-04
7. Ill health interferes with work	26	31	21	29	26	13	—	44	40	01	44	22	17	34	23	41	42	34	17	42
8. Shortness of breath	23	31	22	23	20	11	41	—	54	07	46	20	16	30	22	34	34	28	17	29
9. Heart beats hard	20	32	21	24	21	10	37	53	—	07	43	24	21	35	25	33	34	29	23	29
10. Drinking	03	07	01	08	09	15	-04	03	04	—	05	16	12	07	08	12	02	-05	04	-05
11. Dizziness	28	34	33	30	26	09	38	38	43	07	—	32	24	34	22	34	28	28	22	27
12. Nightmares	17	24	22	19	28	14	15	19	20	13	22	—	23	31	27	29	16	06	11	13
13. Losing weight	15	26	17	36	19	11	10	11	13	12	18	20	—	22	25	32	18	09	22	04
14. Hands tremble	26	37	28	34	23	07	26	31	32	10	34	24	29	—	38	39	26	19	26	19
15. Hands sweat	15	26	22	19	25	15	19	25	24	13	24	24	24	39	—	37	17	09	19	05
16. Can't get going	24	33	21	24	24	23	43	33	33	07	35	20	21	36	30	—	27	15	22	16
17. Pains and ailments	21	22	21	13	21	04	37	28	31	-04	26	07	03	23	20	24	—	37	21	36
18. Healthy enough to do things	18	19	07	15	06	09	38	27	22	-08	23	01	07	21	10	25	33	—	12	29
19. Nervous breakdown	21	39	26	18	16	14	22	17	18	13	25	15	18	24	12	25	09	06	—	14
20. Health trouble	22	26	6	15	18	-01	50	33	32	-10	33	07	02	18	09	28	38	30	17	—

[a] Intercorrelations for 893 men who answered all items are listed *above* the diagonal; intercorrelation for 1,177 women who answered all items are listed *below* the diagonal.

[b] Figures in table are product-moment correlations. Decimal points are omitted in all other figures. All correlations are positive unless otherwise indicated.

factored. Tables 7.2 and 7.3 present the intercorrelation matrices of the twenty symptom items for 1957 and 1976, respectively, with the intercorrelations for men appearing above the diagonal and those for women below the diagonal in both tables. In each case, the intercorrelations are based on only those subjects who responded to all questions. Table 7.4 presents results of four separate factor analyses based on those intercorrelation matrices. Separate principal components analyses[1] were conducted on symptom responses obtained from each group of respondents, extracting all components with eigenvalues greater than or equal to 1.0. Because this principal-components solution extracted only three factors for one group (1957 females), only three factors were rotated to the normalized varimax criterion (an orthogonal rotation algorithm). Following varimax rotation, the three components accounted for 16.2–17.7 percent, 12.9–14.1 percent, and 9.3–11.9 percent of the variance among the original items, respectively.

A comparison of the rotated factor loadings presented by sex and year in table 7.4 reveals a remarkable similarity in the factor structures for men and women both within and across the two survey years. There are some differences, but it is strikingly apparent that items which have high loadings on a given factor for one of the four sex x year groups tend also to have high factor loadings for the other three groups; items with low factor loadings on one of the components for one group tend to have relatively low factor loadings for the others as well. The practical advantage of the similarity in these factor loadings is that it provides a reasonable justification for deriving identical factor scores or indices for men and women in the two survey years. Based in large part on the labels suggested in *Americans View Their Mental Health*, the three factors are designated *Ill Health*,[2] *Psychological Anxiety*, and *Immobilization*.

A fourth factor described in the 1960 volume—*Physical Anxiety*—is excluded here because our replication failed to distinguish it as a separate factor. In retrospect, that factor was the most unstable of the factors emerging in the original study, since items found to load particularly high on *Physical Anxiety* were generally also moderately loaded on the others. In addition, analyses using that factor failed to produce results which differed significantly from those obtained using other factors.

---

[1] In 1957, factors were extracted by the *centroid* method and rotated to a normalized varimax criterion, as programmed for the IBM 650 computer. With the advent of large-capacity, high-speed computers, factor-analysis programs based on the centroid method have rapidly given way to the more popular method of principal axes (see Nunnally, 1967). Using several more "modern" factor-analysis program options available to us, we were not able to replicate precisely the analyses reported in 1960 for the 1957 data. As a result, we decided to abandon that effort, and the principal-components analyses presented here provided by far the most interpretable and consistent results of all the various factor-analytic procedures employed.

[2] The factor labeled *Physical Health* in the 1960 volume is renamed *Ill Health* here to more clearly designate the direction of the component items and the composite index to be described shortly.

TABLE 7.4

Rotated Factor Loadings Derived From Principal Component Factor Analyses of Symptom Items[a] (by sex × year)

Symptom Items	Factor 1 (Ill Health) Men 1957	Men 1976	Women 1957	Women 1976	Factor 2 (Psychological Anxiety) Men 1957	Men 1976	Women 1957	Women 1976	Factor 3 (Immobilization) Men 1957	Men 1976	Women 1957	Women 1976	Commonalities[b] Men 1957	Men 1976	Women 1957	Women 1976
1. Trouble sleeping	26[c]	19	26	22	54	69	65	63	09	03	-07	-05	37	52	50	45
2. Nervousness	31	27	33	29	52	60	59	64	33	28	25	17	48	51	51	53
3. Headaches	18	22	23	13	58	50	58	64	04	20	06	11	37	34	39	44
4. Loss of appetite	17	04	06	17	60	55	64	52	11	27	10	27	40	39	42	37
5. Upset stomach	05	04	21	14	64	57	44	50	-02	26	21	28	41	40	28	34
6. Difficult getting up	-09	-17	-02	-01	15	27	04	27	59	45	63	31	38	31	40	17
7. Ill health interferes with work	71	64	72	70	26	32	25	26	05	14	11	01	57	53	59	56
8. Shortness of breath	72	69	70	65	10	06	12	09	18	28	16	28	56	55	52	51
9. Heart beats hard	63	67	61	63	04	08	19	08	31	32	26	33	49	55	47	51
10. Drinking	-14	-12	-14	-16	00	03	00	-02	53	46	60	57	30	23	38	35
11. Dizziness	47	59	49	50	42	16	40	33	08	33	22	24	40	49	45	42
12. Nightmares	06	21	15	07	48	12	23	27	21	55	38	48	28	37	22	31
13. Losing weight	04	08	-07	-03	42	29	48	37	22	47	28	43	22	31	31	32
14. Hands tremble	33	36	35	35	32	34	18	29	39	42	46	47	37	42	36	43
15. Hands sweat	16	19	21	26	26	15	20	08	61	58	54	62	46	40	38	46
16. Can't get going	40	33	48	43	18	27	25	24	52	54	40	35	46	47	46	41
17. Pains and ailments	51	57	49	62	29	35	25	12	-10	-05	03	-04	35	46	30	41
18. Healthy enough to do things	-63	-64	-65	-61	-06	-04	05	-04	12	12	10	08	41	42	43	38
19. Nervous breakdown	17	16	33	09	33	48	27	56	17	07	25	09	17	26	24	38
20. Health trouble	61	60	66	68	26	26	17	21	-11	-22	-10	-21	45	48	48	55

[a] Principal components analysis extracted: five factors for males, three for females in the 1957 data; and four for both males and females in the 1976 data. Three factors were rotated in normalized varimax rotations for each analysis.

[b] Commonalities indicate the degree to which these three factors account for the variance in response to these items.

As a result, the replicated factor analysis presented here led us to eliminate a relatively unreliable (nonorthogonal) factor. By contrast, the remaining three factors are very distinct in both the 1957 and 1976 data. There are indeed slight differences here and there for men and women or 1957 and 1976, but by and large, the factor structures are strikingly parallel across the four-factor analyses.

Next we derived indices based on selected symptom items which would adequately describe the nature of each factor for all four sex x year groups. We did not want to use statistically derived factor scores in which all twenty items are weighted according to their factor loadings because the use of empirically derived factor loadings based on one particular study hinders widespread use of the resulting measures and because such factor scores frequently lack clear face validity. Thus, as in 1957, we decided to select certain symptom items that we thought best represented each of the three emergent factors and then compute factor scores by adding together responses to the items selected for each symptom factor.

The criteria used in the 1960 monograph for selecting certain symptom items rather than others as representative of a particular factor were that selected items be highly loaded (.40 or higher) on the factor in question and *only* on that factor (i.e., had loadings below .30 on other factors), so that resulting factor indices would be relatively independent of one another. In general, these rather conservative criteria were also applied here, although certain deviations were permitted in order to increase the reliability and/or the face validity of the derived factor indices.

Applying these criteria, the following items were selected to represent the three factors which consistently emerged from the factor analyses reported in table 7.4:

Factor 1: *Ill Health.* Items selected for this factor—interference of ill health with work (7), shortness of breath (8), heart beats hard (9), pains and ailments (17), healthy enough to do things (18), and health trouble (20)—each had loadings of .45 or more on the first factor and no loading higher than .35 on the other two factors. Thus, our measure of ill health is relatively pure, with internal consistency reliability estimates (i.e., Cronbach's [1951] coefficient alpha) ranging from .76 to .77 for the four sex/year groups.

Factor 2: *Psychological Anxiety.* Items representing this factor—trouble sleeping (1), nervousness (2), headaches (3), loss of appetite (4), and upset stomach (5)—all with one exception (1957 women on item 5), had loadings of .50 or greater on factor 2; and factor loadings of .33 or less on the other factors. Although the "nervousness" item in particular showed moderate loadings (.31-.33) on the other two factors, our assessment of this factor still seems relatively pure, with interitem reliability values (coefficient alpha) ranging from .68 to .69.

Factor 3: *Immobilization.* This third factor was somewhat more difficult to represent because the items selected—difficulty getting up in the morning (6), drinking (10), hands sweating (15), and can't get going (16)—seemed more widely discrepant than items which appear to characterize the other two factors. The first three symptoms are essentially pure items on this factor, since they have relatively high loadings on this factor (loadings of .45 or greater, except for women in 1976 on "difficulty getting up"), and relatively low factor loadings (all less than .30) on the others. While the fourth item (can't get going) also loads relatively high on this factor, it also has high loadings on the other two, especially on *Ill Health*. Nevertheless, we include it in this factor score because it has considerably more face validity as a dimension of "immobilization" than as a component of either "ill health" or "psychological anxiety," and because it improves the internal consistency reliability estimates for this measure, which nevertheless remain rather low, ranging from .46 to .50.[3] However, in recognition of the probable confounding (however slight) of these factors by the inclusion of item 16 in factor 3, we will take care in analyses involving the *Immobilization* measure to control for the effects of *Ill Health* and *Psychological Anxiety* on the results observed.

To make some additional judgments about whether our selection of items was appropriate, we further subdivided our sample into various age groups (21–34, 35–54, and 55+) within the sex x year stratification described above and examined patterns of intercorrelations among the selected items within each of these subgroups. In general, intercorrelations among the items selected for each factor are significant and consistent within each subgroup, with one notable exception: the "drinking" item shows a particularly low pattern of intercorrelations with other items in the *Immobilization* factor for older men and women. As it turns out, very few older respondents report that they "ever drink more than they should," resulting in a skewed distribution for this item and hence an attenuation of its capacity to generate reliable correlations with other symptom items. In younger age groups, correlations involving this item are consistently significant, though not strong. Nevertheless, because of its consistently high loading on factor 3, we have included the "drinking" item in the *Immobilization* index.

INTERCORRELATIONS AMONG THE THREE FACTOR SCORES

As noted above, factor indices were derived by adding together the responses to items selected for each symptom factor, with the four response items weighted 1–4 according to increasing reported frequency and yes/no items weighted 4 and 2, respectively (except for item 18,

---

[3] Nunnally (1967, p. 226) suggests that the use of measures with modest reliabilities of .50 or .60 may well suffice in the early stages of research on hypothesized measures of a construct. While our estimates for the other two factors are clearly sufficient according to these criteria, those for the *Immobilization* factor are borderline.

TABLE 7.5

Intercorrelation of Symptom Factor Scores (by sex × year)

		Correlations of:					
		Ill Health with Psychological Anxiety		Ill Health with Immobilization		Immobilization with Psychological Anxiety	
Year	Sex	Number	r	Number	r	Number	r
1957	Men	1,071	.45[a]	1,071	.25	1,070	.37
	Women	1,381	.47	1,382	.30	1,380	.39
1976	Men	946	.39	945	.22	916	.40
	Women	1,283	.40	1,282	.30	1,282	.39

[a] This correlation and all others in this table are highly significant ($p < .0001$) given the size of population on which they are based.

weighted 2 and 4). While an "orthogonal" factor analysis should eliminate factors which are independent of each other (i.e., items which constitute a given factor score should have negligible factor loadings on all the others), we know from table 7.4 and the preceding discussion that this objective was only partially achieved. Thus, we clearly expect some relationship among the three factor scores.

Intercorrelations among the three factor scores are presented by sex and year in table 7.5. As anticipated, these scores are significantly related to one another in all four subgroups. In general, while this pattern of intercorrelations may be viewed as a measure of the extent to which these three indices depart from the ideal of "independence," it may also be viewed as reflecting, in part, the influence of shared-method error (e.g., response style) and, especially, the fact that any given symptom may indeed reflect more than one dimension. Perhaps especially worth noting is the substantial relationship between *Ill Health* and *Psychological Anxiety* and, to a somewhat lesser extent, between *Ill Health* and *Immobilization*. Thus, this pattern of intercorrelations alerts us once again to the advisability of controlling for *Ill Health* when examining relationships involving the other two factor scores.

Nevertheless, in emphasizing relationships among the three indices, one should not overlook the fact that much of the variance in these items is *not* accounted for by these relationships. These factors still appear to reflect three diverse—though interrelated—styles which people use to express or complain about their distress. For example, people reporting frequent symptoms of *Ill Health* are expressing their awareness of being in poor general (physical) health, which may or may not have direct implications for mental health functioning. The fact that physical ill health is indeed strongly correlated with the other more psychological symptoms suggests a definite overlap between experiencing psychological distress and feeling in poor health (see Tessler and Mechanic, 1978). A dynamic interaction between psychological and physical health has long been recognized (e.g., Eastwood and Trevelyan, 1972; Gove and Hughes, 1979).

Psychological Anxiety represents a more direct expression of psychological distress, even though such complaints may also reflect physical difficulties to some degree. Two items in particular (trouble sleeping and nervousness) are usually interpreted as direct reports of psychological difficulties, but they may also have a physical basis. The other symptoms comprising this dimension (headaches, loss of appetite, and upset stomach) are probably best viewed as having both physical and psychological components: i.e., as psychological conditions involving no direct physical precipitants and/or as symptoms having direct health-related causes. Thus, it is not surprising that *Ill Health* and *Psychological Anxiety* are substantially correlated with each other.

A similar difficulty is encountered with regard to *Immobilization*, although two of its component items (drinking too much and, to a lesser extent, difficulty getting up in the morning) had slight negative factor loadings on *Ill Health*. Apparently, persons who admit to either drinking too much or having trouble getting up tend to perceive themselves as being in good health. As we will discover shortly, high symptoms of immobilization are more common among younger people, who in turn perceive themselves as being physically healthy. In contrast, "hands sweating" and "can't get going" show positive correlations with both *Psychological Anxiety* and *Ill Health*.

A plausible hypothesis, based on the patterns of factor loadings and intercorrelations is that *Immobilization* assesses, at least in part, alcoholism-proneness. In this regard, it would be particularly interesting to determine whether alcoholics tend to experience some of the symptoms on this scale more than other people.[4] Consistent with this line of reasoning is the fact that two of the items included only in 1976 (whether people ever drink to reduce tension, and whether their drinking ever caused a problem with family relationships), correlate much more highly with *Immobilization* than with the *Ill Health* and *Psychological Anxiety* factors (see table 7.18).

Summary of Factor Analysis of Symptoms

The statistical technique of factor analysis was applied to the intercorrelations of the responses to the symptom items asked in 1957 and 1976. This technique isolated three groups of items that represented

[4] In particular, it would be critical to discover whether alcoholics report their hands sweat so that they feel "damp and clammy" more than others in the general population. This symptom remains (as it did in 1957) a "mysterious" item on the *Immobilization* factor, but its persistent loading on this factor suggests that it should be included.

clearly different factors of psychological functioning. It was remarkable that these resulting factors were very similar in four different analyses: 1957 men, 1957 women, 1976 men, and 1976 women. The factors and the items which best characterize them are listed below:

> *Ill Health:* interference of ill health with work (item 7 of the symptom check list, see Table 7.1, p. 000); shortness of breath (item 8); hard heartbeats (item 9); pains and ailments (item 17); healthy enough to do things (item 18); health trouble (item 20).
>
> *Psychological Anxiety:* trouble sleeping (item 1); nervousness (item 8); headaches (item 3); loss of appetite (item 4); upset stomach (item 5).
>
> *Immobilization:* difficulty getting up in the morning (item 6); drinking (item 10); hands sweating (item 15); can't get going (item 16).

These factors are somewhat related to one another. In particular, *Ill Health* is a factor which when estimated as a score by adding the above items listed for the factor is also correlated with similarly constructed scores for *Psychological Anxiety* and *Immobilization*. These three symptom scores will be analyzed in the remaining sections of this chapter, each being a different way of thinking about symptoms of distress that people complain about in their everyday lives. Hence, analyzing year, sex, age, and education difference in these scores will very likely produce divergent results for the three factors.

Year, Sex, Age, and Education Related to the Differential Prevalence of Symptom Factors

Let us now turn to the exciting prospect of comparing patterns of symptom scores across a generation. We will first examine year differences in the prevalence of these symptoms, then move on to sex, age, and educational differences in symptom patterns. As in previous chapters, we will highlight differences which emerge as significant from multivariate analyses which simultaneously examine the cross-classification of symptom factors by year, sex, age, and education, including their potential interactions (see table 7.6). Consequently, results discussed in the following few pages are emphasized only if they reflect findings found to be independent of the effects of these other variables. Moreover, because these three scales are significantly correlated with one another, we repeated the multivariate analyses for each symptom score with an additional control for the other two. Unless otherwise indicated, the results we discuss below are also independent of these further refinements.

TABLE 7.6

Summary of Multivariate Analyses of Symptom Scores

| | Relationships Required[a] to Reproduce Observed Cross-classification of Measures (by age × education × year × sex) | | | | |
| | Main Effects[b] | | | | |
Symptoms Scores	Age	Education	Year	Sex	Interaction
Ill Health	Y<MA<O	G>H>C	57<76	M<F[d]	
Psychological Anxiety		G>H>C	57<76	M<F[d]	Age × Year
Immobilization	Y>MA>O	College More Moderate	57<76[c]	M<F[d]	Age × Education (Age × Year)[e]

[a] See footnote a of Table 2.11 for an explanation of "Required."

[b] See footnote a of Table 2.11 for description of "Main Effects."

[c] More "denial" in 1957.

[d] Males "deny" ever having these symptoms more than females.

[e] This interaction not needed when ill-health control is applied.

YEAR DIFFERENCES IN SYMPTOM SCORES

Table 7.7 shows the distributions for the three symptom factors: *Ill Health, Psychological Anxiety,* and *Immobilization* for men and women in 1957 and 1976. In that table we have indicated those scores which are "high." In no way do we wish "high" to indicate *disorder.* We wish a "high" score to be interpreted only in a statistical sense. To achieve a "high" score, a person had to report "pretty often" to at least one of the symptoms that compose each scale. Furthermore, some one who said "not very much" to all of the items on the scale would still have a score less than "high." What is indicated as a "low" score in each of the scales is a value attained when people say "never" to all the items that compose the scale. Within such scores called "low" are undoubtedly many people who deny having any symptoms because they think admitting or having such symptoms would be socially undesirable.

What is clear from the distributions of 1957 and 1976 when subjected to cross-classification analysis by year x sex x age x education is that there is a significant tendency for men and women in 1976 not to have as many as extreme "low" scores in all of the factor scores as did their counterparts in 1957. Furthermore, there is a significant year difference at the higher end of the *Ill Health* and *Psychological Anxiety* scales in the reverse direction: men and women in the new generation reported higher amounts of *Ill Health* and *Psychological Anxiety* than did their counterparts in 1957. This was not true for *Immobilization,* for which the year differences occurred significantly only at the low end of the scale.

These results can be interpreted differentially. They could indicate that more men and women have more of the reported symptoms in

TABLE 7.7

Year Differences in Symptom Scores (by sex)[a]

Symptom Scores	Men		Women	
	1957 (%)	1976 (%)	1957 (%)	1976 (%)
Ill Health Score				
(Low) 9	47	35	34	28
10–11	15	14	15	14
12	16	24	18	20
13–15	12	15	17	20
(High) 16–24	10	12	16	18
	100%	100%	100%	100%
Total Number	1,072	946	1,383	1,285
Psychological Anxiety Score				
(Low) 5	24	14	13	7
6–7	31	28	27	21
8	16	18	18	19
9–10	19	29	23	32
(High) 11–20	10	11	20	21
	100%	100%	100%	100%
Total Number	1,071	948	1,381	1,287
Immobilization Score				
(Low) 4	22	11	16	10
5–6	35	31	32	34
7	13	20	16	19
8–9	11	15	12	16
(High) 9–16	19	22	24	22
	100%	100%	100%	100%
Total Number	1,071	946	1,382	1,284

[a] Distribution omits respondents whose scores are not ascertained because more than one item comprising any given score is missing.

their everyday life experience, or they could mean that fewer men and women are constrained by sanctions against reporting or having symptoms. Both interpretations are possible, especially when we realize that over this generation our culture has become more psychologically sophisticated and hence more alerted to symptoms and less prone to deny their presence. Although we should be cautious about seeing the shift from the "never" category in response to questions about symptoms by itself as a real change in symptoms over the generation, we should also be cautious about seeing it merely as a difference between 1957 and 1976 in styles of reporting. Other data are needed to support the varying interpretations. Even at that, the two major hypotheses may be linked inextricably. If the new generation is more open to la-

TABLE 7.8

"High"[a] Psychological Anxiety Among People
of Different Ages (by year)

Age	Number	1957 (%)	1976 (%)	Number
21–34	759	11	16	809
35–54	1,004	14	18	695
55+	678	22	17	729

[a] Scores of 11–20.

beling experiences of symptoms for themselves and/or reporting these experiences to others, might they also be led to experience *more* of these symptoms? There may be a snowballing effect. Greater openness to acknowledging a symptom may lead to categorization of more experiences within that label. Dynamic psychosomatic processes can introduce interactive effects between labeling and new symptom formation.

The fact that year differences applied throughout the distribution of scores for *Ill Health* and *Psychological Anxiety* in the multivariate analysis but not to the *Immobilization* scale suggests that increased *experience* of ill health and anxiety is more plausible than increased experience of immobilization. We might guess that merely a shift away from the "never" category as a simple response style change would not necessarily affect the experience of *frequent* symptoms. This latter may be going on with *Immobilization*. The increase in immobilization in 1976 may be merely a shift away from denying immobilization symptoms that was more prevalent in 1957. We are harder pressed into giving that interpretation for *Ill Health* or *Psychological Anxiety*.

The increase in *Psychological Anxiety* from 1957 to 1976 needs qualification. We shall see in a subsequent section and in subsequent tables that the general increase in *Psychological Anxiety* across the generation is much more apparent in younger groups in our society than in older groups.[5] Relatively speaking, the oldest group is reporting less *Psychological Anxiety* than did the comparable group a generation ago (see table 7.8). The results for *Psychological Anxiety* are quite in keeping with the results we have found about changes in worries from 1957 to 1976, results showing that younger groups particularly increased about their frequency of worry. Thus, we will have to conclude that this generation has become much more aware of their anxieties, but that the awareness is particularly predominant in young people. The general increase and awareness of ill health has occurred across all age groups between 1957 and 1976.

While there were no overall year differences in the report of *Immobi-*

---

[5] There is a significant age x year interaction in the multivariate analysis for *Psychological Anxiety*.

TABLE 7.9

"High"[a] Immobilization Scores Among People
of Different Ages (by age)

Age	Number	1957 (%)	1976 (%)	Number
21–34	758	30	31	808
35–54	1,005	23	20	692
55+	629	10	14	728

[a] Scores of 9–16.

lization symptoms other than in the decrease in denial, there was an apparent cohort effect. Middle-aged people in 1957 were slightly higher in *Immobilization* relative to the middle-aged in 1976, while the older group in 1976 were slightly higher relative to the older group in 1957. Thus, we seem to be following a cohort: people middle-aged in 1957 who were relatively high in symptoms of *Immobilization* were also relatively high in these symptoms as an older group. These trends can be seen in table 7.9. There are only small but significant differences, which in fact get muddled when the *Ill Health* control is applied to the analysis.[6] Nevertheless, it may be an interesting cohort phenomenon worth considering. As a cohort which was middle-aged in 1957, it was a little late for the newfound energy that the very young generation of postwar mobile people inspired. Perhaps it was a cohort which was "left behind." If they were immobilized (or alcohol prone) as middle-aged people in the late 1950s, they seem to have maintained that mode of adaptation in their older years. We are interpreting this trend as a cohort effect, but this may be an error. There may be ways in which being middle-aged in 1957 and being old in 1976 have particular historical significance, but we find such an interpretation with regard to immobilization a little difficult to ponder. In any case, it is a slight tendency and should not be overly emphasized.

SEX DIFFERENCES

Table 7.7 offers direct confirmation in the analyses of two of the symptom factor scores for the often-quoted finding that women are more likely to report symptoms of distress than men. These results are apparent in both 1957 and 1976 for *Ill Health* and *Psychological Anxiety*. These results are maintained in multivariate analyses of these symptom scales. They are pronounced at every level of reported symptoms. There were significantly more reports of high symptoms in women and low symptoms in men. There is thus no evidence that men's liber-

---

[6] There is a significant age x year interaction for *Immobilization* in the multivariate analysis, but this is no longer needed when *Ill Health* is also used as a contorol.

ation to be more relaxed about masculine stereotypes—stoical denial of symptoms of ill health—has closed any gaps in the male-female comparisons. Nor has there been any abatement of the differences between men and women in *Psychological Anxiety*. This "hysterical" symptom pattern which is stereotypically feminine, remains stronger in women.

Sex differences are found as trends in *Immobilization*, but we hesitate to call them a general sex difference because the multivariate analyses indicated that the trend was only in the denial of symptoms of *Immobilization*, men being more denying than women. That result seems to be accounting for the difference rather than any extreme appearance of high *Immobilization* symptoms among women. That pattern is perplexing because all other evidence suggests that women report *more* symptoms than men. It became clear why this is so. One item on the *Immobilization* scale was, "Do you drink too much?" On that item, many more men report drinking too much "sometimes" or "often" than do women. This fact increased men's *Immobilization* scores. Without that item, sex differences in *Immobilization* would be found. On all of the other items in *Immobilization*, women report higher frequencies than men. Only on the report of overindulging in alcohol do men show higher frequencies. Whether women deny overindulgence as a symptom because it would be socially undesirable to report such an unladylike symptom, or whether indeed women overindulge less because such behavior is a symptom culturally prescribed for men only, is an open question. In our later analyses of drinking vs. drug taking as modes of relieving tension, we will find more women than men reporting the use of drugs or medicines. Perhaps in medicine and drug taking we see a compensatory symptom in women for the greater use of alcohol by men. In addition, we might speculate that among women who are alcohol prone, there may be a number who use another type of overindulgence—overeating—to express their immobilization.

AGE DIFFERENCES

Tables 7.10, 7.11, and 7.12 report age differences in symptom scores. Age by itself seems critical with regard to *Ill Health* and *Immobilization*. *Ill Health* increases with age, as we would naturally expect. In 1957 we had evidence that young people were more likely to be immobilized than middle-aged people, who in turn were more likely to be immobilized than older people. The same holds true for the multivariate analyses of 1976 data. *Immobilization* thus seems to be as powerful a symptom pattern among young people as *Ill Health* is among the elderly.

The multivariate analyses showed that age differences in symptoms depend considerably on both people's educational level and/or the year the interview was done. We already have indicated one of these conditional age differences: young people in 1976 are more likely to be anxious than they were in 1957, and the opposite seems to be true for

Age

Ill Health Scores	21-29 1957 %	21-29 1976 %	30-39 1957 %	30-39 1976 %	40-49 1957 %	40-49 1976 %	50-59 1957 %	50-59 1976 %	60-64 1957 %	60-64 1976 %	65+ 1957 %	65+ 1976 %
Men												
(Low) 9	63	45	53	45	43	42	45	22	46	14	24	21
10-11	11	14	16	12	22	16	14	15	15	11	13	12
12	15	26	18	25	16	21	14	29	14	24	18	19
13-15	10	12	9	11	12	12	12	21	18	24	16	18
(High) 16-24	1	3	4	7	7	9	16	13	6	27	28	30
	100%	100%	100%	100%	100%	100%	100%	100%	100%	100%	100%	100%
Total Number	187	234	250	214	231	155	178	133	65	74	159	136
Women												
(Low) 9	46	40	39	38	35	32	30	22	23	10	14	14
10-11	18	18	15	17	17	11	11	15	11	9	12	7
12	16	23	18	20	22	21	19	18	17	15	16	18
13-15	13	14	18	17	14	23	16	21	21	28	25	25
(High) 16-24	7	5	10	8	12	13	24	24	28	38	33	36
	100%	100%	100%	100%	100%	100%	100%	100%	100%	100%	100%	100%
Total Number	266	316	334	246	284	185	211	201	87	90	192	245

TABLE 7.11
Age Differences in Psychological Anxiety Scores (by Sex × Year)

	Age											
	21–29		30–39		40–49		50–59		60–64		65+	
Psychological Anxiety Scores	1957 %	1976 %	1957 %	1976 %	1957 %	1976 %	1957 %	1976 %	1957 %	1976 %	1957 %	1976 %
Men												
(Low) 5	18	12	21	15	23	13	29	15	33	11	28	16
6–7	39	27	33	27	29	34	30	26	29	13	26	33
8	18	22	15	15	20	17	14	18	15	23	14	13
9–10	20	28	22	33	18	24	16	29	12	38	18	27
(High) 11–20	5	11	9	10	10	12	11	12	11	15	14	11
	100%	100%	100%	100%	100%	100%	100%	100%	100%	100%	100%	100%
Total Number	187	234	250	214	230	155	178	134	65	74	159	137
Women												
(Low) 5	11	8	14	6	15	7	10	6	16	7	12	6
6–7	27	21	25	20	30	19	28	23	24	21	23	23
8	22	21	19	21	15	16	19	18	16	21	14	15
9–10	26	30	24	30	23	34	20	34	20	30	21	36
(High) 11–20	14	20	18	23	17	23	23	19	24	21	30	20
	100%	100%	100%	100%	100%	100%	100%	100%	100%	100%	100%	100%

Age Differences in Immobilization Scores (by Sex × Year)

Age

Immobilization Scores	21-29		30-39		40-49		50-59		60-64		65+	
	1957 %	1976 %	1957 %	1976 %	1957 %	1976 %	1957 %	1976 %	1957 %	1976 %	1957 %	1976 %
Men												
(Low) 4	8	4	18	8	21	10	25	13	42	13	33	27
5-6	32	21	29	28	36	34	43	38	32	36	42	37
7	14	21	16	19	13	24	12	26	15	23	9	12
8-9	18	20	13	17	10	15	9	13	6	10	5	12
(High) 9-11	28	34	24	28	20	17	11	10	5	18	11	13
	100%	100%	100%	100%	100%	100%	100%	100%	100%	100%	100%	100%
Total Number	187	234	249	214	231	154	178	133	65	74	159	137
Women												
(Low) 4	7	6	9	5	18	11	25	11	24	12	27	17
5-6	25	29	32	32	29	34	37	37	36	36	40	38
7	20	19	15	18	13	18	17	19	16	19	17	19
8-9	14	13	13	23	14	13	7	15	13	15	9	15
(High) 9-16	34	33	31	22	26	24	14	18	12	18	7	11
	100%	100%	100%	100%	100%	100%	100%	100%	100%	100%	100%	100%
Total Number	266	315	334	245	284	185	210	201	87	90	92	246

the elderly. We have tried to clarify a parallel phenomenon in our discussion of similar results about worries in chapter 2: young people in 1976 are more worried about their lives than young people in 1957. One explanation could service both results. Chapter 2 argued that young people of today are especially worried because the rules of adequate social behavior are less clear-cut and their futures are not very clearly spelled out. If anything, the opposite holds true for the elderly of today, who now have clearer expectations about retirement and how to live out the rest of their days than the elderly of 1957. The same analysis could apply to the differential impact of the generation on young and old people's *Psychological Anxiety*.

Two other complexities about age differences involve *Immobilization*. We have already discussed the cohort effect: middle-aged people in 1957 seem to be relatively more immobilized and continue to be so when they reach older age in 1976. In addition, there seems to be an age x education interaction for *Immobilization*. That result can be seen in table 7.13 where for older people, and for older people alone, being more educated tends to be associated with being less immobilized. This holds true for 1957 and 1976. We shall hold off commenting on that result until we summarize what we know about *Immobilization* and age.

Age relationships with symptoms seem more complex than we imagined. *Ill Health* is a straightforward symptom pattern that increases with age. *Psychological Anxiety* does not bear any direct relationship with age, but has some interactive relationship with year much as the extent of worries did in chapter 2. *Immobilization* seems to be a symptom pattern found particularly in young people. Why is it a young person's set of symptoms? Perhaps because the young in trying to be active, as-

TABLE 7.13
"High"[a] Immobilization Scores
for People Varying in
Educational Levels (by age)

	Age		
Education	**21-34** (%)	**35-54** (%)	**55+** (%)
Grade School	28 (132)	22 (365)	15 (670)
High School	31 (874)	22 (908)	11 (494)
College	31 (560)	21 (420)	6 (726)

NOTE: Numbers in parentheses are total number of persons in each group.

[a] Scores of 9–16.

sertive people and to make critical decisions often find themselves unable to master these demands.

Frustration of assertiveness can easily turn to the experience of immobilization as a symptom of distress. This phenomenon operates less with older people, who are presumably less geared to assertive action as a dominant theme of their lives. It especially seems to be a symptom pattern less prominent among the more educated elderly. We might argue that older people may have some doubt about how to handle their time—especially their leisure. Only those elderly people who have been given the benefit of education or have the resources for handling leisure both economically and psychologically will have any room for new growth directed toward experiencing new challenges. The less educated elderly might experience the same problems in facing up to issues of leisure that young people might experience facing up to problems about careers and family life during their initiation into the adult life cycle.

EDUCATION DIFFERENCES

Tables 7.14, 7.15, and 7.16 present three sets of data describing education differences for the three symptom scores. Our multivariate analyses indicate that education is powerful in predicting symptoms of *Ill Health* and *Psychological Anxiety*, with the college educated being considerably less likely to report both of these symptoms than other groups and the high school group less likely to report these symptoms than the grade school–educated people. These results are important since they are independent of age and year effects. Thus, these findings confirm previously reported results about status related to symptoms: people in higher status, defined by educational attainment, report fewer physical and psychological symptoms. There is much debate in the literature about what this pattern reflects. The most interesting presentation of this problem is in a paper by Kessler (1979), who suggests that status differences in reactions to stress with symptoms might reflect *current life situation differences, background differences, or mobility differences.* Kessler finds evidence for each of these interpretations.

However one interprets these results, we prefer not to see the findings as evidence of greater disorder in lower-status groups. As other social theorists have suggested, there are differential stresses that people in lower-status positions have contrasted to those of higher-status positions. These stresses may touch upon political issues, economic issues, or any life stresses that are more likely to occur among lower-status groups in our society. Researchers have attempted to equate the level of stress among people of different statuses, and have found that the lower-status groups still show more symptoms.

We find these results misleading because of the difficulty in realisti-

TABLE 7.14
Education Differences in Ill-Health Scores (by sex × year)

Ill-Health Scores	Men										Women									
	Grade School		Some High School		High School Graduate		Some College		College Graduate		Grade School		Some High School		High School Graduate		Some College		College Graduate	
	1957 (%)	1976 (%)	1957 (%)	1976 (%)	1957 (%)	1976 (%)	1957 (%)	1976 (%)	1957 (%)	1976 (%)	1957 (%)	1976 (%)	1957 (%)	1976 (%)	1957 (%)	1976 (%)	1957 (%)	1976 (%)	1957 (%)	1976 (%)
(Low) 9	36	26	45	25	57	34	52	40	54	48	26	11	28	22	42	32	38	35	45	42
10–11	17	10	17	15	13	13	13	16	16	14	13	9	16	12	16	16	13	12	16	19
12	15	19	19	23	14	30	18	24	18	21	15	17	21	20	20	21	20	24	17	17
13–15	14	15	12	21	10	15	14	12	7	12	18	23	20	23	15	20	18	18	12	15
(High) 16–24	18	30	7	16	6	8	3	8	5	5	28	40	15	23	7	11	11	11	10	7
	100%	100%	100%	100%	100%	100%	100%	100%	100%	100%	100%	100%	100%	100%	100%	100%	100%	100%	100%	100%
Total Number	363	143	206	125	255	296	124	197	118	178	435	221	305	218	419	464	123	212	92	166

TABLE 7.15

Education Differences in Psychological Anxiety Scores (by sex × year)

	Men										Women									
	Grade School		Some High School		High School Graduate		Some College		College Graduate		Grade School		Some High School		High School Graduate		Some College		College Graduate	
Psychological Anxiety Scores	1957 (%)	1976 (%)	1957 (%)	1976 (%)	1957 (%)	1976 (%)	1957 (%)	1976 (%)	1957 (%)	1976 (%)	1957 (%)	1976 (%)	1957 (%)	1976 (%)	1957 (%)	1976 (%)	1957 (%)	1976 (%)	1957 (%)	1976 (%)
(Low) 5	27	19	19	12	27	12	16	14	24	12	12	4	10	7	13	7	14	6	21	9
6–7	27	23	33	25	36	28	37	31	27	28	25	23	23	17	31	19	25	24	29	28
8	16	13	17	17	14	19	23	21	17	19	14	10	19	13	19	23	27	22	13	22
9–10	18	28	21	30	14	31	18	26	26	32	20	33	28	37	22	30	20	35	29	29
(High) 11–20	12	17	10	16	9	10	6	8	6	9	29	30	20	26	15	21	14	13	8	12
	100%	100%	100%	100%	100%	100%	100%	100%	100%	100%	100%	100%	100%	100%	100%	100%	100%	100%	100%	100%
Total Number	362	149	206	125	255	296	124	198	118	178	435	222	304	219	418	463	123	212	92	167

TABLE 7.16

Education Differences in Immobilization Scores (by sex × year)

	Men										Women									
	Grade School		Some High School		High School Graduate		Some College		College Graduate		Grade School		Some High School		High School Graduate		Some College		College Graduate	
Immobilization Scores	1957 (%)	1976 (%)	1957 (%)	1976 (%)	1957 (%)	1976 (%)	1957 (%)	1976 (%)	1957 (%)	1976 (%)	1957 (%)	1976 (%)	1957 (%)	1976 (%)	1957 (%)	1976 (%)	1957 (%)	1976 (%)	1957 (%)	1976 (%)
(Low) 4	28	21	23	14	21	11	12	8	12	6	20	16	15	12	14	7	10	13	20	4
5–6	38	33	35	33	35	30	32	27	34	31	35	32	31	30	30	35	32	37	31	35
7	12	14	10	18	12	20	17	21	19	27	15	18	18	17	15	21	17	17	16	17
8–9	7	13	12	18	13	15	17	17	12	14	10	12	13	14	12	17	15	14	13	22
(High) 9–16	15	19	20	17	19	24	22	27	23	22	20	22	23	27	29	20	26	19	20	22
	100%	100%	100%	100%	100%	100%	100%	100%	100%	100%	100%	100%	100%	100%	100%	100%	100%	100%	100%	100%
Total Number	363	149	206	125	254	296	124	197	118	177	435	223	304	218	419	461	123	212	92	166

cally controlling the stress experienced by people in different statuses. Generally, this research counts the number of life events (Holmes and Rahe, 1967) checked from a list. Equating the *pattern* of specific stresses encountered in these life events is not done. Experiencing a debilitating disease is not the same as experiencing a marriage or a birth of a child. Furthermore, people in lower-status groups are less likely to be able to cope with stress for pragmatic reasons. Kessler (1979) suggests that there are certain coping patterns that are more available to the more statusful in our society. For example, easier access to private physicians among the more educated enables them to control symptoms following stress better than the less educated.

With the *Immobilization* symptoms, we do not have a clear-cut status difference. We do find that college educated are more moderate in *Immobilization* symptoms than are either grade school– or high school– educated men and women. The college educated are thus less likely to deny symptoms of *Immobilization* and to feel them very intensely. If we think of *Immobilization* in terms of *alcohol proneness,* we could say that the college educated are particularly able to think of themselves as occasional overindulgers but are less likely than the less educated either to turn to overindulgence as an extreme symptom pattern or to rule alcohol entirely out of their lives. College-educated people clearly have the resources and the credentials which permit them to handle the inevitable anxiety about performance that occurs in our achieving society: the kind of anxiety that may be behind symptoms of immobilization. People who may be stigmatized by their lack of educational attainment may develop more extreme adaptations to their difficulties through *Immobilization* symptoms.

In any case, the results on *Immobilization* and its relationship to education refute the general hypothesis that the higher the status, the higher the strain experienced. It is not so simple with regard to strain expressed through *Immobilization* symptoms. College-educated people are more moderate in *Immobilization,* which means that a sizable group of people of lower status report experiencing many of the symptoms of immobilization, compared to the people of high status.

Let us now turn to results about symptom items used only in 1976.

Analyses of Symptom Items Asked Only in 1976

While we wanted to replicate verbatim the items of the 1957 symptom checklist for the 1976 study, we realized that one of the items—"Do you drink too much?"—was poorly worded. Therefore, in consultation with a number of social scientists, we devised two additional items to elicit symptoms of alcoholism that could be assessed in the 1976 sur-

TABLE 7.17

Three Symptom Items Asked Only in 1976

Items	Alternatives
1. When you feel worried, tense or nervous, do you ever drink alcoholic beverages to help you handle things?	Many Times. Sometimes. Hardly ever. Never.
2. Have there ever been problems between you and anyone in your family (spouse, parent, child, or other close relative) because you drank alcoholic beverages?	Many Times. Sometimes. Hardly ever. Never.
3. When you feel worried, tense or nervous, do you ever take medicines or drugs to help you handle things?	Many Times. Sometimes. Hardly ever. Never.

vey. These items are listed in table 7.17, along with one other, which we devised in parallel fashion to account for potential use of medicines and drugs as a way to relieve tension. The two alcohol items reflected a person's report of using alcohol as a way to relieve tension and reports of alcohol usage as some factor interfering with family relationships (see table 7.17). These two items were similar to one used by other researchers in surveys of alcohol abuse (Cahalan, 1970). We felt that the use of drugs to relieve tension had to include the word "medicines," although we realize that in introducing medicine as a substance which is used for tension relief, we may be confusing a whole group of respondents who would think of prescription medicines used in connection with physical ailments. As a result, the reported use of medicines/drugs to relieve tension is more related to *Ill Health* than the other substance-use items (see table 7.18). Nevertheless, we thought we needed to include the word "medicine" in order to destigmatize the word "drugs" which is an anathema to many adults in our society. Controlling for *Ill Health* symptoms will be critical to our analyses of the substance-use items, especially medicine/drug taking.

Tables 7.20, 7.21, and 7.22 highlight the sex, age, and education differences that we found in the responses to these three questions; each table records demographic differences for one item. Table 7.19 shows the summaries of the cross-classification analyses for each of these items. The cross-classification analyses tells us clearly that age is a relevant factor in reports of all these items[7] as is sex, but education enters into the picture only with respect to the use of alcohol or drugs in the release of tension.[8] These differences are analyzed below in greater detail:

[7] The age effect is not critical with respect to drug use when *Ill Health* is introduced into the cross-classification.

[8] Education differences in drug taking are also not critical when *Ill Health* is introduced into the cross-classification analysis.

TABLE 7.18

Intercorrelations of Substance Items With Symptom Factor Scores

	Substance Item											
	Alcohol Use for Tension				Medicine/Drug Use for Tension				Alcohol Use as Family Problem			
	Men		Women		Men		Women		Men		Women	
Factor Scores	Total Number	r	Total Number	r	Total Number	r	Total Number	r	Total Number	r	Total Number	r
Ill Health	946	.06	1,283	−.01	943	.35[a]	1,276	.38	944	.11[b]	1,281	.07[c]
Psychological Anxiety	947	.17[a]	1,283	.10[b]	944	.31[a]	1,276	.36	945	.14[a]	1,281	.08[c]
Immobilization	946	.34[a]	1,284	.32[a]	943	.19[a]	1,276	.28[a]	944	.20[b]	1,280	.19[a]

[a] $p<.0001$.
[b] $p<.001$.
[c] $p<.01$.

TABLE 7.19

Summary of Multivariate Analyses of 1976 Substance-Use Items

| | Relationships Required[a] to Reproduce Observed Cross-classification of Measures by Age × Education × Sex | | | |
| | Main Effects[b] | | | |
Substance Use Item	Age	Education	Sex	Interaction
Drinking Cause Family Problem	Y,MA>O		M>F	
Drinking to Relieve Tension	MA>Y>O	G<H<C	M>F	
Medicines/ Drugs to Relieve Tension	(Y<MA<O)[c]	(G>H>C)[c]	M<F	

[a] See footnote a of Table 2.11 for an explanation of "Required."

[b] See footnote a of Table 2.11 for a description of "Main Effects."

[c] This effect not needed when ill-health control introduced.

1. *With respect to sex differences,* more men than women report using alcohol as a form of tension release and also that alcohol use creates problems with their families. The differences are quite striking with respect to the use of alcohol to relieve tension. We have many more women than men saying they never used alcohol to relieve tension. This result is counter to the assumption that men find it less socially desirable to admit to the presence of *any* negative state. This is obviously not true for alcohol usage to relieve tension, nor was it true for asking whether they drink too much. More men than women may think it socially desirable to use alcohol to relieve tension. That possibility does not seem to account for why many more women than men said they never have used alcohol to relieve tension. As a result, we would strongly state that alcohol usage as a way to relieve tension is geared for men in our society as a mode of expression of experienced difficulties. Other symptoms in the symptom checklist may be biased toward women's ways of handling problems, but alcohol usage may be the way of responding to stress that is peculiarly masculine. Reported problems with family because of alcohol use are also reported as never being the case by many more women than men. Ninety-three percent of the women in the nation say they never have found alcohol use a problem with their families, whereas 79 percent of men say "never" to that question. In contrast, more women than men report the use of medicine or drugs to relieve tension; 18 percent of women say they sometimes or many times have used medicine or drugs this way while only 11 percent of men do. Drugs and medicines are evidently a more acceptable route for substance abuse for women than men.

2. *With respect to age differences,* we find that drinking that causes family problems and using alcohol as a means for tension release are not at all symptomatic of older people, but are of younger people. Using alco-

TABLE 7.20
Sex, Age, and Education Differences in Reported Alcohol Use for Handling Tension (1976 only)

Differences	Total Number	Reported Alcohol Use — By Percent				Total Percentage
		Never (%)	Hardly Ever (%)	Sometimes (%)	Many Times (%)	
en	947	71	16	12	1	100
omen	1,285	84	11	5	<1	100
nd Age						
en:						
21–29	234	66	21	13	<1	100
30–39	214	70	15	12	3	100
40–49	155	66	19	15	0	100
50–59	133	69	15	15	1	100
60–64	74	79	12	8	1	100
65+	137	87	7	6	<1	100
omen:						
21–29	316	78	15	7	<1	100
30–39	245	75	19	6	<1	100
40–49	185	83	9	8	<1	100
50–59	201	88	8	4	<1	100
60–64	90	96	3	1	0	100
65+	246	94	4	2	0	100
nd Education						
en:						
Grade school	149	77	13	9	1	100
Some high school	125	73	14	11	2	100
High school graduate	296	73	14	12	1	100
Some college	197	72	16	11	2	100
College graduate	178	62	21	16	1	100
omen:						
Grade school	210	94	4	2	0	100
Some high school	190	87	8	5	<1	100
High school graduate	381	83	11	6	<1	100
Some college	168	79	14	6	1	100
College graduate	125	75	20	5	0	100

TABLE 7.21
Sex, Age, and Education Differences in Reported Medicine/Drug Use
for Handling Tension—By Percent (1976 only)

		Reported Medicine/Drug Use				
Differences	Total Number	Never (%)	Hardly Ever (%)	Sometimes (%)	Many Times (%)	To Perce
Sex						
Men	944	76	13	8	3	1
Women	1,278	66	16	15	3	1
Sex and Age						
Men:						
21–29	233	82	11	6	1	1
30–39	214	81	10	8	1	1
40–49	154	71	18	8	3	1
50–59	133	75	15	8	2	1
60–64	74	69	16	7	8	1
65+	136	71	9	15	5	1
Women:						
21–29	316	75	13	10	2	1
30–39	246	69	16	13	2	1
40–49	183	59	20	19	2	1
50–59	198	61	18	18	3	1
60–64	88	57	16	20	7	1
65+	245	60	17	18	5	1
Sex and Education						
Men:						
Grade school	149	71	9	12	8	1
Some high school	124	77	8	10	5	1
High school graduate	295	79	13	6	2	1
Some college	197	80	13	7	<1	1
College graduate	177	72	19	8	1	1
Women:						
Grade school	222	58	15	20	7	1
Some high school	216	61	14	21	4	1
High school graduate	458	64	18	16	2	1
Some college	212	70	19	8	3	1
College graduate	166	76	14	10	<1	1

TABLE 7.22
*Sex, Age, and Education Differences in Reported Problem with Family
Because of Alcohol Use—By Percent (1976 only)*

Differences	Total Number	Reported Family Problem Re: Alcohol				Total Percentage
		Never (%)	Hardly Ever (%)	Sometimes (%)	Many Times (%)	
n	945	79	12	7	2	100
men	1,283	93	4	2	1	100
d Age						
n:						
1–29	233	78	16	5	1	100
0–39	213	79	11	8	2	100
0–49	155	74	16	8	2	100
0–59	133	80	12	7	1	100
0–64	74	76	15	5	4	100
5+	137	88	4	6	2	100
men:						
1–29	316	90	5	3	2	100
0–39	246	91	4	4	1	100
0–49	185	94	4	1	1	100
0–59	200	92	3	4	1	100
0–64	90	94	2	3	1	100
5+	244	96	3	<1	0	100
d Education						
n:						
Grade school	149	78	10	9	3	100
ome high school	124	76	10	9	5	100
High school graduate	296	78	14	7	1	100
ome college	197	81	14	4	1	100
College graduate	177	82	14	4	0	100
men:						
Grade school	221	95	4	1	0	100
ome high school	217	91	3	4	2	100
High school graduate	463	92	4	3	1	100
ome college	212	93	4	2	1	100
College graduate	166	94	2	2	1	100

hol for tension relief is especially prominent in middle-aged groups in our society. The reports of having family problems because of alcohol are as prevalent in the younger as it is in middle-aged groups. Using drugs for tension release is most common in the older group, next most prominent in the middle-aged, and least prevalent in younger groups in our society, but this finding does not withstand the control for *Ill Health*, which obviously is related to the use of drugs and medicine for tension release.

The fact that alcohol usage is most common in the middle-aged in our society as opposed to the younger and older people is an interesting phenonomen. It may take the span from early adulthood to middle adulthood to discover the socialized usage of alcohol as a means of dealing with tension. In young people alcohol is so often associated with *social* partying, where its capacity for tension reduction on a *personal* level may not be relevant. For young people, getting drunk is having a good time; when people get older, getting drunk can be seen as a means for dispelling their anxieties.

3. *With respect to education differences,* we find the more educated in our society are more oriented toward drinking as a way of relieving tension and less oriented toward drug (medicine) taking. The latter, however, is a function of *Ill Health* scores. The less educated in our society do experience more physical health problems. When they consult doctors about these problems, the doctors will prescribe a drug rather than alcohol as a means for handling any psychological reactions embedded in the physical problems. It is important to remember that these results are independent of the relationship of education to age, since education by itself was found to be a significant fact in multivariate analyses of cross-classification data. An immediate explanation might be that alcohol is expensive; hence, the more statusful in our society can more easily buy it. Medicine or drugs can be paid by insurance or by Medicaid. Another explanation might be that higher-status groups develop a special culture of drinking as a way to handle tension. We so easily can picture the affluent having cocktail hours or lunches with cocktails as a means of social and business entertainment. This social form can provide the medium by which people in those groups learn to drink to relieve tension. While we can also picture the lower- or working-class culture of drinking to handle tensions, it may not be as widespread as affluent drinking. Furthermore, it may not be as readily perceived as a coping strategy for handling tension by the lower- or working-class as it is by the more affluent. The camaraderie of drinking may be more often seen as the basis of drinking among the less affluent.

Thus we find a very interesting difference between drinking and medicine/drug taking in our society. We find drinking most clearly associated with the more statusful: men, middle-aged, well-established college-educated people. Medicine/drug taking is associated with the less statusful: women, the older and the less educated in our society.

Little is known about the differential dynamics of drug and alcohol use as a form of tension release, but these results suggest that there may be socialization patterns that allow one or the other to develop in different groups in our society. McClelland and others (1972) have argued that drinking represents a mode of power induction for people. To be under the spell of alcohol momentarily allows people to have a sense of their desired power. We would expect the less statusful in our society to be as alerted to this as a psychological phenomenon as much as the more statusful—if not more so. The fact that the more powerful in our society, compared to the less powerful more often say they use alcohol as a means of tension release suggests that there are mechanisms of control in the social structure not only for keeping real power within the reins of the powerful, but also for keeping the ways of gaining illusions of power and within the groups in power. For example, women are not "permitted" to use alcohol as a form of tension release. They often do covertly, but probably with considerable guilt; drinking is most often seen as a highly masculine and inappropriate form of behavior for women. Unescorted women in bars are often seen as loose women. Thus men maintain their status by permitting only the more statusful (men) the tension release associated with alcohol use. Another example can be seen in the fact that while heavy alcohol drinking in suburban partying is seen almost as a "desired" condition, heavy alcohol drinking in bars is seen as very "low class." We interpret alcohol use in the context in which it occurs, and it is more likely to be socially accepted in more statusful contexts.

Medicine/drug taking as potential tension release seems to be more typical of the less statusful groups in our society. Perhaps because it is seen as a form of tension release that women use, or that sick people use, that this form of relief has been demoted as a symptom pattern in our society. Some social observers have noted that extraordinary anxiety was created by the drug culture of the 1960s and 1970s because it occurred among the more affluent. The powerful might have felt they were being weakened from within, perhaps because of an unconscious fear of emasculation of the elite. The fear associated with drug taking might have thus arisen because drug taking had connotations of anti-masculine and antiestablishment attitudes. Affluent parents of the 1960s and 1970s were much more upset if their children were taking drugs than if they were using alcohol. Clearly, some of their differential reactions depended on the different legal implications of drug and alcohol involvement. In addition, however, downward mobility is associated with drug taking. It is interesting to note in table 7.18 that there are stronger correlations between drug taking as tension release and *Psychological Anxiety* than there is with *Immobilization*. There is also higher correlation between drinking for tension release and *Immobilization* than there was between drinking for tension release and *Psychological Anxiety*. Thus, the more "masculine" general symptom factors of *Immobilization* is associated with drinking and the more "feminine" symptom factors of *Psychological Anxiety* is associated with drug taking.

Whether alcoholism or medicine/drug taking is a greater subjective problem in our society really depends on the normative values associated with each. It is quite clear from these results, however, that it may be more problematic for people in our society to be drug takers than to be alcohol consumers. Part of this conclusion comes from noting the closer association of medicine/drug taking with *Ill Health*. Part of the conclusion comes from realizing that alcoholism as tension release is more clearly identified with more statusful groups in our society. Whether alcohol abuse or medicine/drug abuse is a better indicator of "disorder" on an absolute basis would be much harder to say. We have no direct evidence to support one or the other by our analyses.

Summary

Our analysis of the symptom checklist for both the 1957 and 1976 surveys underscores once more a thesis offered in *Americans View Their Mental Health* but which generally went unheeded in the ensuing efforts to use symptoms to diagnose mental health "problems": *symptoms are multidimensional and hence require multiple measures for adequate assessment of presenting complaints that people have about their well-being.* We have isolated three factors that clarify what some of these dimensions might be: *Ill Health, Psychological Anxiety*, and *Immobilization*. These dimensions are replicated in four factor analyses run separately for men and women's symptoms reported in 1957 and in 1976.

Depending on which of these dimensions are examined, we emerge with different portrayals of which group is feeling more distress. The 1976 respondents generally are higher than the 1957 respondents in *Ill Health* and *Psychological Anxiety*, but not in *Immobilization*. The same pattern holds true for sex and education comparisons: women and the less educated are higher in *Ill Health* and *Psychological Anxiety*, but not generally in *Immobilization*, compared to men and the more educated respectively. While older people are clearly higher in *Ill Health* symptoms than younger people, they are lower in *Immobilization* symptoms and show no difference in *Psychological Anxiety* symptoms. Young people in 1976 have particularly increased in *Psychological Anxiety* relative to young people in 1957.

The additional 1976 symptom items dealing with substance use further underscore the differential measuring of symptoms: men use alcohol for tension release and find that drinking causes family problems more than women; women use medicine/drugs to relieve tension more than men. Drinking to relieve tension is primarily a middle-aged and more educated symptom pattern. While the less educated and older people are more oriented than younger people to medicine or drugs, this seems largely due to their connection with physical health problems.

These findings thus lead us to state again that symptom checklists should not be simply totaled to get a measure of experienced strain. To do so would ignore the potential of getting differential diagnoses that would clarify the psychological dimensions of symptom presentations. If we would concentrate on understanding that psychology rather than on getting a single diagnosis of distress or disorder, we would make better headway in understanding mental health problems for the general population. Pigeonholing men and women as "disordered" has been a goal that has obfuscated work on symptoms. Different dynamics, different prevalence rates, different treatments will emerge for different symptom patterns.

Chapter 8

SELECTED SOCIAL CHARACTERISTICS AND SUBJECTIVE MENTAL HEALTH

POWERED by the multiple-criteria approach to the study of subjective well-being, we have followed many different tracks in the preceding chapters to discover ways in which Americans look at their own mental health. From our initial examination about overall feelings of well-being and self-perception, we moved into territories that examine each of three social roles: marriage, parenthood, and work. In the last chapter, we looked at the ways people report psychological and physical symptoms of well-being. Not only did we move from one area to another without much crossover between areas, but also within each of them we looked at multiple subjective appraisals.

This eclecticism forms a diffuse picture of the subjective state of a people. In some ways we wish to maintain that impression because the philosophical assumption of multiple criteria suggests that there are indeed different consequences of adopting one or another evaluation of psychological well-being. Although future research reports from our study will examine systematically the interrelationships among the variety of reports of well-being that appear in this book, in this chapter we will look for possible integrations of these multiple facets of subjective mental health.

In the first part of this chapter, we will look at sex, age, and education differences in dimensions of subjective mental health. We will summarize how men and women, education groups, and age groups compare in evaluations of their own mental health across the different criteria. In doing so we will try to draw some integrative patterns among the chapters.

We will next present analyses correlating other social characteristics with subjective mental health. We selected social characteristics that are popular in the social science literature that deals with demographic analyses of attitudes and well-being and certain other social facts about people's lives that have a theoretical bearing on subjective mental health. We refer to these characteristics loosely as demographic factors, although the designation does not fit all of the characteristics we examine. For example, *Broken Home Background* (We ask whether disruption in early childhood; whether one or the other or both parents died before the respondent was sixteen, or the respondent's parents were divorced when the respondent was a child) relates to contemporary evaluation of adjustment or mental health. Strictly speaking, this is not a current "demographic" characteristic, but, like other variables we examine, it is a social fact with interesting theoretical implications for certain aspects of well-being. Analyses presented here may also permit integration of the highly differentiated presentations in previous chapters.

We reserve the final chapter of the book for the most interesting integration: the way in which the subjective mental health of the nation as a whole has changed from 1957 to 1976. Some themes in the final chapter on change will incorporate integrations that emerge in the present chapter.

Summary of Sex, Age, and Education Differences in Subjective Mental Health

SEX DIFFERENCES

We cannot look at the array of data amassed in previous chapters focusing on differences between men's and women's reports of well-being without concluding that women are more demoralized than men. From the first chapter about feelings and sources of well-being, to the last chapter on symptom patterns, women, more than men, report difficulties in their daily lives. By and large, this is as true in 1976 as it was in 1957. In only two instances did we find greater problems among men, and both of these occurred at work. Many more men report having experienced some kind of work problem, particularly problems of job selection. Fewer men report their jobs to be satisfying, but that result was significant only in 1957. Otherwise, where there are sex differences (and there are perhaps fewer than we expected), they are in the direction of women finding life more problematic than men. The differences are not always large, but they are consistent.

In the last chapter's discussion of sex differences in symptom reports, we mentioned two common interpretations of sex difference in reported distress. First, we can say that men are more defensive about their life experience than women. They may feel more discomfort in admitting problems to themselves and/or to someone else, even if at some level they are experiencing problems in their lives. Second, we can say that women experience greater objective oppression in a sexist society. The first interpretation alerts us to a defensive or nonintraceptive response style in men; the second to the peculiar life circumstances of women. Obviously, both interpretations may be accurate.

In this summary we will argue that we have indirect evidence that sex differences in subjective mental health are not merely a function of men's relative reluctance to see their lives as problematic and/or to report difficulties to a strange interviewer. Instead, we interpret the pattern of results as indicating that women's life situations confront them with experiences which put them in a more vulnerable position than men, a position that engenders psychological difficulties.

Let us justify this assertion by focusing on results that show fairly substantial differences between men and women in subjective mental health. Women report more worries, more often say they have felt they were going to have a nervous breakdown, report that bad things happen to them more frequently, more frequently feel overwhelmed by bad events when they do happen, say they experience greater inadequacy as parents, and report turning to professional help for personal problems more often than men. Other results buttress this generally gloomier picture of women's subjective lives compared to men's, but these other differences are minor, and hence we do not focus on them. For example, compared to men, women report slightly more psychological anxiety and endorse slightly lower self-evaluation and personal efficacy statements.

Although this pattern of results can be interpreted as men's greater resistance to admitting affective difficulties in life, the coherence of the findings suggests something more: that women, because of their different life circumstances actually encounter more difficulties than men do. We refer specifically to the broad societal demand that women take responsibility for the interpersonal success of marriage and children's socialization. These role demands carry an enormous inherent potential for creating discomfort with people's life situation. To the degree that some people have responsibility for another person's well-being in a life role (marriage or parenthood), to that degree they have less control over their *own* well-being. If gratification depends on the behavior, attitudes, or feelings of another person—a husband or child—then indeed that other person's fortunes and feelings can interfere with a woman's own sense of contentment and pleasure.

One difference between men's and women's subjective experience occurs in feelings of adequacy as a parent. Many more women than men say they experience inadequacy as parents. Such feelings often arise out of the awareness that children are experiencing difficulties. In their roles as mothers, women are expected to be more attuned to children than men are as fathers. Furthermore, even when men become aware of their children's problems, they may compartmentalize the child's difficulty as something that does not directly concern their own competence. Women's assignment to the supportive task of child rearing, we would argue, puts them in a position to experience *through the problems of another person* a variety of events in their *own* life which they code as problematic. Women's responsibility for children induces worries, a sense of being overwhelmed and unable to handle life. Demoralization usually implies that one is out of control, that one cannot handle the future. If, in fact, the future is closely tied to other people—children—and their reactions, women are indeed faced with a future which is beyond their own control. By definition, a future dependent on responses of other people will be more problematic.

If we are right, then the fact that men and women do not differ in their reports of inadequacies in marriage would suggest that it is not the *marital* relationship that induces this feeling of responsibility for another as much as it is the *parent* role. However, we find that in orientation to both the marital and parent role, women are more negative than men and more often feel that a person's life is restricted by these roles. These findings may stem from the fact that women are assigned nurturing obligations in both roles.

We thought that controlling for parent status might shed some light on the hypothesis we are advancing; among those who are not parents, morale differences between men and women would disappear. Our hypothesis may have been too naïve. We will see that sex differences in morale do not in fact disappear when parent status is controlled. Even women who do not have children live in a cultural matrix which mandates that to be a complete person, a woman must bear and assume the responsibility for children. Even childless women in our society (Chodorow, 1974) learn through early socialization to be attuned to others and to base their sense of well-being on the responses of others. Few women are free from the interpersonal orientation that early training for mothering encourages.

A number of other significant differences between men's and women's appraisals of well-being may stem from this differential role assignment to parenting. We find substantial differences between men and women in sources of happiness, unhappiness, and worries. More men than women structure well-being around jobs or communities; more women than men structure well-being around family life, particularly around their relationship with children. These results corroborate the view that the differential assignment to roles in our society has enormous impact on the sources from which men and women derive a sense of well-being.

Social scientists often assume that women see themselves as less competent than men. We find slight support for this assumption. Women report somewhat lower self-esteem and efficacy and somewhat more negative ways in which they differ from other people. However, when we look closely at specific competencies, some of the sex difference breaks down. Among working men and women, for example, we find that women feel slightly *more* competent than men when we control for perceived job difficulty. As we have mentioned previously, women express no greater feelings of inadequacy in the marital role than men do, and in discussing marital problems, women more often than men "blame" their spouses.

This is not to say that there may not be greater self-doubt in women. It could well be that in learning to manage the difficult task of socializing children, women become especially aware of their own inadequacies. We find, for example, that when we ask people how they would like their children to be different from themselves, many more women than men refer to internal attributes, ones we would label personality characteristics. This intraceptive construction of shortcomings may stem from anxieties mothers feel as they attempt to mold the lives of the future generation. Women may become particularly sensitive to their own inadequacies when they are self-consciously trying to induce ideal behavior in children. Thus, the heavier burden of parenting that falls to mothers compared to fathers may lead to greater self-questioning.

There is another possible and related explanation for women's more negative reports of well-being. We have suggested that women reflect on their own shortcomings and other difficulties in life more than men because they are assigned greater responsibility for socializing the young. When well-being is so dependent on another person, morale and self-esteem rely heavily on the other person's "good behavior," and thus is in greater jeopardy. In contrast, men's denial of problems, men's greater cover-up of things that are going badly in their lives, men's higher self-evaluations, may come from their assignment to the role of work. Denial may be especially effective in coping with work problems. The complexity of formal organizations people confront at work can bewilder those who are contemplative about their shortcomings or their larger experience. Perhaps people have to blind themselves to difficulties experienced in a factory, a hospital, or an office in order to efficiently proceed with work. People may have to discount shortcomings in themselves. More working men than women report that what they like best about work is the "impact" they have on the job, while more working women than men report affiliative satisfactions at work. These contrasting orientations to work by men and women follow from their differential role assignment. Furthermore, if men are attending to their impact rather than to affiliative relationships, they may have to deny personal weaknesses or the social hurts that their acts provoke. If men were to attend more to affiliation at work, they would less easily deny the effects people have on one another. Furthermore, they might have to focus on their own shortcomings, which could be devastating for them in the large-scale bureaucratic work settings so typical of current society.

In summary, in looking closely at the patterns of results obtained in previous chapters, we begin to see how sex differences in morale reflect the consequences of differential role assignments in our society. We suggest that the key to the pattern of results is the dominance of the parental role in the life experience of women and the dominance of the work role in the experiences of men. Preoccupation with parenthood seems to contribute to the greater sense of oppression and demoralization in women because women's well-being is contingent upon other people's adjustment and success in life. The concern about impact at work may lead to denial of subjective maladjustment. These interpretations gain support from the results we found plotting reported happiness across the life cycle separately for men and women. Women show a sharp decline in reporting being "very happy" at mid-life, a time when the results of and responsibilities for children are more critically judged than at earlier and later periods of the life cycle. Women's steady decline in reported happiness over the life cycle may correlate with the increasing feminization of their interests—from career-oriented concerns to more interpersonal values. The drop in reported happiness in much older men may also be partially interpreted as a growing "feminization" of their interests, as work goals recede. While Campbell, Converse, and Rodgers (1976) saw little in the way of sex differences in well-being, they generally focused on questions about satisfaction, rather than on questions about feelings of demoralization. In addition, their discussion of the absence of sex differences in reported happiness failed to take account of the life-cycle interaction noted above.

AGE DIFFERENCES

Having observed that men and women differ in their experience of happiness across the life cycle, we begin to focus on the significance of

age for feelings of well-being. As we survey the various findings that
have accumulated in analyses of age differences in previous chapters,
we become aware that people obviously deal with different personal issues when they are young than when they are old. In many ways people in different age groups experience the flow of life differently.
Roles experienced at different ages require different competences, offer different possibilities for gratification, and present varying sources
of dissatisfaction.

It may be easiest to see the differential confrontation of life in younger and older people in the specific facets of well-being emphasized by
younger and older people in response to questions about sources of
happiness, unhappiness, and worry. In their youth, people more often
talk about interpersonal aspects of happiness, unhappiness, and worries. This generalization extends to other results. Compared to older
people, the young more often focus on interactive problems they experience in marriage; their performance of social roles when they think
about their strengths and weaknesses; how adequately they are raising
their children. Younger people are learning to adapt to the responsibilities required of adult social roles. Since they learn about these roles
through interpersonal contacts, they become very much attuned to interpersonal issues in their lives. Interpersonal encounters are the
source of their troubles, as well as the basis of the particular challenges
and joys that they experience in life. For example, younger married
people are very much caught up in issues of interpersonal accommodation in marriage. While they mention relationship aspects of marital
well-being and report frequent physical and conversational exchange
more often than older married people do, they are also more likely to
talk about quarrels and tensions in marriage. Older people seem to
have come to terms with their roles and their adaptation to each other
in marriage, even though new demands in married life occur at later
stages of development. They no longer focus on the particular pleasures derived from interpersonal accommodation in marriage, nor are
they particularly sensitive to the disruptions that marital negotiations
often produce.

One interpretation of these results is that younger people are more
vital, more engaged by experience than older people. In Jahoda's terms
(1958), they show more "positive mental health." Being more engaged,
they reap a greater harvest of both positive and negative consequences.

Another interpretation is possible. Younger people focus on interpersonal aspects of well-being, while older people focus on equally
"vital" but different issues. Older people more often allude to spiritual
aspects of identity when they speak of their own strengths. They also
talk more about their concerns about community than younger people
do. It is as though older people refocus identity from interpersonal relationships to broader social concerns. Older people indicate less need

of social acceptance, and they less often feel inadequate in social roles. While we can interpret this as a diminishing energy for role performance and interpersonal relationships, we can also think of these results as reflecting the fact that older people are more at peace with themselves and more invested in moral and spiritual values.

Older people may evaluate themselves and others for what they *are*, separate from their specific judgment of interpersonal competence. They may accept relationships for what they are, without seeking to change or perfect them. Older parents more than younger parents refer to affiliation as the nicest thing about parenting. It is as if their willingness to appreciate the relationship for what it is and not for what it might be allows them to see the relationship to the child as a critically positive experience. Younger parents are so caught up in dealings with the problems of child rearing, so fixed on socialization for future goals, that they often cannot simply enjoy the pleasures afforded by their relationships to their children. This interpretation does not rank or evaluate the subjective "mental health" of young and old respondents relative to each other.

One of the most interesting results of our age analysis is the somewhat surprising finding: young and old respondents do not differ significantly in self-esteem. The bases of self-evaluation shift as people mature. Personal competence and social role enactment are critical for younger people, while spiritual issues come to the fore as people get older. This is again clearest in response to child rearing. Younger parents are often preoccupied with their inadequacy as agents of socialization, whereas older parents are more accepting of their own limitations as parents.

Adaptation provides a key to understanding the age-related reorientation of self-evaluation and subjective mental health. As people age, they encounter illness and death. Such fundamental problems put other problems into perspective and allow older people to accept and adapt to problems and inadequacies which would have seemed overwhelming at an earlier period in their lives. Older people thus have a perspective that allows them to adapt to issues that create anxiety in the young.

This kind of adaptation in older people can be read into many of the results we have reported. In 1957 and 1976, far fewer older people than younger people say they have had problems for which they could have used professional help, or said that they have felt as though they might have a nervous breakdown. In 1976 older people are less likely than the young to feel overwhelmed when "bad things" happen to them. Older people do not mention bad things happening to them any more than young people do, in spite of the fact that purely as a function of longevity they surely have experienced more "bad things." This adaptation to "bad" experiences must occur in conjunction with the shift in focal concerns as people proceed through the life cycle. This is clear in the ways older and younger people react to work. Older people report far fewer problems at work. The same pattern occurs in marriage and parenting: compared to younger men and women, older men and women less often admit to parental and marital problems.

Part of adaptation to problems experienced in life roles must be the changed time perspective that occurs as people get older. Younger people can put off gratification for some future time. They can be optimistic because they can work toward future goals and see potential change from the past to the present. The past is more immediate for a young person; bad past experiences remain. The young person can project better times in the future. As we age, we begin to put the future into the perspective of time left to live, and we extend past time. Adaptation to bad past events occurs. This hypothesized change in the time perspective of well-being is supported by a number of results. More older than younger people say that the past was happier than the present; they are more likely to see childhood as the happiest time of their lives; they clearly less often anticipate a very happy future. Young people are more oriented to the present and more optimistic about the future. Perhaps younger people are less "satisfied" with their lives because they measure their current lives against some picture of perfect happiness in the future.

This shift in time perspective may be very important in accounting for the people's adaptation as they advance through the life cycle. They learn to put up with difficulties or to see them no longer as being the difficulties they once experienced. Older people are quite naturally bothered by ill-health symptoms. Failing health makes them adapt to other more psychological issues readily. Young people report symptoms of immobilization; they are unable to cope with the present and retreat into inactivity. That is an infrequent symptom among older people; they are not as concerned about the impact of decisions they make on their entire future. Immobilization does not become as great a problem for them primarily because they know their decisions do not have the consequences that younger people think their decisions have for them.

In the marriage and parenthood chapters, we noted that older people are less open than younger people to new conceptions of family roles. Having experienced and accommodated to the roles over a lifetime, older people are more committed to their ways of dealing with life circumstances while younger people are more open to changed ways of coping with adult responsibilities. Younger people are more tolerant of people who decide not to marry or not to have children. This is interpretable as young persons' greater willingness to entertain new ideas about roles to which they have not as yet quite adapted.

In summary, four major interrelated themes emerge from our comparisons of different age groups and their subjective appraisals of their own mental health. First, *young people differ from older people in the issues they confront; a life-cycle difference that makes them focus on different sources and feelings of well-being, but does not necessarily make them evaluate their overall sense of well-being or distress differently.* Second, *young people, contrasted to older people, are more overwhelmed by life circumstances*—perhaps because they expend more energy adapting to or changing their life circumstances than older people, who may be more committed to their pattern of living for the present and future. Third, *older people, contrasted to younger people, have a greater orientation to the past as a source of happiness and less orientation to the future as a time for positive change.* Greater emphasis on the future among young people undoubtedly is related to the fact that young people are especially overwhelmed by present circumstances, because they see the present as critical to the shape of the future. Fourth, *young people are much more open than older people to defining well-being in innovative ways.*

How, then, do we answer the question: Are old or young people better off in subjective adjustment? Different criteria of well-being promote different answers. To the extent that people's subjective appraisal is higher if they perceive positive change in the future, then clearly younger people have advantages over older people in their general subjective appraisals. To the extent that we use adaptation to present life circumstances as a criterion for subjective mental health, then older people have more positive experiences in their life circumstances. Since our appraisal of subjective well-being rests on a number of different criteria, we conclude that younger and older people have both positive and negative aspects of subjective mental health, and that no single evaluation can or should be made.

EDUCATION DIFFERENCES

Compared to people who are less educated, educated men and women in our society feel better about their lives and report a wider array of experiences that enrich their lives. Educational credentials provide access to many social resources. People who have college degrees, and especially those with advanced professional degrees, hold better-paying jobs and gain entry to spheres of influence which allow them to fashion the good life. Furthermore, occupations open to men and women with college diplomas provide reference groups which tell how to proceed with life and how to evaluate experience. These can be very powerful effects, ones that we think pervade many of our findings about ways in which educated men and women differ from the less educated in their presented self-appraisals.

It may be more questionable to assert that schooling itself gives people a more elaborated perspective of life or spawns enriched experiences or more and better understanding of the pleasures of family, work, community or leisure activities. Nevertheless, many would argue that therein lies the critical advantage of higher education. Classrooms *do* teach points of view. Faculty and peers in educational settings provide reference group orientations and new bases for reflecting on the quality of one's life.

Another debatable issue is the direction of causality to be assumed in discussing relationships between education and well-being. It is simplest to take the view that education leads to well-being. One might argue easily that the person who copes more adequately to begin with will more often end up in the ranks of the educated; while the less able person who cannot cope well with life, will not get into the higher grades or continue to college. Filtering of people of differential ability into "proper" educational attainments undoubtedly occurs. Nonetheless, despite meritocratic opportunities, many of our institutions encourage the less educated to remain where they are in spite of ability, and automatically encourage college among the wealthy of our society. Meritocratic goals in American education are only partially fulfilled. In interpreting our results, we thus lean rather heavily on ideas about education affecting well-being rather than vice versa.

The most evident conclusion from relationships of education to indices of subjective mental health is that the less educated in our society are more demoralized. They are less happy about their current life situation, less optimistic about the future, more oriented toward the past as a time when they were happy. One component of this demoralization is that the less educated less often think they can change their life circumstances. The less educated in our society feel themselves lower in overall efficacy, less in control over planning, more helpless in relationships with other people (e.g., they need people to listen to them, accept them). Demoralization may also lie behind the finding that less educated people clearly less often see professional help as relevant to their problems. Perhaps the less educated do not structure their difficulties as relevant for help because they do not see that anything can change the circumstances of their lives.

The roots of demoralization among the less educated in our society probably lie in the special stresses they encounter. They report bad things happening much more often than the educated. In addition, the less educated report being more overwhelmed when bad things *do* happen. These results suggest that the less educated are more demoralized because their experiences with life are more oppressive. They have probably had more frequent experiences with death, illness, and disruptions in education and jobs (Holmes and Rahe, 1967). These experiences place them in greater stress. Furthermore, their lack of education often cuts them off from the resources to cope with stress, both because of their lower financial status and their lack of awareness of channels and opportunities that the more educated easily grasp (Kessler, 1979). The fact that the less educated in our society also experience more ill health and psychological anxiety symptoms indicates that greater stress and demoralization have physical and psychological consequences.

Demoralization also often leads to lower aspirations. Campbell, Converse, and Rodgers (1976) have interpreted the fact that the less educated express just as much satisfaction with life as the higher educated as a case of lowered aspirations. People whose lives offer little learn to adapt but they may pay a considerable cost in physical and psychological symptoms. It is also possible that a doorstep interview cannot get at the underlying experience of painful dissatisfaction that accompanies the demoralization we note. Certainly the picture Rubin draws of the lower working class in our society in *Worlds of Pain* (1976) suggests that beneath a layer of adaptation there lies a more turbulent dissatisfaction with life, a sharper contrast between experience and dreams once held. The fact that less educated people experience anxiety symptoms suggests that while they express satisfaction with their life circumstances, they may have more internal concerns about their lack of fulfillment.

Specific qualities of life experience mentioned by the less educated are quite different from those mentioned by the more highly educated.[1] It is revealing that less educated people report health as a major source of happiness. Compared to others in our society, the uneducated seem more aware of those things in their life that are necessary for survival. They speak less often of interpersonal or role sources of well-being, features of life beyond mere survival. The moderately educated (e.g., the high school graduates) focus more frequently than other groups on family roles as sources of well-being, while the highly educated focus more frequently than other groups on their jobs and their communities. We would interpret this pattern to mean that occupational and civic concerns are probably maximally engaged in the college educated because their jobs and their roles in the community give them more contact with and clear responsibility for civic affairs. Not that the college educated are unconcerned about parenthood and marriage; they are very articulate about these roles. But jobs and community compete with family for time and thought. We thus have a picture of the college educated having a variety of resources entering their considerations of the quality of life, while the high school educated focus more exclusively on home and family experiences.

The specific socialization that occurs in formal and informal settings

---

[1] Although we should always remember that in examining education differences in responses to open-ended questions about well-being, we may be attending to differences in articulateness. The results are so consistent with conceptual understanding of the effects of education, however, that we see the results as substantive despite methodological ambiguity.

experienced by the more educated seems to foster a more highly intraceptive orientation to life than is characteristic of the less educated.
This finding occurs in many contexts in the preceding chapters. More-
educated people focus on personality aspects of self-definition more
than the less educated. Compared to the less educated, they mention
more personal traits in discussing how they differ from other people,
how they would like a child to be different from themselves, and their
strong points. They thus use personality categories in considering various aspects of their self-schema, more than less educated people do.

Furthermore, the more educated use these categories in thinking
about their experience in roles: they think about highly personal satisfactions and dissatisfactions that occur in work; they are especially sensitized to relational aspects of parenting and marriage. Although intraceptiveness alerts them to "problems" and inadequacies in roles, it also
fosters more involved satisfactions.

The positive contribution of intraceptiveness to role experience is
clearest in results about marriage. The more educated express self-
doubts about their own adequacy as spouses and report more problems
in marriage. Yet, compared to those with less education, they also report higher levels of happiness in their marriages. It may be that the
college-educated person more frequently applies standards of excellence to relationship satisfactions and thus has both more problems
and greater marital happiness. They say they experience both physical
and verbal interaction in marriage more frequently and the irritations
of marriage less frequently. We would suggest that these results are not
due entirely to the possibility that each additional level has its own
standard of evaluation of marriage, but may in part be due to the fact
that the more educated, with their intraceptive orientation, have a
greater openness and capactiy to enjoy the experience of marriage.

Education undoubtedly brings opportunities for higher positions in
society, but it may also stimulate a psychological perspective that contributes positively to experience in all life roles. One might argue that
"enriched" experience of work among the college educated simply reflects the fact that they hold more complex jobs which offer greater opportunity for economic and personal fulfillment. In the interpersonal
roles of marriage and parenthood, however, the positive effect of education on well-being may be more subtle. One could argue that those
who earn more feel more comfortable about survival issues and have
time and opportunities for psychological evaluation of experience.
Over and above such a possibility is the fact that the idealization of a
psychological approach to life has clearly been directly and indirectly
encouraged in higher education contexts. Socialized to this ideal, the
college educated approach all roles differently and, as we argued
above, become sensitive to both challenging problems and special joys
of family life that contribute to subjective mental health.

Social Demography and Subjective Mental Health

Beyond the critical variables of sex, age, and education, other social characteristics of men and women are woven into their experience of well-being. We have analyzed thirteen such characteristics which we highlight in this section. Each of the thirteen variables will be analyzed more extensively in future works, but, for the purposes of this book, will provide both basic information about the relationship of the characteristics to subjective mental health, as well as further support for integrative themes developed from our multiple-criteria approach.

Characteristics we have selected for study beyond sex, age, and education can be grouped according to the type of social fact they represent:

1. Economic position in the society: *Income.*
2. Role status: *Parent Status, Marital Status, Employment Status, Occupation (if employed).*
3. Geographic environment: *Region of the Country, Population Density of Place of Residence.*
4. Group identification: *Race, Religion.*
5. Social background during childhood: *Size of Childhood Community, Father's Occupation, Broken Home Background.*
6. Institutional integration into society: *Church Attendance.*

Nowhere is the dual function of this book more apparent than in the presentation of subjective well-being differences among these demographic groups. We have not only a journalistic interest in differences existing in American society in this part of the twentieth century, but also a scientific theoretical commitment to understand the determinants and correlates of subjective well-being. To know that people who live in suburbs are different from people who live in the city is an interesting journalistic fact, but it does not directly tell us much about the processes by which people in these settings come to differ in their appraisal of their own mental health. As a step toward comprehending the differences we find in the patterns of well-being expressed by people in the various categories, we will exert multivariate controls for sex, age, education, and year. So, for example, we find that income differences correlate strongly with different subjective appraisals of well-being. However, when we examine income differences controlling sex, education, and year we reach a slightly different understanding of the way in which income contributes to well-being. Some results relating to income are maintained in spite of controls; others are no longer very strong, suggesting that the interrelationships between income and age, income and education, and income and year may have some critical potential for understanding the dynamics of income–well-being relationships. Our analyses will reflect this double feature. We are intrigued by subjective mental-health differences in the social groupings per se, many of which have policy implications. But we also seek to understand *why* these social facts relate to subjective mental health. Our discussion of each variable will be necessarily brief, but many of them are being analyzed for more extensive separate publications. (See Kulka and Weingarten, 1979, for extended analysis of Broken Home Background.)

Our dual approach to the study of social characteristics and subjective mental health leads us to take slightly different stances on what is a significant result. Statistically significant differences between groups in some of our multivariate analyses turn out to be very small, in light of raw percentage differences among groups. For example, we find that there are a number of significant differences among the regions of the country (Northeast, Midwest, South, and West), but they are small. In our journalistic stance, we would be impressed with the fact that the regions are quite similar. In a social-scientific inquiry, we might be interested in the small differences because they signal some social-environmental characteristics of the regions that are worth exploring.

ANALYSIS STRATEGIES

Because large quantities of data were to be managed in this inquiry, we adopted certain arbitrary analysis procedures to serve both the journalistic and social-scientific inquiries. We first selected from the array of measures presented in chapters 2 through 7 those which produced significant effects in analyses of sex, age, education, and year differences. We then eliminated certain of these measures because of skewed distributions or because the meaning of the measure was not entirely clear. We culled twenty-three measures thought to merit wholesale analysis with respect to each of the social characteristics. They are listed below:[2]

> *General Well-Being* (chapter 2):
>   *Happiness, Worries, Future Morale, Anticipated Nervous Breakdown*
> *Self-Conceptions* (chapter 3):
>   *Positive View of Self, Personality Strengths, Role Shortcomings*
> *Subjective Feelings about Marriage* (chapter 4):
>   *Positive Orientation to Marriage, Restrictiveness of Marriage, Relationship Satisfaction in Marriage, Inadequacy as Spouse*
> *Subjective Feelings about Parenthood* (chapter 5):
>   *Positive Orientation to Parenthood, Restrictiveness of Parenthood, Problems in Raising Children, Inadequacy as Parent*

[2] See the relevant chapter for a detailed account of each measure.

Subjective Feelings about Job (chapter 6):
  Job Satisfaction, Ego Satisfaction in Job, Ego Dissatisfaction in Job
Symptom Factors (chapter 7):
  Psychological Anxiety, Ill Health, Immobilization

As a first appraisal of the relationships of social characteristics to the indicators of subjective well-being, we cross-classified each social characteristic against each of the twenty-three measures of well-being.[3] We looked at the cross-classification separately for 1957 and 1976. If there was any significant effect for either 1957 or 1976, we subjected the data to another analysis, asking whether the relationship was different in 1957 or in 1976. We did this by using log-linear analyses of the cross-classification of a given subjective indicator, by the social characteristic, by year, and asking for the best-fitting, most parsimonious model to explain that three-way classification. If we confirmed that there was a significant social-characteristic effect without distinguishing 1957 from 1976, we classified that effect as a combined-year effect (1957=1976) for that characteristic and tabulated it as such in our summary tables (tables 8.27 and 8.28) at the end of the chapter. If there was an interaction with year, we then listed this fact in the summary table. (We noted that the effect varied in the two years as a year-specific effect.) In the latter case, however, we also looked to see if there was still a potent cross-year social-characteristic effect *independent of difference between years:* even though a relationship between a given social characteristic and a given measure of subjective well-being was different in 1957 and 1976 in some respects, there could still be a general powerful relationship between that social characteristic and the subjective appraisal of mental health. We listed such a pattern as both a combined-year effect and a year-specific effect. Thus we indicate in tables 8.27 and 8.28 at the end of the chapter whether the relationship between a given characteristic and a given subjective appraisal of well-being fit one of four typologies: *no significant effect* whatsoever; a *combined-year effect only* (there was a relationship between the social characteristic and the subjective appraisal of well-being that was parallel in 1957 and 1976); *a year interaction effect with the social characteristic only* (the social characteristic was related to the particular measure of well-being differently in 1957 and in 1976); *both cross-year social-characteristic effect and interaction effect by year* (there was both a powerful general relationship between the social characteristic and the particular measure of subjective well-being apparent in both years, but there was also some specific difference in 1976 contrasted to 1957). In tables 8.27 and 8.28 we also indicate whether any one of the aforementioned results was maintained through log-

---

[3] For four characteristics (Occupation, Marital Status, Parent Status, and Employment Status), we stratified cross-classifications further by sex.

linear analyses when controls for sex, age, education, and year were imposed in a six-variable cross-classification.[4]

We will not concern ourselves much with the ways in which a social characteristic under investigation relates to the subjective measure of well-being through more complicated interactions among sex, age, education, and year. There will be instances where such interactions seem important or intriguing, and we will then attend to them. In the summary table, we note only whether complicated interactions are required for the model that fits the cross-classification. For example, we find that people from the South are *less* likely than others to say that their strong points consist of some personality characteristic. This result is further conditioned by education differences within regions. College-educated Easterners are somewhat different from all other groups, but the pattern of results is not altogether clear, nor, as far as we could tell, very informative about the original finding that the South was different. As a result, we will ignore many such interactions. Sometimes we will probably ignore important complications that accurately reflect the real world. Nevertheless, we see them as too extensive and complex to fit with the summary purpose of this chapter. In later papers we will extend analyses of particular social characteristics and at that point we will attend to more complicated interactive effects.

We are interested in how given social characteristics relate to psychological evaluations of well-being differently in 1957 and 1976. That interaction is crucial to any evaluation of how powerful a given social characteristic is and how much the correlation is conditioned by the particular social environments of 1957 and 1976. Such interactions can be highly informative about the meaning of the social characteristic and the meaning of its relationship to subjective well-being.

When we establish that a result is significant and required in the cross-classification analysis, it is still important to know *how strong* the effect is. The best way to estimate this is to turn to the original cross-classification of the subjective measure of well-being and examine the gross difference there.[5] By doing so, we hope to differentiate results that are significant but not strong from those that are both significant and reflect large differences between levels of the social characteristic. These full cross-classifications are too numerous to present in this

---

[4] In these log-linear analyses of six-way cross-classifications, we asked the following model-testing question: Does the relationship of the social characteristic to the measure of well-being by itself (or in interaction with year) appear as part of the most parsimonious fit (.05), or significantly improve the most parsimonious fit (.05) attained in addition to *using all possible interactive effects on subjective well-being of sex, age, education, and year as variables associated with measures of subjective well-being?* This model testing does not ask for the best model that could be attained; it asks only whether the social characteristic contributes significantly to the distribution of the psychological variable over and above the relationships of sex, age, education, and year (and their interactions) to that variable.

[5] There is clearly some distortion in reporting only cross-tabulations, for variables which had been analyzed for *net* effects in a log-linear six-variable model. We accept this distortion in order to maximize the clarity of data presented.

chapter; only results that survive the age, education, and year controls will be highlighted in tabular presentation, and in some instances we report only representative findings. Further, to reduce the amount of tabular presentation even for selected survivors, we present only certain *levels* of the subjective measure that reflect the difference or lack of difference found. For certain dichotomous measures (such as yes/no response to a question about problems in marriage), singling out one level has no effect on understanding the results. For measures which have more than two levels, truncated presentation may occasionally fail to communicate all of the effect.[6]

INCOME AND SUBJECTIVE MENTAL HEALTH

We begin our analysis of social factors in subjective mental health with an analysis of people's socioeconomic position in the society.

The 1957 study asked only for family income. While we had information on both individual and family income in 1976, we confined analyses to respondents' family income in order to include year differences in our analysis of the effect of income on subjective well-being.[7] We also needed to equate the purchasing power of 1957 and 1976 dollars; hence, respondents' family income for 1957 was converted to its equivalent in 1976 dollars. Since the Consumer Price Index of 1976 almost exactly doubled from 1957, we simply doubled the 1957 income levels to standardize income for the two years. Moreover, because we wished to detect potential differences in the effects of a moderate income, as opposed to either high or low income, we wanted to have enough categories in the middle-income range to permit an examination of possible changes in the inflection of curvilinear relationships at the two time points. Therefore, we divided income into six roughly equivalent groups. The lowest level included those families who earned under $4,000, and the highest level included those families earning more than $20,000; intermediate levels were $4,000–7,999; $8,000–9,999; $10,000–12,499; and $12,500–19,999.

There is a significant difference between family income levels reported in 1957 and 1976. Table 8.1 shows that 30 percent of the 1957 population report the equivalent of $12,500 or more family income, while 47 percent of the 1976 sample report that level. Thus, even after taking into account differences in the purchasing power of 1957 and 1976 dollars, the current generation is clearly more affluent than their counterparts twenty years ago. Ostensibly, then, these results could be

---

[6] We can make available to anyone who is interested the complete cross-tabulation of a given social characteristic with all levels of a given subjective measure of well-being.

[7] As in all of the Survey Research Center's surveys, a respondent is handed a card and asked to select a category which represents family income level, rather than to quote a dollar value directly to the interviewer. These categorizations were different in 1957 and 1976, comparable to the distributions of national incomes at those two times.

TABLE 8.1

Year Differences in Reported
Family Income Converted to
1976 Dollar Values[a]

1976 Dollars	1957 (%)	1976 (%)
<4,000	17	14
4,000– <8,000	23	18
8,000–<10,000	16	9
10,000–<12,500	14	12
12,500–<20,000	22	25
20,000+	8	22
	100%	100%
Total Number	2,396[b]	2,117[b]

[a] Based on doubling 1957 reported incomes to account for the doubling of the Consumer Price Index from 1957 to 1976.

[b] Excludes respondents whose income was not ascertained.

used to test hypotheses offered by Easterlin (1974) about the effects of relative versus absolute income on people's well-being. For example, many of the people classified as high income in 1957 could be classified as middle income in 1976, and many of those considered low in 1976 might have been classified as middle income in 1957. Similarly, many more people are in the richest income groups in 1976 while, in comparison with 1957, members of the current generation are far less numerous in the two "poorest" income groups. Hence, if the Easterlin theory about the effects of relative income on well-being is accurate, we might expect a number of interactions by year in relationships between family income and indicators of subjective well-being, but with differential effects possible at any of the three relative income levels. For instance, we might speculate that negative effects of being in the poorest income group might be *more* salient in 1976, since members of those groups are less numerous, or that the potential positive benefits of being in the highest income groups may have been greater in 1957, when membership in that group was more exclusive.

The relationship between income and subjective mental health is both consistent and strong; it pervades many different assessments of subjective mental health. High income is associated with feeling good about one's life, and low income is associated with feeling bad about one's life on nearly all mental-health indices. Only three of the measures (worrying, positive orientation to parenting, and relationship satisfaction in parenting) fail to show significant income effects. Moreover, over half of the results we note withstand controls for age, sex, education, and year. This is surprising since education and income are so closely associated in our society. We had thought that many income effects would be interpretable as age or education differences, but we seem to be dealing with powerful effects of income itself on mental health.

If we look only at results that withstand controls for sex, age, and education (reported in table 8.2), we find that in both 1957 and 1976 compared to those with low income, people with high incomes (1) report greater present happiness and higher future morale; (2) less often say they have felt as if they might have a nervous breakdown; (3) have a positive orientation toward and see fewer restrictions in marriage; (4) report greater happiness in their own marriages; (5) report greater job satisfaction; and (6) list fewer symptoms of ill health. Thus a wide variety of dimensions of well-being all seem to be affected by—or at least correlated with—income. Although we are dealing only with correlations, it is difficult to avoid considering potential causal links between income and subjective well-being. We might suggest that a happy marriage leads to higher income, but it is more compelling to see higher income leading to marital happiness. More detailed analyses of income and income over the life cycle might clarify the nature of these causal linkages.

Only one result which withstood controls for sex, age, and education points to a negative effect of income on well-being: the higher a person's income, the more likely the person is to report problems in raising children. However, in earlier parts of this book, we have interpreted perceptions of problems in roles not necessarily as a negative experience per se, but rather as a psychological or intraceptive orientation to social roles.

In addition to the foregoing results that withstood controls, many other significant correlations of income with well-being wither when demographic controls are introduced. Most of these are income correlations with psychological orientations to self-perception and to roles. People with high incomes compared to those with low incomes hold a positive view of themselves, see personality strengths in the self, less often focus on role shortcomings, see more problems but also more relationship satisfactions in their own marriages, feel inadequate as parents and spouses, and are ego involved in both satisfactions and dissatisfactions in their work. Furthermore, without the controls, we find that people with low income are particularly high in psychological anxiety. Since controls diminish these effects considerably, we conclude that the powerful relationship of income to education underlies many of these correlations of income to subjective mental health. What alerts people to the more psychological aspects of roles and more intraceptive orientation to well-being is not their income but their education. Likewise, association with educated, not affluent, reference groups teaches people a psychological orientation. Greater wealth and the social resources that wealth produces may not directly be the criti-

TABLE 8.2
Selected Income Differences in Subjective Mental Health

Measure of Subjective Mental Health	Income										
	<$4,000		$4,000-7,999		$8,000-9,999		$10,000-12,499		$12,500-19,499		$20,00
	1957 (%)	1976 (%)	1957 (%)	1976 (%)	1957 (%)	1976 (%)	1957 (%)	1976 (%)	1957 (%)	1976 (%)	1957 (%)
No Year Interaction											
Happiness: Not too happy	23	25	15	17	7	8	9	11	5	6	5
High Future Morale: Very happy	27	24	45	38	54	62	60	55	68	61	61
Experienced Feeling of Nervous Breakdown: Yes	25	26	20	22	18	22	17	25	17	20	17
Orientation to Marriage (in general): Positive	34	30	41	30	44	29	42	25	48	30	52
All restrictive	51	60	46	63	43	62	46	63	41	59	37
Happiness of Own Marriage: Very happy	40	43	38	50	43	50	45	52	55	50	59
Job Satisfaction: Very satisfied	21	15	25	21	32	26	31	27	34	30	47
Ill Health: Very high	31	37	15	23	9	12	9	12	6	8	9
Year Interaction											
Worrying: Always, a lot	40	46	38	47	32	50	33	46	28	46	28
Orientation to Parenting: Positive	52	49	59	45	56	45	53	41	61	71	61
All restrictive	32	41	30	46	32	51	33	47	31	41	32
Problem Raising Children: Yes	72	76	76	72	76	79	78	79	75	82	69
Total Number	407	295	549	380	389	195	323	345	536	518	186

cal factors that affect well-being. We have spoken previously of educational effects on subjective well-being as the product of formal and informal socialization to a psychological orientation to life. To the extent that income overlaps education, we can also speak of the idealization of "psychological man" among the more affluent.

Surprisingly few results suggest that people with high incomes have higher or lower levels of subjective well-being in 1976 than they had in 1957. Those with high income in 1976 tend to be somewhat more introspective and intraceptive than the comparable affluent groups in 1957. We draw this conclusion from the interaction effects of year by income on well-being occurring in a few analyses (see table 8.2). In 1957 people with high income were less worried, were more likely to have a positive, less restrictive orientation to parenthood, and were less likely to report problems in raising children. The affluent are thus somewhat more thoughtful and introspective about their lives in 1976 than they were in 1957, especially in child rearing. To a certain extent, these results confirm the theory of relative income effects on well-being. More people are in the affluent category in 1976, and this fact may contribute a different meaning to affluence. A smaller affluent group may imply a more coherent reference group and clearer directives about how people should perform certain roles. As the group increases, norms may become less coherent simply because greater variety exists within the group. That greater variety may thus induce uncertainty and a greater sense of conflict or confinement in social roles. Nonetheless, the dominant theme in this analysis is that the effects of income are similar in 1957 and 1976.

Campbell (1980) has reviewed a number of studies which plot the relationship between income and happiness and discovers that the 1957 and 1976 surveys reported in this book find a higher correlation than other comparable surveys. He suggests that perhaps the general economic conditions in the country at different points in history affect the overall correlation between incomes and happiness—that in times of general recession, income may figure more critically in people's evaluations of well-being. In spite of these fluctuations, however, we are impressed with the similarity in the pattern of results in 1957 and 1976, which argues for the general power of economic well-being in determining overall subjective well-being.

Surprisingly few results suggest that middle-income groups are significantly different in unique ways from other income groups in either 1957 or 1976. We have some indication that middle-income people see more restrictiveness in the parent role and report more symptoms of immobilization. These results confirm the suggestion that middle-income families experience restriction of freedom particularly in child rearing. Middle-income men and women may have expectations of a full life particularly for their children, but unlike high-income people, do not have the wherewithal to implement these expectations. Planning for children may be the area in which the greatest differentiation of realization of expectations occurs. These results distinguishing the middle-income group are minimal, however, and are overshadowed by the linear effects that dominate most relationships between income and subjective mental health.

In reviewing our results, we can ask whether the strength of relationship between income and well-being comes from the negative impact of low income or the positive effect of high income. It is difficult to draw simple conclusions about this issue. In some measures, it is clear that the biggest differentiation of well-being occurs between low and moderate income, but in other instances the power of the correlation seems to come from the distinction between high and moderate levels. Future analyses may distinguish those subjective experiences which are especially susceptible to very low or very high income. Low income seems to be the major contributor to the strong relationship between income and future morale. People with low income have little optimism about the future. This fact seems to be stronger than the fact that people with very high income are particularly optimistic about the future. On the other hand, happiness in marriage was correlated with income primarily because those with very high incomes are most happy in their marriages. High-income people are also the major contributors to the relationship between income and finding ego satisfactions in work. There is thus some suggestion that being rich affects people in *specific role contexts*—marriage, work—while poverty corrodes one's *general* sense of well-being. Although we hesitate to label this a common pattern, it is a hypothesis worth exploring in order to understand the effects of financial resources on people's well-being.

Many complex interactions of income with both education and age (and some even more complex with year) were difficult to interpret. One, however, stood out as especially interesting: the relationship between income and happiness is most powerful for middle-aged men and women. Linear effects occur in all age groups, but in middle age they are consistently strong, especially in 1976 (table 8.3). There is a significant difference among age groups in the *variance* of income reported. This suggests the possibility that the middle-aged effect may be

TABLE 8.3

Correlations (Gammas) between Income and
Happiness (by age × year)

	1957		1976	
Age	Gamma	Number	Gamma	Number
Young (21–34)	.27	748	.34	787
Middle-aged (35–54)	.30	978	.42	650
Old (55+)	.20	644	.26	644

a variance effect. We examined the findings and found that attenuation of the distribution of income had very little bearing on where the correlations were stronger or weaker in the relationship of income to happiness. We thus feel reasonably safe in saying that middle age is a time, especially in 1976, when income seems to have its most dramatic effects on happiness, and perhaps on other aspects of well-being. We can return to an interpretation of life-cycle differences made in previous chapters. Young people are future building and may not see income as critical to well-being because they can anticipate change in the future. Middle-aged people presumably have "arrived" and can no longer anticipate any change in their social status in the future: thus their present income signifies the quality of their well-being. Older people, aware that they can't "take it with them," are perhaps attending to inner aspects of life and may experience a restructuring of values that deemphasizes financial status as a major determinant of well-being.

PARENT STATUS AND SUBJECTIVE MENTAL HEALTH

Each of the next four sections will consider a different critical role status in our society: parent status, marital status, employment status, and occupation (if employed). Let us consider parent status first.

Hoffman, Thornton, and Manis (1978) report in a national representative study of parents and nonparents the specific advantages people see in having children. Parents are more likely than nonparents to say that children provide love, companionship, stimulation, joy, and fun. Thus, parents are seen as more aware of the potential for loving relationships through children, and more aware of parenting as a stimulating and interesting life function.

Quite contradictory hypotheses can be generated from Rossi's theoretical work (1968), which enumerates difficulties people experience in the transition to parenthood. Rossi asserts that parenthood is often an involuntary state for people despite adequate birth-control methods, and that it is often viewed as irrevocable and overwhelming because of the total responsibility it involves. Rossi points to the plethora of pressures in our society to consider performance of the parental role as natural and automatic. As a result, any difficulties that a mother or father experiences are interpreted as personal inadequacy. In fact, parenthood is a rather poorly defined role which makes people susceptible to countless conflicting norms from "experts" about how to parent. Such problems and contradictions in the role of parent lead us to believe that there may be considerable stress in the role. Results from other surveys (Campbell, Converse, and Rodgers, 1976; Feldman, 1964) suggest that the parent role interferes in many ways with other areas of adjustment—particularly with gratification in marriage.

Chapter 5 highlighted the positive reactions of the role disclosed by mothers and fathers as well as their feelings of inadequacy. Clearly the romantic ideal about parenthood is being questioned much more by people in the 1970s than it was in the 1950s. Therefore we might expect differences in the way the role affected the subjective mental health of people in 1957 in contrast to 1976.

Taking the contradictory hypotheses as representative of current opinion, we had no clear expectation about how parenthood might relate to indicators of subjective mental health, even though past research evidence tends to support the hypothesized negative impact of parenting on marriage.

What are the results of our analyses? We compared all parents, whether or not they were married, with all nonparents, again married or not, on all subjective mental-health indicators. Among the parents are those who are divorced or widowed; among the nonparent group, are single and divorced people, as well as those who are married. In future analyses, we will want to control for marital status, but at present we highlight the gross effects of being a parent in contrast to not being a parent. We are asking whether being a parent in American society is correlated with positive or negative indicators of subjective mental health. In analyses of marital well-being, we will compare only married respondents who are parents or nonparents. Because of this gross categorization of parents vs. nonparents, the control for age in our six-way cross-classification analysis will be particularly crucial.

We can see in table 8.28 that without controls, parent status relates significantly to a number of subjective mental-health indicators, although the findings vary somewhat for men and women. Analyses of the six-way cross-classification, however, produced only two instances in which relationships of parent status to subjective well-being in men and women were critical to the cross-classification. In most of the discussion that follows, therefore, we discuss parents and nonparents without distinguishing between mothers and fathers. In a few instances, we highlight results that seem to be clearer for one sex or the other.

We have a number of significant results that hold up across 1957 and 1976 with controls for age, education, sex, and year. These are reported in table 8.4. Being a parent does correlate with increased strain in both men and women, though this correlation is clearer for women. Mothers and fathers are more likely to say they worry "always" or "a lot," compared to men and women who are not parents. This was true both in 1957 and 1976, but especially in 1976. Forty percent of the fathers in 1976 say they worry "always" or "a lot" compared to 30 percent of childless men. Comparable percentages for mothers and nonmothers are 50 percent and 44 percent, respectively. Mothers are significantly more likely than nonmothers to say that they have at some time or another felt as if they were going to have a nervous breakdown.

Mothers and fathers are not different from nonparents with respect to affective measures of subjective mental health—happiness and fu-

TABLE 8.4
Parent Status and Selected Measures of Mental Health (by sex X year)

Measures of Subjective Mental Health	Year	Men Parent Status		Women Parent Status	
		Has Children (%)	Does Not Have Children (%)	Has Children (%)	Does Not Have Children (%)
No Interaction With Year					
Worrying:					
Always, a lot	1957	28	26	40	36
	1976	40	30	50	44
Nervous Breakdown:					
Yes	1957	12	8	27	15
	1976	13	17	27	19
Negative Orientation to Marriage:					
Negative	1957	19	19	27	18
	1976	25	21	28	27
Restrictive Orientation to Marriage:					
All	1957	42	39	47	40
	1976	59	54	57	53
Marital Problem:					
Yes	1957	45	30	52	34
	1976	60	48	65	52
Relationship Satisfaction in Marriage:					
Yes	1957	39	51	43	55
	1976	50	66	59	79
Freq. Felt Inadequacy as Spouse:					
Never	1957	44	53	42	53
	1976	45	55	44	44
Positive Orientation to Parenthood:					
All positive	1957	63	61	54	56
	1976	49	40	45	22
Ego Satis. Job:					
All	1957	31	29	68	64
	1976	59	57	72	63
Immobilization:					
Never	1957	43	37	30	34
	1976	29	21	23	21
Interaction With Year					
Happiness of Marriage:					
Not happy	1957	28	32	36	34
	1976	19	10	23	10
Restrictiveness of Parenting:					
All restrictive	1957	27	31	31	34
	1976	43	50	41	56
Total Number	1957	848	147	1,105	201
	1976	711	119	1,017	160

ture morale. It is important to keep this in mind because it suggests that the above differences about the felt strain associated with parenthood are less associated with general affective distress in the role than they are with the stresses of being responsible for socializing and caring for another person. Furthermore, this strain does not translate into passivity. Quite the contrary—parents as a group rarely talk about immobilization symptoms of strain (see table 8.4). It is as if parents are activated by the strain of raising children to express symptoms of agitation, but do not translate these symptoms into feelings of unhappiness or symptoms of passivity. Commitment to socializing children and being a role model for them may block the possibility of using immobilization symptoms. Such commitment can also bring considerable joy, despite the strain.

Married parents in our sample are quite different from childless married men and women in their reactions to marriage. Parents clearly have a more negative orientation to their marriages than childless husbands and wives. Table 8.4 shows the dramatic results registered in the greater report of marriage problems in the parents compared to nonparents, in both years, for both men and women. These results further withstand controls for age. Evidently, regardless of age, married couples who have children experience more problems with marriage than childless couples do. Further analyses to detect the kind of marital problems which differentiate parents and childless married people show that childless couples are more likely than couples with children to focus on relationship problems when they mention problems in their marriages. This is especially prevalent among younger men and women. Table 8.5 reports the type of marital problems mentioned by parents and childless men and women. Parents mention more problems in their spouses, themselves, and their general situations (including children), and parents are far less likely to focus on the marital relationship as a problem. This result may give us a clue about the bases of marital difficulties for parents. When children are part of a marriage, new dynamics arise that focus difficulties on aspects of marriage separate from the bond itself. Children can cause husbands and wives to be inattentive to each other (problem attributed to the spouse or the self), or to see the need for more time or money to pursue interests (problems attributed to external situations). Without children, the burden of problems more likely falls on the relationship itself. We suspect that one of the reasons childless couples may not admit to more problems in their marriages is that such admission is tantamount to seeing a problem in the relationship and thus threatens the existence of the bond.

Perhaps the most striking difference between the two groups of married people is that husbands and wives who do not have any children are more likely to report relationship satisfactions from their marriage. In 1976, for example, 66 percent of childless husbands reported relationship satisfaction in marriage compared to only 50 percent of the

TABLE 8.5

Types of Marital Problems Mentioned by Husbands and Wives Who Are Parents or Childless (by year, 21–35 year olds only)

	Men				Women			
	Parents		Childless		Parents		Childless	
Type of Marital Problem Discussed	1957 (%)	1976 (%)	1957 (%)	1976 (%)	1957 (%)	1976 (%)	1957 (%)	1976 (%)
Problem in Relationship	37	37	69	58	33	36	47	39
Problem of Spouse	13	8	0	0	29	22	23	21
Problem in Self	17	9	0	7	8	8	12	6
Problem in Situation	33	46	31	35	30	34	18	33
	100%	100%	100%	100%	100%	100%	100%	100%
Total Number	108	93	13	26	174	188	17	33

married fathers. Comparable figures for childless wives and married mothers were 79 percent and 59 percent, respectively. This very large difference can be interpreted in several ways. Parents may be distracted from their partners because of their investment in their children. Conversely, childless couples can become highly invested in one another.

Still other results point to greater marital difficulties experienced by parents compared to childless couples. Married parents are more likely to feel inadequate as husbands and wives. This is a significantly stronger result among men than women. This imbalance might be due, in part, to the fact that childless women—more than men—feel that not having a child impugns their adult function. Parents also have a more negative orientation to marriage in general than nonparents and see marriage as more restricting. On the whole it is hard not to conclude along with Campbell, Converse, and Rodgers (1976) that children seem to disrupt marital relationships.

One result changed from 1957 to 1976. More parents in 1976 say they are not very happy with their marriage, compared to childless men and women. One interpretation of these results is that in the 1970s married people who did not have children were likely to get divorced if their marriages were not very happy. A second interpretation may reflect the considerable disillusionment over the last generation with the child-rearing ideal for family life. Childless couples may feel less pressure now to have children in order to have a happy marriage. Indeed, many more nonparents in 1976 see the restrictive aspects of being a parent than did nonparents in 1957. This change is not as marked in parents as it is in nonparents. These results are also reported in table 8.4 as an "interaction with year" effect. In sum, there are competing plausible interpretations for the large decline in the unhappy childless husbands and wives from 1957 to 1976. A childless couple in 1976 has greater potential for gratification both because divorce is more readily available if the marriage is not working, and because the burden of feeling outside the norm if one is childless has lessened.

We might emphasize that it would be mistaken to interpret any of these results as the explicit causal connections between having children and marital difficulty. Many people who would seek divorce if they did not have children have resisted because divorce seems more difficult when there are children in the marriage. A joke still in current circulation has it that a ninety-five-year-old couple can finally get divorced because their only child—a seventy-three-year-old son—has died. The fact that people who do not have children can dissolve their troubled marriages more readily is in contrast to marriages where the presence of children poses ongoing problems in the marital relationships.

Quite apart from the difficulties associated with parenting that the data uncover, it is reassuring to know that parents have a more positive orientation to parenthood than do nonparents. Evidently parents are not translating difficulties with the role into explicit negative attitudes. Very likely the difficulties of being a parent underscore the commitment not only to parenting but to the particular children they have borne. Theories of psychological commitment (Tomkins, 1965) and dissonance (Aronson, 1969) suggest that attachments to people, objects, or ideas become stronger when people are faced with unavoidable difficulties. Indeed the parent-child bond may be as rich as it is because of the difficulties we have been noting.

One result in table 8.4 suggests that being a parent may have positive consequences for subjective well-being. Parents—especially mothers— are more likely to obtain ego satsifactions from work than nonparents. These results suggest that parents—again, women in particular—seemingly immerse themselves in the intrinsic benefits of the work role. The childless status of women who are not mothers may raise concern about their adequacy as women. This concern may, in turn, affect how much psychological gratification they extract from the work role traditionally relegated to men in our culture. For mothers, on the other hand, work may be welcomed as psychological fulfillment which compensates for potential limitations of child rearing.

In summary, the analyses suggest that being a parent in American society, especially in 1976, is a somewhat more emotionally disturbing condition for people than not being a parent. Parents have greater experience of strain than nonparents and also greater difficulty in marital relationships. Just two results in our tabulation of parent/nonparent differences in subjective mental health suggest there may be any direct positive consequences of being a parent: parents are less likely to experience feelings of immobilization than nonparents, and they are more likely to get ego gratification from work. The more complicated interactions will be important to follow up in further work. Future work should examine the exact ways in which controls for education and age affect subjective well-being among parents and nonparents in our society. It will be even more important to know how being married, single, divorced, or widowed interacts with the parental status to affect the results we have discussed. Indeed some of the clearest results in this discussion centered on what we obtained by limiting our analysis to married people's reactions. Comparable analyses of marital status may produce new insights about the significance of the parental status in American society.

MARITAL STATUS AND SUBJECTIVE MENTAL HEALTH

We have discussed the effect of marital status on attitudes about marriage in chapter 4. In this chapter we want to ask a different question: what effect does married, single, divorced (separated)[8] or widowed have on general well-being?

Since we are interested in generational differences in the effect of marital status on well-being, it is important to ask whether there are critical year differences in the distributions of marital status. Cross-classification analyses of marital status by age, education, year, and sex indicate that respondents in 1976 are considerably *less likely to be married* and considerably *more likely to be divorced or separated*. (See chapter 9 for a detailed description of these data.) There were more single people in 1976, but this fact is evidently best understood as an age effect.

Age controls are quite critical to our understanding of the correlates of marital status. Older people are more likely to be widowed and less likely to be either married or divorced/separated. Young people are infrequently widowed and are most likely to be single. The education control is critical because, when age is controlled, less educated people are more likely to be widowed. We analyze year differences separately for men and women, but in our cross-classification for age, education, and year, we also cross-classify by sex. These analyses will allow us to test sex differences in marital status effects on well-being as well as any interactions that occur differentially for men and women.

The controls we introduce in analyses of marital status are quite critical. In the 1957 book, we examined marital status without these controls and drew certain conclusions which are clearly vitiated by the controls. In *The Future of Marriage* (1972), Jessie Bernard emphasized

---

[8] For purposes of this chapter, we combined divorced and separated groups. The latter includes only those people who *at the time of the interview* were divorced or separated, but it does not include people who *at some time* in their adult life experienced divorce or separation, but are now married.

TABLE 8.6

Marital Status Comparisons in Selected Measures of Subjective Mental Health
(by age × sex × year)

	Men								Women							
	Married		Single		Widowed		Divorced/ Separated		Married		Single		Widowed		Divorced/ Separated	
Measure of Subjective Mental Health (N)[a] — Age	1957 (%)	1976 (%)	1957 (%)	1976 (%)	1957 (%)	1976 (%)	1957 (%)	1976 (%)	1957 (%)	1976 (%)	1957 (%)	1976 (%)	1957 (%)	1976 (%)	1957 (%)	1976 (%)
21-34	(269)	(225)	(44)	(92)	—	—	(5)	(29)	(269)	(303)	(28)	(88)	(7)	(4)	(38)	(22)
35-54	(404)	(255)	(18)	(16)	(5)	(6)	(23)	(35)	(434)	(277)	(23)	(13)	(45)	(31)	(52)	(65)
54+	(232)	(217)	(20)	(22)	(42)	(40)	(13)	(23)	(156)	(158)	(24)	(25)	(176)	(226)	(19)	(88)
Total	(905)	(697)	(82)	(130)	(47)	(46)	(41)	(87)	(959)	(738)	(75)	(126)	(231)	(261)	(109)	(175)
Future Morale: Very Happy																
21-34	77	72	61	64	—[b]	—[b]	—[b]	72	74	69	57	67	—[b]	—[b]	74	62
35-54	56	54	17	56	—[b]	—[b]	35	37	56	51	48	46	33	39	52	46
55+	31	32	15	23	14	2	31	17	28	35	25	28	17	17	21	21
Total	55	53	40	56	17	11	38	44	59	55	43	57	21	21	50	47
Frequency Feel Inadequate as Parent: A lot																
21-34	11	13	—[c]	—[c]	—[b]	—[b]	—[b]	25	18	22	—[c]	—[c]	—[b]	—[b]	44	24
35-54	15	17	—[c]	—[c]	—[b]	—[b]	67	39	18	16	—[c]	—[c]	30	18	37	30
55+	12	13	—[c]	—[c]	9	3	29	6	16	15	—[c]	—[c]	9	8	20	20
Total	13	15	—[c]	—[c]	8	6	40	26	18	18	—[c]	—[c]	13	10	36	26
Positive Orientation to Self as Different: Positive																
21-34	68	73	56	65	—[b]	—[b]	—[b]	71	58	64	58	70	—[b]	—[b]	62	63
35-54	73	72	50	62	—[b]	—[b]	56	74	68	65	57	80	69	59	67	81
55+	78	67	75	80	86	—[b]	75	65	65	70	84	62	80	74	82	79
Total	73	70	59	66	88	73	61	70	64	66	66	70	79	73	68	73
Ego Dissatisfaction with Job: Yes																
21-34	31	45	61	18	—[b]	—[b]	—[b]	—[b]	27	55	32	64	—[b]	—[b]	21	62
35-54	29	40	12	38	—[b]	—[b]	—[b]	56	26	35	38	29	21	30	22	41
55+	17	38	42	58	17	42	29	55	26	46	43	62	26	30	23	45
Total	27	41	20	58	14	35	23	52	25	39	38	62	26	30	19	32

NOTE: Numbers in parentheses are total number of persons in each group.

[a] Numbers will vary according to measure. Percentage do not ...

differences in the effect of marital status on the subjective well-being of men and women. She used the data to support her thesis that marriage was good for men but had pitfalls for women. Reanalysis of the data with controls only partially supports the position she advanced. The analyses we are about to report suggest that being married makes a positive contribution to feelings of well-being for both sexes, although, as we shall see, there are many more indicators that marriage is good for men than that it is good for women. Nevertheless, we have no evidence in the data that marriage is bad for women. A summary of the multivariate analyses appears in table 8.28 at the end of this chapter.

Our key findings indicate that two statuses—widowhood and being divorced (or separated)—are subjectively bad for both sexes. Divorced/separated men and women are not very happy, according to self-reports, nor are they as hopeful about the future as married people (see table 8.6). They worry more than other groups, more often say they have felt as if they might have a nervous breakdown, and more often report feelings of inadequacy as parents. Not surprisingly, they, along with single people, have a more negative orientation to marriage than do married or widowed people. Divorce may not always have negative effects, but this finding suggests that people who remain divorced and do not remarry, suffer negative feelings of adjustment. The finding holds for both men and women, in both years. Although there is no significant interaction by sex and year, it is interesting to note that 37 percent of women in the divorced/separated status in 1976 report that at one time or another they have felt as if they might have a nervous breakdown. This contrasted to a much lower (24 percent) percentage of women in other status positions in 1976 and a lower percentage in all groups in 1957. This finding may offer a clue about the nature of the difficulties inherent in being divorced. The feeling that one might have a nervous breakdown seems to come from extraordinary pressures of coping. Women in the divorced/separated status must often manage to meet the major responsibilities of child rearing on very low incomes. They feel particularly inadequate as parents (see table 8.6). Divorced men also feel inadequate as parents, but their feelings are kept at a distance. Fathers tend to feel inadequate because they are not close enough to their children, whereas mothers feel inadequate in tolerance and personal controls. The divorced or separated status often implies parenting, and the single-parent role may cause the undue stress that leads to both feelings of inadequacy as a parent and to burdensome worrying. Confronting such feelings, divorced people clearly may begin to think they cannot cope and thus that they might have a nervous breakdown.

The widowed status is also an unhappy one. Widows are as likely as divorced men and women to report being not very happy and having low future morale (see table 8.6). Widows are particularly *unlikely* to see marriage as restrictive. Widows and widowers probably nostalgically remember their previous marital status, which offered more benefits than their present lives. Perhaps the retrospective examination of past married life gives them an anchor for evaluating life, something solid that allows them to cope with their present lives. Widows and widowers more than others (especially the married) take a positive view of the ways in which they differ from other people (see table 8.6). This is an interesting finding: it may mean that people left on their own because of the death of a spouse are confronted for the first time with the necessity of coping with life on their own. The widow who manages money, who for the first time has sole discretion over the use of funds, may discover new competence and gain self-esteem. A widower who must learn to prepare his own food and take care of his own household arrangements for the first time in his life may gain a new or enlarged sense of control. These new realms of involvement though precipitated by tragedy, can induce self-confidence. In the same vein, it is interesting to note that widows and widowers are particularly low in reported immobilization. Evidently the pressures they experience to cope with life circumstances in their solitary state engage them in activity and keep them from developing the symptoms of passive withdrawal implied in the *Immobilization* scale.

Among single people, we find that *Immobilization* scores are strikingly high in comparison to other marital categories. Immobilization is a symptom of the young, but it also seems to be associated with the single status, *when age is controlled.* This finding may speak to the nature of specific problems faced by single people. They are often making decisions about marriage: whether to marry at all, whom to marry, choices and decisions involving commitments and loyalties. We have suggested earlier that *Immobilization* may reflect conflicts and problems around interpersonal commitment. It thus makes considerable sense that *Immobilization* is especially high in single men and women.

Single people stand out in their negative appraisals of both parenthood and marriage. This is not surprising, but is perhaps again most interesting in connection with our interpretation of single people's problems of commitment.

Single people are deeply involved in jobs and work. This is clearly reflected in the fact that single people are more likely to report *ego* dissatisfactions with work (see table 8.6), as though work were the primary locus of identity. Many more single people mention an aspect of work which diminishes their self-identity as the source of job dissatisfaction. Married people, those who are divorced or separated, and the widowed have other roles, such as parenthood, which absorb some of the singular ego involvement in work that we note among single men and women.

Each nonmarried status presents some difficulties. The divorced/separated face the difficulty of overload, the widowed status, the difficulty of having a time orientation too specifically fixed on past life, and single status, the problem of commitment for the future. This leaves the married status as the most comfortable integration into society. Institutions are arranged for the married. Marriage permits easy management of present life circumstances and anticipation of future possibilities. We find that married people report being much happier than other groups, have a more positive orientation to themselves, and are very *unlikely* to have experienced an impending nervous breakdown. In addition, married men, in particular, say they do not worry much. These latter results suggest that Jessie Bernard is correct in her view that men gain a great deal from marriage. Married men report greater well-being than married women, but married women seem to be far better off than women who are not married.

It is surprising and important to realize that we find no clear indications of interactions between marital status and year. Marital status is correlated with aspects of well-being in the same way in both years. We have had some indication that there were different normative responses to marriage and parenthood in 1957 and 1976. For example, results indicated that single people in 1957 were much more positive and felt less restricted by marriage than single people did in 1976. The earlier generation of single people were more caught up in the halo of the married state. Single people in 1976 seemed to be more dubious about marriage. However, with the control for age and education in the log-linear analyses, these results were no longer very striking. The more negative appraisal of marriage by single people in 1976 may be attributable to the increased number of young and more educated people who are single in 1976.

EMPLOYMENT STATUS AND SUBJECTIVE MENTAL HEALTH

Let us now turn to the third role status to be correlated with measures of subjective mental health: employment status.

Between 1957 and 1976, there occurred a "subtle revolution" (Smith, 1979)—the influx into the labor market of women who have every intention of staying there even if they or their families do not "need" the money and even if they deprive men of jobs. At the same time, there was a subtle disengagement of men from work. In chapter 6 we saw that this was especially apparent in older working men of 1976. We argued that older men in the 1970s had enough contact with norms for a new role—retirement—to enable them to socialize themselves anticipatorily to that role and begin to divest themselves of strong involvement with their work identities. We saw less evidence of this in the younger men of 1976. Tamir's (1980) analysis of middle-aged men (40–49) of 1976, however, suggests that they, too, are clearly beginning to question the importance of work and are turning more to familial or general social supports as the major bases of their well-being. Tamir did not analyze the 1957 data. We suspect that the apparent mid-life reevaluation of work might also have been present then, though perhaps less significantly. Over the time between the two studies, men's general investment in work has been seriously questioned, and this cultural change may be particularly absorbed by mid-life people who are, in any case, at a point of reevaluation.

We are thus confronted with paradoxical changes in the culture—as women are investing themselves increasingly in the psychological importance of working, men may be quietly disengaging from the role. A woman being in the work force may thus have had important differential psychological consequences for her in 1976 compared to 1957, and, in turn, these consequences will be very different from what employment status meant for a man in 1957 and in 1976.

We hypothesized that both unemployment and retirement might be less troublesome psychologically for men in 1976 compared to 1957. We were less sure about their significance for women. We also hypothesized that working, in comparison to being a full-time housewife, might make more positive contributions to women's well-being in 1976 than in 1957.

With these hypotheses in mind, we were surprised by the general consistency of the results across both years when we compared people of different work statuses (employed, retired, unemployed, student—for men; employed, housewife, retired, unemployed, student—for women).[9] (See table 8.28 at the end of the chapter.)

Unemployment

For both men and women, in both years, unemployment is clearly associated with troublesome psychological feelings (table 8.7). Unemployed men in both years are especially likely to see themselves as unhappy, pessimistic about their future, and inadequate as husbands. Unemployed women in both years were also especially unhappy, unhappy with their marriages, and likely to see children as burdens. The last finding may indicate that unemployed women see children as obstacles to employment. Men do not usually face this problem.

Because the unemployed are disproportionately represented in different age groups—in the older groups of 1957 and in the younger groups of 1976,[10]—we checked the above trends for all age groups. The results occur in each age group.

---

[9] We allowed the person's own designation of being employed determine his/her categorization as "employed" regardless of how many hours a person worked. In 1976, 97 percent of the men and 89 percent of the women, worked at least twenty hours of work per week.

[10] In 1957, 76 percent of the unemployed men and 74 percent of the unemployed women were 35 or older. The comparable figures in 1976 were 46 percent (men) and 42 percent (women). Thus in 1976, the majority of the unemployed were younger people (21–35).

TABLE 8.7

Selected Comparison of Working vs. Unemployed
on Measures of Subjective Mental Health (by sex × year)

	Men				Women			
	Working		Unemployed		Working		Unemployed	
asure of Subjective Mental Health	1957 (%)	1976 (%)	1957 (%)	1976 (%)	1957 (%)	1976 (%)	1957 (%)	1976 (%)
piness								
Jot Too Happy	8		24		13		30	
		7		34		11		19
ure Morale								
Happier	56		20		55		35	
		57		44		56		57
rital Happiness								
Jot Very Happy	28 (808)		50 (16)		37 (274)		25 (4)	
		18 (568)		24 (17)		20 (314)		56 (27)
quency of Marital Inadequacy								
A Lot	11 (780)		29 (17)		12 (264)		0 (4)	
		11 (55)		18 (17)		12 (311)		22 (27)
trictive Orientation Toward enthood								
All Response Restrictive	28		29		31		50	
		44		63		46		60
Total Number	924	153	25	39	469	599	20	65

NOTE: Numbers in parentheses are total number of persons in each group.

Retirement

In both 1957 and 1976, one significant finding in which retired people stood out in comparison to all others made us rethink our strategy
for analyzing the effects of retirement. Retired men and women were
more likely to report symptoms of physical ill health. This not-too-sur-
prising result alerted us to the fact that any comparisons between retired and working people are not only weighted by the preponderance
of old people in the retired category[11] but also by a large number of retired people with severe health problems. For an adequate test of the
potential effect of retirement, we thus conducted a more limited analy-

[11] The "retired" are entirely confined to 55 and older in 1957, with only a handful in
the 54 and under group in 1976.

TABLE 8.8

Selected Comparisons of Working vs. Retired "Healthy"[a]
Men (55+) on Measures of Subjective Mental Health (by year)

	Working		Retired	
Measure of Subjective Mental Health	**1957 (%)**	**1976 (%)**	**1957 (%)**	**1976 (%)**
Happiness				
Very Happy	36		27	
		32		40
Worries				
Never	20		38	
		12		28
Marital Happiness				
Very Happy	50		51	
		55		65
	(141)	(106)	(37)	(52)
Frequency of Marital Inadequacy				
Never	53		60	
		48		67
	(141)	(106)	(37)	(52)
Anxiety				
In High Third of Distribution	20		22	
		41		24
Total Number	169	169	63	80

NOTE: Numbers in parentheses are total number of persons in each group.

[a] Excludes men who report extreme physical health symptoms in symptom factor score of ill health.

sis which will be confined only to men,[12] fifty-five and older who do not suffer from severe self-diagnosed health problems.

Table 8.8 shows that for that limited sample in 1976, there were some significant differences between retired and working men. Retired men were significantly happier and reported that they never worried more than working men did. More remarkably, retired men's reports of happiness and marital happiness are significantly greater in 1976 than in 1957. We thus have some evidence that retirement is associated with positive adjustment among healthy men—more in 1976 than in 1957. We have no doubt that Medicaid and Medicare, plus the development of retirement plans may have contributed to this shift. In addition, more retired people in 1976 may provide a larger and clearer reference group and an anxiety-reducing perspective on how to adapt to this role.

---

[12] We did not do a parallel analysis with women because such a large proportion of the already small category of women retirees in 1957 (29) also differed so markedly from the employed in family status. In the future, a parallel but somewhat more limited analysis could be done with just the 1976 data.

Housewife vs. Working Woman

In analysis of women's employment status and its effects on subjective mental health, we found little to indicate that being employed versus being a housewife meant something different *and better* for women's subjective mental health in 1976 compared to 1957. Iglehart (1979) concluded much the same in analysis of these same data, but with a sample limited to married women. Our own multivariate analyses, which control for age, education, and year do not control for family status, which is undoubtedly germane to the comparisons. Nevertheless, we obtain some interesting results.

Irrespective of family status, in both years being a full-time housewife has a few positive consequences for well-being compared to being a worker. These results are summarized in table 8.9. (They are presented for different age groups, because that control is essential to seeing some of the trends.) We find that:

1. Housewives do not report being unhappy as often as working women. (This conclusion is not apparently supported in the oldest age group, but further controls for education in the oldest age group help explain this anomaly.)
2. Housewives are less likely to report role-related shortcomings in themselves. Compared to working women, they were less likely to want a daughter to be better educated, to have a better job, or the like.
3. Housewives less often report feelings of inadequacy as mothers. This result is again somewhat less apparent in the older groups. In the boxed comparison in table 8.9, some support for the hypothesized 1976 diminution of the problem of the working role for women can be seen. Working women were no different from housewives in their reports of inadequacy as mothers in the 35–54 year-olds in 1976. They are also less likely to report frequent feelings of parental inadequacy as their counterparts in 1957.

All of these results are small, but generally consistent. There is some indication that working women have some discontents about their lives that housewives do not share.

In addition to the trend indicating that middle-aged working women do not feel as inadequate as mothers in 1976 as they did in 1957, there was another important but complicated result that suggests something different. There was a significant difference in the way working women in the later stage of life react to their marriages (table 8.10). Many more of these women in 1976 see their marriage as "very happy," in contrast both to working women in 1957 *and to housewives.* Some special zest may accrue to these women when they have work as an adjunct to marriage in 1976, a zest that working women in 1957 did not experience and that seems to be absent from the lives of housewives. This seems not to be the case for younger married women who work. While they clearly are less unhappy about their marriages than their counter-

TABLE 8.9

Selected Comparisons of Working Women vs. Full-Time Housewives on Measures of Subjective Mental Health

Measure of Subjective Mental Health	21–34				35–54				55+			
	Working Women		Full-time Housewives		Working Women		Full-time Housewives		Working Women		Full-time Housewives	
	1957 (%)	1976 (%)	1957 (%)	1976 (%)	1957 (%)	1976 (%)	1957 (%)	1976 (%)	1957 (%)	1976 (%)	1957 (%)	1976 (%)
Happiness Not Too Happy	2	10	4	7	13	13	9	5	17	9	21	16
Role Shortcomings No Role Shortcomings	62	75	26	74	59	66	67	71	59	69	69	73
Felt Parental Inadequacy A Lot	30 (37)	29 (136)	18 (264)	16 (137)	29 (107)	19 (190)	16 (162)	20 (132)	12 (74)	18 (83)	11 (140)	11 (184)
Total Number	147	269	287	151	240	220	306	139	78	109	265	214

TABLE 8.10

Working Women's vs. Housewives' Evaluation of Their Marital Happiness;
1957 vs. 1976 (by age)

		1957		1976	
Age	Marital Happiness	Working Women (%)	Housewives (%)	Working Women (%)	Housewives (%)
Young (21–34)	Very Happy	45		48	
			49		58
	Happier Than Average	10		32	
			23		23
	Average; Not Too Happy	45		20	
			28		19
		100%	100%	100%	100%
	Total Number	92	276	259	143
Middle-Aged (35–54)	Very Happy	43		55	
			46		48
	Happier Than Average	24		24	
			20		27
	Average; Not Too Happy	33		21	
			34		25
		100%	100%	100%	100%
	Total Number	156	276	134	128
Old (55+)	Very Happy	25		63	
			38		48
	Happier Than Average	38		17	
			13		30
	Average; Not Too Happy	37		20	
			50		22
		100%	100%	100%	100%
	Total Number	24	127	30	93

parts in 1957, young housewives still surpass them in reported marital happiness. It may be that juggling motherhood with work is so difficult for many of these young women that it reduces marital happiness. For dual-career families, the weight of responsibility for child care still falls most heavily on a woman's shoulders, an inequitable burden that may create marital tension both from her resentment of the burden and from her husband's jealousy of her precious time committed to children rather than to himself. This problem undoubtedly eases as children become more self-sufficient during the woman's middle years, and should be totally absent when women are over fifty-five. This seems to be the case in the age trends for 1976.

We also wondered whether our analyses of the housewives vs. working women might show different effects on general subjective adjustment if we were to control for marital status and for working women's reasons for working. If a woman works only for money, she may resent the role; if she works to escape what is perceived to be the limited world of the housewife, or for more positive reasons, she may show more consistent positive effects of working.

OCCUPATION AND SUBJECTIVE MENTAL HEALTH

Americans View Their Mental Health presented a detailed description of subjective mental health differences among employed people in different occupational categories, the last major role status to be examined in this chapter. Although percentages were not given in *Americans View Their Mental Health*, they were provided in the tabular supplement attached to the book. A close examination of the tabular supplement suggests that differences discussed and highlighted in *Americans View Their Mental Health* were very small. Furthermore, two criticial oversights occurred in the 1957 analysis. First, there was no attempt to distinguish effects of occupational settings on people from educational differences implicitly represented by occupational distinctions. Second, the original volume did not present occupational correlations with well-being for women. The present analysis of the correlation between occupational differences and subjective mental health in both the 1957 and 1976 data will serve to correct these omissions, since we include male-female and education comparisons in the cross-classification of occupational differences in well being. Our current analysis indicates that occupation is not a very powerful predictor of well-being, once we control for sex, year, education, and age differences.

We maintained the original classification of occupations used in *Americans View Their Mental Helath*: professional, managers, clerical, sales, skilled workers, operatives, service workers, laborers, and farmers. This is a common set of distinctions drawn from the literature on occupation. We are aware that all of these categories lump together very different occupational demands. Teachers and medical technicians are grouped together as professionals, along with architects and doctors. This makes for a very gross grouping of occupations under each broad label. There is, however, an implicit prestige hierarchy in the current classification, as well as a blue-collar/white-collar distinction. Implicitly, professionals and managers are at the top of the hierarchy, and service workers and laborers are at the bottom. The blue-collar/white-collar distinction is as follows: white-collar (professional, managers, clerical, sales) and blue-collar (skilled, operatives, service workers, laborers). Farmers are usually considered apart from both the prestige hierarchy and the blue-collar/white-collar distinction.

We have already used these occupational distinctions in talking about the reactions people in different occupations have to their work in chapter 6. This was mostly descriptive and did not include a detailed analysis of interactive controls. In this section we will reconsider some of these data, along with our examination of more general indicators of psychological adjustment, marital well-being, and parental reactions among workers in these different occupations.

We ran initial analyses of occupational differences for 1957 and 1976 *separately* for men and women. Much of the current literature about sexism suggests that the significance of any given job may be different for the two sexes.

In table 8.28 at the end of the chapter, we see that for men and women separately a number of measures of subjective well-being relate to occupation *before* controls for age, education, sex and year are introduced, but very few of these results remain significant when controls are applied. This suggests that we may have overinterpreted differences in the subjective mental health of occupational groups in the 1957 data in *Americans View Their Mental Health*. Not that the measures of subjective well-being of different occupations are identical, but many of those that show clear differences could well have been interpreted as a function of status or age distinctions rather than of specific occupational demands. This finding seems especially true when we realize that the occupational categories themselves are rather gross and implicitly reflect an underlying prestige hierarchy.

Tables 8.11, 8.12, and 8.13 summarize the few significant findings about occupation and subjective mental health that exist when we control for sex, age, education, and year.

Table 8.11 shows that farmers, as a group, are particularly prone to be either very worried or very unworried. More than twice as many farmers, compared to people in other occupational groups, say they worry "all the time"; at the same time, twice as many farmers say they worry "not at all." Although we must also keep in mind the possibility that farmers who say they never worry may actually be denying worries in order to ward off overwhelming concerns, it is still hard to understand these polarized responses by farmers. There are no clear interactions with education or age for the farmers. We tried further controls for region and income to see if we could locate a group of farmers who were particularly worried or farmers who particularly denied being worried. Neither control made any difference. The specific type of farming may determine whether and how much a particular farmer worries. The hazards of climate and market conditions differ for different types of farmers. An additional hypothesis that should be investigated in the future is that the small farmer may be more worried than one who is working in large-scale agribusiness.

Table 8.11 also shows that professional men and women report being happily married more than men and women in other occupations do. In both 1957 and 1976, being a professional man or woman was correlated with having a happy home life. We assume that the status that a profession accords men and women in our society gives them a sense of power which translates positively in marriage. Such status gives people some sense of confidence outside of family arrangements, which in turn may make them less defensive and more accommodating in marriage. People who have real power in the outside world do not have to realize power needs in marriage. They may be tuned to affection rather than power in relationships, and this orientation may make for a happier marriage.

Locksley (1978) explored the possibility that a person's class position related to how she/he reacted to marriage. She found, however, that class (as measured by occupational differences) translated very little into reaction about marriage once education was used as a control. In her analysis of class, however, she grouped people who were actually doing very different kinds of work in the same class. Some professionals were put in the same category with some blue-collar workers because they bore the same type of relationship to labor. Using Wright's (1979) Marxist analysis of occupational factors in defining class, for example, Locksley saw semiautonomous workers as a group that could include professors as well as certain kinds of craft workers.

Our present analysis shows that when we categorize people into the highest social status based on occupation (the professionals), some correlation with happy marital interaction exists. This is not a Marxist analysis of social status, but it suggests that status connected to work affects family life. Rubin's book *Worlds of Pain* (1976) tries to underpin these hypotheses with some concrete accounts of people's demoralized feelings in marriage, which seem to be spinoffs from their dashed dreams about occupational success. But again it is hard from her impressionistic analysis to interpret her results as stemming largely from the effects of men's and women's work, per se. Our more systematic results suggest that the professionals benefit from occupational power and react better to their marriages. That these results are as true for women professionals as they are for men seems important.

Linked to the greater marital happiness of professionals is their

TABLE 8.11

Selected Occupational Differences in Subjective Mental Health (by sex × year)

Measures of Subjective Mental Health	Men 1957 Farmers (%)	Men 1957 All Others (%)	Men 1976 Farmers (%)	Men 1976 All Others (%)	Women 1957 Farmers (%)	Women 1957 All Others (%)	Women 1976 Farmers (%)	Women 1976 All Others (%)
Worries								
All the Time	4	2	13	4	12	5	9	4
A Lot, Sometimes, Not Much	72	87	77	91	88	86	72	92
Never	24	11	10	5	0	9	9	4
	100%	100%	100%	100%	100%	100%	100%	100%
Total Number	78	787	30	668	8	435	11	574

Measures of Subjective Mental Health	Men 1957 Professionals (%)	Men 1957 All Others (%)	Men 1976 Professionals (%)	Men 1976 All Others (%)	Women 1957 Professionals (%)	Women 1957 All Others (%)	Women 1976 Professionals (%)	Women 1976 All Others (%)
Marital Happiness								
Very Happy	62	42	66	52	62	40	58	50
Total Number	100	691	93	469	29	245	67	253
Job Satisfaction								
Very Satisfied	43	29	33	26	57	36	44	27
Total Number	113	778	131	608	54	395	114	496

TABLE 8.12

Occupation Differences in Mentioned Ego Job Satisfaction Only
(by sex × year)

| | Percent Mentioning Ego Job Satisfaction Only | | | | Total Number[a] | | | |
| | Men | | Women | | Men | | Women | |
Occupation	1957	1976	1957	1976	1957	1976	1957	1976
Professionals	80		89		112		54	
		82		82		129		111
Managers	72		86		112		36	
		76		85		117		40
Clerical Workers	43		69		53		122	
		71		69		42		185
Salespersons	67		80		51		30	
		71		73		41		26
Skilled Workers	56		86		198		7	
		63		50		160		10
Operatives	46		41		154		69	
		49		51		112		67
Service Workers	40		73		55		99	
		74		68		43		130
Laborers	48		50		40		2	
		47		50		32		4
Farmers	65		60		77		5	
		61		46		31		11

[a] Excludes respondents who are not ascertainable on Job Satisfaction.

TABLE 8.13

Percentage of College Educated vs. Less Educated
Who Mention Ego Dissatisfaction Among Sales
and Other Occupations Combined (by year)

| | Salespeople | | All Other Occupations | |
	1957 (%)	1976 (%)	1957 (%)	1976 (%)
College Educated	46	55	39	62
	(22)	(38)	(255)	(492)
Less Educated	30	38	24	30
	(11)	(27)	(1005)	(817)

NOTE: Numbers in parentheses are total number of persons in each group.

greater job satisfaction. We noted this fact in chapter 6, but it is high-lighted in juxtaposition with the finding of marital happiness among professionals. In contrast with all other groups (controlling for age, education, sex and year of interview), professionals report being very satisfied with their work. This is as true for women as it is for men, and it is as true in 1976 as it was in 1957. Furthermore, professional men and women stand out in reporting ego satisfactions in their work, as is shown in table 8.12, although managers are also relatively high in such reports. We can develop a picture of the professional who gets par-ticular satisfaction from his or her psychological investments at work (ego satisfactions) and then goes home to a family, relaxed and self-confident. In addition, the professional may experience less family strain because of the general status her/his occupation provides his/her family. Furthermore, involvement with work may compete with family involvements as a focal concern for life satisfaction. As a result, we might say that professional men and women take on such complex and interesting challenges in work that they are less over-whelmed by inevitable conflicts that exist in marriage.

There is one other result about the degree of ego satisfaction felt by people who work in various kinds of occupations: a very interesting change has occurred in the way men in certain occupations construct their satisfaction from work. Men in clerical and service work are find-ing much greater ego satisfaction in 1976 than they did in 1957. This change largely reflects the fact that men in 1957 were particularly un-gratified in these positions. How do we account for these changes? One speculation about these results is that the greater press for androgyny and equal treatment of men and women in the workplace may have made men in clerical and in service work less upset about being in women-dominated work settings. If this interpretation is accurate, these changes for male clerical and service workers are among the few results that suggest that sex-role shifts have had some effects on the way men and women react to their subjective mental health. Another possible explanation for the pattern of results is that more men in 1976 were in the higher-status positions of clerical or service organizations. This might well have been the case if the clerical and service settings have become bureaucratized over the generation, as most organizations have.

The final result which shows occupational differences in well-being also involves some complicated interactions. In both 1957 and 1976, less educated people in sales express more ego dissatisfaction with their work than did less educated people in other occupational settings. This is not consistently the case with college-educated people in sales. They are no more ego dissatisfied with their work than college-educated peo-ple in other occupations. One can ask, are less educated people in sales likely to be in particularly demeaning positions? Could it be that they are in low-status saleswork, where the customer is always right, and bosses and supervisors even righter?[13]

In summary, analyses contrasting people from different occupational groups in 1957 and 1976 on measures of subjective well-being produce a paltry set of results. We conclude that occupation, per se, has very little bearing on subjective mental health. Most of the few significant results we found are confined to specific reactions to work itself. The effects of jobs apparently do not go beyond the confines of work and reactions to it, and do not translate into more generalized concerns or other role reactions. The two exceptions to this conclusion have to do with the greater worry and denial of worry found among farmers, and the unusual marital happiness found in professional men and women. Aside from these two results, we could easily conclude that occupations have little impact on people's *general* well-being. Because we found many results that described occupational differences to be originally significant but no longer significant when sex, education, and age are used as controls, we suggest that some of the occupational differences reported in our previous volume and by others (Caplan et al., 1975; Kahn et al., 1964) may be attributable to other aspects of people's lives: their age and their social status in society, which may be a more critical feature of occupations than are occupational demands per se. For example, many people promoted to higher-status jobs in an organization move into jobs that carry heavy responsibility. While we can assume that increased responsibility increases strain, we should also remember that older people are often promoted into the more statusful jobs. While some of the vulnerability felt in these new roles may be a function of increased responsibilities, some of the new vulnerabilities from work may be a function of changes in the life stage. Men with general feelings of inadequacy at mid-life might very well see what formerly may have been "challenging work" as "stressful," regardless of any shift in real job responsibilities.

This is not to say that more refined analyses of occupational variables should not produce critical differentiations about subjective mental health. Work by Kahn et al. (1964) and Caplan et al. (1975) produce impressive support for the general hypotheses that role stress, role ambiguity, role conflict, and role overload at work have powerful effects on people's experience and well-being. Further analyses on these data using more psychologically defined bases of job categorization are called for.

---

[13] We have found in our simpler analyses that there was a year interaction with ego dissatisfaction measure that was different in 1957 and 1976. With this more complicated cross-classification analysis, we find that it is education that makes the difference. Hence we feel the year differences are most accounted for by the fact that there are more college-educated people in 1976 than there were in 1957.

REGIONAL DIFFERENCES AND SUBJECTIVE MENTAL HEALTH

We now shift gears from considering social roles whose effects on subjective experience are usually analyzed in psychological terms to considering geographical factors—region and population density— whose effects are more often analyzed in physical terms.

In *Americans View Their Mental Health,* regional differences were examined but quickly dismissed because they were very small. In the analyses to follow, we find small differences among regions of the country. Some of them, however, are so consistent across 1957 and 1976 that they are more noteworthy than those from the 1957 study alone. As a result, we present them in more detail in this section.

How can we think about regional differences in subjective mental health? Many complex factors are involved in describing the regions of the country. While physical, climate, and population-density differences of the various regions no doubt have effects, they are perhaps less important than a number of social characteristics of these regions. Regional differences in population density, for instance, are not just a matter of variations in physical crowding, but include a number of social-interactive differences. Densely populated areas often contain highly cosmopolitan world perspectives, but they can also generate competitiveness as well as some degree of social distrust and anomie.

Other social differences among regions emerge from their historical origins. The South has always been politically and culturally distinct from the rest of the country. The West has represented a mecca for adventuresome migration in the nineteenth century as well as in the twentieth. The East has been identified with the older social elite and also as the home of countless migrant groups. The Midwest is the bastion of agricultural traditionalism.

Speculation about what the different regions might yield on indices of subjective mental health may interest people who are involved in geographic and physical environmental effects on well-being, as well as historians interested in psychological reactions that might characterize regions which differ in economic mobility, migration, or political patterns. We project no specific hypotheses and wish simply to present the data that show consistency in both 1957 and 1976.

We differentiated the eight regions listed below. Under each we indicate the states representing that region in which we have sample points.

New England
   Connecticut, Maine, Massachusetts
Middle Atlantic States
   New Jersey, New York, Pennsylvania
East North Central
   Illinois, Indiana, Michigan, Ohio, Wisconsin

West North Central
   Iowa, Kansas, Minnesota, Missouri, Nebraska, South Dakota
Solid South
   Alabama, Arkansas, Florida, Georgia, Louisiana, Mississippi, North Carolina, South Carolina, Texas, Virginia
Border States
   Kentucky, Maryland, Oklahoma, Tennessee, Washington, D. C., West Virginia
Mountain States
   Arizona, Colorado, Idaho, New Mexico, Utah
Pacific States
   California, Oregon, Washington

Initially, two general points of information must be made. First, from 1957 to 1976, the population of two of the regions increased: the Border States, and the Pacific States. Second, while the regions of the country differ somewhat in distributions of age and education (e.g., in the South there are many more older uneducated people), cross-classification analysis by age and education rules out any bias that might exist in our analyses of different regions of the country.

We find very little variation in regional effects between our two studies. Table 8.27 at the end of this chapter shows that most of the significant differences in well-being by region remain consistent from 1957 to 1976. We will therefore concentrate on results that show consistency from 1957 to 1976. Results that differ for the two years are not easily understandable, and since even these significant results represent very small differences, we feel that they do not warrant extended discussion.

Significant regional effects *without* the controls for sex, age, and education generally remain significant as well in our six-way cross-classification. Table 8.14 records all results that survive controls. We present selected parts of the distributions of measures of subjective mental health to indicate where important differences occur.

Of the eight regions designated, four yield significant findings on more than one measure of subjective adjustment. We will concentrate on these four regions. Compared to people from other regions, New England residents allude to personality strengths, more from the East North Central report not worrying, and more respondents from the West North Central area report being very happy. Since no other results accompany these trends, we will not highlight them in our analysis. There were no results indicating that residents of the Mountain States differed from any other region in the country. The four regions that displayed consistent results across several measures of adjustment are the Middle Atlantic States, the Solid South, the Border States, and the Pacific States. For each of them we characterize the pattern of reactions, singling out the significant results that describe the region. Table 8.14 highlights distinctive findings for the regions.

TABLE 8.14
Selected Regional Differences in Subjective Mental Health (by year)

Measure of Subjective Mental Health	Year	New England (%)	Middle Atlantic (%)	East North Central (%)	West North Central (%)	Solid South (%)	Border South (%)	Mountains (%)	Pacific (%)
Year Interaction									
Worrying:									
Always	1957	4	10	2	2	3	9	2	5
	1976	2	4	2	4	4	2	4	2
Future Morale:									
Very happy	1957	59	54	51	50	52	36	40	54
	1976	52	46	52	50	46	43	51	53
Personality Strong Points:									
Yes	1957	58	53	48	47	45	44	47	44
	1976	68	59	62	58	55	52	62	64
Positive View of Marriage:									
Yes	1957	43	40	48	40	41	40	43	52
	1976	31	31	30	31	32	22	33	32
Marriage Problems:									
Yes	1957	38	41	51	46	45	49	52	50
	1976	67	53	63	52	61	64	67	68
Feel Inadequacy as Spouse:									
A lot	1957	7	11	11	11	12	12	10	23
	1976	9	12	13	10	10	13	11	15
Restrictiveness of Parenthood:									
All response restrictive	1957	27	33	30	24	33	29	31	30
	1976	40	54	42	47	43	49	35	42
Problems in Raising Children:									
Yes	1957	68	70	70	76	77	84	76	81
	1976	74	74	80	67	75	82	77	85
Felt Inadequacy as Parent:									
Never	1957	64	67	50	45	48	60	59	34
	1976	44	48	39	49	52	51	31	38
Job Satisfaction: Ambivalent, neutral, dissatisfied	1957	25	26	23	20	16	31	26	26
	1976	28	29	27	24	24	24	28	28
Ego Dissatisfaction on Job:									
Yes	1957	24	29	27	33	24	24	24	34
	1976	51	51	45	41	36	45	66	48
Psychological Anxiety:									
Very high	1957	8	17	12	15	17	25	18	16
	1976	16	20	16	17	17	21	15	12
Ill Health:									
Very high	1957	10	12	9	19	13	28	14	15
	1976	11	16	14	18	17	18	15	12
Total Number	1957	181	445	441	275	648	115	104	251
	1976	140	340	409	238	577	172	74	314

Middle Atlantic States

In this highly urbanized area, an interesting pattern emerged which can be characterized as containing elements of both anxiety and denial of problems. Men and women from the Middle Atlantic States report a high degree of worry. More than in any other region of the country, a sizable group say they worry "all the time": 10 percent said this in 1957, 4 percent say this in 1976. Furthermore, people from this region are more likely to feel that parenthood is restrictive: 33 percent of Mid-Atlantic residents in 1957 gave nothing but restrictive responses in thinking about how parenthood changes a person's life; 54 percent gave such responses in that region of the country in 1976. This represented the highest percentage of respondents in any region of the country to give this restrictive orientation to parenthood. We think that perhaps some of their heightened worrying has to do with raising children in an urban environment.

Accompanying their anxiety, people in this region show active denial of difficulties in both marriage and parenthood. More than people in any other region, married people in this region tend to say they do not have any marital problems and never feel inadequate as parents. This presents a very interesting pattern when coupled with the heightened anxiety in this Mid-Atlantic region. Could it be that this pattern reflects the style of coping in urban America? People experience anxiety from living in a complex, stressful, heterogeneous urban environment, especially in relation to child raising, but perhaps adjust to that anxiety by denying the existence of problems in their interpersonal life—as if there were a compensatory depersonalization of anxiety. To live in the city, perhaps people have to retreat a bit from personalized concerns and define anxiety in more abstract, impersonal ways, including seeing the city as a hostile environment in which to bring up children. Coping with both environmental and personal anxiety may be too overwhelming. We will find the same pattern of results emerging when we investigate place of residence: people residing in metropolitan areas in the United States seem to show the same kind of anxiety, the same kind of orientation to children, and the same denial of marital unhappiness that people in the Mid-Atlantic States show. This suggests that people in the Middle Atlantic region may typify the urban experience more than others due to heavy population density. The reference groups for these metropolitan residents may be only other urban dwellers.

The Solid South

Results which distinguish people residing in the Solid South from other areas point to the South as a region which discourages a psychological orientation to experience. On what do we base this conclusion? When asked about their strong points, people in the Solid South are less likely than people in the rest of the country to mention personal aspects of the self. Their strengths are seen in more virtuous terms, or in more role-related terms, but not in the terms of personality. Accordingly, psychological orientation to self-perceptions has not taken as strong a hold on the experience of Southerners as for other people in the country. Southerners are also less likely to mention ego dissatisfactions with work than people elsewhere. We have interpreted this measure as indicating ego *involvement* with work. When speaking of job dissatisfaction, Southerners are more likely to mention *extrinsic* rather than psychological factors. With regard to overall job satisfactions, they are also less likely than people in other regions of the country to mention negative responses (i.e., some ambivalence, feeling neutral about work, or direct statements of dissatisfaction). Such compliance about jobs may again indicate a lack of introspective orientation to experience.

The fact that men and women in the Solid South show these differences both in 1957 and 1976 reinforces the notion that it may be a general regional phenomenon. In fact, some results indicate a shift from 1957 to 1976, making the Solid South even less introspective than in 1957. Parents in the Solid South were more likely to discuss feelings of inadequacy in parenting in 1957 than they are in 1976. (This was a significant year interaction found in cross-classification analysis.) Furthermore, on the question about personal shortcomings, people in the Solid South in 1976 are more likely to mention some aspect of role performance than they were in 1957. Again, this was not true for any other region of the country. We can therefore conclude that the nonpsychological orientation that appeared in the South in 1957 is even more strongly represented in 1976. Some of this attitude could reflect the continual migrations of people away from the South to the more cosmopolitan North. Some of it may be interpreted as a defensively nonpsychological orientation that occurred as desegregation efforts intensified during the 1960s and 1970s.

The Border States

The third distinctive grouping resides in the Border States. Culturally and geographically, these are Southern states, but they have a Northern orientation. One important sampling point in this regional group is Washington, D.C., a strikingly heterogeneous city in regard to its orientation to both the South and the North. Of all regions of the country, the Border area has more people who clearly admit to difficulties in their subjective experience. Men and women in the Border States seem particularly low in morale about the future, particularly high in reports of symptoms of both psychological anxiety and ill health. These results are consistent in both 1957 and 1976. To interpret these findings, we examined the relationship between region and income and found that the Border States have a high percentage of very-low-income people. In 1957, 37 percent of respondents reported family incomes of less than $4,000 (in 1976 dollars). This compared to 10 percent at that level in other regions. Comparable figures in 1976 were 19 percent for the Border States and 14 percent for the rest of the country. While some sections of the Solid South, which also has a large "poor" group, have experienced an economic boom (e.g., Florida and Texas), the states which comprise our sample of Border States have not had an economic resurgence. The low morale and high symptoms of anxiety in the Border States may be a function of general economic deprivation in these states, a deprivation that might set the tone of living for even the more well-to-do and educated in that region.

The Pacific States

California, Oregon, and Washington have become the meccas for people discontented with the climate and style of life of more traditional urban societies in other parts of the country. The West has experienced an enormous increase in population during the period between 1957 and 1976. Part of this increase had to do with people searching for new psychological horizons as the old territories were found wanting. And indeed a psychological orientation to experience—the desire for deeper and richer interpersonal connections—characterizes the different response of the people from the Pacific States. Residents of the Pacific States feel most inadequate as parents, most inadequate as spouses, and see more problems in child rearing compared to people in other regions of the country. Lest we think of this pattern as symptomatic of a generally negative psychological condition, there is, coupled with this pattern of negative concerns about family roles, a distinctly positive orientation to marriage in this population. In both years, but especially in 1957, more people in the Pacific region revealed a positive orientation to the changes marriage brings. We would say that this translates into Westerners being conditioned more rapidly than people elsewhere to a psychological orientation to roles, both negative features of roles as well as their psychological benefits. Further, these results withstand controls for age and education, a fact that is important to keep in mind because the West has the youngest and most educated respondents of all the regions.

The general statement can be made that the psychological orientation to subjective experience of well-being is alive and well in the West. This conclusion should not be surprising in light of the fact that many avant-garde psychologically oriented growth and alternate-lifestyle groups have incubated in the Pacific region. California has probably led the way in introducing the country to new types of understanding in contrast to other regions, although the results are not strikingly different for any one region. That the results are consistent across 1957 and 1976 speaks of fairly persistent regional effects. Whether this is due to climate, migration pattern, historical setting, reference groups, or population density is difficult to assess. The fact that the results remain stable when we control for age and education suggests that the predominance of any type of social group in a particular region may establish a frame of reference for the subjective experience of other people in the region. Accordingly, urban attitudes may be typical of Middle Atlantic people, whether or not they live in the city. Poor people's attitudes toward their well-being may be more typical of people in the Border States, whether or not they are poor. The young and more educated orientation may be more typical of the Pacific West, whether or not people are young and well educated. That the psychological orientations of dominant groups in a region may come to be the frame of reference adopted by most people who reside in that area is a hypothesis worthy of more careful testing in further research.

POPULATION DENSITY URBANIZATION AND SUBJECTIVE MENTAL HEALTH

Along with the traditional migration of rural populations to cities, a countermigration from the central city to the suburbs developed in America after World War II. Migrations of farm populations and particularly the movement of blacks from the rural South to cities in the Northeast and Midwest continued during and after the war. The migration supplied labor to the war industries which offered productive opportunities at a time when many farm workers lost employment because of farm mechanization.

The suburban and exurban movement reflected other changes in our society and its myths. Veterans returning from war turned inward toward family life as an arena of palpable meaning and significance. Pronatal norms and the feminine mystique assumed dominance in our national myths. The booming automobile industry provided the means of mobility that allowed families to move farther from the workplace and shrank distances to conceivable commutes. The bedroom community made up of women and children and weekend husband/fathers focused attention and activities around children and children's developmental needs. Schools and their quality, and easy access to child-oriented organizations and activities became dominant considerations in the choice of residence for millions of families. Sennett (1970), Slater (1976), and other social observers detect fear of difference and attraction to homogeneity behind the middle-class flight from the cities. Whether such forces were operating consciously or not, the outcome was certainly there: suburban communities clustered people by age and income and car ownership. The cities were left to the very rich and the poor.

Two opposing myths about urbanization have vied for dominance in American thought. On the one hand, the nineteenth-century image of America as a "go-getter" nation pictured the city as the seat of opportunity to which the brightest and most courageous young people were drawn. This view stimulated theories of selective migration, a form of social Darwinism, which said that the brightest and fittest left the farm and the dull or fearful remained there or in small towns.

On the other side of our ambivalence was the view of the city as the corrupter of innocence, the center of vice and human degradation. Good youngsters could be corrupted or ground down by the dangers of the city and its inhumanity. While many of the best youngsters would be drawn by opportunities, and while some of these would indeed find their fortunes, others would founder in anonymous, competitive, dangerous city life. A different, more complicated view of selective migration accompanied this conception of city life. In this view, the city would draw both the most promising and those who were deviant and needed the cover of urban anonymity to survive.

Epidemiological studies of mental illness tended to follow and support the more complex view. Schizophrenia—along with criminality—tended to show highest incidence in the central city, in the oldest, most poverty-ridden, socially disorganized neighborhoods, with rates diminishing as one moved through concentric rings toward the outer reaches of the city and into the suburbs.

In our data we can differentiate between metropolitan areas, suburbs, cities, small towns, and rural regions. We cannot, however, distinguish inner-city from outer-ring neighborhoods and cannot therefore reproduce analyses which make such distinctions.

What can we say about the settings we do differentiate? How does an urban environment affect mental health? How does city life differ from rural life and from interaction in small towns, nonmetropolitan cities, or suburbs? Complexity and density of social interaction are major differences. Stimulation—sheer sensory input—and complexity of choices and decisions distinguish urban life.

City life also tends to differentiate and fractionate people's lives. Small-town and rural people live and work among people they know and by whom they are known. The fact that roles overlap, that one's boss may also be one's neighbor and will almost certainly be a member of one's church and parent-teacher organization, lends a seamless quality to life and to identity. There is no stimulus to vary one's behavior or self-presentation when the audience is constant. On the other hand, the anonymity of city life, may stimulate greater variation in behavior from one role to another, particularly when the larger world is cast as dangerous and competitive and the family is seen as a safe haven. The city provokes greater "self-presentation" and emphasizes the use of surface qualities like charm and assertiveness to make one's way in a competitive, threatening world.

Both settings imply challenges and hazards to personal integration. The less populated rural setting may be simpler and more coherent, but people can never escape notice or experiment with different ways of being themselves. The city allows considerable self-differentiation, but

TABLE 8.15
Selected Population Density Differences in Subjective Mental Health (by year)

Measure of Subjective Mental Health	Metro 1957 (%)	Metro 1976 (%)	Suburb 1957 (%)	Suburb 1976 (%)	Small City 1957 (%)	Small City 1976 (%)	Town 1957 (%)	Town 1976 (%)	Rural 1957 (%)	Rural 1976 (%)
Happiness										
Very Happy	29	22	38	32	34	30	36	32	35	32
Not Too Happy	18	17	8	10	10	12	10	9	11	11
Worry										
Always, A Lot	45	52	31	47	32	48	31	44	34	42
Not Much, Never	48	46	61	46	61	46	62	47	60	51
Future Morale										
Very Optimistic	51	46	56	50	56	50	51	50	48	46
Pessimistic	9	13	6	8	7	8	8	10	12	15
Experienced Nervous Breakdown										
Yes	23	25	16	30	17	24	16	23	22	25
Positive View of Self										
Yes	69	80	71	78	65	77	72	72	67	72
Sees Personality Strengths										
Yes	50	58	51	61	46	62	52	61	43	54
Orientation Toward Marriage										
Positive	40	27	50	29	46	29	44	32	40	33
Negative	31	33	23	31	21	28	20	27	25	26
Restrictiveness of Marriage										
Very Restrictive	46	60	39	59	42	61	43	57	49	58
Not Restrictive At All	21	15	26	14	23	14	23	15	20	15
Mentions Relationship Satisfaction in Marriage										
Yes	37	71	40	63	41	61	45	52	45	54
Inadequacy as a Spouse										
A Lot, Often	11	9	18	16	12	12	11	10	11	12
Sometimes, Rarely	32	37	33	39	49	44	47	44	47	46
Never	57	54	50	45	39	44	42	46	42	43

TABLE 8.15 (continued)
Selected Population Density Differences in Subjective Mental Health (by year)

Measure of Subjective Mental Health	Population Density									
	Metro		Suburb		Small City		Town		Rural	
	1957 (%)	1976 (%)	1957 (%)	1976 (%)	1957 (%)	1976 (%)	1957 (%)	1976 (%)	1957 (%)	1976 (%)
Positive Orientation Toward Parenthood Positive	55	33	62	37	62	49	58	44	54	47
Restrictiveness/ Parenthood Very Restrictive	33	63	31	46	26	40	28	45	34	42
Not Restrictive At All	37	19	35	15	38	21	36	24	33	22
Problems in Raising Own Children Yes	71	76	77	79	75	77	73	78	76	75
Relationship Satisfaction in Parenthood Mentioned	31	43	44	34	38	44	41	42	42	40
Felt Inadequate As Parent A Lot, Often	18	15	23	19	17	15	12	15	16	18
Never	62	67	48	54	53	48	51	51	51	52
Job Satisfaction Very Satisfied	27	34	34	34	39	31	31	24	29	25
Not Very Satisfied	27	25	25	26	20	27	22	29	20	22
Ego Satisfaction in Work Ego	57	71	67	66	59	70	66	72	63	63
Extrinsic	22	6	13	16	16	14	11	14	18	20
Ego Dissatisfaction in Work Ego	42	55	37	50	39	47	32	43	29	39
Extrinsic	48	24	57	34	54	35	51	37	58	46
Psychological Anxiety High	38	40	33	44	34	50	34	47	42	52
Ill Health High	25	31	23	28	27	31	29	34	33	39
Total Number	324	159	324	343	385	456	702	724	716	543

it may impose greater demands for integration and for withstanding high levels of stress.

The Dohrenwends, in reviewing epidemiological research, conclude that metropolitan life is more hazardous to mental health (Dohrenwend and Dohrenwend, 1974). It should be noted, however, that the findings on which they base this conclusion are not consistent.

In our data, rural-urban differences appear in analyses of mental health and role experience and expectations. Most of the differences withstand our imposition of controls for age, education, and sex (see table 8.27), but a few drop out in the more complex analysis. The remaining ones are in table 8.15.

Urbanization shows a somewhat mixed relationship to mental-health measures and measures of well-being. People living in metropolitan areas score lower on psychological anxiety than all other groups, while rural residents score highest. In both of these cases, education interacts with urbanization so that more educated people in large cities are especially low on anxiety and less educated farm dwellers are especially high.

Farm residents, particularly those with little education, also score high on our index of physical ill-health. But in this case large-city dwellers along with people in smaller cities and towns score most often in the middle range on symptoms; the suburban group reports fewest physical symptoms.

Although they have fewer anxiety symptoms than other groups, respondents who live in metropolitan cities report worrying more than those who live in less densely populated areas, and they are also less likely to report overall happiness with their present lives. On the happiness question, there is a significant interaction between urbanization and education: among big-city residents, the grade school–educated are happier than those who have a high school education. In small towns, on the other hand, the high school–educated are happier than those who have only grade-school education. Among farm dwellers, it is the college educated who stand out as especially happy with their lives.

Future morale—the expectation that life will be better in the future—is lower among farm residents than among people in other settings, but this finding is evidently a function of age and education since it is no longer significant when controls are imposed.

Metropolitan residents present, on the average, a more positive self-image than any of the other groups. Farm dwellers are least likely to allude to personality strengths when asked to describe ways in which they differ from other people.

Overall, then, our findings on well-being in relation to urbanization do not correspond closely to the generalization made by the Dohrenwends from older studies. City dwellers do not show more symptoms than those from rural areas. They worry and report somewhat less happiness in their current lives, but on both psychological anxiety and physical ill health, city dwellers are more symptom-free than their counterparts in rural settings. And city dwellers show stronger self-concepts than farm residents.

When we shift focus to the experience and performance of roles, we again find evidence of a strong self-concept among people living in metropolitan cities: they are lowest of all groups in reporting that they feel inadequate or have experienced problems in their family roles—either spouse or parent—and when they describe job dissatisfactions, the metropolitan city residents are most likely of all groups to allude to ego dissatisfactions stemming from some failure of work to provide opportunities for self-expression or maximum use of their talents and abilities. We should recall that previous analyses have supported an interpretation of such job dissatisfactions as the assertion of self, an imposition of self-oriented criteria reflecting a strong sense of self.

Heightened individuality and self-orientation can also be seen in city residents' relatively negative orientation to marriage and parenthood. They more often describe the changes effected in life by marriage and parenthood as restricting, as though they were more invested in individual pursuits and freedom and therefore also more aware of the restrictions imposed on individual freedom by the encumbering roles that make them interdependent with other people. They are just as happy with their marriages as people in less urbanized settings, and in 1976, in particular, they are more likely to refer to the *relationship* with their spouse when they speak of satisfactions with marriage. But they are more aware of (and some would say realistic about) the ways in which both marriage and parenthood obstruct or limit individual freedom.

Farm residents do not often stand out as distinctive in analysis of roles. They are more likely than any other residence group to report having problems with their children and to refer to extrinsic aspects of work when they think of sources of job dissatisfaction. Aside from these two responses, rural respondents are in the middle group in response to life roles: they are moderately positive toward marriage, parenthood, and work. They feel moderately adequate in their family roles, and they do not see them as especially restrictive or enlarging.

Respondents who live in the suburbs show a more distinctive pattern than the rural group in their response to roles. They are highly satisfied with their jobs and also apparently more highly invested in work than any other group. When asked what they like most about their jobs, the suburban group mentions more sources of satisfaction than rural dwellers *or* city residents.

In family roles, respondents from the suburbs are moderately happy in their marriages and have a moderately positive view of marriage, but they are most likely of any group to say that they have feelings of inadequacy as spouses. They are moderately positive in their attitude toward parenthood and are less likely than city dwellers to think of parenthood as restricting. Again, as parents, they say that they experience a sense of inadequacy more often than rural or city residents. It is also noteworthy that suburbanites are less positively disposed toward parenthood in 1976 than they were in 1957; in 1976 they less often refer to the relationship with their children as the nicest thing about being a parent.

We interpret these findings as reflecting a certain disaffection with the suburban dream. Parents who moved to suburban communities under the sway of strong familistic norms and ideals—looking for a safe and perfect environment in which to live a life of close family relationships centered around children—may not have found the safe haven they desired. Separation of home and work often requires difficult choices and creates conflict between family and work obligations. The cost of suburban life and aspirations may have led inevitably to giving first priority to work. Certainly, work focuses a good deal of satisfaction in this group and apparently claims a high degree of their commitment. Ironically, suburban adults who chose their residence pattern with family goals preeminent end up feeling inadequate in their family roles.

RACE AND SUBJECTIVE MENTAL HEALTH

Two critical sources of group identities are race and religion. We will analyze the contribution of each to subjective well-being.

Americans View Their Mental Health did not analyze race comparisons. The number of blacks in the standard national sample is small—between 150 and 250 in all—and with the limited analytic methods available at that time, it was not possible to impose the controls for income or education necessary to conduct meaningful analysis without reducing cell sizes beyond acceptable limits. Rather than risking misleading or unreliable conclusions, the authors relinquished race as an analytic variable. With new multivariate techniques, we are now able to conduct analyses by race and, while they must still be taken with some caution because of the limited size of our black sample, the results are consistent and interesting enough to allow some generalizations.

The years between 1957 and 1976 witnessed significant changes in the legal, social, and educational situation of black Americans. The Supreme Court had made its historic decision against segregation, and a civil rights movement developed in its wake. Sit-ins and boycotts, urban riots, court-ordered changes in school districts, busing—all became issues during the twenty years intervening between our two studies. The civil rights movement shifted to northern cities, and the whole society became deeply involved in an inexorable, revolutionary movement toward an egalitarian society. A backlash, or countermovement in opposition to these thrusts, threatened at many points to obstruct democratic change. Affirmative-action legislation—acts passed to facilitate decisions of the courts and ensure equal access to educational and occupational opportunities—has met with extraordinary resistance.

Yet some change has been realized. Blacks have achieved and used greater educational opportunities. Black middle-class and professional groups have grown and have been able to lay claim to a significant power in the political institutions of American society. In turn, black leaders have used their power and the public forums of Congress and the press to maintain pressure for greater democratization. Equality between minority populations and the dominant majority is not yet a fact, but it is a more vivid, effective, and imposing ideal than at any previous point in American history. Racism continues to be a dominant fact of American life, but the range of its effectiveness has been significantly reduced, constrained by law.

What effect has the egalitarian thrust—the opening of our culture— had on the lives of blacks? Do we find evidence of major changes in blacks' evaluation of subjective well-being, life experience, and experience in roles? The answer is complicated by the fact that race is systematically related to status characteristics such as access to education and income. Despite changes in their legal status, blacks continue to be disproportionately poor and uneducated compared to whites. Insofar as education, occupation, and income are powerfully determined by home background, blacks in our samples—even the youngest groups in the 1976 sample—did not grow up in homes that had equal access to the resources that assure educational and occupational achievement. Discrimination is still pervasive in the job market. In all, then, changes in the law have not yet effected sweeping changes in differential chances for success.

With a larger sample of blacks in each year, we could detect changes that have occurred. However, the confounding of education level or occupation or income with race in our small sample severely handicaps our analysis. Education and income are powerfully related to well-being. When we filter out these effects and look at race effects *net* of such status factors, we are straining our analytic techniques, given the small size of the black sample. It takes a very large year difference to achieve significance when group size is small. When we control income and/or education, we simply do not have enough left to reach significance.

By and large, blacks' sense of self and subjective adjustment show the same significant changes over the twenty years as white respondents' do. That is, only with four measures is there any significant race x year interaction needed in the multivariate analyses (see table 8.27 at the end of the chapter), and strong enough to withstand a test of significance when education is factored out of the effect. Let us examine each of these, the data for which appear in table 8.16 along with an exten-

TABLE 8.16
Race Related to Selected Measures of Subjective Mental Health (by year)

Measure of Subjective Mental Health	White 1957 (%)	White 1976 (%)	Black 1957 (%)	Black 1976 (%)
piness				
ery Happy	36	36	22	25
ot Too Happy	10	11	23	28
ries				
ways, A Lot	34	44	36	50
ot Much	48	42	45	37
ever	11	6	11	7
re Morale				
ery Happy	51	49	58	47
appy	21	20	23	23
ot Happy	9	11	13	11
ot Ascertained	19	20	16	21
ve Self-concept				
sitive	69	73	71	72
egative	18	15	17	19
nal Strong Points				
ention	49	61	35	50
coming—Role				
s	42	32	47	58
tation to Marriage				
sitive	44	32	38	21
egative	23	28	29	27
Restrictive is Marriage				
Restrictive	44	57	50	71
ot Restrictive	22	15	25	10
al Happiness				
ppy	47	54	38	36
ot Happy	32	19	42	34
iage Problem				
s	45	64	55	72
ionship Satisfaction				
s	43	58	34	54
quacy as Spouse				
Lot	12	12	14	9
me, Rarely	45	45	30	34
ver	43	47	57	68

Measure of Subjective Mental Health	White 1957 (%)	White 1976 (%)	Black 1957 (%)	Black 1976 (%)
Orientation toward Children				
Positive	59	44	47	43
Negative	22	29	27	25
Restrictiveness—Children				
All Restrictive	29	44	42	52
Not Restrictive	36	21	32	19
Problems with Children				
Yes	74	77	81	75
Relationship Satisfaction				
Yes	37	37	34	33
Inadequate Parent				
A Lot	16	17	20	15
Some	32	40	16	22
Never	51	43	63	63
Job Satisfaction				
Very	32	28	30	26
Not	22	26	26	29
Source of Job Satisfaction				
Ego	63	69	51	64
Extrinsic	15	14	23	23
Source of Job Dissatisfaction				
Ego	28	47	19	26
Extrinsic	46	38	53	40
No Dissatisfaction	26	15	28	34
Psychological Anxiety				
High (11–20)	15	17	18	19
Physical Ill Health				
High (13–24)	29	34	27	32
Immobilization				
High (5–8)	24	21	17	17
Nervous Breakdown				
Have Felt	19	21	22	21
Total Number	2,164	1,918	188	242

sive survey of race comparisons in a number of other measures of subjective adjustment.

First, a very critical one. In 1957, race did not strongly affect people's reference to role shortcomings, but in 1976 such reference increased in the black group and decreased among whites. The question asks respondents how they would like their children to be different from themselves. Many of the role references concerned the wish that one's child would achieve higher educational status. As we noted in chapter 3, the large increase in college-educated people in the population has generally decreased people's sense of educational deficiency and with it the desire to see one's children transcend one's own educational attainment. Clearly the increase in college education did not occur equally in blacks and whites. Many more black adults are in the high school–educated group and wish their children to reach the college level that they missed. Nevertheless, the fact that the proportion of black adults voicing such a hope has increased while their education has also increased, seems to reflect a significant change in the outlook and expectation of black adults compared to whites.

Two measures of attitudes toward marriage show a race-by-year effect. In 1957 whites were slightly more positive (and less negative) toward marriage than blacks. In 1976 the difference at the positive end of the scale has increased and the difference at the negative end has disappeared. Blacks have become increasingly of a mixed mind—some would say realistic—about marriage. They recognize that marriage enlarges life, but also restricts freedom. Compared to whites, they are less often completely positive about marriage, but in 1976 they are no more likely than whites to see marriage as *only* limiting (see table 8.16). We will amplify this year difference more fully below when we discuss race differences in reactions to marriage.

One other measure shows a race-by-year effect: the increased report of ego-invested dissatisfaction about work has occurred primarily among whites. For many blacks, evidently the major psychological issue about work is to have a secure job. The increased affluence of American society between 1957 and 1976 enormously increased the unmet psychological expectations about work for whites, but evidently not for blacks. This phenomenon probably reflects the continued inequity that exists for mobility of blacks in our society (Duncan, 1969).

Aside from these differential shifts over time, the two racial groups change in very similar ways. There are minor differences in worries and future morale indicating a worsening of life conditions for the black population, but they are not significant. Further research with larger black samples is needed before we can assess change more reliably.[14]

---

[14] A major survey of the black population is currently underway at the Survey Research Center under the direction of Philip Bowman, James Jackson, and Gerald Gurin. When that study is analyzed, we will gain very significant new knowledge.

When education is controlled—that is, when race is analyzed aside from education—we find some race differences in life experience and satisfaction, but no consistent or large differences in strain—in long-term psychological consequences of life-stress. Stress is apparent in responses of blacks to all of the major life roles we considered in this study, but these stresses are apparently handled in ways that do not convert them into major psychic strain. Through internal psychological strength and social supports, blacks manage to assign problems accurately to the reality in which they lie or at least limit their disruptive effects to certain roles and relationships without allowing them to pervade the sense of self and identity. No signs of demoralization mark the picture that develops from black respondents' self-assessment and experience of life.

We find, for example, no association between race and self-esteem (table 8.16). Black and white respondents do not differ in having experienced an impending nervous breakdown. They have equal optimism about the future, equal psychological anxiety, and equal physical health. The single symptom factor on which difference occurs is *Immobilization,* and in this case it is the white group—particularly young whites—who report greater immobilization. If we consider this symptom factor to reflect internalization of conflict in the form of indecision and blocking, it makes good sense that it should be more common among whites. The forces blocking action for black youth—discrimination, unemployment, lack of access—are *external,* palpably so. Black youths do not experience them as internal forces inhibiting action and do not express the conflict between impulse and inhibition—both internally conceived and, in a real sense, balanced—as immobility, the inability to get going.

Blacks admit to worrying more than whites. The latter finding, however, disappears when we impose controls for education and income; it thus probably reflects the lesser economic and opportunity resources available to blacks.

Table 8.16 shows that white respondents report greater overall hap-

TABLE 8.17

Race Differences in Reports of Being "Very Happy" (by year × age)

	1957				1976			
	Whites		Blacks		Whites		Blacks	
ge	Total Number Whites	Percent "Very Happy"	Percent "Very Happy"	Total Number Blacks	Total Number Whites	Percent "Very Happy"	Percent "Very Happy"	Total Number Blacks
-34	664	42	19	59	482	36	9	87
-54	878	38	22	87	587	34	21	82
+	613	27	29	42	649	28	27	71

piness about the way their lives are going. These are powerful results which withstand tests for controls on age, education, sex, and year. In the multivariate analysis, however, a very critical interaction with age was also discovered. It is highlighted in table 8.17. Young blacks are dramatically less happy than young whites; middle-aged blacks are also less happy, but the differential is diminished; and older blacks are about as happy as older whites. What accounts for this interaction? The most plausible explanation is that given the higher mortality of blacks in the United States, surviving blacks have been especially resourceful in being able to cope with the differential opportunities afforded blacks in American society. Their resourcefulness accentuates their well-being. They are true "survivors." Young blacks most directly come up against the obstacles for fashioning the good life. Some lower their aspirations as they get older, but some may literally not survive. This is not just because of their relatively lower level of education. These results hold up controlling on education. The inequitable opportunities for whites and blacks to establish dignified and secure positions in our society undoubtedly contribute to these findings.

White respondents indicate a somewhat stronger sense of self through their more frequent allusion to individuated personality strong points and the groups differ in response to the question about how they would like their children to be different from themselves. Whites give fewer role shortcomings than blacks, and whites give fewer role responses in 1976, while blacks increase in role shortcomings in 1976. Since these answers often refer specifically to educational shortcomings, we can view the pattern of change as a reflection of change in actual educational status and expectations. As we noted earlier, the population as a whole—particularly the dominant white population—has become much more highly educated by 1976 and therefore feels less pressure to see their children go farther in school. For the black population, on the other hand, real educational opportunity has opened only during the last twenty years; thus many adults can now hope that the next generation will achieve greater educational status than they have.

Aside from these few differences in overall orientation to life and the self, most race differences seem to occur in marriage. White respondents are more positive toward the idea of marriage, while blacks more often see marriage as *only* restricting. Whites report greater happiness in their own marriages, and white men, in particular, say that their marriages are very happy. The one finding that runs counter to this picture of married life is that white respondents are also more likely to say that they feel *some* inadequacy as spouses. It must be added, however, that this finding applies only to white women, with white men very often denying any sense of inadequacy.

Neither the parent role nor the work role yields as many race differences as marriage. Blacks more often construe parenting—just as they do marriage—as bringing restrictions to their lives. It is as though any interdependence brings with it a certain encumbrance of their freedom and choices. Here we find whites reporting a sense of inadequacy in this case as parents more often than blacks—though, again, white males do not report inadequacy as commonly as white females. Aside from these differences, blacks and whites equally often experience both problems with children and relationship satisfactions in parenting.

Results of analysis of job questions reveal that job satisfactions focus somewhat differently for the two groups: whites speak of ego satisfactions somewhat more, while blacks more often refer to extrinsic satisfactions like pay and good working conditions. Whites allude more often to ego dissatisfactions with work, a response we have taken as a sign of investment and self-assertion—an indication of high expectations for one's work.

What do we make of this pattern? Two general observations seem justified: one is that the experience of being black in a society dominated by whites does *not*, as is sometimes incorrectly assumed, lead to deep and corrosive personal demoralization. Blacks live with greater stress, but they have the personal and social resources to maintain a perspective which keeps the stress external, does not permit it to become internalized or to disrupt personal integration.

Second, marriage is especially vulnerable to the stresses that American blacks experience. The heritage of poverty and certain cultural traditions have created a family structure that deemphasizes sexual division of labor and stresses flexible and substitutable role assumption. When people struggle for subsistence, they cannot and do not assign a whole gender group exclusive responsibility for child raising and home maintenance. Both women and men work in the productive economy and the work of the home. Activities of family maintenance and child raising are treated as auxiliary functions, to be managed on the side in the time left over from the work of survival, and to be shared more or less equally by all.

If egalitarian family structures have dominated family life among black Americans, at the same time it has meant a family structure that deviated from dominant social ideals during much of recent history. As educated white middle-class women began to press for a role in the productive labor force, black women found the call to work somewhat ironic. As Toni Morrison and other black women have made clear, the goal of whites of freeing women to enter the labor force did not look like an enormous gain to many black women, who would first like to be able to win the choice to work or stay at home with their children.

During the fifties and later, the collective moral force that was exerted to keep white women in the role of full-time homemaking and child raising, was destructive to families who were forced into or who chose other patterns. It made these marriages vulnerable and increased the likelihood that life stress would manifest itself in marital conflict. The fact that marriage—and, to a smaller extent, parenting—are viewed as a mixture of pleasure and restriction is a comparatively mild expression of strain. The further finding that blacks feel inadequate in these roles less often—compared to whites—indicates again that negative features are kept in perspective as part of the role and are not allowed to spill over or become internalized as part of the self.

RELIGION DIFFERENCES IN SUBJECTIVE MENTAL HEALTH

Another source of group identity in American culture is religious affiliation. Although for some people this affiliation is not a critical basis for self-anchoring, for others it is a primary commitment, one that, like being black in our society, may have significant impact on certain feelings and sources of well-being or distress. *Americans View Their Mental Health* compared the subjective mental health of Protestant versus Catholics. In this volume, we will make certain distinctions within the Protestant group and will include two additional groups: Jews and people who hold no religious preference. Distinctions among Protestant groups were made as follows: Baptists, Methodists, Lutherans, Presbyterians, Fundamentalist groups (largely composed of Pentecostal, Church of Christ, Primitive Baptist) and a combined "other Protestant" category (Episcopalian, Congregational, and general "Protestant"). These distinctions among Protestant groups were drawn largely because the groups so defined included large enough samples to warrant special consideration. In the case of the Fundamentalist groups, we include those sects which profess an evangelical, personal relationship to religion.

Comparing the distributions for 1957 and 1976 we find that the largest change in any of the groups occurs in the No Preference Group. Only 57 people in the 1957 sample professed no religious preference at all, while 225 people did so in 1976. The very large change in this category is testimony to the shift in religious orientation that has occurred over this generation. A further indication of this change in religiosity will be considered when we look at *Frequency of Church Attendance* in a later section. We will see that there are many more infrequent church-goers in 1976 compared to 1957.

The distinctions among Protestant groups reflect ethnic, regional, and social-status differences, as well as variations in theological positions. On the basis of Andrew Greeley's book, *The Denominational Society* (1972), we can trace various social and religious evolutions in Protestant denominational groups that may have implications for the way members of these groups structure well-being. Table 8.18 presents important demographic differences among these groups, as well as Catholics and Jews, as of 1957.

The *Baptist* group, with strongest membership in the South, takes a

TABLE 8.18

Selected Demographic Characteristics of Major American Denominations in 1957 Census Sample

Demographic Characteristic	Catholic	Baptist	Methodist	Lutheran	Presbyterian	Episcopalian	Jewish
Percentage of population	25	21	14	7	6	3	3
Percentage college educated	17	10	20	20	34	45	44
Percentage white	95	76	91	99	98	94	99
Percentage professional and business	23	15	24	24	31	37	51
Percentage living East and Midwest	78	33	53	76	56	50	90
Percentage earning more than $7,000	47	26	42	49	60	64	69
Percentage living in cities over 500,000	51	19	21	28	30	41	80
Percentage weekly church attendance[a]	68	37	34	43	36	31	22

[a] FN missing.

relatively restrictive orientation to impulse control and a clear focus on issues of sin. Although dogma is not supposed to be powerful in the church, literal interpretations of the Bible abound. Conservativism often characterizes Southern Baptists because theirs is the religious orientation of the majority in many communities in the South. Conventional beliefs in these communities undoubtedly influence how people structure choices in life. Glock and Stark (1965) found that along with Lutherans and Fundamentalists, Baptists were among the most highly conservative in their unquestioned beliefs about the nature of God and religion.

Fundamentalist groups are especially oriented toward primitive expressiveness and personal voluntarism in church participation. There is a directness in the way people of the church express their communion with symbols of their religion. Baptists share in the more direct personal voluntarism, but perhaps because of their dominance in many communities, Baptists may develop more ritualized conventionality. We expect that with their highly personal orientation to religion, Fundamentalists may also be very individual in the way they structure their well-being. We expect Fundamentalists to be the most difficult group to characterize with regard to subjective well-being.

Methodism and *Presbyterianism* are religions deriving from the British Isles and today are likely to be associated with middle-class orientations. Members of the Methodist and Presbyterian churches often make use of the church as a vehicle for general civic participation rather than for social control, as they once did. Glock and Stark (1965) found the Methodists among the most liberal in religious beliefs. While originating in England, Methodism got its big spurt from American revivalism in the nineteenth century. As Methodists became more dominant and successful in American life, Methodism lost some of its revivalistic fervor and became more conventionally tied to the middle-class way of life. Revivalism today finds its clearest expression in Fundamentalist groups. Presbyterians are probably more clearly tied to the original British connection and have retained a stalwart middle-class and upper middle-class orientation to life.

While both Methodists and Presbyterians are highly involved in the more general political and civic participation of the larger community, *Lutherans* are more insulated from general political involvement. This segregation of church from the political life of the nation has been a basic Lutheran tenet. Furthermore, Lutheranism derives primarily from Northern European countries and maintains some of these ethnic loyalties. It has maintained fairly restrictive guidelines for its members, unlike most Methodist and Presbyterian groups who have moved left of center in religious orientation. In this respect, the Lutherans are more like the Baptists. The Lutheran church is extremely well organized, with its own parochial-school system in this country, although it has suffered some severe splits in the liberal-conservative battles within the church structure.

One way to characterize the differences among these five religious groups is to consider how much personal investment there seems to be in the religious doctrine of the groups. On the extreme end we would put Fundamentalism; its religious orientation attracts a very personal involvement with theology as a way of expressing concerns about life in a personal way. Next, we would see Baptists and Lutherans, who are also individually involved with church structure, with a fairly personal interpretation of the relationship to religion and to God, but with clear conventional guidelines for behavior within that structure. As a result, role obligations for being a good Baptist or a good Lutheran must be implicitly codified, more so than for Fundamentalists. Baptists and Lutherans are generally conservative groups, and thus they depend on role obligations to structure their lives. Finally, we would see Methodists and Presbyterians as financially better off and less involved in religious guidelines for participation. Members of these groups are given considerable freedom and active encouragement to participate in civic and political life in a more general sense. We thus see Methodism and Presbyterianism as giving less structure to the style of life that people encounter.

In summary, we hypothesize that Fundamentalism would contribute to subjective well-being in allowing individual adaptations to flourish. Of all the Protestant churches, the Baptist and Lutheran would most explicitly affect styles of adjustment, because for a variety of reasons conventionality is such a marked feature of these churches. Methodism and Presbyterianism would contribute least because these more liberal denominations are so clearly oriented to participation in the general civic life of the society that broader middle-class conventions take on a more dominant socialization function than the individual church.

The American Catholic (Greeley, 1977) gives an all-encompassing picture of the historical and sociological understanding of *Catholics* in modern American society. Coming as nineteenth- and twentieth-century immigrant ethnic groups to this largely Protestant country, they developed a fear of Protestantism and clear group loyalty to handle this fear. Greeley sees this initial reaction to being an American Catholic in this country as becoming much less dominant in the twentieth century as American Catholics adapted to the pressure for success in the society. His book traces the successful adaptation of Catholics to the educational and occupational structure of American society. Contrary to many speculations about American Catholics, they have adapted well, and at this point are among the most educated groups in American society. Greeley sees this adaptation as having occurred because American Catholic Irish and Italian families provided the kind of support that children needed to adapt successfully to work in society as they became adults. This may have had as much to do with the ethnic identity of being Irish or being Italian as it did being Catholic, but Greeley implies in his book that being Catholic also softened the authoritarian structure of Irish and Italian Catholic families, made them less forbidding, and allowed the growth of trust in these groups while unameliorated authoritarianism in families of other religious groups led to fear and suspicion. The notion that authority can be loving toward the disobedient child comes fairly directly out of the Catholic theological understanding of the nature of sin and forgiveness. The lack of supportiveness in authoritarian Protestant homes reflects a more abstract, less forgiving orientation to sin. Whatever the explanation, it is clear that Catholic families have provided a supportive environment for socialization. There is thus a highly focused orientation to family in Catholics, who maintain close and long-term contact with family members. They often live in the same cities and neighborhoods with each other, much more so than do Jewish or Protestant families. This difference may play an important role in the way Catholics structure well-being.

Jews are clearly the most achieving ethnic or religious group which immigrated to this country. From demographic comparisons among different religious groups in table 8.18, we find Jews as a group to be highly educated and strongly represented in professional and business occupations. They are also clearly urban-dwelling people. Thus we have a picture of the Jews as a group very successfully adapted to middle- and upper-middle-class urban life in America. They have quickly moved from an immigrant position low in socio-economic status to being among the highest in American life. Part of this quick change has been attributed to a family structure that permits mobility away from the family: a democratic orientation to decision making within the family, and a strong emphasis on independence training. This kind of pressure for achievement may make the movement into and success within the occupational world dominant themes in Jewish people's orientation to their well-being. This is not to say that close family ties are unimportant to Jews. Indeed, until very recently, the divorce rate among Jews was very low. One study has shown that Jews, in spite of being in very high-prestige time-absorbing occupations, are very dutiful about visiting their parents (Greeley, 1971).

What about those people who express *No Religious Preference?* This category includes people who are explicitly atheistic or agnostic as well as those who fall in the category by default. We cannot accurately distinguish these groups. Our assumption is that people who would express no religious preference by default are perhaps those who are not well integrated in their communities. Such an anomic position is perhaps less true of atheistic and agnostic men and women. Nevertheless, we recognize that people who profess no religious affiliation may have difficulty in adapting to a religiously committed society. Religious commitments reflect social commitments. Lack of religious commitments may reflect lack of social support in the community to which one belongs. Thus we expect that people with no religious preference may experience more difficulty in psychological adjustment than affiliated people.

What are the results? A look at table 8.27 at the end of this chapter shows that there are many differences among religious groups in subjective feelings of mental health, even with age, education, sex, and year controlled, although it is clear that some differences disappear when the controls are introduced. Looking at results which withstand controls (table 8.19), we found that the Protestants that stand out as different from others are the Baptists, with some differences distinguishing Fundamentalists. Jews, Catholics, and those with no preference also show distinctive styles of well-being. In the paragraphs below, we will thus limit our characterization to these groups.

Baptists

The pattern of results distinguishing Baptists from other groups on measures of subjective mental health suggests that Baptists are not low in mental-health indicators but lack subjective experiences of *positive* mental health (Jahoda, 1958). They are more likely to mention role shortcomings in their perceptions of themselves, but are not likely to speak of personality strengths when talking about their strong points. We get the picture of people who are not very oriented toward their own uniqueness. They lack a special sense of identity. Furthermore, they are neutral about the effects of marriage and feel that marriage tends to restrict people. In their perceptions of their own inadequacies as marital partners, they neither deny that they feel inadequate nor think they experience such inadequacies very often. There is a general blandness to the Baptists' psychological life; they are neither very positive nor very negative in their orientation to themselves or their marriages. As we have noted, most Baptist respondents in our sample are from Southern Baptist communities, where their religion is the dominant force in the community. It could be that the homogeneity of the setting encourages a lack of psychological orientation to experience and a conventionality about their lives.

The one positive feature of Baptists' subjective well-being—one that is distinct from other groups—is their emphasis on relationships with their children. Baptists report that the nice thing about raising their children is the parent-child bond. The one really negative perception of self in Baptists is a slightly but significantly higher report of extreme anxiety, especially among the youngest and oldest Baptists.

In summary, we see Baptists as a group who are relatively colorless in their own perceptions of well-being, a group that emphasizes neither their positive nor negative experiences. This subdued morale may not imply extraordinary oppression, but it indicates very little zest for worldly activities. The only exception to this picture is an evident fondness for children which pervades the parental responses of Baptist men and women.

Catholics

In contrast, Catholics do not present a subdued picture of well-being, but one that is characterized by active denial of maladjustment. More than any other religious group, Catholics are on the denial side of indicators of subjective mental health (see table 8.19). They are more likely to say that they do not know what will happen to them in the future. They tend to deny ever feeling they might have a nervous breakdown. They say they have never felt marital or parental inadequacy. Furthermore, they deny ever experiencing symptoms of anxiety. This pattern of denial suggests that Catholics, as a group, use religious identification to ward off difficulties in their lives. Identification with the church and church ritual—especially confession—may be mechanisms for handling disturbing feelings. Their religious orientation offers Catholics institutional support for well-being. They use the formal structure of the church as a way to cope with difficulties, perhaps to the point of denying that any difficulties exist.

Identification with the church requires Catholics to be deeply committed to the institution of marriage. As a group, they show an interesting pattern of response to questions about marriage. On the one hand, Catholics, compared to other religious groups, see marriage as quite re-

TABLE 8.19
Selected Religion Differences in Subjective Mental Health (by year)

Measures of Subjective Mental Health	Baptist 1957 (%)	Baptist 1976 (%)	Methodist 1957 (%)	Methodist 1976 (%)	Lutheran 1957 (%)	Lutheran 1976 (%)	Presbyterian 1957 (%)	Presbyterian 1976 (%)	Fundamentalist 1957 (%)	Fundamentalist 1976 (%)	Other Protestant Groups 1957 (%)	Other Protestant Groups 1976 (%)	Catholic 1957 (%)	Catholic 1976 (%)	Jewish 1957 (%)	Jewish 1976 (%)	No Preference 1957 (%)	No Preference 1976 (%)
No Year Interaction																		
Happiness: "Not too happy"	16	12	7	8	6	9	14	8	9	10	8	11	12	10	16	19	14	13
Worrying: "Always," "a lot"	38	45	31	41	24	41	30	35	31	42	31	45	36	48	51	51	37	47
Experience Feelings of Nervous Breakdown: Yes	22	23	17	19	16	17	19	19	26	25	18	23	16	16	21	30	14	22
Personality Strength in Self: Yes	44	52	51	62	46	64	52	60	42	57	49	64	50	59	60	67	47	63
Orientation to Marriage: Negative	24	25	17	27	24	28	22	24	22	26	18	24	28	31	22	32	36	35
Neutral	36	47	35	39	36	45	27	35	32	40	34	43	31	41	38	35	26	34
Orientation to Marriage: All changes restricting	51	64	40	58	47	55	33	54	38	59	38	53	47	61	42	50	52	56
Happiness in Marriage: "Not too happy"	36	26	30	20	32	20	25	20	37	21	30	17	32	16	19	32	38	23
Frequency Feel Inadequacy as Spouse: Never	41	44	39	44	36	45	41	44	36	38	40	42	59	52	54	47	41	44
Often	12	10	12	10	13	10	12	9	14	12	14	14	10	9	6	15	19	20

Religion

Measures of Subjective Mental Health	Baptist 1957 (%)	Baptist 1976 (%)	Methodist 1957 (%)	Methodist 1976 (%)	Lutheran 1957 (%)	Lutheran 1976 (%)	Presbyterian 1957 (%)	Presbyterian 1976 (%)	Fundamentalist 1957 (%)	Fundamentalist 1976 (%)	Other Protestant Groups 1957 (%)	Other Protestant Groups 1976 (%)	Catholic 1957 (%)	Catholic 1976 (%)	Jewish 1957 (%)	Jewish 1976 (%)	No Preference 1957 (%)	No Preference 1976 (%)
Relationship with Child Nicest Thing about Parenting: Yes	41	40	37	42	39	27	42	41	35	38	38	35	31	35	25	31	35	30
Frequency Felt Inadequate as Parent: Never	49	48	48	44	40	43	53	39	51	45	52	34	63	52	63	54	41	44
Psychological Anxiety: Very high	19	18	16	15	10	15	15	11	18	22	10	15	15	17	21	16	10	16
Interaction with Year Future Morale: Not happy	12	14	8	13	6	8	12	9	9	10	10	8	6	10	6	4	21	12
Future not ascertained	19	20	16	21	14	14	14	14	19	24	18	25	22	19	18	30	14	19
Role Shortcomings in Self: Yes	45	45	39	34	47	32	38	17	43	32	36	26	44	30	35	24	47	24
Dissatisfaction Seen in Job: Ego	21	37	33	35	30	34	30	40	24	37	32	51	25	52	41	62	36	54
Extrinsic only	54	39	44	46	48	49	39	48	46	46	41	33	48	30	26	19	44	34
Total Number	525	473	398	246	200	147	162	101	222	207	242	269	542	504	91	57	57	225

strictive and binding. On the other hand, they, along with Jews, are highest in reports of marital happiness. Seeing marriage as both restrictive *and* happy represents a peculiar combination. Accepting the restrictions of marriage may, in their belief structure, be seen as a way to guarantee subjective well-being. As we noted earlier, supportive Catholic family life experienced in childhood may serve as a model for Catholic adults when they become parents. However authoritarian a Catholic family may be, its supportiveness may preserve people's sense of self.

Jews

Were it not for the fact that Jews also report that their marriages are very happy, we would conclude from the patterns of results distinctive for Jews that they are in pretty bad psychological shape. Compared to other religious groups, Jews say that they are *not happy* (especially high school–educated Jews), that they *worry a lot*, that they often experience feelings of nervous breakdown (see table 8.19). This affective distress may reflect a culturally derived emotional lability. A number of studies have indicated that Jews are not taught to be stoical or tolerant of pain. Their ready admission to difficulty may reflect subcultural norms encouraging expressiveness. Such an interpretation leads to the prediction that Jews will see both the positive and the negative features of life more clearly than other groups. The one result that speaks to positive aspects of their life is the finding that Jews are very happy in their marriages. This factor, combined with their admitting negative feelings (unhappiness, worries), leads us to think that there is a cultural style among Jews to be open to feelings.

Another finding about Jews distinctive from other groups should be highlighted: Jews are the group most likely to mention intrinsic job dissatisfaction. Of all religious groups, they are most likely to focus on psychological aspects of their jobs when asked to discuss difficulties they find in their work. Their emotional lability seems to extend to the work arena. This result may also reflect the strong investment Jews have in achievement and the occupational structure which makes them sensitive to psychological aspects of work. They are especially involved in work as a source of gratification. Given the low incidence of difficulties Jews report about marriage and parenting and their emphasis on ego dissatisfaction in work, one might suggest that work is the area undermining Jews' general morale (i.e., worries, unhappiness, feelings of nervous breakdown). The fact that high school–educated Jews stood out as being discontented is further evidence for such an interpretation. Jews who do not follow the usual success route of going to college and becoming professionals may feel ungratified by life. Given subcultural values, lack of success may present special difficulties for the high school–educated Jew in our society.

No-Preference People

The religious category of No Preference clearly reveals the lowest morale of all groups. The pattern of results in table 8.19 is clear-cut. They report that they are not very happy more often than other groups, and they are especially negative about their marriages and feel especially inadequate as husbands and wives. In addition, people who profess no religious orientation give the most pessimistic picture about their future. More than any other group, they say that their future will be unhappy. Nevertheless, it is hard to know whether this means that people are in bad psychological states because they have been disillusioned with religious faith or that the absence of religious faith induces a negative orientation. But it is clear that lack of religious affiliation is correlated with negative appraisal of well-being.

Our guess is that professing no religious preference is a way for most people to indicate that they are not attached to religious institutions. In so doing, they fail to secure the easy access to affiliative relationships available to those who affirm a religious faith together. It may be difficult in our very complex society to exist without religious faith; not so much because of the rituals or the belief systems that such faith affords, but because of the contact and easy communication with others that religious adherence allows. Religious practice makes people part of a group, and group belonging may be hard to come by in advanced industrial societies like ours. Even if they do not attend church, religious adherents can identify with a group; such identification may produce social consciousness and support that help affirm their social selves.

We have covered a lot of ground in considering interpretations that might account for why religious groups differ from each other on subjective mental-health indicators. Further examination of religious groups will be presented in future reports.

SOCIAL BACKGROUND (SIZE OF CHILDHOOD COMMUNITY, FATHER'S OCCUPATION) AND SUBJECTIVE MENTAL HEALTH

We had originally expected to look at the *size of the community in which the respondent grew up* and the *occupation of respondent's father* as two separate social background factors. The size of childhood community was presumed to be a measure of the degree of social contact and/or social isolation experienced during early socialization. Father's occupation was thought to entail something more: the social status of the respondent while growing up. Although we expected these two social-background characteristics to produce different results in relationships to subjective mental health, the results in table 8.27 showed they had very similar effects. People who come from rural backgrounds, in particular, seem quite distinct from all other groups, and those whose fathers were farmers seemed distinct from all other groups. Thus, the results from the two variables reflected a single phenomenon: people from rural backgrounds evaluate their adult subjective mental health more negatively than people who come from other backgrounds. Certain other findings make the two variables somewhat more distinct, but most of the findings about these two social-background variables can be considered together.

When we consider the impact that size of the childhood community might have on subjective mental health, we are immediately inclined to assume that different-sized communities provide different kinds of information about society. Isolated rural life is removed from highly organized activities. People growing up in farming communities generally are confronted with fewer decisions in planning and transacting their daily lives. By contrast, people from metropolitan areas are very often assaulted with complex decisions and physical and social stimulation. There is, if anything, too much input. One coping style that might be socialized in children raised in the city is to blot out some of this information; another may be to attempt to be vigilant to all the kinds of stimulation, which might in turn encourage an overly sensitive, potentially paranoid orientation to life. By contrast, growing up in a small town or city might mean socialization at a pace well suited to the information and decision-making capacity of children. Does this moderation train people to be maximally adaptive to whatever community they may experience as adults?

There is little empirical or theoretical work to rely on in hypothesizing how size of community might affect one's well-being. The Dohrenwend and Dohrenwend (1974) review of social and cultural factors affecting psychopathology leans in the direction of assuming greater adjustment difficulty in highly urbanized areas, but their conclusions are based largely on studies from countries other than the United States. Lynn Lofland (1973) has suggested that the simpler expectations for social integration among people who come from a smaller-sized community may be dysfunctional in an urban world. As we become more urbanized, perhaps the best adaptation will be made by people who have experienced urban society when they were young.

The measure of size of childhood community is very inexact and subjective. We asked all respondents, "Were you brought up mostly on a farm, in a town, in a small city, or in a large city?" It was left to the respondents to judge whether the size of the community they grew up in was small or large. The distinction between a town and a small city must indeed be subjective. Nevertheless, the nomenclature used in this question seems sufficiently distinct for most Americans to provide a reasonably reliable measure.

Asking people about their father's occupation[15] gets at something

---

[15] Or the occupation of the person who was head of the household if the respondent grew up without a father.

presumably very different. We asked all respodnents: "What kind of work did your father do for a living while you were growing up?"[16] The same code that was used to identify occupation of respondent was also used to ascertain father's occupation. Because there was less articulation of occupation for respondents' fathers contrasted to the respondents' own, we collapsed some original occupational categories: clerical and sales workers were combined, and all farmers, whether managers, laborers, or independent farmers were combined. Occupational categories reflect a status hierarchy ranging from highest white-collar (professional), to lowest blue-collar work (unskilled). In relation to subjective mental health (with respondent's own education controlled), father's occupation looks like a measure of the embedded values of families. Farming families seem to represent a very special socialization context which produces distinctive effects on subjective well-being.

Pearlin and Kohn (1966) offer some insights about how occupational groups prepare children for the kind of work they will do. They suggest that people from white-collar work settings prepare children to be autonomous and independent, while blue-collar workers are more likely to train children to be obedient. Pearlin and Kohn do not discuss the socialization consequences of growing up in a farm family. Indeed, the impact of farmers on their children is not commonly examined in the socialization literature. This literature focuses on social mobility and usually excludes people from farm backgrounds. One of our objectives in asking the question, "Is there any generalized correlation between the occupation of one's father with one's own adult subjective well-being?" was to attend to this very large group.

In table 8.27, at the end of this chapter, we see that for both father's occupation and size of childhood community, there are many significant relationships with measure of subjective mental health, with only year controlled. With the addition of age, education, and sex as controls, many of these results are no longer significant. This is doubtless due to the fact that both of the social background factors are related to current age and current educational status of the respondent. People from rural backgrounds are much more likely in 1957 and 1976 to be older and less educated than those who grew up in towns or cities. Similarly, people whose fathers are professionals or managers are more likely to be highly educated than people whose fathers had other occupations. Among the results that persist, most fall into a generalized pattern: people from rural backgrounds are more negative in their appraisal of well-being than those from other backgrounds. Several results involve complicated interactions with sex, education, year, and age, and these are indicated in table 8.27. In this chapter, however, we discuss only the more direct results.

---

[16] The interviewer was instructed to ask for the job of the head of household if the father was not present when the respondent grew up.

TABLE 8.20

*Selected Comparisons of Subjective Mental Health of Respondents
Who Grew Up in Different Sized Communities (by year)*

	Size of Community in Childhood							
	Rural		Town		Small City		Large City	
Measure of Subjective Mental Health	1957 (%)	1976 (%)	1957 (%)	1976 (%)	1957 (%)	1976 (%)	1957 (%)	1976 (%)
No Interaction with Year								
Future Morale:	12		8		5		6	
Not happy		13		10		8		9
Sees Personality Strengths:	42		51		55		53	
Yes		52		60		63		65
Marital Happiness:[a]	40		29		26		25	
Not happy		25		19		16		16
Job Satisfaction:								
Moderately	53		44		39		44[b]	
satisfied (neither very satisfied nor unsatisfied)		54		45		45		36[b]
Ego Dissatisfaction from Work Mentioned:	22		28		37		30	
Yes		32		48		48		55
Total Number	989	745	568	536	362	413	468	527

[a] There are some very complex interaction effects with year and size of community in childhood and marital happiness, but no simple ones.

[b] There is a significant interaction by year effect found in the decreased percentage of respondents from large city backgrounds who report being moderately satisfied with their job from 1957 to 1976, while other groups increased.

Table 8.20 shows the results that highlight the relationship of the size of childhood community to present subjective well-being; Table 8.21 indicates the parallel results for father's occupation. The results support the idea that people from rural backgrounds have a more difficult time compared to other groups. They are less optimistic about the future, less often refer to their personality strengths, more often say their marriages are not too happy, are only moderately satisfied (neither very satisfied nor very dissatisfied) with their jobs, and are less likely to report ego dissatisfactions in work. Furthermore, we found a significant interaction involving age, size of childhood community, and present happiness. While as many young people from rural backgrounds speak of being happy or unhappy as young people from other backgrounds, middle-aged and older people from rural backgrounds are much more likely to say they are unhappy than people from other backgrounds. This distinction between the younger group and the middle-aged or older group parallels results on marital happiness. Many more middle-aged and older men and women from rural back-

TABLE 8.21

Respondents' Fathers' Occupation Related to Selected Measures of Subjective Mental Health (by year)

Measure of Subjective Mental Health	Father's Occupation													
	Professionals		Managers		Clericals/ Salespersons		Craftspersons		Operatives/ Service Workers		Farmers		Unskilled Laborers	
	1957 (%)	1976 (%)	1957 (%)	1976 (%)	1957 (%)	1976 (%)	1957 (%)	1976 (%)	1957 (%)	1976 (%)	1957 (%)	1976 (%)	1957 (%)	1976 (%)
Happiness														
Very Happy	46	38	46	35	40	41	36	32	38	26	29	28	28	38
Not Too Happy	9	7	8	7	5	5	12	9	9	14	13	12	13	13
Future Morale														
Not Very Happy	7	7	4	6	2	6	9	10	6	10	13	15	7	8
Positive View of Self														
Neutral	9	12	11	14	11	14	12	16	16	17	14	24	14	18
Sees Personality Strength														
Yes	59	73	54	63	60	66	55	66	46	59	41	48	43	56
Marital Happiness														
Very Happy	63	59	63	63	54	53	47	53	47	51	40	47	40	60
Job Satisfaction[a]														
Moderately Satisfied (neither very satisfied nor unsatisfied)	38	38	39	47	39	39	50	40	46	41	51[a]	60[a]	33	46
Ill Health														
Very High	9	3	8	13	10	8	10	8	15	17	18	23	12	17

[a] There is also a year interaction effect that is critical: respondents whose fathers were farmers were especially moderately satisfied in 1976.

grounds report marital unhappiness than do their age peers from other backgrounds. Although young people from rural backgrounds report less marital happiness than young people from other backgrounds, the difference is not as great as it is for the middle-aged or older group.

These findings suggest the interesting interpretation that younger people from rural backgrounds are more hopeful about potential change as they move away from the farm to either towns or cities. But this adaptation to town and city may be more difficult for people from a rural background than for those who have grown up elsewhere. By middle and older age, disillusionment has set in to counter their hopes and ambitions.

Some of the results about job difficulties experienced by people from farm backgrounds suggest that the hopes held by young people about changing their occupations and finding satisfying and secure work different from farming affects all aspects of their psychological lives. The finding that people from rural backgrounds are moderately satisfied about work—neither very satisfied or very dissatisfied—suggests a strong commitment to find satisfaction in the movement away from the farm, no matter how inadequate the alternative proved to be. For many people, movement from the farm may represent a committed act of assertion; one to which they pay allegiance in identity. When these commitments fail, it may be very difficult for them to talk about dissatisfaction with work. That people from a rural background are less likely than people from other backgrounds to mention ego dissatisfactions suggests that they are psychologically uninvolved in their work, and that they report moderate levels of satisfaction simply as a form of compliance with having to work for a living at a job below what they expected when they left the farm.

Some other rather complex results show that people from other than rural backgrounds also show signs of strain, but since these are not consistent across a number of variables, we do not highlight them here.

Father's occupation in relationship to reported subjective well-being yields results consistent with these concerning rural background: people whose fathers were farmers less often see personality opnengths in themselves, less often say that their marriages are very happy, and more often are moderately satisfied with their jobs.

Additional results underscored in table 8.21 need discussion. The sons and daughters of managers, (business people, executives, or people working in large corporations) report their lives as being most affectively sound. In three measures which ask about happiness (present happiness, future morale, and marital happiness), the sons and daughters of managers turn out to be the most happy. By contrast, people from rural backgrounds are ill prepared for the exigencies of urban social life. More isolated, more concerned about the self and the independence of the self in decisions, farmers do not socialize their children into making the type of decisions relevant to organizational contexts, where mutual decision-making is more common. In contrast, the sons and daughters of managers are more likely to be taught by parents to take organizational life into account rather directly. Professionals who work in organizations are more likely to be semi-autonomous in decision-making, while managers are more directly dependent on others and develop interactive skills. As the sons and daughters of blue-collar workers are taught to be obedient, so the sons and daughters of managers are taught to be other-directed in an organizational society. Assuming that the major structure of American society is most efficiently run by that kind of organizationally oriented person, then, more than likely, the sons and daughters of managers are best adapted for it and accordingly, experience greater happiness.

Miller and Swanson (1960) long ago spoke of the distinction between an entrepreneurial and bureaucratic orientation. Farmers may be a vestigial social group in the terms of commitment to an explicitly entrepreneurial orientation; managers may be the clearest example of people committed to a bureaucratic orientation. People socialized in the entrepreneurial context but working in a bureaucratic society may be mismatched with their social environments; those trained to bureaucratic positions in a bureaucratic society are ideally matched.

Two other results: sons and daughters of operatives and service workers report the greatest experience of ill health. It is apparent from table 8.21 that children of farmers and unskilled laborers also are relatively high in poor health. When age and education controls are applied, however, operatives and semiskilled workers stand out as being distinctly different from all other groups. For example, among young people whose fathers were operatives and semiskilled workers, 10 percent in 1957 and 8 percent in 1976 were in the extreme-ill-health category. Only 5 percent of other groups in 1957 and 3 percent in 1976 shared these extreme symptoms. The same pattern exists for other age groups. Might it be that sons and daughters who grow up in the socialization context of lower-status industrial, blue-collar settings experience the most disruption in physical needs of childhood such as nutrition? If so, consequences may be seen in their ill health as adults.

Finally, the sons and daughters of unskilled laborers are those most likely to report being not too happy. This may be the group that Lillian Rubin writes of in *Worlds of Pain* (1976)—people from very poor backgrounds who live as adults in settings not very far removed from their early lower-class backgrounds. Their inability to move out of the lower class may well be one of the conditions leading to lack of happiness.

Interesting as these results are, they will be of even more interest in connection with respondents' own present occupation. Analysis of occupational mobility from generation to generation may prove to be a most interesting variable related to psychological well-being.

THE INNER AMERICAN

BROKEN HOME BACKGROUND AND SUBJECTIVE MENTAL HEALTH

Developmental psychologists have generated much interest in the effects of disrupted home background on people's psychological adaptation. They have been particularly interested in whether a childhood experience of family dissolution by divorce or separation causes mental-health problems in adulthood. Recent acceleration in divorce rates has prompted concern about this question. Does parental divorce harm children? Developmental psychologists also argue that the death of a parent during the early formative years may have long-lasting traumatic consequences for psychological well-being. In the 1957 sample, we found little to argue for the long-term consequences of having experienced such disruption as a child, and the same is true for the 1976 study.

In this analysis, we group people on the basis of responses to two questions: "Did you always live together with your real parents up to the time you were sixteen years old?" (If no was the answer to the above question) "What happened?" From these two questions we code whether the respondent had experienced the death of one or both parents, or parental divorce (or separation). In table 8.27 we see that even without controls for age, education, sex, and year, very few results indicate that disrupted and intact groups differ much on measures of subjective mental health. With the controls introduced, only four measures show any significant difference among groups (table 8.22). People from divorced and separated homes are most likely of all groups to say that at one time or another they have experienced feelings of nervous breakdown, and they report symptoms of psychological anxiety and immobilization. Although it is not easily apparent from table 8.22, it is also true that people who experienced the death of one or both parents before they were sixteen are somewhat more likely than those from intact families to experience these negative states as adults, but not as much as those from homes disrupted by divorce or separation. Furthermore, men and women who come from homes disrupted by divorce or separation are more likely than men and women who come from intact families or had experienced death of a parent while they were growing up to state that they have experienced difficulties in their *own* marriages. This last result suggests that having experienced difficulties in the marriage of their parents while they were growing up causes people to become especially sensitized to marital problems in their own lives.

This is the sum of significant results distinguishing the three groups. Elsewhere, Kulka and Weingarten (1979) present a comparable analysis of these data although not quite as completely controlled as we report in this chapter, and indicate that while a few significant results distinguish the groups, they are most impressed by the lack of differences in light of the dire consequences of early disrupted home life suggested

TABLE 8.22

Selected Subjective Mental Health Comparisons Among People Who Experienced Parental Divorce (or Separation), Parental Death, or Intact Home Life While Growing Up (by year)

	Early Home Life Experience					
	Parental Divorce (Separation)		Parental Death		Intact Home	
Measures of Subjective Mental Health	1957 (%)	1976 (%)	1957 (%)	1976 (%)	1957 (%)	1976 (%)
No Year Interaction						
Experience feeling of Nervous Breakdown:						
Yes	31		20		18	
		29		19		20
Experience Problem in Own Marriage:	62		47		45	
	(90)		(235)		(1,435)	
Yes		72		53		61
		(118)		(142)		(1,094)
Psychological Anxiety:						
Very High	19		17		15	
		23		17		16
Immobilization:						
Very High	33		24		23	
		24		16		20
Total Number	123	191	351	243	1,915	1,742

NOTE: Numbers in parentheses are total number of persons in each group.

in theoretical writings. Kulka and Weingarten argue that the results may be interpreted to mean that adult socialization experiences have as many consequences for mental health as do formative experiences. No doubt, early disruption in childhood has some lasting effects, but they are evidently not as powerful as often hypothesized. As young people mature into adults, encounter experiences with others, and adapt to the social world of their own families and their own relationships, they compensate for difficulties experienced in early family life. We might speculate that, as increasing divorce rates make it more normative to experience a disrupted home life, people may be even less affected by the event. With more people in that status, clearer socialization rules may evolve to facilitate the adaptation of children of divorcing parents.

CHURCH ATTENDANCE AND SUBJECTIVE MENTAL HEALTH

We have seen that men and women who express no preference in religious beliefs tend to evaluate their subjective mental health negatively. Among these people are those who are actively atheistic or agnostic and those who lack religious beliefs by default. In either case, no religious preference can be interpreted as a lack of integration to the social community. And it is this lack of integration that may lie behind perceived mental distress.

We carry this idea one step further in analysis of the relationship of perceived distress to church attendance, for which we expect similar results: low church attendance should be related to negative subjective mental health. And again, rather than interpreting differences in church attendance as differences in religiosity, we interpret them as different levels of social integration.

We asked all people in the sample: "About how often do you usually attend religious services? More than once a week, once a week, two or three times a month, once a month, a few times a year or less, or never?" For our analyses, we combined the two middle categories (two or three times a month, and once a month) into one category (monthly or a few times a month). Our contention is that, aside from people who tell us they go to church more than once a week, people who report a given level of church attendance tell us more about their integration and identification with a particular social group than about their degree of religious commitment. Of course, for many people, frequent church attendance reflects powerful religious commitment. For many more, however, it speaks of commitment to the ritual accompaniments of group identity. We thus hesitate to label church attendance as a measure of religiosity. Other people doing research in religion and behavior have made a similar distinction between public and private religious commitment (e.g., Stark, 1968).

Because church attendance will be read as a measure of public commitment to a group, we would further interpret the level of church attendance as a reflection of *general* social integration. Religious public commitments are perhaps the most striking means used by people to identify with larger institutions in the society. Church attendance is a public act; it tells the world where people belong and with whom they associate. Presence or absence in church is a noteworthy piece of information noted by both church members and nonmembers who are aware of people's comings and goings at specified times. The church is often the community center, the structure which organizes social life. In certain areas, church attendance represents the major form of public integration; the church and its activities represent the central gathering place for people. Therefore, we will look at church attendance as the degree to which people are committed to integration in their community. Lack of church attendance can be read as a sign of lack of integration, and regular church attendance as a sign of very explicit and active ties to the social order. Men and women who attend church more than once a week may be demonstrating clear *religious* behavior. Therefore, we will examine that group separately from the others for any indication that intense religiousity may be a factor in subjective mental health. Furthermore, the once-a-week attenders may be a distinct group. Their pattern may reflect a style of integration explicitly bound by ritual and social prescription. Such dutiful church attenders should include people who are more attuned to social commitments than to idiosyncratic reactions to life experience.

Controls for sex, age, education, and year have clear and highly significant relationships to church attendance. Women are much more faithful churchgoers than men. Table 8.23 shows that in both 1957 and 1976, more women than men attend church regularly. However, an interesting interaction appears in the data: more women were active church attenders in 1957 than in 1976. Whereas both men and women over the generation have become less regular in their church attendance, this dropoff is much more apparent in the women's data than in the men's. Men and women are becoming more alike on the frequency of church attendance. Perhaps this decrease in women's church attendance was one of the consequences of the women's movement. Women may have increased their obligations to society more dramatically over this generation than men have. The women's movement advocated that women attend to self-development. Women's sharp decline in church attendance may reflect an increased involvement in individualized forms of adaptation.

Age differences also appear in church attendance in both 1957 and 1976. Younger people are less likely to attend church than older people. If we look at changes in different age groups in 1957 and 1976 as reflections of cohort phenomena (graphed in table 8.23), we see an important shift. The people who were young in 1957 and became middle-aged in 1976 show a decrease in church attendance. Perhaps that cohort became more separated from the church as a ritual form of social integration. This is not true of the cohorts who were middle-aged in 1957 and became elderly in 1976. They show no change whatsoever in frequency of church attendance. Perhaps in previous generations there would have been *increases* in the frequency of church attendance as people moved from middle- to old age. The *lack* of increase in the cohorts who were middle-aged in 1957 and elderly in 1976 might suggest that they too were affected by the disillusionment with attending church as a form of adaptation to the social order. The most striking finding is in the dramatic drop-off in weekly church attendance among young people in 1976 compared to 1957. Thirty-five percent of the people who were 21 to 34 in 1957 were regular church attenders. On the other side of the coin, 23 percent of the young people in 1976 say they never attend church during the year whereas there were only 8 percent in that category in 1957. This is a dramatic shift among young adults. This disillusionment with the church as a form of social commitment has many ramifications in our results.

The same trend is reflected in education differences in 1957 and

TABLE 8.23

Sex, Age, Education, and Religion Differences in Church Attendance: 1957 vs. 1976

Social Characteristic	More Than Once a Week 1957	More Than Once a Week 1976	Weekly 1957	Weekly 1976	Few Times a Month 1957	Few Times a Month 1976	Few Times a Year 1957	Few Times a Year 1976	Never 1957	Never 1976	Total Percentage	Total Number
Sex												
Men	9	9	28	22	22	16	28	32	13	21	100	1,070
											100	947
Women	15	3	38	28	22	18	19	26	6	15	100	1,375
											100	1,287
Age												
21–34	9[a]	8	35	19	25	16	24	34	7	23	100	757
	14[b]		33		23		22		8		100	804
35–54		12		25		20		28		15	100	999
											100	691
55 and older	14	15	34	32	18	17	23	22	11	14	100	678
											100	737
Education												
Grade school	12	14	29	30	24	18	24	22	11	16	100	799
											100	377
High school	12	11	35	26	21	18	24	29	8	16	100	1,178
											100	1,098
College	12	11	41	22	20	17	18	30	9	20	100	454
											100	752
Religion												
Baptists	15	18	26	23	31	23	21	28	7	8	100	524
											100	472
Methodists	6	7	21	23	27	23	29	35	7	11	100	396
											100	245
Lutheran	6	3	34	33	30	27	26	27	4	10	100	199
											100	146
Presbyterian	6	2	33	26	19	24	30	37	12	11	100	162
											100	98
Fundamentalists	23	34	32	19	15	16	24	22	6	9	100	220
											100	204
All Other Protestants	7	13	24	18	22	17	32	32	15	20	100	240
											100	258
Catholics	18	8	57	43	12	14	9	24	4	11	100	542
											100	502
Jewish	2	4	7	7	22	9	48	58	21	23	100	91
											100	52

1976. While we see no remarkable changes in church attendance among grade school–educated between 1957 and 1976, we see a dropoff in attendance in both the high school and the college groups. Most remarkable is the dropoff in church attendance among the college educated. Forty-one percent of the college educated in 1957 were regular church attenders, while only 22 percent were regular church attenders in 1976. This result is partially a function of the fact that among the college educated we have a large group of young people, but the young college-educated people in 1957 were also regular church attenders. There is no doubt, therefore, that young adults in 1976 march to a much different drummer with respect to social integration through church attendance. Apparently for these people, the style of adaptation in our society is much more dependent on personal integration than social integration. The comfort that church attendance represents either as a social or religious commitment is evidently not an assumed form of adaptation for the young in our society today.

The pattern of results we have noted in church attendance is especially noticeable among Catholics (see table 8.23), who show a remarkable drop in regular church attendance over the generation. In Catholicism, more clearly than in other religions, church attendance means commitment to outside authoritative obligation. With secularization and abandonment of the Latin service, perhaps some of the mystery of the church obligation has waned. In addition, the church's conservative edicts on birth control and abortion have reduced faith in the social authority of the church since they were so clearly at odds with the feelings of church members (see Greeley, 1977). At any rate, for all religious groups and perhaps especially for Catholics, the meaning of church attendance has shifted from a behavior that emphasizes social obligations to a behavior that is seen to conflict with personal goals. Furthermore, as our society has moved away from social commitment to more personal styles of integration, nonattendance at church may represent a somewhat different fact about a person in 1976 than it did in 1957. In 1976, not attending church may be less clearly contrary to social norms than it once was.

Thus we have a dual set of expectations about the impact of church attendance (as a measure of social integration) on subjective well-being. On the one hand, as the 1957 results suggested, we would expect that the more people attend church, the more they are integrated into the social system. Their commitments to social groups are underscored, and hence they experience easier adaptation to the social world. We suspect that some of these forces operate in 1976, too. However, over the generation, the shift toward more personal styles of adaptation and increased suspicion of ritualized forms may mean that nonattendance reflects a new style of integrating into a more diffuse and secular society. Furthermore, some people who attend church frequently in 1976 may often feel at odds with dominant social values in the media or other social institutions. As a result, we are aware that church attendance may relate to subjective well-being differently in 1957 and 1976.

In *Americans View Their Mental Health,* church attendance was run separately for Catholics and Protestants. We felt that the meaning of church attendance might be different for the two major religious groups. We decided not to institute that control in our analysis since we are more explicitly using church attendance as a measure of general social integration, whatever the religious belief held, and not as a measure of a commitment to a specific religious system. Nevertheless, we felt it was important to examine the effect of church attendance on subjective mental health of Catholics and Protestants separately. In one major set of analyses which follows, we will look at the difference between Catholics and Protestants in the relationship of church attendance to well-being.

Turning to results which look at the general relationship of church attendance to subjective mental health, we find that many indicators of well-being relate to church attendance both without demographic controls and also when controls for sex, age, and education are instituted in the six-way cross-classification. Furthermore, table 8.27 at the end of the chapter highlights four critical results that suggest differences in the way church attendance relates to subjective well-being in the two years. In summary preview of these results, most of which are reported in selected comparisons in table 8.24, we can say that church attendance as a measure of social integration has many positive correlates with subjective well-being. The more that people are integrated by church attendance, the more likely they are to report feeling good about their subjective mental health. This is true both in 1976 and 1957.

However, in 1976, certain results relating church attendance to well-being are more muted. We should also note that there are many complicated interactions which must be taken into account in understanding the relationship of church attendance to subjective mental health, besides the ones we discuss. Education, year, sex, and age all contribute in complicated ways to these relationships, but none of them is striking. The sophisticated reader will realize that detailed analysis of the effects of church attendance on subjective well-being might uncover a much more complex picture of the relationships than what we will discuss. Following our usual procedure, we will highlight only results which show the main effects of church attendance on subjective mental health over and above some of these more complicated interactions.

On indicators of affective morale, we have clear results showing that the more frequently people attend church, the more likely they are to report satisfaction or happiness with their experience. These results can be found in reports of general happiness, marital happiness, positive orientation toward parenthood, and satisfaction with work. As an example of the linear effects, the reader might focus on the relationship of church attendance to marital happiness (table 8.24). A clear lin-

TABLE 8.24
Church Attendance Related to Selected Measured of Subjective Mental Health

Measure of Subjective Mental Health	Church Attendance									
	More Than Once a Week		Weekly		Few Times a Month; Monthly		Few Times a Year		Never	
	1957 (%)	1976 (%)	1957 (%)	1976 (%)	1957 (%)	1976 (%)	1957 (%)	1976 (%)	1957 (%)	1976 (%)
No Year Interaction										
Happiness:										
Very Happy	41	40	39	34	31	29	33	31	23	24
Nervous: Breakdown Feelings										
Yes	19	22	16	16	20	22	20	23	19	27
Happiness in Marriage:										
Happy	54	59	51	57	47	49	39	53	36	47
Positive-Negative Orientation to Church:										
Negative	19	21	23	26	21	27	21	31	30	35
Relationship Satisfaction with Children:										
Yes	36	38	36	40	36	39	38	35	33	27
Felt Inadequacy as Parent:										
A lot	16	14	14	14	18	11	16	19	17	24
Job Satisfaction:										
Very satisfied	42	37	35	33	28	29	26	25	28	22
Psychological Anxiety:										
Very high	15	15	13	16	16	19	17	17	21	18
Ill Health:										
Very high	14	16	10	19	14	14	15	12	18	16
Interaction with Year										
Future Morale:										
Not too happy	9	10	7	12	11	9	9	9	12	13
Role Shortcomings:										
Yes	37	31	42	34	44	43	41	30	46	25
Negative Orientation to Marriage:										
Positive	49	36	43	33	42	32	44	26	34	29
Negative	20	19	24	22	22	28	23	33	33	36
Felt Inadequacy as spouse:										
A lot	10	15	11	8	9	6	14	12	19	19
Total Number	295	259	834	559	536	390	562	634	218	392

ear decline occurs in reports of marital happiness: people who attend church more than once a week report being happy in their marriage more frequently than those who attend regularly, who in turn report being more happy than monthly attenders, and so on. These results are apparent even when controls for age, education, sex, and year are imposed.

A question introduced in examining relationships between happiness and church attendance in both 1957 and 1976 was whether the relationship might differ for people in different-sized communities. We controlled for place of residence (metropolitan, suburb, small city, town, rural), and found (see table 8.25) that the correlation between church attendance and happiness in small towns, suburbs, and rural areas is larger than in metropolitan areas. These results suggest that church attendance is a more distinct act of integration in smaller, more homogeneous communities. People are more aware of attendance in a rural area or in a small town. Absence from church can be more easily read as a mark of lack of faith or commitment to a social group. Attendance or absence may not be so obvious in more urbanized areas. Furthermore, other options for group identity which can ward off feelings of discomfort from not attending church exist in more urban areas. People in small towns and rural areas may be more dependent on church attendance as a means of demonstrating social integration.

On indicators of strain (rather than indicators of affective morale), regular church attenders are distinctive. People who attend church once a week tend to reject having had feelings of impending nervous breakdown and are least likely to be high in psychological anxiety (table 8.24). People who attend church regularly are also least likely to report worrying all the time and most likely to say they worry very little. This pattern suggests that people who attend church regularly have control over feelings of strain in their lives. Whether there is any causal connection between these two is open to further investigation. It can be argued that people who attend church regularly control feelings of

TABLE 8.25

Correlation (gamma) Between Church Attendance and Reported Happiness (by place of residence × year)

Place of Residence	1957		1976	
	Numbers	gamma	Numbers	gamma
Metropolitan City	322	.10	158	.10
Suburb	319	.15[a]	341	.24[b]
City	384	.11	446	.04
Town	698	.12[b]	714	.13[b]
Rural Area	713	.23[c]	513	.13[b]

[a] $P < .05$ [b] $P < .01$ [c] $P < .001$

strain, but attending church on a regular basis may also relieve strain. Regular church attendance has declined remarkably in the American population, especially among the young, the college educated, and the Catholics, indicating that the capacity of regular church attendance to provide defensive adaptation to strain may have weakened. We have some slight evidence of this in the interaction between year and regular church attendance. We find that regular church attenders in 1976 are much less likely to report that they expect the future to be happy, compared to a regular church attenders in 1957. These results have two different interpretations. Over the generation, regular church attendance either has lost some of its capacity to ward off anxiety about the future, or has become less characteristic of people who are not anxious in their daily lives.

A number of results showing significant effects of church attendance on subjective well-being highlight the negative feelings experienced by nonchurchgoers. These results duplicate findings we report below about lack of religious preference: less frequent church attenders are more unhappy, find their marriages unhappy, say parenting is negative, and find their jobs unsatisfying. Other findings about people's reactions to family roles confirm the fact that infrequent church attenders are especially distressed about their marriages and their children. In these results, both the infrequent church attenders and those who never attend church stand out in their negative subjective mental health appraisals compared to all other groups. However, frequent church attenders do not stand out particularly as being positive in their appraisal compared to moderate church attenders. For example, people who never attend church are least likely to see the relationships with children as the nicest thing about parenting. They are also most likely to feel inadequate both as parents and spouses, and are most likely to feel negative about changes that marriage brings to people's lives. The sum of these results highlights the lack of social integration that nonattenders feel at a societal level and at a more deeply personal level within their families. The interdependence of feelings of family integration with feelings of societal integration must be very complex. It would be useful to make analyses to ferret out potential causal linkages.

Findings in the 1957 survey indicating that Catholics and Protestants differed in how church attendance related to certain contextual aspects of marital and parental experience provide a clue about how personal and societal integration may be related differently in different groups. We followed up these findings for the 1976 survey. Only one set of results seemed constant for both years: married Catholics and Protestants differed in how church attendance related to their naming their relationship to their spouse as the nicest thing about their marriages (table 8.26). For Catholics, the more infrequently they attend church, the more likely they are to mention relationship aspects of their marriages.

TABLE 8.26

Catholic-Protestant Differences in the Relationship of Church Attendance to Reporting the Marital Relationship as Nicest Thing About Marriage (by year)

	Church Attendance									
	More Than Once a Week		Weekly		Monthly: Few Times a Month		Few Times a Year		Never	
	1957 (%)	1976 (%)	1957 (%)	1976 (%)	1957 (%)	1976 (%)	1957 (%)	1976 (%)	1957 (%)	1976 (%)
Catholic	26 (66)	43 (28)	36 (253)	51 (139)	39 (54)	41 (49)	49 (39)	69 (80)	64 (14)	56 (27)
Protestant	58 (143)	59 (142)	42 (368)	53 (202)	46 (345)	55 (180)	40 (355)	58 (286)	46 (83)	57 (94)

NOTE: Numbers in parentheses are total number of persons in each group.

For Protestants the reverse is true: the more frequently they attend church, the more likely they are to mention relationship aspects of marriage. Thus we have a replication of a pattern of findings highlighted in *Americans View Their Mental Health:* Catholics who are frequent church attenders are *less* invested in the personal relationships of marriage and parenting than nonattenders, while the opposite is true for Protestants. This is the only result that consistently supported this view in both years. Other measures that supported this view in 1957 did not in 1976. The Catholic church has become more secularized about the psychological nature of church functions, and it may be that the distinction between organizational and personalistic orientations in the Catholic-Protestant difference has begun to disappear.

One interesting interactive result with year is reported in table 8.24. Among those who never attend church, we find a very significant decline in the report of role shortcomings. In 1957, people who never attended church were very likely to mention some aspect of their social roles as a shortcoming; in 1976, very few of them report such role shortcomings. This shift in awareness of role shortcomings as negative aspects of self may reflect the difference in the meaning of church attendance in 1957 and 1976. In 1957, it may have been the clearer measure of a lack of social integration. People who did not feel they had the appropriate role credentials to be an adult member of society were among those who did not attend church. In 1976, however, with the increased orientation away from social obligations, many more people who are not attending church may be adopting a new norm for adaptation to the society, away from institutional obligations in behavior like church attendance, toward greater psychological absorption in self-fulfillment. Being psychological may be a new *social* obligation. Although this significant interaction withstands the control for education, we might interpret these results as emerging from the enormous increase in college training over the generation. People going to college over this generation have shifted to the psychological approach to life and have turned away from church attendance. These people have helped establish the new *social* expectations of a psychological orientation to life.

One interesting result that seemed to come up only among the devout was the relative increase from 1957 to 1976 in reports of inadequacies as spouses. Thus, over the generation, the devout have evidently become more psychological in appraising their marriages. The result is further understood by the large decrease among devout Catholics in 1976 who tend to be people who deny their inadequacies as husbands and wives. Thus, even among those who attend church frequently, there has been an intrusion of secularization into experience. The comfort of the church will undoubtedly increasingly take a psychological approach. The authoritative comfort from religious ritual and mystery may become less effective, but the social integration that church attendance provides apparently remains. Results from our survey suggest, however, that this function is somewhat muted in 1976 because of the new norms for psychological approaches to problems which may be becoming part of church orientation, but are still more characteristic of people who forgo the social bonds of attending church. Perhaps not attending church in our increasingly heterogenous urban society is no longer as clearly diagnostic of lack of social bonds as it once was.

Summary

As much as each of the analyses of the subjective correlates of the social/demographic characteristics explored in this chapter has produced a rich variety of conclusions, too extensive to be summarized adequately, not all of them have reflected powerful effects. Some of them are based on small differences. We should once again stop and differentiate major from minor results.

We are impressed with the special power of the three characteristics systematically explored in this book: sex, age, and education. Alone or in combination, they generate more substantial findings than most of the other characteristics, even when these other characteristics are *not* controlled for sex, age, and education. The only other social characteristics that approach the power of sex, age, and education are income and church attendance. Besides the general importance of these five social characteristics are special groups of Americans who stand out as being particularly distressed about their lives: divorced men and women, people who live in or come from rural environments, and the unemployed. These special groups, in turn, are relatively poor groups and hence may be reflecting the burden of having low incomes in an affluent society, rather than the specific consequences of these statuses in our society. Following are capsule summaries of critical differences in subjective mental health associated with each of the social characteristics, but we will distinguish those characteristics which yield powerful effects from those which yield only small but consistent results. In these summaries, readers can refer to tables 8.27 and 8.28, which bring together the various multivariate analyses that served as the bases of our discussion of each section of this chapter.

POWERFUL SOCIAL CORRELATES OF SUBJECTIVE MENTAL HEALTH

The three social characteristics that we systematically analyzed in this book—sex, age, and education—are clearly vital factors in differentiating people's subjective mental health.

Sex differences in many indicators suggest that women are experiencing considerably more feelings of strain in their lives, although there are no extensive sex differences in measures of morale or self-esteem. These findings can be interpreted as showing both that men are more reticent about voicing their complaints about their lives, and that the major role assignments—of women to parenting and men to work—carry with them differential vulnerabilities.

A number of features of subjective life characterize the way different *age* groups view their mental health. Younger men and women quite naturally look to different bases of gratification or frustration in accounting for their inner life and have different time perspectives in making their evaluations. Younger people experience more strain, while older people are more adapted to what life holds for them. In this sense, younger people are more distressed; but, in another sense, they are more open to change and more optimistic about their future.

Education differences in subjective well-being are very powerful: the more educated clearly have more resources for feelings of well-being; the less educated experience greater demoralization. People with different educational attainments also focus on different facets of well-being: the least educated on health and economic issues; the moderately educated on family roles; the most educated on their jobs, their communities, and issues of self-fulfillment.

Another status characteristic—*income*—has powerful effects on subjective mental health, independent of education. Having economic security and affluence are critical aspects of high morale in practically all dimensions of self-appraisal. These findings undoubtedly also account for certain groups standing out in our delineation of other social factors: the unemployed, divorced women, and people who live in or come from rural environments, all of whom also have relatively low family incomes.

The final social characteristic that generates powerful correlates with subjective mental health is *church attendance*. Regular church attenders and people who do not attend church at all are vastly different from each other in their reports of the quality of their lives. Compared to those who do not attend church, regular church attenders think their lives are going well. While these results can be interpreted differentially, the most plausible explanation depends on interpreting church attendance as a measure of social integration. People who attend church regularly may be more clearly bonded to their communities, a bonding which must give people that affirmation of self that enhances the value and meaning of their lives. Without that kind of institutional bonding, social meaning is more difficult.

OTHER SIGNIFICANT BUT LESS POWERFUL SOCIAL CORRELATES OF SUBJECTIVE MENTAL HEALTH

Other Status Effects

While people's education and income are the most powerful measures of social status that correlate with subjective mental health, other social characteristics also seem to affect people's well-being because of their partial connection to status.

Some of the *race* differences in subjective well-being can be interpreted as reflecting the relatively low status assigned by whites to blacks, over and above issues of education, occupation or income. Young blacks, in particular, report not being very happy, which is not surprising considering the inequities in the opportunities for economic status granted to them. Blacks also judge the institutions of marriage and their own marriages more negatively than whites. Their comments are not surprising, considering the difficulties blacks face in maintaining harmony between family patterns and a world that provides few opportunities for statusful work.

There were few correlates of *occupation* to subjective mental health once education was controlled. One group showed some additional significant effects. Professionals were especially positive about their marriages and jobs. The special status accorded the professionals in our society undoubtedly has implications for their appreciation of work and also the impact this status might have on their marital interactions.

Group Identity Effects

In light of the inequities facing blacks, it may be important to understand why there are so few significant differences in subjective well-being between blacks and whites. We suggest that the supports of group identity can give blacks the personal strengths that provide buff-

TABLE 8.27

Summary of Significant Combined-Year[a] and Year-Specific[b] Demographic Effects
Found in Relating Selected Demographic Characteristics to Selected Measures of Subjective Mental Health

Social-Demographic Characteristic

Measures of Subjective Mental Health	Income		Population Density		Region		Broken Home Background		Father's Occupation		Size of Childhood Community		Race		Religion		Church Attendance	
	Combined Year Effects	Year Specific Effects	Combined Year Effects	Year Specific Effects	Combined Year Effects	Year Specific Effects	Combined Year Effects	Year Specific Effects	Combined Year Effects	Year Specific Effects	Combined Year Effects	Year Specific Effects	Combined Year Effects	Year Specific Effects	Combined Year Effects	Year Specific Effects	Combined Year Effects	Year Specific Effects
General Well-Being																		
Happiness	✓ [c,d]		✓ [c,d]		✓ [c]				✓ [c]	✓	✓ [d]		✓ [c,d]		✓ [c,d]		✓ [c]	
Worrying	✓ [c]	✓	✓ [c]		✓ [c]		✓		✓	✓	✓ [c]	✓ [c]			✓ [c,d]		✓ [d]	✓ [d]
High Future Morale	✓ [c]		✓ [d]	✓	✓ [c]	✓	✓ [c]		✓ [c]		✓ [c]				✓ [c]	✓ [c]	✓ [c,d]	
Nervous-Breakdown Feelings	✓ [c]										✓				✓ [c]			
Self-Conceptions																		
Positive View of Self	✓	✓ [c]	✓ [d]		✓ [c]				✓ [c]		✓		✓ [c]	✓ [c]	✓ [c]		✓ [c]	✓ [c]
Personality Strength (mentioned)	✓ [d]		✓ [c]		✓	✓			✓ [c]		✓		✓ [c]		✓ [c]	✓ [c]	✓ [c]	✓ [c]
Role Shortcoming (mentioned)	✓				✓				✓ [d]				✓ [c]	✓ [c]	✓ [c]			
Reactions Re: Marriage																		
Positive Orientation to Marriage	✓ [d]		✓ [c]						✓ [c,d]				✓ [c]	✓ [c]	✓ [c]		✓ [c]	✓ [c]
Restrictive Orientation to Marriage	✓ [d]	✓ [d]							✓				✓ [c]	✓ [c]	✓ [c]		✓ [c]	✓ [c]
Marital Happiness	✓ [c]								✓ [c]		✓ [c]		✓ [c,d]		✓ [c]		✓ [c]	

Marital Relationship Satisfaction (mentioned)

Frequency of Marital Inadequacy Feelings

Reactions Re: Parenthood

Positive Orientation to Parenthood

Restrictive Orientation to Parenthood

Parenting Problems

Parental Relationship Satisfaction (mentioned)

Frequency of Parental Inadequacy Feelings

Reactions Re: Job

Job Satisfaction

Ego Job Satisfaction (mentioned)

Ego Job Dissatisfaction (mentioned)

Symptoms

Psychological Anxiety

Ill Health

Immobilization

[a] A significant combined year effects is checked (✓) under two conditions: (1) When the relationship between a given demographic characteristic (DC) and a given measure of subjective mental health (SMH) is required to reproduce the cross-classification of SMH × DC × Year in the most parsimonious model (p > .05) detected by log-linear analyses; or (2) when there is a significant year-specific effect (see footnote b below) but the lambdas page ▮ for explanation) testing the combined year effects *net of the year-specific effect* detect highly significant differences (p < .01).

[b] A significant year-specific effect is checked (✓) when the interaction of a given demographic characteristic (CDC) with both year and a given measure of subjective mental health (SMH) is required to reproduce the cross-classification of SMH × DC × Year in the most parsimonious model (p > .05) detection by log-linear analyses.

[c] Effect persists when sex, age, and education controls are introduced in a six-way cross-classification: measure of subjective mental health × demographic characteristic × year × sex × age × education. [Criteria for persistence are: (1) effect itself is needed in most parsimonious model (p > .05) adds to fit; (2) effect is nested in a higher-order effect, but lambdas testing the effect *net of the higher-order effect* detects highly significant differences (p < .01)]

[d] A complex higher-order interaction with sex, age, and education exists.

TABLE 8.28
Summary of Significant Combined-Year[a] and Year-Specific[b] Demographic Effects Found in Relating Selected Demographic Characteristics to Selected Measures of Subjective Mental Health (by sex)

Measures of Subjective Mental Health	Occupation				Marital Status				Parent Status				Employment Status			
	Men		Women		Men		Women		Men		Women		Men		Women	
	Combined Year Effects	Year Specific Effects	Combined Year Effects	Year Specific Effects	Combined Year Effects	Year Specific Effects	Combined Year Effects	Year Specific Effects	Combined Year Effects	Year Specific Effects	Combined Year Effects	Year Specific Effects	Combined Year Effects	Year Specific Effects	Combined Year Effects	Year Specific Effects
General Well-Being																
Happiness	√[c]				√[c]		√[c]		√[c]				√[c]		√[c]	
Worrying	√		√		√[c]		√[c]						√[c]		√	√
High Future Morale	√		√		√[c]		√[c]	√			√[c]		√[c]	√	√	√
Nervous-breakdown Feelings					√[c]		√[c]			√	√[c,d]		√	√		√
Self-Conceptions																
Positive View of Self	√	√	√		√		√[c]			√						
Personality Strength (mentioned)	√		√				√									
Role Shortcoming (mentioned)	√		√													
Reactions Re: Marriage																
Positive Orientation to Marriage	√[c]				√[c]		√[c]	√		√	√[c]		√			
Restrictive Orientation to Marriage					√[c]		√[c]	√			√[c]					
Marital Happiness	√		√[c]		—[e]	—	—	—	√[c]		√[c]				√[d]	√
Marital Problems	√				—	—	—	—	√[c]		√[c]					
Marital Relationship Satisfaction (mentioned)					—	—	—	—	√[c]		√[c] √[c]		√			
Frequency of Marital Inadequacy Feelings					—		—	—	√[c]		√[c]		√[c]			

Reactions Re: Parenthood

- Positive Orientation to Parenthood
- Restrictive Orientation to Parenthood
- Parenting Problems
- Parental Relationship Satisfaction (mentioned)
- Frequency of Parental Inadequacy Feelings

Reactions Re: Job

- Job Satisfaction
- Ego Job Satisfaction (mentioned)
- Ego Job Dissatisfaction (mentioned)

Symptoms

- Psychological Anxiety
- Ill Health
- Immobilization

---

[a] A significant combined year effects is checked (✓) under two conditions: (1) When the relationship between a given demographic characteristic (DC) and a given measure of subjective mental health (SMH) is required to reproduce the cross-classification of SMH × DC × Year in the most parsimonious model($p > .05$) detected by log-linear analyses, *or* (2) when there is a significant year-specific effect (see footnote b below) but the lambdas (see chapter 2, page 67 for explanation) testing the combined year effects *net of the year-specific effect* detect highly significant differences ($p < .01$).

[b] A significant year-specific effect is checked (✓) when the interaction of a given demographic characteristic (CDC) with both year and a given measure of subjective mental health (SMH) is required to reproduce the cross-classification of SMH × DC × Year in the most parsimonious model ($p > .05$) detection by log-linear analyses.

[c] Effect persists when sex, age, and education controls are introduced in a six-way cross-classification: measure of subjective mental health × demographic characteristic × year × sex × age × education. [Criteria for persistence are: (1) effect itself is needed in most parsimonious model ($p > .05$) adds to fit; (2) effect is nested in a higher-order effect, but lambdas testing the effect *net of the higher-order effect* detects highly significant level differences ($p < .01$)]

[d] A complex higher-order interaction with sex, age, and education exists.

[e] A signifies an inappropriate comparison.

ers against symptoms of distress, lowered self-esteem, and feelings of inadequacy in marriage.

Other group-identity processes are probably involved in certain religions appearing distinctive in their patterns of responses to measures of subjective well-being. Baptists are prone to be bland about their psychological experiences; Catholics, to deny certain feelings of distress; and Jews, to be expressive about their discontents. Jews also seem to focus on psychological fulfillment through statusful work, which may account for why moderately educated Jews in our society report being particularly unhappy.

Role Status Effects

The correlates of *parental, marital,* and *employment statuses* with subjective mental health are not striking. The most significant results indicate problems of loss of roles for people. The unemployed, the divorced, and the widowed have lower morale than most other groups. In this connection, it is hard to assess the impact of retirement on people: many people retire because of poor health, which has its concomitant effects on subjective mental health. Among relatively healthy male retirees, however, we find greater subjective well-being than among working men of the same age, and especially in 1976.

Role overload is probably the basis of some other scattered results relating role status to subjective mental health. Compared to nonparents, parents experience both more general strain and greater disruptions to their marital relationships. Compared to married women, divorced women show heightened anxiety and lowered morale. Contrasted to housewives, working women have somewhat lower morale and feelings of self-doubt about their family-role adequacies. In all these findings, we can see groups which have to juggle many different responsibilities suffering more strain than groups with lighter loads.

Compared to other marital statuses, single people report more symptoms of immobilization. These results may reflect problems of commitment among single people rather than problems of ongoing life circumstances.

Geographic Effects

Both *region of the country* and *population density* as measures of geographic or physical environment have consistent but minor correlations with subjective experience. The effects of a particular *region* are parallel to the psychological adaptations of groups distinctive to that region. Middle-Atlantic residents show patterns of psychological wariness that are distinctive to many urban dwellers typical of their region (New Yorkers, Philadelphians, and others); they report high psychological anxiety, deny problems in family roles, but see having children as burdensome. The Solid South is comparatively unpsychological in its approach to the quality of experience, which in turn is characteristic of Baptists, who are well represented in the South. The Border States are relatively low in morale and high in psychological and physical symptoms—a combination frequently found among poor people, many of whom inhabit that region. And the Pacific region is relatively psychological in its orientation to its own mental health—which, in turn, is typical of the great number of young and college-educated men and women who make up its population.

The analysis of *population density* yields a number of results. Rural people make relatively demoralized appraisals of their own mental health. As mentioned earlier, some of this phenomenon may be read as the concentration of low-status people in rural areas. As noted above, urban dwellers have a kind of psychological wariness. Suburbanites seem to be especially invested in their work, but they find parenthood problematic. This result is especially apparent in 1976, suggesting that the 1950s' and 1960s' idealization of the suburbs as a protected place to bring up children has been questioned in the suburbanites' own evaluation of their lives in the 1970s.

Social Background Effects

Aside from the clear status effects that can be read into why people from rural and farming backgrounds have considerably poorer views of their own mental health, there are only minimal results relating *size of childhood community* and *father's occupation* to measures of subjective well-being. There are some provocative findings to suggest that people growing up in homes of managers (people attuned to bureaucracies) are more adapted than others to their present life circumstances. In addition, people growing up in a blue-collar, industrial setting have slightly more symptoms of ill health.

As in 1957, *broken-home background* in the 1976 study has not as much impact on subjective mental health as the clinical literature on the topic suggests. The clearest results suggest that experiencing a divorce of one's own mother and father makes people more generally anxious, and sensitive to problems in their own marriages.

All of the results that we have highlighted in this chapter emerge from multivariate analyses that detect the effects of these social characteristics independent of year, age, sex, and education differences, and their interactions. Although there are some important differences in the way some of these characteristics are related to subjective mental health in 1976 compared to 1957, the effects we have discussed are remarkably consistent over the generation.

Chapter 9

COPING WITH PROBLEMS AND SOCIAL SUPPORT

IN the preceding chapters, we have looked at various aspects of American adults' subjective experience. We have noted that the tone of much of that experience is positive; that we are an optimistic people who derive significant satisfaction from life and from performance of important life roles: work, marriage, and parenthood. We also noted in chapter 7 that only a small minority of the population experience symptoms serious enough and often enough to signal serious problems of adjustment.

Yet, because we were concerned with life stress, we highlighted responses to questions about problems encountered, inadequacies felt in life roles and in general functioning, including items from the inventory of psychological symptoms. Dealing with these negative features of adjustment could leave a reader with the sense that American people experience a great deal of difficulty with life, despite their verbal optimism and our conclusions about their overall well-being.

We have also made a good deal of findings that speak to a general loosening of people's social integration, a reduction in the meaning and satisfaction they find in assuming and performing roles in a social organization. Asked to define themselves, our 1976 respondents allude less often to positions they fill, roles they perform, compared to respondents in 1957.

In part to balance what may appear an overly negative view of the subjective experience of American adults, or exaggerated picture of the state of organized social life, we want now to look briefly at the methods and resources available to people as they confront problems of daily living. To what extent do people turn to friendship and kin resources to support them when they meet problems? Do they rely on people with whom they can share difficult issues, worries, unhappy periods? What other resources and techniques do people use to manage difficult periods? Do they pray? Deny problems? Use direct action to solve them? Do they think of using professional help?

On the basis of data about coping and social support, we should be able to see what resources people have for coping with problems and to evaluate whether these resources are sufficient for managing the problems they face. Knowing that a person has friends and kin who can help in difficult times tells us something very important about that person's life quality and subjective experience. We can think of this analysis, then, as revealing another facet of that experience. The bulk of this chapter focuses on responses to two questions from which both styles of coping and sources of informal social supports were drawn. One question asked about coping with worries:

> If something is on your mind that is bothering you or worrying you and you do not know what to do about it, what do you usually do? (If respondent mentioned talking with someone, the interviewer asked or noted who the supporting person was. If the respondent did not mention talking with someone, the interviewer asked: Do you ever talk it over with anyone? Who is that?)

The question used to assess styles of coping and social support for periods of unhappiness was:

> One of the things we would like to know is how people face the unhappy period in their lives. Thinking of unhappiness you have had to face, what are some of the things that have helped you in these times?

Unlike the question about worries, respondents were not probed specifically for whether they talked over unhappiness with anyone if they did not spontaneously mention it.

In addition to these direct measures of adaptation and social support, we also used more indirect assessments of people's potential for adaptation. We described and used very simple measures of social integration that can be seen as a social context in which many styles of adaptation occur, including the use of social support. Specifically, we examined how men and women in 1957 and 1976 responded to ques-

TABLE 9.1

Items Used to Assess Social Context for Coping, Styles of Adaptation, and Quality of Support for Ways of Dealing with Worries and Periods of Unhappiness

Measure	Question
Social Context for Coping	
Visiting	...About how often do you get together with friends or relatives—I mean things like going out together or visiting in each other's homes? (Would you say more than once a week, once a week, a few times a month, once a month, or less than once a month?)
Membership in Organizations	Are you a member of any clubs and organizations— like a lodge, PTA, a community group or any other kind of group?" (Yes/No)
Marital Status	Are you married, separated, divorced, widowed, or have you never been married?
Styles of Adaptation and *Quality of Support*	(For worries): If something is on your mind that's bothering you or worrying you and you don't know what to do about it, what do you usually do? (For unhappiness): One of the things we'd like to know, is how people face the unhappy periods in their lives. Thinking of unhappiness you've had to face, what are some of the things that have helped you in those times?

tions about visiting with friends and relatives, and membership in organizations. We also used marital status as an indirect index of social integration.

Measures of Social Context for Coping, Styles of Adaptation, and Quality of Social Support for Handling Problems

Table 9.1 lists all the measures used in this chapter to assess the social context for coping and the styles of adaptation and social support people use to handle worries and periods of unhappiness.

MEASURES OF SOCIAL CONTEXT FOR COPING

To elicit the feelings of connectedness that people experience through visiting, the following question was asked:

About how often do you get together with friends or relatives—I mean things like going out together or visiting in each other's homes? (Would you say more than once a week, once a week, a few times a month, once a month, or less than once a month?)

To assess potential integration people experience through membership in organizations, the following direct question was asked:

Are you a member of any clubs and/or organizations, like a lodge, PTA, community group, or any kind of group? If yes, what are they?

To assess marital status, we asked the following question:

Are you married, separated, divorced, widowed, or have you never been married?

We were particularly interested in whether any of the nonmarried statuses define contexts for different styles of social support. One assumes that each marital status implies a different type of support environment: single people are more likely to be involved with families of origin, more so than divorced/separated or widowed people, who, in turn, often have children for support. Friendships may also be more central to nonmarried people than to married people.

MEASURES OF STYLES OF ADAPTATION

Parallel codes were adopted to assess styles of adaptation for periods of unhappiness and for worries. This allowed us to compare how people adapt to worries with how they adapt to periods of unhappiness. Chapter 2 suggested that "worries" represent life circumstances that evoke coping responses more often than do "periods of unhappiness." Worries are states of disequilibrium oriented toward the future. Periods of unhappiness, however, are low points in morale that do not necessarily have a future referent.

Coding distinctions used to assess styles of coping broke down into five broad categories. The first, *passive reactions,* included denial of the problem (e.g., forget about the worry or the period of unhappiness); *displacement* (e.g., worry about something else or notice how unhappy other people are); doing nothing, and continuing the tension (e.g., just keep on worrying). The second major category included *religious means* for dealing with difficulty, the most critical of which was prayer (e.g., praying or turning to the Bible or trusting in God). The third category, *coping response,* applied when people said they did something about their worries or their periods of unhappiness or actively searched for means to alleviate the difficulty. The fourth category, *informal social support,* was coded when the respondent mentioned talking things over with or seeking help from family, friends, neighbors, or the like. And the fifth category, *formal support,* was coded if the respondent mentioned a formal resource, such as clergy, doctor, or psychiatrist. By and large, we looked at first responses only. Since many people mention either prayer or informal support seeking as a second response, we kept special count of whether either was mentioned as a first *or* second response to the query about ways of dealing with worries and periods of unhappiness.

MEASURES OF QUALITY OF SOCIAL SUPPORT

Eight major categories of social support sought by people were used: (1) spouse only mentioned; (2) parent only; (3) children only; (4) family in general (or combinations of more than one type of family member, such as spouse and child, or some other family member not mentioned above); (5) clergy; (6) doctor; (7) mental health specialist; and (8) non-mental-health specialist, which included a generalized catch-all category of other people that were not coded as mental health specialists or as informal resources (such as a lawyer or a teacher or a group that the person belongs to).

Since there was a specific probe for people who were turned to when respondents were worried if they did not spontaneously mention a helping resource, we kept track of the resources mentioned by people when they were probed. We could thereby distinguish between spontaneous responses and those given only in response to a specific probe for helping resources. We assume that spontaneous responses are especially salient. Responses to the probe, however, give us more complete data about the nature of the potential support networks people have. So many respondents gave only one response to the question about people they turn to, that we set up code categories to capture information about *sole sources* of counsel during worries and periods of unhappiness. We specifically coded whether parents, children, and spouse were turned to as the *only* resource.[1]

In addition, we did some grouping to get a more general measure of how much a family member or in what combinations family members are used as a resource by people in 1957 and 1976. We grouped all family responses under one category and asked whether a family member was used as a sole resource in combination with other social supports or not reported at all as a resource. We used the same sort of coding of

---

[1] There was one difficulty with that decision. Since we have a code for the responses that cover family members in general, lumped with responses of combinations of family members, it was difficult to get a clear estimate of how much a spouse, a child, or a parent would be used in general by people as a resource. If a person mentioned talking to a spouse and mother, his/her responses would be coded in this general family category. We could not recover the piece of information—that he/she talked to his/her spouse. The "family" category is a catch-all that does not permit refined differentiations. Since the data were coded in that way for 1957, the same code was repeated again in 1976.

two responses with regard to whether friends were ever used for worries or periods of unhappiness.

Year Differences in Ways of Dealing with Personal Problems

Before we examine generational shifts in the ways people cope with their everyday life problems, we thought it important to contrast the social integrative context in 1957 and 1976 in which coping and social support occur. Just how integrated were people into the social order in 1957 and 1976? We will answer that question only indirectly, by looking at visiting, organizational membership, and marital differences for men and women in 1957 and 1976.

SOCIAL CONTEXT FOR COPING

Table 9.2 presents differences between the 1957 and 1976 respondents' social contexts for coping and social support. We find only one really striking difference in these comparisons. More of the 1957 respondents were married: 76 percent of the men and women in 1957 were married, but only 64 percent of the 1976 sample were married. There were more single and more divorced or separated people in 1976. A later cross-classification analysis of marital status (table 9.9) will show that the increases hold up only for the divorced/separated comparison when sex, age, and education are controlled. Having a much younger cohort in 1976 compared to 1957 accounts for the higher incidence of single people in the 1976 sample.

If marriage is a social bond that automatically enables people to help each other easily, the 1976 population was at a considerable disadvantage. That the 1976 sample is more populated with divorced, single, and separated men and women rather than married people, means that in 1976 fewer people had that easy access both to a spouse as a social support and to the networks of relationships evolving from the institution of marriage. We would speculate that more people in 1976 had to work at creating their own social networks for dealing with personal problems.

The multiple classification analyses in table 9.9 indicate that there are significant differences in informal visiting and the number of organizations mentioned by the 1976 and 1957 populations, but these differences are relatively small in the year comparisons in table 9.2. There is a significant tendency for the 1976 population to visit less and to belong to fewer organizations. Seven percent more of the 1976 population visit with friends and relatives less than weekly. Seven percent more of the 1976 population belong to no organizations at all.

TABLE 9.2
*Year Differences in Social Context
for Informal Support*

	1957 (%)	1976 (%)
Informal Visiting		
More than weekly	31	31
Weekly	34	27
More than once a month	16	20
Once a month or less	19	22
	100%	100%
Total Number	2,452	2,253
Number of Organizations Mentioned		
None	50	57
One	26	22
Two	13	11
Three or more	11	10
	100%	100%
Total Number	2,440	2,257
Marital Status		
Married	76	64
Single	6	11
Widowed	12	14
Divorced/separated	6	11
	100%	100%
Total Number	2,460	2,262

All in all, the social integrative context for coping with problems put the 1976 population at a potential disadvantage compared to the 1957 population. In 1976 men and women found themselves in fewer ritualized informal supportive relationships (visiting) and in fewer formal relationships that gave them institutional bases for social support (marriage, organiations). They had less access to social arrangements in everyday experiences than did people in the more tightly organized society of 1957. Not only were the 1976 men and women less likely to be married, but they were also somewhat less inclined to participate in the formal life of organizations and the informal life of visiting families and friends. In 1976 men and women had fewer easily available contexts for obtaining support. Knowing this disadvantage for the 1976 population, we are curious about how they handle problems. Do they actually make use of fewer supports than people in 1957? As we shall see, our results run counter to this hypothesis.

TABLE 9.3

Year Differences in Ways of Handling Worries and Periods of Unhappiness (First-Mentioned Responses Only)

Methods of Handling Personal Difficulties	Worries		Periods of Unhappiness	
	1957 (%)	1976 (%)	1957 (%)	1976 (%)
Passive Reactions				
Denial or Displacement	18	12	15	15
Do Nothing	10	9	7	6
Continues Tension	6	5	1	2
Coping Reactions				
Do Something About It	14	17	7	8
Informal Help-Seeking	25	35	20	28
Formal Help-Seeking	3	2	2	2
Help-Seeking, Not Ascertained				
Formal or Informal	2	1	3	5
Prayer	16	14	32	23
Other	2	1	5	6
Inappropriate: Respondent				
Never Worried or Unhappy	2	1	4	1
Not Ascertained	2	3	4	4
	100%	100%	100%	100%
Total Number	2,460	2,264	2,460	2,264

STYLES OF ADAPTATION TO WORRIES AND UNHAPPINESS

Table 9.3 presents data on ways the generations deal with worries and periods of unhappiness. The clearest year differences regarding worries indicate that the 1976 population is *less* passive in the way they respond. They are *more* likely either to turn to informal support or to do something active about their worries. Twenty-five percent of the 1957 population used some kind of informal support for dealing with worries; this has increased to 35 percent in 1976. While the social integrative context for support in 1976 reduced potential available supports, *more* rather than fewer people engaged in support-seeking behavior. Table 9.4, which indicates the percentage of people who report seeking support in at least one of two responses, shows that from 1957 to 1976 there has been an increase from 35 percent to 48 percent in the number of people mentioning seeking some kind of help from another person when they are worried.

Using prayer as a way to handle worries has not changed much from 1957 to 1976, whether we look at only the first response as listed in table 9.3 or two responses (table 9.5). Eighteen percent of the 1957 population said they pray when they worry; 17 percent in 1976. The result

TABLE 9.4

*Year Differences in Seeking Informal Support as Way
to Handle Worries (Spontaneous and Probed) and
Periods of Unhappiness (two responses coded)*

Source	Spontaneously Mentioned for Worries		Probed and Spontaneously Mentioned for Worries		Spontaneously Mentioned for Periods of Unhappiness	
	1957 (%)	1976 (%)	1957 (%)	1976 (%)	1957 (%)	1976 (%)
Mentioning seeking informal support	35	48	81	86	37	50
Total Number[a]	2,350	2,187	2,350	2,187	2,264	2,194

[a] Excludes respondents who were not ascertained.

TABLE 9.5

*Year Differences in Use of Prayer as Way to Handle Worries
and Periods of Unhappiness (two responses)*

	Worries		Periods of Unhappiness	
	1957 (%)	1976 (%)	1957 (%)	1976 (%)
Using Prayer	18	17	42	31
Total Number[a]	2,350	2,187	2,264	2,194

[a] Excludes respondents who were not ascertained.

will be quite different when we look at the use of prayer for periods of unhappiness.

Thus, the critical result seems to be that the 1976 population deals with worries by talking to people about their problems much more than people did in 1957. While in 1957 more people did nothing about these problems, men and women in 1976 at least talked over their worries with others. To the degree that other people can provide information, comfort, or affirmation of one's own ideas, then talking with them can be seen as an effective means of dealing with worries—certainly more effective than doing nothing.

A slightly different picture emerges when we look at the way the 1957 and 1976 populations handle periods of unhappiness. In table 9.3 there is not much evidence of change in frequency of passive reactions to unhappiness. While there is a slight increase in turning to other people during periods of unhappiness, the remarkable difference is the decline in the use of prayer. If we look at mention of prayer over *two* responses in table 9.5, we see that while 42 percent of the population in 1957 mention prayer as a way to handle unhappiness, this is true for only 31 percent in 1976. By contrast, analyses of two mentions of informal support seeking (table 9.4) reveal a sizable increase. Thirty-seven percent of the 1957 population turned to other people as a way to handle periods of unhappiness, and by 1976 this was true for exactly one-half of the population. Thus the 1976 population reported more use of other people in periods of unhappiness, but did not pray as much as the 1957 population. Whether that is a shift from a more passive style of coping with problems to a more active one is open to various interpretations. People with strong religious values may see prayer as a truly effective, active response to distress; people without religious orientations may view prayer as a resigned, passive way of dealing with problems. We have very little information about the specific effectiveness of prayer for maintaining well-being although we will attempt such an analysis at the end of the chapter. All we can say at this point is that while the earlier population used prayer to deal with periods of unhappiness more than any other coping mechanism, it is much less true of the 1976 population, for whom seeking social support is the most popular way of adapting to unhappiness.

Why has there been a decrease in the use of prayer for unhapiness in 1976, but not for worries? We would suggest that prayer in times of worry is a very goal-oriented response, a way to alleviate or ward off specific anxiety. This instrumentality of prayer might be common among deeply religious people, whose number may have remained relatively constant from 1957 to 1976. On the other hand, prayer in times of unhappiness may be much more a search for solace, therapy, or communion, even among the moderately religious. And that type of response may have diminished as a coping mechanism in 1976, both because the number of moderately committed religious people has diminished and because the number of clergy who invoke prayer as a way to deal with unhappiness has diminished as churches have become increasingly secularized and infused with psychologizing therapies.

Men and women in 1976 thus frequently turn to other people in times of worry and unhappiness. This pattern is much clearer in 1976 than it was in 1957. Formal support as a way of dealing with worries and unhappiness is mentioned infrequently in both years. We conclude that seeking informal support is *the* critical coping style people in the new generation adopt to deal with everyday life problems.

QUALITY OF SOCIAL SUPPORT

Table 9.6 lists the percentage of people in each year who sought help for their problems through various types of informal and formal resources. It is quite clear that the major resource used by people to talk

TABLE 9.6

Year Differences in Sources of Outside Help About Worries (Spontaneously and Probed)
and Periods of Unhappiness (first mentioned response only)

	Spontaneously Mentioned for Worries		Probed and Spontaneously Mentioned for Worries		Spontaneously Mentioned for Periods of Unhappiness	
	1957 (%)	1976 (%)	1957 (%)	1976 (%)	1957 (%)	1976 (%)
Informal						
Spouse Only	56	41	51	48	17	13
Parents Only	4	6	4	5	9	6
Children Only	3	4	5	5	4	3
"Family"; Family Combined with Above; Other Family Members	8	14	11	15	16	28
Friends, Neighbors	12	24	14	25	32	31
Other Acquaintances	1	2	2	3	1	1
Formal						
Clergy	4	2	3	2	5	1
Doctor	4	3	2	2	3	1
Mental Health Specialist	1	1	<1	1	1	2
Nonmental-Health Specialist	3	2	2	2	1	8
Not Ascertained	4	1	6	2	11	6
	100%	100%	100%	100%	100%	100%
Total Number[a]	726	871	2,013	1,903	615	786

[a] Based on number who sought help.

over their worries is their spouse alone. That is true for about half of the help seekers in both generations whether one computes the results based on only the spontaneously mentioned responses to worries or includes people who mention resources when specifically probed. Looking at only married respondents, in fact, we find that about 60 percent of the respondents in both years mention their spouses alone as their resource for handling worries. In the overall year comparison, however, the sole use of the spouse as resource has declined somewhat in 1976. In the new generation, more people evidently turn to other people as well as their marriage partner for help with their worries. We will see that this broadening of support sources in 1976 is a general theme. People in the new generation not only use *more* informal resources, but those they use are more varied in their relationship to the respondent.

This generalization can also be made about the differences between 1957 and 1976 in how people handle periods of unhappiness. More people in 1976 report their family, combinations of family members, or combinations of family and friends as resources for periods of unhappiness. By contrast, more people in 1957 referred only to a specific family resource. Thus, in 1976, we have an apparent increase in the variety of people used for support in periods of unhappiness as well as in ways people handle worries.

While there is a decline in the proportion of clergy and doctors in the support networks of people who seek help for periods of unhappiness, there is a corresponding increase in the use of mental-health specialists and non-mental-health specialists. The more specialized support found in both mental-health and non-mental-health experts is drawing people away from the more traditional formal support found in the clergy and in the medical professions. For our purposes in describing *informal* coping styles used by people in periods of unhappiness, however, the critical result is that, as with worries, people evidently now turn to a *variety* of resources.

This shift to combined patterns of informal support is further highlighted in our data when we analyze *two* mentions rather than just one. These appear in table 9.7 and allow the following conclusions: (1) exclusive dependence on the spouse and the family as a resource for handling periods of worries or unhappiness has decreased considerably from 1957 to 1976; (2) reliance on family in general has decreased and reliance on friends has risen.

These two conclusions are very important: they highlight the general characteristics of support networks for 1976 in contrast to 1957. With many more people unmarried, with many more people staying single longer or divorcing, a heavy reliance on friends emerges as a style of support. Nonrelated people's dependence on one another has become more characteristic of the support systems of the American population in 1976. The decline in family support is not strong but is significantly

TABLE 9.7
*Year Differences in Selected Types of Informal Help Sought
among Those Who Sought Help about Worries (Spontaneous and Probed)
and Periods of Unhappiness (two responses coded)*

Source	Spontaneously Mentioned for Worries		Probed and Spontaneously Mentioned for Worries		Spontaneously Mentioned for Periods of Unhappiness	
	1957 (%)	1976 (%)	1957 (%)	1976 (%)	1957 (%)	1976 (%)
Spouse Only						
Yes	57	42	54	41	20	14
Family Only[a]						
Yes	60	53	63	54	40	35
Family[a] in Combination with Others						
Yes	15	18	12	16	17	25
No Family						
Yes	20	27	19	28	33	34
Friend						
Yes	20	33	19	32	37	44
Total Number	832	1,047	2,019	1,905	615	786

[a] Could include spouse along with others in family.

present. We can view the declining use of prayer as a source of coping with unhappiness as another indication that people rely more on close interpersonal connections and are not tied to formal institutional ways of handling difficulties. The increased importance of friends is surprising in light of the overall year differences showing that fewer people in 1976 belonged to organizations and spent time visiting. It is likely that the support systems involving friends rather than family come not from formal organizations (such as the church, or business, or social clubs), nor from ritualized formal visiting that might more typically characterize obligatory family exchanges. It very likely comes from people developing ties in their informal associations at work or in their neighborhoods.

We wonder whether the promise of support that comes from reliance on close interpersonal ties is more than can be realized. Families who depend on one another are given institutionalized mechanisms for support. Friends do not have easy built-in ways to manage support. In our mobile society, a friend may be bewildered about how to comfort someone over loss of a parent whom the friend did not even know. A friend may not know how to react to the divorce of a couple both of

TABLE 9.8

Year Differences in Selected Types of Informal Help Sought
among Those Who Sought Help about Worries (Spontaneous and Probed)
and Periods of Unhappiness (two responses coded; married respondents only)

Source	Spontaneously Mentioned for Worries		Probed and Spontaneously Mentioned for Worries		Spontaneously Mentioned for Periods of Unhappiness	
	1957 (%)	1976 (%)	1957 (%)	1976 (%)	1957 (%)	1976 (%)
Spouse Only						
Yes	70	64	68	62	26	20
Family Only[a]						
Yes	68	64	70	65	43	43
Family[a] in Combination With Others						
Yes	15	18	12	16	16	24
No Family						
Yes	13	16	12	16	29	27
Friend						
Yes	14	23	13	22	34	39
Total Number	682	688	1,587	1,241	488	534

[a] Could include spouse along with others in family.

whom have been his/her friends. In contrast, family loyalties are near-ly always clear.

We also wonder whether the results we have been discussing are en-tirely due to the fact that people are less likely to be married in 1976. We reran year differences in selective types of informal help across two responses for married respondents only (table 9.8) and found virtually the same pattern of results that occurred in the whole sample. For example, for married people, the use of friends as social support for worries increased from 14 percent to 23 percent from 1957 to 1976; an increase from 34 percent to 39 percent occurs in use of friends during periods of unhappiness. The spouse as the only support has decreased across the two mentions from 70 percent to 64 percent among those who spontaneously mention some support for worries and from 26 per-cent to 20 percent for those who spontaneously mention some help for periods of unhappiness. Close interpersonal ties, whether in marriage, family relationships, or friendship, seem to be sought for support in the newer generation. Ritually structured support in family relation-ships is not given up entirely, but is probably used more selectively.

Multivariate Analyses of Informal Support

Multivariate analyses summarizing main and interactive effects of sex, age, education, and year are reported in three different tables. The first (table 9.9) summarizes the multivariate analyses of the measures of social context. The next two summarize multivariate analyses of ways of handling worries and periods of unhappiness, for first responses only (table 9.10) and for two mentions where they were analyzed (table 9.11).[2] These tables together will provide a mechanism for detecting qualifications needed about year differences we have highlighted and will alert us to sex, age, and education differences in ways of handling problems and the nature of social support.

QUALIFICATIONS OF YEAR DIFFERENCES AS RESULT OF MULTIVARIATE
ANALYSES

Are there ways in which we erred in attending or not attending to year differences in the previous sections which should be qualified as a result of the multivariate analyses in tables 9.9 to 9.11? We need to qualify little of what has been said. There is a surprising lack of change in year differences produced by including control variables.

Only two findings alert us to different year comparisons. One is that there are proportionately more young, unmarried people in 1976 than there were in 1957. Twelve percent of men and women who were 21–29 in 1957 were never married; 28 percent of the comparable group in 1976 were never married. This reminds us that in 1976 we have a particularly large cohort of young people who had not (yet) turned to marriage as a formal institution for social support.

The second qualification also involves young people. Although young people generally pray less in periods of unhappiness, and people in 1976 pray less with regard to these times of difficulty; the young people in 1976 particularly "underutilize" prayer as a solution to periods of unhappiness. Perhaps, as the American people as a whole became disenchanted with religious forms and more attracted to direct interpersonal social supports as a way of coping with life difficulties, young people socialized as children during the generation of religious disenchantment may have been particularly susceptible to this view. Older groups in 1976 may have been less affected by the social pressure to abandon prayer as a mode of coping because they had experienced early socialization to use prayer for dealing with misfortune. Older

[2]Analyses were also carried out for the probed and spontaneously mentioned sources of support for worries. Although the probed data gave us a larger proportion of people mentioning any type of support, in no instance did the probed data yield results that contradicted those from spontaneous responses. This is an interesting methodological finding in and of itself, and seems to justify simplifying our presentation by attending only to spontaneous mention or help for worries.

TABLE 9.9

Summary of Multivariate Analyses of Social Context For Coping

	Relationship(s) Required[a] to Reproduce Observed Cross-Classification of Measures by Age × Education × Year × Sex				
	Main Effects[d]				
Social Context For	**Age**	**Education**	**Year**	**Sex**	**Interaction**
Visiting					
Men	—[b]	—[b]	—[b]	M<F	—[b]
Women	Y>MA,O	G<H<C	57>76	—[c]	
Belongs to No Organizations	Y>MA,O	G<H<C	57>76	—[c]	
Men	—[b]	—[b]	—[b]		—[b]
Women	Y>MA,O	G>H>C	57<76	—[c]	
		G>H>C	57<76	—[c]	Age × Education
					Age × Education; Age × Year
Marital Status					
Married	Y,MA>O		57>76	M>F	
Single	Y>MA,O			M>F	
Widowed	Y<MA,O	G<H<C		F>M	
Divorced/Separated	Y,MA>O		57<76		

[a] See Footnote a of Table 2.11 for an explanation of "Required."

[b] Cross-classification is run separately for men and women because a complex four-way interaction involving both the measure of well-being and sex needed to explain the five-variable cross-classification.

[c] Sex effects inappropriate in disaggregated data.

[d] See Footnote a of Table 2.11 for discussion of description of "Main Effects."

TABLE 9.10

Summary of Multivariate Analyses of Spontaneously Mentioned Ways of Handling Worries and Periods of Unhappiness (first responses only)

Ways of Handling Worries and Unhappiness	Relationship(s) Required[a] to Reproduce Observed Cross-Classification of Measures by Age × Education × Year × Sex				
	Main Effect[b]				Interaction
	Age	Education	Year	Sex	
A. Worries					
Overall Assessment:					
Passive		G>H>C	57>76	M>F	
Prayer	Y<MA<O	G>H>C		M<F	
Coping		G<H<C		M>F	
Informal help	Y>MA>O	G<C<H	57<76	M<F	
Sources of Help:					
Friends			57<76		
Acquaintances				M<F	
Parents only	Y>MA>O				
Children only	Y<MA<O				
Clergy			57>76		
Doctor	Y<MA<O				
B. Periods of Unhappiness					
Overall Assessment:					Age × Year
Passive				M>F	
Prayer	Y<MA<O	G,H>C	57>76	M<F	
Coping		G<H<C		M>F	
Informal help	Y>MA>O		57<76	M<F	
Sources of Help:					
Spouse only				M>F	
Parents only	Y>MA>O				
Children only	Y<MA<O			M<F	
"Family"			57<76		
Clergy			57>76		
Doctor	Y<MA<O		57>76		
Mental health specialist			57<76		
Non-mental health specialist	Y>MA,O		57<76		

[a] See Footnote a of Table 2.11 for an explanation of "Required."

[b] See Footnote a of Table 2.11 for discussion of description of "Main Effects."

TABLE 9.11

Summary of Multivariate Analyses of Ways of Handling Worries and Periods of Unhappiness (two responses coded)

Ways of Handling Worries and Periods of Unhappiness	Relationship(s) Required[a] to Reproduce Observed Cross-Classification of Measures by Age × Education × Year × Sex[b]				
	Main Effect[c]				
	Age	Education	Year	Sex	Interaction
A. Worries					
Prayer:	—[d]	—[d]	—[d]	M<F	—[d]
Men	Y<MA,O	G>H,C		—[b]	
Women	Y<MA<O	G>H>C	57>76	—[b]	
Help Sought?	Y>MA>O	G<H,C	57<76	M<F	
Sources of Help:[e]					
Spouse only sought (married only)			57>76	M>F	
Family sought			57>76		
family only		H>G>C			
family in combination		G<H<C	57<76		
no family		G>H>C	57<76	M<F	
Friend sought		G,H<C			
B. Periods of Unhappiness					
Prayer:	—[d]	—[d]	—[d]	M<F	—[d]
Men	Y<MA,O		57>76	—[b]	
Women	Y<MA<O	G,H>C	57>76	—[b]	
Help Sought?	Y>MA>O		57<76	M<F	
Sources of Help:[e]					
Spouse only sought (married only)			57<76		
Family sought:					
family only		G,H>C			
family in combination		G<H<C	57<76	M<F	
no family		G>H,C			
Friend sought	Y>MA,O		57<76		

[a] See Footnote a of Table 2.11 for an explanation of "Required."

[b] Sex effects inappropriate in disaggregated data.

[c] See Footnote a of Table 2.11 for discussion of description of "Main Effects."

[d] Cross-classification is run separately for men and women because a complex four-way interaction involving both the measure of well-being and sex needed to explain the five-variable cross-classification.

[e] For those who sought help.

people in 1976, having been taught earlier to pray, may continue to use prayer from time to time in spite of general disillusionment with religion. Younger groups, never having been socialized in religious rituals, rarely use religion as a mode of adaptation to their difficulties. In 1957, 33 percent of the youngest group (from 21 to 29) reported that they used prayer during periods of unhappiness; the comparable figure for 1976 youngest groups is 19 percent.

Overall, the youngest group in the 1976 sample might be characterized as the group which has developed no strong bonds to formal institutions of any kind. As we have indicated at many points earlier in this chapter and in other chapters, the new generation has called into question a number of formalized modes of reacting, perhaps to their own detriment, at times, but nevertheless in a style that is consistent with a new value orientation that stresses individualized and interpersonal styles of dealing with psychological distress and life challenges.

Aside from these two results brought to our attention through the multivariate analyses, the other findings summarized in these tables generally confirm statements we have made about year differences in social supports and ways of dealing with life problems. The tables once again underscore the fact that more people are turning to informal resources as a way of dealing with their problems, are less passive about the way they handle problems, are less likely to use prayer as a way of dealing with difficulties, are more likely to use a variety of resources rather than any single resource, and are *less* likely to be in situations that permit easy access to formal social support such as ritual visiting and membership in formal groups. One result that needs further underscoring is that men and women in 1976 are more likely to turn to non-mental-health specialists as well as mental-health specialists in dealing with periods if unhappiness. When we examine resources included in the group of non-mental-health specialists, we see that they are largely semiformal therapeutic groups of various sorts: encounter groups, T-groups, Alcoholics Anonymous, and the like. Thus, even though there has been a reduction in the participation in formal organizations by the new generation of people, organizations that might have brought social support very easily, there has been some movement toward these more structured therapeutic informal groups as a way of dealing with life crises. It is hard to categorize these groups as being either professional or informal since they are usually characterized as self-help groups.

Sex Differences in Informal Coping with Problems

In both 1957 and 1976, slightly more women than men talked about visiting friends and family frequently, while equal numbers of women and men report belonging to formal organizations. Table 9.12 (selected sex comparisons in informal support) shows that 68 percent of the women in 1957 and 60 percent of the women in 1976 said they visited friends and family weekly or more frequently. Comparable percentages for men are 62 percent in 1957 and 56 percent in 1976. This is not a large difference, but clearly one that suggests that women are somewhat more affiliative in their daily lives and informal contacts. Another finding presented in table 9.12 is that in both 1957 and 1976 more men than women in our samples were married.[3] Thus, with regard to marital status, we observe the important fact that a large majority of men are married and their wives can provide readily available, albeit occasionally ritualized, social support. While the majority of women in our samples are also married, many fewer of them are in that position than men. Paradoxically, however, slightly more men than women are also single. The most striking result from the examination of sex differences in marital status (table 9.12) is the large proportion of widowed women in both 1957 and 1976.

Twenty percent of the women in our 1976 sample are widowed. This is a very interesting piece of data in relation to social support. Many people (Berardo, 1976; Lopata, 1973) have pointed out that widowhood is an ambiguous status for everyone: the widow herself and also her friends and family. There are no clear directives for the widow or her friends and family to establish social networks she may need after her husband has died. Having earlier established a social network as a couple, the widowed person may wish to maintain that same network but experience constraints about doing so. It is as if the social network engaged by a couple is oriented toward *couples* and unable to include someone who is just "part" of the unit that made up the network in a prior time. This further suggests that older women might have somewhat more difficult times maintaining social-support networks than older men, who are more likely to be married.

We find it difficult to draw firm conclusions about the social context for support and ways of handling problems available differentially for men and women. On the one hand, women are slightly more involved in informal social contacts. On the other hand, more men than women are married, which, in itself, affords them greater access to the most critical social support available in human relationships.

[3] We should remind ourselves that our samples are residential samples and thus many nonmarried men and women who are in more institutionalized settings may not be represented.

TABLE 9.12
Selected Sex Differences in the Social Context for Coping, Style of Adaptation and Social Support Used for Problems of Worries, and Periods of Unhappiness (by year)

	1957		1976	
Measure	Men (%)	Women (%)	Men (%)	Women (%)
A. Social Context for Coping				
Visiting:				
Weekly or more	62	68	56	60
Marital Status:				
Married	84	73	73	57
Single	8	6	14	10
Widowed	5	17	5	20
Divorced/separated	3	4	8	13
B. Style of Adaptation				
Handling Worries:				
One Mention:				
Passive	38	30	30	23
Coping	21	9	27	13
Two Mentions:				
Prayer	9	26	10	22
Seek help	32	38	41	52
Handling Unhappiness:				
One Mention:				
Passive	27	20	25	20
Coping	10	5	11	5
Two Mentions:				
Prayer	30	50	23	37
Seek help	34	40	46	53
C. Social Support (for those who seek help)				
Worries:				
Spouse only	69	70	72	58
(married only)	(288)	(394)	(272)	(416)
Friends	15	23	32	34
	(324)	(508)	(376)	(671)
Unhappiness:				
Children only	17	4	2	6
	(303)	(483)	(253)	(359)
Total Number[a]	1,077	1,483	960	1,304

NOTE: Numbers in parentheses are total number of persons in each group.

[a] The numbers will vary somewhat depending on number of nonascertained responses in a particular computation of percentages; the NS for the sex comparisons on social support are listed in parentheses in the table because the percentages are based only on those who sought help.

The results in table 9.12 that highlight critical sex differences in styles of adapting to problems also show other paradoxical patterns. Although men are clearly more passive in the way they handle worries and unhappiness (e.g., do nothing; don't think about it), they are also clearly much more likely to cope (do something about it). Women are much more likely to seek help from others or to turn to prayer as ways to handle these problems. In chapter 2 we learned that more women than men have sought formal help for personal problems. Thus we have a picture of men compared to women. Although they report "doing something" about their problems more than women do, they do not easily avail themselves of one of the critical forms of coping available to people: talking things over with a formal or informal resource. Nor do they as easily make use of prayer. As a result, they either do something very direct or do nothing at all about what worries them or causes them unhappiness.

It is clear that women turn more often to informal sources of help. While 52 percent of the women in 1976 turn to some help for handling worries, only 41 percent of the men do. If we view prayer as a form of help, then men are less likely to use that informal help as well (see table 9.12). Without seeking help from either loved ones or professionals, men either cope directly on their own, try to banish thoughts about their problems from their minds, or end up doing nothing.

We find additional sex differences in coping styles when we look further at the quality of the social support for people who seek help. Married men are more likely to turn to their spouse *alone* as a way of dealing with worries. In 1976 that was particularly apparent: 72 percent of married men who sought help said they spoke to their wives and their wives alone in handling their worries, while this was true for only 58 percent of the married women who sought some support. Women are more likely to use friends as a source of help, a result that meshes well with the fact that they visit friends and neighbors more than men do. Women just talk more to people including their friends than men do; men, if they talk, often talk only to their wives. Men depend heavily on their marriages to handle their difficulties.

One further minor result: more women than men turn to their children in times of unhappiness. Not very many men and women report children as a resource for handling periods of unhappiness. In 1976, 1 percent of the male help-seekers and 4 percent of the female help-seekers talked to their children. These results could be explained by the fact that more women than men experience the death of a spouse. And in these times particularly, women may turn to children as a source of help. However, we looked at the results only for married men and women and found that the sex difference remains. Married women talk to their children during periods of unhappiness more than married men do.

TABLE 9.13

Education Differences in the Use of Prayer for Coping with Problems of Worries or Periods of Unhappiness (by sex × year)

		Education									
		Grade School		Some High School		High School Graduate		Some College		College Graduate	
Use of Prayer	Sex	1957 (%)	1976 (%)	1957 (%)	1976 (%)	1957 (%)	1976 (%)	1957 (%)	1976 (%)	1957 (%)	1976 (%)
For Worries	Men	15	17	8	10	4	9	5	11	7	7
	Women	32	35	28	25	20	19	22	17	17	12
For Unhappiness	Men	31	20	26	24	27	24	34	21	36	26
	Women	58	47	48	42	49	35	40	30	44	26
Total Number[a]	Men	367	154	206	125	255	299	124	198	118	178
	Women	435	226	305	222	419	467	123	212	92	168

[a] Numbers vary somewhat depending on the nonascertained responses in a particular computation of percentage.

An interesting phenomenon also worth mentioning is the differential effect that education seems to have on whether or not men and women turn to prayer in times of worries and unhappiness. These results are reported in table 9.13. The significant interactions in table 9.10 suggest that while grade school men pray considerably more than other men as a way to cope with problems or worries, there is not much difference between high school– and college-educated men. This seems not to be so for women, who show a gradual decline in the use of prayer with greater education in both 1957 and 1976. This same result seems to be true for women in their reports of how they handle periods of unhappiness: the more educated they are, the less likely they are to turn to prayer to deal with unhappiness. For men, there is little relationship between education and turning to prayer in times of unhappiness. These results can be looked at in a different frame: while in both years there is very little difference between male and female college graduates' use of prayer to cope with periods of unhappiness, there are very large sex differences in the less educated groups in both years.

What can we conclude from this pattern of results? We think it points primarily to the effects college education has on women's ways of dealing with problems. We assume that prayer is a way of coping among people who feel personally powerless. A college education is a means by which women become more confident about their own competence and autonomy. It also brings them closer to power positions in our society either through the marriages it helps them secure or the occupations it helps them enter. Men, except for those who are poorly educated, are automatically given a certain degree of power through occupational activity Thus, poorly educated men and less-than-college-educated women share that sense of powerlessness that fosters the use of prayer for spiritual guidance during personal troubles.

AGE DIFFERENCES IN INFORMAL COPING WITH PROBLEMS

Table 9.14 presents selected comparisons of age groups in the social contexts they experience for coping, styles of adaptation they use for dealing with problems, and the quality of their social support. These results summarize the major age differences found in the multivariate analyses compiled in tables 9.9 to 9.11.

First, let us look at age differences in the social context for coping. For all of the assessments of social context, we considered men and women together. Although there were slight differences in the way age related to some of the social context variables for the two sexes, these were not strong enough to warrant specific attention.

Younger people visit more often with friends and relatives than older people do, but are less likely to belong to organizations. Thus one

TABLE 9.14

Selected Age Differences in the Social Context for Coping, Style of Adaptation and Social Support Used for Coping with Problems of Worries and Periods of Unhappiness (by year)

Measure	21-29 1957 (%)	21-29 1976 (%)	30-39 1957 (%)	30-39 1976 (%)	40-49 1957 (%)	40-49 1976 (%)	50-59 1957 (%)	50-59 1976 (%)	60-64 1957 (%)	60-64 1976 (%)	65+ 1957 (%)	65+ 1976 (%)
Number[a]	(453)	(553)	(584)	(463)	(515)	(341)	(390)	(342)	(153)	(169)	(353)	(397)
A. Social Context for Coping												
Visiting: Weekly or more	81	70	68	57	60	56	64	53	60	46	55	55
Number of Organizations: Belong to none	59	67	40	51	46	54	46	51	58	55	59	57
Marital Status: Married	81	60	88	74	85	79	73	73	65	57	45	37
Single	12	28	5	9	4	3	6	4	5	8	8	6
Widowed	1	4	1	1	4	5	14	12	25	25	43	51
Divorced/separated	6	12	6	16	7	13	7	11	5	10	4	6

B. Style of Adaptation

Handling Worries: Two mentions												
prayer	8	7	14	12	18	18	27	20	21	26	30	29
help sought	51	62	43	52	34	47	26	42	23	38	26	31
Handling Unhappiness: Two mentions												
prayer	33	19	39	26	43	34	47	37	46	42	48	40
help sought	49	62	40	53	34	51	33	45	32	43	28	37

C. Social Support (for those who sought help)

Worries:												
Parents only	7	12	6	8	2	2	0	1	0	0	0	0
Children only	0	0	1	0	2	2	5	6	15	12	16	19
Number	(203)	(300)	(218)	(199)	(141)	(128)	(80)	(109)	(27)	(41)	(55)	(94)
Unhappiness:												
Parents only	16	11	7	8	9	5	5	4	7	2	3	0
Children only	1	1	1	2	3	2	9	4	11	7	8	0
Nonmental-health specialist	1	1	2	0	0	4	1	4	7	7	0	6
Number	(155)	(249)	(165)	(171)	(117)	(116)	(85)	(102)	(28)	(42)	(59)	(101)

[a] Numbers vary somewhat depending on nonascertained responses in a particular computation of percentage; the numbers for the age comparison in social support are listed in parentheses in the table because these percentages are based only on those who sought help.

might expect the styles of coping of young people to be more geared to the informal social context, and the styles of coping of the older people to be more tied to established community sources of support. This is very important because informal resources people obtain through visiting and the like are self-initiated—a style appropriate to the young, while the formal social supports that come from organized groups may come more directly from membership itself and less from self-initiated activity—a style appropriate for older people. For example, belonging to a church is a critical credential for certain kinds of support around such crises as death or illness in the family. Organized groups within churches often visit members who are ill or in the hopsital. It is usually a prescription for the clergy to visit the sick and attend the mourning. Such problems occur more frequently in the lives of older or elderly people. In another sense, self-initiated informal contact seems more appropriate for young people and organizational membership more appropriate for older people. Men and women affirm their well-being by participating effectively with others. As people age and their easy access to and energy for participating informally with others are reduced—children leave home, parents and lifetime friends die—organizational membership may compensate for diminished everyday connection to others.

Age is clearly critical in determining another social context factor for coping: marital status. Although the following findings sound like demographic truisms, they should be kept in mind as we think about age difference in social support. Older people are more likely to be widowed than young people. As discussed earlier, widowhood as a role status can present complications to social support. Young people are clearly more likely to be single and therefore lack the easy access to a committed personal relationship with someone of the opposite sex. Far different circumstances prevail for middle-aged people who generally are married, or at least not single. There are slight year differences in the age group which contains the most divorced and separated people, but these results seem unimportant. The critical result among this array of findings is the simple fact that there are many more widows and widowers at older ages. Of those sixty-five and older, 63 percent of the women and 14 percent of the men are widowed. In passing, we should note this very strong sex difference in the marital status of the elderly: the majority of elderly women are without husbands; the majority of elderly men are still married.

Let us now look at styles of adaptation across the life cycle. It is quite clear in table 9.14 that older age groups in both years are more likely to use prayer to handle both worries and unhappiness and are less likely to seek outside help from either informal or formal sources. For example, in 1976, 29 percent of the oldest age group report using prayer for worries where only 22 percent of the youngest age group do; 62 percent of the youngest group, in turn, use outside help compared to 31 percent of the older group.

We know from examing readiness for self-referral to professionals in chapter 2 that older people are less likely to turn for help in times of stress. We argue that elderly people are skeptical about the possibility that seeking formal help will change things. This is underscored in our analysis of informal resources. Older people are clearly less likely than younger people to report turning to other people (either family or friends) in times of difficulty, worries, or unhappiness. Among people 21 to 29 in 1976, 62 percent say they sought help in times of unhappiness; 37 percent of the people 65 years and older say they sought such help.

The reduced tendency of older people to seek help may not be entirely a function of their seeing their reduced potential for change. Other factors may also play a part. Rejecting both formal and informal resources may be possible for older people because they are aware of their own "wisdom." Their accumulated experience may shift their focus from other people as sources of help to their own potential for self-reliant coping. One can also argue that fewer resources are available to people as they move through the life cycle. Parents die; spouses and friends die. Nevertheless, as significant people are lost, other family members and friends may fill the vacuum.

Neither the increased wisdom of older people nor the sheer loss of supportive people in their world seems to be sufficient bases for the remarkable drop in the use of the social support among older people. Another explanation seems required. We suggest two general explanations, one which makes the assumption that we can use cross-sectional age differences to infer life-cycle changes, and the other which requires that we look at adaptation styles in birth cohorts.

Let us first assume that the repeated age results in 1957 and 1976 reflect an important general shift in adaptation styles of people across the life cycle. We would suggest the following: as people get older, they become aware of the limitations of outside resources for handling the worries and unhappiness that life presents. Either older people become increasingly disappointed in the capacity of others to help, or the specific problems faced by people as they get older are not ones that can be easily resolved by other people's support. Is there not a limit to the comfort that a sympathetic person communicates during times of mourning? Another person may lack resources to comfort someone facing the death of a spouse or child. As people experience more serious difficulties in life, the more limited comfort or sympathy may seem. The more people realize that failing health and mortality cannot be changed or affected by the assurances of other people, the less they may seek support from social networks. Thus, it is not just growing disillusionment with people as willing helpers, but the increased realization that for the critical issues facing the aged, other people can offer only limited support.

In contrast, one can speculate about the increased turning to "otherworldly" beliefs for handling problems among the elderly—turning to religion and prayer. These spiritual solutions to problems may become more relevant as more serious problems with aging are encountered and greater disillusionment with social support occurs. Perhaps there is no direct relationship between the decline in using social support for handling problems and increased turning to prayer, but clearly there could be an indirect connection between the two. The fact that the data presented in table 9.14 demonstrate a *gradual* linear increase in the use of prayer to handle problems in both 1957 and 1976 as one moves across the life cycle suggests that turning to prayer is not a coping mechanism that develops suddenly when people vividly face the issue of dying. Furthermore, the gradual linear increase with age in the use of prayer mirrors the gradual linear decline with age in the use of social support.

Now let us look at these data in relation to birth cohort. The groups are reconstituted as cohorts in table 9.15. We are impressed with the results that aside from a few comparisons, *cohorts are very consistent in their use of either prayer or support seeking as styles of adaptation.* There is a remarkable consistency in each cohort's tendency to talk over worries with someone or pray when unhappy, regardless of the point at which the assessment was made—in 1957 or nineteen years later in 1976. These patterns strongly suggest that these are styles learned early—in childhood or adolescent socialization. Each era may generate a style by historical circumstances. As we have become a more affluent, secular, and psychological culture, we have apparently increasingly socialized our adolescents to pray less and talk more. This interpretation has to be modified for the cohort results about using prayer for handling worries, which can be interpreted more easily as a developmental change.

Regardless of whether we interpret the finding as developmental or as a cohort phenomenon, in either year the different age groups are characteristically social or nonsocial (prayer) in their adaptation to worries and unhappiness. Anyone who wants to help people take advantage of "natural" coping styles will have to take these results into account.

Finally, let us examine the kind of social support used by people of different ages who actually seek help in times of worries or unhappiness. Table 9.14 presents one set of results which, while not earthshaking, is critical to keep in mind as we plot the social-support patterns for people across the life cycle: younger people are more likely to turn to their parents alone as a source of support, and older people are more likely to turn to their children alone as a source of support during times of difficulties. The availability of parents as a source for young adults and the availability of children as a resource for older adults are

TABLE 9.15

Birth Cohort Differences in the Use of Prayer and Support-Seeking for Worries and Periods of Unhappiness (two mentions, by year)

	Year	Cohort 1 (Born 1928-1936)		Cohort 2 (Born 1918-1927)		Cohort 3 (Born 1908-1917)		Cohort 4 (Born 1898-1907)		Cohort 5 (Born Before 1897)	
Style of Adaptation		1957 (%)	1976 (%)	1957 (%)	1976 (%)	1957 (%)	1976 (%)	1957 (%)	1976 (%)	1957 (%)	1976 (%)
For Handling Worries											
Prayer		8	19 [a]	14	20 [a]	18	25 [a]	27	33	27	31
Support-Seeking		51	47	43	42	34	36	26	30	21	27
Total Number		440	329	570	327	496	295	372	168	461	64
For Periods of Unhappiness											
Prayer		33	34	39	37	42	40	47	41	48	41
Support-Seeking		49	51	40	45	34	42 [a]	33	38	30	29
Total Number		411	325	545	324	478	289	364	167	454	66

[a] Percentage difference in box is significant ($p < .05$).

structured into life-cycle changes. As parents die, they are no longer available. As people move into families of procreation from their families of origin, men and women turn to their spouses as major sources of support. As people move through the life cycle and children become more available as responsible others, they, too, can be a source of support for older people. It would be interesting to find out more about respondents who consistently use family ties as their only source of support as they move through the life course. Do young people who turn to parents as their only resource have something in common with middle-aged people who rely on their spouses and older people who turn to the children as sole supports during times of worry and periods of unhappiness?

A further result in table 9.14 bears mentioning: younger people, especially in 1976, tended to select a group of helpers during periods of unhappiness that were labeled as non-mental-health specialists. Many of these were not people but "groups," such as encounter groups and other semitherapeutic groups, which young people, particularly in 1976, report as being of help to them during periods of unhappiness. This resource should not be dismissed; it is a new mode of establishing group support when friendship and family supports are not sufficient or do not fulfill the needs that young people especially have. These quickly established therapeutic groups may have special value for younger men and women in times of crisis.

Education Differences in Informal Coping with Problems

Table 9.16 summarizes critical education differences found in 1957 and 1976 in respondents' informal coping patterns. Multivariate analyses for coping (tables 9.9 and 9.10) underpin these results.

Omitted from table 9.16 is one finding already presented: educated people tend to pray less in times of worry or unhappiness. The results reported earlier in table 9.13 show that the change from high school to college education for women is critical in producing a decrease in the use of prayer as a way of handling difficulties, while such a change does not occur between the high school and college men. These results can be reexamined in the context of status differences independent of sex differences. We clearly see in these results that the higher their status in our society, the less likely men and women are to use prayer to deal with difficulties. We have already suggested why this may be so. Prayer may be a form of coping for people who have less direct actual power in the society. We might think of prayer as a search for help from outside the existing social structure. The less power people have in society, the less they may want or be able to use available social structures (either friendships, families, or formal structures) to handle and cope with the problems of life. This kind of interpretation is supported in the finding that less educated people generally participate less directly in the informal and formal settings that we used to measure social integration. Table 9.16 shows that more educated people visit friends and families a lot more than the less educated. Furthermore, the more educated participate in many more formal organizations. More educated people in our society are also less likely to be widowed. Thus, they less often confront the difficulties of establishing a social life in a society that disadvantages the nonmarried.

In addition to the greater use of prayer among people of lower status in our society, we note other styles of coping that are more typical of the uneducated. Table 9.16 shows that less educated people more often react passively to worries and less often take direct coping action about worries and unhappiness. In particular, they are less likely to seek help for their worries from other people. The results are not as dramatic for periods of unhappiness, yet they are significant. Again we would argue that these data reflect the fact that people with higher education are granted power in the system. Perhaps people are *less* likely to turn to others for help when they lack power. It is almost as if credentials of status (e.g., education) are necessary for people to feel comfortable about asking for help even in times of personal trouble. Asking for help from a position of weakness implies that the help seeker has few resources to offer in exchange for help given. This conceptualization is reminiscent of Blau's insightful discussion of social exchange in organizational life (Blau, 1960), in which he suggests that people of less status are less willing to enter into interaction with people of higher status because they feel disadvantaged in power in the social interaction. An alternative to people's feeling powerless in interpersonal relationships, even when they are distressed, is to avoid these interactions altogether, perhaps especially when they would normally ask for help.

Turning to the specific types of social support sought by people who have used help, we find that especially in 1976 people of higher status use friends in times of worry more than do people of lower status. More statusful people are more likely to see people outside the family in combination with family members in their social networks for times of worries. The lowest educational groups tend either not to seek any family help at all, or to use their family as the only resource in times of unhappiness or worries. We cannot resist the interpretation that people of lower status have less varied resources available for times of crisis.

We must conclude that education, as it marks status in life as well as potential for enlisting resources from a social network, has a profound effect on styles of coping and on the way people structure their social supports. The educated turn to others more. It may be that others are more available to them, but it may be that the educated are more comfortable in enlisting others and know better how to do it. The less edu-

TABLE 9.16

Selected Education Differences in the Social Context for Coping, Style of Adaptation, and Social Support Used for Problems of Worries and Periods of Unhappiness (by year)

	Education									
	Grade School		Some High School		High School Graduate		Some College		College Graduate	
Measure	1957 (%)	1976 (%)	1957 (%)	1976 (%)	1957 (%)	1976 (%)	1957 (%)	1976 (%)	1957 (%)	1976 (%)
A. Social Context for Coping										
Visiting:										
Less than monthly	27	30	17	22	15	20	15	20	15	18
Number of Organizations:										
Belong to 2 or more	10	10	19	12	30	19	41	27	58	39
Marital Status:										
Widowed	20	34	9	16	6	10	8	9	4	2
B. Style of Adaptation										
Handling Worries:										
One mention										
passive	41	34	32	26	30	24	26	23	30	23
coping	8	9	14	16	16	16	26	21	21	23
Two mentions										
help sought	26	34	36	44	43	51	38	48	42	57
Handling Unhappiness:										
One mention										
coping	6	4	6	5	6	8	6	10	13	11
Two mentions										
help sought	31		39		41		4?		39	

C. Social Support (for those who sought help)

Worries:										
Family sought										
family only	54	59	64	57	66	57	57	45	54	44
family in combination with others	10	11	14	12	15	13	23	22	19	29
no family	32	29	16	30	15	27	17	29	20	24
Friends sought	23	27	17	29	19	31	16	40	22	40
Total Number[a]	(192)	(123)	(174)	(150)	(285)	(383)	(92)	(196)	(86)	(194)
Unhappiness:										
Family sought										
family only	40	37	42	35	40	40	35	29	35	32
family in combination with others	9	17	17	31	20	24	24	29	21	25
no family	42	40	32	30	29	30	27	35	31	37
Total Number[a]	(170)	(102)	(144)	(131)	(195)	(291)	(70)	(147)	(52)	(148)

[a] Numbers vary somewhat depending on nonascertained responses in a particular computation of percentage; the numbers for the education comparison in social support are listed in parentheses in the table because these percentages are based only on those who sought help.

cated either do nothing, do not cope with the problems that arise, or use prayer as a method of dealing with troubles, turning to some spiritual guidance outside of the social network in which their lower social status is not particularly valued. When people of lower social status do invoke a helping system, it tends to be limited and less varied than that used by higher-status people who have access to a larger variety of channels for social support.

Social/Demographic Factors and Informal Coping with Problems

In addition to seeing how sex, age, and education might affect the ways in which people deal with personal difficulties and the context for such coping, we investigated the role of other social and demographic factors. We followed the same analysis strategies used in the last chapter. We performed multivariate analyses relating each of the characteristics studied in that chapter to two measures of coping: whether the person reported seeking help from someone when worried (*talking when worried*) and whether the person said she/he prayed during periods of unhappiness (*praying when unhappy*) with a person's sex, age, education, and year, as well as with each demographic variable. Two measures of social context for coping were also analyzed similarly: frequency of reported visiting with friends and relatives (*visiting*) and number of organizations in which the respondent reports being a member (*number of organizations*). These four measures give us a range of factors. *Talking when worried* gives us an indication of spontaneous social-support seeking for day-to-day problems, while *visiting* gives us an indication of the context out of which support can occur. *Praying when unhappy* taps a religious mode of dealing with problems. *Number of organizations* is a contextual measure of formal integration settings that can promote both social support and religious coping.

A summary of major results from these multivariate analyses appears in table 9.17. For each measure, we have checked the demographic or social characteristic for which a significant effect occurs, independent of *sex, age, education (and year differences) and their interactions.*[4] We also show an abbreviated summary of the effect. (For example, the first effect checked as a significant main effect is income under praying when unhappy and it is summarized as "Low > High," indicating that low-

---

[4]As in chapter 8, a main effect is checked if it is needed in the model that best reproduces the contingency table. It is also checked if it is nested in a significant interaction but as a net effect in a lambda comparison (see chapter 2, p. 67), significant at $p < .01$.

income people pray more when unhappy than do high-income people.) There are many significant interactions—sometimes very complex ones. We summarize only those which are easily understood and meaningful.

Most of the significant main effects are also tabulated in distributions in tables 9.18 and 9.19. We will not review all of these, but will highlight some in the integration of findings which follows. We see three major themes in these results. Let us discuss each in turn.

1. *Prayer as a means of handling problems is a coping style of impoverished groups, and, as such, represents a resignation to life, a retreat from any sense of direct personal efficacy in the social world, an expression of hope through spiritual as opposed to social salvation.* Although parts of this statement sound like truisms, the entire pattern gives us some new understanding of the meaning of resignation among the disadvantaged in our society, and perhaps in any society.

Our conclusion is based on the following facts: compared to people with high incomes, the very poor in both years pray more when unhappy, talk less when worried, and are less integrated in social contexts which offer access to social support (i.e., they visit less with friends and relatives and belong to fewer formal organizations). This is not to say that it is the common pattern for *all* poor people. The majority of the poor do not, in fact, show this style of resignation. But it is a coping pattern more likely to evolve among the poor rather than the rich.

These conclusions are derived not only from analyses of income, but also from other demographic findings: educational differences in the preceding section and other results in tables 9.18 and 9.19. This pattern of resignation is especially apparent in people from the South more than other regions, and in blacks more than whites. Southerners and blacks are heavily represented in impoverished groups. Parts of the pattern are also apparent in other groups that are typically but not consistently poor. Fundamentalists and Baptists, generally poor Protestant denominations, are the groups most committed to prayer (table 9.19). People who come from rural backgrounds or whose fathers were farmers are often among the poorest groups in America and they are also particularly *un*likely to talk worries over with other people (table 9.19). Although we can interpret the latter result as reflecting another theme that will be discussed below—people whose life situations do not permit easy access to other people will not use social styles to cope with personal difficulties—the fact that many people from rural backgrounds were also socialized in impoverished circumstances might also contribute to their asocial pattern of resignation.

The causal matrix for the correlation of poverty and resignation has been the topic of considerable political debate. Black political activists in the 1960s and 1970s often asserted that religious resignation interferes with the social acts that might eventually secure a better economic and political position for blacks in our society. Resignation can lead

TABLE 9.17

Summary of Multivariate Analyses of Selected Measures of Informal Coping and Social Context for Coping

Demographic Variables	Informal Coping			
	Praying When Unhappy		**Talking When Worried**	
	Main Effect	**Interaction**	**Main Effect**	**Interaction**
Economic Position Income	(X) Low>High		(X) Low<High	(X) Complex

Role Status
  Occupation
  Employment Status				

Marital Status	(X) widows>others		(X) married>others	
Parental Status		(X) with sex		
Geographic Social Environment Region	(X) Solid South> others> Mid-Atlantic, Pacific	(X) Complex with age × year	(X) Mid-Atlantic> others> Solid South	
Place of Residence	(X) Rural>others> metropolitan areas		(X) Rural< others	(X) Complex with year
Group Identification Race	(X) Black> White	(X) especially strong in less educated Blacks	(X) Whites> Blacks	(X) with year: Whites> Blacks in 1957
Religion	(X) Fundamentalists, Baptists> others> Jews, no preference	(X) with education	(X) Jews>others >Baptists	
Social Background Size of Birthplace	(X) large city <all others	(X) with education	(X) small city >others >rural	(X) with age
Father's Occupation	(X) Children of farmers> all others		(X) children of farmers< all others	(X) complex with education
Broken Home Background			(X) children of divorce< others< children of parents who died	
Social Integration Church Attendance	(X) freq.> less freq.	(X) with age: less strong in older groups (X) with education		(X) with sex: men who attend church once a week talk more than other men

| Social Context for Coping | | | |
| Visiting | | Organizational Membership | |
Main Effect	Interaction	Main Effect	Interaction
(X) Low<High		(X) Low<High	
			(X) with age: employed men unemployed
	(X) with age: young single> young married	(X) married> unmarried	
			(X) with age: young parents non-parents
(X) Solid South >others	(X) Complex	(X) West Northcentral >others> Solid South	(X) Complex with age
(X) Small city, towns>others		(X) Small city, town >suburb, rural >metropolitan area	
	(X) Complex		(X) Complex with year
(X) Lutheran >others >no pref.	(X) with year	(X) Lutheran, Methodist, Jew>others> Baptist, Fundamentalist, no preference	
(X) Never< All others		(X) Freq.> Less freq.	

TABLE 9.18
Selected Social-Demographic Comparisons on Visiting and Organizational Membership

	Total Number[a]		Visiting More than once/week		Visiting Less than once/month		Organizational Memb None	
Social-Demographic Characteristic	1957	1976	1957 (%)	1976 (%)	1957 (%)	1976 (%)	1957 (%)	1976 (%)
Income, (1976 dollars)								
under 4000	407	295	28	35	28	27	69	74
4000–7999	549	380	31	31	21	24	59	68
8000–9999	389	195	33	34	16	13	50	56
10,000–12,499	323	245	33	33	15	16	45	60
12,500–19,999	536	518	31	32	17	18	35	49
20,000 and over	186	474	36	27	16	23	28	42
Marital Status								
Married	1,871	1,436	No Relationship				47	54
Single	158	256					56	64
Widowed	280	308					60	60
Divorced/Separated	151	262					53	63
Region								
New England	181	140	29	33	20	13	46	59
Middle Atlantic	445	340	30	28	22	24	50	56
East N. Central	441	409	26	28	19	24	49	52
West N. Central	275	238	29	32	18	16	42	49
Solid South	648	577	36	35	16	22	53	64
Border States	115	172	24	31	26	23	56	64
Mountain States	104	74	32	34	25	24	50	53
Pacific States	251	314	39	30	18	23	49	53
Place of Residence								
Metropolitan	325	166	28	27	18	21	60	67
Suburbs	326	350	35	28	21	23	51	49
Small Cities	385	461	31	38	19	19	44	55
Towns	704	737	33	33	17	21	56	56
Rural Areas	720	550	29	27	21	25	51	62
Religion								
Baptists	525	473	30	28	18	23	58	63
Methodists	398	246	34	31	16	24	44	48
Lutherans	200	147	32	29	17	9	44	48
Presbyterians	162	101	29	40	22	17	41	40
Fundamentalists	222	207	34	28	20	25	53	64
Other Protestants	242	269	35	31	21	24	44	54
Catholics	542	504	27	35	22	20	50	58
Jews	91	57	40	34	16	16	42	36
No Preference	57	227	28	32	25	26	68	66
Church Attendance								
More than Once/Week	295	259	40	32	17	20	39	57
Once/Week	834	559	31	32	18	20	42	47
Few Times/Month	536	390	30	29	15	18	51	58
Few Times/Year	562	634	30	32	22	22	57	57
Never	218	392	27	30	31	27	68	67

[a] Numbers will vary somewhat because of the number of people not ascertained.

TABLE 9.19
*Selected Social-Demographic Comparisons in Praying When Unhappy
and Talking When Worried (by year)*

Social-Demographic Characteristic	Total Number[a]		Praying When Unhappy		Talking When Worried	
	1957	1976	1957 (%)	1976 (%)	1957 (%)	1976 (%)
Income, (1976 dollars)						
under 4000	407	295	52	42	20	36
4000–7999	549	380	40	30	32	42
8000–9999	389	195	42	33	36	50
10,000–12,499	323	245	39	29	45	49
12,500–19,999	536	518	38	29	43	53
20,000 and over	186	474	35	26	38	53
Marital Status						
Married	1,871	1,436	40	30	38	49
Single	158	256	36	16	32	53
Widowed	280	308	54	49	24	36
Divorced/Separated	151	262	45	22	28	46
Region						
New England	181	140	40	26	37	53
Middle Atlantic	445	340	35	23	41	53
East N. Central	441	409	40	35	38	49
West N. Central	275	238	46	31	33	43
Solid South	648	577	48	39	32	45
Border States	115	172	46	32	26	41
Mountain States	104	74	38	30	44	49
Pacific States	251	314	37	22	32	48
Place of Residence						
Metropolitan Area	325	166	35	20	39	52
Suburbs	326	350	40	25	34	55
Small Cities	385	461	45	36	43	46
Towns	704	737	42	30	35	47
Rural Areas	720	550	44	35	31	44
Race						
White	2,170	1,953	40	30	37	48
Black	190	245	57	41	21	43
Religion						
Baptists	525	473	46	41	30	42
Methodists	398	246	42	36	35	44
Lutherans	200	147	46	36	41	52
Presbyterians	162	101	34	24	31	61
Fundamentalists	222	207	50	44	33	41
Other Protestants	242	269	37	32	33	47
Catholics	542	504	46	29	40	54
Jewish	91	57	12	2	49	65
No Preference	57	227	9	4	29	45
Size of Birthplace						
Country/Farm	989	745	45	37	30	38
Town	568	536	44	31	34	52
Small City	362	413	38	27	45	55
Large City	468	527	36	25	38	51

TABLE 9.19 (continued)
Selected Social-Demographic Comparisons in Praying When Unhappy
and Talking When Worried (by year)

Social-Demographic Characteristic	Total Number[a]		Praying When Unhappy		Talking When Worried	
	1957	1976	1957 (%)	1976 (%)	1957 (%)	1976 (%)
Father's Occupation						
Professionals	136	152	41	22	38	58
Managers	271	274	40	25	37	48
Clerical/Sales Workers	120	114	39	24	40	58
Crafts Workers	362	402	39	28	43	50
Operatives	321	330	41	29	40	49
Farmers	903	500	46	45	29	37
Laborers	128	110	38	31	37	42
Broken Home Background						
Parents Divorced/ Separated	123	191	No Relationship		29	48
Parent(s) Died	351	243			38	51
Intact Home	1,915	1,746			36	48
Church Attendance						
More than Once a Week	295	259	73	72	No Relationship	
Once/Week	834	559	50	45		
Few Times/Month	536	390	38	34		
Few Times/Year	562	634	26	13		
Never	218	392	17	9		

[a] Numbers will vary somewhat because of the number of people whose responses were not ascertained, especially people who said they never worried or were never unhappy.

to continued poverty, poverty to continued resignation—an encapsulated system, one that may be difficult to undo.

2. *Using informal social support as a way to cope with personal problems partially depends on the opportunities provided for such supports in the groups people are identified with, or in the critical roles that define their lives.* As much as people might want to talk over a personal problem with a friend or relative, or even an acquaintance, social opportunities for such support may be lacking for one reason or another. This is a simpleminded but important principle to recognize in considering how various social-demographic groups differ in their use of social support in dealing with either worries or major crises in their lives.

Belonging to certain groups or residing in places with certain population densities might make social supports easily available; belonging to other groups or living in other places might make social support less accessible. We think that this kind of explanation underlies a number of findings. For example:

(a) *People who live in small cities—not in the most densely populated metro-*

politan regions nor in rural areas—have the most integrated context for social support. It is in the small cities that people report visiting and belonging to formal organizations most frequently (see table 9.18) and use social support most. Compared to all other groups, people who live in rural areas are less likely to report talking to someone when worried (table 9.19). Rural people have less social contact and hence less opportunity to talk, but, as we discussed above, people in rural areas may also assume the resigned style of poor people, since so many of them are impoverished. People in small but not metropolitan cities are active social-support seekers, which alerts us to the possibility that such cities optimize the opportunity for personal social contact. The largest cities may be so large, their institutions so bureaucratized and impersonal, that the psychologically available field for supportive interaction is considerably reduced. Big-city dwellers are people least active in organizations. The suburbs and small towns may also create a greater sense of social isolation from available support, compared to the somewhat more densely populated small city. The sense of neighborhood (Warren, 1976) as a place for group support may evolve in places that are of some optimal density. The neighborhoods of very large cities may be too dense; those of small towns or suburbs may be too small or nonexistent.

The effect is also apparent in comparisons made among people who come from different childhood residential backgrounds (table 9.19). People who come from small cities are the most likely to talk when worried. In this case, one would speak of a socialization effect: people who had more opportunities to talk over worries in the social environments in which they grew up have been reinforced to use that style as adults.

(b) *The South maintains a distinctive style of social integration, characterized by a high degree of personalism.* In most of the social comparisons we have drawn, the two context measures (*visiting* and *organizational membership*) are highly related. High income, education, membership in the Lutheran church and regular church attendance, and residence in small cities all relate to social integration on *both* indices. But our findings on geographic region are different: Southerners are especially high on visiting with friends and relatives, but particularly low on membership in formal organizations (see table 9.18). We would suggest that the South has maintained a unique cultural pattern that stems from its agrarian past. This pattern emphasizes social integrating based on kinship and other personal and particularistic ties. Until *recent* inmigration and industrial development, the South had been less affected than other sections of the country by the social patterns of industrial, urban society—universalistic, contractual interaction among strangers—and had been able to hold on to a separate coherent cultural pattern, closely tied to its agrarian past. This pattern still manifests itself in a unique style of social integration.

(c) *Lutherans surpass all other religious groups in their integrated social context.* They visit with friends and relatives frequently and are particularly likely to belong to social organizations (table 9.18). We return again to our depiction of Lutherans as an insulated group with an extensive parochial school system, a group that protects itself from too much contact with "sinful" outsiders who do not have the true faith. Their religious chauvinism sets up an enclave within the larger system that encourages close interaction in the in-group. The increased secularization of Catholicism over the past fifty years probably interfered with a similar phenomenon among Catholics.

(d) *Men who attend church regularly are especially likely to talk over their worries with someone.* This is not apparent for women. This finding may mean that many regular church-attending men use church attendance as a demonstration of their social integration. In the process, they underscore their commitments to family life and to community ties, and thus increase the opportunity to make social contact when they are worried. For women, church attendance may have a less exclusively social integrative meaning and thus less bearing on opportunities for social support.

Aside from participation in certain social groups, people's *involvement with certain critical role situations may also promote easy use of social support* for coping with problems. We support this conclusion with a number of findings below:

(e) *Married men and women, compared to any of the nonmarried people, have more overall social interaction and social support; they are more likely to talk to someone when they are worried, and to belong to formal organizations.* Marriage affords people easy access to a member of the other sex in a role that prescribes that easy access. Being married also entails additional opportunities for social integration and support (in-laws, children, spouse's friends) not automatically available to nonmarried people. However, marriage can also restrict social interaction at certain stages. Among the youngest age group, single people report more visiting than their married peers. Visiting is certainly functional for single people in providing a social life and opportunities to meet potential marriage partners. On the other hand, marriage may at first absorb and supply all of the young couples' social needs. The differences between marital status groups diminishes in the older age groups.[5] For certain marital statuses, there may be reason to think the status might be ignored or even engender avoidance by others.

---

[5] Although there was no significant interaction by year indicated in our multivariate analysis, there was an interesting trend for the young single people's rates of visiting family and friends to decrease (59 percent to 52 percent) while the young divorced's rates to increase (34 percent to 56 percent). These results speak to certain changes in the social expectation for these nonmarried statuses. More single people are now openly living with members of the opposite sex. Their lives might follow the visiting patterns of married people. More divorced people feel less stigmatized by their status and thus may feel more comfortable about an active social life.

(f) *People who experienced parental divorce during childhood are less likely than people whose childhood family life was intact, to talk out a worry as a coping strategy for adult personal problems; they are especially less likely to use this strategy in comparison to people who experienced the death of one or both of their parents during childhood (table 9.19).* These differences may reflect differential reinforcement of "talking it out" in early family roles. Families are often especially sensitive to children's needs to talk when they have experienced death of a parent at an early age. Quite the opposite may be true for a family's treatment of children of divorce. They may avoid talking about the child's concerns because of the guilt the parents and family experience about the divorce.

3. *Certain groups act as pace-setters in our society: groups which are sensitive to new models of adaptation for the social problems that emerge as new technologies and patterns of living also change.* As pace-setters, these groups reject the traditional modes of coping (prayer) and quickly take on the modes recommended by psychological experts. "Talking it out," both with professionals and with friends or relatives, has certainly been highly recommended by experts since Freud introduced psychoanalysis as a treatment for neurosis. To bottle up feelings, to avoid sharing thoughts (however erroneous or antisocial) has been thought to be bad for the psychological soul. Psychoanalysis is intended to make the unconscious conscious through directed talk with an expert. The analyst uses the transference relationship to make formerly suppressed ideas available for constructive rather than neurotic living. This same general assumption lies behind more recent expert counsel about engaging a natural support system to help weather crises. Talking will reduce tension somehow—perhaps because it will bring reassurance or love when people are feeling particularly bereft of friends or family; perhaps because it gives people new insights about problems they were not able to solve rationally; perhaps because it may lead to more extreme assumptions that the more one talks, the better one feels, or, the more people that one talks to, the better one feels.

Given this portrayal of the latest view of how to cope with personal problems, it is not surprising that we find certain groups especially tuned into this therapeutic regimen. In our prior depiction of informal coping styles among the more educated in both samples—their reliance on informal support and their lack of reliance on prayer—their easy engagement of a large support system, we had hints of this pace-setter interpretation of group differences. We also find evidence for the interpretation of results about other groups. For example:

(a) *People living in the Mid-Atlantic and Pacific Coast regions of the country are the least oriented of all regional groups to prayer, and they are especially oriented to talking to others about worries (table 9.19).* Since New York City and California are the areas where fashionable therapeutic strategies are first promulgated, we are not surprised by these findings.

(b) *Metropolitan areas contain fewer people who say they have prayed dur-*

ing unhappy times than any other residential area (table 9.19)   Again, we would interpret these findings with the pace-setter explanation. Big-city people are especially attuned to modern ways of adapting.

(c) *Jews are more likely to talk over their worries than are members of any other religious groups.*   There are traditional elements in Judaism as a this-worldly religion which promote talking as a general style of adaptation. For example, the Jewish ritual of mourning, the *shiva,* requires immediate socializing with friends after the death of a loved one. Jews in most Western countries who have been given opportunities to partake of the general social order have also tended to be among the pace-setters for developing modern modes of adaptation. We see their greater use of talking when worried as partially a function of their pace-setting orientation to life.

TABLE 9.20

Relationship of Talking When Worried to Selected Measures of Well Being (1976 only)

	Talking When Worried		
Measure of Well-Being	Yes (Spontaneously Mentioned) (%)	Yes (Mentioned only when probed) (%)	No (%)
Psychological Anxiety			
Very low[a]	9	7	18
Very high	16	12	18
	$\chi^2_{(8)} = 34.49\ p<.00001$[b]		
Ill Health			
Very high	13	15	24
	$\chi^2_{(8)} = 32.36\ p<.0001$		
Happiness			
Not too happy	8	13	15
	$\chi^2_{(4)} = 21.62\ p<.0002$		
Self-Esteem			
Low	31	33	37
	$\chi^2_{(4)} = 11.44\ p<.03$		
Zest			
Low	32	36	44
	$\chi^2_{(4)} = 16.07\ p<.003$		
Total Number	1,048	846	299

[a] For simplicity, critical comparisons are tabulated in each row of this table.

[b] χ^2s are computed on *entire* classification of measure of well-being; degrees of freedom in parenthesis indicate levels used.

Is Social Support Good for Subjective Mental Health?

Having examined changes in styles of informal social support in the national population as well as how men and women of various age and education levels differ in these styles, we still can raise the critical question: Is informal social support good for people's well-being? We clearly have no way to get at the direct causal connection between support and well-being, and evidence for the causal linkage from *any* underlying source is not yet in (Heller, 1978). Nevertheless, we can ask whether social support and well-being are even correlated in the national sample. Are Americans who use informal support systems likely to report being psychologically better off than people who do not? Are people who turn to more—rather than fewer—people for crises especially likely to report psychological problems or difficulties? Or are they especially unlikely to say that they are troubled people? A close examination of such questions warrants a full monograph. For now, let us present a quick appraisal of these questions for the American population at large, with some critical demographic controls introduced.

We selected one measure of informal help-seeking: whether a person talks with anyone when worried (*talking when worried*). For this measure, we made a further distinction between those people who spontaneously said they talked to others when they are worried and those people who said they spoke to others only when specifically probed. We then selected five varied measures of well-being: two symptom factors (*Psychological Anxiety* and *Ill Health*);[6] and three reported feelings about the self (*Happiness*,[7] *Self-esteem*,[8] and *Zest*[9]). These five measures comprise a variety of dimensions of well-being with which to explore the relationship of social support to subjective mental health.

We then correlated the two measures of social support to the five measures of well-being. These analyses were done for the 1976 population only, because the indices of *Self-esteem* and *Zest* are available only in the 1976 sample. These results are summarized in table 9.20. We present truncated sections of cross-tabulations to highlight critical findings.

There are clear relationships between *talking when worried* and measures of psychological well-being. Compared to people who do not talk to others in times of worry, talkers (especially those who spontaneously report talking to others) tend to be: lower in *Ill Health*, higher in reported happiness, less likely to be on the "depressed" side of the *Zest* scale, and higher in *Self-Esteem*. All of these results would argue that

---

[6] See chapter 7.
[7] See chapter 2.
[8] See chapter 3.
[9] See chapter 2.

informal help-seeking and talking to people in times of worry have favorable mental-health correlates.

However, it is also true that people who are *not* talkers in times of worry are *more* likely to be very *low* in *Psychological Anxiety*. This result suggests that help seekers may have unfavorable mental-health correlates since they tend to report more psychological anxiety. Indeed, this result would support the theoretical analysis that Schachter (1959) offers about the relationship of affiliation to anxiety. His theory and research suggest that help seeking often occurs because people are unsure of themselves and are experiencing heightened anxiety. But our result showing that people who say that they do *not* speak to anyone in times of worry are also relatively low in anxiety, has another interpretation. Being very low in *Psychological Anxiety* generally means that a person has said "never" to all items asking about anxiety symptoms. It seems reasonable to argue that those who say "never" to all of these symptoms are *denying* such concerns, since it is unlikely that people never experience some feeling of nervousness, some slight trouble in getting to sleep, and so forth. Perhaps people who do not seek help when they are worried are also especially prone to deny their problems of anxiety. As a result, we can argue that it is not that help seekers are more anxiety prone, but that non-help-seekers are more likely to deny experiencing anxiety. This latter interpretation fits better with the other positive indicators of well-being among people who do talk to others in times of worry.

Multivariate analyses of these results relating talking to others in times of worry to measures of psychological well-being reveal that not all of them survive controls for sex, age, and education. Only the result regarding the correlation of *talking when worried* and *Self-Esteem* remains as a clear-cut finding.[10] The correlations of *talking when worried* to *Psychological Anxiety* and *Happiness* remain only marginally significant.[11] The results relating social support to *Ill Health* and *Zest* are no longer critical in the demographically controlled cross-classification of these variables. Thus, the overall relationships between seeking support by talking to others when worried and psychological well-being are greatly diminished when sex, age, and education controls are applied. We must recall that these variables are intimately connected to both help-seeking behavior and psychological well-being measures. As a result, log-linear analyses suggest that although there is an overall relationship between *talking when worried* and psychological well-being, the findings may be partially understood by remembering that *talking when worried*, high *Zest*, and low *Ill Health* all appear much more frequently among the college educated. The demographic controls do not

[10] It remains as an independent effect needed in the most parsimonious model, one with the simplest terms which produces a .05 level of fit.

[11] At the .01 level of confidence, they significantly improve the most parsimonious fitted model accounting for the variable, *talking when worried*, in the log-linear analysis.

TABLE 9.21
Relationship of Seeking Support When Worried (Talking) to Zest
(by Education, 1976 only)

	Education					
	Grade School		High School		College	
	Talk When Worried[a]		Talk When Worried[a]		Talk When Worried[a]	
Zest	Yes (%)	No (%)	Yes (%)	No (%)	Yes (%)	No (%)
Low	54	54	36	34	20	31
Moderate	24	26	30	29	32	28
High	22	20	34	37	48	41
	100%	100%	100%	100%	100%	100%
Total Number	118	222	525	544	384	354

[a]Spontaneous mention only.

vitiate a possible relationship between social support and *Zest,* or social support and health, but they do raise some question about the strength of the association.

There was one very important exception to the conclusion that the relationship between *Zest* and support-seeking is largely explainable by demographic control variables. When we apply multivariate analyses only to the simpler categorization of people—those who mention talking when worried spontaneously vs. all others—we find that low *Zest* (or depressed state) was distinctly more apparent among people who do not report talking over worries, *but only among college-educated men and women.*[12] These findings are reported in table 9.21. Here we see why we no longer have a dramatic difference in *Zest* scores between talkers and nontalkers after controlling for education. Grade school–educated people whether they talk or not are low in *Zest,* compared to the more educated groups. Within the college-educated group, however, talkers are clearly less likely to report low *Zest* than nontalkers. This finding is very provocative. It alerts us to two possibilities about the limitations to the value of social support for well-being.

First, certain styles of social support may not be effective in groups which do not particularly value that style. The college educated are socialized to talk over problems. That norm may be less pronounced in less educated groups, which may even suggest to their members that, since there is not much to do about worries, it would be best to forget them and not hassle other people with such concerns. Where problem-solving talk is not valued, it may even be negatively reinforced. And

[12] A support x zest x education interaction effect significantly ($p < .05$) added to the most parsimonious fitted model.

people who talk do so only under very desperate conditions which may be beyond help through talking.

A second possible limitation to the value of support seeking is suggested by the differential relationship of talking to *Zest* among different education groups. Talking about worries in groups where there are no easy ways to cope with the problems of life may indeed exacerbate people's anxieties—not only for the support seeker, but also for the person who is asked to help. Misery may like company, but only to a point. When solutions to economic or health or even interpersonal woes are unavailable, perhaps the best choice is to deny the problem to oneself and to others, and to seek support in shared activity rather than in disclosure of worries.

These results suggest that there may be problems for which the use of help from others reflects deliberate pragmatic problem-solving; for other problems, seeking help may represent desperation—a lack of capacity to cope with a specific problem or a more emotionally laden withdrawal from life. Most people probably need other people in both of these two very different senses, but different people face different kinds of problems or may employ the two styles of support differentially. Perhaps happy people tend to seek more support than unhappy people, as our data suggest, because happy people face only the kinds of problems in which social support clearly offers a means of rational coping with difficulties. Perhaps people who have not confided in others in times of worry are low in *Anxiety* because they have never felt desperate about their concerns.

In any case, we have no overall answer to the initial question posed: Is social support good for well-being? Some of the results support the utility of social support, but most of them—especially when demographic controls are introduced—do not support it one way or the other. In one instance, we find social support beneficial only for the college-educated. The most reasonable conclusion is social support seems generally positive. Refinements to that conclusion will have to be conditioned by more elaborate analyses of the specific characteristics of people, as well as the types of life problems they face.

Is Praying Good for Subjective Mental Health?

We can also ask whether praying is associated with well-being. Chapter 8 indicated that church attendance correlates positively with a number of measures of well-being, but our explanation for the results rests on thinking of churchgoing as a sign of social integration rather than a sign of religious coping with problems. Using the measure of *praying*

TABLE 9.22

Relationship of Use of Prayer During Unhappy Periods to
Selected Measures of Well-Being (1976 only)

Measure of Well-Being	Prays When Unhappy	
	Yes (%)	No (%)
Happiness		
Very happy[a]	35	29
$X^2_{(2)} = 8.35\ p < .02$[b]		
Self-Esteem		
High	42	44
$X^2_{(2)} = 1.07$, not significant		
Psychological Anxiety		
Low	30	35
$X^2_{(4)} = 14.46\ p < .01$		
Ill Health		
High	19	14
$X^2_{(4)} = 17.90\ p < .01$		
Zest		
Low	30	39
$X^2_{(2)} = 8.35\ p < .02$		
Total Number	649	1,492

[a] For simplicity, only critical highlights are tabulated in each row of this table.

[b] X^2 is computed on entire cross-classification of well-being and prayer with degrees of freedom in parentheses.

when unhappy, we come closer to a direct analysis of the impact of religious coping styles on subjective mental health.

A limited analysis parallel to the one in the previous section was made relating *praying when unhappy* to five well-being measures for the 1976 sample. Results presented in table 9.22 indicate very inconsistent tendencies. Two measures suggest that praying relates to positive feelings of well-being (*Happiness, Zest*); two, to negative feelings (*Psychological Anxiety* and *Ill Health* symptoms); and one, to neither positive nor negative (no relationship to *Self-Esteem*). Only the positive associations of prayer with *Happiness* and *Zest* withstand multivariate tests:[13] people who pray during periods of unhappiness report being happier and report fewer symptoms of depression (low *Zest*) than people who do not. Thus, at least in the affect domain, we have evidence that prayer during unhappy periods is used by people who are generally happier and less depressed. The results are not strong, but they are significant. We can only suggest that for many of these people, prayer is a

[13] Psychological Reaction x Praying x Sex x Age x Education, analyzed by log-linear analyses.

sign of resignation to uncontrollable problems; a resignation that may make them less vulnerable to remorse about their own ineptitudes. They are then able to carry on with some pleasure and without depression. When lack of control over such serious events as death, illness, and accidents is recognized, and is thought to be in the hands of God, then in some way people can avoid the sense of personal helplessness that pervades their feelings of unhappiness or depression (Seligman, 1975). Wortman and Silver (1980) have built such a model for victims of rape and accidents. People who pray during periods of unhappiness may be avoiding the onus of personal responsibility for uncontrollable events.

Year Differences in the Importance of Talking or Praying for Personal Happiness

Having found both *talking when worried* and *praying when unhappy* to be associated with happiness in 1976, we may ask whether this was more or less true in 1957. Multivariate analyses of year, sex, age, and education controls on the relationship yielded overall significant relationships of these coping styles to happiness in both years. The relationship of praying to reported happiness is remarkably similar in both years (see table 9.23). The relationship of *talking when worried* to happiness is also significant in 1957; indeed, it was stronger in 1957 than in 1976. These analyses also reveal many complicated interactions. The most dramatic difference between 1957 and 1976 is the comparison of

TABLE 9.23
Relationship of Social Support and Praying
When Unhappy to Happiness (by year)

	Social Support				Prayer			
	1957		1976		1957		1976	
	Talking When Worried		Talking When Worried		Praying When Unhappy		Praying When Unhappy	
Happiness	Yes (%)	No (%)	Yes (%)	No (%)	Yes (%)	No (%)	Yes (%)	No (%)
"Very Happy"	43	30	34	28	37	32	35	29
"Pretty Happy"	49	57	57	59	52	57	55	60
"Not too Happy"	8	13	9	13	12	11	10	11
	100%	100%	100%	100%	100%	100%	100%	100
Total Number	830	1,513	1,027	1,119	939	1,316	649	14

middle-aged men in the two eras. In 1957 they demonstrated the general phenomenon: people who talk when worried tend to be very happy, and those who do not tend to be only pretty happy or unhappy. In 1976 this association is no longer apparent for middle-aged men. Either their social support no longer comforts them, or they no longer seek social support when unhappy, or both may be true. Perhaps more men in the 1976 sample have faced the "mid-life crisis." This transitional crisis in values for men in the 1970s was not so clearly part of the picture for men in earlier times. Solutions to mid-life problems may arise out of soul searching that neither demands, nor is helped by, other people's advice.

Summary

This generation has seen a profound change in the degree to which people seek and use informal help to deal with problems in everyday life: worries and unhappiness. While people in the earlier generation were more likely to see no solutions to problems they faced, to have a sense of resignation about their miseries, members of the new generation, both young and old, see some possible guidance and help in talking intimately with other people. We have seen the rise of professional help-seeking over the generation, and we also see a rise in this informal discussing of difficulties, worries, and unhappiness. With the decline of normal structured institutional ways of dealing with problems—especially through membership in groups such as churches—more people make use of intimate relationships as an arena for working out problems. Rather than seeking just one resource, people now tend to ask a number of different kinds of people for advice and counsel. Where the family or the spouse was once the sole resource turned to in times of difficulty, the social network is more extensive for respondents in 1976. All that we have said about year differences can also be applied to sex, age, and education differences. The trends to greater variety and to more help-seeking through informal channels are truer of women, of the more educated, and of younger people. Multiple-classification analyses suggest that these results are *net of each other*; each variable provides some additional information about differences in informal social support.

Throughout this chapter, we have highlighted the fact that changes in social support from 1957 to 1976 grow out of a changed matrix of interaction typified by much less ritual visiting and participation in formal organizations and much less use of the marital relationship as the sole anchoring focus for life. The new generation not only seeks more varied and more extensive interactions with people, but does it out of a context that is in some ways less socially integrated. The 1976 sample visits less with family and friends, they belong to fewer organizations, including church, and they are less likely to be married. All of the superstructures for easy social access have diminished; as a result, in order to obtain affirmation and support from others, people must be more self-directed and initiating. Perhaps people are disillusioned with ritualized, formalized channels for seeking help. Perhaps formal structures were taken for granted and consequently failed to provide the closer interpersonal exchange that gives people a lift when they are in difficulty. Perhaps the shift away from formal organizations, marriage, ritualized visiting, has to do with a search for a more protective and personal social support. In any case, people in 1976 seek more informal social way of dealing with life problems in spite of—or perhaps because of—the disadvantage of being in a more diffuse, less tightly organized society. We wonder whether this search has been effective, or whether it is merely a substitute for the easier supports that are customarily available to people in a more traditional society.

Two sets of data make us skeptical about informal social support as a panacea. While talking over worries is as powerfully related to feelings of happiness in 1976 as it was in 1957, in one particular group—middle-aged men—we see some disruption in the connection. Perhaps men who are solving problems of mid-life require an internal dialogue, so that the social coping styles may indeed be ineffective.

Another result makes us dubious about the therapeutic value of social support for all people. College-educated people are the only ones who show a clear positive connection between talking out worries and lack of depression. The less educated do not show the pattern; for them, social coping may be neither valued nor effective in bringing about changes in their lives. Indeed, the belief that they would—and the realization that they do not—might even exacerbate feelings of depression.

Chapter 10

CONCLUSIONS

OUR multiple-criteria approach to studying subjective mental health and the ways in which people cope with life problems has brought us an ever-widening understanding of alternative psychological reactions people have to both stresses and gratifications of everyday life. We have looked at people's sense of general well-being, their self-perceptions, their experiences in marriage, parenthood, and work, their reported patterns of symptoms, and finally their use of social support in times of stress. As we cover an ever-widening spectrum of feelings and methods of coping with problems, we may begin to forget where we have been and what it all adds up to. Like professional bird-watchers who attend to detailed differences in plumage or identify certain species of birds, we have sought certain refinements in each of the chapters to which many readers may be indifferent. Like amateur bird-watchers, most readers may be interested in more general distinctions. They may ask: overall, have people's adjustments and resources for solving psychological problems changed over the generation of 1957 to 1976? Is there evidence of dramatic social change in the way that Americans view their mental health? Can we say anything about the direction that the country is taking with regard to its own psychological well-being?

1957 and 1976 Compared

In this chapter, we return to these broad questions and present answers we have given implicitly in various chapters of this book. We wish this compilation to be more than a list. We have done some hard thinking about integrative themes that characterize both changes and stable elements in our subjective life experience. We also see potential directions that we are taking with regard to our own psychological health.

Some of the changes we have observed, while significant in a statistical sense, and independent of changes that age and education changes alone might have brought over the two years, are *very small*. We should remember that. These minimal differences may be worth social scientists' attention, and they may be prognostic of more dramatic changes in the future—but now they are still only small changes. As a result, we will start our integrative account of what has changed in Americans' view of their mental health with what we see as the most dramatic changes in the subjective appraisals of the nation from 1957 to 1976. In later sections, we integrate smaller changes that have occurred.

At the end of this chapter, we will attempt to present the general implications of our findings about the state of the nation's subjective well-being in 1976. Interwoven in some of our discussion will be results showing remarkable stability from 1957 to 1976; a stability we think should command as much interest on the part of social scientists and practitioners as do the changes we highlight. Some of these stable features reflect psychological processes for which we might have expected change. We will take special note of these "surprises."

CRITICAL GENERATIONAL CHANGES IN SUBJECTIVE MENTAL HEALTH

Increased Concern About an Uncertain Future

A number of results suggest that there has been a generational shift in the degree to which people feel they can rely on the future as a time to expect better things—or at least more stable things—to occur in their lives. Two related findings stand out: in 1976 young people report increased symptoms of psychological anxiety and greater frequency of worrying than did the young in 1957. Although there has been a general increase in anxiety symptoms and worrying in all groups in our society, it is particularly true of the young. We interpret this to mean that while young people in 1957 had a clear future to which they directed their psychological lives, young people in 1976 are much more uncertain about their future lives. Uncertainty is a psychological problem that has many consequences. Worrying may be the coping response people make to issues of uncertainty. The more general deleterious reaction to uncertainty is found in symptoms of anxiety: nervousness, feeling irritated and tense, sleeplessness, and the like—all of which have increased in young people much more than they have in other groups. Although nowhere in the results do young people tell us directly that they are anxious or worried about the future, it is not difficult to interpret their concerns as being connected to that uncertainty.

The job market for young people is unclear. Family roles—both marriage and parenthood—are in transition. Commitments to family and work are harder for young people to make than they once were. The culture at large is probably more uncertain about these issues, but the most profound consequences of this uncertainty would be in young people, who have a longer future at stake. More of their future depends on commitments they make now.

The Movement from Social to Personal Integration of Well-Being

In many of the chapters investigating changes in subjective mental health, we were aware of an important change that has occurred in the responses of the newer generation. We have discussed this change in many ways, but it can be stated simply: there has been a shift from a *socially* integrated paradigm for structuring well-being, to a more *personal* or *individuated* paradigm for structuring well-being. We see the 1957 population taking much more comfort in culture and the 1976 population gathering much more strength in its own personal adaptations to the world. We see this very general theme in a number of different ways which we will summarize below as three types of changes that have occurred in people's responses to questions of their well-being and coping styles: (1) the diminution of role standards as the basis for defining adjustment; (2) increased focus on self-expressiveness and self-direction in social life; (3) a shift in concern from social organizational integration to interpersonal intimacy. Let us discuss important results that made us conclude that these changes have occurred over the recent generation.

The diminution of role standards as forces for defining adjustment. Although we had indications in chapter 2 that people were using roles of marriage, parenthood, and work less frequently as anchors for their general feelings of adjustment, these results were not very striking, and we reserve discussion of them to a later section. The most dramatic changes that occurred and reflect role standards becoming less figural for people's evaluations of themselves emerge from investigation of normative expectations for marriage and parenthood. In questions asking how a person's life is changed by becoming a parent, there is a clear decrease in the unconditional positive regard that Americans have for parenthood. Fewer people in 1976 thought that parenthood totally enriched people with important positive experiences. The same was true for the way Americans in 1976 saw the changes that marriage brings; they were much more open to the negative facets of the role than people were in 1957. Furthermore, more people in 1976 thought it was quite all right for young people to decide not to get married at all. These results suggest to us that the whole culture is moving away from seeing the roles of marriage and parenthood as critically defining prerequisites for personal adjustment. Americans have become more open to more individualized and abstract bases for well-being. They now feel much more restricted by role assignments that enforce patterns of life or are too rigidly defined.

An increase in Americans' self-expressive and self-directive reactions to their adjustment.   While we think that people's new investment in self-expression and self-fulfillment is one that pervades all of life, the clearest support for this generalization comes from the important changes in reactions to work in 1957 and 1976. There are many large shifts in people's responses to work which suggest that men and women are more concerned about their own individuation in jobs. A surprisingly strong change occurred both in people's perception of their jobs as requiring a lot of ability and in their perception of themselves as being very competent at their work. Furthermore, many more men and women report what we have called "ego dissatisfactions" with their work: many more people now, compared to a generation ago, focus on things having to do with their own personal involvement with their jobs when they speak of their dissatisfactions.

There was also a dramatic rise in the percentage of women committed to work: more working women in 1976 said they would continue working even if they did not need the money. A related dramatic change for women is the markedly decreased satisfaction with the housewife role. This change in focus from the housewife role to the job role is another instance of increased attention to self-fulfillment that has pervaded psychological changes in the current generation. Many women express it as wanting not to be "just a housewife," but to go out and do something in the job world, as if working were a vehicle for finding a more individuated expressive potential.

The value of self-efficacy and self-expression at work may be so powerful that it forces people to distort their work experiences. We have some evidence for this important hypothesis: there is a higher correlation in 1957 than in 1976 between perceived difficulties of work and the *actual* challenge of work (assessed through categorization of the job from the *Dictionary of Occupational Titles*). This change in correlations between actual and perceived difficulty in work may be a function of the importance that people have learned to attach to finding their potential at work. If achievement fulfillment is lacking, people in 1976 are more likely than people in 1957 to distort their own perception of their activities. We have no direct evidence for this change in distortion, but it is our inference from the change in correlation between actual and perceived difficulty of work.

Shift from integration through social organizations to integration through interpersonal intimacy.   One of the most dramatic findings in our study is the degree to which people in 1976 now talk to friends and other people in their support system about their worries and periods of unhappiness. Not only do they report such help-seeking much more often than they did in 1957, but when they do seek out help of this sort, they are more likely to select a *variety* of such people. Where in 1957 many married people depended solely on their spouse for help with their problems, many more married people now talk both to the spouse and to a friend or other family members as well.

Coordinated with this general rise in intimate help-seeking is the decline in the use of prayer as a vehicle for handling worries and unhappiness. The decline in the use of prayer occurs in all groups, but is especially marked in young people in 1976. This shift from prayer to more intimate help-seeking as a way of dealing with problems is a clear example of the shift away from more organized formal institutionalized forms of integrating to the social world to a much more personal form through intimate interpersonal relationships. Prayer as a mechanism for coping with problems usually implies that people are tied into a larger social institution (i.e., religious institution), which offers adherents structured techniques for coping with or overcoming life problems.

We also see a dramatic shift from formal interpretations of integration to more interpersonal intimate ones in parents' perceptions of their own inadequacies. There has been a very large shift toward seeing parental inadequacies in terms of affiliative relationships with children. This result is especially true of men. How much time parents spend with children and how well parents get along with their children are of much greater concern in 1976 than they were in 1957. More standardized *formal* role requirements (physical care, provision, financial support) were less salient in parents' concerns in the 1970s; issues of intimacy, as the basis of integration with children, are more powerful in the newer generation.

These three different findings—showing the diminution of role standards for defining adjustment, increased orientation to self-expression and self-directedness in social life, and increased use of interpersonal intimacy rather than social organization integration as the basis for ties to the social world—all illustrate the general theme of a shift from the comfort of society and social integration to personal growth as a way of defining well-being. Later we will list many other results that illustrate this general theme and the three subthemes discussed above. The results just reported are the most dramatic.

An Increase in the Psychological Approach to Understanding One's Own Behavior

A review of *Americans View Their Mental Health* in the *Atlantic Monthly* (Rolo, 1961), suggested that the book was ushering in a new era of interpreting the ideal for adjustment as "Psychological Man." That ideal might have been the authors' bias in interpreting the 1957 results, but it surely was the beginning of a new cultural norm: one that accounts for a strong change that occurred in people's responses to their own well-being from 1957 to 1976. It is clear from the data that men and women have become much more psychological in their thinking about themselves and attempting to understand their own lives. The most dramatic findings illustrating this theme come from two sources: the increase in formal help-seeking and the decrease in people's denial of problems in their lives.

A very large change has occurred in the use of professional facilities for personal problems, and especially the use of mental-health facilities. These results, discussed in Book 2 cut across almost all groups. Formal help-seeking for problems can be read as a desire to achieve a psychological understanding of people's own behavior, in the belief that such understanding will facilitate solutions. However misguided this faith in mental-health experts may have been, it reflects the national investment in such expert help as a resource for conquering obstacles to the good life.

There were remarkable decreases in the number of people who say they have never had any marriage problems, or they have never had any problems raising their children, or they have never had problems at work. We do not interpret this to mean that the problematic nature of these roles has necessarily increased, but that *denial* of problems was more common in 1957. Sensitization to problems often reflects an increased psychological orientation to the context of these problems. Many other results support this conclusion. Many fewer people today say they do not know how often they have felt inadequate as a parent or as a spouse. In 1976 people evidently have thought about these issues more. This declining rate of denial is further reflected in clear reductions in the report of never experiencing symptoms in response to the symptom checklist. Many fewer respondents in the 1976 study use the category "never" when asked about various psychological and psychosomatic symptoms. Whether this decrease in denial of problems or symptoms contributes in some way to an actual increased experience of problems or symptoms is an open question. Once people remove a barrier to the experience of a problem, sensitization alone may create new problems. This phenomenon may be particularly pronounced in interpersonal roles, where interactive problems can snowball. Once a married person is free to talk about a problem, his/her spouse may talk more, which may generate new problems.

Significant But Smaller Generational Changes

The important generational shifts highlighted in the previous section are summarized under five integrated themes. Other smaller but significant results also support these major themes. In this section, we present further ripples inspired by the major psychological changes that seem to have occurred over the generation.

Smaller Changes Indicating Uncertainty About the Future

More people in the 1976 generation said that they worried about their children, or their jobs than did people in the 1957 sample. Worries about children and jobs usually entail some concern about the future. In the case of children, parents wonder what is to become of their sons or daughters, whether they are doing well in school, or associating with the proper values or people. Workers wonder what will happen to their jobs in light of uncertainty in the economic conditions of the society. Some of this increased worry about children and jobs may be a function of our increased wish to have life under our control, coupled with a realization that our children and our jobs have become increasingly susceptible to social changes that occur in the larger society. Many parents now recognize that the peer society or television have become dominant forces in their children's world and have taken out of their hands some of the socializing control they once had. And many parents are probably worried about the fact and worried about the future that it might imply for their children. Furthermore, people well trained for certain jobs often find themselves in outmoded jobs— at least more so now than in 1957. The technological shifts that occur in the society can undermine a profession or a skill to which a person has been highly committed. Such change causes uncertainty about specific jobs and about the nature of work and livelihood in the future.

In analyses of specific questions asked about the future, we were indeed surprised that, although there was no obvious overall change from 1957 to 1976 in people's optimism about the future, when we controlled for demographic differences between 1957 and 1976, and particularly when we accounted for the proportionally more educated and younger people in 1976 than in 1957, it became apparent that in 1976 *fewer* people were optimistic about the future than in 1957. The 1976 sample had more educated and more younger people, who, in turn, are people who are likely to be more optimistic than less educated, older people. When we controlled for these factors, we found a significant tendency for people to be *less* optimistic in 1976 than they were in 1957.

It is almost as if the future is not the perspective that is frequently taken for thinking about well-being. If a future is uncertain, then why not discard it as something upon which to build general adjustment? In this respect, it was interesting to note that people who were unhappy in 1976 were less likely than people in 1957 to think that their future would be unhappy, too. For the new generation, if people are unable to find happiness in the present, it may not mean that they will be unhappy in the future. More people in 1957 were probably staking out their present happiness in terms of what they *thought their future happiness would be like.* Hence there was more correlation between their future perspective and their present happiness in 1957 than there was in 1976. We take this as further evidence that the time span for considering personal well-being has become more uncertain and hence much more narrow in focus for the general population in 1976.

The one exception to this conclusion about how critical the future is for people's well-being is the significant expectations of retirement that seem to color men's orientation to their well-being—especially in relationship to their jobs when they are middle-aged. There is some evidence that there is more disengagement from work in the 1976 population of older working men than was true in 1957. More men now may think about their future goals as retirees than they once did. It is a future prospect they actively consider which allows them to resocialize themselves for that expectation. Indeed, a *role* for retirement may be developing which presents certain kinds of rules and sanctions which permit people to anticipate their own socialization to the role while they are still at work.

Smaller Changes Indicating a Shift from Social Integrative Bases of Well-Being to Personal Growth Bases

The diminution of role standards. In our analysis of the schema that people use in defining their strong points and weaknesses, we find a considerable decline in status or role sources. In particular, there is a significant decline in people saying they would like their son (or daughter) to be more educated than they are. In the schema people use to portray how they are different from other people, we find a decrease in references to occupations and to their marital status. These role and status anchors for the definitions of self have thus become less critical in the 1976 population. Other results about definitions of personal well-being dovetail with these decreases in the use of role categories for self-definition. While there has been some slight decrease in how much people refer to their marriage spontaneously as a source of well-being, the more important result is that people are more likely to report *their own personal* characteristics as a source of their happiness. Not many in the population do, but there is significant change in that direction.

Increase in concern for self-expression and self-direction. For us to assert that people are becoming more oriented to their own self-fulfillment in their life circumstances makes us sound as if we were joining the bandwagon to indict the current population for their "narcissism." As people become much more heavily involved in themselves, they may no longer be involved in their society. And indeed, to some extent, that is part of the picture. Nevertheless, we hesitate to interpret the change simply as a regression to primary or secondary narcissism. Rather, we see it as a social development in a very affluent society. Concerns about self-development occur when society moves to a level of complexity that makes ease in social integration more difficult. To the degree that work life and family life have been no longer simply and ritually worked out for people, to the degree that more choices are open to people in selecting careers or family situations to which they can see themselves committed over a lifetime, there is an inevitable refocusing on the self. We do not see it as a disintegration of values, but as an adaptation that people have made to a complexity of choice in a heterogeneous society. Indeed a heightened concern about choice, self-direction, and self-sufficiency can be a potential positive contributor to subjective well-being in many ways. From 1957 to 1976 there are significant changes in the following: seeing oneself as different from other people in a more positive light, seeing oneself as less needy of being liked by others, seeing oneself as less needy of having other people listen to what one is saying, seeing oneself as generally more efficacious. This pattern seems to indicate a much more positive regard for oneself and a much less involved interest in how other people react to the self. This self-sufficiency may be seen as a fault, but it may also be seen as a value which has been directly espoused in our society from a very early point in American life. Indeed, many more people in the 1976 population look at their own independence as a source of their well-being. This American value has been around for a long time; it has become more highly articulated and elaborated in recent times.

As our society moves to a more pluralistic grouping of roles and more ambiguous role standards, self-reliance becomes even more important. This is no more clearly highlighted than in the case of older people in the society of 1976 who have joined the rest of the population in seeking self-sufficiency as a crucial life value for well-being more than older people in 1957. In order to maintain a separate household, to keep from becoming a burden on the idealized nuclear family, to avoid the conjectured or realistic horrors of institutional life of a nursing home or a hospital, older people have a strong involvement in remaining independent and clearly responsible for their own lives. Thus we see the focus on personal growth and personal integration as very adaptive to the changes in life's circumstances that have come about in our society. More people say that they are unhappy about their interpersonal circumstances and the nature of their community and national life. Thus, social integration does not provide the basis for well-being that it once may have, and people have to rely more on their own personal rules for well-being. It is interesting to us that even among older people there is less involvement in children as a source of happiness in 1976 than there once was. Disappointments the elderly may feel in how responsive their children are to their changing needs during aging perhaps have engendered a defiant, defensive disengagement from children as a resource.

If there has been an increase in valuing self-sufficiency, why do we find *more* people in 1976 seeking formal and informal support for personal problems? The increase in *formal* support-seeking can be seen as a reflection of a very different change: the growth of a psychological orientation. The increase in *informal* support-seeking, however, is a phenomenon that may fit well into the increased value for self-sufficiency. In 1976 compared to 1957, there was much less dependence on a *specific individual*—such as a spouse or a child—for handling everyday problems or the distress of critical life events. There is thus an increased orientation to seeking support from a *variety* of resources, or a decrease in overdependence on some individual source. This shift may enhance self-sufficiency. Having a variety of social supports perpares people for the circumstances of living if they were to lose the support of any one individual and need to survive alone. The likelihood of divorce, the increased possibility of women spending many years as widows, the increased numbers of single parents, are circumstances which make an orientation to self-sufficiency, accompanied by an extensive social network, adaptive.

We were surprised to find that many more husbands and wives in 1976 were happy about their marriages than they were in 1957. This result is perhaps best understood in the context of the increased orientation to self-fulfillment and self-expression. The increased divorce rate suggests that people who were not finding personal gratification in marriage are now freer to move out of that relationship. The value on self-enrichment in relationships is often sufficient to disentangle a man or woman from a relationship that is unsatisfactory. As a result, we would argue, the value for self-expression may have contributed to the increased divorce rate, but we may now have many fewer marriages in our current society that are very unsatisfactory over a long period of time.

We see the greatest effect of this orientation to self-development in analysis of the work role. Compared to 1957, many more people in 1976 talk about achievement and power gratification from work; the expectation of self-actualization in jobs was on the upswing. On the other hand, there is greater expressed dissatisfaction in 1976 with the work environment because relationships between people at work are not satisfactory. Furthermore, there is a decline from 1957 to 1976 in the response that work is satisfying because it is "interesting" work to do. Thus, the press for self-fulfillment—at least as it is enacted in the work setting—may have reduced the subjective pleasures that people get in experiencing work as intrinsically "interesting," as well as the subjective pleasure from being part of a group working together. The focus on self may diminish the focus on the value of the work for its own sake and may reduce people's capacity to see the pleasures of social interaction in their work environment. Self-development in work may compete with the ease of social integration that occurs in work settings when people are less oriented toward self-fulfillment.

In summary, we feel this 1957–1976 shift from more social integrative pleasures to more self-expressive and self-fulfilling pleasures has had both positive and negative consequences for subjective well-being. On the one hand, the attention to personal fulfillment has made men and women in the 1976 sample somewhat more positive about their own self-pictures, perhaps more flexible about their commitments to unsatisfactory marriages, more open to adopting interpersonal support systems which are adaptive in a very complex society that presents difficulties in social integration. On the other hand, this orientation to self creates some incompatibility with maintaining totally satisfactory social ties with people. We see this incompatibility arising in the workplace. It also arises in marriages to the extent that people dissolve marriages quickly without sufficiently honoring the commitments to couplehood.

Increased emphasis on interpersonal intimacy as opposed to social organization as a means of integration. We have many different pieces of data to support the general conclusion that interpersonal intimacy has become a vehicle for personal fulfillment much more in 1976 than it was in 1957. Contrariwise, social organizational commitments have become less important as a basis for personal fulfillment. As evidence of the decline in organizational commitments, people belong to fewer organizations in 1976 than they did in 1957. In addition, fewer people in 1976 participate in what we view as ritualized visiting with family and friends. As evidence of the stronger interest in 1976 in intimate interpersonal relationships, husbands and wives refer more often in 1976 to relationship aspects of marriage when asked about the nicest things about their marriages. And there has been a considerable rise in how much people refer to interpersonal difficulties as a source of the feeling that they might have a nervous breakdown. In 1957 many more people refer to concrete outside events—e.g., death of a loved one or a financial collapse—as the source of such feelings. Furthermore, there is more attention in 1976 to interpersonal sources of unhappiness. Thus, an increased salience of interpersonal intimacy as a basis of well-being runs through a number of the results that we have reported in various chapters.

What can we say about the fact that formal participation in the society has decreased and more intimate, interpersonal ways of dealing with one's social life have increased? Or, to put it more abstractly, the movement from a social organizational form of integration to society, to a more personal and intimate one? It is hard to judge whether this shift is for better or for worse. In many ways, a sharp focus on interpersonal integration can enrich awareness of social life. People committed to more formal roles often cannot take the time to let the nuances of affection and power touch their consciousness. The people in Thornton Wilder's sentimental *Our Town* do not see their love for each other as they are caught in enacting the demands of their lives. This play evokes powerful empathic understanding in Americans. Nevertheless, the ritualized experiences in social organizations may provide a kind of automatic guarantee of self-affirmation. The attention to close personal interaction puts a greater burden on individuals to enhance their interpersonal lives. Furthermore, in this new form of integration, interpersonal intimacy becomes a self-conscious arena for achievement rather than an automatic social activity that is more or less part and parcel of the social life provided by institutionalized attachments. More people now "work at" intimacy rather than experience it as a spontaneous reaction to their relationships with others. There is a growing sense that people are lucky if interpersonal relationships work out. There are comforts to be had from social organizations and commitments to the larger social structure which are not necessarily or easily available through close ties.

Smaller Changes Indicating Increased Psychological Approach to Understanding One's Own Behavior

In addition to findings indicating that more American men and women in 1976 were aware of problems in their life roles and took a more psychological approach to help-seeking behaviors, a number of smaller results support the general thesis that Americans over this generation have become highly psychological in their orientation to their lives.

Much of this further evidence comes from the way Americans responded in 1976 to questions about self-perceptions. Many more Americans were able in later generations to articulate perceived differences from other people (that is, their own uniqueness from most other people); many more Americans referred to personal strong points rather than role-related bases for strength; many more Americans alluded to personal characteristics or traits in describing their own shortcomings.

This increased psychological orientation is not unrelated to the changes noted in previous sections documenting the swing from social to personal integrations of well-being. As people become more personal in their approach to adaptation to life, they become more psychological in their orientation to understanding behaviors. The more people give situational (organizational) explanations of behavior, the more likely they are to use their understanding of social structure or social roles as perceived causal determinants of human action. The more psychological they are in explaining behaviors, the less tied they are to social roles as the source of behaviors. We would expect more people these days to say that someone acted in a particular way because of the kind of person s/he was, not because s/he was middle-class, black, a woman, or the like.

To the extent that this more psychological approach allows people insights about factors producing problems that can also lead to change, this new psychological approach may be seen as a benefit for subjective mental health. To the extent that this more psychological approach puts an unrealistic and unmodifiable bind on people, then a psychological approach may be a negative force on subjective mental health. Nowhere is this clearer than in the Gurin, Gurin, Lao, and Beattie's (1969) approach to the differences between blacks who interpret the lack of movement of blacks in the society to problems in the system (a social approach to explanation) in contrast to those who attributed it to some personal incompetence in blacks themselves (a much more psychological orientation to understanding human behavior). These researchers found that blacks who have attributed the causes of discrimination to the system are more successful in the achievement realm than are people who hold more personal attributions of responsibility. Thus we keep open the question of whether increased psychologizing about human behavior has an ultimate positive or negative consequence in general well-being. Our guess is that for some people it has positive consequences and for other people it has more negative consequences, depending on how optimistic they are about modifying their own behavior.

ARE SOME OF THE CHANGES IN SUBJECTIVE MENTAL HEALTH COHORT PHENOMENA?

Whenever we examine social change, we must always be sensitive to the possibility that what we see as change might very well be a result of the movement of cohorts through time, as well as the introduction of a totally different birth cohort. The changes we observe could be the result of the diminished ranks of the older cohort in the earlier study, and/or the introduction of a new cohort in 1976, rather than changes within people moving through time over the generation. Analyses presented in earlier chapters were also examined for such potential cohort phenomena. Most results that we discussed seemed to occur in all of the birth cohorts examined, and hence represented a general cultural shift, rather than phenomena specific to one or two cohorts.

However, there are five results which are perhaps better interpreted as cohort phenomena, rather than general cultural change. Two have to do with help seeking; one with people's orientation toward children; one with people's orientation toward marriage; the last, with women's orientation to work.

In examining informal help-seeking behaviors, we saw that some groups moving through time seemed to remain constant in their responses, even though we have evidence of general generational change.

We found that young people in 1957 who became the middle-aged people in 1976 and the middle-aged people in 1957 who became the older people in 1976 were relatively constant in their use of informal helping for handling worries and unhappiness. If we examine the percentage of people who turn to friends and family in periods of unhappiness or worry, we find the percentages constant in cohorts who were young in 1957 and middle-aged in 1976, and those who were middle-aged in 1957 and old in 1976. This finding suggests that some help-seeking orientations may remain as relatively constant expressive coping styles. Why, then, did we find such a remarkable shift in overall comparisons? Probably because the general cultural infatuation with personal informality as a way to seek support for difficulties was especially consonant for the very youngest groups in the new generation and was especially dissonant for the older group in 1957, which was much smaller in 1976. Although we obviously have a cultural shift in the view of informal support as a way of coping with problems, we thus also have evidence of some consistency in the way people utilize such a coping style once they adopt it during their youth.

We also saw an interesting cohort effect with regard to formal help-seeking. People who were middle-aged in 1957 were just as likely to seek professional help in 1976 as they were in 1957. What we have seen as a general cultural shift toward formal help-seeking does not seem to have affected that group of people who were middle-aged in 1957 and became the elderly of 1976. They seem to have been immune to the increased cultural dependence on expert guidance for dealing with psychological problems. Younger cohorts thus seem to have been most easily socialized to the new norm for turning to mental-health specialists. While we see a large general change in formal help-seeking, we should remember that the change affected younger people in particular. If we wish to increase formal help-seeking, we need to attend to the fact that attitudes toward professional mental-health resources may not be changed easily in the elderly. Of course, it could also be that therapeutic interventions in the recent generation were not designed to address the problems of the elderly. Perhaps, as we recognize that fact, we can make therapeutic intervention more appropriate to the elderly and hence socialize the elderly to take advantage of professionals in their efforts to cope with problems.

Another set of results easily interpretable as a cohort phenomenon centers around different cohorts' involvement with parenthood. While most Americans show a diminished involvement with parenthood, the remarkably strong orientation to children that characterized young people in 1957 remains strong in their middle age. As the culture came to see the baby boom and population growth as threats to national and world economies, and as the revolution against the feminine mystique proliferated from a handful of middle-class housewives in the 1960s to women in all groups in the 1970s, there was a general reevaluation of parenthood and motherhood, in particular. A more negative orientation toward parenthood developed, a general questioning of whether total involvement with children was the route to happiness. Nevertheless, young people in the 1950s and early 1960s who produced the babies that contributed to the overflow of young adults in the economy in the 1970s had to live with their involvement with children. They were deeply committed to raising children as an expression of life goals. As the whole culture moved away from the style, they may have become defensively involved in their own choices and commitments. In many of the results about people's orientation toward children, we find that this cohort of mothers and fathers remained strongly fixed on parenthood as a way of organizing their lives.

A fourth important cohort effect can be read into the data about changes that marriage brings and the view of someone who chooses not to marry—changes most striking in the young men and women of 1976. This is truly a different cohort with regard to attitudes toward family roles, most clearly distinguished in the nonchalance of young single women in 1976 about a woman who decides not to marry. Young women in 1957 were extremely negative about such a choice.

The last noteworthy cohort effect is also among young women in 1976. They are distinctly committed to working, not very satisfied about housework, and much more vocal about dissatisfactions with their jobs. The women's movement seems clearly to have affected this new cohort.

In the material examined in the chapters of this book, there may be many other results that could be interpreted better as cohort phenomena than as generational shifts, but these are the ones that stand out. Although we were alert to the possibility of cohort effects, it became clear in analyses that we were more often dealing with changes in normative values and orientations that permeate the whole society. The changes discussed in previous sections were generally not located in only one cohort. We were surprised by this, since the life-span developmental literature points to the power of cohort analyses. We conclude that where cohort effects occur in subjective mental-health indices, the measures probably reflect either expressive styles or value commitments made in late adolescence or early adulthood as part of young people's consolidation of values. This early commitment may be impervious to further social change. A few middle-aged men and women may do a turnaround in their commitments to social roles, but they are probably unusual people.

Many of our measures deal with reactive feelings which come from people's integration of their ongoing lives. These "reactive" measures are (by definition) responsive to historical change and are less dependent on very personalized commitments made in adolescence or early adulthood. We do not see most of the measures used in our studies as "personality" measures in the sense that they assess long-term dispositions that people form early and maintain relatively intact throughout life. Rather, we see our measures of adjustment as reactive to life situations as people move through history and the life cycle.

CONSISTENCY IN WELL-BEING FROM 1957 TO 1976

In our comparisons of the earlier and later generation, we have focused on measures that *differed* in 1976 compared to 1957. Therefore we should return to the more general question: Is there a great deal of change in the findings about subjective adjustment from the earlier to the later year, or are things just about the same? There is remarkable consistency in the way men and women respond to questions about their well-being in 1957 and 1976. *Overall, changes are small; often there is no change at all.*

With hindsight we can rationalize this lack of change, but we were initially surprised by the consistency in many indices of subjective mental health from 1957 to 1976. Some consistent results are more surprising than others.

We were especially surprised by the lack of change in men's overall job satisfaction. By and large, people in 1957 and 1976 give very comparable responses about how satisfied or dissatisfied they are with work. We had every expectation that there would have been a substantial decrease in job satisfaction as competition for jobs increased and the nature of work had presumably been degraded. As a corollary to our hypothesis that job satisfaction would be lower in 1976, we also expected that men would show a decline in work commitment. We thus expected a general decrease in the psychological value of work in American society; we thought that heightened job pressure would make people think twice about the value of work. Not so. There was essentially no change in the psychological value of work for men.

How do we account for this lack of change? One hypothesis worth exploring focuses on sex-role change in American life. Perhaps as men have become less involved in work, women have become particularly invested in jobs. This initial cross-over shift in work investment for men and women may have reinforced the involvement with work that men had begun to lose. It was probably a threat to men for women to enter the labor force and to develop a commitment to work as the focus of self-expression. In turn, men may have recharged their own involvements with work.

Another surprising consistency was the relatively stable distribution of responses in both years to questions about inadequacy in the spouse role. We had thought that the increased focus on interpersonal life and the increased difficulties in marriages in American society would have consequences on the confidence people felt about their performance as husbands and wives. This seems not to be the case. Although there is a large increase in perceived problems in marriage, there is no comparable increase in inadequacies in performing the marital role. We can only suggest that the interpersonal orientation that has become so dominant a theme in American life has for some reason *reduced* the *personal* sense of responsibility people have in performing these roles. We would have anticipated that increased orientation to marital performance would have engendered increased feelings of inadequacy about it. Could it be that the new vision of marital role difficulties as a *system of interpersonal communication problems* rather than ones in which one spouse or the other is at fault, *reduces guilt* that men and women feel about marital difficulties? Perhaps the increased *interpersonal* focus on life problems reduces the onus of responsibility for incompetence that may once have existed in marital or other interpersonal situations. As it becomes more normative to think about interpersonal difficulties in both marriage and parenthood, perhaps difficulties can be thought of as *system* problems, rather than personal flaws.

Many notable differences in people's responses to questions about subjective well-being concerned evaluations of what roles might mean for people in general, rather than specific reactions to *being* in the role. These results suggest that normative changes, or shifts in evaluations of life circumstances for a generalized "other," are more likely to be dramatized in a generational study like this, than very *personal* reactions to life circumstances. The power of human adaptation to different settings is remarkable. People's happiness, satisfaction, feelings of competence or incompetence, and self-esteem are perhaps ultimately dependent on what is available at a *given point of history*. Thus, if there is a greater burden on people to perform a given role such as marriage or parenthood in the normative expectations of the society, people quickly adapt to that and judge their satisfactions or dissatisfactions relative to other people who are performing within that normative climate. The power of reference-group adaptations to norms is especially important in people's evaluation of their own self-esteem, their own feelings of happiness and unhappiness. Grandmothers and grandfathers would become very anxious if they had to confront the challenges of the new sex roles required of men and women in younger marriages today; they adapted to a very different set of expectations about the nature of marriage and parenthood. Their own responses to their marriages are based on how *other older people* respond to their lives and their particular life circumstances. Their comfort and anxiety are embedded in their own reference groups.

We might think that there are certain kinds of stresses in our social environments which change so dramatically that they induce problems of adaptation for everyone, and hence induce dramatic changes in psychological strain. Evidently, we have not reached such points of stress that adaptation to reference-group perspectives on styles of coping does not occur. It would not be difficult to conclude that the social embeddedness of all of our life experiences becomes the basis of our adaptive strength. The year 1957 was a sociohistorically different context for evaluating well-being than was 1976. And it is within those contexts that psychological adjustment occurs. Happiness, feelings of adequacy, self-esteem, are all evaluated by people in sociohistorical context. People have little sense of the *absolute* potential for their own mental health. They constantly judge their lives in comparison to others. The general lack of change we see can be interpreted as reflecting the great power of humans to adapt to whatever social context exists at a given moment in their development. Values may change over a period of time, and indeed we find in analysis of other data from these two national surveys (Veroff, Depner, Kulka and Douvan, 1980) that there have been remarkable changes in the underlying motives of American adults from 1957 to 1976. Both men and women in our society are much more oriented to power than they were in 1957. Men show a remarkable decline in affiliative motivation during that time period, while women show a remarkable increase in achievement motivation. This is not the place to discuss these changes, but only to note that some underlying values for well-being may show dramatic changes over a generation. The subjective appraisal of how well someone is faring within any given value system may remain relatively constant because that appraisal is so dependent on comparing one's life with other people who comprise the present relevant reference group.

The State of Subjective Mental Health in 1976

Having explored differences in results from 1957 to 1976, as well as noting remarkable stability in many measures, we can still try to answer the more limited question of how this country was faring in subjective well-being and ways of coping with problems in 1976, regardless of any comparisons with 1957. In this analysis, we use measures in the 1976 data that were not available in the 1957 sample. Overall, we conclude that we are doing well according to the measures amassed in this study. We are generally a happy culture, lacking in anxiety, satisfied with our jobs, happy in our marriages, armed with positive orientations to ourselves, and buttressed by social support for problems we encounter. Let us review each of the chapters very briefly and highlight results which lead us to the general conclusion that we as a nation are doing well in subjective mental health. We will also highlight results that point to certain difficulties we encounter in our everyday lives.

GENERAL SOURCES AND FEELINGS OF WELL-BEING

We seem to be a happy society although we are somewhat worried about the future. Our happiness seems to be largely contingent upon interpersonal issues. Contentment in marriage is a very strong basis of well-being. While most of us respond to life as offering zestful opportunities, a substantial group of people (19 percent) select responses indicating considerable depression about their existence. We should not discount that small group. An increasing sense of alienation from life experience might occur over the next twenty years. We have much evidence from our studies that most of our adjustments depend on highly personal adaptations rather than on cultural ones. Comfort from culture has seriously eroded between 1957 and 1976. Under those circumstances, the people who do not make the interpersonal accommodation required for adjustment, for one reason or another, would find living in our society a very isolated and detached experience.

We are still an optimistic people. We think well about our future and are not especially nostalgic about the past as having been a better time. Most of us refuse to say we are completely satisfied with life, an indication that we recognize some future changes that could make life even more satisfying. We would characterize our general adjustment as one that selects the present as a general time orientation, but holds some hope for future change that might make things even better. Increased worries and psychological anxiety that are apparent, compared to the previous generation, suggest that this future optimism may be dwindling.

SELF-PERCEPTIONS

As a people, we are fairly confident about our own efficacy. Most of us are willing to talk about our strengths. When we do so, most of us talk about personal rather than external qualities and conditions. Most of us can talk about how we are different from other people, and when we do, we are likely to give positive characteristics rather than negative ones. In talking about our weaknesses, however, we are also more alerted to internal matters than external bases of difficulties. We see ourselves as capable of planning for the future, as able to control our lives. We do not see ourselves needing people to make us feel better. Responding to a direct question about self-esteem, we hedge somewhat more. We are unwilling to talk of ourselves in extremely praiseworthy terms as worthwhile people—especially in doing things well compared to others. Whether this reflects our modesty in social comparison or a general lack of confidence when we compare ourselves to others is an open question. We consider both interpretations plausible. To the extent that the results reflect a questioning of overall competence in competitive comparisons with other people, we may want to ask where such questioning comes from. We would note that our school systems and our vocational ladders are ones where comparisons are constantly demanded in judging how well we are doing. This focus on comparison cannot help but translate into some doubts people in our society have about the adequacy of their own lives.

MARRIAGE

We are a family-centered society. Family roles—marriage and parenthood—yield high value for most people; compared to work or leisure activities, they are clearly more central to self-definition.

Most married people invest in marriage and derive both support and satisfaction in the relationship with their partners. They report their marriages to be happy, and they feel reasonably adequate in their own performance as husbands and wives. Depner (1978) has reported findings from analysis of these data which indicate that satisfaction in the marriage role contributes very heavily—more so than satisfaction in work or parenting—to overall life satisfaction. We have seen that married people use their spouses very heavily as a support in times of trouble and worry. For most men, the marriage relationship is the major source of interpersonal gratification and emotional expression, particularly given diminished interpersonal satisfactions in work and parenthood.

The fact that marriage is generally highly important and the source of much satisfaction does not exempt it from problems. In fact, its crucial role in life—particularly for men—may, in itself, contribute to problems in the relationship. When so much rides on a single role and a single relationship, anxiety is likely to run high and to act in some ways as an obstacle to realizing the ease and intimacy people seek in marriage. The high incidence of divorce and tolerance in societal norms toward single and divorced statuses have also contributed to the recognition of marriage problems. When divorce was not an alternative to be considered realistically, when the norms in large segments of the population held that marriage was indissoluble, people probably adjusted without thought to problems and difficulties which now lead to divorce, or at least to help seeking. When there is no way out, human beings adapt. When the way out becomes visible—when people see their friends and relatives choosing divorce—they become more aware of problems in their own marriages.

Yet recognizing problems is not inevitably the precursor to divorce. Many married people recognize that they have had serious problems in their marriages, but have somehow managed to withstand the problem—with or without formal help—and have maintained their marriages. This willingness to admit problems which in earlier generations would have been denied seems to be a sign of strength. The experience of working out problems in a relationship can lead to greater intimacy and understanding between a couple and may, in the final analysis, contribute to the happiness which is so strikingly present in Americans' responses to their own marital experience.

PARENTHOOD

Parenthood, like marriage, is very important in the life view, identity, and values of people who choose to become parents or who blunder into parenthood. Norms about parenthood are neither strong nor rigid, and we can assume that most people who are parents—particularly younger parents in our population—have actively chosen the role rather than being forced into it through the pressure of pronatal norms. Young, highly educated people are postponing parenthood and a small proportion will probably elect not to have children at all. Those who do become parents, then, will probably find the role satisfying and meaningful if only for dissonance-reducing reasons.

Our data indicate that in 1976 most parents find their children to be a source of meaning and satisfaction. However, they also recognize that parenthood—like all really involving roles and relationships—is not perfect. When we ask people to describe changes that children bring to a person's life, the modal answer is a mixture of joy and enlargement, on the one hand, and problems and anxiety on the other. Most parents have a differentiated view of the experience rather than a glossy, romantic view. Again we see this as a strength, since an unconditioned positive conception of parenthood would seem to be at variance with reality and thus to be based on defensive denial.

A significant minority of respondents in 1976 feel inadequate as parents because they have not managed to develop as warm and open interpersonal relations with their children as they would like, or think somehow they should have. We interpret this sense of discomfort, in part, as a transition phenomenon, one to which men are particularly vulnerable. As the father role has lost some of its grounding and significance from traditional authority—a victim of the culture's struggles and ambivalence about authority and the nature of authority of any kind—men have sought to replace authority-based interaction with interpersonal warmth and closeness. And it has not always worked. Because of their own socialization and the demands of the traditional male role, but perhaps also because of a misunderstanding of the realities of the parent role, they have tried to be friends with their children, but have not succeeded in this effort to the extent they wish to.

A large subgroup of parents consists of women raising children alone. These women face extraordinary difficulties. Many of them are existing on or near poverty levels, and they reflect this harsh reality in their answers to the question about inadequacies in parenthood. They often say they feel inadequate because they cannot provide well enough for their children's real needs. This group includes a significant minority of mothers who seem to be really stressed and unhappy with parenthood—saying, for example, that having children has only restrictive effects on a person's life, and that they do not feel close to their children. But most of the women who are single parents feel much more positive about parenthood: they see it as an enlarging, satisfying experience and a central element in their lives and self-definition.

WORK

As a people, we are surprisingly committed to and satisfied with our work. Very few people admit to being dissatisfied, ambivalent, or even neutral about their jobs. Most people say the work they do is challenging and interesting when they are asked to think about the issue. Although many people's commitment to work reflects the need to structure time, fewer people in 1976 give that kind of response than people did in 1957. This suggests that in 1976 people are more personally committed to work than people once were. Work as a way to structure time is still the major way people think of commitment to work, but it is decreasing. While work remains an involved role for most men and women in our society, it nevertheless pales as a role involvement compared to family roles, as noted in the previous sections. Furthermore, Depner (1978) has found that job satisfaction is not as critical as marital satisfaction in contributing to overall satisfaction with life.

In thinking about types of job satisfaction and job dissatisfaction, 1976 workers report characteristics that clearly reflect high ego-involvement with work. People are more demanding in their psychological approach to work than ever before, and they are more ego-involved with work satisfactions than with their reported dissatisfactions. People are more likely to represent their satisfactions as tied to the intrinsic nature of work or to relationships with people at work, than to extrinsic factors. When they speak of dissatisfactions, fewer people mention these intrinsic or interpersonal qualities of work. Extrinsic factors such as money and hard conditions are the critical issues in job dissatisfaction.

Most people think they are very good at what they do, and that what they do is relatively demanding. These results may be examples of people adjusting to whatever they are required to adapt to. They see their work as demanding, *whatever that work is*, and they see themselves as competent at work, *whatever the demands are*. A good proportion (about 20 percent) of American workers are aware of difficulties in the social fabric of their work setting, many more than there were in 1957. This change alerts us to the possibility that the critical feature of the work environment that needs attention now with regard to subjective well-being is not increased challenge from work, as *Work in America* suggested, but increased humanization of people's relationships to each other at work.

SYMPTOMS

A minority of American men and women in our society report a high frequency of physical, psychological, or psychosomatic symptoms. More women than men report a high frequency of symptoms that would unmistakably be coded as indicating distress. Furthermore, only a fairly small proportion of men and women report frequent use of alcohol, medicines, or drugs to handle tension. The highest report of alcohol use is in middle-aged men, 15 percent of whom report that they use alcohol to relieve tension "sometimes" or "many times." Older women are particularly prone to use medicines or drugs to relieve tension. Twenty percent of American women sixty-five or older report using medicines or drugs to relieve tension "sometimes" or "many times." But these are small segments of the population; ones which may need specific attention with respect to substance abuse. We can hardly say that substance abuse is a style broadly adopted to cope with psychological difficulties in our society.

COPING WITH PROBLEMS AND SOCIAL SUPPORTS

Our dominant mode of adapting to worries or periods of unhappiness is talking to someone about our troubles. We are a very social people who rely on interpersonal contacts with others to help us cope with life's problems. Prayer is a fairly common response to periods of worries and unhappiness but less so than it once was. A fairly large group of people (over 20 percent in 1976) responds to worries and periods of unhappiness by doing nothing or trying to forget the problem. This kind of passive, denying way of handling difficulties is probably harmful in most instances. Even so, it is hard to assess whether denial may be the best means people have for coping with some problems.

Although more than a third of the American population have turned to professional help for some kind of personal problem at some time in their lives, very few mention these resources for problems they encounter in their everyday lives. Rather, we have developed and diversified our interpersonal sources of help for worries and periods of unhappiness. Husbands and wives are still a dominant resource for married people, but we use many other resources—both family and friends—in periods of worry and periods of unhappiness. Turning to friends has increased over the generation at the same time that marriage and participation in formal organizations have become less common. We suspect that informal mechanisms people use for dealing with problems will increasingly supplant the more ritualized forms of organizational, family, or marital support. Perhaps these informal networks will serve people well. Person-to-person helping can be the most direct and human form of interaction. Nonetheless, participation in formal organizations, in role-governed exchange in marriage, and ritual contact with friends and family can provide continuity, social stability, and comfort in troubled times. And our findings indicate that these supports are used less by American adults now than they were twenty years ago. We take this as another indication that formal role structures have weakened in our society, have lost some of their compelling force, comfort, and stability in people's lives.

Appendix A

1976 INTERVIEW SCHEDULE

GUIDE FOR DETECTING QUESTIONS IN THE 1976
INTERVIEW SCHEDULE THAT WERE ALSO PART
OF THE 1957 INTERVIEW SCHEDULE

Question prefix	Information Designated about 1957 Interview
*	Identical question asked in the 1957 study
*⅓	Identical question asked of one-third of the 1957 sample
*(M)	Identical question asked of men only in the 1957 sample
*(M)⅓	Identical question asked of one-third of men only in the 1957 sample
*(H)	Identical question asked of housewives only in the 1957 sample
#	Approximate question asked in the 1957 study
#(W)	Approximate question asked of women only in the 1957 sample

¹X, Y, Z represented random two-thirds of the total 1976 sample.

*Introduction: Read to *Everyone*

The Survey Research Center has been asked to make a study of the stresses and strains of modern living. There have been a lot of changes in our way of living over the past fifty years or so. These changes have brought this country to the highest standard of living in the world. But a great many people are concerned about whether or not there are problems involved in the rapid pace of our present life. Doctors, educators, religious leaders, and other experts are interested in finding out how people feel about this question.

Of course this interview is completely voluntary. If we should come to any question you don't want to answer, let me know and we'll skip over it. I think you'll find the questions interesting and will want to give them careful thought.

TIME NOW_____

Section A: Leisure and Social Support

One of the things we'd like to know is how people spend their time.

*A1.   For instance—how do you usually spend your time when your work is done—what kind of things do you do, both at home and away from home?_____

_____
_____
_____
_____

*A2.   Are you a member of any (other) clubs and organizations—like a lodge, PTA, a community group, or any other kind of group?

1. YES   5. NO ──────▶ GO TO A3

*A2a.   What are they?_____
_____
_____

A3. (CARD A) How much of your free time do you usually spend doing things to help or please other people? Would you say that you spend *most, a lot, some, a little,* or *none* of your free time doing such things?

1. MOST	2. A LOT	3. SOME	4. A LITTLE	5. NONE

A4. Do you wish that you spent *more* of your free time doing things to help or please other people, *less time,* or do you *like it the way it is?*

1. MORE TIME	5. LESS TIME	3. LIKE IT IS

A5. (CARD A) Next, how much of your free time do you spend doing things that challenge you? Would you say that you spend *most, a lot, some, a little,* or *none* of your free time doing such things?

1. MOST	2. A LOT	3. SOME	4. A LITTLE	5. NONE

A6. Do you wish that you spent *more* of your free time doing things that challenge you, *less time,* or do you *like it the way it is?*

1. MORE TIME	5. LESS TIME	3. LIKE IT IS

A7. Now a couple of questions about neighbors. About how many of your neighbors do you know well enough to visit or call on? Would you say you have *many, several, a few,* or *none* that you know well enough to visit or call on?

1. MANY	2. SEVERAL	4. A FEW	5. NONE	7. R SAYS HAS *NO* NEIGHBORS

TURN TO A9

A8. (CARD B) About how often do you visit with any of your neighbors, either at their homes or at your own? (Would you say *more than once a week, once a week, a few times a month, once a month,* or *less than once a month?*)

MORE 1. THAN ONCE A WEEK	ONCE 2. A WEEK	A FEW 3. TIMES A MONTH	ONCE 4. A MONTH	LESS 5. THAN ONCE A MONTH	6. NEVER

*A9. (CARD B) Here are a few questions about your friends and relatives. First, about how often do you get together with friends or relatives—I mean things like going out together or visiting each other's homes? (Would you say *more than once a week, once a week, a few times a month, once a month,* or *less than once a month?*)

MORE 1. THAN ONCE A WEEK	ONCE 2. A WEEK	A FEW 3. TIMES A MONTH	ONCE 4. A MONTH	LESS 5. THAN ONCE A MONTH	6. NEVER

A10. Now, think of the friends and relatives you feel free to talk with about your worries and problems or can count on for advice and help—would you say you have *many, several, a few,* or *no* such friends or relatives?

1. MANY	2. SEVERAL	4. A FEW	5. NONE

A11. (CARD C) How often, if ever, have you talked with friends or relatives about your problems when you were worried or asked them for advice or help—*very often, often, sometimes, rarely,* or *never?*

1. VERY OFTEN	2. OFTEN	3. SOMETIMES	4. RARELY	5. NEVER

*A12. Do you feel you have as many friends as you want, or would you like to have more friends?

| 1. AS MANY FRIENDS AS WANTS | 5. WOULD LIKE MORE FRIENDS |

A13. INTERVIEWER CHECKPOINT

☐ 1. COVER SHEET IS FORM "X" OR "Y" ⟶ TURN TO SECTION B
☐ 2. COVER SHEET IS FORM "Z" ⟶ TURN TO SECTION C

Section B: Picture Stories

*Another thing we want to find out is what people think of situations that may come up in life. I'm going to show you some pictures of these situations and ask you to think of stories to go with them. The situations won't be clearly one thing or another—so feel free to think of any story you want to. (SHOW SET OF MALE PICTURES TO MEN; FEMALE PICTURES TO WOMEN.)

(SHOW PICTURE 1)

*For example, here's the first picture. I'd like you to spend a few moments thinking of a story to go with it. To get at the story you're thinking of I'll ask you questions like: Who are these people? What do they want? and so on. Just answer with anything that comes to mind. There are no right or wrong answers.

*B1. Who are these people? What are they doing?_____

*B1a. What has led up to this—what went on before?_____

*B1b. What do they want—how do they feel?_____

*B1c. What will happen—how will it end?_____

(SHOW PICTURE 2)

*B2. Who are these people? What are they doing?_____

*B2a. What has led up to this—what went on before?_____

*B2b. What do they want—how do they feel?_____

_____

_____

_____

*B2c. What will happen—how will it end?_____

_____

_____

_____

(SHOW PICTURE 3)

*B3. Who are these people? What are they doing?_____

_____

_____

_____

*B3a. What has led up to this—what went on before?_____

_____

_____

_____

*B3b. What do they want—how do they feel?_____

_____

_____

_____

*B3c. What will happen—how will it end?_____

_____

_____

_____

(SHOW PICTURE 4)

*B4. Who is this person? What is (he/she) doing?_____

_____

_____

_____

*B4a. What has led up to this—what went on before?_____

_____

_____

_____

*B4b. What does (he/she) want—how does (he/she) feel?_____

_____

_____

_____

*B4c. What will happen—how will it end?_____

_____

_____

_____

(SHOW PICTURE 5)

*B5.   Who are these people? What are they doing?_____

_____

_____

_____

_____

    *B5a.   What has led up to this—what went on before?_____

        _____

        _____

        _____

    *B5b.   What do they want—how do they feel?_____

        _____

        _____

        _____

        _____

    *B5c.   What will happen—how will it end?_____

        _____

        _____

        _____

(SHOW PICTURE 6)

*B6.   Who are these people? What are they doing?_____

_____

_____

_____

    *B6a.   What has led up to this—what went on before?_____

        _____

        _____

        _____

    *B6b.   What do they want—how do they feel?_____

        _____

        _____

        _____

    *B6c.   What will happen—how will it end?_____

        _____

        _____

        _____

Section C: Worries and Unhappiness

One of the things we're interested in is what people think about these days.

    *C1.   Everybody has some things he worries about more or less. What kinds of things do you
        worry about most?

        _____

        _____

        _____

*C2. Do you worry about such things a lot, or not very much? _____
_____
_____

*C3. If something is on your mind that's bothering you or worrying you, and you don't know what to do about it, what do you usually do?
_____
_____

*C4. INTERVIEWER CHECKPOINT

☐ 1. R MENTIONS "TALK IT OVER"—
       PERSON MENTIONED ————▶ TURN TO C5
  ☐ 2. R MENTIONS "TALK IT OVER"—PERSON *NOT* MENTIONED
    ☐ 3. R DOESN'T MENTION "TALK IT OVER" ————▶ GO TO C4b

C4a. Who do you talk it over with? (RELATIONSHIP TO R)
_____
TURN TO C5

C4b. Do you ever talk it over with anyone?

1. YES; DEPENDS   5. NO
                    TURN TO C5

C4c. Who is that? (RELATIONSHIP TO R)
_____
TURN TO C5

*C5. Now I'd like you to think about your whole life—how things are now, how they were ten years ago, how they were when you were a little (boy/girl). What do you think of as the happiest time of your life? (IF R MENTIONS SINGLE EVENT, PROBE: I don't mean just a particular day or single happening, but a whole period of your life.)
_____
_____

(IF R MENTIONS "PRESENT" TIME AS HAPPIEST OR BOTH A PRESENT AND PAST TIME.)
*C5a. Why is this a happy time—what are some of the things that you feel pretty happy about these days? (PROBE FOR FULL RESPONSES.)
_____
_____
_____

GO TO C6

(IF R MENTIONS "PAST" TIME ONLY AS HAPPIEST.)
*C5b. How about the way things are today—what are some of the things you feel pretty happy about these days? (PROBE FOR FULL RESPONSES.)
_____
_____
_____

*C6.   Everyone has things about their life they're not completely happy about. What are some of the things that you're not too happy about these days? (PROBE FOR FULL RESPONSES.)

_____
_____
_____
_____
_____
_____

*C7.   Thinking now of the way things were in the *past*, what do you think of as the most unhappy time of your life? (PROBE FOR WHOLE PERIOD OF R'S LIFE.)

_____
_____

  *C7a. Why do you think of that as an unhappy time? (Can you tell me more about that time?)

_____
_____
_____
_____
_____
_____

*C8.   Taking things all together, how would you say things are these days—would you say you're *very happy, pretty happy,* or *not too happy* these days?

| 1. VERY HAPPY | 3. PRETTY HAPPY | 5. NOT TOO HAPPY |

*C9.   Compared to your life today, how do you think things will be 5 or 10 years from now—do you think things will be happier for you than they are now, not quite as happy, or what?

_____
_____

C10.   Compared to your life today, how were things 5 or 6 years ago—were things happier for you then than they are now, not quite as happy, or what?

_____
_____

*C11. One of the things we'd like to know, is how people face the unhappy periods in their lives. Thinking of unhappiness you've had to face, what are some of the things that have helped you in those times?

_____
_____
_____

Section D: Self-Perceptions

Now, we'd like to ask you some other questions about yourself.

*D1.   People are the same in many ways, but no two people are exactly alike. What are some of the ways in which you're different from most other people?

_____
_____
_____

*D2.   Many people when they think about their children, would like them to be different from themselves in some ways. If you had a (son/daughter—SAME SEX AS R), how would you like (him/her) to be different from you?

_____
_____
_____

*D3. How about your good points? What would you say were your strongest points?

_____
_____
_____
_____

(P. 1, RESPONDENT BOOKLET) Now I'd like you to look at the first page of this booklet which tells about some of the ways in which different people describe themselves. After each statement, would you please check the category that applies to you. Please let me know when you have finished this page.

(HAND R THE RESPONDENT BOOKLET TURNED TO D4 AND D5. AFTER R FILLS OUT AND RE-TURNS IT, TURN TO D6.)

> INTERVIEWER: IF R HAS A READING OR SEEING PROBLEM, USE THE QUESTION-NAIRE AS USUAL: READ EACH STATEMENT AND THE RESPONSE CATEGORIES AND CHECK R'S CHOICE.

SAMPLE OF
RESPONDENT BOOKLET

D4. How often do you feel:

	A LITTLE OR NONE OF THE TIME	SOME OF THE TIME	A GOOD PART OF THE TIME	ALL OR MOST OF THE TIME
a. My mind is as clear as it used to be.				
b. I find it easy to do the things I used to.				
c. My life is interesting.				
d. I feel that I am useful and needed.				
e. My life is pretty full.				
f. I feel hopeful about the future.				

D5. How often are these true for you:

	OFTEN TRUE	SOMETIMES TRUE	RARELY TRUE	NEVER TRUE
a. I feel that I am a person of worth, at least as much as others.				
b. I am able to do things as well as most other people.				
c. On the whole, I feel good about myself.				

D6. When you make plans ahead, do you usually get to *carry out things the way you expected,* or do things usually come up to make you *change your plans?*

1. THINGS WORK OUT AS EXPECTED	5. HAVE TO CHANGE PLANS	8. DON'T KNOW

D7. Some people feel they *can run their lives* much the way they want to; others feel the *problems of life are sometimes too big* for them. Which one are you most like?

| 1. CAN RUN OWN LIFE | 5. PROBLEMS OF LIFE TOO BIG | 8. DON'T KNOW |

D8. In general, how satisfying do you find the way you're spending your life these days? Would you call it *completely satisfying, pretty satisfying* or *not very satisfying?*

| 1. COMPLETELY SATISFYING | 3. PRETTY SATISFYING | 5. NOT VERY SATISFYING | 8. DON'T KNOW |

D9. INTERVIEWER CHECKPOINT

☐ 1. COVER SHEET IS FORM "X" ──────▶ TURN TO SECTION F
☐ 2. COVER SHEET IS FORM "Y" OR "Z" ──────▶ TURN TO SECTION E

Section E: Personal Preferences

Now I'd like to ask you about your preferences for certain things. Keep in mind that there are no right or wrong answers.

E1. (CARD D) Which of the three things on this card is *truest* for you—I would like to have more friends, I would like to do better at what I try, or I would like to have more people pay attention to my point of view?

| 1. I WOULD LIKE TO HAVE MORE FRIENDS |

| 2. I WOULD LIKE TO DO BETTER AT WHAT I TRY |

| 3. I WOULD LIKE TO HAVE MORE PEOPLE PAY ATTENTION TO MY POINT OF VIEW |

E2. (CARD D) Which of these three is *least* true for you?

| 1. I WOULD LIKE TO HAVE MORE FRIENDS |

| 2. I WOULD LIKE TO DO BETTER AT WHAT I TRY |

| 3. I WOULD LIKE TO HAVE MORE PEOPLE PAY ATTENTION TO MY POINT OF VIEW |

E3. (CARD E) Now looking at the next card—what kind of job would you want the *most*—a job where you had to think for yourself, a job where the people you work with are a nice group, or a job where you have a lot to say in what's going on?

| 1. A JOB WHERE YOU HAD TO THINK FOR YOURSELF |

| 2. A JOB WHERE THE PEOPLE YOU WORK WITH ARE A NICE GROUP |

| 3. A JOB WHERE YOU HAVE A LOT TO SAY IN WHAT'S GOING ON |

E4. (CARD E) Which of these three would you want *least?*

> 1. A JOB WHERE YOU HAD TO THINK FOR YOURSELF

> 2. A JOB WHERE THE PEOPLE YOU WORK WITH ARE A NICE GROUP

> 3. A JOB WHERE YOU HAVE A LOT TO SAY IN WHAT'S GOING ON

E5. Now I'll read some statements people use to describe other people. Suppose you were to hear them. Which of the following would you *most* like to overhear about yourself—(his/her) opinion carries a lot of weight among people who know (him/her), *or* people like to live next door to (him/her)?

> 1. (HIS/HER) OPINION CARRIES A LOT OF WEIGHT

> 2. PEOPLE LIKE TO LIVE NEXT DOOR TO (HIM/HER)

E6. Now which of these would you rather hear about yourself—other people like (him/her) very much, *or* (he/she) can do anything (he/she) sets (his/her) mind on doing?

> 1. OTHER PEOPLE LIKE (HIM/HER) VERY MUCH

> 2. (HE/SHE) CAN DO ANYTHING (HE/SHE) SETS (HIS/HER) MIND ON DOING

E7. Now these two. (He/She) is fun to have at a party, *or* people like to go to (him/her) for advice on important matters?

> 1. (HE/SHE) IS FUN TO HAVE AT A PARTY

> 2. PEOPLE LIKE TO GO TO (HIM/HER) FOR ADVICE ON IMPORTANT MATTERS

> INTERVIEWER: QUESTIONS E8–E10 SHOULD BE ASKED OF *EVERYONE,* REGARDLESS OF WORK, PARENTAL, OR MARITAL STATUS.

E8. Now, for each pair of statements I read, please tell me which one you would rather overhear *a friend* say about you. First, which of these—(he/she) is a fine (father/mother), *or* (he/she) is excellent at the work (he/she) does?

> 1. (HE/SHE) IS A FINE (FATHER/MOTHER)

> 2. (HE/SHE) IS EXCELLENT AT THE WORK (HE/SHE) DOES

E9. How about these two—(he/she) is a fine (father/mother), *or* (he/she) is a fine (husband/wife)?

> 1. (HE/SHE) IS A FINE (FATHER/MOTHER)

> 2. (HE/SHE) IS A FINE (HUSBAND/WIFE)

E10. And which of these two would you rather overhear—(he/she) is a fine (husband/wife), *or* (he/she) is excellent at the work (he/she) does?

> 1. (HE/SHE) IS A FINE (HUSBAND/WIFE)

> 2. (HE/SHE) IS EXCELLENT AT THE WORK (HE/SHE) DOES

Section F: Marriage

Now I'd like to ask you some questions about marriage.

*F1. First thinking about a (man's/woman's—SAME SEX AS RESPONDENT) life. How is a (man's/woman's—SAME SEX AS RESPONDENT) life changed by being married? (PROBE FOR FEELINGS.)

---

*⅓ F2. Suppose all you knew about a (man/woman—SAME SEX AS RESPONDENT) was that (he/she) didn't want to get married. What would you guess (he/she) was like? (PROBE FOR FULL RESPONSES.)

> IF ANSWER IN TERMS OF NEVER ASKED, NEVER MET A PERSON TO MARRY, ETC.: Well, suppose (he/she) had plenty of chances to get married, but just didn't want to?

F3. How about a (man/woman—*OPPOSITE* SEX FROM RESPONDENT)? Suppose all you knew about a (man/woman) was that (he/she) didn't want to get married. What would you guess (he/she) was like? (PROBE FOR FULL RESPONSES.)

> IF ANSWER IN TERMS OF NEVER ASKED, NEVER MET A PERSON TO MARRY, ETC.: Well, suppose (he/she) had plenty of chances to get married, but just didn't want to?

---

*F4. Are you married, separated, divorced, widowed, or have you never been married?

> ☐ R VOLUNTEERS THAT (HE/SHE) IS LIVING WITH SOMEONE OF OPPOSITE SEX (ALSO CHECK APPROPRIATE BOX BELOW AND FOLLOW SKIP INSTRUCTION.)

1. MARRIED, (INCLUDING SPOUSE AWAY IN SERVICE)	2. SEPARATED	3. DIVORCED	4. WIDOWED	5. NEVER MARRIED, SINGLE
TURN TO F5	TURN TO F17		TURN TO F23	TURN TO F27

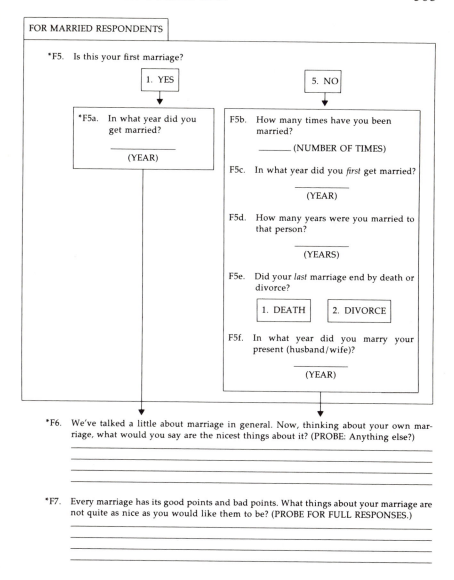

FOR MARRIED RESPONDENTS

*F5. Is this your first marriage?

1. YES

5. NO

*F5a. In what year did you
get married?

———————
(YEAR)

F5b. How many times have you been
married?

——— (NUMBER OF TIMES)

F5c. In what year did you *first* get married?

———————
(YEAR)

F5d. How many years were you married to
that person?

———————
(YEARS)

F5e. Did your *last* marriage end by death or
divorce?

1. DEATH   2. DIVORCE

F5f. In what year did you marry your
present (husband/wife)?

———————
(YEAR)

*F6. We've talked a little about marriage in general. Now, thinking about your own mar-
riage, what would you say are the nicest things about it? (PROBE: Anything else?)
_____
_____
_____
_____

*F7. Every marriage has its good points and bad points. What things about your marriage are
not quite as nice as you would like them to be? (PROBE FOR FULL RESPONSES.)
_____
_____
_____

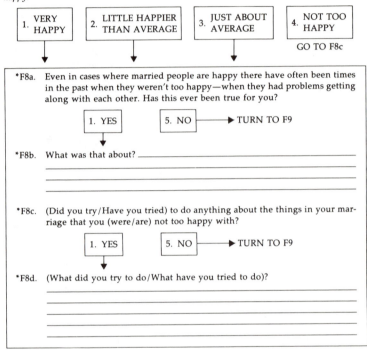

FOR MARRIED RESPONDENTS

*F8. Taking things all together, how would you describe your marriage—would you say your marriage was *very happy, a little happier than average, just about average, or not too happy?*

1. VERY HAPPY	2. LITTLE HAPPIER THAN AVERAGE	3. JUST ABOUT AVERAGE	4. NOT TOO HAPPY

GO TO F8c

*F8a. Even in cases where married people are happy there have often been times in the past when they weren't too happy—when they had problems getting along with each other. Has this ever been true for you?

1. YES   5. NO ⟶ TURN TO F9

*F8b. What was that about? _____
_____
_____

*F8c. (Did you try/Have you tried) to do anything about the things in your marriage that you (were/are) not too happy with?

1. YES   5. NO ⟶ TURN TO F9

*F8d. (What did you try to do/What have you tried to do)?
_____
_____
_____
_____

FOR MARRIED RESPONDENTS

*F9. Many (men/women—SAME SEX AS RESPONDENT) feel that they're not as good (husbands/wives) as they would like to be. Have you ever felt this way?

1. YES   5. NO ⟶ GO TO F10

*F9a. What kinds of things make you feel this way? (PROBE FOR FULL RESPONSES.)
_____
_____
_____

*F9b. Do you feel this way a lot of times, or only once in a while?
_____
_____
_____

F10.   Now I'm going to read you a couple of things that married couples sometimes do together.

(CARD F) First, how often have you and your (husband/wife) chatted with one another in the past 2 weeks? Would you say *many times, sometimes, hardly ever,* or *never?*

| 1. MANY TIMES | 2. SOMETIMES | 3. HARDLY EVER | 4. NEVER |

F11.   (CARD F) How about: Been physically affectionate with one another? How often have you and your (husband/wife) been physically affectionate with one another in the past 2 weeks? (Would you say *many times, sometimes, hardly ever,* or *never?*

| 1. MANY TIMES | 2. SOMETIMES | 3. HARDLY EVER | 4. NEVER |

FOR MARRIED RESPONDENTS

F12.   We are also interested in work that has to be done around the house—like cooking, cleaning and laundry. Who would you say does *more* of the housework in your family—you, your (husband/wife) or both about equal?

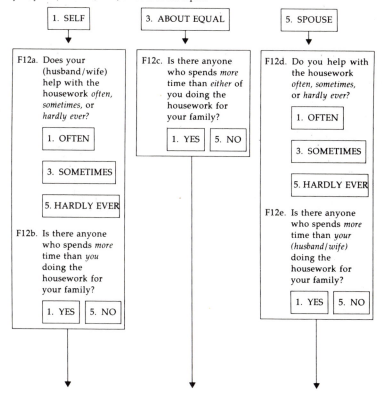

(RESPONDENT BOOKLET) Now would you look at this list which tells about troubles and complaints some people have. (HAND R RESPONDENT BOOKLET, F13, AND PENCIL.) For each one, would you check the answer which tells how often you have had this trouble or complaint: *often, sometimes, rarely,* or *never.* Please let me know when you have finished this page. (WHEN R RETURNS BOOKLET, TURN TO F14.)

SAMPLE OF
RESPONDENT BOOKLET

F13. How often have you:

	OFTEN	SOMETIMES	RARELY	NEVER
a. Been irritated with or resentful toward what your spouse did or didn't do.				
b. Been upset about how you and your spouse were getting along in the sexual part of your life.				
c. Wished your spouse talked more about how (he/she) feels or thinks.				
d. Felt tense from fighting, arguing or disagreeing with your spouse.				
e. Wished that your spouse understood you better.				

FOR MARRIED RESPONDENTS

F14. Some married people think of themselves as two separate people who make a life together. Others think of themselves as a couple, it being very hard to describe one person without the other. Which best describes your marriage—the "two separate people" way, or the "couple" way?

1. TWO SEPARATE PEOPLE   5. COUPLE

F15. All and all, who would you say gets more out of being married—you, your (husband/wife), or both about equal?

1. SELF   5. SPOUSE   3. ABOUT EQUAL

F16. Some people think that divorce is often the best solution when people can't seem to work out their marriage problems. Other people think divorce is never the best solution. Would you say divorce is *often, sometimes, rarely,* or *never* the best solution?

1. OFTEN   2. SOMETIMES   3. RARELY   4. NEVER

TURN TO SECTION G

FOR DIVORCED/SEPARATED RESPONDENTS

F17. In what year were you (divorced/separated)? (IF R HAS BEEN DIVORCED MORE THAN ONCE, RECORD LAST TIME ONLY.)

_____ YEAR

F18. In what year did you marry that person?

_____ YEAR

*F19. We've talked a little about marriages in general. Now, thinking about your own marriage, what were some of the problems in your marriage? (PROBE UNLESS R IS RESISTANT.)

_____
_____
_____
_____

*F20. What did you and your (husband/wife) try to do to work things out? (IF R MENTIONS TALKING TO SOMEONE, PROBE FOR WHOM.)

_____
_____
_____
_____

F21. Was that your first marriage?

| 1. YES | | 5. NO |

TURN TO F22

F21a. How many times have you been married?

_____ NUMBER OF TIMES

F21b. Did any of your other marriages end in divorce?

| 1. YES | | 5. NO |

F21c. In what year did you *first* get married?

_____ YEAR

F21d. How many years were you married to that person?

_____ YEARS

FOR DIVORCED/SEPARATED RESPONDENTS

F22. Do you think you'll ever marry again?

| 1. YES | 3. MAYBE; PROBABLY | 5. NO | 8. DON'T KNOW |

TURN TO SECTION G

F22a. Do you have specific plans to marry in the near future?

| 1. YES | | 5. NO |

F22b. What are the main reasons you don't think you'll marry again?

_____
_____
_____
_____

TURN TO SECTION G

FOR WIDOWED RESPONDENTS

F23. In what year did your (husband/wife) die? (MOST RECENT SPOUSE IF WIDOWED MORE THAN ONCE.)

_____ YEAR

F24. In what year did you and (he/she) get married?

_____ YEAR

F25. When your (husband/wife) died what helped you the most? (PROBE FOR MORE THAN ONE SOURCE.)

_____
_____
_____
_____
_____
_____

F26. Was that your first marriage?

| 1. YES | 5. NO |

TURN TO SECTION G

F26a. How many times have you been married?

_____ NUMBER OF TIMES

F26b. In what year did you *first* get married?

_____ YEAR

F26c. How many years were you married to that person?

_____ YEARS

TURN TO SECTION G

FOR SINGLE, NEVER MARRIED RESPONDENTS

F27. Do you think you'll ever get married?

| 1. YES | MAYBE; 3. DEPENDS; PROBABLY | 5. NO | 8. DON'T KNOW |

TURN TO SECTION G

F27a. Do you have specific plans to marry in the near future?

| 1. YES | 5. NO |

F27b. What are the main reasons you think you won't get married?

_____
_____
_____
_____

TURN TO SECTION G

Section G: Parenthood

(ASK EVERYONE)

And now I'd like to ask you some questions about children.

*G1. First, thinking about a (man's/woman's—SAME SEX AS RESPONDENT) life, how is a (man's/woman's—SAME SEX AS RESPONDENT) life changed by having children? (PROBE FOR FEELINGS.)

_____
_____
_____
_____

*G2. What would you say is the nicest thing about having children? (PROBE FOR FULL RESPONSES.)

_____
_____
_____
_____

G3. How do you feel about couples who decide to have no children at all?

_____
_____
_____
_____

G4. INTERVIEWER CHECKPOINT

☐ 1. R IS MARRIED OR NEVER MARRIED ———→ TURN TO G5
☐ 2. R IS SINGLE, NEVER MARRIED ———→ TURN TO SECTION H

*G5. Do you have any children?

| 1. YES | | 5. NO |

G5a. Do you expect to have any children?

| 1. YES | 3. MAYBE; DEPENDS; PROBABLY | 5. NO |

TURN TO SECTION H

*G5b. How many children have you had? _____ NUMBER OF CHILDREN

*G5c. Would you tell me whether they're boys or girls, how old they are, and whether they're living with you or away from home?
(WRITE DOWN IN ORDER OF MENTION)

CHILD NUMBER	SEX	AGE	CHILD LIVES WITH R, AWAY, OR IS DEAD?		
1			1. WITH R	2. AWAY	3. DEAD
2			1. WITH R	2. AWAY	3. DEAD
3			1. WITH R	2. AWAY	3. DEAD
4			1. WITH R	2. AWAY	3. DEAD
5			1. WITH R	2. AWAY	3. DEAD
6			1. WITH R	2. AWAY	3. DEAD
7			1. WITH R	2. AWAY	3. DEAD
8			1. WITH R	2. AWAY	3. DEAD

G5d. Are there any other children you have helped to raise who you may not have mentioned—like a child who died, an adopted child, or a child from a previous marriage?

| 1. YES | | 5. NO |——▶ TURN TO G6

G5e. Would you tell me whether they're boys or girls, how old they are, and whether they're living with you or someplace else?
(WRITE DOWN IN ORDER OF MENTION)

CHILD NUMBER	SEX	AGE	CHILD LIVES WITH R, AWAY, OR IS DEAD?		
1			1. WITH R	2. AWAY	3. DEAD
2			1. WITH R	2. AWAY	3. DEAD
3			1. WITH R	2. AWAY	3. DEAD
4			1. WITH R	2. AWAY	3. DEAD
5			1. WITH R	2. AWAY	3. DEAD
6			1. WITH R	2. AWAY	3. DEAD
7			1. WITH R	2. AWAY	3. DEAD
8			1. WITH R	2. AWAY	3. DEAD

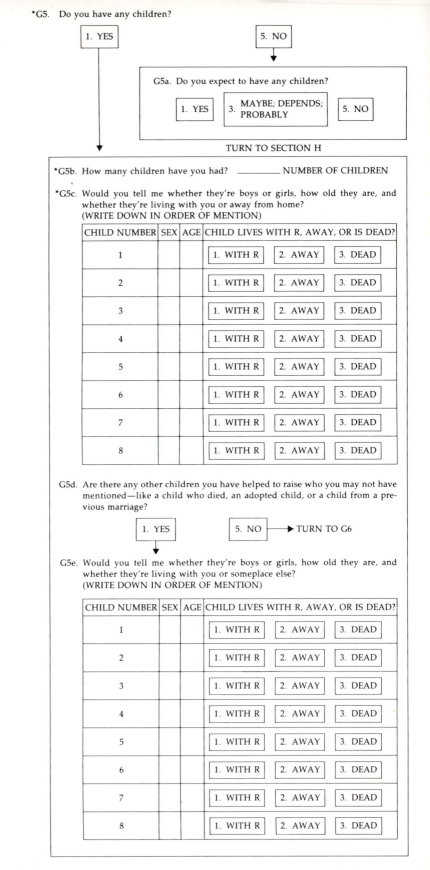

G6. In what year did you first become a parent?

_____ YEAR

*G7. Do you expect to have any more children?

| 1. YES | | 3. MAYBE; DEPENDS; PROBABLY | | 5. NO |

*G8. Most parents have had some problems in raising their children. What are the main problems you've had in raising your child(ren)? (PROBE FOR FULL RESPONSES.)

_____
_____
_____
_____
_____
_____

*G9. Many (men/women—SAME SEX AS RESPONDENT) feel that they're not as good (fathers/mothers—SAME SEX AS RESPONDENT) as they would like to be. Have you ever felt this way?

| 1. YES | | 5. NO | ➞ TURN TO G10 |

*G9a. What kinds of things have made you feel this way? (PROBE FOR FULL RESPONSES.)

_____
_____
_____

*G9b. Have you felt this way a lot of times, or only once in a while?

_____
_____

G10. Some people say that having children does not leave them enough time for other things they want to do. Would you say that having children prevents (prevented) you from doing things you want(ed) to do *often, sometimes, rarely,* or *never*?

| 1. OFTEN | | 2. SOMETIMES | | 3. RARELY | | 4. NEVER |

G11. Some people say that having children brings a husband and wife closer together. Others feel that having children makes a husband and wife less close. How do you feel about that? Do you feel that children have brought you and your (husband/wife) *closer together* or *farther apart*?

| 1. CLOSER TOGETHER | | 5. FARTHER APART | | 3. SOME OF BOTH | | 6. NO DIFFERENCE |

G12. INTERVIEWER CHECKPOINT: R IS:

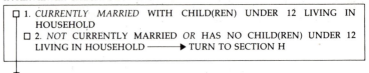

□ 1. *CURRENTLY MARRIED* WITH CHILD(REN) UNDER 12 LIVING IN HOUSEHOLD
□ 2. *NOT* CURRENTLY MARRIED *OR* HAS NO CHILD(REN) UNDER 12 LIVING IN HOUSEHOLD ──────▶ TURN TO SECTION H

G13. Who in your family would you say spends *more* time taking care of the child(ren)—you, your (husband/wife) or both about equal?

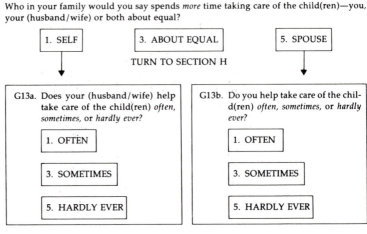

| 1. SELF | 3. ABOUT EQUAL | 5. SPOUSE |

TURN TO SECTION H

G13a. Does your (husband/wife) help take care of the child(ren) *often, sometimes,* or *hardly ever?*

1. OFTEN

3. SOMETIMES

5. HARDLY EVER

G13b. Do you help take care of the child(ren) *often, sometimes,* or *hardly ever?*

1. OFTEN

3. SOMETIMES

5. HARDLY EVER

#H1. Now I'd like to talk to you about your work. Are you working now, unemployed,

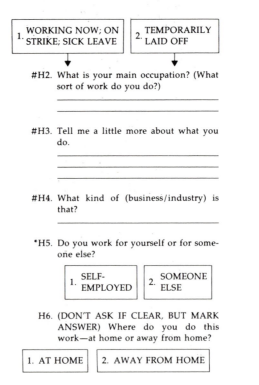

1. WORKING NOW; ON STRIKE; SICK LEAVE   2. TEMPORARILY LAID OFF

#H2. What is your main occupation? (What sort of work do you do?)
_____
_____

#H3. Tell me a little more about what you do.
_____
_____
_____

#H4. What kind of (business/industry) is that?
_____

*H5. Do you work for yourself or for someone else?

1. SELF-EMPLOYED   2. SOMEONE ELSE

H6. (DON'T ASK IF CLEAR, BUT MARK ANSWER) Where do you do this work—at home or away from home?

1. AT HOME   2. AWAY FROM HOME

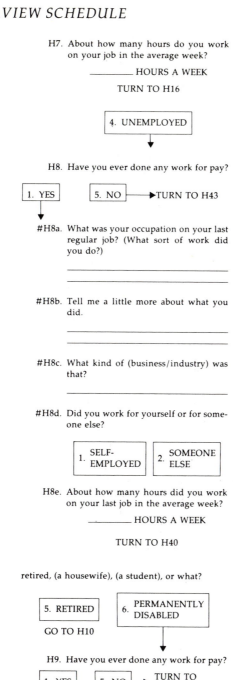

H7. About how many hours do you work on your job in the average week?

——————— HOURS A WEEK

TURN TO H16

4. UNEMPLOYED

H8. Have you ever done any work for pay?

1. YES

5. NO ——► TURN TO H43

#H8a. What was your occupation on your last regular job? (What sort of work did you do?)

————————————————————
————————————————————

#H8b. Tell me a little more about what you did.

————————————————————
————————————————————

#H8c. What kind of (business/industry) was that?

————————————————————

#H8d. Did you work for yourself or for someone else?

1. SELF-EMPLOYED

2. SOMEONE ELSE

H8e. About how many hours did you work on your last job in the average week?

——————— HOURS A WEEK

TURN TO H40

retired, (a housewife), (a student), or what?

5. RETIRED

GO TO H10

6. PERMANENTLY DISABLED

H9. Have you ever done any work for pay?

1. YES

5. NO ——► TURN TO SECTION J

#H10. What was your main occupation before you (retired/became disabled)? (What sort of work did you do?)

————————————————————
————————————————————

#H11. Tell me a little more about what you did.

_____

_____

#H12. What kind of (business/industry) was that?

_____

#H13. Did you work for yourself or for someone else?

| 1. SELF-EMPLOYED | 2. SOMEONE ELSE |

H14. INTERVIEWER CHECKPOINT

☐ 1. R IS RETIRED ──────▶ TURN TO H44

☐ 2. R IS DISABLED

H14a. Are you doing *any* work for pay at the present time?

| 1. YES | 5. NO |

GO BACK TO H2   TURN TO
"WORKING NOW"   SECTION J

| 7. HOUSEWIFE | 8. STUDENT |

#H15. Are you doing *any* work for pay at the present time?

| 1. YES | 5. NO |

GO BACK TO H2
"WORKING NOW"

H15a. Have you ever done any work for pay?

| 1. YES | 5. NO |

GO TO H15d

H15b. When did you leave your last regular job? (IF LESS THAN TWO YEARS, GET MONTH.)

_____ YEAR   _____ MONTH

H15c. What happened—why did you leave it?

_____
_____
_____
_____

H15d. INTERVIEWER CHECKPOINT

☐ 1. R IS HOUSEWIFE——▶ TURN TO H49

☐ 2. R IS STUDENT——▶ TURN TO SECTION J

ASK ALL PEOPLE WORKING FULL OR PART TIME

*(M)H16. How long have you been doing this kind of work?

_____ YEARS

*H17. Taking into consideration all the things about your job, how satisfied or dissatisfied are you with it?

_____
_____
_____

*H18. What things do you particularly like about the job? _____
_____
_____
_____

*H19. What things don't you like about the job? _____
_____
_____
_____

*H20. Regardless of how much you like your job, is there any other kind of work you'd rather be doing?

| 1. YES | | 5. NO | ——▶ TURN TO H21 |

*H20a. What is that? _____
_____
_____

ASK ALL PEOPLE WORKING FULL OR PART TIME

H21. Taking everything into consideration, how likely is it that you will make a genuine effort to find a new job within the next year—*very likely, somewhat likely,* or *not at all likely?*

| 1. VERY LIKELY | 3. SOMEWHAT LIKELY | 5. NOT AT ALL LIKELY |

*(M)H22. If you didn't have to work to make a living, do you think you would work anyway?
#(W)

| 1. YES | 3. MAYBE; PROBABLY | 5. NO | 8. DON'T KNOW |

GO TO H23

*H22a. What would be your reasons for going on working?

_____
_____
_____
_____

H22b. Why would you *not* continue to work?

_____
_____
_____
_____

*(M)H23.   Have you ever had any problems with your work—times when you couldn't work or weren't getting along on the job, or didn't know what kind of work you wanted to do?

| 1. YES | | 5. NO | ──▶ GO TO H24 |

*(M)H23a.   What was that about? _____

_____

_____

_____

H24.   Do you feel that the demands of your work ever interfere with the demands of your family?

| 1. YES | | 3. SOMETIMES | | 5. NO |

ASK ALL PEOPLE WORKING FULL OR PART TIME

H25.   Next are some things that might describe a person's job. First, how much does your job allow you to make a lot of decisions on your own? Would you say *a lot, somewhat, a little, or not at all?*

| 1. A LOT | | 2. SOMEWHAT | | 3. A LITTLE | | 4. NOT AT ALL |

H26.   How much say do you have over what happens on your job? Would you say *a lot, some, a little,* or *none?*

| 1. A LOT | | 2. SOME | | 3. A LITTLE | | 4. NONE |

(CARD G) Here are some more things that might describe a person's job. Please tell me *how true* each is of *your* (main) job, using one of the answers on this card.

	VERY TRUE (1)	SOMEWHAT TRUE (2)	NOT VERY TRUE (3)	NOT AT ALL TRUE (4)
H27. The first one is: The work is interesting. Is this *very true, somewhat true, not very true* or *not at all true* of your job?				
H28. The next one is: I am given a lot of chances to talk with the people I work with. (Is this *very true, somewhat true, not very true* or *not at all true* of your job?)				
H29. I am given a chance to do the things I do best. (Is this *very true, somewhat true, not very true* or *not at all true* of your job?)				

*(M)⅓H30.   What does it take to do a really good job at the kind of work you do?

_____

_____

ASK ALL PEOPLE WORKING FULL OR PART TIME

*(M)½H31. How much *ability* do you think it takes to do a really good job at the kind of work you do?

_____

_____

*(M)½H32. How good would you say you are at doing this kind of work—would you say you were *very good, a little better than average, just average,* or *not very good?*

| 1. VERY GOOD | 2. A LITTLE BETTER THAN AVERAGE | 3. JUST AVERAGE | 4. NOT VERY GOOD |

*(M)H33. Do you have any people working under (for) you?

| 1. YES | | 5. NO | ───▶ GO TO H34

*(M)H33a. How many?

_____ NUMBER OF PEOPLE

H34. INTERVIEWER CHECKPOINT

☐ 1. R IS SELF-EMPLOYED────────▶ TURN TO H37
☐ 2. R IS *NOT* SELF-EMPLOYED────────▶ TURN TO H35

WORKING FULL OR PART TIME

(IF R IS *NOT* SELF-EMPLOYED)

*(M) H35. Do you work under anyone—a supervisor or anyone in charge of your work?

| 1. YES | | 5. NO | ───▶ GO TO H36

*(M)H35a. Just how much does (he/she) have to do with you and your work?

_____

_____

*(M) H36. Outside of the people working over you or under you, do you work with any other person or people?

| 1. YES | | 5. NO | ───▶ GO TO H37

*(M)H36a. How do you like the people you work with? _____

_____

_____

H37. INTERVIEWER CHECKPOINT

☐ 1. R IS MALE ──────▶ TURN TO SECTION J
2. R IS FEMALE

*(H)H38. Different people feel differently about taking care of a home—I don't mean taking care of the children, but things like cooking and sewing and keeping house. Some women look on these things as just a job that has to be done—other women really enjoy them. How do you feel about this?

_____

_____

_____

WOMEN WORKING FULL OR PART TIME

H39. INTERVIEWER CHECKPOINT

☐ 1. R HAS CHILD(REN) UNDER 12 LIVING IN HOUSEHOLD
☐ 2. R HAS *NO* CHILD(REN) UNDER 12 LIVING IN
HOUSEHOLD ———▶ TURN TO SECTION J

H39a. How (are the children/is the child) taken care of while you are at work?

_____
_____

H39b. (IF R MENTIONS SCHOOL *ONLY*) What about the time (he/she isn't) (they aren't) in school?

_____
_____

TURN TO SECTION J

R IS UNEMPLOYED

*H40. When did you leave your last job? _____

*H41. What happened—why did you leave it? (DON'T PROBE IF R IS RESISTANT.)

_____
_____
_____

*H42. Do you expect to have much trouble getting another job?

| 1. YES | | 5. NO |

H43. Have you been looking for work during the past month?

| 1. YES | | 5. NO | ———▶ GO TO H43b

H43a. What have you been doing in the last month to find work?

_____
_____
_____

TURN TO SECTION J

H43b. Do you want a regular job now, either full or part-time?

| 1. YES | 3. MAYBE—IT DEPENDS | 5. NO | 8. DON'T KNOW |

H43c. What are the reasons you are not looking for work? (DON'T PROBE IF R IS RESISTANT.)

_____
_____
_____

H43d. Do you intend to look for work of any kind in the next 12 months?

| 1. YES | | 5. NO |

| 3. DEPENDS | 8. DON'T KNOW |

TURN TO SECTION J

R IS RETIRED

H44. In what year did you retire? (IF LESS THAN TWO YEARS, PROBE: In what month was that?)

_____ YEAR _____ MONTH

*H45. Why did you retire? _____
_____

H45a. (IF NOT CLEAR) Did you have to retire, or is this something that you wanted to do?
_____

*H46. In what way has retirement made a difference in your life?
_____
_____
_____

*H46a. Could you tell me more about these changes and what they have meant in your life?
_____
_____
_____

*H47. When you think of the days when you were working, what do you miss most?
_____
_____
_____

H48. Are you doing *any* work for pay at the present time?

1. YES	5. NO	──► TURN TO
TURN *BACK* TO H2		SECTION J
"WORKING NOW"		

R IS A HOUSEWIFE

*H49. Different people feel differently about taking care of a home—I don't mean taking care of the children, but things like cooking and sewing and keeping house. Some women look on these things as just a job that has to be done—other women really enjoy them. How do you feel about this?
_____
_____
_____

*H50. Have you ever wanted a career?

| 1. YES | 5. NO | ──► GO TO H51 |

*H50a. What kind of career? _____
_____
_____

H51. What are the main reasons you aren't working at present?
_____
_____
_____

*H52. Are you planning to go to work in the future?

| 1. YES | | 5. NO | ──▶ TURN TO SECTION J |

*H52a. Women have different reasons for working. What would be your main reasons for working? (PROBE FOR FULL RESPONSES.)

_____
_____
_____
_____

*H52b. What kind of work do you think you will do? _____
_____
_____
_____

H52c. Are you looking for work at the present time?

| 1. YES | | 5. NO |

TURN TO SECTION J

Section J: Role Comparisons

J1. (CARD H) Here is a list of things that many people look for or want out of life. Please study the list carefully, then tell me which *two* of these things are *most* important to you in *your* life.

(CHECK TWO)

01. SENSE OF BELONGING	06. FUN AND ENJOYMENT IN LIFE
02. EXCITEMENT	07. SECURITY
03. WARM RELATIONSHIPS WITH OTHERS	08. SELF-RESPECT
04. SELF-FULFILLMENT	09. A SENSE OF ACCOMPLISHMENT
05. BEING WELL-RESPECTED	

J2. (CARD H) And of these two, which *one* is *most* important to you in your life?

(CHECK ONE)

01. SENSE OF BELONGING	06. FUN AND ENJOYMENT IN LIFE
02. EXCITEMENT	07. SECURITY
03. WARM RELATIONSHIPS WITH OTHERS	08. SELF-RESPECT
04. SELF-FULFILLMENT	09. A SENSE OF ACCOMPLISHMENT
05. BEING WELL-RESPECTED	

NOTE TO INTERVIEWER: COPY HERE THE VALUE SELECTED BY R IN J2:
_____ . SUBSTITUTE THIS
PHRASE FOR "MOST IMPORTANT VALUE" IN QUESTIONS J3a-J3e.

J3. (CARD J) Now I'd like to ask you how much various things in your life either have led or would lead to (MOST IMPORTANT VALUE).

QUESTIONS J3a-J3e SHOULD BE ASKED OF *EVERYONE*	VERY LITTLE (1)	A LITTLE (2)	SOME (3)	A LOT (4)	A GREAT DEAL (5)
a. First, how much have the things you do in your *leisure* time led to (MOST IMPORTANT VALUE) in your life— *(very little, a little, some, a lot, or a great deal)?*					
b. How much has the work you do in and around the house led to (MOST IMPORTANT VALUE) in your life— *(very little, a little, some, a lot, or a great deal)?*					
c. How much (has/would/did) *work at a job* (led/lead) to (MOST IMPORTANT VALUE) in your life?					
d. How about being married? How much (has/would/did) *being married* (led/lead) to (MOST IMPORTANT VALUE) in your life?					
e. What about being a (father/mother)? How much (has/would) being a parent (led/lead) to (MOST IMPORTANT VALUE) in your life?					

J4. (CARD K) Some things in our lives are very satisfying to one person, while another may not find them satisfying at all. I'd like to ask how much satisfaction you have gotten or would get from some of these different things.

QUESTIONS J4a-J4e SHOULD BE ASKED OF *EVERYONE*	GREAT SATIS- FACTION (1)	SOME SATIS- FACTION (2)	LITTLE SATIS- FACTION (3)	NO SATIS- FACTION (4)
a. First, consider the *things you do in your leisure time.* All in all, would you say you have gotten *great* satisfaction, *some* satisfaction, *a little* satisfaction, or *no* satisfaction from the things that you do in your leisure time?				
b. How about the *work you do in and around the house?* (Would you say you have gotten *great, some, a little,* or *no* satisfaction?)				
c. How much satisfaction (have you gotten/would you get/did you get) out of work at a job?				
d. What about *being married?* How much satisfaction (have you gotten/would you get/did you get) from being married?				
e. How much satisfaction (have you gotten/would you get/did you get) out of being a (father/mother)?				

Section K: Symptoms

*Now, some questions about your health.

*K1. Do you have any particular physical or health trouble?

| 1. YES | | 5. NO | → GO TO K2 |

*K1a. What is that? _____

_____
_____ _____
_____
_____

*K2. (RESPONDENT BOOKLET) Here is a list which tells about different troubles and complaints people have. After each one would you check the answer which tells how often you have had this trouble or complaint. Please let me know when you have finished the page. (HAND RESPONDENT BOOKLET TURNED TO Qs K2 AND K3, AND PENCIL.) (AFTER R FILLS OUT AND RETURNS BOOKLET, TURN TO K4.)

*K2. How often have you had the following?

	NEARLY ALL THE TIME	PRETTY OFTEN	NOT VERY MUCH	NEVER
*a. Do you ever have any trouble getting to sleep or staying asleep?				
*b. Have you ever been bothered by nervousness, feeling fidgety and tense?				
*c. Are you ever troubled by headaches or pains in the head?				
*d. Do you have loss of appetite?				
*e. How often are you bothered by having an upset stomach?				
*f. Do you find it difficult to get up in the morning?				

*K3. How often have you had the following?

	MANY TIMES	SOME-TIMES	HARDLY EVER	NEVER
*a. Has any ill health affected the amount of work you do?				
*b. Have you ever been bothered by shortness of breath when you were not exercising or working hard?				
*c. Have you ever been bothered by your heart beating hard?				
*d. Do you ever drink more than you should?				
*e. Have you ever had spells of dizziness?				
*f. Are you ever bothered by nightmares?				
*g. Do you tend to lose weight when you have something important bothering you?				
*h. Do your hands ever tremble enough to bother you?				
*i. Are you troubled by your hands sweating so that you feel damp and clammy?				
*j. Have there ever been times when you couldn't take care of things because you just couldn't get going?				
k. When you feel worried, tense or nervous, do you ever drink alcoholic beverages to help you handle things?				
l. Have there ever been problems between you and anyone in your family (spouse, parent, child, or other close relative) because you drank alcoholic beverages?				
m. When you feel worried, tense or nervous, do you ever take medicines or drugs to help you handle things?				

TURN TO K4

*K4. Here are some more questions like those you've filled out. This time just answer "Yes" or "No." Do you feel you are bothered by all sorts of pains and ailments in different parts of your body?

| 1. YES | | 5. NO |

*K5. For the most part, do you feel healthy enough to carry out the things that you would like to do?

| 1. YES | | 5. NO |

*K6. Have you ever felt that you were going to have a nervous breakdown?

| 1. YES | | 5. NO |——▶ TURN TO K7

---

*K6a. Could you tell me about when you felt this way? What was it about?

_____

_____

_____

_____

*K6b. What did you do about it?

_____

_____

_____

K7. (CARD M) Now here is something different. I have some statements here that describe the way some people are and feel. I'll read them one at a time and you just tell me how true they are for you—whether they're *very true* for you, *pretty true*, *not very true*, or *not true at all*.

	VERY TRUE (1)	PRETTY TRUE (2)	NOT VERY TRUE (3)	NOT TRUE AT ALL (4)
*K7a. I have always felt pretty sure my life would work out the way I wanted it to.				
K7b. No one cares much what happens to me.				
*K7c. I often wish that people would listen to me more.				
*K7d. I often wish that people liked me more than they do.				
K7e. These days I really don't know who I can count on for help.				

Section M: Formal Help-Seeking

Problems often come up in life. Sometimes they're personal problems—people are very unhappy, or nervous and irritable all the time. Sometimes they're problems in a marriage—a husband and wife just can't get along with each other. Or, sometimes it's a personal problem with a child or a job. I'd like to ask you a few questions now about what you think a person might do to handle problems like these.

*M1.   For instance, let's suppose you had a lot of personal problems and you're very unhappy all the time. Let's suppose you've been that way for a long time, and it isn't getting any better. What do you think you'd do about it?

_____
_____
_____
_____

M2.   INTERVIEWER CHECKPOINT

> ☐ 1. R IS CURRENTLY MARRIED
>   ☐ 2. R IS NOT CURRENTLY MARRIED ⟶ TURN TO M4

*M3.   Suppose it was a problem in your marriage—you and your (husband/wife) just couldn't get along with each other. What do you think you would do about it?

_____
_____

ASK EVERYONE

*M4.   Sometimes when people have problems like this, they go someplace for help. Sometimes they go to a doctor or a minister. Sometimes they go to a special place for handling personal problems—like a psychiatrist or a marriage counselor, or social agency or clinic. How about you—have you ever gone anywhere like that for advice and help with any personal problems?

| 1. YES | | 5. NO |——▶ TURN TO M5 |

---

*M4a.   What was that about? _____

_____

_____

_____

*M4b.   Where did you go for help? _____

_____

_____

_____

*M4c.   INTERVIEWER CHECKPOINT

☐ 1. IN M4b R MENTIONS PERSON *ONLY*
☐ 2. IN M4b R MENTIONS PLACE ——————▶ GO TO M4e

*M4d.   Is that person connected with an agency, place, or other organization?

| 1. YES | | 5. NO |——▶ TURN TO M4f |

*M4e.   Can you tell me the type of place it was? _____

_____

#M4f.   How did you know to go there? That is, how did you know about that (person/place)?

_____

_____

_____

_____

*M4g.   What did they do—how did they try to help you? _____

_____

_____

_____

*M4h.   How did it turn out—do you think it helped you in any way?

_____

_____

_____

TURN TO M6

IF R SAID "NO" TO M4

*M5. Can you think of anything that's happened to you, any problems you've had in the past, where going to someone like this might have helped you in any way?

1. YES

5. NO

*M5a. What do you have in mind— what was it about?

_____
_____
_____
_____
_____

*M5b. What did you do about it?

_____
_____
_____

*M5c. Who do you think might have helped you with that?

_____
_____
_____
_____

*M5d. Why do you suppose that you didn't go for help?

_____
_____
_____
_____

*M5e. Do you think you could ever have a personal problem that got so bad that you might want to go someplace for help—or do you think you could always handle things like that yourself?

_____
_____
_____

TURN TO M6

TURN TO M6

ASK EVERYONE

M6. Has any member of your family or a close friend ever gone to a special place for handling personal problems—like a psychiatrist or a marriage counselor, or a social agency or clinic?

1. YES

5. NO

M7. Over their lives most people have something bad happen to them or to someone they love. By that I mean things like getting sick, losing a job, or being in trouble with the police. Or like when someone dies, leaves, or disappoints you. Or maybe just something important you wanted to happen didn't happen. Compared with most other people you know, have *things like this* happened to you *a lot, some, not much,* or *hardly ever?*

1. A LOT

2. SOME

3. NOT MUCH

4. HARDLY EVER

M8. When things like these have happened to you, have there been times when you found it very hard to handle? That is, when you couldn't sleep, or stayed away from people, or felt so depressed or nervous that you couldn't do much of anything?

| 1. YES | | 5. NO |

*M8a. Would you say you felt that way *many times, sometimes,* or just *once in a while?*

| 1. MANY TIMES |

| 3. SOMETIMES |

| 5. JUST ONCE IN A WHILE |

M8b. Now think about the last time you felt that way. What was it about?

_____
_____
_____
_____

M8c. Now think about the last time something really bad happened to you. What was it about?

_____
_____
_____
_____
_____
_____

M8d. How long ago did that happen?

_____ | YEARS | MONTHS | WEEKS | DAYS | AGO | IT'S HAPPENING RIGHT NOW
NUMBER

(CHECK ONE)

M9. (CARD N) When things like that happen some people like to talk it over with other people. (HAND R CARD.) Did you talk to any of *these* people about that matter? For each person, choose the *one* description that fits them best. If more than one person you talked to fits the *same* description (like friend or relative), please tell me.

CARD N

A. HUSBAND

B. WIFE

C. SON

D. DAUGHTER

E. FATHER

F. MOTHER

G. BROTHER

H. SISTER

I. OTHER RELATIVE OR FAMILY MEMBER (PLEASE SPECIFY)

J. FRIEND

K. NEIGHBOR

L. CO-WORKER

☐ CHECK HERE IF R SAYS "TALKED TO NO ONE" ON THE LIST. THEN TURN TO M10

PERSON:

M9a. Is that person male or female?

	M9a. Is that person male or female?	
1.	1. MALE	2. FEMALE
2.	1. MALE	2. FEMALE
3.	1. MALE	2. FEMALE
4.	1. MALE	2. FEMALE
5.	1. MALE	2. FEMALE
6.	1. MALE	2. FEMALE
7.	1. MALE	2. FEMALE
8.	1. MALE	2. FEMALE

M9b. Is (he/she) older than you are, younger, or about the same?	M9c. (CARD P) Which of the things on this card happened when you talked with (him/her)? You can choose *more than one*. *(CHECK ALL THAT APPLY.)* a. listened to me b. cheered or comforted me c. talked things out d. told me who else to see e. showed me a new way to look at things f. gave me advice g. helped me take action	M9d. How much did it help to talk? Would you say it: helped a lot? helped some? or was it not much help?
1. OLDER 5. YOUNGER 3. SAME	a b c d e f g	1. A LOT 3. SOME 5. NOT MUCH
1. OLDER 5. YOUNGER 3. SAME	a b c d e f g	1. A LOT 3. SOME 5. NOT MUCH
1. OLDER 5. YOUNGER 3. SAME	a b c d e f g	1. A LOT 3. SOME 5. NOT MUCH
1. OLDER 5. YOUNGER 3. SAME	a b c d e f g	1. A LOT 3. SOME 5. NOT MUCH
1. OLDER 5. YOUNGER 3. SAME	a b c d e f g	1. A LOT 3. SOME 5. NOT MUCH
1. OLDER 5. YOUNGER 3. SAME	a b c d e f g	1. A LOT 3. SOME 5. NOT MUCH
1. OLDER 5. YOUNGER 3. SAME	a b c d e f g	1. A LOT 3. SOME 5. NOT MUCH
1. OLDER 5. YOUNGER 3. SAME	a b c d e f g	1. A LOT 3. SOME 5. NOT MUCH

M10. (CARD S) Now how about these people? Did you talk to any of these people about that matter? Again, for each person, choose the *one* description that fits them best. If more than one person you talked to fits the same description, please tell me.

CARD S	☐ CHECK HERE IF R SAYS "TALKED TO NO ONE" ON THE LIST. THEN TURN TO SECTION N OCCUPATION OF *PROFESSIONAL:*	M10a. Is that person connected with an agency, clinic, or other organization?	M10b. (IF YES TO M10a) Do you remember the name of the place, or the kind of place it was? (What is it?) (ENTER NAME OR TYPE OF PLACE)
M. PSYCHIATRIST N. PSYCHOLOGIST O. SOCIAL WORKER P. COUNSELOR Q. DOCTOR R. NURSE S. CLERGYMAN T. TEACHER U. POLICE V. LAWYER W. OTHER PROFESSIONAL (PLEASE SPECIFY)	1.	1. YES 5. NO 8. DK	
	2.	1. YES 5. NO 8. DK	
	3.	1. YES 5. NO 8. DK	
	4.	1. YES 5. NO 8. DK	
	5.	1. YES 5. NO 8. DK	
	6.	1. YES 5. NO 8. DK	
	7.	1. YES 5. NO 8. DK	
	8.	1. YES 5. NO 8. DK	

M10c. How did you know to go to that person?	M10d. (CARD P) Which of the things on this card happened when you talked with that person? You can choose *more than one. (CHECK ALL THAT APPLY.)* a. listened to me b. cheered or comforted me c. talked things out d. told me who else to see e. showed me a new way to look at things f. gave me advice g. helped me take action	M10e. How much did it help to talk? Would you say it: helped a lot? helped some? or was it not much help?
	a b c d e f g	1. A LOT 3. SOME 5. NOT MUCH
	a b c d e f g	1. A LOT 3. SOME 5. NOT MUCH
	a b c d e f g	1. A LOT 3. SOME 5. NOT MUCH
	a b c d e f g	1. A LOT 3. SOME 5. NOT MUCH
	a b c d e f g	1. A LOT 3. SOME 5. NOT MUCH
	a b c d e f g	1. A LOT 3. SOME 5. NOT MUCH
	a b c d e f g	1. A LOT 3. SOME 5. NOT MUCH
	a b c d e f g	1. A LOT 3. SOME 5. NOT MUCH

Section N: Personal Data

Now we have finished the regular part of the interview. We need a few facts about you, like age, education, and so on, so that we can compare the ideas of men with those of women, older people with younger people, and one group with another.

#N1. First, what is your date of birth? _____/_____/_____
                                            MONTH   DAY   YEAR

*N2. Where were you born?

   STATE (OR COUNTRY IF NOT U.S.A.)_____

N3. And where did you live mostly while you were growing up?

   STATE (OR COUNTRY IF NOT U.S.A.)_____

*N4. Were you brought up mostly in the country, in a town, in a small city, or in a large city?

| 1. COUNTRY | 2. TOWN | 3. SMALL CITY | 4. LARGE CITY |

N5. What was your religious background when you were growing up—Protestant, Roman Catholic, Jewish, or something else?

| PROTESTANT | 200. ROMAN CATHOLIC | 300. JEWISH | 800. NONE, NO PREFERENCE | OTHER: SPECIFY _____ |

GO TO N6

N5a. What church or denomination was that?

_____

N6. What is the original nationality of your family on your father's side? (IF R SAYS, "AMERICAN," PROBE: What was it before coming to the United States?)

_____ ORIGINAL NATIONALITY

N7. How many brothers and sisters did you have while you were growing up?

_____ NUMBER | 00. NONE |——▶ GO TO N8

N7a. Were you the oldest, the youngest, or what?

| 1. OLDEST | 5. YOUNGEST | 3. IN BETWEEN |

*N8. Did you always live together with both of your *real* parents up to the time you were 16 years old?

| 1. YES | 5. NO |

TURN TO N9

---

*N8a. What happened? _____

_____

*N8b. How old were you when it happened?

_____ YEARS OLD

N8c. Who was the head of your family or household most of the time while you were growing up?

| 1. FATHER | 2. MOTHER | OTHER MALE: _____ (SPECIFY) | OTHER FEMALE: _____ (SPECIFY) |

---

*N9. (ASK N9–N13 ABOUT FATHER OR OTHER HEAD MENTIONED IN N8c.) Now a few questions about your father (the person who was head of your family while you were growing up). First, what kind of work did (he/she) do for a living while you were growing up? (What was (his/her) main occupation?)

_____

#N10. Can you tell me a little more about what (he/she) did on (his/her) job?

_____

_____

#N11. What kind of (business/industry) was that? _____

_____

#N12. Did (he/she) work for (himself/herself), or for someone else?

| 1. SELF-EMPLOYED | 2. SOMEONE ELSE |

N13. What was the highest grade of school or year of college (he/she) completed?

| GRADES OF SCHOOL | | | | | | | | | | | | | COLLEGE | | | | |
| 00 | 01 | 02 | 03 | 04 | 05 | 06 | 07 | 08 | 09 | 10 | 11 | 12 | 13 | 14 | 15 | 16 | 17+ |

TURN TO N14

DON'T KNOW

N13a. Would you guess that (he/she) had *less than seven years* of school, *between seven and twelve years* of school, *finished high school*, or had *some schooling past high school?*

| LESS THAN 1. SEVEN YEARS | BETWEEN SEVEN 2. AND TWELVE YEARS | FINISHED 3. HIGH SCHOOL | SOME SCHOOLING 4. PAST HIGH SCHOOL |

N14. INTERVIEWER CHECKPOINT

N9–N13 WERE ASKED ABOUT:

☐ 1. R'S FATHER
☐ 2. OTHER MALE HEAD
☐ 3. OTHER FEMALE HEAD
☐ 4. R'S MOTHER ⟶ TURN TO N17

N15. Other than being a housewife, did your mother have a job while you were growing up?

| 1. YES | | 5. NO |

N16. What was the highest grade of school or year of college *your mother* completed?

| GRADES OF SCHOOL | COLLEGE |
| 00 01 02 03 04 05 06 07 08 09 10 11 12 | 13 14 15 16 17+ |

TURN TO N17

DON'T KNOW

N16a. Would you guess that she had *less than seven years* of school, *between seven and twelve years* of school, *finished high school*, or had *some schooling past high school?*

| LESS THAN 1. SEVEN YEARS | BETWEEN SEVEN 2. AND TWELVE YEARS | FINISHED 3. HIGH SCHOOL | SOME SCHOOLING 4. PAST HIGH SCHOOL |

#N17. What is the highest grade of school or year of college you have completed?

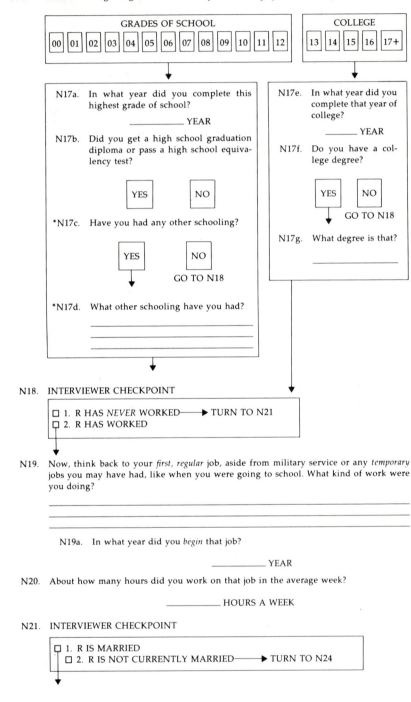

GRADES OF SCHOOL	COLLEGE
00 01 02 03 04 05 06 07 08 09 10 11 12	13 14 15 16 17+

N17a. In what year did you complete this highest grade of school?

_____ YEAR

N17b. Did you get a high school graduation diploma or pass a high school equivalency test?

YES   NO

*N17c. Have you had any other schooling?

YES   NO

GO TO N18

*N17d. What other schooling have you had?

_____
_____
_____

N17e. In what year did you complete that year of college?

_____ YEAR

N17f. Do you have a college degree?

YES   NO

GO TO N18

N17g. What degree is that?

_____

N18. INTERVIEWER CHECKPOINT

☐ 1. R HAS *NEVER* WORKED ⟶ TURN TO N21
☐ 2. R HAS WORKED

N19. Now, think back to your *first, regular* job, aside from military service or any *temporary* jobs you may have had, like when you were going to school. What kind of work were you doing?

_____
_____
_____

N19a. In what year did you *begin* that job?

_____ YEAR

N20. About how many hours did you work on that job in the average week?

_____ HOURS A WEEK

N21. INTERVIEWER CHECKPOINT

☐ 1. R IS MARRIED
☐ 2. R IS NOT CURRENTLY MARRIED ⟶ TURN TO N24

N22. And what is the highest grade of school or year of college your (husband/wife) has completed?

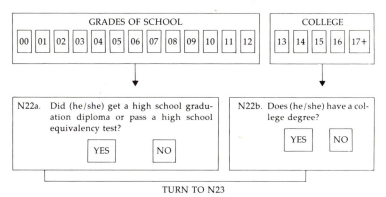

GRADES OF SCHOOL	COLLEGE
00 01 02 03 04 05 06 07 08 09 10 11 12	13 14 15 16 17+

N22a. Did (he/she) get a high school graduation diploma or pass a high school equivalency test?

YES   NO

N22b. Does (he/she) have a college degree?

YES   NO

TURN TO N23

#N23. Is your (husband/wife) doing any work for pay at the present time?

1. YES   5. NO

N23a. Has (he/she) done any work for pay in the past twelve months?

1. YES   5. NO ➞ TURN TO N24

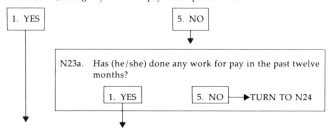

*N23b. What kind of work (does/did) (he/she) do? (What [is/was] [his/her] main occupation?)

_____

#N23c. Please tell me a little more about what (he/she) (does/did) on (his/her) job.

_____
_____

#N23d. What kind of (business/industry) is that?

_____

N23e. (Does/Did) (he/she) work for (himself/herself) or for someone else?

1. SELF-EMPLOYED   2. SOMEONE ELSE

(IF R IS *MALE* WITH CHILD(REN) UNDER 12 LIVING IN HOUSEHOLD)
N23f. How (are the children/is the child) taken care of while your wife is at work?

_____
_____

N23g. (IF R MENTIONS IN SCHOOL *ONLY*) What about the time ([he/she] isn't/ they aren't) in school?

_____
_____

#N24. (CARD T) In this survey of people all over the country, we are trying to get a clear picture of people's financial situations. Taking into consideration all sources of income, about what do you think your total income will be this year (1976) for yourself and your immediate family? Just give me the letter on the card.

01	A. LESS THAN $1,000	07	G. $6,000–$6,999	13	M. $12,500–$14,999
02	B. $1,000–$1,999	08	H. $7,000–$7,999	14	N. $15,000–$17,499
03	C. $2,000–$2,999	09	I. $8,000–$8,999	15	O. $17,500–$19,999
04	D. $3,000–$3,999	10	J. $9,000–$9,999	16	P. $20,000–$24,999
05	E. $4,000–$4,999	11	K. $10,000–$10,999	17	Q. $25,000–$34,999
06	F. $5,000–$5,999	12	L. $11,000–$12,499	18	R. $35,000 AND OVER

N25. (CARD T) How much of this total will you yourself earn this year? (Just give me the letter on the card.)

01	A	04	D	07	G	10	J	13	M	16	P
02	B	05	E	08	H	11	K	14	N	17	Q
03	C	06	F	09	I	12	L	15	O	18	R

#N26. Is your current religious preference Protestant, Roman Catholic, Jewish or something else?

| PROTESTANT | 200. ROMAN CATHOLIC | 300. JEWISH | 800. NONE, NO PREFERENCE | OTHER: SPECIFY _____ _____ |

TURN TO N27

#N26a. What church or denomination is that? _____

*N27. About how often do you usually attend religious services?

| 1. MORE THAN ONCE A WEEK | 2. ONCE A WEEK | 3. TWO OR THREE TIMES A MONTH | 4. ONCE A MONTH | 5. A FEW TIMES A YEAR OR LESS | 6. NEVER |

N28. How long have you lived in (INSERT NAME OF PRESENT COMMUNITY OR OF TOWNSHIP IF RURAL)_____? (IF LESS THAN TWO YEARS, GET NUMBER OF MONTHS.)

_____ YEARS _____ MONTHS, OR SINCE: _____

N29. And finally, how many telephones, counting extensions, do you have in your (house/apartment)?

| 0 | 1 | 2 | 3 | 4 | 5 | MORE THAN 5, SPECIFY _____ |

TIME NOW _____

This completes the interview. Thank you very much for your help. When we have finished this survey we would like to send you some of our findings as a way of thanking you for your time. (HAND R A REPORT REQUEST CARD AND EXPLAIN ITS USE. BE SURE TO WRITE IN "MODERN LIVING" AS THE PROJECT.) We may also want to come back in a few months to talk with you or another member of your family to see if any of your opinions or your situation have changed.

Section S: Interviewer Observation

*S1. Respondent's sex is:
| 1. MALE | 2. FEMALE |

#S2. Respondent's racial or ethnic group is:

| 1. WHITE | 2. BLACK | 3. ORIENTAL | 4. CHICANO; PUERTO RICAN; MEXICAN- OR SPANISH-AMERICAN |

| 5. AMERICAN INDIAN | OTHER (SPECIFY): _____ |

S3. Other persons present at interview were (CHECK MORE THAN ONE BOX IF NECESSARY):

| NONE | CHILDREN UNDER 6 | OLDER CHILDREN | SPOUSE | OTHER RELATIVES | OTHER ADULTS |

GO TO S5

S4. How much do you feel the presence of other person(s) influenced the answers given by respondent?

| 1. A GREAT DEAL | 2. SOME | 3. VERY LITTLE | 4. NONE |

#S5. Overall, how great was R's interest in the interview?

| 1. VERY HIGH | 2. ABOVE AVERAGE | 3. AVERAGE | 4. BELOW AVERAGE | 5. VERY LOW |

S6. Did the respondent seem to find the interview too long?

| 1. YES | 5. NO |

S7. Type of structure in which family lives?

| 01. TRAILER |

| 02. DETACHED SINGLE FAMILY HOUSE |

| 03. 2-FAMILY HOUSE, 2 UNITS SIDE BY SIDE |

| 04. 2-FAMILY HOUSE, 2 UNITS ONE ABOVE THE OTHER |

| 05. DETACHED 3-4 FAMILY HOUSE |

| 06. ROW HOUSE (3 OR MORE UNITS IN AN ATTACHED ROW) |

07. APARTMENT HOUSE (5 OR MORE UNITS, 3 STORIES OR LESS)

08. APARTMENT HOUSE (5 OR MORE UNITS, 4 STORIES OR MORE)

09. APARTMENT IN A PARTLY COMMERCIAL STRUCTURE

10. OTHER: _____
                    (SPECIFY)

S8. Number of stories in the structure, not counting basement:

| 1 | | 2 | | 3 | | MORE THAN 3: _____ |
                                        (SPECIFY)

S9. COPY INFORMATION FROM COVER SHEET

	*(a) Household member by relationship to Head	(b) Sex	(c) Age	(e) Enter "R" to Identify Respondent
PERSONS 21 YEARS OR OLDER				
PERSONS UNDER 21				

S10. *THUMBNAIL SKETCH:*

Appendix B

SAMPLE DESIGN AND SAMPLING VARIABILITY

Sample Designs for the 1957 and 1976 Surveys

The sample designs for the two surveys have a high degree of correspondence: each is a national multistage, area probability sample of housing units and adults at a particular point in time. Each is a study of persons twenty-one years of age or older living in housing units within the coterminous United States exclusive of housing units on military reservations.[1] In the first stage of sampling, the two studies included with certainty the twelve major metropolitan areas of the United States in addition to a probability selection of other metropolitan areas and nonmetropolitan counties or county groups. The samples progressed

---

[1] In both surveys the Survey Research Center was using the dwelling unit definition formulated by the U.S. Bureau of the Census and reported in *1950 Census of Housing*, Vol. I, Part I, Washington, D.C.: U.S. Government Printing Office, 1953, p. XVI. Persons living in a dwelling unit comprise a household. Persons in nondwelling unit quarters—such as large rooming houses, residential clubs, transient accommodations, barracks for workers, accommodations for inmates of institutions, and general hospitals—were excluded from both studies.

along the same path of stratification and selection from the first to the final stage of sampling. In the last two stages, clusters of approximately four housing units were identified, and from each sample household one eligible person was objectively selected to be interviewed (Kish, 1949). If after repeated calls no one was at home, or the designated respondent was not at home or refused to be interviewed, no substitution was made. Further details of the sample designs are presented in Gurin, Veroff, and Feld (1960) and Kish and Hess (1965) for the 1957 and 1976 surveys, respectively.

Differences in the two samples occur in both the number of sample areas and in the number of designated respondents. For the 1957 survey, the metropolitan areas and counties, exclusive of the 12 major areas, were assigned to 54 strata, while in 1976 that number was increased to 62. Each stratum was represented by one primary area selected with probability proportionate to the population reported in the preceding census, bringing the total number of sample areas to 66 in 1957 and 74 in 1976. Thirty of the 54 primary areas in the 1957 sample were also in the 1976 sample. The remainder of the study population was represented by 24 sample areas in 1957 and 32 in 1976. Population growth over the two decades explains, in part, the rationale for increasing the number of sample areas. A further consideration was to effect some improvement in the precision of regional estimates from the SRC sample. The 1957 survey was designed to yield about 2,500 interviews, the second survey about 2,300. The overall sampling rates for housing units were one in 16,360 for the first study and one in 20,960 for the second. The achieved numbers of interviews were 2,460 and 2,264, with response rates of 84 and 71 percent, respectively.

Although each household had an equal chance of selection into the sample, adults within households had different probabilities of selection according to the number of eligible persons within the household. The chance of a person being selected for interview is inversely proportional to the number of eligible household members. Thus, to counter the biasing effects of these inequalities, data for each respondent should be weighted by the number of eligible persons in the housing unit. However, the use of such variable weights to calculate sample estimates increases the complexities of data processing to some degree, and experience has shown that the preponderance of dwellings with one to three eligible members (and particularly those with two eligible members) is so large that weighted results generally resemble unweighted results quite closely.

As a precaution in this study, however, both weighted and unweighted estimates for a number of variables of primary importance to the research were examined. Specifically, weighted and unweighted percentage distributions for the twenty-four subjective measures selected for demographic analysis in chapter 8 were compared for both the 1957 and 1976 samples. In all cases, differences between weighted and unweighted percentages are well within sampling error, usually differing by less than one percentage point. Although similar comparisons on demographic variables (such as those presented in table 1.1 in chapter 1) yield somewhat larger differences, estimation of distributions on such variables was not a primary goal of the research. Consequently, the bias resulting from the use of unweighted data was judged to be negligible, and all analyses presented in this report are based on unweighted data.

Sampling Error

ERRORS IN SAMPLE SURVEY ESTIMATES

Properly conducted sample interview surveys yield useful estimates, but they do not yield exact values. Errors and biases arise from several sources. These include sampling errors and nonsampling errors, which in turn include interviewer errors and biases, response errors, nonresponse bias, and processing errors. By design, sampling variability can be estimated from the sample data. Other types of errors are not as readily recognized and measured. Even though data collection procedures can be designed to measure interviewer variability, that type of design is employed infrequently and was not a part of these surveys. Comparisons with estimates from other sources, or record checks may reveal the magnitude of response errors. While nonresponse (failure to obtain an interview with a designated respondent) can be counted, the effects often remain unknown.

With some types of sample estimates, such as aggregates, it is essential to make adjustments for missing data in order to avoid serious underestimates of population totals, or to avoid distorted estimates of the distribution of the population by economic and demographic variables. When attitudes and opinions are the primary research interest, however, often little is known about population parameters and researchers have been reluctant to assume that nonrespondents share the same opinions and attitudes as their responding neighbors. Therefore, data in this report were not adjusted for total or item nonresponse.

FACTORS AFFECTING THE SIZE OF SAMPLING ERRORS

If a list of all household members meeting criteria for eligibility had been available and a simple random sample of those persons had been selected, the calculation of sampling errors would be simplified greatly. When simple random sampling has been used to choose respondents, the sampling error of estimated percentages depends on two major factors: the magnitude of the percentage and the number of respondents. Since a simple random sample of eligible persons could not be achieved, the samples were clustered in a limited number of geographic locations. This clustering lowers data collection costs, but yields higher sampling errors than a simple random sample. At the same time, the 1957 and 1976 samples were both highly stratified, a technique that tends to lower sampling errors. Moreover, some variables of research interest may not be evenly distributed among eligible persons, so in some cases the sample may have too many or too few of certain classes of respondents.

The formulas used to calculate sampling errors for this report take into consideration the various factors affecting the precision of sample estimates (Kish and Hess, 1959, 1965). All of the factors affect the final outcome of sample estimates and their sampling errors in unknown ways. Therefore, it is to be recognized that values presented in tables B.1 and B.2 offer guidance to the interpretation of sampling error but do not give the exact sampling error for a specific percentage or percentage difference.

ESTIMATING SAMPLING ERROR OF PERCENTAGES

This discussion is limited to sampling errors of percentages because many survey findings are presented as percentages, and their sampling errors are more easily summarized than the sampling errors of more complex estimates. If the latter are required, it is best to calculate the sampling variability of the particular estimates being analyzed.

Sample statistics reflect random variations which arise in interviewing only a fraction of the population. The distribution of individuals selected for a sample will usually differ from that of the population. As a result, the proportion of respondents having a given attitude, opinion, or some other characteristic will usually be somewhat larger or smaller—by an unknown amount—than the population value: the value that would have been obtained if the entire population had been in-

TABLE B.1
Approximate Sampling Errors of Percentages[a]
(in percentages)

Reported Percentages	Number of Interviews											
	2,500	2,250	2,000	1,750	1,500	1,250	1,000	750	500	400	300	200
50	2.4	2.5	2.6	2.8	3.0	3.2	3.5	3.9	4.8	5.2	5.9	7.1
30 or 70	2.2	2.3	2.4	2.6	2.7	2.9	3.2	3.6	4.4	4.8	5.4	6.5
20 or 80	1.9	2.0	2.1	2.2	2.4	2.5	2.8	3.2	3.8	4.2	4.7	5.7
10 or 90	1.4	1.5	1.6	1.7	1.8	1.9	2.1	2.4	2.9	3.1	3.5	4.3
5 or 95	1.1	1.1	1.2	1.2	1.3	1.4	1.5	1.7	2.1	2.3	2.6	3.1

[a] The figures in this table represent *two* standard errors. Hence, for most items the chances are 95 in 100 that the value being estir within a range equal to the reported percentage, plus or minus the sampling error.

terviewed using the same survey instrument and data-collection procedures during the same time period. The population value may differ from the "true value" because of nonsampling errors which would affect an attempt at complete enumeration as well as a sample survey.

TABLE B.2

Approximate Sampling Errors of Difference[a]
(in percentages)

Size of Subgroups	For percentages from 35% to 65%								
	2000	1500	1000	700	500	400	300	200	100
2,000	3.6	3.9	4.3	4.8	5.4	5.8	6.4	7.5	10.1
1,500		4.2	4.6	5.0	5.6	6.0	6.6	7.7	10.2
1,000			4.9	5.4	5.9	6.3	6.8	7.9	10.4
700				5.8	6.3	6.6	7.2	8.2	10.6
500					6.7	7.1	7.6	8.6	10.9
400						7.4	7.9	8.8	11.1
300							8.3	9.2	11.4
200								10.0	12.1
100									13.9
For percentages around 20% and 80%									
2,000	2.9	3.1	3.4	3.8	4.3	4.6	5.1	6.0	8.1
1,500		3.3	3.7	4.0	4.5	4.8	5.3	6.2	8.2
1,000			4.0	4.3	4.7	5.0	5.5	6.3	8.3
700				4.6	5.0	5.3	5.7	6.6	8.5
500					5.4	5.6	6.1	6.8	8.7
400						5.9	6.3	7.0	8.9
300							6.7	7.3	9.1
200								8.0	9.7
100									11.1
For percentages around 10% and 90%									
2,000	2.1	2.3	2.6	2.9	3.2	3.5	3.8	4.5	6.1
1,500		2.5	2.7	3.0	3.4	3.6	4.0	4.6	6.1
1,000			3.0	3.2	3.5	3.8	4.1	4.8	6.2
700				3.5	3.8	4.0	4.3	4.9	6.4
500					4.0	4.2	4.5	5.1	6.5
400						4.4	4.7	5.3	6.7
300							5.0	5.5	6.9
200								6.0	7.3
100									8.3
2,000	1.6	1.7	1.9	2.1	2.3	2.5	2.8	3.3	4.4
1,500		1.8	2.0	2.2	2.4	2.6	2.9	3.4	4.5
1,000			2.2	2.3	2.6	2.7	3.0	3.5	4.5
700				2.5	2.7	2.9	3.1	3.6	4.6
500					2.9	3.1	3.3	3.7	4.8
400						3.2	3.4	3.8	4.8
300							3.6	4.0	5.0
200								4.4	5.3
100									6.0

[a] The values shown are the differences required for significance (two standard errors) in comparisons of percentages derived from two different surveys and from two different subgroups of the same survey.

The sampling error is a measure of the expected variation of a sample statistic from the corresponding population value. It does not measure the actual error of a particular estimate but leads to statements in terms of confidence intervals that are correct in a specified proportion of cases over the long run. The estimates of sampling errors presented in table B.1 are *two standard errors,* a measure frequently chosen in social research to obtain a 95 percent level of confidence. A statement that the range of sampling error on either side of the sample value includes the population value will be correct 95 times out of 100 and incorrect 5 times out of 100 in the long run. If a greater degree of confidence is required, a wider range should be used. Most of the time, however, the actual error of sampling will be less than the sampling error just defined. In about 68 cases out of every 100, range of one-half of the sampling error on either side of the sample estimate can be expected to include the population value.

To illustrate, the survey estimate that 51 percent of the 546 people in their twenties in 1976 report worrying "a lot or always" is subject to a sampling error of about 4.8 percentage points (by interpolation from table B.1). Thus, the statement that the interval 46.2 to 55.8 percent includes the population value has 95 in 100 chances of being correct and 5 chances of being incorrect. The chances are 68 in 100 that the range of 48.6 to 53.4 percent includes the population value. It is impractical to calculate the sampling error for every sample estimate when there are hundreds of such statistics. Hence, the sampling errors presented in table B.1 are average values derived from a large number of calculations for the two samples; 1957 and 1976. Some of the survey statistics calculated had larger and some had smaller sampling errors than those shown in the table.

The estimates of sampling errors themselves are subject to the vagaries of sampling. Therefore, the approximate sampling errors provided in table B.1 should be regarded as just that: approximations. If more precise estimates of sampling error are required, calculations of sampling error should be made for the specific statistic. In particular, regional estimates and those for domains that concentrate in a limited number of primary areas (SMSAs or non-SMSAs) may be subject to higher sampling errors than those presented in table B.1. Special calculations can be made for those estimates.

SAMPLING ERROR OF DIFFERENCES

Of greater interest than the sampling error of percentages is the sampling error of the differences between percentages for two different surveys or from two different subgroups of the same survey. Factors affecting individual percentages affect their differences in a similar but more complex manner. The sampling errors of many comparisons within each of the surveys and between the two surveys were calculated using formulas that take those complexities into account (Kish and Hess, 1959, 1965). The average values given in table B.2 may be used for either type of comparison, although, on the basis of comparisons made in this and some previous studies conducted at the Survey Research Center, there is a tendency for sampling errors of year-to-year differences in the same group (e.g., men) to be somewhat smaller than those applicable to differences between two groups from the same survey (e.g., men and women). The table is not appropriate when overlapping subgroups (the same respondents appearing in both subgroups) are compared. However, the sampling error of that kind of estimate can be calculated when the need is established.

An illustration may aid the understanding of table B.2 and its uses. Let us suppose that we are interested in the difference between the 51 percent of 546 young adults in 1976 and the 32 percent of those in their twenties in 1957 (453) who worry "a lot or always." By inspecting the section of table B.2 for percentages from 35 to 65 percent, and locating the intersection of the row for 500 and the column for 400, we see that the average sampling error (two standard errors) is 7.1 percent. Since the observed difference of 19 percent far exceeds the average sampling error, we may say that the chances are at least 95 in 100 that in the populations as a whole—and not only in our samples—young adults in 1976 are more likely to frequently worry than their counterparts in 1957.

Appendix C

STRATEGIES OF MULTIVARIATE ANALYSIS

Throughout this volume, log-linear and hierarchical models, as described by Goodman (1978) and others (Bishop, Fienberg, and Holland, 1975; Davis, 1974; Fienberg, 1977; Reynolds, 1977), are routinely used for significance tests in multivariate contingency tables, most commonly in multivariate analyses involving sex, age, education, and year—the standard filter or control variables used to differentiate respondents in each chapter of the book. Our use of log-linear analysis in that regard follows the general lead of Davis (1975) and the Duncans (Duncan, 1975; Duncan and Duncan, 1978; Duncan and Evers, 1975), who demonstrate the substantial analytic rigor to be gained by using log-linear models for studying social change by survey replication.

In the current research, our choice of the log-linear approach was guided by two major considerations. First, log-linear and hierarchical models represent a powerful system of novel techniques for analyzing *qualitative* or *categorical* data, and *Americans View Their Mental Health* (perhaps to a greater extent than any national survey conducted either before or since) is almost entirely an investigation of categorical data, since it relies heavily on open-ended questions or codes and a concomitant presentation of results in both bivariate and multivariate contingency tables.

Second, the log-linear analysis approach is especially well suited to address several key multivariate research questions of particular interest in the replication study. As noted by Davis (1974), the system provides at least three important significance tests not previously readily available to the average researcher: (1) tests for the significance of a partial association (e.g., whether or not a year difference vanishes when education is controlled), regardless of the number of categories or level of measurement in the associated variables or controls; (2) a test for the significance of interactions (specifications) where the control variable has many categories, including higher-order interactions involving a combination of control variables; and (3) general significance tests which permit relatively succinct statements about the structure and nature of relationships in a multivariate contingency table, including tests of significance for log-linear effect coefficients corresponding to specific cells in a table. Hence, log-linear and hierarchical models are especially useful for answering questions like: (1) to what extent are significant changes in attitudes, behaviors, and characteristics observed between the two survey years due to shifts in demographic characteristics (e.g., age and education) of the population over that period; (2) to what extent do such changes vary in intensity within various populations (e.g., educational) subgroups; and (3) to what extent have there been significant changes in the nature of strength of relationships between the two survey years (e.g., are various significant subgroups of the population becoming more or less alike in their attitudes and behaviors)?

Based on its capacity to elegantly address these major analytic questions, it is perhaps not surprising that log-linear hierarchical modeling systems have gradually emerged as a favored means of analyzing qualitative data in survey replications (see, however, Davis, 1978; Grizzle, Starmer, and Koch, 1969). Nevertheless, the development of log-linear analysis has been far from a one-man show, a factor which has predictably resulted in substantial differences in both notation and strategy. In general, the statistical analyses described in this research follow the Goodman (1978) system, using the ECTA computer program developed and distributed by Fay and Goodman, but even among those using the Goodman system, there are important differences in strategy, interpretation, and presentation, and the present research is no exception. Consequently, this appendix will illustrate the specific log-linear hierarchical analysis strategies used in this research by providing several examples of the types of analyses used throughout the book so that the interested reader may better understand the analytic assumptions which underlie the major multivariate conclusions stated in the texts. For a detailed and comprehensive exposition of the fundamental concepts and techniques underlying the Goodman system (including alternative analytic strategies), the reader is referred to the literature cited above.

Central to the log-linear method is a sequential modeling process, by which the researcher attempts to explain what is going on in a multiway contingency table. Based on hypotheses about the relationships among variables in the table, the researcher employs an iterative procedure to calculate maximum likelihood estimates of the expected frequencies in each cell of the table. The process involves a series of decisions which ultimately allows determining which dimensions of a contingency table (e.g., relationships among variables) are necessary and sufficient to reproduce the observed cell frequencies; i.e., how much a given table can be collapsed without losing important information. The maximum likelihood-ratio chi-square (LR_χ^2) statistic is used to assess the goodness of fit between cell frequencies expected under a given model and those actually observed. A nonsignificant (e.g., $p >$ .05) LR_χ^2, indicating little discrepancy between expected and observed frequencies, implies that a model fits the data well. By deriving a "best-fitting" model for a given table, researchers are able to determine which of several possible relationships represented in the table must be taken into account in order to explain the data structure; or, more specifically, whether an effect of interest is included in that model.

Although several basic approaches for selecting a "best-fitting" model (i.e., a model which most accurately and parsimoniously fits the structure of data in a contingency table) have been proposed in the literature, the basic selection strategies used in this research involve a "bracketing" process, whereby researchers fit models of uniform order (e.g., all marginal (univariate), all bivariate, or all trivariate relationships) to find a model with terms of $r-1$ that fits the data *poorly* (i.e., yields a significant LR_χ^2) and a model with terms of order r that fits the data *too well* (i.e., yields a nonsignificant LR_χ^2 and has several unnecessary parameters).[1]

Under the assumption that the simplest, best-fitting model falls somewhere within the region bracketed by these two models which do and do not fit the data well (since the bracketing process tells us that at least one r-level effect but no effect more complex than level r is needed to describe cell frequencies), one then employs either a *forward* (stepwise-up) *selection* procedure, whereby one adds terms one at a time to the model with terms $r-1$ until the model fits, or a *backward* (stepwise-down) *elimination* of redundant terms from the model with terms of order r until no more terms can be excluded without significantly

[1] For example, for a given table with three or more variables, a model containing all third-order (trivariate) terms (i.e., all interactions of variables taken three at a time) might fit the data too well (e.g., $\rho > .25$), while a model with all second-order (bivariate) terms (all associations between variables taken two at a time) yields a significant difference between observed frequencies and those expected under the model.

decreasing the fit, or a combination of both, to find an intermediate model containing one or more terms of order r. Once no more terms of order r can be added or deleted, a similar stepwise-down procedure is executed to insure that no effects of order $r-1$ or $r-2$ are unnecessary.

In this research, both forward-selection and backward-elimination procedures were used in model fitting, generally in combination. In addition, two possible criteria of "fit" were employed: one absolute and one relative. Under the first criterion, a model was said to fit if the discrepancy between the model and actual data was not statistically significant at a prespecified alpha level, arbitrarily chosen at .05 for this study. A second criterion emphasized, instead, significant *improvement* or *reduction* in fit compared with a base model, based on a test of significance for the difference between likelihood-ratio chi-square statistics for the two models in question, again with an alpha level set at .05. Under the first criterion, terms are added until researchers obtain a model yielding a LR_{χ}^2 greater than .05 or deleted until the associated LR_{χ}^2 drops below .05. Under the second criterion, however, terms that result in a significant improvement in fit ($p < .05$) over a base model are sequentially added, even *after* achieving a model with a LR_{χ}^2 greater than .05, until no further terms can be added that produce a significant improvement in fit, or, in a stepwise-down procedure, are deleted until no further terms can be eliminated without resulting in a significant *reduction* in fit.

Regardless of how a best-fitting model, is derived, for most survey data analyses, it is necessary to supplement these basic significance tests used in model selection with some additional tests of significance and descriptive statistics to simplify the interpretation of statistical findings based on log-linear analysis. In essence, the model-fitting process alerts us to the existence of statistically significant effects, but tells us nothing about the nature, direction, or magnitude of those relationships. To aid in our interpretation of complex multivariate tables, log-linear effect coefficients—equivalent to Goodman's (1978) lambdas (λ) and taus (τ) and Fienberg's (1977) "u-terms" were computed for each final model using the ECTA program. Since these log-linear effect coefficients are similar to analysis of variance effects, we are able to test whether they are statistically different from zero. By attending to the pattern of statistically significant λ coefficients associated with a given relationship, we are better able to describe the direction of that association, or, in the case of a higher-order interaction, we are better able to specify the precise nature of that interaction.

However, even these statistics are limited in their capacity to convey the magnitude of these relationships (see Page, 1977). The particular utility of calculating and interpreting *odds ratios*—to which log-linear effect coefficients bear a direct functional relationship has been amply demonstrated by Page (1977) and Duncan and Duncan (1978). However, in the interest of continuity with the previous reporting of the

1957 data (Gurin, Veroff, and Feld, 1960), we decided to provide conventional percentage tables rather than adopt the odds ratio approach.

Let us turn now to some specific examples of our use of log-linear and hierarchical models for multivariate contingency table analysis in this book. Basically, three distinct types of analysis were conducted: (1) five-variable log-linear analyses of the cross-classification of key dependent measures in each chapter by sex, age, education, and year (except for measures assessed only in 1976, which reduced the problem to a four-dimension cross-classification; (2) three-variable analyses of the cross-classifications of multiple indicators of subjective mental health and selected social characteristics by year; and (3) six-variable analyses of the cross-classifications of these same indicators of subjective adjustment and selected social characteristics by sex, age, education, and year.

Example 1: A Five-Variable Table

Table C.1 presents the results of the log-linear analysis of the cross-classification of "Worries" (W) by sex (S), age (A), education (E) and year (Y). All of the models presented assume (W) as the dependent variable and thereby routinely fit the marginals (SAEY), the relationships among all independent variables. Finding the best-fitting model should ascertain whether sex, age, education, and year differences in worries, or higher-order interactions among these predictors, are necessary to adequately describe the pattern of frequencies in the cross-classification table of these variables. The criterion of selection in these tables is the most parsimonious model (over and above a base model

TABLE C.1

*Log-Linear Hierarchical Models of Effects of Sex (S), Age (A),
Education (E) and Year (Y) on "Worries" (W)*

Fitted Models (all include SAEY)	LRχ^2	df	ρ
1. (W)	446.34	105	.000
2. (WS) (WA) (WE) (WY)	145.57	87	.000
3. (WSA) (WSE) (WSY) (WAE) (WAY) (WEY)	63.87	48	.062
4. (WSA) (WE) (WY)	144.36	81	.000
5. (WSE) (WA) (WY)	139.87	81	.000
6. (WSY) (WA) (WE)	145.49	84	.000
7. (WAE) (WS) (WY)	126.45	75	.000
8. (WAY) (WS) (WE)	102.04	81	.057
9. (WEY) (WS) (WA)	131.37	81	.001
10. (WAY) (WS)	144.13	87	.000
11. (WAY) (WE)	175.22	84	.000

which includes all relationships among the independent variables) which generates expected frequencies which do not significantly deviate from those actually observed (e.g., yields a LR_{χ}^2 with $\rho > .05$). We first present the models with terms of uniform order used to find the original base model with terms of $r-1$ (in this case, the model which includes all bivariate relationships). Next we add terms of order r (three-variable interactions) one at a time in an attempt to find a simpler intermediate model which fits the data at our prespecified criterion. Having achieved that goal with a model containing only one term of order r (one trivariate), models omitting each remaining bivariate (order $r-1$) were fit to determine whether they were really necessary.

The best-fitting model derived from this process is (WAY) (WS) (WE), indicating that sex and education are related to worries independent of age and year, while the relationship of age to worries differs significantly by year (or, alternatively, year changes in reported worries differ significantly by age). Having established the significance of these main and interactive effects of sex, age, education, and year on worries, log-linear effect parameter estimates for this best-fitting model (H_8) were computed and examined to determine the precise nature or direction of these significant effects. Table C.2 presents estimates of Goodman's lambda (λ) parameters and their standard errors for each of the effects included in that model.

These results, which are summarized in table 2.11 of chapter 2, indicate that: (1) men report worrying less than women; (2) young people worry more than older adults; (3) less educated people worry more than the highly educated; and (4) adults in 1976 apparently worry more often than people in 1957. These main effects for age and year must be qualified, however, because they are couched within a significant age x year interaction, which indicates that these main effects are conditional. Throughout the book such main effects are reported and interpreted only when the lambda coefficients corresponding to these relationships are statistically significant at the .01 level, a criterion which is met by each of these effects. In addition, however, the parameters describing a significant age x year interaction in table C.2 indicate that: (1) the significant increase in worries from 1957 to 1976 is especially marked among young adults; and (2) that the negative relationship between age and frequency of worry is stronger in 1976 than in 1957.

Example 2: A Three-Variable Table

Two other types of log-linear analysis were used only in chapter 8, in which several sociodemographic variables were related to selected measures of subjective adjustment. Multivariate analyses of these varia-

TABLE C.2

Estimates of Log-Linear Parameters (λs) Describing the Effects of
Sex (S), Age (A), Education (E), and Year (Y) on "Worries" (W)[a]

	How Much R Worries			
Predictor	A lot; Always	Sometimes; Hardly Ever	Never	NA
Sex				
Male[b]	−.204[c]	.000	.222[c]	−.018
	(.038)[d]	(.037)	(.066)	(.065)
Age				
21–34	.273[c]	.162[c]	−.412[c]	−.023
	(.061)	(.060)	(.114)	(.105)
35–54	.003	−.031	.029	−.001
	(.050)	(.048)	(.084)	(.085)
55 and over	−.275[c]	−.131[c]	.383[c]	.024
	(.051)	(.048)	(.080)	(.086)
Education				
Grade School	.078	−.189[c]	.123	−.013
	(.061)	(.061)	(.112)	(.106)
High School	.036	.002	−.002	−.037
	(.046)	(.044)	(.078)	(.079)
College	−.114[e]	.187[c]	−.121	.049
	(.054)	(.050)	(.089)	(.090)
Year				
1957[b]	−.191[c]	.034	.287[c]	−.130[e]
	(.038)	(.037)	(.066)	(.065)
Age × Year (1957[b])				
21–34	−.163[c]	.061	.103	−.001
	(.061)	(.060)	(.114)	(.105)
35–54	−.002	.062	−.024	−.035
	(.050)	(.048)	(.084)	(.085)
55 and over	.165[c]	−.123[c]	−.078	.036
	(.051)	(.048)	(.080)	(.086)

[a] Based on best fitting model from table C.1: (WAY) (WS) (WE) (SAEY).

[b] Since sex and year are two-level variables, parameter estimates for females and 1976 respondents are identical to those for males and 1957 respondents, but opposite in sign.

[c] $p < .01$.

[d] Numbers in parentheses are standard errors of the lambda coefficients.

[e] $p < .05$.

bles proceeded in two distinct stages: (1) a three-variable analysis of the cross-classification of the subjective adjustment indicator of interest by a social characteristic and year, to determine whether the relationship between that characteristic and the mental-health indicator differed significantly by year; and (2) a six-variable analysis of these same three variables along with sex, age, education, and year, to assess whether or not the adjustment by sociodemographic characteristic relationship persists when the latter predictors are controlled and/or whether such relationships differ significantly by sex, age, education, and year (this time with the other predictors held constant).

An example of the first type of analysis is presented in table C.3, which presents the results of a three-variable log-linear analysis of the cross-classification of "perceived role shortcomings" by family income and year. In this case, a model which includes all bivariate relationships (notably those between role shortcomings and income and year, respectively) generates expected frequencies which differ significantly from those observed, implying that a year x income interaction is required to fit the data well. The nature of that interaction is indicated by the parameter estimates for the saturated model (RIY) presented in table C.4. Main effects for year and income indicate that people in 1957 were more likely to mention role shortcomings than adults in 1976, and that high-income people are less likely than the less affluent to mention such shortcomings. However, the significant interaction reflects that this income relationship was statistically significant *only in 1957*. In 1976, no reliable relationship is apparent between income and the mention of role shortcomings. In addition, when a six-variable analysis was conducted similar to that to be described next, this income x year interaction was found to persist even when sex, age, and (especially) education were controlled.

Example 3: A Six-Variable Table

As noted above, six-variable analyses were conducted to determine whether or not relationships between demographic characteristics and subjective adjustment (including interaction by year) persisted when sex, age, and education were controlled and to determine whether such relationships were conditioned by sex, age, and/or education. Table C.5 presents the results of a log-linear analysis of the cross-classification of "psychological anxiety" (P) by income (I), sex (S), age (A), edu-

TABLE C.3
Log-Linear Hierarchical Models
of Effects of Income (I) and
Year (Y) on "Perceived Role
Shortcomings" (R)

Fitted Models	LRχ^2	df	ρ
1. (R) (IY)	72.77	11	.000
2. (RI) (RY) (IY)	13.48	5	.019
3. (RIY)	—	—	—

TABLE C.4

Estimates of Log-Linear Parameters (λs)
Describing the Effects of Income (I) and
Year (Y) on "Perceived Role
Shortcomings" (R) [a]

Predictor	Role Shortcomings Mentioned	
Income		
<$4,000	.042	(.039)[b]
$4,000–7,999	.046	(.035)
$8.000–9,999	.099[c]	(.042)
$10,000–12,499	.003	(.042)
$12,500–19,999	−.004	(.033)
$20,000 and over	−.187[d]	(.046)
Year		
1957[e]	.083[d]	(.018)
Income × Year (1957[e]		
<$4,000	−.066	(.039)
$4,000–7,999	.019	(.035)
$8,000–9,999	.041	(.042)
$10,000–12,499	.044	(.042)
$12,500–19,999	.074[c]	(.033)
$20,000 and over	.112[c]	(.046)

[a] Based on saturated model: (RIY).

[b] Numbers in parentheses are standard errors of the lambda coefficients.

[c] $p < .05$.

[d] $p < .01$.

[e] Since year is a two-level variable, parameter estimates for 1976 respondents are identical to those for 1957 respondents, but opposite in sign.

TABLE C.5

Log-Linear Hierarchical Models
of Effects of Income (I), Sex (S), Age (A),
Education (E) and Year (Y) on "Psychological
Anxiety" (P)

Fitted Models	LRχ^2	df	ρ
1. (PSAEY) (ISAEY)	751.77	720	.204
2. (PI) (PSAEY) (ISAEY)	722.22	700	.272
Difference $\chi^2(H_1) - \chi^2(H_2)$	28.22	20	$>.05$

cation (E), and year (Y). A previous three-variable analysis of the cross-classification of psychological anxiety by income and year, similar to that summarized in table C.3, revealed no significant income by year interaction, but a significant main effect of income in both survey years: low-income adults in both 1957 and 1976 were more likely than higher-income respondents to report high levels of psychological anxiety. Since the relationship of psychological anxiety and income is that of foremost interest in table C.5, marginals specifying all relationships between anxiety and the four control variables (PSAEY) and between income and these same variables (ISAEY) are routinely fitted for all models in these six-variable analyses. Table C.5 shows that a model specifying *only* these "constant" terms fits the observed pattern of frequencies in this table quite well, and that adding the bivariate relationship between income and anxiety does not significantly improve that fit. Thus we concluded in chapter 8 that the consistent relationship between income and anxiety observed in both 1957 and 1976 is accounted for by the relatively strong relationship between income and education (the latter also being a strong correlate of psychological anxiety).

A more complex example of a six-variable problem is presented in table C.6, which presents a similar analysis of the cross-classification of reported "happiness" (H) by income (I), sex (S), age (A), education (E) and year (Y). Once again, since our focus is on the income-happiness relationship, two "constant" terms are fit: (HSAEY) and (ISAEY). Using the bracketing procedure described above, we determine that a model

TABLE C.6

Log-Linear Hierarchical Models of Effects of Income
(I), Sex (S), Age (A), Education (E), and Year (Y) on
"Reports of Happiness" (H)

Fitted Models (all models fit: HSAEY and ISAEY)	LRχ^2	df	ρ
1. (HSAEY) (ISAEY)	602.11	360	.000
2. (HI)	407.68	350	.018
3. (HIS) (HIA) (HIE) (HIY)	319.18	290	.115
4. (HIS)	396.21	340	.019
5. (HIA)	364.89	330	.090
6. (HIE)	375.91	330	.041
7. (HIY)	399.38	340	.014
8. (HIA) (HIS)	354.83	320	.088
9. (HIA) (HIE)	337.84	310	.133
10. (HIA) (HIY)	356.19	320	.080
Differences			
$\chi^2(H_5) - \chi^2(H_8)$	10.06	10	p>.30
$\chi^2(H_5) - \chi^2(H_9)$	27.05	20	p>.10
$\chi^2(H_5) - \chi^2(H_{10})$	8.70	10	p>.50

including only the bivariate relationship (H_2) fits poorly, while a model containing all three-way interactions (H_3) fits the data too well; it probably has some unnecessary parameters. By a forward-selection process which adds three-way interactions to model H_2 one at a time (H_4–H_7), we arrive at an intermediate model (H_5) that provides the greatest improvement in fit and therefore becomes a new base model. Since the addition of each of the remaining trivariates in turn (models H_8–H_{10}) does not result in a significant improvement in fit, model H_5—which specifies an income x age interaction—is designated the best-fitting model. A previous three-way analysis of the happiness-income relationship by year indicated that to a similar extent in both survey years (e.g., no year interaction), people with high incomes reported greater levels of happiness. Based on our examination of the log-linear effect parameters (not presented here) for model H_5 in table C.6 we were able to specify in chapter 8 that this positive relationship between income and happiness is strongest among middle-aged men and women.

References

Anderson, O. W., and Andersen, R. M. Patterns of use of health services. In H. E. Freeman, S. Levine, and L. G. Reeder (eds.), *Handbook of medical sociology* (2d ed.). Englewood Cliffs, N.J.: Prentice-Hall, 1972.

Andrews, F. M., and Withey, S. B. *Social indicators of well-being.* New York: Plenum Press, 1976.

Aronson, E. The theory of cognitive dissonance: A current perspective. In L. Berkowitz (ed.), *Advances in experimental social psychology* (vol. 4). New York: Academic Press, 1969.

Bane, M. S. *Here to Stay.* New York: Basic Books, 1976.

Berardo F. *Social adaptation to widowhood among a rural-urban aged population.* Pullman, Washington: Washington State University (Washington Agricultural Experiment Station Bulletin 689), 1976.

Bernard, J. *The future of marriage.* New York: Bantam Books, 1972.

Bettelheim, B. Untying the family. *The Center Magazine,* vol. IX, Sept.–Oct. 1976, 5–9.

Bishop, Y. M. M., Fienberg, S. E., and Holland, P. W. *Discrete multivariate analysis: Theory and practice.* Cambridge, Mass.: MIT Press, 1975.

Blau, P. M. A theory of social integration. *American Journal of Sociology,* 1960, *65,* 545–56.

Blum, J. D. On changes in psychiatric diagnosis over time. *American Psychologist,* 1978, *33,* 1017–31.

Blumenthal, M. D., Dillman, T. E., and Bongort, K. *Relationships of demographic variables and mental health indices to satisfaction and functioning.* Technical Memo (NIH Grant #20707), Survey Research Center, 1974.

Braverman, H. *Labor and monopoly capital: The degradation of work in the twentieth century.* New York: Monthly Review Press, 1975.

Bronfenbrenner, U. *The ecology of human development: Experiments by nature and design.* Cambridge, Mass.: Harvard University Press, 1979.

Butler, M. C., and Jones, A. P. The Health Opinion Survey reconsidered: Dimensionality, reliability, and validity. *Journal of Clinical Psychology,* 1979, *35*(3), 554–59.

Cahalan, D. *Problem drinkers.* San Francisco: Jossey-Bass, 1970.

Campbell, A. *Sense of well-being in America: Recent patterns and trends.* New York: McGraw-Hill, 1980.

Campbell, A., Converse, P. E., and Rodgers, W. L. *The quality of American life.* New York: Russell Sage, 1976.

Caplan, R. D., Cobb, S., French, J. R. P., Jr., Harrison, R. V., and Pinneau, S. R. *Job demands and worker health: Main effects and occupational differences.* Cincinnati: National Institute for Occupational Safety and Health, HEW Publication No. (NIOSH) 75–160, April 1975.

Chodorow, N. Family structure and feminine personality. In M. Rosaldo and L. Lamphere (eds.), *Woman, culture and society.* Stanford, California: Stanford University Press, 1974, 43–66.

Clancy K., and Gove, W. Sex differences in mental illness: An analysis of response bias in self-reports. *American Journal of Sociology,* 1974, *80,* 205–16.

Collins, G. The good news about 1984. *Psychology Today,* 1979, *12* (8), 34–48.

Cooley, C. H. *Human nature and the social order.* New York: Scribner's, 1902.

Crandall, V. C. Sex differences in expectancy of intellectual and academic reinforcement. In C. S. Smith (ed.), *Achievement-related motives in children.* New York: Russell Sage, 1969.

Crandell, D. L., and Dohrenwend, B. P. Some relations among psychiatric symptoms, organic illness, and social class. *The American Journal of Psychiatry*, 1967, *123*, 1527–38.

Cronbach, L. Coefficient alpha and the internal structure of tests. *Psychometrika*, 1951, *16*, 297–334.

Davis, J. A. Hierarchical models for significance tests in multivariate contingency tables: An exegesis of Goodman's recent papers. In H. L. Costner (ed.), *Sociological methodology 1973–1974*. San Francisco: Jossey-Bass, 1974.

Davis, J. A. The log-linear analysis of survey replications. In K. C. Land, and S. Spilerman (eds.), *Social indicator models*. New York: Russell Sage, 1975.

Davis, J. A. Studying categorical data over time. *Social Science Research*, 1978, *7*, 151–79.

Deci, E. L. *Intrinsic motivation*. New York: Plenum Press, 1975.

Depner, C. *"Adult roles and subjective evaluation of life quality."* Ph. D. dissertation, University of Michigan, 1968.

Dohrenwend, B. P. Socio-cultural and social psychological factors in the genesis of mental disorders. *Journal of Health and Social Behavior*, 1975, *16*, 365–92.

Dohrenwend, B. P., and Dohrenwend, B. S. Social and cultural influences in psychopathology. In M. R. Rosenzweig and L. W. Porter (eds.), *Annual Review of Psychology* (vol. 25). Palo Alto, California: Annual Review, Inc., 1974, 417–52.

Dohrenwend, B. P., and Dohrenwend, B. S. *Social status and psychological disorder: A causal inquiry*. New York: John Wiley, 1969.

Douvan, E. *Changes in the family and later life stages*. Paper presented at the meeting of the Gerontological Society, Dallas, November, 1978.

Duncan, B., and Duncan, O. D. *Sex typing and social roles: A research report*. New York: Academic Press, 1978.

Duncan, B., and Evers, M. Measuring change in attitudes toward women's work. In K. C. Land and S. Spilerman (eds.), *Social indicator models*. New York: Russell Sage, 1975.

Duncan, O. D. The inheritance of poverty or the inheritance of race? In D. P. Moynihan (ed.), *On understanding poverty*. New York: Basic Books, 1969.

Duncan, O. D. Measuring social change via replication of surveys. In K. C. Land and S. Spilerman (eds.), *Social indicator models*. New York: Russell Sage, 1975.

Easterlin, R. A. Does economic growth improve the human lot? Some empirical evidence, *Nations and households in economic growth*. New York: Academic Press, 1974, 89–125.

Eastwood, M. R. and Trevelyan, M. H. Relationship between physical and psychiatric disorder. *Psychological Medicine*, 1972, *2*, 363–72.

Feldman, H. *Development of the husband-wife relationship: A research report*. Ithaca, New York: Cornell University Press, 1964.

Fienberg, S. E. *The analysis of cross-classified categorical data*. Cambridge, Mass.: MIT Press, 1977.

Garson, B. *All the livelong day: The meaning and demeaning of routine work*. New York: Penguin, 1977.

Glock, C. Y., and Stark, R. *Religion and society in tension*. Chicago: Rand McNally & Co., 1965.

Goodman, L. A. *Analyzing qualitative categorical data: Log-linear models and latent structure analysis*. Cambridge, Mass.: Abt Books, 1978.

Gourash, N. Help-seeking: A review of the literature. *American Journal of Community Psychology*, 1978, *6*(5), 413–23.

Gove, W. R. Sex differences in mental illness among adult men and women: An evaluation of four questions raised regarding the evidence on the higher rates of women. *Social Science and Medicine*, 1978, *12B*, 187–98.

Gove, W. R., and Geerken, M. R. Response bias in surveys of mental health: An empirical investigation. *American Journal of Sociology*, 1977, *82*(6), 1289–1317.

Gove, W. R., and Hughes, M. Possible causes of the apparent sex differences in physical health: An empirical investigation. *American Sociological Review*, 1979, *44*, 126–46.

Gove, W. R., McCorkel, J., Fain, T., and Hughes, M. D. Response bias in community surveys of mental health: Systematic bias or random noise? *Social Science and Medicine*, 1976, *10*, 497–502.

Gove, W. R., and Tudor, J. Adult sex roles and mental illness. *American Journal of Sociology*, 1973, *78*, 50–73.

Greeley, A. M. *The American Catholic: A social portrait*. New York: Basic Books, 1977.

Greeley, A. M. *The denominational society*. Glenview, Illinois: Scott, Foresman and Company, 1972.

Greeley, A. M. *Why can't they be more like us?* New York: E. P. Dutton & Co., 1971.

Grizzle, J. E., Starmer, C. F., and Koch, G. G. Analysis of categorical data by linear models. *Biometrics*, 1969, *25*, 489–504.

Gurin, G., Veroff, J., and Feld, S. C. *Americans view their mental health.* New York: Basic Books, 1960.

Gurin, P., Gurin, G., Lao, R., and Beattie, M. Internal-external control in the motivational dynamics of Negro youth. *Journal of Social Issues*, 1969, *25*, 29–53.

Gutmann, D. An exploration of ego configuration in middle and later life. In B. Neugarten (ed.), *Personality in middle and later life.* New York: Atherton, 1968.

Heller, K. The effects of social support: prevention and treatment implications. In A. P. Goldsten and F. H. Kanfer (eds.), *Maximizing treatment gains: Transfer enhancement in psychotherapy.* New York: Academic Press, 1978.

Hinkle, L. E., and Wolff, H. G. Health and the social environment. In A. M. Leighton, J. A. Clausen, and R. N. Wilson (eds.), *Exploration in social psychiatry.* New York: Basic Books, 1957.

Hochschild, A. R. The sociology of feeling and emotion: Selected possibilities. In M. Millman and R. M. Kanter (eds.), *Another voice.* Garden City, New York: Anchor, 1975.

Hoffman, L. W., Thornton, A., and Manis, J. B. The value of children to parents in the United States. *Journal of Population*, 1978, *1*, 91–131.

Holmes, T. H., and Rahe, R. H. The social readjustment scale. *Journal of Psychosomatic Research*, 1967, *11*, 213–18.

Horner, M. S. Toward an understanding of achievement-related conflicts in women. *Journal of Social Issues*, 1972, *28*, 157–76.

House, J. S. *The relationship of intrinsic and extrinsic work motivations to occupational stress and coronary heart disease risk.* Unpublished doctoral dissertation, University of Michigan, 1972.

Iglehart, A. P. *Married women and work: 1957 and 1976.* Lexington, Kentucky: Lexington Books, 1979.

Jahoda, M. *Current conceptions of positive mental health.* New York: Basic Books, 1958.

Jegede, R. O. Psychometric characteristics of the Health Opinion Survey. *Psychological Reports*, 1977, *40*, 1160–62.

Kahn, R. L., Wolfe, D. M., Quinn, R. P., Snoek, J. D., and Rosenthal, R. A. *Organizational stress: Studies in role conflict and ambiguity.* New York: John Wiley, 1964.

Katz, D., and Kahn, R. L. *The social psychology of organizations* (2d ed.). New York: John Wiley, 1978.

Kelley, H. H. The processes of causal attribution. *American Psychologist*, 1973, *28*, 107–28.

Kessler, R. C. Stress, social status, and psychological distress. *Journal of Health and Social Behavior*, 1979, *20*, 259–72.

Kipnis, D. M. Inner direction, other direction, and achievement motivation. *Human Development*, 1974, *17*, 321–43.

Kish, L. A procedure for objective respondent selection within the household. *Journal of the American Statistical Association*, 1949, *44*, 380–87.

Kish, L. *Survey sampling.* New York: John Wiley, 1965.

Kish, L., and Hess, I. On variances of ratios and their differences in multi-stage samples. *Journal of the American Statistical Association*, 1959, *54*, 416–46.

Kish, L., and Hess, I. *The Survey Research Center's national sample of dwellings.* Ann Arbor, Michigan: Institute for Social Research, University of Michigan, 1965.

Kornhauser, A. W. *Mental health of the industrial worker.* New York: John Wiley, 1965.

Kulka, R. A., Veroff, J., and Douvan, E. Social class and the use of professional help for personal problems: 1957 and 1976. *Journal of Health and Social Behavior*, 1979, *20*, 2–17.

Kulka, R. A., and Weingarten, H. The long-term effects of parental divorce in childhood on adult adjustment. *Journal of Social Issues*, 1979, *35*, 50–78.

Langner, T. S. A twenty-two item screening score of psychiatric symptoms indicating impairment. *Journal of Health and Social Behavior*, 1962, *3*, 269–76.

Lasch, C. *The culture of narcissism.* New York: Norton, 1979.

Lasch, C. *Haven in a heartless world: The family besieged.* New York: Basic Books, 1977.

Lawler, E. E., III. *Motivation in work organizations.* Monterey, Calif.: Brooks/Cole, 1973.

Leighton, D. C., Harding, J. S., Macklin, D. B., Macmillan, A. M. and Leighton, A. H. *The character of danger.* New York: Basic Books, 1963.

Locksley, A. *The effects of occupational experience on marital attitudes.* Unpublished doctoral dissertation, University of Michigan, 1978.

Locksley, A., and Douvan, E. Problem behavior in adolescents. In E. Gomberg and V. Franks (eds.), *Sex differences in disordered behavior*. New York: Brunner-Mazel, 1979.

Lofland, L. H. *A world of strangers: Order and action in urban public space*. New York: Basic Books, 1973.

Lopata, H. Z. *Widowhood in an American city*. Cambridge: Shenkman, 1973.

McClelland, D. C., Davis, W. N., Kalin, R., and Wanner, E. *The drinking man*. New York: Free Press, 1972.

Macmillan, A. M. The Health Opinion Survey: Technique for estimating prevalence of psychoneurotic and related types of disorder in communities. *Psychological Reports*, 1957, *3*, 325–39.

Mead, G. H. *Mind, self and society*. Chicago: University of Chicago Press, 1934.

Meile, R. L. The 22-item index of psychophysiological disorder: Psychological or organic symptoms? *Social Science and Medicine*, 1972, *6*, 125–35.

Miller, D. R., and Swanson, G. E. *Inner conflict and defense*. New York: Holt, 1960.

Morgan, J., and Duncan, G. J. *Five thousand American families: Patterns of economic progress (Vol. 5)*: Components of change in family well-being. Ann Arbor: Institute for Social Research, 1977.

Myers, J. K., and Bean, L. L. *A decade later: A follow-up of social class and mental illness*. New York: John Wiley, 1968.

Myers, J. K., Lindenthal, J. J. and Pepper, M. P. Life events and psychiatric impairment. *Journal of Nervous and Mental Disease*, 1971, *152*, 149–57.

Neugarten, B. L. *Middle age and aging*. Chicago: University of Chicago Press, 1968(a).

Neugarten, B. L. The awareness of middle age. In B. L. Neugarten (ed.), *Middle age and aging*. Chicago: University of Chicago Press, 1968(b).

Neugarten, B. L., and Datan, N. Sociological perspectives on the life cycle. In P. B. Baltes and K. W. Schaie (eds.), *Life-span developmental psychology: Personality and socialization*. New York: Academic Press, 1973.

Neugarten, B. L., and Gutmann, D. L. Age-sex roles and personality in middle age: A thematic apperception study. In B. L. Neugarten (ed), *Middle age and aging*. Chicago: University of Chicago Press, 1968.

Norland, S., and Weirath, T. Validating the Langner Scale: A critical review. *Social Problems*, 1978, *26*(2), 223–31.

Nunnally, J. C. *Psychometric theory*. New York: McGraw-Hill, 1967.

Orr, J. B. The changing family: A social ethical perspective. In V. Tufte and B. Myerhoff (eds.), *Changing images of the family*. New Haven: Yale University Press, 1980.

Ortner, S. B. Is female to male as nature is to culture? In M. Z. Rosaldo and L. Lamphere (eds.), *Woman, culture and society*, Stanford, Calif.: Stanford University Press, 1974.

Page, W. F. Interpretation of Goodman's log-linear model effects: An odds ratio approach. *Sociological Methods and Research*, 1977, *5*(4), 419–35.

Parsons, J. E., Ruble, D. N., Hodges, K. L., and Smale, A. W. Cognitive-developmental factors in emerging sex differences in achievement-related expectancies. *Journal of Social Issues*, 1976, *32*, 47–61.

Pearlin, L., and Kohn, M. Social class, occupation, and parental values: A cross-national study. *American Sociological Review*, 1966, *31*, 466–79.

Phillips, D., and Clancy, K. Response bias in field studies of mental illness. *American Sociological Review*, 1970, *35*, 503–15.

Phillips, D., and Clancy, K. Some effects of 'social desirability' in survey studies. *American Journal of Sociology*, 1972, *77*, 921–40.

Phillips, D., and Segal, B. Sexual status and psychiatric symptoms. *American Sociological Review*, 1969, *34*, 58–72.

Porter, L. W., Lawler, E. E., and Hackman, J. R. *Behavior in organizations*. New York: McGraw-Hill, 1975.

Quinn, R. P. and Shepard, L. J. *The 1972–73 Quality of Employment Survey*. Ann Arbor, Michigan: Survey Research Center, Institute for Social Research, 1975.

Quinn, R. P., and Staines, G. L. *The 1977 Quality of Employment Survey: Descriptive statistics with comparison data from the 1969–1970 and 1972–1973 surveys*. Ann Arbor, Mich.: Survey Research Center, Institute for Social Research, 1979.

Reynolds, H. T. *The analysis of cross-classification*. New York: Free Press, 1977.

Rokeach, M. The nature of human values. New York: Free Press, 1973.

Rolo, C. J. Are Americans well adjusted? *The Atlantic Monthly*, 1960, *207*, 59–63.

Rosenberg, M. *Society and the adolescent self-image*. Princeton, N.J.: Princeton University Press, 1965.

Rossi, A. S. Transition to parenthood. *Journal of Marriage and the Family*, 1968, *30*, 26–39.

Rotter, J. B. Generalized expectancies for internal vs. external control of reinforcement. *Psychological Monographs*, 1966, *80* (whole No. 609).

Rubin, L. *Worlds of pain*. New York: Basic Books, 1976.

Salaman, G. *Community and occupation*. New York: Cambridge University Press, 1974.

Sawhill, I. V. *Income transfers and family structure*. Washington, D.C.: Urban Institute, 1975.

Schachter, S. *The psychology of affiliation*. Stanford, Calif.: Stanford University Press, 1959.

Schwartz, C. C., Myers, J. K., and Astrachan, B. M. Comparing three measures of mental status: A note on the validity of estimates of psychological disorder in the community. *Journal of Health and Social Behavior*, 1973, *14*, 265–73.

Seiler, L. H. The 22-item scale used in field studies of mental illness: A question of method, a question of substance, and a question of theory. *Journal of Health and Social Behavior*, 1973, *14*, 252–64.

Seiler, L. H., and Summers, G. F. Toward an interpretation of items used in field studies of mental illness. *Social Science and Medicine*, 1974, *8*, 459–67.

Seligman, M. E. P. *Helplessness: On depression, development, and death*. San Francisco: Freeman, 1975.

Sennett, R. The brutality of modern families. In R. Sennett (ed.), *The uses of disorder: Personal identity and city life*. New York: Knopf, 1970.

Shanas, E., and Maddox, G. L. Aging, health and the organization of health resources. In R. H. Binstock and E. Shanas (eds.), *Handbook of aging and the social sciences*. New York: Van Nostrand, 1976.

Shepherd, M., Cooper, B., Brown, A. C., and Kalton, G. W. *Psychiatric illness in general practice*. London: Oxford University Press, 1966.

Slater, P. *The pursuit of loneliness* (rev. ed.). Boston: Beacon Press, 1976.

Smith, R. E. (ed.). *The subtle revolution*. Washington, D.C.: The Urban Institute, 1979.

Spiro, H. R., Siassi, I., and Crocetti, G. M. What gets surveyed in a psychiatric survey? A case study of the MacMillan index. *Journal of Nervous and Mental Disease*, 1972, *152*, 105–14.

Srole, L., Langner, T. S., Michael, S. T., Opler, M. K., and Rennie, T. A. C. *Mental health in the metropolis: The Midtown Study*. New York: McGraw-Hill, 1962.

Star, S. A. The screening of psychoneurotics in the army: Technical development of tests. In S. A. Stouffer, L. Guttman, E. A. Suchman, P. F. Lazarsfeld, S. A. Star, and J. A. Clausen. *Measurement and prediction* (Vol. 4). Princeton, N.J.: Princeton University Press, 1950.

Stark, R. Age and faith: A changing outlook or an old process. *Sociological Analysis*, 1968, *29*, 1–10.

Tamir, L. M. *The transition to middle age: Men in their forties*. Unpublished doctoral dissertation, University of Michigan, 1980.

Temme, L. V. *Occupation: Meanings and measures*. Washington, D.C.: Bureau of Social Science Research, Inc., 1975.

Tessler, R., and Mechanic, D. Psychological distress and perceived health status. *Journal of Health and Social Behavior*, 1978, *19*(3), 254–62.

Thoits, P., and Hannan, M. Income and psychological distress: The impact of an income maintenance experiment. *Journal of Health and Social Behavior*, 1979, *20*(2), 120–38.

Tomkins, S. S. The psychology of commitment. In S. S. Tomkins and C. Izard (eds.), *Affect, cognition, and personality*. New York: Springer, 1965.

Tousignant, M., Denis, G., and Lachapelle, R. Some considerations concerning the validity and use of the Health Opinion Survey. *Journal of Health and Social Behavior*, 1974, *15*, 241–52.

United States Department of Labor. *Dictionary of occupational titles* (3d ed.). Washington, D.C.: U.S. Government Printing Office, 1965.

Veroff, J. Social comparison and the development of achievement motivation. In C. S. Smith (ed.), *Achievement-related motives in children*. New York: Russell Sage, 1969.

Veroff, J., Atkinson, J. W., Feld, S., and Gurin, G. The use of thematic apperception to assess motivation in a nationwide interview study. *Psychological Monographs*, 1960, *74* (whole No. 499).

Veroff, J., Depner, C., Kulka, R., and Douvan, E. A comparison of American motives: 1957–1976. *Journal of Personality and Social Psychology*, 1980, *39*, 1249–62.

Veroff, J., and Feld, S. C. *Marriage and work in America*. New York: Van Nostrand Reinhold, 1970.

Veroff, J. B. The dynamics of help-seeking in men and women: A national survey study. *Psychiatry*, in press.

Warren, D. I. *Neighborhood and community contexts in help seeking, problem coping and mental health: Data analysis monograph*. Manuscript prepared for NIMH Grant #MH 24982, 1976.

Work in America: Report of a special task force to the Secretary of Health, Education and Welfare. Cambridge, Mass.: MIT Press, 1973.

Wortman, C. B., and Silver, R. Coping and undersirable life events. In M. E. P. Seligman and J. Garber (eds.)., *Human helplessness: Theory and applications*. New York: Academic Press, 1980.

Wright, E. *Class structure and income determination*. New York: Academic Press, 1979.

Zung, W. W. A self-rating depression scale. *Archives of General Psychology*, 1965, *12*, 63–70.

Index

466, 473; and anxiety, 421, 422, 429, 433, 454, 455, 461, 462, 463, 469, 471, 472, 545; and children, 385, 392–95, 397–400, 403, 421, 422, 425, 428, 431, 433, 434; and church attendance, 35; 455–65, 467, 468–69; and divorce, 401n8, 402, 403, 404, 454, 455, 466; and economic conditions, 385, and ego, 397, 402, 404, 416, 417, 421, 423, 428, 433, 450, 469, 471; and happiness, 9, 386, 392, 394, 396, 397, 406, 407, 408, 410, 411, 415, 417, 421, 427, 433, 444, 451, 452, 461, 462, 468–71; and ill health, 387, 392, 407, 433, 451, 461, 469, 471; and immobilization, 387, 397, 404, 433, 455, 469, 471, 472; and income, 389, 390, 392–95, 466–69; and marriage, 385, 387n3, 389, 391, 392, 394, 396–405, 401n8, 407, 408, 411, 414, 417, 421, 427, 430, 433, 450, 454, 455, 468–72, 546; and morale, 386, 391, 392, 402, 407, 427, 433, 434, 445, 450, 451, 452, 461, 468–71; and multivariate analyses, 432; and nervous breakdown, 386, 392, 397, 427, 433, 444, 455, 461, 468–71; and parenthood, 385, 387n3, 392, 395–401, 403, 410, 428, 433, 469–72, 543, 546, 547–48; and personality, 421, 423, 427, 450, 451, 468–71; and population density, 425–32, 468, 469, 473; and praying, 522–24; and race, 385, 468–69, 431–38, 467, 468–69; and regions, 419–25, 468–69, 472–73; and religion, 385, 438–47, 458, 468–69; and roles, 385, 391, 393, 394, 395, 468–72; and satisfaction, 397; and self-perception, 545; and social background, 447–50, 452–53; and urbanization, 425–32; and well-being, 385, 389, 390, 393, 394, 403, 405, 409, 412, 413, 431, 453, 468–72; and widowhood, 402, 404; and work, 385, 387, 391, 392, 394, 395, 405–18, 428, 429, 433, 448–51, 452, 461, 467–73; and worries, 386, 392, 397, 408, 415, 421, 427, 433, 444, 446, 471; year differences in, 388–93, 388n4, 396, 397, 399–403, 406, 407, 409, 410, 411, 413, 415, 416, 417, 418n13, 454, 462, 468–71, 473

Summers, G. F., 333

Survey Research Center, 27–28, 242, 243, 244, 389n7, 434n14, 552, 601n1, 607; Quality of Employment surveys, 249, 250–51, 320

Swanson, G. E., 453

sweating, 338, 339, 340, 342, 344, 346

symptom patterns, 330–71; and age, 347, 348, 350, 351, 352, 353–55; and education, 337, 347, 348, 352, 356–62; factor analysis summary, 346–47, 348; factor analysis of twenty symptoms, 337–46; and gender, 335, 347, 348, 349, 361–55; multivariate analyses of, 364, 368; studies of, 330–32; summary on, 370–71; and

year differences, 341–45, 347–51, 353–55, 358–60; *see also* symptoms

symptoms: and age, 337, 348, 350, 351, 362, 364–68; and alcohol, 362, 365–71; of anxiety, 8, 333, 341–48, 350, 350n5, 351, 352, 354, 356, 357, 359, 363, 368, 369, 370, 383; appetite as, 338–42, 346; breath shortness as, 338, 339, 340, 342; denial of, 352; differential reports of, 10; dizziness as, 338, 339, 340, 342; drinking as, 338, 339, 340, 342, 344, 346; and drugs, 362, 362n7; 363, 364, 365, 368–71, 549; and education, 337, 348, 356–62, 364–68; and ethnicity, 8–9; and happiness, 9; and ill health, 341, 341n2; 342–53, 356, 357, 358, 362, 362n7–8; 363, 368, 370; and immobilization, 333, 342–52, 356, 360, 361, 363, 369, 370; interview on, 582–84; and multivariate analyses, 348, 350, 351; nervous breakdown as, 338, 339, 340, 342; nervousness as, 338, 339, 340, 342, 346; nightmares as, 338, 339, 340, 342; overlapping of, 45; physical condition as, 333, 338–42, 371; psychosomatic, 330, 530, 547; sleep as, 338, 339, 340, 342, 346, 528; stomach upset as, 338, 339, 340, 342, 346; sweating as, 338, 339, 340, 342, 344, 346; and validity, 343, 344; and weight, 338, 339, 342; year differences in, 341–45, 347–51, 353–55, 356–60; *see also* symptom patterns

talking: and coping, 524, 525; and worries, 518–22, 520n11; *see also* chatting

Tamir, L. M., 405

teaching: and morality, 221; and parenthood, 204; *see also* education

technology and politics, 5

Temme, L. V., 301n4

Tessler, R., 345

T-group, 21, 492

Thoits, P., 334

Thornton, A., 208, 395

time: and change, 33; and feelings of well-being, 36–37; and subjective mental health, 36, 37; and work, 256; *see also* year differences

Tomkins, S. S., 400

Tousignant, M., 330, 332, 333

transference, 517

Trevelyan, M. H., 334, 346

Tudor, J., 332

unconscious, 517; and cognitive distortions, 43

unhappiness, 549; and adolescence, 40, 60, 62; and age, 70, 378; and children, 40–48,